T0395923

# Text and Textuality in Early Medieval Iberia

# Text and Textuality in Early Medieval Iberia

## The Written and The World, 711–1031

GRAHAM BARRETT

OXFORD
UNIVERSITY PRESS

Great Clarendon Street, Oxford, OX2 6DP,
United Kingdom

Oxford University Press is a department of the University of Oxford.
It furthers the University's objective of excellence in research, scholarship,
and education by publishing worldwide. Oxford is a registered trade mark of
Oxford University Press in the UK and in certain other countries

Published in the United States of America by Oxford University Press
198 Madison Avenue, New York, NY 10016, United States of America

British Library Cataloguing in Publication Data
Data available

Library of Congress Control Number: 2022944889

ISBN 978-0-19-289537-0

DOI: 10.1093/oso/9780192895370.001.0001

Printed and bound by
CPI Group (UK) Ltd, Croydon, CR0 4YY

Links to third party websites are provided by Oxford in good faith and
for information only. Oxford disclaims any responsibility for the materials
contained in any third party website referenced in this work.

*Simon Barton*
*(1962–2017)*

*Mark Whittow*
*(1957–2017)*

*Peter Linehan*
*(1943–2020)*

At last came the end of Don Quixote, after he had received all the sacraments and execrated the books of chivalry with manifold and convincing arguments. The scribe was present there, and said that he had never read in any book of chivalry that any knight-errant had died in his bed so serenely and in so Christian a manner as Don Quixote: and he, with the sympathies and tears of those who looked on, gave out his spirit – that is to say, he died. And when the priest saw this, he asked of the scribe to prepare for him a written record of how the good Alonso Quixano, commonly called Don Quixote de La Mancha, had departed from this life, and died of natural causes; and he was asking for this testimony lest any author, other than Cide Hamete Benengeli, should falsely raise him from the dead and make endless accounts of his exploits.

Miguel de Cervantes Saavedra,
*Don Quixote de La Mancha*, II.74

# Preface

This book has been a while in the making, and remains in many ways unsatisfactory. I have always found it easier to define what it is not than what it is: while its focus is the Latin charters of the kingdoms of Asturias-León and Navarra in the early Middle Ages, it is neither a palaeographic nor a diplomatic nor a linguistic study of material normally treated in one of those terms, and my approach is neither legal nor institutional nor social nor cultural, at least in the strict sense of those traditions. I have instead attempted something at once simpler and more difficult, but which has seemed to me the precondition for all such enquiries of a higher order. This is a sociocultural study of the interface between the written and the world: my aim is to trace the lifecycle of the charters and the network of texts in which they were embedded as a step towards finding their place in the society and culture which we use them to describe. I hope to convey some sense of not the literacy but the textuality of early medieval Iberia, its inscription in writing, and thereby provide a point of departure for its historical study.

Preparing such a study has at times felt like a Sisyphean labour. The charters which I have assembled into a database are divided up amongst many archives in Spain and Portugal; visiting each of them in turn, or where impractical scanning digital images kindly supplied by understanding archivists instead, has been the work of a decade. Ironically, tracking down the printed editions in which they are published has been no easier an undertaking, and remains a chimeric dream. Certain of these publications have such an exiguous presence in libraries that consulting them conveys something of the experience of samizdat literature. There is no one critical introduction to the whole corpus and few translations to provide any apprenticeship in often difficult texts, access to archival material varies widely, not always explicably, editions differ in date, quality, and coverage by region and from archive to archive, and some charters still await cataloguing, let alone publication. My hope here is not only to lay groundwork for a new way of reading the documentation of early medieval Iberia, but also to lower the bar to entry as best I can for students and scholars approaching this material for the first time.

Some explanatory notes are in order for what follows. The foundation of this book is a survey of all, or very nearly all, the charters of early medieval Iberia, excluding Catalunya for the sake of manageability, and I should say up front that I employ the term 'Iberia' with that limited compass. In the main body I provide illustrative extracts from the texts themselves as often as possible, and as an aid to comprehension I have paraphrased each one in parentheses rather than translating directly, because (for me at least) the Latin tends often to elude precise rendering into English. In the footnotes, I cite a representative range of charters for each of my points, rather than all possible examples, simply because this would make a book which is long as is unending. It is also partly a control, as I am bound to have misinterpreted some of the charters, or missed new scholarship.

There are a number of systems of abbreviation in use for the major collections in the corpus, but I have devised my own in an attempt to offer an immediately recognisable sign for each archive as a guide to the reader. Where this short form is followed by a comma, it refers to introductory material from that edition; without a comma, it designates a document or series of documents. For the sake of economy, I employ these abbreviations to refer to the charter in its physical as well as its edited form, but in the cases where I discuss script, layout, or other material aspects of presentation in detail I have provided full archival referencing in the list of figures. For the same reason, all citations of literature are in the shortest form possible, author surname and distinguishing noun from the title, and the full entry can be consulted in the bibliography. For the sake of clarity rather than literary elegance, I have quoted the New International Version for all verses of Scripture, and the corresponding numbering (applicable to the Psalms). On the problem of proper names, in the end I have employed the modernised Spanish or Portuguese equivalent wherever there is a sizeable historiography. For all other names, including unidentified places, I use that in the document, though even this approach is bound to be inconsistent, since they are often spelled multiply within a text, leaving the nominative case, if there was one, unfathomable.

Handling such a large corpus of material inevitably poses a problem of how to present it manageably. To escape as best I can the Scylla of generalising anecdote and the Charybdis of plodding exhaustiveness, I have distilled the charters into tables and charts illustrating the main aspects which I then treat in detail. The tables are explained in the course of discussion, but the charts call for a brief introduction here. As historians we are in the business of change over time, but the charters are distributed unevenly from year to year, so to say that there is a greater number of examples of some phenomenon in one year than in another risks reflecting this distribution back at the reader without understanding what lies behind the trend. In other words, if the total number of lay charters, for instance, increases over time, this may only be the product of the total number of charters rising at that rate, rather than any social or cultural change in documentary practice. By way of correction, all graphic representations of the data in this book are given not in absolute numbers but as proportions of all charters surviving for a given year. The other distorting factor when dealing with documentation is forgery, and so each chart has three lines to convey full context. The thin solid line denotes the rate per year for genuine charters only, the thin dashed line includes false charters, and the thick solid line indicates a five-year moving average based on the annual rate for authentic charters. For clarity, however, the more complex charts comparing multiple trends show the moving average alone.

In many ways this book is the product of the effort of others; certainly my own share in it is the result of the immeasurable support which I have enjoyed over the long years of its gestation. I owe my start in the field to the inspiration of Nick Everett and Mark Meyerson in Toronto, but it was Chris Wickham who guided me through my doctorate at Oxford with his unflagging encouragement and boundless wisdom, and I had the great good fortune to benefit from the generous criticism of Wendy Davies and the late Simon Barton as thesis examiners.

In helping me to bring that initial effort to publication, I must thank my colleagues at Balliol College and St John's College, Oxford, the Institute of Historical Research, London, and the University of Lincoln, as well as the Bodleian Library, Oxford, the British Library, London, the Archivo Catedralicio de León, the Consejo Superior de Investigaciones Científicas and Archivo Histórico Nacional (AHN), Madrid, and the Arquivo Nacional da Torre do Tombo (ANTT), Lisbon. Of the many colleagues and collaborators whom I have been privileged to rely upon while writing this book, I wish particularly to thank Julio Escalona Monge and Eduardo Manzano Moreno for their welcome to Spain and their countless acts of kindness since then, as well as Álvaro Carvajal Castro, Ainoa Castro Correa, André Evangelista Marques, David Peterson, José Carlos Sánchez-Pardo, Jamie Wood, and Roger Wright for much stimulating discussion and comradeship. Above and beyond the call of duty, Roger Collins read through the final manuscript with patience and surpassing acumen. As stout yeomen of soundness, my friends Oren Margolis, Robert Portass, Matthew Walker, and George

Woudhuysen have sustained me in all things, and I am truly blessed by my parents David Barrett and Virginia Robeson, my sister Meredith, and the gift of Emma Cayley, my partner. Now and ever, they have all my gratitude, and all my love. This book is dedicated to the memory of three dearly departed mentors—Simon Barton, Mark Whittow, and Peter Linehan—whose friendship and counsel I miss no less for the passage of time.

Leeds
February 2022

# Table of Contents

# List of Figures

# Introduction

## Literacy as Textuality

The study of literacy should justify itself. What relation does the written record of the past have to the world which it seems to describe for us? Why was it made, and why does it survive? This is, or should be, the study of literacy: asking our sources the question of their own existence, and investigating how texts—and text itself—mattered. The challenge is that it can so easily become a simple survey, a catalogue of everything set down in writing, rather than a critical examination of what was written when, by and for whom, and why. Maybe a new word is needed to capture this orientation: in ordinary usage 'literacy' is the antithesis of 'illiteracy', but it can range well beyond the ability to read and write, to denote a familiarity with certain skills or knowledge. Recognising this by speaking of 'literacies' only draws out the point, that the term is an empty vessel, to be filled with cultural priorities of the moment and used to measure their attainment in society, whether past or present.[1] For as long as there have been Middle Ages, the question of literacy has been asked by the standards of Antiquity and the Renaissance, but reluctance to query the question itself has directed the search for an answer towards description and evaluation by those terms, away from definition and analysis within the sociocultural framework of the period. This keeps us in the business of measuring surface phenomena, the survival of Classical literary culture and education. What we need is a more basic enquiry, to map out the foundations. Before we can securely make use of what text we have, we must find its home in the society which produced it: the 'textuality' of that society is an index of the intersection and interaction of the written with the world.

Until recently there was little argument that medieval literacy should be understood as continuity with one aspect of the ancient world. What gauged it was the relative degree not of the ability to read and write, but of the

---

[1] Crain, 'Histories', 467–70; Grundmann, '*Litteratus*', 56–125; *cf.* Woolf, 'Literacy', 46–68.

*Text and Textuality in Early Medieval Iberia: The Written and The World, 711–1031*. Graham Barrett, Oxford University Press. © Graham Barrett 2023. DOI: 10.1093/oso/9780192895370.003.0001

cultivation of the Classics, especially by the laity. At the end of this grand tradition stands the work of Pierre Riché, delineating the decline of the urban schools of grammar and rhetoric which provided the foundation for educated culture in secular Roman society, and the subsequent rise of the monastic *schola* which retained solely those aspects of the Classical curriculum useful for studying Scripture, and confined itself to teaching the clergy and to a lesser extent a court élite. Change came through dichotomy: by the eighth century *Romanitas* had yielded to *Germanitas* and 'written civilisation had been destroyed', admittedly surviving in debased form in the monasteries but hardly meriting the name.[2] The problem here is not one of method or results; there is no point pretending that the early Middle Ages rivalled the late Republic in literary glories. The partiality of such studies is their limiting factor, the identification of literacy with one special literature. For how else to explain the economic determinism which lies behind them? Henri Pirenne had argued that bureaucratic administration by literate laymen survived the barbarian invasions, yet once the rise of Islam had 'closed the Mediterranean', bringing about the disappearance of commerce and cities, the schools which underpinned this system followed. In the Carolingian world, the clergy monopolised learning and provided such managerial skills as were needed, while the laity remained illiterate.[3] This has become a universal iron law: absent commercial and urban dynamism, clergy and laity must represent literacy and orality respectively.[4] But it is based on a limited case, in that Roman literacy, the gift of the grammarian, was both contingent on the demands of bureaucracy and served to provide the imperial élite with a shared identity, privileged because difficult to obtain without an expensive education.[5] In other words, it is a particular construction of literacy for a specific context. Should we still be thinking with the fall of Rome? Did the heirs to Rome need the same cultural tools? Did urban schools, or any schools, have a role in their literacy? Did cities or citizens? Did politics or commerce?[6]

How one answers these questions depends in large part on the type of evidence which one studies, and the major change came with a turn from literature to documentation. At the beginning of this new tradition stands

---

[2] Riché, *Education*, 495; Riché, *Écoles*, 11–46; *cf.* Thompson, *Literacy*; Marrou, *History*, 439–65.

[3] Pirenne, *Mohammed*, 118–44, 236–85.

[4] Cipolla, *Literacy*, 8, 42; Auerbach, *Language*, 23; Curtius, *Literature*, 25; Parkes, 'Literacy', 2, 556–61; Barrow, 'Churches', 127–52; Graff, 'Literacy', 12–37.

[5] Kaster, *Guardians*, 15–31; Heather, 'Literacy', 177–98.    [6] Stenger, 'Cities', 1–23.

the work of Michael Clanchy, who traced in an instant classic of historiography how the Norman kings of England secured their conquered realm through bureaucratic government, driving a greater and more general use of written records and as a by-product promoting trust in them. Oral and tactile modes—dictation, reading out loud, documentary seals—offered means by which the illiterate could participate indirectly but effectively in writing, such that personal literacy mattered less than willingness to engage with the written word. Over time, this combination of trust and access resulted in a shift from reliance on memory to documentation as the primary form of legal evidence.[7] As a case study it is revolutionary, but even more significant is the approach: literacy defined not by Classics, but by working outwards from its manifestations to motivations and meanings, subordinating the question of how much to those of what and why. Yet rather than that former tradition, the prompt came from another iron law, the technological determinism which attributed the creation of a reading public to the agency of the printing press.[8] The result is an unduly schematic contrast between the 'new literacy' of a vindicated high Middle Ages, where government reached all citizens, and the 'old literacy' guarded jealously by a religious caste. With some new actors, the model remains dichotomous, an early medieval clergy who restricted literacy versus the Norman state which generalised it by routinising authority through bureaucracy.[9]

For the centuries between the Romans and Normans, one obstacle remained the Latin language itself, assumed to be unintelligible to the lay vernaculars. But this presumption of illiteracy has been undermined by the seminal work of Roger Wright, who has argued for a broad variation amongst evolving spoken Romance dialects allied to a single conservative written standard, not unlike the continuum holding together the spoken and written registers of modern English, French, or Arabic. If Latin was the written vernacular of early medieval western Europe, texts were comprehensible when read aloud; only with archaising reforms to orthography and pronunciation by the Carolingians did writing and speaking begin to diverge in regions under their immediate influence.[10] Wholesale reappraisal of the early Middle Ages beckoned, and the first to take the lead was

---

[7] Clanchy, *Memory*.

[8] Eisenstein, *Press*, 129–59; Eisenstein, *Revolution*, 102–20; *cf.* Chaytor, *Script*, 1–4, 115–41; Febvre and Martin, *Coming*, 248–332; Clanchy, *Looking Back*, § 2.

[9] Weber, *Economy*, 1, 226–55.

[10] Wright, *Latin*; Wright, *Study*, esp. 3–17; *cf.* Banniard, *Communication*, 305–68; Böhmer, 'Literacy', 115–64.

Rosamond McKitterick, making the case that the written word was not limited to an ecclesiastical élite, but part of everyday life for the laity in the Carolingian world, even in its eastern Germanic lands where bilingualism was the norm. Government exploited documentation in administration, witnessed by a tremendous growth in the number of charters and manuscripts during the period and the many well-worn legal codices which survive; legislation cannot have been merely minutes of oral pronouncements recorded by clerics for internal use or symbols of the Roman legislative tradition. Inevitably for this field the focus came to rest on vindicating the efficacy of the state and the vitality of court culture, but the key finding is that the clergy promoted rather than constrained a wider use of texts. Charters from St Gall reveal how the monastery provided scribes for transactions taking place in its environs, and in turn how members of the laity who were not themselves literate nonetheless found it necessary to make complex social and logistical arrangements to facilitate engaging in written modes of business.[11] There was a bias for, rather than against, literacy in the early medieval period, and we should approach it with the same.

Over the past 30 years there has been a comprehensive reassessment of literacy in the early Middle Ages.[12] From the work of successive generations of scholars ready to recast the era more positively, we have learned that literacy, both literary and documentary, was less confined to cities and clerics than previously supposed, while formal distinctions drawn from legal history such as dispositive versus probative mattered less in practice. Where there was no strong pre-existing habit of recourse to text, procedures developed over time to enable and encourage use of written records by the laity; they never displaced oral forms of transaction, but instead were complementary, and equally important.[13] The need to understand how Latin could be more than an obstacle to comprehension has become apparent, and we can see how it stimulated vernacular literacy including in zones which had been marginal to the Roman world such as Ireland.[14] For periods which have traditionally been written down (or off), an overdue stock-taking of what survives and what is lost has forced a re-evaluation: even the Lombards, 'quintessential barbarians', have been cleared of blame for

---

[11] McKitterick, *Carolingians*; McKitterick, 'Latin', 135–7; McKitterick, 'Law-Books', 13–27; McKitterick, *Charlemagne*, esp. 214–380; *cf.* Wormald and Nelson (eds), *Intellectuals*.

[12] Costambeys and Innes, 'Introduction', 1–11.

[13] Smith, *Europe*, 13–50; Everett, 'Literacy', 362–85.

[14] Johnston, *Literacy*, 1–26, 157–76; *cf.* Gretsch, 'Literacy', 273–94; Gilbert and Harris, 'Word', 149–78.

terminating lay literacy in Italy, by moving beyond tabulating signatures on charters to assessing the wider utility of written law for participants in court cases, whatever their personal abilities, and the enduring epigraphic habit as a written means of self-promotion.[15] Once historians lowered their sights from Classics to charters, the mirage of an illiterate early medieval laity was bound to clear. But where do we go from here? Cataloguing uses and users of the written word has served its purpose, and anyone who now predicates a thesis on absence of evidence which may yet be discovered or reassessed does so at some risk.[16] The problem is that difficulty of transcending description, which can demonstrate little beyond presence or absence, rise or fall, however the quarry is redefined. And how can we be certain that what we have compiled is more than anecdotal? What if our conclusions are merely a shorthand for what has been preserved?

The field is at something of an impasse because it has resisted articulating a purpose for itself which is not in some sense an index of culture. Scholarship is expansive on survey but reticent when it comes to the fundamental question of why, tending to imply correlation between dynamic government and prevalent literacy, though shying away from the logical inverse; the Carolingians are the Normans of the early Middle Ages, other dynasties lesser imitations.[17] Yet when Simon Franklin looked at the high medieval birchbark letters from Novgorod, he found routine and casual literacy, scarcely the preserve of a mandarin class, more at home amidst the diversity of informal writing in the Roman world. No developed state or administration engendered this, though the environment was urban: instead, use of the written word seems simply to have been a personal choice.[18] The question remains open for discussion. One way forward has been offered by Gerd Althoff, who argued that ritual, governed by *Spielregeln* or 'rules of the game', stood in for an absence of literate capacities in Ottonian society, and urged the study of ceremony and gesture in their place.[19] Taking the cue, Marco Mostert has directed the invaluable *Utrecht Studies in Medieval Literacy* in quest of the 'relative importance' of literacy amongst other forms of communication.[20] Published volumes, however,

---

[15] Everett, *Literacy*; cf. Wickham, *Italy*, 124–7.     [16] Garrison, 'Mentality', 69–99.

[17] McKitterick (ed.), *Uses*, 319–33; Davis, *Practice*, 293–335; Britnell, 'Bureaucracy', 413–34; cf. Vessey, 'Literacy', 152–8.

[18] Franklin, 'Literacy', 1–11, 25–6, 36–8; Franklin, *Writing*, 129–86; cf. Bagnall, *Writing*, esp. 117–37.

[19] Althoff, *Family*, 136, 162–3; Althoff, *Rules*, esp. 3–15; cf. Buc, *Dangers*, 248–61.

[20] Mostert, 'Approaches', 15–37; Mostert, *Bibliography*.

have largely resisted 'attempts at rehabilitating early medieval pragmatic literacy': some inventory documentation, others trace the passage 'from memory to written record' across later medieval Europe under the influence of state formation, urbanisation, or trade.[21] There have been fascinating explorations of the entanglement of orality and literacy, but arguments that writing, speech, and ritual were 'equally valid' tools spark minimal joy.[22] Even redefined as a communicative mode, the study of literacy can so easily slip into listing literature, counting enough of the chosen cultural products to endorse a period or place. As with the renaissances being discovered in the most unpromising environments, if literacy is any writing and any writing proves literacy, what can we do with what we are doing?[23]

Like the rise of Late Antiquity in the historiography, the 'literacy industry' finds its mark everywhere, and is contented. We naturally want our own patch of history to be highly literate, because that means complexity and sophistication.[24] The mid-twentieth century saw an extraordinary debate about the 'consequences of literacy', which Jack Goody identified as the cognitive ability to distinguish past from present: Greece gave birth to logical analysis because this is predicated on widespread personal alphabetic literacy, while in those literate societies where it failed to emerge some active restriction such as a complex script or 'caste literacy' is invariably to blame.[25] The object was neutral premises for the 'rise of the West', but 'technologies of the intellect' leave little manoeuvring room for the historian; if the stated consequences seem absent, one simply identifies the limiting factor. In the Middle Ages, the subordination of literacy to religious tradition restricted the Classical golden age of a literate laity, but when it was reborn in later medieval England, all the major historical innovations in administration, the economy, and religion were 'recapitulated', going through the motions of literacy and its further consequences.[26] The technological determinism now comes across as naïve, and was driven by developments in communications media presaging the computing revolution.[27] Walter Ong pronounced 'interiorised' literacy to be 'absolutely necessary' for human consciousness to

---

[21] Adamska and Mostert (eds), *Development*, 34–6; but see *e.g.* Heidecker (ed.), *Charters*; Mostert and Barnwell (eds), *Process*; Koziol, *Politics*; Adamska and Mostert (eds), *Communication*.

[22] Egmond, *Saints*, 198–200; see Rankovic, Melve, and Mundal (eds), *Continuum*; Garrison, Orbán, and Mostert (eds), *Language*.

[23] Goody, *Renaissances*.    [24] Ward-Perkins, *Fall*, 1–10; Wickham, *Inheritance*, 3–12.

[25] Goody and Watt, 'Consequences', 33–49, 67–8; Goody, *Interface*, 105–7.

[26] Goody, *Domestication*, 16–18, 146–7; Goody, *Logic*, 176.

[27] Thomas, *Literacy*, 16–18; Cole and Cole, 'Rethinking', 305–24.

reach its 'fuller potentials', and coined the term 'residual orality' to describe transitional societies such as the Middle Ages in which writing took place in an oral psychological setting, memorised and recycled back into a world of speech.[28] Yet behind the pseudo-science is the familiar, inescapable association of literacy with development.

The assumption underlying 'consequences' is that literacy plays a fixed, independent role in society. Scholars have in the past made much of mixed idioms like 'the Bible says', or the survival of oral formulaic poetry, or persistent reliance on memory, as indices of relative literacy in medieval Europe, as if conventions of speech and cultural practices can be mapped straightforwardly onto cognitive states.[29] Insofar as these have been explored by experiment, however, any observable mental change is a function not of literacy itself, but of the specific form of schooling in it: agency lies with the uses made of the technology, rather than with the technology itself.[30] We might formulate these as 'autonomous' and 'ideological' models; any given tool offers constraints and opportunities, but how they are dealt with is the business of social organisation, and technology, far from neutral, is the product of human actions, social and cultural processes which shape its forms and functions.[31] If the nature of a medium acts to structure its surroundings through the arrangements put in place to use it, the 'message' of the written word becomes the means of its usage, rather than any signifier of development.[32] How did medieval society use the written word? The consequences follow from the how, not from the written word; its historical study is an enquiry into sociocultural organisation. When literacy is looked at in this way, orality and memory are components of the measures which enabled its employment. One need not agree with Michael Richter that writing in the early Middle Ages was nothing but an artificial clerical gloss on a world of speech to recognise a valuable warning against assuming the accessibility or representativeness of text.[33]

No one can seriously argue that a majority, or even a sizeable minority, could read and write in the period. Beyond reading and writing, social memory provided the means to retain information and commemorate the

---

[28] Ong, *Orality*, 7–15.
[29] O'Brien O'Keeffe, *Song*, 4–22, 191–2; Carruthers, *Book*, 1–17, 274–337; cf. Camille, 'Seeing', 27–8.
[30] Scribner and Cole, *Psychology*, esp. 113–60; Olson, 'Tradition', 289–304.
[31] Street, *Literacy*, 65, 96; Finnegan, *Literacy*, 6–12, 175–8; Chartier, *Forms*, 6–24; Treharne and Willan, *Text Technologies*, 1–31.
[32] McLuhan, *Media*, 7–21.
[33] Richter, *Formation*, 45–77; Richter, *Tradition*; cf. Richter, 'Word', 103–19.

past, but when we explore how it functioned as a counterpart to text, we realise that both recalling and speaking were in constant contact with reading and writing, and mutually influential.[34] If oral and literate modes complemented each other, the question becomes how they were integrated—through what intermediary actors in possession of the necessary skills, through what processes of dialogue—rather than which of them mattered more. The most illuminating recent studies have consequently been those not focussed on literacy as such, but on the situation of literacy, or textuality: which seek a home for the written word in specific contexts of use, such as the settlement of disputes, the control and management of land, gift-giving and the creation of relationships, or the continuous but changing archival practices of the laity. Whereas the predominance of ecclesiastical estates in the documentary record has customarily been taken to reflect a clerical monopoly of literacy, and the use of oral procedures in court cases as proof of the decline of lay literacy, the work of the 'Bucknell Group' especially has elucidated how written evidence nonetheless played a key role for all parties in defending ownership and resolving differences, as it had in the late Roman world.[35] Wherever we encounter argument we find documentation introduced by oral and ritual processes, read aloud, sworn on oath, often proving decisive. The old opposition of laity and clergy has come in for a rethink, in a world before the Gregorian Reform where the interests and actions of both were entangled in the affairs of a proprietary Church.[36]

What remains is to move from the particular to the general, to think through what role literacy played in a whole society, and how that society shaped itself to it. Yet before we do so, we need to step back and decentre the actual, physical presence of text from the study of its usage. One of the most fruitful insights into medieval literacy is the model of the 'textual community', first formulated by Brian Stock to describe certain heretical movements in the later Middle Ages. This refers to groups whose thoughts and actions were founded on their reading of a particular set of texts or, absent the texts themselves, the guidance of a 'literate interpreter' who enabled the group to internalise them.[37] Supposedly this social configuration could not have existed in earlier centuries because of lesser literacy,

---

[34] Fentress and Wickham, *Memory*, 145–6, 170–2; Innes, 'Memory', 5–34.

[35] Davies and Fouracre (eds), *Settlement*, 212–14; Davies and Fouracre (eds), *Property*, 251–60, 266–71; Davies and Fouracre (eds), *Languages*, 242–7, 254–61; *cf.* Brown *et al.* (eds), *Culture*, 363–76.

[36] Wood, *Church*, esp. 851–82; Nelson, 'Review', 355–74; *cf.* Hamilton, *Church*, esp. 60–118.

[37] Stock, *Implications*, 3–49, 522–3; *cf.* Biller and Hudson (eds), *Heresy*.

but the evidence given for that is the probative rather than dispositive role of charters; if a text need not be involved, at least first-hand, surely what must matter is whether the written word can be demonstrated to have been accepted into the framework for social behaviour, and how it then operated in practice.[38] More simply, the 'textual community' is a model for the integration of literacy and orality. The written word was communicated and disseminated via speech, whatever the type of text; medieval writing often had public recital as well as private reading in mind.[39] Once we grant the coexistence of primary and secondary or first-hand and second-hand literacy, a text can be accessed not only by a literate but also by an illiterate through a literate: assessing who 'read' what and how is crucial to understanding the full meaning of the written record.[40] If text can serve to frame behaviour – 'acting textually' – regardless of immediate presence, channels to text become one part of the sociocultural study of literacy as textuality.

This is not remotely intended as a comprehensive survey of a vast literature, merely to chart the idiosyncratic course of reading which has led to the present study.[41] For the 'textual community' as stated does not go far enough. The import of social memory is that a 'literate interpreter' need not personally have been literate to transmit an originally written code to a group: once the first transmission of the text took place, its content could be communicated amongst illiterates thereafter—spoken, internalised, recalled. Literacy can be tertiary in the sense that the rules of a text can be operative at several removes from the text itself, even if the literal content of that text has been attenuated over the course of its dissemination. How many actions in modern life are governed by our vague sense of what is provided or required by some written law? Can we even be sure why we think so? Yet how can we truly assess the significance of the written word without taking this full reach into account? One step in the right direction is to let go of the singularity of text. The linguistic turn in philosophy gave us the term 'intertextuality' to describe the state of each text being a product of other texts, a transposition of their systems of signs into one of its own. The reader is the space where all references to other texts which constitute a given text are interpreted; whatever the authorial intention, the reader constructs the meaning of a text by recognising and acknowledging a

---

[38]   Haines-Eitzen, 'Communities', 246–53; Klausmann, 'Communities', 71–88.

[39]   Green, 'Orality', 277; Green, *Listening*, esp. 270–315; Saenger, *Space*, 1–17; O'Brien O'Keeffe, 'Listening', 17–36.

[40]   Bäuml, 'Varieties', 237–47; Schaefer, 'Orality', 287–311.

[41]   Briggs, 'Literacy', 397–420; Melve, 'Literacy', 143–97; McKitterick, 'Charters', 22–67.

combination of codes residing within its intertextuality.[42] The point in plain English is that we shall still miss the full scope of literacy even if we extend our horizon to the written word in primary, secondary, and tertiary modes of access and use. What other texts gave each text its total meaning—and how? Texts circulated not only in copies, and through reading aloud, and by retention in memory, but also as intertextualities: as quotations, citations, allusions, a network of texts contributing to the signification of each individual text. Only by identifying the sources involved and tracing the connections amongst them can we go beneath the surface to map the underlying written structure of society.

## The Case Study

This essay in the study of textuality focusses on the Christian kingdoms of Asturias-León and Navarra, which I have chosen because of their rich but still underexploited source material. When Muslim invaders conquered the Visigothic kingdom in 711, the northern third or quarter of the Peninsula was left to go its own way, and soon became home to independent polities (see Appendix 1).[43] Traditionally, simplistically, this began with the legendary battle of Covadonga (718/22), where freedom fighter 'Don' Pelayo confronted a punishment detail of 'Moors' despatched from al-Andalus in the south, and in victory took the first step in eight centuries of *Reconquista*, culminating in the reconquest of Granada in 1492.[44] In reality, his kingdom of Asturias was a modest and local affair, safe in the fastness of the Cantabrian Mountains, and only came into its own under Alfonso II (791–842), who expanded west and south into Galicia and eastwards into the Basque Country. His successors, notably Alfonso III (866–910), made further inroads into Muslim-held as well as autonomous territory, and by the reign of Fruela II (924–25) the kingdom was based at León, below the mountains on the edge of the Meseta Central plateau and the Duero River basin. To the east, meanwhile, the county of Castilla was developing under intermittent royal oversight as a militarised frontier facing al-Andalus. Beginning with Fernán González (931/32–70), its counts began to be

---

[42] Barthes, 'Work', 155–64; Barthes, 'Theory', 31–47; *cf.* Kristeva, *Desire*, 36–63; Martínez Alfaro, 'Intertextuality', 268–85.

[43] Collins, *Conquest*; Isla Frez, *Edad*; Collins, *Caliphs*; Portass, 'Spain', 176–225.

[44] Linehan, *History*, 1–21, 95–127; Kosto, 'Reconquest', 93–116; García-Sanjuán, 'Conquest', 185–96.

increasingly assertive in their independence, but for the moment they remained one more ambitious regional aristocracy amongst many.[45] Farther east still, in the foothills of the Pyrenees, Charlemagne had established a Carolingian presence from 778 which developed into the Catalan counties of the 'Spanish March', but amidst their struggles with al-Andalus, a Basque chieftain named Íñigo Arista came to power in Pamplona by the 820s. In the early tenth century, this kingdom of Navarra emerged fully from Muslim overlordship as the eastern counterpart to León.[46]

With military, political, and dynastic vicissitudes, the configuration remained broadly stable until the collapse of the Islamic caliphate based at Córdoba in 1031. This transformed the geopolitical situation fundamentally, fracturing al-Andalus into a constellation of *taifa* or 'faction' statelets and altering the calculus of Christian reconquest; six years later, by killing his brother-in-law, Fernando I (1037–65) created a new entity of León-Castilla.[47] As such, the early medieval centuries from 711 to 1031 are readily delimited as a discrete period of study, but they present an unusual profile in terms of primary sources.[48] For narrative we are reliant on two versions of a chronicle running from the accession of the Visigothic king Wamba in 672 to the death of the Asturian king Ordoño I in 866, seemingly emanating from the courts of the sons of Alfonso III in the 910s, and from a generation earlier the related chronicle, or more accurately miscellany, of Albelda, produced perhaps in La Rioja; one prominent feature which all three share is an ideology of the ruling dynasty of Asturias-León as the successors to and ultimately the foreordained restorers of the Visigothic kingdom.[49] Essentially that is all until Sampiro, royal notary, picked up the narrative thread with his own chronicle early in the eleventh century, while for the county of Castilla and the kingdom of Navarra we have only the most skeletal of notes in sundry genealogies and annals of around the same date.[50] In the genre of theology there are the *opera* of Beatus of the Liébana (d. 800?), an outlier from the late eighth century: his interventions in the

---

[45] Estepa Díez, 'Castilla', 261–78; Escalona and Reyes, 'Change', 153–83.

[46] Larrea Conde, 'Reino', 279–308.

[47] Wasserstein, *Rise*; Scales, *Fall*; Viñayo González, *Fernando*; García-Sanjuán, 'Replication', 64–85.

[48] Díaz y Díaz, *Index*, 101–95; Martín, *Sources*, esp. 142–67; Codoñer (ed.), *Hispania*, esp. 227–95.

[49] Gil Fernández, Moralejo, and Ruiz de la Peña, *Crónicas*, 113–88; Bonnaz, 'Aspects', 81–99; Isla, 'Monarchy', 41–56; Besga Marroquín, *Orígenes*, 433–44; Barrett, 'Hispania', 81–6; see now Gil, *Chronica*, 383–484.

[50] Pérez de Urbel, *Sampiro*, 275–346; Martín, '*Annales*', 206–12; Lacarra, 'Textos', 204–65; see now Estévez Sola, *Chronica*, 177–95.

controversy over the Adoptionist heresy and his mammoth commentary on Revelation, which lived on in a heritage of exquisitely illustrated manuscripts.[51] There is also a handful of hagiography, some contemporary, some late antique in subject, and a wealth of liturgical texts in the Visigothic-Mozarabic tradition.[52] Deserving greater study too is a small but significant number of inscriptions.[53] Ironically, however, the largest body of Latin literary sources comes from al-Andalus, where in the mid-ninth century the martyrs of Córdoba and their circle exchanged letters, attempted poetry, and wrote bleak polemics denouncing cultural assimilation and its consequences for their language.[54]

In contrast to the Visigoths, who issued laws, compiled codes, held Church councils, and promulgated canons with gay abandon, neither Asturias-León nor Navarra has left us any original normative sources until the very end of the period. What does survive is a remarkable corpus of four thousand Latin charters, mainly recording land transactions, distributed highly unevenly across Galicia and Portugal in the west, Castilla, Navarra, La Rioja, and Aragón in the east, and between them Asturias, León, and Cantabria. The Catalan counties lie outside the bounds of this case study, a distinct cultural space looking northwards to Francia, but they would add another six thousand charters or more, and there are many points of comparison.[55] Foremost is the simple fact that, in both regions, diplomatic material accounts for by far the majority of the written evidence from the early Middle Ages; one cannot easily fall back on literature as a proxy for 'literacy'. In one sense, it is altogether inaccurate to call this corpus from Asturias-León and Navarra underexploited, in that it has provided a foundation for rich traditions of scholarship in socioeconomic history and linguistics. Yet when the charters have been studied rather than used as sources, they have typically been examined through the focal lens of 'pure' palaeography or diplomatic, necessary and valuable but (at least for

---

[51] Löfstedt, *Elipandum*; Gryson and Bièvre, *Tractatus*; Sáenz-López Pérez, *Maps*; Williams, *Visions*.

[52] Fábrega Grau, *Pasionario*; Riesco Chueca, *Pasionario*; Zapke (ed.), *Hispania*; see now Yarza Urquiola, *Passionarium*.

[53] García Lobo and Martín López, 'Inscripciones', 87–108; Pereira García, 'Epigrafía', 267–302; see *e.g.* Diego Santos, *Inscripciones*; Azkarate Garai-Olaun and García Camino, *Estelas*; Barroca, *Epigrafia*; Pérez González, 'Latín', 341–84.

[54] Gil, *Corpus*; Millet-Gérard, *Chrétiens*; Herrera Roldán, *Cultura*; see now Gil, *Scriptores*.

[55] Zimmermann, *Écrire*; Bowman, *Landmarks*, 1–29, 228–47; Kosto, *Agreements*, 268–94; Jarrett, 'Comparing', 89–126; Chandler, *Catalonia*, 1–23; *cf.* Tischler, 'Carolingian', 111–33.

historians) auxiliary approaches.[56] What I intend to pursue here is the sociocultural history of the corpus of documentation, by posing three basic questions: what there is, how it relates to the world around it, and to what degree each element of it intersects and interacts with other texts.

What then is the context from which these charters emerged? Looking back, scholars have long recognised the Romanised literary and legal culture of the Visigothic kingdom, its learned bishops and its aspirations to bureaucracy, but until recently this was the view from the top, a normative portrait painted by laws and canons telling us how it ought to be.[57] There are few surviving documents from the period: five parchment originals, all very incomplete, and six later copies, three in medieval books and three from the sixteenth century.[58] However, since the discovery and publication (still ongoing) of the *pizarras* or 'slates', some 163 more or less fragmentary texts and uncounted numerical inscriptions scattered across the northern Meseta, we have a complementary view from ground level, and can see varied uses made of the written word for land management, legal affairs, elementary education, and in devotional practice throughout the sixth and seventh centuries, essentially in the middle of nowhere.[59] While much about these slates remains debated, they should at least force us to reconsider the institutionalisation of literacy: despite no evidence for formal schools in the area, a basic and broadly diffused access to the written word clearly obtained, and the inhabitants of one corner of the post-imperial world were able to maintain it in ordinary and everyday usage.[60] Literary culture may have relied on urban schools, but literacy could evidently exist and endure in the absence of those structures. And indeed, if the collapse of the Roman state had no 'automatic' effect on literacy, why should that other great historiographical caesura, the Muslim conquest of 711, have been any different?[61] We should presume neither continuity nor discontinuity in using the written word, decouple its history from high politics, and let the

---

[56] Mendo Carmona, *Escritura*, esp. 1, 219–348; Mendo Carmona, 'Escritura', 179–210; *cf.* Castillo Gómez and Sáez, 'Paleografía', 133–68; Sáez and Castillo Gómez, 'Signo', 155–68.

[57] Riché, *Education*, 246–65, 274–9, 281–2, 285–90, 293–303, 352–60; Collins, 'Literacy', 114–18; Díaz and Valverde, 'Strength', 59–93; *cf.* Handley, *Death*, 166–80.

[58] See *ChLA* 114, 1–5; Corcoran, 'Donation', 215–21; Tomás-Faci and Martín-Iglesias, 'Documentos', 261–86; Tomás-Faci, 'Transmission', 303–14; Martin and Larrea (eds), *Chartes*.

[59] Velázquez Soriano, *Pizarras*; see Velázquez Soriano, 'Pizarras', 129–32; Velázquez Soriano, 'Cultura', 185–95, 208–9; Collins, *Visigothic Spain*, 170–3; Wickham, *Framing*, 223–6; Velázquez Soriano, 'Ardesie', 31–45; Fernández Cadenas, 'Review', 1–27.

[60] Akinnaso, 'Schooling', esp. 78–82; Barrett, 'Librarian', 44–53.

[61] Davies, 'Ages', 70; Hillgarth, *Visigoths*, 57–81; *cf.* Wright, 'Latin', 35–54.

evidence guide us to how, when, and why the need for it or the means of accessing it changed over time.

Studies of literacy in early medieval Iberia are broadly in agreement on a high degree of continuity from the Visigothic period. In a series of pioneering essays, Roger Collins has argued that although the clergy were responsible for the writing, the laity made active use of charters, while lay judges referred regularly to their working copies of the Visigothic code in court cases.[62] These conclusions have been definitively drawn out by Wendy Davies, who in two milestones of scholarship demonstrates the significant incidence of peasants and peasant communities as actors in the documentation, and probes how disputes were managed in the absence of a strong state or clear jurisdictions by courts and actors relying on shared norms and procedures derived from Visigothic law.[63] The same elements are reflected too in a range of identifiable lay archives, speaking to the continuing utility of the written record long after the moment of its creation.[64] There otherwise remains, however, a tendency in the literature to survey the sources before veering off into education and literary culture.[65] Where charters are kept in focus, the question of when has been broached, an increasing use over time, but only outline thoughts on how and why have been hazarded, a nebulous feudalisation in which the written word aided the growth of seigneurial power.[66] This is to confuse what is recorded in charters—transactions and relationships—with the decision to record them in written form. Both accepting a textual way of doing things and choosing which texts to employ are cultural decisions; both arranging to use texts and determining how textually to act in a given context are social processes. There is yet much scope here for a study of literacy as textuality, asking whether documentation mattered, and if so, how and why. By thinking socioculturally we can realise not a rule but particularities: moments when writing seemed advantageous, systems to enable access, fragments of text framing discourse and action. In what follows, by tracing the lifecycle of charters and the network

---

[62] Collins, 'Visigothic Law', 85–104; Collins, 'Law', 489–512; Collins, 'Literacy', 122–33; Collins, *Law*, §§ V–VI, XV; Collins, *Early Medieval Spain*, 241–3, 252–63.

[63] Davies, *Acts*, esp. 189–213; Davies, *Windows*; see now Davies, *Spain*.

[64] Mendo Carmona, *Escritura*, 1, 145–59; Kosto, 'Practices', 259–82.

[65] Alturo Perucho, 'Sistema', 31–61; Quilis Merín, 'Lectura', 162–9; Díaz y Díaz, 'Cultura literaria', 195–204; Casado de Otaola, 'Escribir', 113–77; Sánchez Prieto, 'Aprender', 3–34; Calleja-Puerta, 'Notas', 16–21; *cf.* García Andreva, 'Enseñanza', 473–506.

[66] Casado de Otaola, 'Cultura', 35–55; Sierra Macarrón, 'Escritura', 249–74; Sierra Macarrón, 'Aumento', 2, 119–31; Sierra Macarrón, 'Producción', 99–120.

of texts in which they were embedded, I hope to convey a sense of the textuality of early medieval Iberia, its inscription in the written word.[67]

The study of literacy should be the study of textuality—the biography of text. What did it do, what uses of the written word are revealed by or can be inferred from the surviving material, and what factors may have determined that role for it? All these functions represent what was made possible by the ability to use the written word, and therefore how that ability shaped the structures of society. We must ascertain what constituted access, be it personal literacy of some kind or contact with literates, then who had access and how they gained and exercised their access, to complement an image of the functions of the written word with an idea of its functioning. We must map mental landscapes: to what degree were users of texts conversant with and shaped by other texts and norms originating in texts? Here I treat the corpus of charters as a text, to ask of it the basic historical questions of author, audience, composition, and sources: a mantra of how, who, where, when, what, and why. The closest comparison is to 'paperwork studies', querying the basic fact of a mass of writing and its relation to the world around it.[68] What did text want, and how did it get it?[69] The study of literacy matters because it seeks to understand why literacy mattered: the role of the written word in the workings of society, what was done with it and by whom, how attitudes were formed and actions framed by it—how the presence of this technology ramified in society.[70] If our entrance into the past is a portal of partial and scattered texts, even to peer through we must first see how they lived in their environs, how they shaped and were shaped by them.[71] This interface between the written and the world is a point of departure into what lies behind and beyond the text.

[67] Bertrand, *Documenting*, 5–14, 23–79, 273–329.
[68] Kafka, *Demon*, esp. 9–18; Gitelman, *Knowledge*, 1–20; *cf.* Bedos-Rezak, 'Sources', 313–43; Chartier, *Inscription*, vii–xii.
[69] Mitchell, *Pictures*, 28–56.
[70] Olson, *World*, esp. 257–82; Olson, 'Literacy', 385–403.
[71] Chastang, 'Archéologie', 245–69; *cf.* Chartier, 'Monde', 1505–20.

# PART I

# THE LIFECYCLE

I looked again, and there before me was a flying scroll. He asked me, 'What do you see?' I answered, 'I see a flying scroll, twenty cubits long and ten cubits wide.' And he said to me, 'This is the curse that is going out over the whole land; for according to what it says on one side, every thief will be banished, and according to what it says on the other, everyone who swears falsely will be banished. The Lord Almighty declares, "I will send it out, and it will enter the house of the thief and the house of anyone who swears falsely by my name. It will remain in that house and destroy it completely, both its timbers and its stones."'

Zechariah 5:1–4

# 1

# Archival Voices

The lifecycle of the charters has yet to run its course. Early medieval birth gave way to centuries of changing hands, passage from archive to archive, until their only homes were ecclesiastical and state institutions. The decisive moment in this process came only with the *Desamortización* or 'Dissolution': all monasteries in Spain, though not the cathedrals, were dissolved by law in 1835–7, their property expropriated, and their collections of charters, cartularies, and codices eventually transferred to the Archivo Histórico Nacional at Madrid (founded in 1866), or else gathered in regional or local repositories, with many lost in transit or to simple neglect.[1] The similar process begun a year earlier in Portugal was carried out with considerably greater efficiency, centralising monastic archives at the Arquivo Nacional da Torre do Tombo in Lisbon (an institution dating back to 1378), though again not without losses.[2] Transmission of this material from past to present has quieted many of the voices which originally spoke through it, and we must try to hear them anew. The charters record interactions between thousands of granters and recipients, and if we group those delivered to the same recipients we can reconstruct hundreds of early medieval archives—institutional and personal, ecclesiastical and lay—now subsumed into barely two dozen major cathedral or monastic collections which together constitute almost the whole of the corpus. Many charters too were issued to individuals attested only once, pointing to an expansive hinterland beyond what remains; but all survive because they were incorporated into one of those ecclesiastical archives, a concentration and distillation largely complete by the high Middle Ages.

Prior to the 'Dissolution', there had already been three other decisive moments in the transmission of the charters which reflect and affect the content and form of what has been preserved.[3] The first, of course, came

---

[1] Hevia Ballina (ed.), *Desamortización*; Campos y Fernández de Sevilla (ed.), *Desamortización*; Cruz Herranz, 'Sección', 373–432; Cruz Herranz, *Archivo*, 267–84; cf. Martí Bonet (ed.), *Guía*.

[2] Silveira, 'Desamortización', 29–60; Linehan, *España*, 'Introduction'.

[3] See Geary, *Phantoms*, 177–81; Bouchard, *Rewriting*, 9–86.

*Text and Textuality in Early Medieval Iberia: The Written and The World, 711–1031.* Graham Barrett, Oxford University Press. © Graham Barrett 2023. DOI: 10.1093/oso/9780192895370.003.0002

after each scribe had written out each text, when it was handed over to the beneficiary for archiving; a sizeable minority of the charters survive as parchment originals, despite many subsequent changes of hands. But the majority are extant as copies in manuscript cartularies, firstly of the late eleventh or twelfth century, compiled amidst political and cultural crisis in León-Castilla, when safeguarding title to property was paramount for religious institutions. The balance exist only as extracts or summaries in paper indices, prepared in the seventeenth or eighteenth century during a period of archival reform and reorganisation. Collectively this process is one not only of transmission, however, but also of concentration and distillation. Criteria of selection and transcription applied at these moments condition the corpus: what to retain, what to copy, what to register, what to discard or destroy, each answer to each question has bequeathed to us a partial history. The Church and its lands are the main concerns of our charters, because the Church is what has endured, and its agents have winnowed down the documents in reflection of its priorities and interests; we have to reimagine the textuality of that time with respect for all these limits.[4] In defining the corpus of charters for study, I have cast the widest possible net, to control by comparison and contrast for particularities which can distort the overall picture, and vagaries which can frustrate understanding a single text taken on its own. In short, this is a study of all surviving (and published) charters from early medieval Iberia between 711 and 1031.

## The Corpus

The challenge in any investigation of literacy is to balance survey and anecdote, the macroscopic overview with the microscopic analysis. To that end I have assembled a corpus of all major archival collections from the period, with many minor additions (see Figure 1.1).[5] This comprehensive treatment of the material is frustratingly less normal than it ought to be; with a handful of distinguished exceptions, scholars ordinarily take into account the full range of documentation from

---

[4] Mendo Carmona, 'Cartulario', 119–37; Sáez, 'Origen', 12–15; Herrero de la Fuente, 'Cartularios', 111–52; Sánchez Mairena, 'Propuestas', 1, 217–30; Calleja-Puerta, 'Cartularios', 187–97; Cruz Herranz, 'Archivo', 177–230; Escalona, 'Cartularios, memoria', 163–203; Agúndez San Miguel and García de Cortázar, 'Cartularios', 211–27.

[5] García de Cortázar, Munita, and Fortún (eds), *CODIPHIS*; Malalana Ureña, *Año*, 2, 185–204; Martín, *Sources*, 252–62.

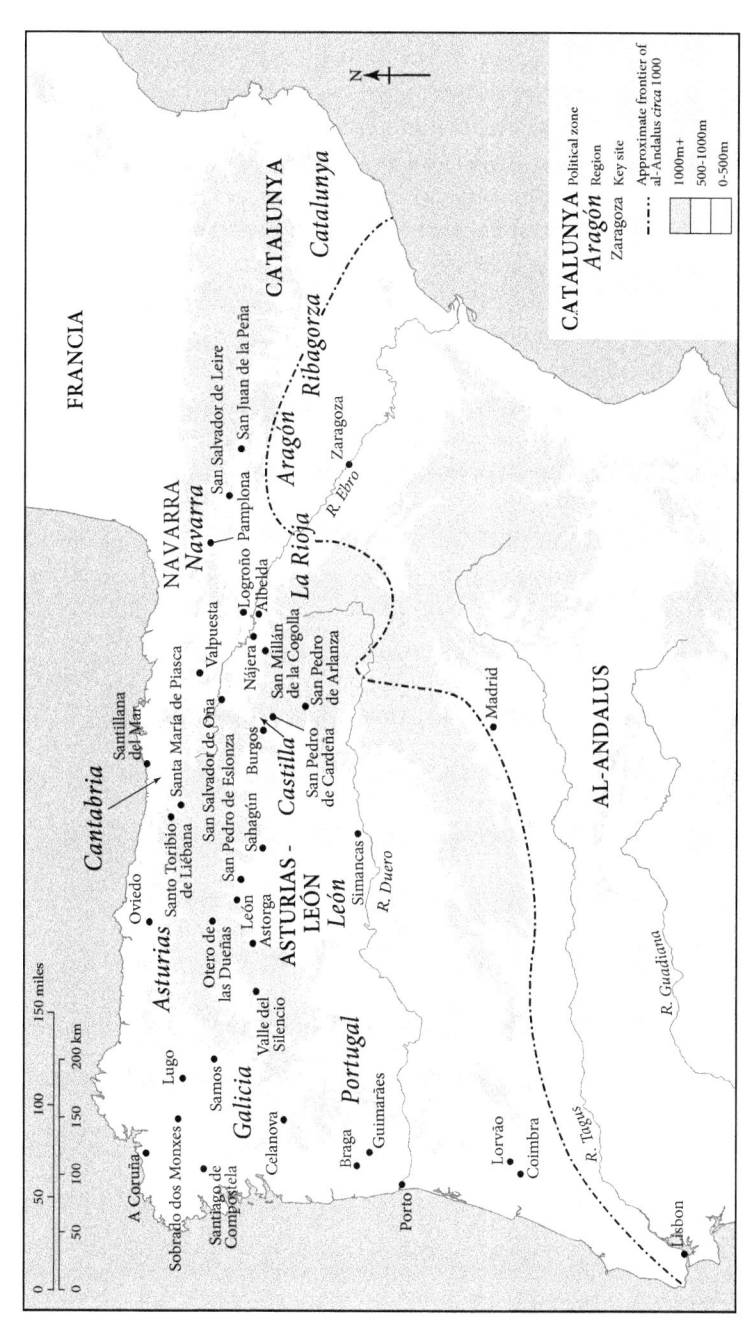

**Figure 1.1** Major Archival Collections and Repositories for Early Medieval Iberia

Asturias-León and Navarra only in dealing with royal diplomas or the origins of Spanish.[6] In the nearly two centuries since the *Desamortización*, cataloguing and editing of charters from early medieval Iberia have proceeded fitfully and unevenly, but now near completion, if not perfection.[7] The problem for the student or scholar approaching this material for the first time is the high bar to entry: there is no single critical introduction to the corpus as a whole, and few translations to provide any apprenticeship in texts which are often difficult.[8] Characteristically, publication is also highly regionalised, varying widely in date, method, quality, and coverage from archive to archive; a not trivial number of charters from Galicia, Portugal, and Castilla still await publication.[9] But what we now have in print is at least 95% of what there is, barring major new finds. For ease of reference and as a tool for comparison, I have organised these archives by geography into three groups (see Figure 1.2). The only real difficulty of delimitation arises in the east, which blurs into Catalunya. Charters from Aragón intermittently use Frankish regnal dating, looking to the Carolingian world, but since those from the Ribagorza region do so consistently, I treat that as the eastern boundary of the corpus.[10] What

| West | Centre | East |
| --- | --- | --- |
| Galicia | Asturias | Aragón |
| Portugal | Cantabria | Castilla |
| | León | La Rioja |
| | | Navarra |

**Figure 1.2**  Regional Groupings of Archives and Charters

[6]  *Floriano*, 1, 17–18; Bastardas Parera, *Particularidades*, xxxiii–xxxix; Menéndez Pidal, *Orígenes*, xii–xv; *cf.* Davies, *Acts*, 22–6; Davies, *Windows*, 10–17.

[7]  García de Cortázar, Munita, and Fortún (eds), *CODIPHIS*, 19–86; Ruiz de la Peña Solar and Sanz Fuentes, 'Instrumentos', 781–9; Díaz de Bustamante, 'Trabajos', 2, 349–64; Calleja-Puerta *et al.*, 'Edición', 205–9.

[8]  Carvajal Castro, Marques, Barrett, *et al.*, 'Approach', 1–18; see *e.g.* González and Tejada y Ramiro, *Colección*, 3, 18–84; Rodríguez Muñoz, García Leal, and López Álvarez, *Colección*, 1, 95–119, 131–44, 149–53; Barrett, 'Book', 251–4.

[9]  Castro, *Colección*, 9–16; Marques, 'Inventário', 1, 705–18; Peterson, 'Estratos', 217–18; Boullón Agrelo, 'Edición', 79–81; *cf.* Pérez González, 'Edición', 1017–39.

[10]  Serrano y Sanz, *Noticias*; Abadal y Vinyals, *Comtats*; Martín Duque, *Obarra*; Corral Lafuente, *Alaón*; Ubieto Arteta, *Obarra*; Grau Quiroga, *Roda*; Tomás-Faci, *Montañas*, esp. 23–107. I also exclude papal bulls from the corpus, since the only authentic examples from this period pertain to Catalunya: see Kehr, *Papsturkunden*; Berger *et al.*, *Papsturkunden*; Mansilla, *Documentación*; Berger and Domínguez Sánchez, *Iberia*.

follows is a preliminary 'texts and transmission' for the documentation of early medieval Iberia, describing what we have and how it has reached us.[11]

## Centre: Asturias

The early kingdom of Asturias had its capital, if that is the right word for what was in effect a petty statelet in the process of inventing itself, first at Cangas de Onís, then at Pravia, and finally at Oviedo from the reign of Alfonso II (791–842).[12] The cathedral of San Salvador stood from 812 as the episcopal see of Oviedo, and its archive has consequently invited much critical attention for what light it can cast upon these formative centuries.[13] Many of the most celebrated documents, including multiple bulls from a Pope John purporting to raise the city to metropolitan status, are problematic, if not outright falsifications; the 'great' forger-bishop Pelayo of Oviedo (1098/1102–30, 1142–3) discarded, improved, or rewrote much in his turbulent career.[14] The relevant holdings include a set of parchments, beginning with a charter of one Fakilo from 803, amongst the earliest originals surviving from the period, and the testament of Alfonso II, a curious tenth-century copy written on the first half of a manuscript of eight folios, apparently the start of some aborted compilation.[15] There are also two cartularies, the more important of which is the *Liber Testamentorum*, a codex of 113 folios and 84 charters, primarily donations, from 812 to 1118; it was written around the latter date by two hands in Visigothic script and adorned with noted miniatures of the royal donors. Bishop Pelayo was responsible for its genesis, seeking supporting documentation for the independence and pre-eminence of his see, hence the copyists transcribed their sources with little fidelity, altering language, form, and content.[16] The second Oviedo cartulary is the deluxe *Regla Colorada*, a manuscript of 158 folios written in a Gothic

---

[11] See Reynolds (ed.), *Texts*; for reasons of space I shall limit myself here to describing only those archival collections of at least 20 charters.

[12] On Asturias see Sanz Fuentes and Calleja-Puerta, *Escrito*; García Leal, 'Documentación', 2, 73–154.

[13] Castro Valdés and Ríos González, 'Origen', esp. 67–84; González González, 'Ciudad', 363–87.

[14] *Oviedo*, vii–viii; Zimmermann, *Papsturkunden*, 1, 6; *Documentación*, 98–101; Floriano Llorente, 'Crítica', 1, 69–80; Valdés Gallego, 'Donación', 243–55; Deswarte, 'Metrópoli', 153–66.

[15] Rodríguez Díaz, 'Notas', 71–8; Sanz Fuentes, 'Documento', 1, 32; García Arias and Miranda Duque, *Documentos*, 7–8; *ChLA* 114, 25.

[16] Fernández Conde, *Libro*, 81–8, 373–6; Rodríguez Díaz *et al.*, *Liber*, 1, 13–143; Valdés Gallego, *Liber*, 29–56, 435–42; Henriet and Sirantoine, 'Église', 172–88.

bookhand around 1384 by Juan Rubio, a cleric; all but one of its nine early medieval texts are forgeries.[17] To these may now be added eight archival notices from a late eighteenth-century inventory, bare summaries of documents long since lost.[18] In total the collection amounts to 53 charters from 803 to 1031, but most of this is a veil drawn by Bishop Pelayo over the earlier history of Oviedo and Asturias.

The monastery of San Vicente de Oviedo seems to pre-date the cathedral by at least a generation, but its foundational charter of 781 survives in a twelfth-century interpolated copy, making it hard to be sure. When Alfonso II rebuilt the episcopal church in 812, the monastery was incorporated into its walls: tenth-century charters call San Vicente *ante altares* (literally, 'before the altars') of San Salvador, and it did not consistently have its own abbot, implying dependency akin to that of San Paio de Anteltares on Santiago de Compostela.[19] The archive is modest in size: with no cartulary, its early medieval holdings run to 30 parchments, now held at the monastery of San Pelayo de Oviedo, which preserve 30 charters ranging in date from 781 to 1028.[20] As the majority of them are originals, the collection offers a valuable authentic counterweight to the larger, more renowned, but more problematic cathedral archive.[21]

## Cantabria

To the east of Asturias, mountainous Cantabria was bound up with its earliest history through the person of Alfonso I (739–57), supposedly the son of a royal 'Duke Pedro' of the Cantabrians.[22] The monastery of Santo Toribio de Liébana offers the main documentation for the region: though traditionally founded by Santo Toribio of Astorga in the fifth century, nothing certain is known of its origins, and it first appears in the early ninth century under the name of San Martín de Turieno, retaining this dedication into the eleventh.

---

[17] Rodríguez Díaz, *Regla*, 3–6, 83–5, 145–51, 272–3.

[18] Calleja-Puerta, 'Noticias', 541–70.

[19] Sanz Fuentes, 'Lenguaje', 1, 126–8, 151–2; Calleja-Puerta and Sanz Fuentes, 'Fundaciones', 9–41; Castro Valdés and Ríos González, 'Origen', esp. 60–7.

[20] *San Vicente*, 8–13; Serrano, *Vicente*, vii–xiii, 13–15; García Arias and Miranda Duque, *Documentos*, 8, 12; *cf.* Jennings, *Study*.

[21] For Asturias, noting the number of early medieval charters in parentheses, see also *Corniana* (1); *Obona* (6); *San Pelayo* (1); *Vermudo III* (1 (no. 5)); Floriano, *Belmonte* (1); García Leal, *Monasterio* (1); García Leal, *Registro* (1); Pérez Rodríguez, 'Aspecto', 527–46 (1).

[22] Escalona, 'Memories', 223–62; on Cantabria see García de Cortázar (ed.), *Memoria*; Grijuela Gil, 'María', 75–104; Portass, *World*, 29–114.

During the abbacy of Opila in the mid-tenth century, the monastery subsumed many of its neighbours (and their archives), including San Salvador de Villeña, formerly the more important abbey, and many smaller institutions otherwise unknown. The collection also incorporates the charters of the local aristocrats Bagaudano and his wife Faquilona, parents to Opila, which he inherited with the ample patrimony recorded in them and left in turn to his monastery, constituting its lay prehistory.[23] The nucleus of the archive is at Madrid, but parchments and codices were also left behind at the 'Dissolution'. This applies to a portion of the cartulary of Santo Toribio, a codex of 76 folios written in a Gothic bookhand, containing 237 charters from 790 to 1316: commissioned around the latter year by the prior in reorganising the monastery, its copyist had poor Latin and made numerous erroneous transcriptions, especially of dates, but just one early medieval original survives as a control.[24] The collection runs to 82 charters dating from 790 to 1028, and divides neatly into three successive blocs, reflecting the documentation first of Villeña, then of Bagaudano, Faquilona, and family, and finally of Turieno itself.

The next largest Cantabrian monastery, Santillana del Mar, is first attested in 962 and was properly established only with the pact signed by Abbot Indulfo and 50 brothers in 980. The early medieval archive has two components: five parchments held at the former abbey and in the diocesan archive, transmitting five originals and two copies between them, and the *Libro de Regla*, a cartulary of 64 folios, two of them now lost, with 94 documents from 870 to 1202. This codex is written in a Gothic bookhand of the first half of the thirteenth century, reproducing the monograms and signs of scribes, but some 20 documents are incomplete and a third incorrectly dated or undated, complicating their use.[25] The collection consists of 41 charters dating between 870 and 1031, and in marked contrast to Santo Toribio traces with singular focus the growth of the monastic patrimony from the mid-tenth century.[26]

[23] *Liébana*, ix–xxi; Gautier-Dalché, 'Domaine', 65–6; Montenegro Valentín, *María*, 21–34.

[24] *Liébana*, xxii, xxvi–xxix, xxxviii–xli; Blasco Martínez, *Cartularios*, 14–24, 34–44; Montenegro Valentín, *María*, 24–6.

[25] *Santillana*, 71–3; Jusué, *Libro*, v–vi; Blasco Martínez, *Cartularios*, 189–209; Díez Herrera, 'Abadía', 15–23; Blasco, 'Aproximación', 78–80, 98–107.

[26] For Cantabria see also *Piasca*, 237–50 (8); *Puerto* (7).

## León

The kingdom of Asturias first expanded southwards from the Cantabrian Mountains in the reign of Ordoño I (850–66), who 'repopulated' what the chronicles claim to have been the 'deserted' basin of the Duero River—a claim which has occasioned intense debate about colonisation, settlement, and historiographical discourse.[27] After the king had conquered, or 'reconquered', the city of León, he re-founded the cathedral, and when the centre of gravity of the kingdom shifted here on the death of Alfonso III (866–910), this became the episcopal see of the new capital.[28] The archive makes up nearly a quarter of the corpus of charters from early medieval Iberia, in part because it was never dissolved, but also because it incorporates collections from monasteries and churches in the diocese absorbed into its patrimony during the eleventh and twelfth centuries.[29] The holdings are comprised of about 330 parchments, almost all originals, including perhaps the earliest to survive, the diploma of King Silo from 775, a later acquisition; the next oldest is a diploma of Ordoño I himself from 860.[30]

The second element of the collection is the *Tumbo de León*, a cartulary of 474 folios containing 1007 charters, written in Caroline minuscule by a canon named Juan Pérez; the latest entry original to the compilation dates to 1124, indicating that it was assembled under Bishop Diego, before 1130. The *Tumbo de León* is arranged by institutional provenance, the see and 16 monasteries; this may reflect archival organisation, facilitating the division of rents between the bishop and the chapter, which held the monastic lands as prebends. After the Council of Burgos officially replaced the Mozarabic liturgy with the Roman rite in 1080, and the Council of León substituted Caroline for Visigothic script in 1090, early medieval originals gradually ceased to be legible, and new copies became necessary, while successive councils at León and Santiago in 1114 enjoined churches to vindicate property and records stolen amidst the unrest of the reign of Urraca (1109–26).[31] Together these imperatives gave rise to a 'golden age' of cartularies, and with it of opportunity for forgery. Yet comparison of the 64 charters surviving as

---

[27] Sánchez-Albornoz, *Despoblación*; cf. Mínguez, 'Despoblación', 169–82; Escudero Manzano, '"Despoblación"', 151–72; Escalona and Martín Viso, 'Life', 21–51.

[28] On León see Carvajal Castro, *Máscara*; Larrea, 'Estado', 181–98.

[29] Pérez, 'Churches', 195–212.

[30] *ChLA* 114, 11–12; *León*, 1, xxi–xxv, lxxx–lxxxii, 2, x–xi, 3, ix–xv; Millares Carlo, *Diploma*, 29–49; Ser Quijano, *Documentación*, 9–10, 29–30; García Leal, *Diploma*, 31–70, 227–38.

[31] Castro Correa, 'Leaving', 631–64.

both originals and copies in the *Tumbo de León* reveals that most observable tampering is (at least for the historian) minor, confined to updating language and omitting signs. The copyist on occasion modified the number or condition of confirmers and witnesses, elaborated boundaries, or misread a date, but he was broadly faithful, even tracing monograms, which helps to differentiate amongst persons with like names.[32]

The cathedral archive of León consists of 895 charters from 767 to 1031, containing within it many smaller collections. The monastery of Abellar, founded sometime before 905, accounts for a fifth of the total, while another tenth come from Cillanueva and Rozuela, both dedicated to Santos Justo y Pastor and often mistaken, including by the *Tumbo* scribe, for one institution uniting two houses; their dates of foundation are unknown, but Cillanueva is first attested around 914, Rozuela in 932, and their overlapping documentation includes without doubt the most famous list of cheeses ever written, an early example of proto-Romance. The see of Santa María contributes just 6% of its own holdings, and Santiago de León, an urban monastery founded by 917, the same figure.[33] But more than a tenth of the charters share one of 32 members of the laity as recipient, demonstrating the fact of early medieval lay archives. And almost a fifth have singly attested parties, with no guide to provenance: unless religious houses acted as local depositories to store such documents, the property recorded must later have come into the possession of the see, and with it originally multiple archives.[34]

The monastery of Sahagún may be of Visigothic origin, but Alfonso III seems to have restored it during his conquest of the Cea valley, and a grant which he made in 904 is its first reliable attestation.[35] This is the largest single Leonese archive, reflecting the peerless wealth which Sahagún attained in the tenth century, and it survives remarkably intact, comprised of over 150 parchments and a cartulary held at Madrid. Almost three-quarters of the parchments are originals, while the remaining copies include early medieval

[32] Ser Quijano, *Documentación*, 20, 26, 32; *León*, 1, xxv–xxix, lxv–lxvii, lxxx–lxxxii, 3, ix–xi, xxviii–xxix; Pérez González, 'Originales', 239–65; Fernández Flórez, 'Huella', 1, 171–5, 191–210; Fernández Catón, '"Tumbo"', 422–34.

[33] *León*, 1, xxii–xxiii, 2, xi–xii, 3, xiii–xv; Rodríguez Fernández, *Monasterio*, 36, 48; Yáñez Cifuentes, *Monasterio*, 55, 72–3; Carbajo Serrano, *Monasterio*, 34–6, 102–5; Lagunas, 'Abadesas', 813; Fernández Catón, 'Nodicia', 1, 37–45, 69–73, 84–5; and see *Documentos selectos* 1b.

[34] *León*, 3, xiii–xv.

[35] Mínguez Fernández, *Dominio*, 217; Carriedo Tejedo, 'Orígenes', 83–7; Agúndez San Miguel, *Memoria*, 35–72.

versions made in the mid- to late tenth of transactions only provisionally recorded at the time (or not at all), and others of the twelfth century.[36] There is also a set of originals from the monastery of Piasca in the Liébana, a tenth-century foundation absorbed into Sahagún by 1109; to these must be added five early medieval documents transmitted by its parchment and paper cartularies, from the mid-twelfth and eighteenth century respectively.[37] The cartulary known as the *Becerro Gótico* of Sahagún consists of 246 folios containing 994 charters from 904 to 1110, and was created in the same 'golden age' as the *Tumbo de León*.[38] Written in the latter year by Munio Díaz, a priest in the monastic scriptorium, in Visigothic-Caroline transitional script, the contents are arranged into nine books by geography, perhaps reflecting organisation in the archive. The *Becerro Gótico* preserves the majority of the documents of Sahagún, and a comparison with 47 also surviving as originals reveals that the copyist intervened much more than at León, particularly to make improvements to language and standardise diplomatic formulas; he often copied monograms and signs, but intermittently reduced confirmers and witnesses or modified their status, even substituting himself in as scribe at times, a source of some confusion.[39] Conditioned by these factors, the collection consists of 432 charters from 857 to 1031, beginning with a series of early originals from Piasca.[40] While it includes a number of smaller clerical and lay archives, it is overall less variegated than León, more focussed on the documentation of Sahagún.

Similarly to León, the cathedral of Astorga was restored after the conquest of the city by Ordoño I, and its archive consists mainly of charters from monasteries absorbed by it in the course of the eleventh to early twelfth century. Of these, the monk-bishop San Genadio (d. 936) founded or re-founded San Andrés de Montes, Santa Leocadia de Castañeda, and Santiago de Peñalba, amongst others, in the late ninth and early tenth centuries, fostering a dense religious life in El Bierzo. Clustered in the Valle del Silencio ('Valley of Silence'), these houses have given the equally evocative

---

[36] *Sahagún*, 1, 9–14, 2, xii, xx–xxxv, lxvi, lxx–lxxi, 4, 3–5; Romera Iruela, 'Refacciones', 185–98; Fernández Catón, *Index*, 1, 17–22; Fernández Flórez, 'Fondo', 133–46.

[37] *Piasca*, 11–14; Montenegro Valentín, *María*, 11–13, 41–9, 113–16; Cantero Mediavilla, 'Cartulario', 1, 499–504.

[38] Agúndez San Miguel, 'Escritura', 261–85; Agúndez San Miguel, 'Reacción', 99–117.

[39] *Sahagún*, 1, 10–11, 2, xxii–xxiii, xxxiv–xxxvii; Shailor, 'Sahagún', 41–61; Romera Iruela, 'Becerro', 23–4, 41; Romera Iruela, 'Refacciones', 196; Fernández Flórez and Herrero de la Fuente, 'Libertades', 306–19; Fernández Flórez, 'Huella', 171–5, 179–91; Fernández Catón, ' "Tumbo" ', 416–22; Fernández Flórez, 'Fondo', 128–9; Serna Serna, 'Munio', 431–6; Pérez González, 'Características', 593–629; Herrero de la Fuente, '*Becerro*', 61–80.

[40] *ChLA* 114, 6–9.

name of Thebaid to the region, after the cradle of coenobitic monasticism in Upper Egypt.[41] Yet what may have been correspondingly dense early medieval documentation survives only in silhouette: the archive was fired first by an Ecta Rapinatiz in 1028 amidst a struggle for the episcopate, and again by the British during the Peninsular War (1807–14), such that there are now just ten contemporary parchments.[42] We are reliant on early modern archival indices, primarily one from the eighteenth century, held at Madrid, with 2,000 notices. Half refer to parchments, half to two cartularies, also lost, for another layer of transmission; a reorganised copy of this index and six other codices yield a further tranche of documents. Caution is needed, because many notices are misdated, and the same charter often appears in more than one manuscript, or even multiply in the same codex bearing different dates. The editors of this collection did heroic work, but took a decision to publish every entry as if unique, which forces the user first to sort out misdated and duplicate charters (see Appendix 2).[43] Once done, the archive of Astorga amounts to 243 charters from 857 to 1031, including a colourful series of forgeries concerning the see of Simancas.[44] Notable blocs come from the cathedral, the monastery of San Adrián del Valle, first attested in 922, and the sometime episcopal residence of San Dictino de Astorga, restored in 921/2, as well as other Genadian establishments.[45] But in such attenuated form, often a bare summary, these charters are mostly limited to skeletal testimony of documentary practice.

The monastery of Otero de las Dueñas was established in 1230, but its founder was a descendant of two Leonese counts from the turn of the millennium, and their archives, united by the marriage of their children, formed a part of its endowment. Fruela Muñoz was the son of Munio Fernández, and relocated from Asturias to Viñayo, while Pedro Flaínez was born to Flaíno Muñoz, and based himself in Valdoré, both immediately north of León; their charters document the acquisition and management of their estates in these zones.[46] The collection is unique too in comprising

---

[41] *Astorga*, 13–14, 21–2; Quintana Prieto, 'Fundaciones', 56–76; Quintana Prieto, 'Tebaida', 77; Quintana Prieto, 'Obispado', 170–3; Quintana Prieto, *Siglos IX y X*; Martínez Tejera, 'Cenobios', 87–108; Martín Viso, 'Monasterios', 9–38; Testón Turiel, 'Genadio', 35–58.

[42] *Astorga* 361; Quintana Prieto, *Siglo XI*, 9–26, 588–90.

[43] *Astorga*, 15–20, 27–8, 31–2; Sánchez Mairena, 'Tumbos', 23–64; *cf.* Durany Castrillo and Rodríguez González, 'Puntualizaciones', 275–8, 281–4; Domínguez Sánchez, 'Puntualizaciones', 298–302.

[44] Deswarte, 'Restaurer', 83–106.

[45] Quintana Prieto, 'Fundaciones', 56–76; Quintana Prieto, 'Tebaida', 84–5; Quintana Prieto, 'Miguel', 71–3; Quintana Prieto, 'Monasterios', 212–17, 258–68.

[46] *Otero*, 21–3; Prieto Prieto, 'Fruela', 21; García Leal, *Archivo*.

about 200 parchments, almost all originals, and no cartulary; partly owing to academic theft, it is now fragmented into four blocs, and though three have returned to the diocesan and cathedral archives in León, the Fondo Torbado is lost except for two sets of photographs and transcripts of rather murky provenance.[47] All told there are 196 charters from 854 to 1031: the earliest, a sale by Ordoño I rewritten in 1020, is held in private hands, while the families of Fruela Muñoz and Pedro Flaínez together account for more than half of the total.[48] With other lay archives and just a handful of documents from local churches and clergy, the collection is our prime resource for studying the (aristocratic) laity.

The last major Leonese archive belongs to the monastery of San Pedro de Eslonza, founded sometime in the late ninth century, contemporary with the restoration of Sahagún. After the 'Dissolution', the archive was moved to Madrid; some charters which went astray were reintegrated in stages around 1900, but others are in the diocesan archive of León. The collection includes a book, begun in 1576, indexing the monastic archive and mentioning a lost medieval cartulary, but omissions and errors in its composition complicate identifying the documents described. As with León, Sahagún, and Otero, there are numerous originals, some 24 from the period, including the only original diplomas of García I (910–14).[49] In total the archive of Eslonza consists of 33 charters dating from between 912 and 1006.[50]

## West: Galicia

The kings of Asturias were active in Galicia from at least the mid-eighth century, but it was not until the reign of Alfonso II in the early ninth that the region began to come fully under royal authority. The emirs ruling at Córdoba had only ever enjoyed transitory control over the northwest after the initial Muslim conquest, and in the ensuing vacuum a powerful local aristocracy had developed, remaining a force to be reckoned with even in

---

[47]  *Otero*, 10–19; Ser Quijano, *Colección*, 14–16; García Leal, 'Colección', 591–8.
[48]  *Otero*, 25–9, 33–4; Ser Quijano, *Colección*, 17; Sánchez-Albornoz, 'Serie', 327–8; Fernández Flórez, 'Purello', 167–81.
[49]  *Eslonza*, 11–30, 33–5; and see *Documentos 2*.
[50]  For León see also *Benevívere* (1); *Carracedo* (5); *Carrizo* (1); *Castañeda* (11); *Cozuelos* (5); *Diócesis* (1); *Entrepeñas* (2); *Escalada* (1); *Montes* (13); *San Isidoro* (2); *San Isidro* (18); *Valladolid* (5); *Vega* (4); Castro Toledo, *Tordesillas* (3); Echániz Sans, *Salamanca* (1); unfortunately, Domínguez Maestro, *Cartulario*, has proven inaccessible.

the Leonese period.[51] The monastery of Celanova was founded in 936, when the scion of one such family, Fruela Gutiérrez, donated a *villa* to his brother the future San Rosendo (d. 977) in order for him to establish a religious community; by 942 he had finished its construction and provided it with a handsome endowment. The history of Celanova is tied inextricably to this magnate dynasty, relations of the kings of León: its earlier charters document the previous generation, Gutier and his wife Ilduara, building up the patrimony, but they gradually fade from view, in a process for the most part complete by the later tenth century.[52] The collection is limited to the *Tumbo de Celanova*, a cartulary of 198 folios now held at Madrid, with 578 charters from 842 to 1165. Compiled amidst and after the gradual transition away from Visigothic script, it is the work of numerous hands in twelfth-century Caroline scripts, and errors of transcription testify to declining familiarity with the earlier writing system. Some of the copyists, however, have made a real effort to reproduce monograms, signs, and confirmations from the originals, especially of the foundational charters and other high-status documents (see Figure 1.3).[53]

The *Tumbo de Celanova* is distinctive for its early medieval documentary inventories, seemingly proto-cartularies, and the codex itself is a fusion of three cartulary projects carried out during the twelfth century, bound together in the seventeenth. The original organisation put donations from Rosendo and family up front, and the rest of the charters sorted in blocs by geography, typology, and protagonist; in the second project, each regional bloc concluded with the record of a pertinent inventory or lawsuit, speaking to the assorted threats facing the monastic estates in the high Middle Ages, which the monastery was endeavouring to counter by memorialising its holy founder.[54] The cartulary has been edited twice, but in neither case altogether satisfactorily: once down to 1006 only, once completely but marred by errors of reading and dating. The editors also handle the inventories differently, one presenting each transaction separately, in nearly unusable

---

[51] On Galicia see Barreiro Fernández, Portela Silva, and Pallares Méndez, *Inventario*, 11–14; Fernández de Viana y Vieites, 'Fuentes', 1–7; Tato Plaza and Boullón Agrelo, 'Fontes', 709–70; Castro, *Colección*, 9–16; Portass, 'Quiet', 283–306; Portass, *World*, 115–93.

[52] Sáez, 'Ascendientes'; Carzolio de Rossi, 'Participación', 5–59; Pallares Méndez, *Ilduara*, 90–100; Carriedo Tejedo, 'Familia', 103–23.

[53] Castro Correa, 'Script', 203–42; *cf.* Castro Correa, 'Study', 25–35.

[54] *Celanova*, 1, 7–11, 3, 6; *Celanova*, x–xx; Gallego, *Archivo*, 25, 43–6; Andrade Cernadas, 'Tumbo', 75–7; Andrade Cernadas, 'Apuntos', 271–3, 276; Sáez and Gutiérrez García-Muñoz, 'Interpretación', 2, 1005–8; Sáez and Gutiérrez García-Muñoz, 'Austeridad', 216–22; Sáez, 'Origen', 12–13, 19–20.

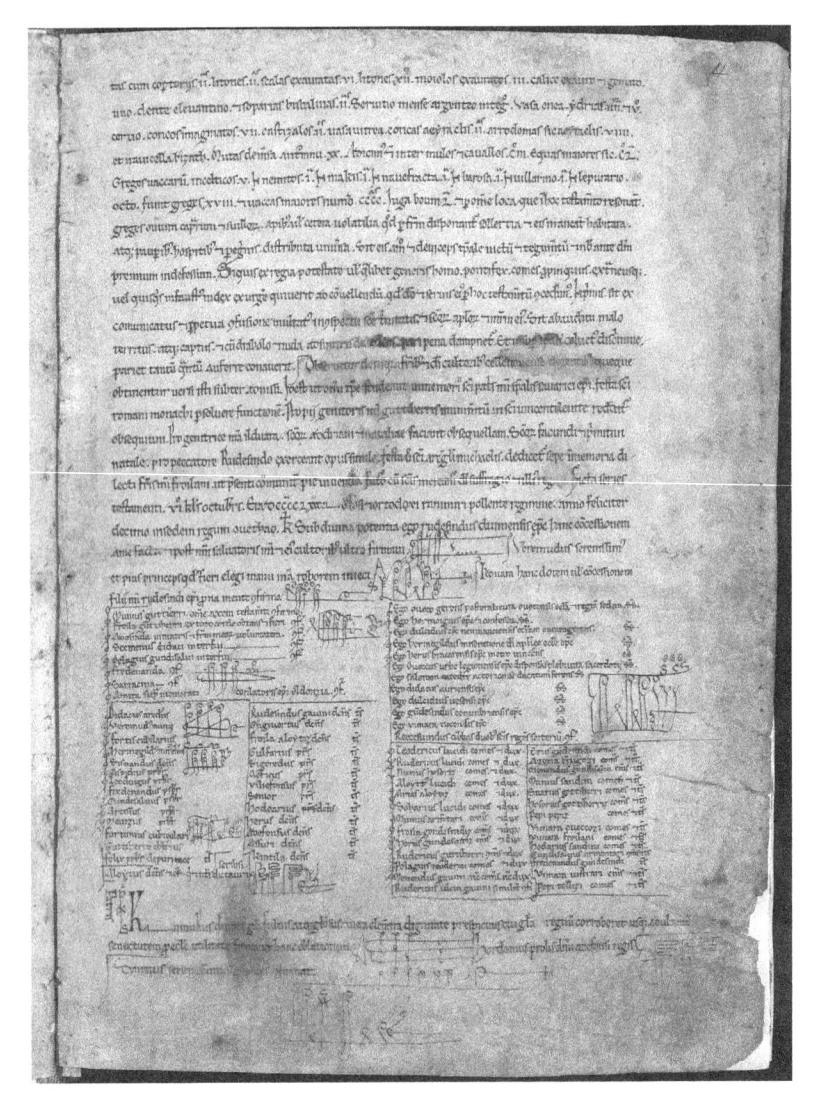

**Figure 1.3**  Cartulary copy, reproducing monograms and confirmations: *Celanova* 72 (Tumbo de Celanova, Madrid, AHN, Códices, L.986, fol. 4r: Ministerio de Cultura y Deporte. Archivo Histórico Nacional. CODICES,L.986)

units of mostly uncertain date, the other retaining the manuscript layout unchanged, in unwieldy blocs of unbroken text.[55] Reconciling these to the degree possible (see Appendix 3), the collection contains 383 charters from 842 to 1031, and after Sahagún forms the second-largest monastic archive from early medieval Iberia.

The next major body of charters comes from A Coruña, but it is editorial shorthand for the archives of three monasteries in this province. In the early Middle Ages, the largest was San Lourenzo de Carboeiro, traditionally (albeit uncertainly) founded by the counts of Deza in 926–36. The establishment of San Martiño Pinario is obscure, but it was initially at the chapel of Santa María de La Corticela, now part of the cathedral church of Santiago de Compostela; it is first attested at its present, separate site in three problematic charters from 911–12. In a similar vein, San Paio de Anteáltares, which appears in a doubtful text of 899, was built into the cathedral complex, serving to provide liturgical services at the tomb of the Apostle James.[56] The three archives came together at Pinario in the late fifteenth century; in the eighteenth, lamentably, its archivists affixed backing paper to the oldest parchments for 'conservation', causing ongoing deterioration. Now divided amongst various Galician public and ecclesiastical archives, the collection consists of about 60 parchments, while another 70 texts, and readings of damaged exemplars, are to be found in early modern indices and *regesta*, not unlike the cathedral archive of Astorga and with all its attendant problems.[57] Overall there are 136 charters from 788 to 1031, the earliest our first known lay transaction though apparently not an original, but much of this collection exists only in outline.

To the northeast of Santiago, the monastery of Sobrado dos Monxes was founded by Hermegildo Aloítiz (variously spelled) and his wife Paterna in 952, and it soon became the second most important foundation in Galicia. Count of Présaras and *majordomo* to Ramiro II (931–51), he endowed it with his lands, and even retired there; the family, notably his son Bishop Sisnando of Iria Flavia, kept control of Sobrado into the eleventh century, notwithstanding the extinction of the direct line in 977. As with the family of Rosendo at Celanova, indeed in competition with them, this was a

---

[55] *Celanova*, 1, 13–15, 23–33, 2, 8–10, 3, 5; Fernández de Viana y Vieites, 'Edición', 231–6; Andrade Cernadas, 'Recordando', 77–82.

[56] *Coruña*, 1, 5–6; Lucas Álvarez, 'Carboeiro', 549–58; Freire Camaniel, 'Documentos'; Lucas Álvarez, *Anteáltares*, 13–16; Lucas Álvarez, *Pinario*, 9–16; Abal, 'Monasterio', 75; Suárez González, 'Memoria', 77–93.

[57] *Coruña*, 1, 6–25; López Alsina, *Ciudad*, 26–31; Gallon, 'Falsifier', 285–301.

proprietorial strategy as well as an act of piety, and there is crossover between the two networks in the archives. The Sobrado collection too preserves its lay prehistory, which accounts for over half the early medieval charters, primarily a record of its founders and their ancestors amassing the estate.[58] There are two cartularies, now held at Madrid, of 169 and 198 folios respectively, which total 986 charters from 787 to 1252 and are published in an unfinished posthumous edition.[59] As is surely true of other cartularies which now present as unitary entities, they conceal within them a far more complex codicological stratigraphy: successively bound and rebound to suit the needs of the moment, they attained their present form in the late sixteenth or early seventeenth century. The shorter cartulary is made up of 14 heterogeneous sectors, the longer nine, a library of sub-cartularies, with repetition of texts across them. Compilation began in the last quarter of the twelfth century with two books, one documenting the earlier history of Sobrado, the other continuing from the arrival of the Cistercians in 1142, roughly 90 folios redistributed between the two volumes; thereafter came a further 15 books, each organised topographically for use in administration, though some summary headers are incomplete. Numerous pre-Gothic hands, expertly reproducing signs and subscriptions, are evident even within sectors, and date to as late as the mid-thirteenth century.[60] Transmitted in this elaborate form, the collection offers us 129 charters from 787 to 1031: anticipating the Asturian hegemony in Galicia, it is by far the richest for that earliest period. The monastery itself is a late arrival, and the archive forms a western counterpart to Otero as a major source for lay documentary practice.

The monastery of Samos has solid Visigothic origins, but its history after the Muslim conquest is enmeshed in the controversial narrative of the 'Mozarabic migration'. Even if not demonstrably false, the remarkable series of royal restorations of the monastery to religious immigrants from al-Andalus is long overdue for reassessment. Samos is also notable in that its earlier abbots seem to have wielded a kind of quasi-episcopal power over a congregation of dependent houses, the model of monasticism characteristic

[58] *Sobrado*, 1, 10–11; Portela Silva and Pallares Méndez, 'Mosteiros', 52–60; Pallares Méndez, *Monasterio*, 71–6, 255–77; Pérez de Urbel, 'Rosendo', 99–108; Sierra Macarrón, 'Aumento', 120–7; Sierra Macarrón, 'Tipologías', 2, 1029–35; Escudero Manzano, 'Condes', 197–213.

[59] *Sobrado*, 1, 7–13; *Celanova*, 1, 6; Pallares Méndez, *Monasterio*, xxv–xxx; Boullón Agrelo, *Antroponimia*, 465–78.

[60] Suárez González, 'Notas', 39–59; Suárez González, 'Volver', 157–61; *cf.* Suárez González, 'Cartulario', 69–101, on the analogous cartulary of San Martín de Castañeda (late twelfth to mid-thirteenth century).

of Fructuosus of Braga (d. 665) and his followers, while its later abbots appear to have overlapped in office, unless this is an artefact of textual problems.[61] The most important component of the archive is the *Tumbo de Samos*, which resurfaced fortuitously in 1984 after a lengthy absence. It contains 96 folios, plus three or more now lost, with 250 charters from 785 to 1200, and a few additions; it is the work of a single hand in a late Caroline script of the early thirteenth century, but the binding dates from the fifteenth, and there are indications of some loss of folios within the manuscript as bound. Four early medieval texts in the cartulary are also preserved as originals or copies at Madrid, with another 12 documents, including a few originals, recently re-edited separately.[62] The collection overall comprises 106 charters from 785 to 1031, centred on the monastery almost exclusively and often featuring a distinctly picaresque quality of narrative composition.

Until very recently, one last major Galician archive remained to be edited, belonging to the cathedral of Santa María de Lugo, but this is now accessible essentially *in toto* thanks to three key publications. Much of the earliest history of the see, starting with the career of its semi-mythical re-founder Bishop Odoario in the eighth century, is shrouded by documentary interpolation, manipulation, and outright forgery, arising from high medieval litigation with its neighbours Ourense and Braga (both restored to episcopal status around 1070), but even so it is clear that Lugo enjoyed royal favour from at least the reign of Alfonso II, including responsibility for 'repopulating' those later rival sees in the wake of the Muslim conquest.[63] For the early Middle Ages, the joy of the collection is 49 originals and 13 copies written in Visigothic script, divided between Madrid and Lugo.[64] Complementing these parchments is the *Tumbo Viejo*, now held in Madrid, a codex of 74 folios copied around 1231 in a Gothic script by Juan Pérez, a cleric of Lugo. He laboured to produce faithful transcriptions of 145 documents, albeit often without success and on occasion omitting whole witness lists; later in the thirteenth century two additions were made, and sundry late medieval documents have since then been bound in with the rest, but there is a core of 26 early medieval charters, and eight of these also survive

---

[61] *Samos*, 20–4; Sánchez-Albornoz, 'Documentos', 147–60; Mundó, 'Inscripción', 157–64; Arias, 'Monasterio', 275–311; García de Cortázar, 'Memoria', 89–94; Díaz Martínez, '*Regula*', 117–35; Zwanzig, 'Heidenheim', 269–95.

[62] *Samos*, 7–20; *Lugo*, 2, 555–94 (1–7); Arias, 'Informe', 163–70; Suárez González, 'Volver', 153–7.

[63] *Lugo*, 1, 15–25; *Costa*, 1, 45–83, 195–223; David, *Études*, 119–84; Pastor Díaz de Garayo and Castro Correa, *Presuras*, 29–56.

[64] *Lugo*, 1, 31–7.

as originals.[65] The balance of the archive, its later parchment and manuscript copies, was transcribed and annotated by the canon archivist Ventura Cañizares del Rey (d. 1940), who planned a *colección diplomática* of the diocese including documents from both the cathedral and the other main Galician collections; his published papers contain 73 texts from our period, seven unavailable elsewhere.[66] The combined cathedral archive of Lugo as such consists of 87 charters from 745 to 1030 (see Appendix 4): it is the single richest source of originals surviving from Galicia, and the 17 documents from the Asturian period rank amongst the most important witnesses to its earliest medieval history.

When the tomb of the Apostle James at Compostela was discovered (or invented) in the reign of Alfonso II, according to the traditional story, the king rushed to the site, founded a church, and merged with it the ancient bishopric of Iria Flavia, just to the southwest. As an offset to the powerful and restive Galician aristocracy, the cathedral of Santiago profited from royal largesse, and it was grandly rebuilt by Alfonso III. This narrative of miraculous ascent and prestigious patronage is the sole interest of the cartularies comprising its early medieval archive, curated or contrived in the high Middle Ages when Compostela had become not only an archiepiscopal see but also the terminus of a pilgrimage route spanning the Peninsula and Pyrenees.[67] The main cartulary, written in Caroline script, is known as *Tumbo A*, and consists of 71 folios with 165 charters from 834 to 1255. The preface indicates that it was composed in 1129 at the commission of Archbishop Diego Gelmírez (1100–40), who had planned for the whole archive to be transcribed in five books by type of granter, but we have only this one of royal privileges. While the first 100 were written by three or four scribes in a single stage, the last 65 are additions from the late twelfth and thirteenth centuries; the diplomas are ordered by date, grouped by reign, and a miniature heads each bloc, making the cartulary a deluxe compendium of the past patrons of Santiago and their acts, designed to inspire in Alfonso VII (1126–57) a similar generosity.[68] As with the cathedral archive of Oviedo, the earliest diplomas from Compostela are much criticised, but

---

[65] *Tumbo Viejo*, 11–21; Sánchez Mairena, 'Metodología', 533–48.

[66] *Cañizares*, 1, 13–16.

[67] Barreiro Somoza, *Señorío*, 21–6, 66–7; López Alsina, *Ciudad*, 105–51; Fernández Conde and Alonso Álvarez (eds), *Reyes*.

[68] *Santiago*, 11–12, 29–38, 42–54; Portela Pazos, *Anotaciones*; Fletcher, *Catapult*, 262–5; Díaz y Díaz, 'Tumbos', 9–24; Fernández Catón, *Tumbo*, 74–96, 259–86; López Alsina, *Ciudad*, 27–36, 43.

they lack the hyperbole of the Oviedo forgeries. The unique diplomatic formulations may be due, at least in part, to *Tumbo A* being a presentation copy in which textual fidelity was a secondary consideration: the formulas of confirmers are minimised so that their names line up neatly in twin columns, and the scribe is named only twice for symmetry. The gift by Alfonso II of three miles around the episcopal church has raised great suspicion, and yet the *Votos de Santiago*, the most gratuitous fake, is only found in *Tumbo B*, dating to 1326. Caution is needed, of course, but this material should not simply be dismissed out of hand.[69] The collection consists of 73 charters from 834 to 1030, predominantly high status and focussed on tracing the relations of the Asturian and Leonese kings to Santiago, and to an extent with Galician society.[70]

## Portugal

An important new county was born in 868, when Vímara Peres, nobleman of the court of Alfonso III, struck south to the Duero River and conquered the town of Portus Cale (Porto; whence 'Portugal'), soon after founding Vimaranis (modern Guimarães) in his own name. As a frontier zone, it was the interface between Galicia to the north of the Miño and al-Andalus to the south of the Mondego; like Castilla it was home to a local aristocracy which grew more ambitious and autonomous over time, and came to overshadow the Leonese kings of the later tenth century, but it did not gain formal independence until 1139–43.[71] By the late nineteenth century, the Academia das Ciências de Lisboa had edited all Portuguese charters then known from the early Middle Ages in the *Portugaliae Monumenta Historica* series, modelled on the *Monumenta Germaniae Historica* and directed by the great liberal man of letters Alexandre Herculano (d. 1877).[72] With few

---

[69] *Tumbo B* 236; *Santiago*, 40–1; Barreiro Somoza, *Señorío*, 43–58; López Alsina, *Ciudad*, 31–47.

[70] For Galicia see also *Bóveda* (2); *Caaveiro* (8); *Chouzán* (4); *Lourenzá* (10); *Meira* (4); *Melón* (1); *Mondoñedo* (7); *Oseira* (1); *Ourense* (4); *Pallares* (3); *Pino* (2); *Pombeiro* (3); *Ramiro II* (1 (no. 42)); *Rocas* (1); *San Clodio* (1); *San Esteban* (1); *Tumbo B* (3); *Tumbo C* (1); Montero Díaz, *Jubia* (2); Lucas Álvarez, 'Camanzo', 273–380 (1); Lucas Álvarez and Lucas Domínguez, *Ramirás* (1); Rodríguez Fernández, *Pino* (2); Lucas Álvarez, 'Documentos', 267–76 (1); Cal Pardo, 'Viveiro', 11–226 (1); Fernández de Viana y Vieites, *Pantón* (1); Romaní Martínez and Otero Piñeyro Maseda, 'Dozón', 27–77 (1); Lucas Álvarez, 'Cis', 603–728 (3); Rodríguez Muñiz, *Cristina* (3).

[71] On Portugal see Branco, 'Portugal', 533–625; Lay, *Kings*, esp. 6–8.

[72] Vasconcelos e Sousa and Boissellier, 'Bilan', 214–15.

major omissions, it remains the edition of reference, though for many of its individual component archives it has been superseded by newer editions with better readings and corrected dates (see Appendix 5). As published, the corpus has two principal components: some 120 parchments held at Lisbon, and seven cartularies with 180 early medieval charters between them.[73] Of the parchments, all but a handful are originals, the earliest, from the monastic archive of São Pedro de Cete, dating to 882. Amongst other lesser houses, the collection comprises significant blocs of material from Moreira, Pedroso, and Pendorada, clustered around Porto, monasteries founded late in or after our period but transmitting prior documentation, as well as the early medieval foundations of Lorvão and Arouca, and the episcopal archive of Coimbra, but a new catalogue and edition are needed.[74]

Of the cartularies, the most important codex is the *Liber Testamentorum* of Lorvão, a monastery near Coimbra founded in the late ninth century and, in a unique case of 'reverse' *Reconquista*, under Islamic rule after 988 until the definitive conquest of the Mondego basin by Fernando I in 1064.[75] The 48 folios contain two brief chronicles and 86 charters from 777 (certainly in error) to 1117, plus later additions, and were written by one main copyist with five contributors in a Visigothic-Caroline transitional script dateable to around 1119, when Lorvão was restored after a momentary suppression; the manuscript transmits more than 60 early medieval documents, but the fidelity of transcription is low, so they must be read with care.[76] The *Livro Preto* of Coimbra itself contributes another 60 charters, mostly originating from monastic and aristocratic archives later absorbed by the episcopal see, since the bishops were only titular until the reconquest of the city. The codex consists of 255 folios with 663 charters from 773 (again, surely misdated) to 1217, and was written by numerous hands over the twelfth and thirteenth centuries, when the diocese faced challenges for its lands; here the copyists were more faithful to their sources, except in transcribing witness lists.[77] The third manuscript, the remarkable *Livro de Mumadona*, is the closest we have to a surviving lay cartulary. In its present form it seems to be a copy

---

[73] Guerra, *Diplomas*, 27–44; Emiliano and Pedro, 'Inventário'; Rodrigues, 'Cartulários', 2, 305–42; Gomes, 'Editions', 25–43; Marques, 'Inventário', 705–18; *cf.* Sacks, *Latinity*, vi.

[74] Emiliano, 'Documento', 7–42; *ChLA* 114, 31; *Santos*, 311–25; *Junqueira*, 1, 23–48, 2, 15–19 (1–4); Lange, *Studien*, 1–78.

[75] Aillet, 'Chrétiens', 27–49; Branco, 'Reis', 2, 27–80.

[76] Coelho, 'Análise', 3, 387–405; Nascimento, 'Liber', 2, 161–92; Ruiz Asencio, 'Copistas', 2, 193–220; Herrero de la Fuente and Fernández Flórez, '"Liber"', 2, 244–5, 252–61, 274–304; *cf.* Furtado, 'Writing', 160–1, 162–3.

[77] *Coimbra*, xv–xxviii, ccxxxi–ccxxxii; Morujão, 'Livro', 7–43.

made in the early thirteenth to fourteenth century of a compilation, now lost, from no later than 1135; written in Gothic script, its 60 folios preserve 70 texts from 873 to 1115.[78] The manuscript takes its name from Mumadona Dias (d. 968), ruling widow of the count of Portugal, who in 950 established and endowed the monastery of Guimarães and built a castle to defend it from Viking attack. Her family and foundation form the focus of the cartulary, which contributes a further 30 early medieval documents to the running total.[79] The remaining four codices pertain to the see of Porto and to the tenth-century foundations of Paço de Sousa, Arouca, and Grijó, but are less significant in numbers for this period.[80] By far the most notable omission from *Portugaliae Monumenta Historica*, however, is one final manuscript, the *Liber Fidei* of the cathedral of Braga, now held at the Arquivo Distrital. Possibly the greatest, certainly the largest cartulary of medieval Portugal, it is made up of over 260 folios containing 954 documents arranged by episcopate. The first 157 folios, written by multiple hands in a Caroline–Gothic transitional script, had been completed as of 1221, but reproduce (with continuations) an earlier cartulary which was in existence by the mid-twelfth century; the balance of the codex was finished in 1254. The initial sector contains all 33 early medieval charters, including a run of forgeries concerning the relations of Braga and Ourense, both suppressed until 1070, with the diocese of Lugo, but otherwise predominantly individual transactions involving members of the local laity and clergy.[81] In that sense this is representative of the substantial and diverse collection from Portugal: consisting all told of 313 charters from 773 to 1031, it has only just begun to be exploited for its many and rich ecclesiastical and lay archives.[82]

## East: Aragón

The county of Aragón in the central Pyrenees emerges into the historical record in the ninth century, during the first half of which it drifted out of Carolingian overlordship and into the orbit of the kingdom of Navarra.

---

[78] *Guimarães*, xxxi–lxv, lxxix–lxxxiv; Ferreira, *Livro*, v–xiv.

[79] Cardozo, 'Testamento', 279–98; Mattoso, 'Famílias', 136–49.

[80] *Porto* (1); *Grijó* (2); *Arouca* (4); *Paço de Sousa* (4); *cf.* Castro, 'Documento', 2, 647–52.

[81] *Braga*, 1, 17–25; Costa, *Liber*, 1, xi–xx; Marques, '*Liber*', esp. 453–61; Marques, *Representação*, 7–25.

[82] For Portugal see also *Azevedo* (2); *Costa*, 2, 367–501 (1); *Crasto* (1); *Fernando I* (1); *Pedro* (2); Conde de São Payo, 'Documentos', 136–55 (1); Madahil, *Aveiro* (1).

By 922, when the local dynasty of counts died out, it had come under direct rule from Pamplona, though it retained a separate administrative identity.[83] Our major source of evidence for this period is the monastic archive of San Juan de la Peña, according to hagiographical legend founded in the eighth century by San Voto, and plausibly built in the tenth, but first securely attested only in 1025; a donation by Sancho III (1004–35) implies that he had either established or restored it. The early medieval archive is an umbrella for a dense monastic life which flourished in Aragón under Carolingian influence: the houses of Cillas, founded in 828, Fuenfría, in about 850, Cercito, perhaps around the same date, and Navasal, extant from 893, all of them absorbed by San Juan in the mid-eleventh century, yet over-written by numerous forgeries in the collection inventing a tenth-century history of royal favour for San Juan itself.[84] There are two main components to the archive: 30 parchments, mostly copies, now at Madrid, which include a 'mini-cartulary' of five charters of the ninth to the eleventh century from Cercito, and the *Libro Gótico*, held in Zaragoza, a composite cartulary of 123 folios bound in the sixteenth century, containing 311 charters from 828 to 1216. The sector of 39 folios in Visigothic script is the oldest cartulary surviving from Iberia, work of a scribe active in the mid-eleventh century, copying texts from 948 to 1061, and another who created the index; there-after other hands added in further early medieval charters. The originally separate sector in Caroline script, from the late eleventh or early twelfth century, spans 959 to 1095, but again with additions, making both sectors cumulative registers.[85] The archive overall consists of 55 charters from 828 to 1031, but the lamentable standard edition impedes handling these often problematic documents with any real confidence.[86]

## Castilla

The development of the county of Castilla began in earnest in the mid-ninth century, and its second count Diego Rodríguez (*ca.* 873–85) founded a border outpost which became the regional capital of Burgos in 884. Just to the

---

[83]  On Aragón see Ubieto Arteta, *Historia*, 5–32.

[84]  *San Juan*, 1, 7–9, 11–12; Lapeña Paul, *Monasterio*, 23–39, 46–53; Larrea, 'Documentación'.

[85]  Canellas López, 'Cartulario', 1, 206–17; Lapeña Paul, *Monasterio*, 17–22; Bádenas Población, 'Índice', 335–58; *cf.* Laliena Corbera, 'Documentos', 378.

[86]  For Aragón see also *Fanlo* (3); *Huesca* (11); *Siresa* (11); *Sobrarbe* (11); Arco, 'Jaca', 47–98 (1); Serrano y Sanz, 'Notas', 254–65 (1); Ubieto Arteta, *Serós* (1); Ubieto Arteta, *Jaca* (1).

southeast the most important monastery of the region, San Pedro de Cardeña, appears fully formed from 902, presumably having been established in the campaign of 'repopulation' under Alfonso III.[87] Castilla remained a militarised frontier zone, and some two hundred monks are supposed to have died in a Muslim raid traditionally dated to 934, though they were not officially canonised as martyrs until the early modern era; the monastery benefitted from consistent comital favour, and in return provided a mausoleum for García Fernández (970–95).[88] The archive is lost except for the *Becerro Gótico*, a codex of 99 folios containing 367 charters from 899 to 1085, substantially written by a single scribe in Visigothic-Caroline transitional script, but with five other hands occasionally contributing. Compiled a year after the date of the latest document, it is the second-earliest cartulary from Iberia to survive: the design is functional, the charters organised geographically for use, with the exception of an initial bloc of comital diplomas (many of them forgeries). The copyists even reproduced hundreds of monograms and signs from their sources, but may have omitted the day from the dating clause, as a quarter of the charters are dated to the first of the month, and they are so homogeneous in formulation that some streamlining seems indicated.[89] The *Becerro Gótico* is complemented by papers of an eighteenth-century archivist which transmit six further documents from a lost cartulary of the thirteenth century.[90] The collection reflects the great wealth of the monastery: consisting of 233 charters from 899 to 1031, it the largest for early medieval Castilla, amounting to more than all its other archives combined.

Almost a century before the establishment of Cardeña, the bishopric and monastery of Valpuesta was founded in 804, to the northeast beyond the Ebro River. At least, so claim two forged diplomas, which recount how Alfonso II sent a Bishop Juan to 'repopulate' the region, and he settled at an 'abandoned' church; the bishops, however, are not securely attested until the late ninth century or at the monastery until the tenth.[91] Before the

[87] On Castilla see Martínez Díez, *Condado*, 2, 749–68.

[88] *Cardeña*, 29–100; Serrano, *Cardeña*, viii–ix, xxxix–xl; Carzolio de Rossi, 'Formación', 79–81; Moreta Velayos, *Monasterio*, 19–23, 60; Martínez Díez, *Colección*, 7–8; Ortiz Espinosa, 'Mártires', 109–34.

[89] *Cardeña*, 101–374 (esp. 122, 181, 244); Sánchez-Albornoz, 'Falsificaciones', 336–45; Moreta Velayos, *Monasterio*, 14–15, 136–40; Fernández Flórez, '*Becerro*', 21–39; Serna Serna, 'Validations', 41–60.

[90] Serrano, *Cardeña*, xii–xiv; Martínez Díez, *Colección*, 9–17; Cruz Herranz, '"Libro"', 139–62.

[91] Cantera Burgos, 'Documento', 3–15; Ruiz de Loizaga, *Iglesia*, 73–4, 113–18; Ibáñez García, 'Privilegio', 149–74; Linage Conde, 'Repoblación', 213–28.

absorption of Valpuesta into the see of Burgos in 1088, there is a substantial archive comprised of two cartularies held at Madrid. The more important of these is the *Becerro Gótico*: now 103 folios, since its initial few are missing, with 178 charters from 804 to 1138, plus additions. Yet to conceive of it as a single discrete cartulary is entirely inaccurate, for it is the product of 34 different scribes, 22 of them writing in Visigothic scripts of the tenth and eleventh centuries, 12 in Caroline scripts of the late eleventh and twelfth. The *Becerro Gótico*, begun sometime in the eleventh century in unknown circumstances, is in fact a motley assemblage of originals, groups of copies, and even a subsidiary cartulary of the mid-eleventh from the monastery of Buezo de Bureba, with a dossier of charters related to a wildfire in 949; as such, there are multiple versions of many texts in different sectors of the codex. The *Becerro Galicano* is the second component of the archive, but less important, the work of a canon of Valpuesta who copied out 138 documents from the earlier cartulary in 1236.[92] All told, we have 49 charters from 804 to 1030, and the initial forgeries aside these include numerous small transactions of great interest.

The third major monastic archive of Castilla was nearly lost, when the *Becerro* of San Pedro de Arlanza vanished in the Civil War (1936–9), but the contents had fortuitously been transcribed and published by the medievalist Luciano Serrano (d. 1944) in 1925. Preserved in this form only, the cartulary can nonetheless be reconstructed in detail: there were 97 charters in it, dating from 912 to 1156, with several additions, and it was put together in three stages, a first thematic project around 1120–35, a second proceeding in chronological order in 1150–65 or so, and an appendix. The several stages explain the duplicate charters of foundation, both dated to 912, but one granted by Gonzalo Téllez (d. *ca.* 915), the other by his nephew Fernán González (931/2–70). The former provided the model for the latter, a forgery of the mid-twelfth century added to the front of the *Becerro* in stage two; Arlanza was usurping the narrative of the origins of Castilla then coalescing around the count, who is interred at the monastery, and the cartulary contains many other such falsifications.[93] Recently, however, the original of one comital diploma from 937 has been identified, and for these formative years of the monastery we also have a handful of important eighteenth-century

---

[92] *Valpuesta*, 1, 41–105, 107–37, 157–67; Fernández Flórez, 'Paleografía', 81–94; Ruiz Asencio, 'Cartularios', 1–19; Peterson, 'Incendio', 139–64.

[93] *Arlanza*, vii–xi, xv; Escalona Monge and Azcárate Aguilar-Amat, 'Fuente', 450–4, 462–73; Escalona Monge, Azcárate Aguilar-Amat, and Larrañaga Zulueta, 'Crítica', 2, 162–206.

copies made by Liciniano Sáez (d. 1809), archivist of Silos, and assorted early modern archival notices of ten more documents, bringing the collection to a very respectable total of 39 charters from 824 to 1026.[94]

The last early medieval foundation of the Castilian counts was the monastery of San Salvador de Oña, established by Sancho García (995–1017) for his daughter Tigridia in 1011, after the example of García Fernández at Covarrubias. Curiously the endowment charter pre-dates by a fortnight the transaction through which he acquired the *villa*, but there is evidence of much later mischief in the initial records of this house, designed to downplay the presence of women as well as their role in its governance, and such textual problems are the inevitable result.[95] Oña soon became a focus for Castilian political identity—its founder was interred in the monastery, as was his son—but major expansion of the estates came later, and the early medieval archive is modest: 20 parchments held at Madrid, and some early modern notices, with nothing from the period in the fourteenth-century cartulary.[96] The collection is limited to 24 charters from 822 to 1029, mostly at the later end, many overlapping and suspect.[97]

## La Rioja

Like the county of Castilla, the territory of La Rioja in the Ebro valley was a frontier zone, and its mountainous southern reaches formed a part of the Upper March of al-Andalus until the Navarrese king Sancho Garcés I (905–25) conquered them in 923, moving his capital from Pamplona to Nájera. But into the eleventh century it was also a border zone between the encroaching influence of the Castilian counts and the kingdom of Navarra, and briefly home to an evanescent sub-kingdom based at Viguera.[98] The

---

[94] Maté Sadornil, 'Padre', 93–110; Escalona, Velázquez Soriano, and Juárez Benítez, 'Identification', 259–88; Juárez Benítez, *Colección*, esp. 79–120, 266–94, 523–5, 585–606.

[95] *Oña*, x, xxx; Zabalza Duque, 'Hallazgo', 325–32; Olmedo Bernal, *Abadía*, 19, 28–51; Reyes Téllez, 'Orígenes', 32–51; Agúndez San Miguel, 'Memoria femenina', 239–55.

[96] *Oña*, ix, xxxi, xxxv–xxxvii, xl; Torrens Álvarez et al., *Documentación*, 1–28; cf. Olmeda Bernal, *Abadía*, 10–13, 51–75; Blasco Martínez, 'Códice', 70–1; Vivancos Gómez, 'Documentación', 52–81.

[97] For Castilla see also *Aguilar* (2); *Burgos* (13); *Concejo* (2); *Covarrubias* (15); *Fernando I* (4); *Husillos* (10); *Peñafiel* (5); *Silos* (7); Martínez Díez, 'Ibeas' (2); Martín Postigo, *Cárdaba* (2); Hernández, *Toledo* (1); Cantera Burgos and Andrío Gonzalo, *Miranda* (1); Velasco Bayón et al., *Cuéllar*, 1 (1); Martínez Llorente and Trullén Galve, 'Carta' (1).

[98] On La Rioja see E. Sáinz Ripa, 'Patrimonio', 291–306; García Turza, 'Espacios', 483–92; Peterson, 'Fronteras', 7–35; cf. Cañade Juste, 'Ramiro', 21–38.

foremost monastery of the region, San Millán de la Cogolla, is dedicated to a sixth-century hermit and located at the cave where he lived, but there is no genuine record of its existence until 932; the intervening centuries were later bridged by apocryphal lists of abbots and charters.[99] The principal element of its archive is the *Becerro Galicano*, a cartulary of 246 folios containing 740 documentary units from 759 to 1194, plus more than 30 additions, written in Caroline script around 1196 and still held at the monastery. One has to speak of 'documentary units' because a quarter of the entries in the index to the manuscript are not individual charters but blocs of texts: often related in location or personnel, at times miscellaneous, they tend to be lists of acquisitions, seemingly inherited from the *Becerro Gótico*, a lost earlier cartulary which may be partially reconstructed through archival notices from the eighteenth century. Handling the blocs as they are or breaking them up yields radically contrasting results, and by adopting the former approach the new digital edition has published 140 units with content falling in the period from 759 to 1031, where its predecessor had printed 196 charters by rashly attempting the latter technique.[100]

The *Becerro Galicano* of San Millán is organised by geography, but groups together the estates of filial houses regardless of their various locations, and situates each bloc by the first property to be identified in it; the underlying structure tracks the diocesan boundaries of the early eleventh century, apparently to demonstrate the seniority of the monastery over the dioceses impinging on it by evoking a golden age when its abbots doubled as the bishops of Nájera and Álava.[101] The archive is famed for its forgeries, emanating out of twelfth-century litigation: the egregious *Votos de San Millán* which prefaces the cartulary, many though not necessarily all of the boilerplate charters of foundation, endowment, and absorption for the smaller houses later incorporated by the monastery, and serial donations supposedly granted by kings of Navarra and counts of Castilla.[102] When these, up to a third of the collection, are discounted, a humbler reality of small-scale transaction remains. The monastery accounts for only a third of the

---

[99] García de Cortázar, *Dominio*, 13–14, 24–8, 41–4, 64–74, 116–43, 156–62, 319–23; Ubieto Arteta, 'Años', 181–200; Zaragoza i Pascual, 'Abadologio', 188–91.

[100] *San Millán*, 'Critical edition'; Ubieto Arteta, *Millán*, 9–198; García Andreva, *Becerro*, 44–82; Peterson, '*Becerro*', 147–73.

[101] Peterson, 'Reescribiendo', 654–80; García Andreva, *Becerro*, 13–43; Peterson, 'Rebranding', 184–203; Peterson, 'Order', 119–34.

[102] Ubieto Arteta, 'Votos', 1, 304–24; Martínez Díez, 'Monasterio', 8–52; Martínez Díez, 'Emeterio', 7–8; Azcárate Aguilar-Amat *et al.*, 'Volver', 373–82; Peterson, 'Mentiras', 295–314.

charters, a quarter belong to San Juan de Hiniestra, founded in 947, and a tenth each to the houses of San Esteban de Salcedo and San Miguel de Pedroso.

The other great monastery of La Rioja was San Martín de Albelda, founded in 924 by Sancho Garcés I in thanksgiving for his victorious conquest of Nájera and Viguera, at least according to a twelfth-century forgery. It existed by 925, in any case, and the kings of Navarra enlisted it in the 'repopulation' of their realm. García Sánchez I (925–70) attended the consecration in 947, and royal patronage may explain how the scriptorium of Albelda became, alongside that of San Millán, a major centre of book production.[103] The monastery was subsumed into Santa María de La Redonda in 1435: this institution, 'co-cathedral' of Logroño, is home to some of its parchments, including the second-earliest charter from the east surviving as an original, written by the calligrapher and illuminator Vigila, which documents the incorporation of San Prudencio de Monte Laturce into Albelda in 950. The other element of the archive, now held at Simancas, is a manuscript from 1501 reproducing seven folios in Visigothic script, in all probability a monastic cartulary.[104] This modest collection consists of 32 charters from 921 to 1024, dominated equally by the Navarrese kings and the agents of the monastery.[105]

## Navarra

Coming finally to the kingdom of Navarra itself, the sole archive of any size belongs to San Salvador de Leire (or Leyre), nestled in the sierra to the southeast of Pamplona.[106] The monastery was described by Eulogius of Córdoba in 848, and the relics of Nunilo and Alodia, child apostates from Islam martyred at Huesca, were translated to it around the same date, or perhaps a generation later. Leire had a close relationship with the Navarrese ruling dynasty: at least two kings were received into the monastic *familia*, and it served for a time as a kind of royal pantheon, while its abbot doubled as the bishop of Pamplona from the early eleventh century.[107] Yet the

---

[103] Bishko, 'Salvus', 559–65; Díaz y Díaz, *Libros*, esp. 53–85; Lázaro Ruiz, 'Monasterio', 354–71, 380–1.

[104] *Albelda*, 5; Sáinz Ripa, *Colección*, 7–8; García Turza, *Prudencio*, 15–16.

[105] For La Rioja see also *Nájera* (4); Rodríguez de Lama, *Colección* (3); García Turza, *Valvanera* (1).

[106] On Navarra see Larrea, *Navarre*, 161–337; Lacarra, *Historia*, 19–74.

[107] Fortún Pérez de Ciriza, *Leire*, 38–50, 73–97; Christys, *Christians*, 68–79.

collection is confined to a dozen parchment copies, the majority of them in a single *pancarta* from the late eleventh century, and the *Becerro Antiguo*, a codex of 137 folios with 277 charters from 842 to 1202, which was written by various hands in Caroline scripts over three stages in the twelfth and thirteenth centuries; all but a handful of these are royal diplomas, tampered with or forged outright for use against the bishop of Pamplona in litigation of the high Middle Ages.[108] As such the main archive for early medieval Navarra, seemingly with 22 charters from 842 to 1024, is largely the partisan product of another era, and its history in this period substantially unreliable, if not wholly unknowable.[109]

## Transmission

Constituted as such, the corpus of documentation from early medieval Iberia consists of 4,095 charters: this total is adjusted for the many inevitable overlaps amongst the editions, where the same charter has been duplicated in multiple publications because it is present in more than one archive or relevant to more than one collection.[110] The foregoing treatment of texts and transmission makes clear that means of survival have conditioned the content and composition of the corpus, and this factor must always be taken into account when making generalisations. In order to assemble an overview classification of the sources, I have drawn on the judgements of the editors, together with critical reappraisals and new discoveries, but there are notable difficulties involved. What is an original? It easy to say a charter preserved in the form in which the scribe first wrote it, yet how close must that act of writing be in time and space to the transaction itself? We may disqualify a text in a cartulary of centuries later, even if this is when it was first recorded, but where to draw the line? Contemporary copies made soon after the fact are scarcely distinguishable from originals, and may have been an integral part of the documentary process. Charters too are often preserved in multiple sources; I have noted them all, categorising each one by its earliest form. This classification is thus a gross simplification of a complex picture, but even so offers valuable context (see Figure 1.4).

---

[108] *Leire*, xii–xxx; Ubieto Arteta, 'Tipo', 409–22; Lopetegui Semperena, 'Preámbulos', 353–83.
[109] For Navarra see also *Elorrio* (1); *Irache* (4); *Pamplona* (11); Banús y Aguirre, *Fuero* (1).
[110] See García de Cortázar, Munita, and Fortún, *CODIPHIS*, 1, 15–16, for the contrary approach.

| | Original | | Copy | | Cartulary | | Other | | Overall | |
|---|---|---|---|---|---|---|---|---|---|---|
| | # | % | # | % | # | % | # | % | # | % |
| Total | 888 | 22 | 261 | 6 | 2438 | 60 | 507 | 12 | 4095 | 100 |
| Region | | | | | | | | | | |
| West | 210 | 24 | 84 | 32 | 881 | 36 | 109 | 21 | 1284 | 31 |
| Centre | 658 | 74 | 102 | 39 | 1005 | 41 | 322 | 64 | 2088 | 51 |
| East | 20 | 2 | 75 | 29 | 552 | 23 | 76 | 15 | 723 | 18 |
| Personnel | | | | | | | | | | |
| Royal | 62 | 7 | 90 | 34 | 299 | 12 | 70 | 14 | 522 | 13 |
| Comital | 3 | 0 | 18 | 7 | 41 | 2 | 9 | 2 | 71 | 2 |
| Ecclesiastical | 449 | 51 | 134 | 51 | 1763 | 72 | 364 | 72 | 2710 | 66 |
| Lay | 369 | 42 | 18 | 7 | 330 | 14 | 52 | 10 | 769 | 19 |
| Typology | | | | | | | | | | |
| Donation | 367 | 41 | 184 | 70 | 1316 | 54 | 344 | 68 | 2212 | 54 |
| Sale | 444 | 50 | 35 | 13 | 879 | 36 | 111 | 22 | 1469 | 36 |
| Other | 76 | 9 | 42 | 16 | 242 | 10 | 51 | 10 | 411 | 10 |
| Complexity | | | | | | | | | | |
| Simple | 587 | 66 | 141 | 54 | 1695 | 70 | 373 | 74 | 2797 | 68 |
| Complex | 300 | 34 | 120 | 46 | 740 | 30 | 132 | 26 | 1292 | 32 |
| Diplomatic | | | | | | | | | | |
| Authentic | 886 | 100 | 152 | 58 | 2277 | 93 | 465 | 92 | 3781 | 92 |
| Suspicious | 1 | 0 | 9 | 3 | 10 | 0 | 4 | 1 | 24 | 1 |
| Interpolated | 1 | 0 | 22 | 8 | 27 | 1 | 7 | 1 | 57 | 1 |
| Falsified | 0 | 0 | 74 | 28 | 123 | 5 | 30 | 6 | 227 | 6 |

**Figure 1.4** Palaeography

Just over a fifth of the charters survive as originals, of which 136 (3%) are also transcribed in cartularies; comparatively few have been preserved as single-sheet copies, and of these some 95 (2%) are duplicated in cartularies. By far the majority of the corpus, three-fifths of the total, is transmitted in the first instance by cartulary copies, with all the potential hazards of that medium in terms of selection, intervention, and fabrication, while slightly over a tenth exist in other, more attenuated forms, including 163 (4%) early modern copies and 318 (8%) archival notices. But how does transmission map onto the material itself?

Originals are concentrated in the centre, especially at León, Otero, and Sahagún, with many in Portugal as well, but the east has almost none. Correspondingly, the west and east rely more on copies of all kinds, particularly in cartularies, which for many archives account for nearly every surviving charter. Each source type has its own profile, and crucially there is a relationship between originals and lay charters, whereas copies of all kinds preserve royal, comital, and ecclesiastical documents at a concomitantly greater rate. This suggests that the total number of lay charters, reflecting archival priorities at the religious institutions which have transmitted the corpus, underrepresents actual lay documentary use; it also means that we are less informed about the laity in the west and above all the east than in the centre. For typology of transaction, similarly, originals preserve more sales, copies more donations and other acts, implying that, for a real sense of the relative incidence, we need to rebalance in favour of the former to compensate for the bias of transmission towards the latter. It should occasion no surprise to find a correlation between both single-sheet and cartulary copies and forgery. In terms of change over time, finally, the proportion of originals roughly doubles at the expense of other sources across the Leonese period (when numbers are sufficient to track trends), making up nearly a third of the total by 1031. If we consider the profile of originals, we know progressively more about the laity as the decades pass (see Figure 1.5).

Related to the sources of the corpus is the question of authenticity, but this is easier to ask than to answer. Identifying interpolation or falsification in the documentation presents the problem of how much standardisation to expect, and the challenge of discriminating amongst alterations made by copyists to form or content has been compounded in certain contexts by a

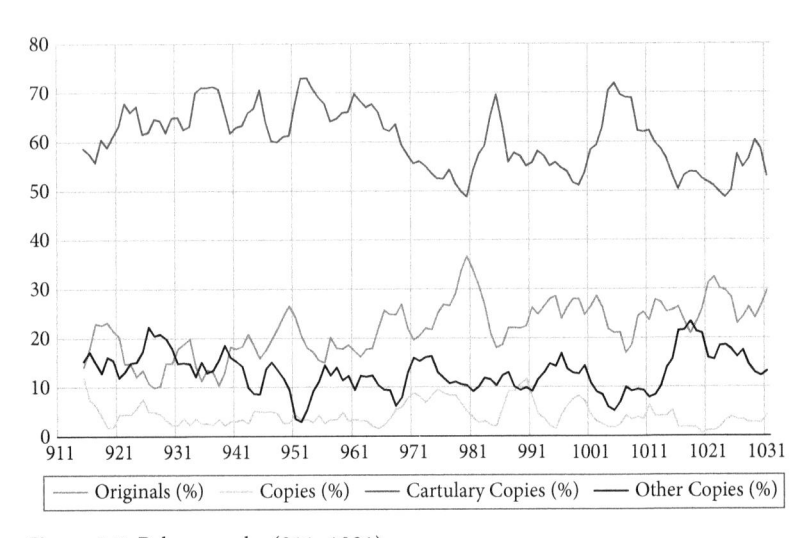

**Figure 1.5** Palaeography (911–1031)

sentimental desire to retain venerable historical traditions. For this overview I have deferred in the main to the judgements of editors and the standard guides, erring on the side of caution in cases of disagreement, but rigorous criticism remains lacking for the east (see Figure 1.6).[111]

Reassuringly, somewhat over nine-tenths of the charters have been judged authentic, in the sense of showing no appreciable signs of alteration since the moment of their creation; the relationship between this original form and the 'real events' which it describes, of course, is another, more complicated question. Even with a cautious approach the rate of forgery is modest at just

| | Authentic | | Suspicious | | Interpolated | | Falsified | | Overall | |
|---|---|---|---|---|---|---|---|---|---|---|
| | # | % | # | % | # | % | # | % | # | % |
| Total | 3781 | 92 | 24 | 1 | 57 | 1 | 227 | 6 | 4095 | 100 |
| Region | | | | | | | | | | |
| West | 1216 | 32 | 4 | 17 | 26 | 46 | 35 | 15 | 1284 | 31 |
| Centre | 1991 | 53 | 8 | 33 | 16 | 28 | 71 | 31 | 2088 | 51 |
| East | 574 | 15 | 12 | 50 | 15 | 26 | 121 | 53 | 723 | 18 |
| Personnel | | | | | | | | | | |
| Royal | 348 | 9 | 12 | 50 | 22 | 39 | 140 | 62 | 522 | 13 |
| Comital | 25 | 1 | 7 | 29 | 4 | 7 | 35 | 15 | 71 | 2 |
| Ecclesiastical | 2618 | 69 | 5 | 21 | 30 | 53 | 52 | 23 | 2710 | 66 |
| Lay | 767 | 20 | 0 | 0 | 1 | 2 | 0 | 0 | 769 | 19 |
| Typology | | | | | | | | | | |
| Donation | 1968 | 52 | 19 | 79 | 43 | 75 | 178 | 78 | 2212 | 54 |
| Sale | 1467 | 39 | 0 | 0 | 1 | 2 | 1 | 0 | 1469 | 36 |
| Other | 344 | 9 | 5 | 21 | 13 | 23 | 47 | 21 | 411 | 10 |
| Complexity | | | | | | | | | | |
| Simple | 2625 | 69 | 15 | 63 | 26 | 46 | 130 | 57 | 2797 | 68 |
| Complex | 1151 | 30 | 9 | 38 | 31 | 54 | 96 | 42 | 1292 | 32 |
| Palaeography | | | | | | | | | | |
| Original | 886 | 23 | 1 | 4 | 1 | 2 | 0 | 0 | 888 | 22 |
| Copy | 152 | 4 | 9 | 38 | 22 | 39 | 74 | 33 | 261 | 6 |
| Cartulary | 2277 | 60 | 10 | 42 | 27 | 47 | 123 | 54 | 2438 | 60 |
| Other | 465 | 12 | 4 | 17 | 7 | 12 | 30 | 13 | 507 | 12 |

**Figure 1.6** Diplomatic

[111] Fernández de Viana y Vieites, 'Problemas', 2, 45–9; Sanz Fuentes, 'Lenguaje', 119–20; see *Floriano*; Ubieto Arteta, *Documentos reales*; *Documentación*, 92–202; Zabalza Duque, *Colección*, 97–568; Jimeno Aranguren and Pescador Medrano, *Colección*; Díaz Salvado, *Falsos*, 5–41, 209–11, 715–18.

over one in 20, while inconclusive suspicions have been raised or anachronistic interpolations detected in the remainder. These inauthentic charters have a distinctive profile: most common in the east, at San Juan, San Millán, and Leire, as well as in the cathedral archive of Oviedo, the majority royal and especially Castilian comital diplomas. High-status granters, chiefly the forerunners of the kings of León-Castilla in the 'golden age' of forgery during the high Middle Ages, are the obvious choice for legitimising spurious acts, whereas few ecclesiastical and no lay charters are false. Virtually all such charters take the form of donations or confirmations, which can easily be expanded in scope and enhanced with imposing words; most of these are transmitted in either cartulary or single-sheet copies, the latter especially, which often come in the form of 'pseudo-originals' disguised by an archaising or imitative script.[112] Forgeries are scattered across the early medieval period, but in identifiable blocs corresponding to the reigns of certain kings and counts: Alfonso III in the late ninth century and Ordoño II in the 920s, then García Sánchez I and Fernán González in the 940s–950s, Ramiro III and García Fernández in the 970s, Sancho Garcés II in the 990s, and finally Sancho III from the 1010s. All except the hapless Ramiro III, likely mistaken for Ramiro II, were known for conquests or benefactions, and could lend their authority to doubtful inventions (see Figure 1.7).

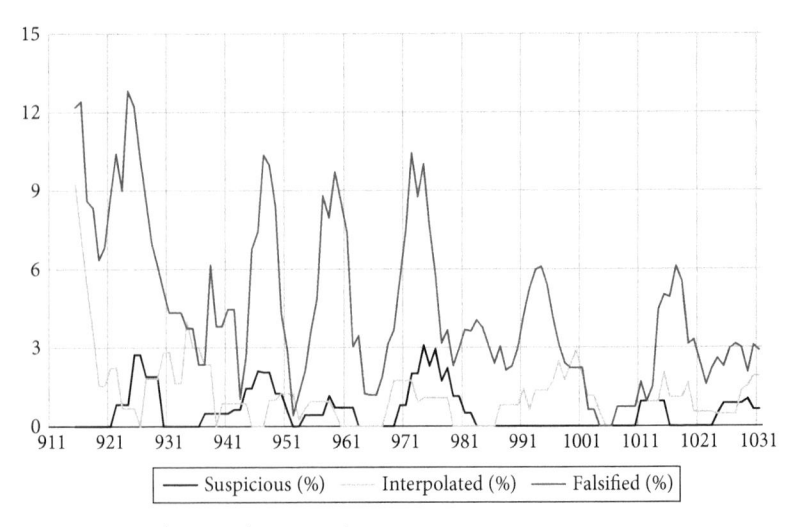

**Figure 1.7** Diplomatic (911–1031)

[112] Vezin, 'Écritures', 61–5.

The greatest advantage of treating the corpus as a whole is the firm foundation which this provides for comparison between regions normally studied in isolation.[113] The first point to note is that the numbers are radically imbalanced: over half of the charters come from the centre, leaving just under a third from the west and a fifth from the east (see Figure 1.8). As we have already seen, not only can we say less about the east, but also less securely, given the far higher incidence of forgery there than elsewhere; in parallel, while the centre is rich in originals, both the east and the west are more reliant on cartulary copies.[114] Sharp differences too can be seen in

| | West | | Centre | | East | | Overall | |
|---|---|---|---|---|---|---|---|---|
| | # | % | # | % | # | % | # | % |
| Total | 1284 | 31 | 2088 | 51 | 723 | 18 | 4095 | 100 |
| Personnel | | | | | | | | |
| Royal | 182 | 14 | 210 | 10 | 130 | 18 | 522 | 13 |
| Comital | 0 | 0 | 4 | 0 | 67 | 9 | 71 | 2 |
| Ecclesiastical | 833 | 65 | 1387 | 66 | 490 | 68 | 2710 | 66 |
| Lay | 256 | 20 | 481 | 23 | 32 | 4 | 769 | 19 |
| Typology | | | | | | | | |
| Donation | 700 | 55 | 1021 | 49 | 491 | 68 | 2212 | 54 |
| Sale | 403 | 31 | 926 | 44 | 140 | 19 | 1469 | 36 |
| Other | 180 | 14 | 140 | 7 | 91 | 13 | 411 | 10 |
| Complexity | | | | | | | | |
| Simple | 745 | 58 | 1516 | 73 | 536 | 74 | 2797 | 68 |
| Complex | 536 | 42 | 570 | 27 | 186 | 26 | 1292 | 32 |
| Palaeography | | | | | | | | |
| Original | 210 | 16 | 658 | 32 | 20 | 3 | 888 | 22 |
| Copy | 84 | 7 | 102 | 5 | 75 | 10 | 261 | 6 |
| Cartulary | 881 | 69 | 1005 | 48 | 552 | 76 | 2438 | 60 |
| Other | 109 | 8 | 322 | 15 | 76 | 11 | 507 | 12 |
| Diplomatic | | | | | | | | |
| Authentic | 1216 | 95 | 1991 | 95 | 574 | 79 | 3781 | 92 |
| Suspicious | 4 | 0 | 8 | 0 | 12 | 2 | 24 | 1 |
| Interpolated | 26 | 2 | 16 | 1 | 15 | 2 | 57 | 1 |
| Falsified | 35 | 3 | 71 | 3 | 121 | 17 | 227 | 6 |

**Figure 1.8** Region

[113] Wickham, 'Problems', 5–28.
[114] Pastor Díaz de Garayo, 'Testimonios', 355–79; Escalona, 'Cartularios', 132–5.

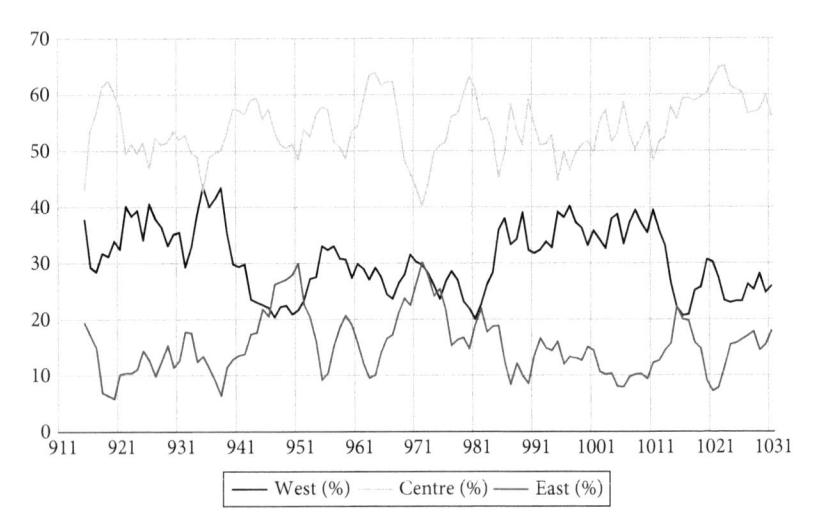

**Figure 1.9**  Region (911–1031)

personnel, as royal diplomas are more prominent in the west and east, and comital diplomas basically limited to the east. The geographical distribution of ecclesiastical charters shows no special weighting, whereas lay charters, which are notably overrepresented in the centre, are next to absent from the east. And in terms of documentary typology, the centre stands out for an approaching even total of donations and sales, unlike the east and west where the former outnumber the latter quite considerably. As such we can speak of regional profiles in sources, authenticity, agents, and transactions, indicating regionalised documentary practice. Indeed, there are distinct patterns in the chronological distribution across the Leonese period, for while the eastern numbers hover within the range of a tenth to a fifth of the total, central and western rates fluctuate in alternation and gradually diverge, from just slightly apart at the outset to twice as many charters in the centre as in the west by the end (see Figure 1.9).

## Chronology

There was change over time amongst the regions of early medieval Iberia, and it will be our business to understand what this entailed. But doing so requires stepping back to ask the fundamental question: why write a charter at all? Literacy tends to be studied in terms of development, progress from lesser to greater use of the written word, or regression in times of crisis.

Where the direction seems positive, the process—whether its impetus is perceived to be 'top-down' or 'ground-up'—is normally presented as a transition towards a 'literate society', however defined; the phenomenon and its causation are observed and explained primarily at the gross level. It is necessary to take stock of the overall shape of things, the general pattern, but this must be in service of more detailed analysis, with sensitivity to underlying trends and exceptions. The mistake is to interpret documentation as a straightforward index of literacy: what we have are rather instances of individuals and institutions deciding to engage in certain transactions in written form and preserve their records. We cannot take the plain fact of the documentation for granted, even if it does so itself: insofar as there is a 'rhetoric of literacy' articulated in the preambles to the charters, it is the banal need to preserve an account for the future, to write it down, to make it last, and more elaborate justifications are often a giveaway of later forgery.[115] To the makers of the written record, making a written record was normal, self-evident in purpose; we have to work outwards from the charters to their reasons for being.[116]

The documentary habit was no innovation. There are a handful of charters from the first generation after the Muslim conquest of Iberia in 711, all more or less certainly forged, but the documentary record picks up as early as 745 with a donation from Lugo, albeit one which raises some doubts for its implication in the Odoario legend.[117] As in the more richly documented Catalan counties, the eighth century is simply the horizon of preservation, giving way to a wealth of charters surviving as originals in the ninth.[118] There is little interruption in practice from the Visigothic period, when the written word was part of everyday life, and the surest proof of continuity is that the charters of Asturias-León and Navarra are immediately comparable with their predecessors on slate, parchment, paper, or in *formulae*, from the sixth century to the first decade of the eighth—standardisation of script and form pre-dates the picking up of the early medieval documentary record.[119]

---

[115] See *e.g. Coruña* 9; *Burgos* 2; Laffón Álvarez, 'Arenga', 136–46; D'Emilio, 'Charter', 285–92; Calleja-Puerta, 'Valor', 179–202; *cf.* Herrero Jiménez, 'Arenga', 2, 365–406.

[116] Zimmermann, *Écrire*, 1, 9–112.

[117] *Floriano* 1–5; *Caaveiro* 15; *Lugo* 1; Vázquez de Parga, 'Documentos', 641–4, 665–8; D'Emilio, 'Legend', 47–83.

[118] *ChLA* 114, 6–10, 12–32; Alturo and Alaix, *ChLA* 112, 1–5, 8–18, 21–48; Alturo and Alaix, *ChLA* 113, 1–47.

[119] *FV*, esp. 1–3, 6–9, 15–16, 21–3, 27, 30, 39, 45; Canellas López, *Diplomática*; Fernández Flórez, *Elaboración*, 13–122; Díaz de Bustamente, 'Pizarras', 129–36; Velázquez Soriano, 'Escritura', 15–53; Herrero de la Fuente and Fernández Flórez, 'Escritura', 55–104; *cf.* Díaz y Díaz, 'Document', 52–71; García Leal, *Diploma*, 181–2.

Writing a transaction down was not a novelty but normality, the way to do business. What can be said of the chronological distribution of the documentation after it picks up? Broadly the number of charters grows over time, but far from linearly, and both features call for explanation. What follows will place these trends in the context of the 'grand narrative' of early medieval Iberia: of course, evidence outside the corpus is fleeting, and the exercise runs the risk of reductionist circularity, fitting everything into a few outline chronicles since they are all we have. It should also be borne in mind that state formation in the period was not simply 'top-down' imposition of power as the chronicles often claim, but a process of negotiation between central powers and a range of regional and local actors with differing interests and remits of authority.[120] But let us first take stock of the broad contours of documentation, and then consider where we may need to look next.

By number of charters, the Asturian period can be divided into two phases, from 711 to 850 and from 850 to 910. The eighth-century kingdom, however culturally sophisticated it was and whatever campaigns, 'depopulation', and resettlement Alfonso I carried out, has left little written record.[121] Whether reflecting reality or erasure of what came before, charters are first preserved in any real number under Alfonso II in the earlier ninth century (see Figure 1.10). After a rough beginning facing Muslim incursions and a palatine revolt, his reign is associated with stability and prosperity, which one may well see as circumstances more favourable to the production and survival of documentation: development of Oviedo as royal capital, first signs of a conscious restoration of Visigothic culture, and patronage of the cult of Santiago at Compostela.[122] Numbers then begin to increase steadily if modestly from 850 onwards. Ordoño I won early victories over both the Basques and the Banu Qasi dynasts of the Upper March, before conquering Tuy, Astorga, León, and Amaya; his son and successor Alfonso III channelled the energies of Galician magnates into taking territory from Ourense to Coimbra. Once he had driven off punitive expeditions from Córdoba and the emir sued for peace in 883/4, the remainder of his rule was devoted to internal development, 'repopulating' Zamora and restoring Simancas, Dueñas, Toro, Burgos, and Castrojeriz.[123] Expansion and consolidation

---

[120] Castellanos and Martín Viso 'Articulation', 19–42; Escalona, 'Archaeology', 40–8.
[121] See Díaz y Díaz, *Asturias*, 149–60.
[122] Ruiz de la Peña Solar, 'Monarquía', 46–60, 75–88; Ruiz de la Peña Solar, 'Rey', 42–61.
[123] Ruiz de la Peña Solar, 'Monarquía', 95–127; Ruiz de la Peña Solar, 'Rey', 61–84.

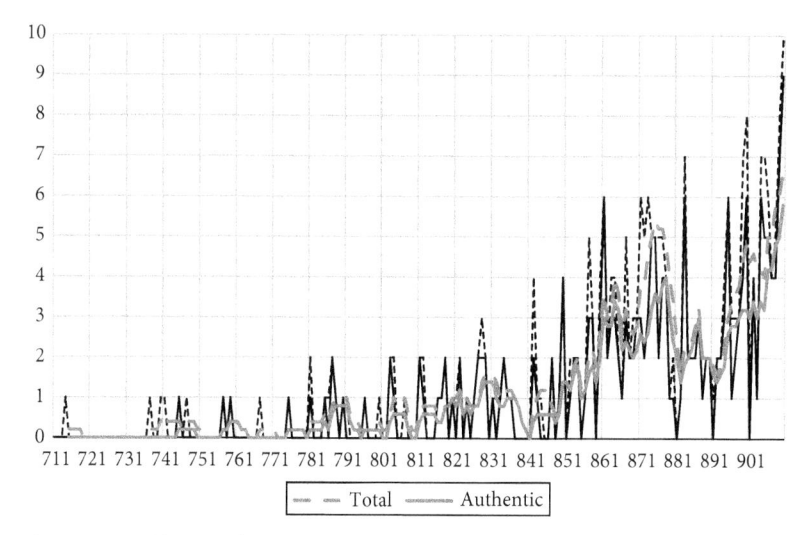

**Figure 1.10** Charters (711–910)

favour more transaction and transmission, yet neither as such provides a new reason to write anything down which would not be operable in more troubled times.

In total, some 276 charters survive from the Asturian kingdom, less than a tenth of the corpus (7%); the balance of 3,819 charters (93%) comes from the Leonese period. These can be divided into three phases: to 965, characterised by steady increase, to 998, by dramatic regression and stagnation, and to 1031, by gradual if partial recovery (see Figure 1.11). The upward trend of phase one corresponds with some territorial expansion. Ordoño II won a great victory at San Esteban de Gormaz in 917 and helped Sancho Garcés I conquer La Rioja in 923, while Ramiro II defeated Abd al-Rahman III at Simancas in 939, bringing Salamanca into the realm, but the balance of power was overall in or near equilibrium. What stability and security fostered was the foundation of new religious institutions, and the expansion of others founded in the immediately preceding decades: the trend reflects at least in part the growth of their archives.[124] Interestingly, the pronounced trough in 957–9 maps onto the overthrow of Sancho I 'the Fat' by Ordoño IV 'the Bad' and his restoration, but a case would still need to be made as to how and why high politics could have depressed

---

[124] *Ramiro II*, 339–90; Rodríguez Fernández, 'Monarquía', 174–88, 266–89.

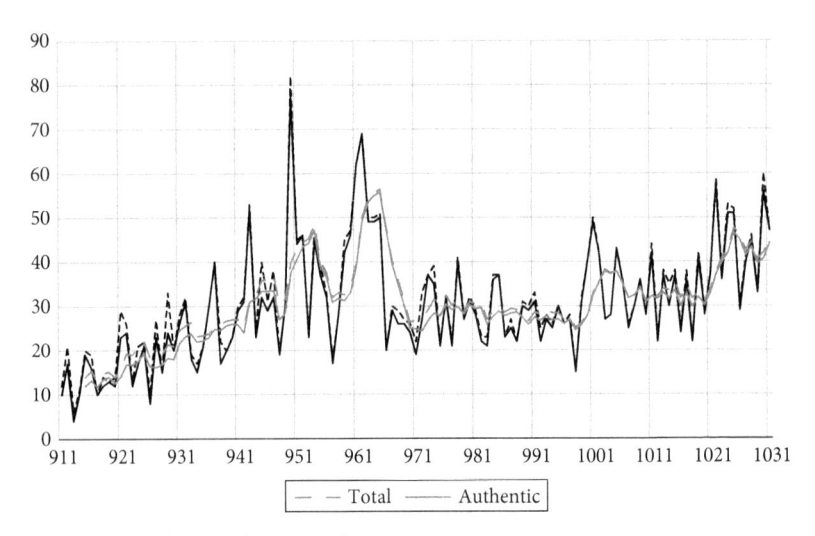

**Figure 1.11**   Charters (911–1031)

documentary practice.[125] The second phase too aligns with the reigns of Ramiro III and Vermudo II, starting with another noticeable dip between 966 and 971, years which saw an uprising of the Galician aristocracy and a protracted Viking incursion, but the numbers remain flat thereafter. Both reigns had a share of internal instability and external insecurity: Galician potentates elevated Vermudo II to the throne, sparking civil war, while he himself later faced widespread noble revolts and had to take refuge back in Galicia. Both kings also faced a resurgent and aggressive caliphate under the leadership of al-Mansur, who launched more than 20 campaigns in the reign of Ramiro III, reaching León in 982, and almost 30 under his successor, razing the capital in 986, its bastions in 994, and sacking Astorga in 996 and Santiago in 997.[126] This is definitely a context which we might expect to have affected transaction and documentation, yet if so it should have had the same effect on the preservation of prior documentation as well.

The disconnect stems from the fact that charters are not in the first instance 'political' texts, but records of social and economic transactions, as logical to be carried out in moments of crisis as in times of peace, or even

---

[125] Rodríguez Fernández, *Sancho*, 20–50, 149–74; Rodríguez Fernández, 'Monarquía', 308–30; Ceballos-Escalera y Gila, *Ordoño*, 95–128.
[126] Ruiz Asencio, 'Campañas', 31–64; Ruiz Asencio, 'Rebeliones', 215–41; Rodríguez Fernández, *Sancho*, 86–104; Rodríguez Fernández, 'Monarquía', 331–70; Ceballos-Escalera y Gila, *Ordoño*, 129–95; Martínez Sopena, 'Reyes', 137–40; Mínguez Fernández, *España*, 183–7.

more so. Military contexts can at most suggest reasons for greater or lesser preservation, though even here it would strain credibility to imagine such no doubt serious campaigns destroying all archives everywhere. The known political history contributes limiting or conditioning rather than explanatory factors; what it fails to answer is the question of why charters were written at all. In phase three, we find an erratic recovery, coinciding with the reign of Alfonso V, under the regency of his mother Elvira initially, then the Galician count Menendo González. An uptick begins amidst the final major invasions by al-Mansur, reason enough to rethink the link between military and documentary activity, but an ensuing decline fits the difficult years of 1005 to 1014, which witnessed Muslim raids into Castilla, Viking attacks in Galicia and along the Duero, and aristocratic uprisings throughout León. As the caliphate in the south began heading downhill rapidly from 1009/10, a turning point for the north came in 1017, when the king took action to rebuild and restore his realm, enacting the conciliar legislation known as the *Fuero de León*. Together with local privileges to incentivise repopulation of the capital city and ensure its supply and defence, the decree included provisions applicable to the whole kingdom, aiming to end four decades of internal disorder by favouring the uppermost social strata. One of these provisions confirmed that documentation was the most secure title to property, and went on to insist on its inviolability and necessity, the first explicit sign of 'top-down' promotion of the documentary habit in early medieval Iberia.[127] From this point the numbers increase, and they continue to rise into the first years of the youthful and ultimately short-lived Vermudo III.

In the broadest and most generous terms the chronology of the charters mostly fits in with contemporary events, as far as we know them, without those events sufficing to account for the fact of the charters. After all, no narrative of ambitious royal government lies behind the documentation until perhaps the very end of the period, and only at its beginning is there a dynamic of territorial expansion, which soon gives way to general equilibrium. In a sense, the overall numbers with their ups and downs are simply the sum of many archival histories and their individual vicissitudes. Yet this is hardly an explanation: the central institutions of these collections, the great monasteries and churches, each charted a course of prosperity and

---

[127] *Alfonso V*, 31–111; Martínez Díez, 'Tradición', 155–72 (2); Mendo Carmona, 'Pensamiento', 1, 591–626; *cf.* Rodríguez Fernández, 'Monarquía', 374–408; Fernández del Pozo, *Alfonso*, 15–143, 231–56; Fernández Flórez, *Elaboración*, 82–92; Martínez Sopena, 'Reyes', 141–6.

poverty, recorded in their documents, but in only a few cases (Sahagún, Celanova, Cardeña, to name three) do they account for all or nearly all the charters in their own archives. How do we explain the other cases—and the other charters? Nor if we look more closely do the total numbers rise neatly in concert with the foundation and development of these institutions: we might expect a generation of prior records documenting the formation of the endowment, yet at both Sobrado and Celanova the pre-monastic charters date back much farther into the past. Conversely, the Sahagún collection just begins with the monastery already there, established (the earlier Piasca series entered the archive later). And what about Otero? No religious foundation here at all, not for centuries. Even accepting the particularities of the archives which comprise the corpus, the question remains: why are there more or less charters over time? Conditioned by stability and prosperity, expansion and consolidation, internal instability, external insecurity, and finally with a bit of pressure from above, why should the total number, albeit irregularly, be growing? For an answer we need to explore the actors and actions of our texts.

## Actors

Since every charter is the product of a decision made by one or more of its parties to have it written down, who are the personnel involved? Based on a preliminary, provisional identification of the granters and recipients by type, I have assigned one of four categories to each document: royal, comital, ecclesiastical, lay (non-royal and non-comital). This is an act of simplification: if a king is a participant, I have classified the charter as royal, subdividing the category with reference to the other party, or if a (Castilian) count, as comital, unless the other party is a king, and if a member of the clergy, as ecclesiastical, unless a king or count figures, while 'lay charters' are those which feature the laity alone.[128] Determining the social identity of granter or recipient is tolerably straightforward when an explicit title is used, but this kind of labelling is inconsistent, and its absence does not necessarily justify categorising a party as lay. Epithets such as *famulus Dei* and *ancilla Domini* (servant of God, handmaid of the Lord) complicate matters, for while they sometimes denote members of the Church, they also

---

[128]   Kosto, 'Laymen', 53–6; Kosto, 'Practices', 262–8.

often function as simple honorifics recognising piety, just as a distinction between *frater* and *germanus* (spiritual versus blood brother, properly speaking) is not always transparently made.[129] These ambiguities can to a degree be controlled for by cross-referencing, identifying ecclesiastics, for example, who are only given a title on occasion, but one then confronts the further difficulty of deciding if two like names stand for the same person. For consistency, I have classified bearers of such equivocal labels as lay unless there is manifest evidence to the contrary, but a large margin for error remains, and is unavoidable. This presentation is also a gross simplification of the range of granters and recipients. Women play a prominent role of their own in the documentary process, building up estates and making benefactions.[130] This has a parallel of sorts in the phenomenon of 'double monasteries' of men and women, which should remind us that the gender divide is more blurred in this period than we might think.[131] The unexpected involvement as parties of peasant proprietors, labourers, and even those labelled 'slaves' (whatever this terminology, which encompassed multiple forms of unfreedom and servitude in the Visigothic period, denoted in the early Middle Ages) serves to underline the expansive scope of social participation in the text.[132] Acts undertaken by an entire family or a whole village too bear witness to a communal stake in documentation.[133] Each of these cases commands closer study; what I aim to provide here is merely an indicative overview.

Speaking of granters and recipients as if unitary entities is furthermore to simplify the array of channels through which they could engage in written business. All manner of agents acted for granters, whether designated representatives of kings, counts, bishops, or lay men and women, or monks like Cresconius of Celanova or Velasco of Cardeña designated to act as purchaser for the monastery; in such cases the party represented might not

---

[129] Zumkeller, 'Gebrauch', 437–45; Cantera Montenegro and Mendo Carmona, 'Antroponimia', 2, 1329–42; Arias y Alonso, 'Expresión', 11–35.

[130] Loring García, 'Poder', 603–15; Sierra Macarrón, 'Presencia', 47–57; Pallares, 'Señoras', 1, 423–42; Davies, *Acts*, 164–81; *cf.* Gómez Rabal, 'Mujeres', 261–77; Bowman, 'Record', esp. 205–7.

[131] Orlandis, 'Monasterios dúplices', 66–88; Rodríguez Castillo, 'Monasterios', 8–21.

[132] Sánchez-Albornoz, 'Siervos', 3, 1523–611; Davies, 'Status', esp. 243; Laliena Corbera, 'Documentos', 371–4; Carzolio de Rossi, 'Reflexiones', 29–50; Carzolio de Rossi, 'Antroponimia', 305–13; Martín Duque, '"Señores"', 386–95; Davies, *Acts*, 16–22, 189–93; Portass, *World*, 141–9; *cf.* Díaz Martínez, 'Sumisión', 507–24; Castellanos, *Kingdom*, 30–58; Lenski, 'Slavery', 251–80.

[133] Escalona, '"Señores"', 129; Davies, *Acts*, 198–202.

even be present at the transaction.[134] He or she could even be dead: when a testamentary executor carried out the last wishes of a deceased party, the latter is often formally identified as fellow granter.[135] In the land of the living there were various other more informal stand-ins as well, under the label of *personarius* (representative) or similar, but a reason for their appointment is seldom given. Disputes in particular involved a host of actors beyond appellant and respondent, who typically deputised an *assertor* or *responsor* (advocate) to represent them rather than acting *pro se*, while the *iudices* (judges) were in theory the most important but in practice the most elusive figures in attendance; their precise role in the proceedings is not always clear, but it appears to have been procedural as often as determinative. Judges were assisted by the *saio* (bailiff), a sort of officer of the court who orchestrated the stages of the settlement process, received oaths or oversaw ordeals, and seized or restored property.[136] Resolutions were also reached with input from others acting almost like jurors: *boni homines* (good men), the better members of the community.[137] And both transactions and disputes could employ guarantors or sureties, frequently labelled *fideiussores* ('requesters of trust'), as pledges to secure future acts or appearances by the parties.[138] Many others were involved; but to retain focus on the granting and receiving of documentation, I have included only those contributing directly to one of the two actions in this simple tabulation of charter personnel (see Figure 1.12).

Royal diplomas account for somewhat over a tenth of the total corpus, the majority granted to religious institutions or individuals, but also including 48 (1%) to members of the laity. The counts of Castilla are represented in a bare fraction of the documents, again mostly granted to ecclesiastics: treating them separately from those of other aristocracies may seem an artefact of historiographical tradition, but they use the comital title the most consistently and their diplomas have been the object of the greatest manipulation, so it is worth keeping them apart, if only to test their difference.[139] By far the

---

[134]  Carzolio de Rossi, 'Cresconio', 225–79; Cruz, 'Velasco', 251–66.

[135]  Merêa, 'Executor', 2, 1–54.

[136]  Martínez Díez, 'Instituciones', 75–7, 156–61; Collins, 'Law', 506–8; Collins, 'Visigothic Law', 86; Prieto Morera, 'Proceso', 424–501; Davies, 'Judges', 193–203; González González, 'Jueces', 1–20; *cf.* Bowman, *Landmarks*, 81–115.

[137]  Carlé, 'Homines', 133–68; Estepa Díez, *Estructura*, 255–66; Davies, 'Homines', 60–72; *cf.* Nehlsen-von Stryk, *Homines*.

[138]  Martínez Díez, 'Terminología', 1, 248–50; Davies, 'Suretyship', 138–52; Arvizu y Galarraga, 'Fianzas', 15–44; *cf.* Kosto, *Agreements*, 124–34; Forrest, *Men*, 33–62.

[139]  Zabalza Duque, *Colección*, 73; Davies, *Windows*, 20–6.

| | Royal | | Comital | | Ecclesiastical | | Lay | | Overall | |
|---|---|---|---|---|---|---|---|---|---|---|
| | # | % | # | % | # | % | # | % | # | % |
| Total | 522 | 13 | 71 | 2 | 2710 | 66 | 769 | 19 | 4095 | 100 |
| *Region* | | | | | | | | | | |
| West | 182 | 35 | 0 | 0 | 833 | 31 | 256 | 33 | 1284 | 31 |
| Centre | 210 | 40 | 4 | 6 | 1387 | 51 | 481 | 63 | 2088 | 51 |
| East | 130 | 25 | 67 | 94 | 490 | 18 | 32 | 4 | 723 | 18 |
| *Typology* | | | | | | | | | | |
| Donation | 406 | 78 | 53 | 75 | 1536 | 57 | 208 | 27 | 2212 | 54 |
| Sale | 20 | 4 | 3 | 4 | 927 | 34 | 511 | 66 | 1469 | 36 |
| Other | 95 | 18 | 15 | 21 | 247 | 9 | 50 | 7 | 411 | 10 |
| *Complexity* | | | | | | | | | | |
| Simple | 280 | 54 | 48 | 68 | 1915 | 71 | 539 | 70 | 2797 | 68 |
| Complex | 241 | 46 | 23 | 32 | 793 | 29 | 230 | 30 | 1292 | 32 |
| *Palaeography* | | | | | | | | | | |
| Original | 62 | 12 | 3 | 4 | 449 | 17 | 369 | 48 | 888 | 22 |
| Copy | 90 | 17 | 18 | 25 | 134 | 5 | 18 | 2 | 261 | 6 |
| Cartulary | 299 | 57 | 41 | 58 | 1763 | 65 | 330 | 43 | 2438 | 60 |
| Other | 70 | 13 | 9 | 13 | 364 | 13 | 52 | 7 | 507 | 12 |
| *Diplomatic* | | | | | | | | | | |
| Authentic | 348 | 67 | 25 | 35 | 2618 | 97 | 767 | 100 | 3781 | 92 |
| Suspicious | 12 | 2 | 7 | 10 | 5 | 0 | 0 | 0 | 24 | 1 |
| Interpolated | 22 | 4 | 4 | 6 | 30 | 1 | 1 | 0 | 57 | 1 |
| Falsified | 140 | 27 | 35 | 49 | 52 | 2 | 0 | 0 | 227 | 6 |

**Figure 1.12** Personnel

bulk of the corpus is ecclesiastical: fully two-thirds of the charters involve a cathedral, monastery, church, or some member of the clergy. Of this subset about two-thirds in turn (1,726 in total, or 42% overall) were granted to ecclesiastics by lay men or women, recording the steady gathering of property into the hands of the Church, while just under a third (860, or 21%) feature ecclesiastics alone, leaving 119 (3%) of the charters issued to lay men or women by ecclesiastics, notable even so given the legal inalienability of Church property. It is worth underlining the figure of 769 charters, equivalent to 19% of the corpus, with both lay granters and lay recipients. By whatever channels of transfer of property these have survived down to the present in ecclesiastical archives, they witness by the very fact of their existence and number a significant participation by the laity in modes of documentary practice.

Royal diplomas are most numerous in the centre, but if we account for the totals from each region they are distributed relatively evenly. Comital diplomas are essentially limited to the east, though a handful are preserved in Cantabrian collections. Ecclesiastical charters are more or less ubiquitous, but there is a decided difference in the case of lay charters, most of which come from the centre, followed by the west; hardly any have been preserved from the east. As we have seen, means of preservation are crucial: whereas royal and comital diplomas mainly survive in single-sheet or cartulary copies, and ecclesiastical charters track the overall breakdown by transmission, lay charters are uniquely more likely to survive as originals than as cartulary copies. We have the most in the centre, at the archives of León and Otero, and in Portugal; the east, with so few originals, has transmitted hardly any. In parallel, it is royal and comital diplomas, in keeping with their prestige, which account for the majority of forgeries, while ecclesiastical charters are false less often in comparison, and lay charters are as a rule authentic. We can also identify at a glance distinctive documentary habits: in what survives, kings and counts primarily grant donations or confirmations, whereas ecclesiastical charters vary, about three-fifths recording donations and a third sales, with a residue of other types. Lay practice stands out again, expressed in sales over twice as often as donations: indeed, sales by the laity make up more than a third of all sales in the corpus, over-representing lay charters.[140] Royal and comital society was one of giving; the Church received, the laity bought and sold.

This impression of distinctive practices is confirmed by the chronological distribution of the documentation broken down by personnel. The numbers for the Asturian kingdom are slight for trends, but the overall trajectory for the Leonese period is quite clear (see Figure 1.13). Royal diplomas 'begin' in 775, and while their weighting in the corpus peaks in the first third of the tenth century, they continue to comprise about 10% of the total. From this perspective, there is no identifiable narrative of pressure from above, an ambitious bureaucracy promoting use of the written word. Royal diplomas are essentially background noise, however voluble, and the same is true of comital diplomas, a negligible fraction of the annual numbers which feature in a few short bursts of monastic foundation. Ecclesiastical charters display the most readily comprehensible trendline: for almost the whole Leonese period they account for over half the total,

---

[140] Kosto, 'Laymen', 47–53.

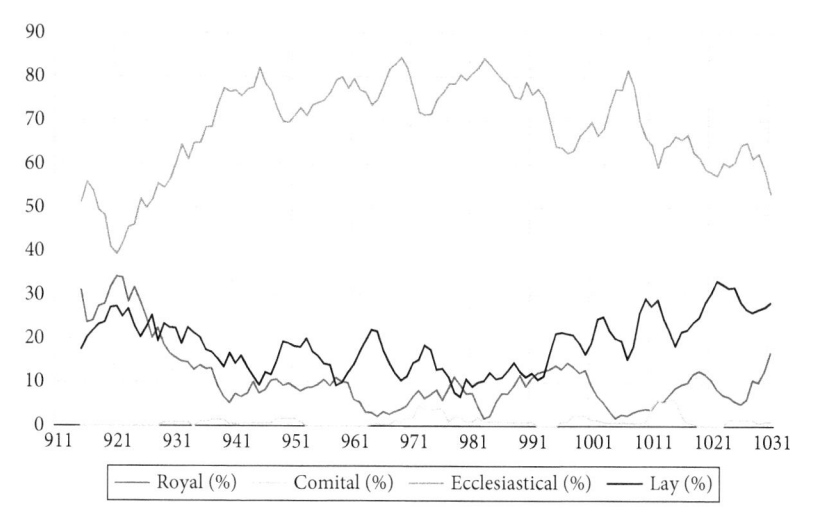

**Figure 1.13** Personnel (911–1031)

and reflect the establishment and expansion of the great monasteries and their estates by increasing radically as a proportion of the whole in the early tenth century. Yet it is striking that as we move later in the tenth and into the eleventh, this predominance begins to give way to lay charters, which become more common with each passing year from the mid-970s. Our first surviving lay charter takes us all the way back to 788, a sale of some property in Galicia for the price of seven cows, and is in fact the sixth-earliest authentic charter to be preserved overall. This makes a strong case for continuity of documentary practice from the Visigothic period even at humbler levels of society, but also against any *a priori* assumption that the habit of using the written word at such levels was either a response to demands made by royal bureaucracy or the 'trickling down' of ecclesiastical practice.[141] At the outset of the Leonese period, the number of lay charters is underpinned by the records of Hermegildo and Paterna, amassing the future estates of Sobrado, and at its close by the Otero archives of the Flaínez and Muñoz families. In between there has been a twofold rise to 30% of the corpus: the dynamic is ever greater recourse by the laity to the written word over time.

---

[141] *Coruña* 1.

## Actions

If we are going to understand why charters were written for whom they were written, we need to establish the purposes for which they were written, and to this end I have further categorised the documentation by typology. In any such enterprise there is risk of becoming lost in particularity or strangled by technicality, and so, while maintaining much of the rigid terminology of traditional diplomatic, I have given absolute priority to function over form, aiming to provide a simple and transparent summary of what charters did.[142] The corpus can be classified under three broad headings: there are 2,212 charters of donation, accounting for just over half of the total, and 1,469 sales, for just over a third, while the remaining 411 (10%) of the texts are miscellaneous records of other transactions as well as statements involving no transaction of any kind. Virtually all the charters concern landed property, but this is what led people to preserve them across the centuries; we cannot conclude from it that land alone is what drew people to use the written word. Two main goals are achieved by resorting to documentation. The first is to make a lasting record: principally in the form of establishing title to property, more broadly in any kind of account or narrative, and most of the charters fit this description. The second is to regulate, by setting out contractual terms or through listing a series of rules: such charters presume ongoing and active application for things written down. No surprises; these are basic functions of writing, and we can see how they were realised (see Figure 1.14).[143]

Most donations are plain statements of gift, documenting only the fact of it, and these account for just over a quarter of the corpus. But the next largest subset, amounting to around a tenth, includes circumstantial details, contextual explanations, or specific contractual obligations; the details are as varied as happenstance, and quite frequently encompass judicial proceedings settled by compulsory gift from the losing party. Kings granted both simple and complex donations similarly to non-royals, and though the latter can be distinguished by a longer text and greater solemnity, real diplomatic differences between documentation with 'private' or 'public' orientation are

---

[142]  Canellas López, *Diplomática*, 45–80; *Documentación*, 237–61; Riesco Terrero, 'Diplomática', 385–416, 494–541; Zabalza Duque, *Colección*, 73–86; *León*, 1, xxxv–lxiv; *Sahagún*, 2, xxxvii–lxii; and see Floriano, *Curso*; Marín Martínez, *Paleografía*.

[143]  Sierra Macarrón, 'Producción', 103–10.

| | Donation | | Sale | | Other | | Overall | |
|---|---|---|---|---|---|---|---|---|
| | # | % | # | % | # | % | # | % |
| Total | 2212 | 54 | 1469 | 36 | 411 | 10 | 4095 | 100 |
| Region | | | | | | | | |
| West | 700 | 32 | 403 | 27 | 180 | 44 | 1284 | 31 |
| Centre | 1021 | 46 | 926 | 63 | 140 | 34 | 2088 | 51 |
| East | 491 | 22 | 140 | 10 | 91 | 22 | 723 | 18 |
| Personnel | | | | | | | | |
| Royal | 406 | 18 | 20 | 1 | 95 | 23 | 522 | 13 |
| Comital | 53 | 2 | 3 | 0 | 15 | 4 | 71 | 2 |
| Ecclesiastical | 1536 | 69 | 927 | 63 | 247 | 60 | 2710 | 66 |
| Lay | 208 | 9 | 511 | 35 | 50 | 12 | 769 | 19 |
| Complexity | | | | | | | | |
| Simple | 1395 | 63 | 1343 | 91 | 59 | 14 | 2797 | 68 |
| Complex | 815 | 37 | 126 | 9 | 351 | 85 | 1292 | 32 |
| Palaeography | | | | | | | | |
| Original | 367 | 17 | 444 | 30 | 76 | 18 | 888 | 22 |
| Copy | 184 | 8 | 35 | 2 | 42 | 10 | 261 | 6 |
| Cartulary | 1316 | 59 | 879 | 60 | 242 | 59 | 2438 | 60 |
| Other | 344 | 16 | 111 | 8 | 51 | 12 | 507 | 12 |
| Diplomatic | | | | | | | | |
| Authentic | 1968 | 89 | 1467 | 100 | 344 | 84 | 3781 | 92 |
| Suspicious | 19 | 1 | 0 | 0 | 5 | 1 | 24 | 1 |
| Interpolated | 43 | 2 | 1 | 0 | 13 | 3 | 57 | 1 |
| Falsified | 178 | 8 | 1 | 0 | 47 | 11 | 227 | 6 |

**Figure 1.14** Typology

relatively insignificant.[144] Another important subset of 155, making up 4% of the corpus, consists of testaments with a particular condition of taking effect *post mortem*, deferred application which assumes retention of the document until its enforcement at death. Until then the property partly or wholly remained with the donor, at least formally, probably putting the recipient under lifetime obligation; the terms could be left unstated, as in a simple pious donation, or spelled out in the details of a complex gift.[145] The

[144] Martínez Díez, 'Instituciones', 148–51; *Documentación*, 238–44; Martínez Díez, 'Terminología', 233–5; Davies, 'Buying', 401–6; Davies, *Acts*, 30–5, 93–5, 113–30, 143–54; Carvajal Castro, *Máscara*, 57–90.

[145] Rubio, '"Donationes"', 1–32; Arvizu y Galarraga, *Disposición*, 129–31, 187–211; Sáez Sánchez, 'Donaciones', 1245–54; Vogel, *Kontinuitäten*, 54–106; *cf.* Udina i Abelló, *Successió*, esp. 128–30, 135–45.

next most common type, extant in 47 cases, is the unusual mechanism unique to Iberia of *perfiliatio* (son-making), by which the granter formally adopted the recipient in order to bequeath property, a legal fiction creating a lasting bond between the parties.[146] But there are also many more rarely instanced categories and objectives of donation: to bestow a dowry, to secure burial for oneself, to grant a *fuero* or set of local privileges and immunities, or to make an *unitas* (literally, a 'unity') or joint transfer of ecclesiastical property, as well as other 'multi-functional' charters.[147]

Such a schematic presentation tells only a part of the story. Donation did not always straightforwardly transfer title to property: a verb such as *incommuniare* (to make common) seems to imply arrangement of shared ownership, another kind of bond between the parties, as much the object of record as the land.[148] These charters forged and made lasting accounts of relationships, including entry into a monastery or patronage, and (occasionally) the lease or usufruct of property by dependants; the practice of reciprocal countergift bears out that donation entailed more than simply land changing hands.[149] They also preserved stories and formalised identities: long preambles commemorating pious foundations or restorations are in essence 'house histories', written memories of benefactions, just as more personal narratives can be 'family histories', benefactors memorialising themselves.[150] Reading such passages as preamble may miss the point: the record was as much of place or person as ownership. What needed setting down, conversely, might also be negative: absolution of a debt, discharge of a judicial obligation, or settlement of a dispute. This involved transfer of property, but from the perspective of the granter the value of the text was as proof that the matter had been closed.[151] At the same time, charters of donation established regulations as well, obviously in the case of a *fuero*, but much more often in the attached terms, whether kings transferring settlement rights by the controversial formula *ad populandum* (to settle?) or jurisdictional rights over a *mandamentum* or *mandationem*, an administrative or seigneurial sphere of operations. Many ordinary gifts have a proviso under a phrase

---

[146] Cruz, 'Considerações', 407–78; Merêa, 'Perfilhação', 119–26; Barbero and Vigil, *Formación*, 379–94; Martínez Díez, 'Terminología', 244–8.

[147] Orlandis, 'Elección', 5–49; Martínez Díez, 'Terminología', 243–4, 269–70.

[148] Isla Frez, 'Relaciones', 5–18; Davies, *Acts*, 80–7.

[149] Orlandis, ' "Familiaritas" ', 95–279; García de Valdeavellano, ' "Renovo" ', 408–48; Davies, *Acts*, 52–61; Davies, 'Reciprocity', 67–82; Davies, 'Gift', 231–5; Davies, 'Notions', 272–5; García Lozano, 'Typologies', 111–24.

[150] See *e.g. León* 432, 701, 803.

[151] Davies, 'Buying', 407–10; Davies, 'Gift', 229–30.

such as *sub ratione servata* (stipulating that), outlining some limits or conditions on the use of the property.[152] In both the goals achieved by resorting to documentation in all these cases, charters were more than moments, and had enduring implications as records of relationships, histories, identities, and rules.

Sales present fewer varieties, as the overwhelming majority, some nine-tenths of all such transactions or just over one-third of the total corpus, are simple statements. Only 112 records of sale (3% overall) offer circumstance or context, normally the outcome of judicial proceedings where the penalty has been formulated thus instead of as the more usual donation. Exchanges differ from sales, in transactional terms, only in the stated price being landed property rather than moveables or monetary units, and few of these are attested. Both were looser categories than we might imagine, in that sale can be present in the same charter as exchange but more commonly overlaps with donation or other types of record.[153] The remaining charters are a miscellaneous lot encompassing both transactions and statements, together making up a tenth of the corpus. The most numerous record dispute settlements, though separating these from the many complex donations and sales which document payment of a judicial penalty is in practice somewhat artificial. Accounts of settling disputes subordinate the material outcome to the narrative, participating in the creation of an official record: if it were solely a matter of documenting title, they could more simply take the form of donations, sales, or confirmations to the victorious party, but many describe the proceedings step by step, setting out arguments and stages of proof leading to resolution.[154] Closure depended on more than a simple record of ownership; the means of obtaining it and the consensus of all parties to it counted.

This 'catch-all' third category demonstrates, despite its diversity, the twin function of charters to record and to regulate. The *placitum* (a written agreement) could emerge from the same densely textual framework of dispute settlement, but others are standalone contractual arrangements, and this sense of the term preserves a late Roman legal definition, whereas in the rest of the early medieval west it designated an assembly, typically

---

[152] Ayala Martínez, 'Relaciones', 200–32; Martínez Díez, 'Terminología', 266–8; Martínez Díez, 'Servidumbre', 1, 641–7; Carvajal Castro, *Máscara*, 154–62.

[153] Fernández Espinar, 'Compraventa', 293–528; Martínez Díez, 'Instituciones', 151–5; Davies, 'Sale', 149–74; Casado Quintanilla, 'Pan', 1, 163–98; Martínez Díez, 'Terminología', 235–8; Davies, *Acts*, 135–8, 156–60; Davies, 'Gift', 223–9; Davies, 'Notions', 275–8; Davies, 'Exchange', 471–89.

[154] Balzaretti, 'Narratives', 11–37; Foot, 'Charters', 39–65.

judicial.[155] Another typology peculiar to Iberia with similarly contractual force is the monastic pact, a legacy of Visigothic monasticism by which abbots and monks bound themselves to each other under certain conditions and obligations.[156] While monastic pacts and *placita* had implications for property, they also presume the ongoing relevance of text, in the same way as the noteworthy subset of confirmations renewed both past transactions and their records. Typically the gift of new granters to the original recipients or successors, these represent a strategy to safeguard ownership by regular recognition or addition to it: nothing necessarily changed hands, but a relationship between past and present granter and recipient was renewed by way of property, even with a further element of story-telling of the land and its proprietors. Beyond these are charters with multiple functions, such as the unique *colmellum divisionis* (literally, 'column of division', perhaps a sorting process), a tool for the inventory and allocation of aristocratic patrimonies; and other narratives and texts with anywhere from secondary to no proprietorial content at all like the famous autobiographical narrative of Odoíno Vermúdez from 982 and the controversial letter of Alfonso III to the clergy of Tours in 906.[157] Finally, there are also as many as 63 inventories and *notitiae* (2% overall), lists of anything from cows to cheese and charters which employ the written word to administer as much as to record.[158] They offer a fleeting glimpse of more occasional and varied uses for text beyond documenting transaction in land.[159]

Assessing the relationship between typology and other features can reinforce some of the conclusions suggested by consideration of personnel. Donations and sales are both most common in the centre, less so in the west, and least in the east; the miscellaneous charters are the outliers, proportionately overrepresented in the west compared with elsewhere, which is something to bear in mind. Neither donation nor sale seems especially associated with one or another means of transmission, but again the 'other' type stands out as linked particularly to cartulary copies, also the form in

---

[155] Martínez Díez, 'Instituciones', 154–6; Petit, *Fiadores*, 130–3; Prieto Morera, 'Proceso', 386–401; Davies and Fouracre (eds), *Settlement*, 273; Martínez Díez, 'Terminología', 250–5; Davies, *Windows*, 35–55, 279–83; *cf.* Kosto, *Agreements*, 78–120.

[156] Martínez Díez, 'Terminología, 269–70; Létinier, 'Naturaleza', 49–66.

[157] Muñiz López, 'Rosendo', 229–37, 253–4; Rodríguez Baixeras, *Historia*; Pick, *Daughter*, 132–5; Fletcher, *Catapult*, 317–23; Henriet, 'Lettre', 155–66; *cf.* Bowman, 'Written Record', 173–80.

[158] *Pedro*, 571–644; García Leal, 'Inventario', 327–42; Morala Rodríguez, 'Nodicia', 2, 2019–32.

[159] See Marques, Carvajal Castro, and Barrett (eds), *Charters*.

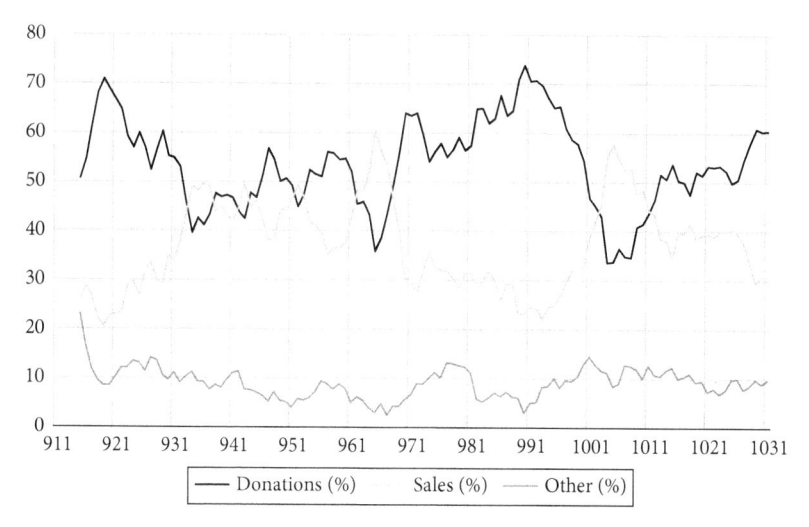

**Figure 1.15** Typology (911–1031)

which most western documentation survives. Donations are the most likely to be forged, followed at a distance by miscellaneous charters, whereas all but two sales seem to be authentic. There is no real reason why a false sale should not make good title to property, but the correlation is a function of the personnel profile of transaction, in that donations account for the majority of royal and comital diplomas. While the association with ecclesiastical charters, making up nearly two-fifths of the corpus, is unsurprising, lay donation is unexpectedly well attested, at least considered as a fraction of charters involving the laity, and was evidently not exclusive to the interaction of lay men and women with the clergy.[160] But whereas sales are around a third of ecclesiastical charters, they comprise two-thirds of the charters of the laity, as their typical mode of business. Equally clear is the connection of 'other' charters with kings and ecclesiastics, readily explicable by the issuing of confirmations.

More unexpected is the chronology of transaction. All three categories are in evidence in the Asturian kingdom, but clear trends emerge during the Leonese period (see Figure 1.15). Donations and sales play out an inverse relationship, fluctuating in alternation, with donations peaking in the early and late tenth century and the early eleventh, while sales briefly overtake them in the 930s, 950s, 960s, and 1010s. Apart from an

---

[160] Davies, *Acts*, 139–43, 154–6.

initial spike, the proportion of 'other' charters in the corpus essentially hovers at or below 10%. There is a macroeconomic history of transaction here to write, but for our purposes what is key to note is that sales are only a percentage point or two more common at the end of the Leonese period than at the outset; in contrast, the incidence of donations has risen over the same timespan by ten points.[161] Since lay charters become more regular from 911 to 1031, the laity are engaging more regularly in acts of donation, a transaction formerly more common to other groups in society.

When operating at this level, there is a danger of being led astray by some underlying *mutation documentaire*, a change in the formulation of the written record which gives a false impression of fundamental transformation, or conceals it.[162] As a (very) crude control I have devised a category of 'documentary complexity' to provide some notice of whether the form of the charters changed over time. Documents which state a transaction plainly, with at most formulaic contextualisation, I have labelled 'simple', and those which offer justifications or outline conditions I have branded 'complex'; the miscellaneous other types are the only ones to present any real challenge for classification, but the difference between a simple statement of confirmation and a complex monastic pact can and should be recognised (see Figure 1.16). Simple charters outnumber complex charters by more than two to one. Complex charters are proportionately more common in the west and centre, less in the east; they are slightly more likely to be forged, while transmission is not apparently a major factor. Rather unexpectedly, transactions involving members of the clergy are more often simple than in the case of other personnel types, perhaps a reflection of the routine quality of many ecclesiastical donations, while royal charters have the highest incidence of complexity, fitting their greater propensity for elaboration. Lay charters are simple and complex at a little over the overall ratio of two to one, meaning that their documentary practice is not atypical in this regard, though sales are ordinarily simple in form. The chronological distribution fills out this picture (see Figure 1.17). Simple and complex charters represent almost the same fractions of the total corpus in 911 as in 1031: the relative incidence fluctuates in a range of about 20%, but it is not trending in any consistent direction. Where does this leave us? The major change which

---

[161] Ayala Martínez *et al.*, *Economía*, 57–74, 257–74; Portass, 'Beginnings'; *cf.* Ubieto Arteta, *Ciclos*, esp. 55–60, 117–21.

[162] Barthélemy, 'Mutation', 767–77; Bedos-Rezak, 'Sources', 320–1; Barthélemy, *Serf*, 12–36; West, 'Meaning', 71–87.

| | Simple | | Complex | | Overall | |
|---|---|---|---|---|---|---|
| | # | % | # | % | # | % |
| Total | 2797 | 68 | 1292 | 32 | 4095 | 100 |
| Region | | | | | | |
| West | 745 | 27 | 536 | 41 | 1284 | 31 |
| Centre | 1516 | 54 | 570 | 44 | 2088 | 51 |
| East | 536 | 19 | 186 | 14 | 723 | 18 |
| Personnel | | | | | | |
| Royal | 280 | 10 | 241 | 19 | 522 | 13 |
| Comital | 48 | 2 | 23 | 2 | 71 | 2 |
| Ecclesiastical | 1915 | 68 | 793 | 61 | 2710 | 66 |
| Lay | 539 | 19 | 230 | 18 | 769 | 19 |
| Typology | | | | | | |
| Donation | 1395 | 50 | 815 | 63 | 2212 | 54 |
| Sale | 1343 | 48 | 126 | 10 | 1469 | 36 |
| Other | 59 | 2 | 351 | 27 | 411 | 10 |
| Palaeography | | | | | | |
| Original | 587 | 21 | 300 | 23 | 888 | 22 |
| Copy | 141 | 5 | 120 | 9 | 261 | 6 |
| Cartulary | 1695 | 61 | 740 | 57 | 2438 | 60 |
| Other | 373 | 13 | 132 | 10 | 507 | 12 |
| Diplomatic | | | | | | |
| Authentic | 2625 | 94 | 1151 | 89 | 3781 | 92 |
| Suspicious | 15 | 1 | 9 | 1 | 24 | 1 |
| Interpolated | 26 | 1 | 31 | 2 | 57 | 1 |
| Falsified | 130 | 5 | 96 | 7 | 227 | 6 |

**Figure 1.16** Complexity

we have observed in the charters falls under the rubric of personnel. Across the early Middle Ages, we have more and better evidence for lay participation in the written record, while the written record itself remained much the same in typology and complexity; the laity were moving into types and complexities of documentation formerly more common to kings, counts, and the clergy. Lay literacy, in other words, was expanding. The question left to answer is why.

## Textual Memories

We have two paradigms for explaining medieval literacy, 'top-down' or bureaucratic pressure and 'ground-up' or personal choice. In a sense the one

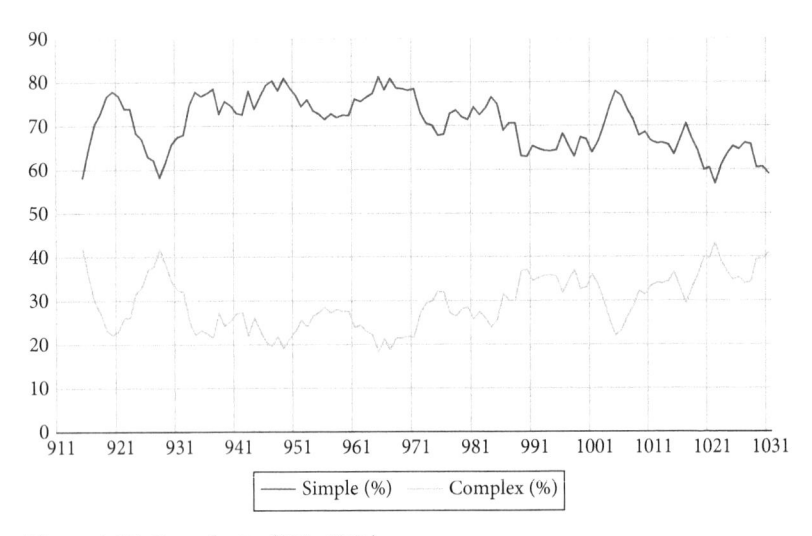

**Figure 1.17** Complexity (911–1031)

is a limited case of the other: for a person to make the decision in favour of the written word, its use must be incentivised, its utility demonstrated, and while strong government can accomplish this by ratcheting up the demands of bureaucracy, it is only one possible means of doing so. There was no strong government in early medieval Iberia, yet there was a profusion of documentation, growing in size and scope over time. The outline of an answer to the question of why can bring our two paradigms together. We have a rare opportunity to see the transition from memory to written record playing out 'live' thanks to an exceptionally dense set of charters from the monastery of Celanova, which made 31 acquisitions in the Galician village of Rabal da Igrexa, less than ten kilometres away, in the years between 956 and 974, plus another 14 transactions in the village from 987 to 1031.[163] The earlier subset is the more interesting: a concentration of some 22 charters date to 961 and 962, shining a particularly bright light on the workings of a small communal world.[164] Until this series, the village is unattested: if charters were in use here before 956, they were not being retained, since none is incorporated into the monastic archive, whereas for many other properties

---

[163] *Celanova* 116–18, 125, 128–41, 143, 145–52, 162–3, 173, 178, 201, 211, 227, 232, 234, 244, 262, 269, 329, 337, 339, 362, 376, 382.
[164] Pallares Méndez, *Ilduara*, 38–47; Pallares Méndez and Portela Silva, '*Villa*', 13–43; Sánchez-Pardo, 'Estrategias', 168–77; Portass, 'Rethinking', esp. 96–103; López Sabatel, '*Villa*', 78–100.

Celanova has preserved documentation from prior to when it came into ownership of them. We are not likely to be looking at first contact with writing: the Visigothic slates and formulaic standardisation from the earliest post-Visigothic charters both caution us to expect at least some continuity of documentary practice even in remote and rural areas. What we can observe is a shifting balance towards use and retention of charters, practice and place not so much coming into contact as developing a more intimate relationship, which can model how documentation diffused more generally in Iberia.

The earlier subset of Rabal charters depicts a community which, before the arrival of the monastery, was able and accustomed to guarantee title to property by means of memory, without need for recourse to the written word. All but three of the 31 charters record sales by villagers to Abbot Rosendo and Celanova, each identifying and delimiting the land involved by one or more of three methods. Most commonly this meant specifying landmarks, such as paths or streams, hedges or fences, springs or wells, and local named spots, which bordered the property.[165] Complementary practices included enumerating neighbours and listing some or all previous owners, providing a chain of ownership.[166] Note the reliance on the physical and the personal: in the village, features of the terrain and members of the community, both generally known, offered sufficient precision to designate property, and before the coming of Celanova transaction doubtless proceeded on these bases. The charters are also witnessed by members of the village, and their names and roles are important to note. Some had a stake in the transaction: they are amongst those recorded as neighbours or prior owners, including the descendants of prior owners.[167] All parties to each sale had a clear interest in getting the nod from such relevant figures, and in binding their approval to it. In total some 165 individuals (or at least 165 different names) witness the 45 charters from Rabal, but in the earlier subset 18 of them appear on a recurrent basis, ranging from four to 15 times each (see Figure 1.18).

Who are these people? They are the means by which title to property was lodged in communal memory: identified and delimited by recognisable features of the land itself and with reference to relevant persons past and present, it was implanted in the consciousness of certain 'interested observers',

---

[165] See *e.g. Celanova* 138, 141, 143, 162.
[166] *Celanova* 117, 131–7, 139–40, 145–51, 163, 178.
[167] *Celanova* 131–5, 146, 173.

*Celanova*

| Witness | 116 | 117 | 118 | 125 | 128 | 129 | 130 | 131 | 132 | 133 | 134 | 135 | 136 | 137 | 138 | 139 | 140 | 141 | 143 | 145 | 146 | 147 | 148 | 149 | 150 | 151 | 152 | 162 | 163 | 173 | 178 |
|---|---|---|---|---|---|---|---|---|---|---|---|---|---|---|---|---|---|---|---|---|---|---|---|---|---|---|---|---|---|---|---|
| Gundesindo | | X | X | | X | X | X | X | X | X | X | | | X | X | X | X | X | X | | X | X | | | | X | X | | | | |
| Vistremirus | X | X | X | | X | X | X | X | X | X | X | X | | X | X | X | X | X | X | | X | X | | | | | X | | | | |
| Mito Gundesindi | | | X | | X | X | X | X | X | X | X | X | | X | X | X | X | X | X | X | X | | | | | | X | | | | |
| Asoi | X | | X | | X | X | X | X | X | X | X | X | | X | X | X | | X | X | | X | X | | | | | | | | X | |
| Argemirus | | | X | | X | X | X | X | X | X | | | | | | X | | | | | | | | | | | | | | | |
| Itila | | X | | | | X | X | X | X | X | | | | X | | | | X | X | | X | | | | | | | | | | |
| Ascarigo | | X | | | X | X | X | X | X | X | | | | X | | | | X | X | | X | | | | | | | | | | |
| Ragiane | | X | | | X | X | X | X | X | X | | | | | | | | X | | | | | | | | | | | | | |
| Rando | | X | | | | X | X | X | X | | | | | | | | | | | | | | | | | | | | | | |
| Sisiverto | | X | | | | | | | | | | | X | X | | | | | X | X | X | X | X | | | | X | | | | |
| Gunderigo | | | | | X | X | X | X | X | X | | X | | | | | | X | X | X | X | | | | | | | X | | | |
| Recesindo | | | X | | X | | | | | | X | X | | | | | X | | | | | | | | | | X | | | | |
| Argemirus | | | X | | X | | | | | | | X | | | | | X | | | | | | | | | | | | | | |
| Berane | | | X | | X | | | | | | | | | | X | X | | X | X | | | | | | | | X | | | | |
| Cindo | | | | | X | | | | | | | X | X | X | | | | | | X | | | | | | | | | | | |
| Vimara Ragianiz | | | | | X | X | X | X | | X | | | | | | | | | | | | | | | | | | | | | |

| Witness | Total |
|---|---|
| Gundesindo | 15 |
| Vistremirus | 14 |
| Mito Gundesindi | 13 |
| Asoi | 12 |
| Argemirus | 7 |
| Itila | 7 |
| Ascarigo | 6 |
| Ragiane | 6 |
| Rando | 6 |
| Sisiverto | 6 |
| Gunderigo | 6 |
| Recesindo | 5 |
| Argemirus | 5 |
| Berane | 4 |
| Cindo | 4 |
| Vimara Ragianiz | 4 |

**Figure 1.18** Witnesses to Rabal Charters

a crucial group of other villagers, guardians of memory or, in less grand terms, those who were habitually present at transactions. Some of them must have been local élites or the possessors of some elevated status within the village. Gundesindo and Mito Gundesindi witness 15 and 13 charters respectively, while Ragiane and Vimara Ragianiz witness six and four, in both cases seemingly fathers passing on their responsibility for remembering to sons.[168] Two more occasional witnesses, Argemirus and Recesindo, are intermittently given the devotional title *confessus*, frustratingly vague in meaning and without any institutional affiliation; a certain Summiro, the local *ferrario* (blacksmith), witnessed one transaction in 961, but otherwise neither the occupation nor the standing of these personages is stated.[169] Significantly, the four most regular witnesses, who make from 12 to 15 appearances each, are all untitled—they were simply those who saw and remembered.

The arrival of Celanova in Rabal introduced an imbalance. The charters which reveal for us the life of the village were produced for the monastery in the course of its acquisitions, but who wrote them? The only scribe named in the earlier subset, Nepotianus, is also attested as a *frater* (brother, generally, or a monk?) who had planted a vineyard there for Celanova.[170] In other words, he was a monastic agent transplanted into the village, where he wrote at least one of its title deeds. But it is not a stereotypical case of literate clergy arriving amongst the illiterate: there were religious institutions in Rabal, present in the prehistory of the charters, a monastery of San Pelayo and a church of San Mamede.[171] Mirus seems to have been priest of the latter, and made three charters of sale to Celanova; when he identifies the former owners of one of his vineyards, he makes no mention of having acquired it by charter.[172] Enmeshed in the community and its memory, these institutions did not need written title to property any more than did the other villagers. Celanova, in contrast, purchased by charter, not only out of its own habitual practice but also because it lacked such a base in communal remembering to secure and perpetuate its rights of ownership through those means. The monastery also went about documenting earlier transactions which had not been documented. In 961, the previous owner of some land being sold to it was called on to confirm the charter of sale, as

[168] Pastor, *Resistencias*, 33–7.
[169] *Celanova* 136; Torres Rodríguez, ' "Confessus" ', 154–74.
[170] *Celanova* 128, 141.
[171] *Celanova* 125, 130, 136, 143, 163.
[172] *Celanova* 130, 135, 143.

if to create a 'retrospective charter' of her own prior unwritten alienation of the property, and thereby to prevent her from ever reclaiming it by appeal to memory.[173] And as Celanova amassed more holdings in Rabal, it began referencing its own documentation, noting in an exchange of 974 the pair of charters by which it had acquired that property in 956 and 961, even naming their granters.[174] Until this point the village had been 'unwritten', but the monastery was casting it into a written framework. In their charters the monks had lasting proof of ownership, all but guaranteed to win out, as we shall see, in the event of a dispute. To restore the balance, self-interest would have brought the villagers to adopt the written record themselves.

We might call this a 'lateral diffusion' model of literacy. Exposure to charters which conferred definite advantages on their users should be expected to engender the adoption of documentary practice and stimulate the development of documentary habits in new quarters. And if we apply this model to the contours of our corpus, the expansion of estates becomes the driver of documentation in early medieval Iberia. Who owned these estates matters less than their habit of building, maintaining, and defending them by charter: from the beginning of the Leonese period, we observe both ecclesiastics and lay aristocrats doing so right across the north, not least the founders of Celanova.[175] Rather than a single channel of bureaucratic pressure from above, the story is of incentive from many directions, countless local instances of institutions and individuals acquiring written title to property, and giving their neighbours a reason to turn to text: as estates grew, landowners entered into communities where memory had sufficed, and a new balance was struck in favour of charters.[176] These communities were not meeting with the written word for the first time—they had been accustomed to it for long centuries. Royal government was not demanding or diffusing the documentary habit, nor was the typology or complexity of charters notably changing. The written word was settling more deeply into local society, amongst the laity, villagers, and the peasantry. Exposed to its uses, they gained reason to use it. As we turn to look at the charter in practice, we shall see it promote not only its own use but also the use of other written authorities, drawing on and projecting a network of texts, reliably proving

---

[173] *Celanova* 134.
[174] *Celanova* 178.
[175] Carlé, 'Propiedad', 1–224; Carzolio de Rossi, 'Propiedad', 59–112; Ayala Martínez, 'Relaciones', 140–9, 179–85; Davies, *Acts*, 207–13; Carvajal Castro, *Máscara*, 208–16; cf. Carvajal Castro, 'Use', 325–49.
[176] Escalona, 'Knowledge', 351–79.

the surest means of gaining and defending title to property. Once actors had cause to carry out their actions in charters, all else followed: like the ups and downs of contemporary political and military history, the personal literacy of any actor was a constraint, only that. Once text had been shown to confer advantage, arrangements for access were made, and the scope of charters in society broadened and deepened over time, a process which we can still apprehend despite the partial and selective channels of transmission which have brought them down to the present day.

# 2
# Creating

The charter may be a product of the society and culture which it describes, but it need not be representative of either even so. What if our corpus amounts to notes in the margins of a world which worked otherwise? We need to make all the basic reportorial enquiries before a charter, or indeed anything written, can serve as evidence for the world without its text. The questions of what and why are fundamental, but only the beginning. Who wrote our charters, by what means, in what context? How were they made known more generally—if they were? This chapter is dedicated to the who, how, when, and where of the documentation. When we look for agents of literacy in early medieval Iberia, we find that primary literacy, first-hand or personal writing and reading, is nearly invisible amongst both the parties and witnesses to the transactions, and so in this society of secondary or second-hand literacy, where making use of the written word by proxy was the norm, scribes become our quarry. And yet those objects of our search remain persistently elusive, retaining an anonymity which belies the centrality of their role. They were more than humble functionaries, but how much more? If we pursue for whom they wrote, we can identify a broad network of scribes spanning every level of society. We can trace their working methods, operating within a framework of standardised language derived from earlier charters, but also showing signs of regionalism, localism, individualism in customising formulaic texts to concrete moments. At the same time, scribes were players in a more complex drama, a dynamic relationship with parties and witnesses which unfolds over the preparation and placement of the charter on parchment, its relationship in time to the transaction which it documents, and the context of confirmation, location as well as audience. Charters emerge as far from simple records of transactions: they are convergences of people and place, context and content, reaching beyond text to the realm of speaking and hearing. In seeking a home for the charter, we find a whole society organised around the written word at one remove, expecting and arranging to use it by gathering, watching, and listening.

*Text and Textuality in Early Medieval Iberia: The Written and The World, 711–1031.* Graham Barrett,
Oxford University Press. © Graham Barrett 2023. DOI: 10.1093/oso/9780192895370.003.0003

## Agents

One venerable approach to medieval literacy is 'counting crosses', using the marks of confirmation made by parties and witnesses to charters as an index of direct engagement with written records. There are difficulties, not least where the evidence survives in cartularies or other secondary forms of transmission, but it can nonetheless provide a valuable steer.[1] Take the Leonese monastery of Sahagún, for which we have 84 originals surviving from the early Middle Ages: in almost 70% of them, both names and corresponding crosses, where present, of all granters and witnesses were written in by the same hand as the main text—by the scribe himself. There are few unquestionable occurrences of autograph names, and just one clear-cut case, in the monastic pact signed by the nuns of Santa María de Piasca in 941, which while of course significant cannot be assumed to reflect the practices of wider society (see Figure 2.1).[2] There could be autograph monograms or crosses on as many as ten documents, but the marks are too exiguous for conclusive palaeographic analysis.[3] Much the same profile describes the other principal collections of originals, including the archives of León, Otero, Lugo, and Portugal: personal involvement in written confirmation was not the cultural norm, regardless of social standing, occupation, or clerical status, and when practised at all generally took the form of making a simple cross or even just adding in some dots to adorn one prepared by the scribe.[4]

The fact that both those whom we might expect to be literate and those we might not are found equally rarely writing their own names or crosses on charters points us to a cultural practice rather than a social reality of illiteracy. Petrus *gramaticus* (*sic*: 'Pedro the grammarian'), when it came his turn to witness the testament of Bishop Fronimio of León in 928, scrawled SSS for *subscripsi* ('I have undersigned'), and left the rest to the scribe.[5] Even allowing for a few outliers like the famous Petaus (*fl.* 184–7), a village clerk in Egypt who was essentially illiterate, it strains credibility to imagine that

---

[1] Collins, 'Literacy', 125; Casado de Otaola, 'Escribir', 118–22; Everett, 'Literacy', 363; Declercq, 'Action', 55–73.

[2] *Sahagún* 79; Cavero Domínguez, 'Monasticism', 27–8; *cf. Sahagún* 39, 87, 153, 242; Jarrett, 'Nuns', 125–52.

[3] *Sahagún* 33, 155, 165, 170, 250, 253, 257, 269, 281, 302.

[4] See *e.g. Lugo* 52; Pereira, 'Symboles', 491–502; Mendo Carmona, 'Suscripción', 207–27; Mendo Carmona, *Escritura*, 1, 381–5, 2, 1–220; *cf.* Conde and Trenchs Odena, 'Signos', 443–52; Ghignoli, 'Writing', 20–3.

[5] *León* 76; Mendo Carmona, *Escritura*, 1, 384, 2, 51.

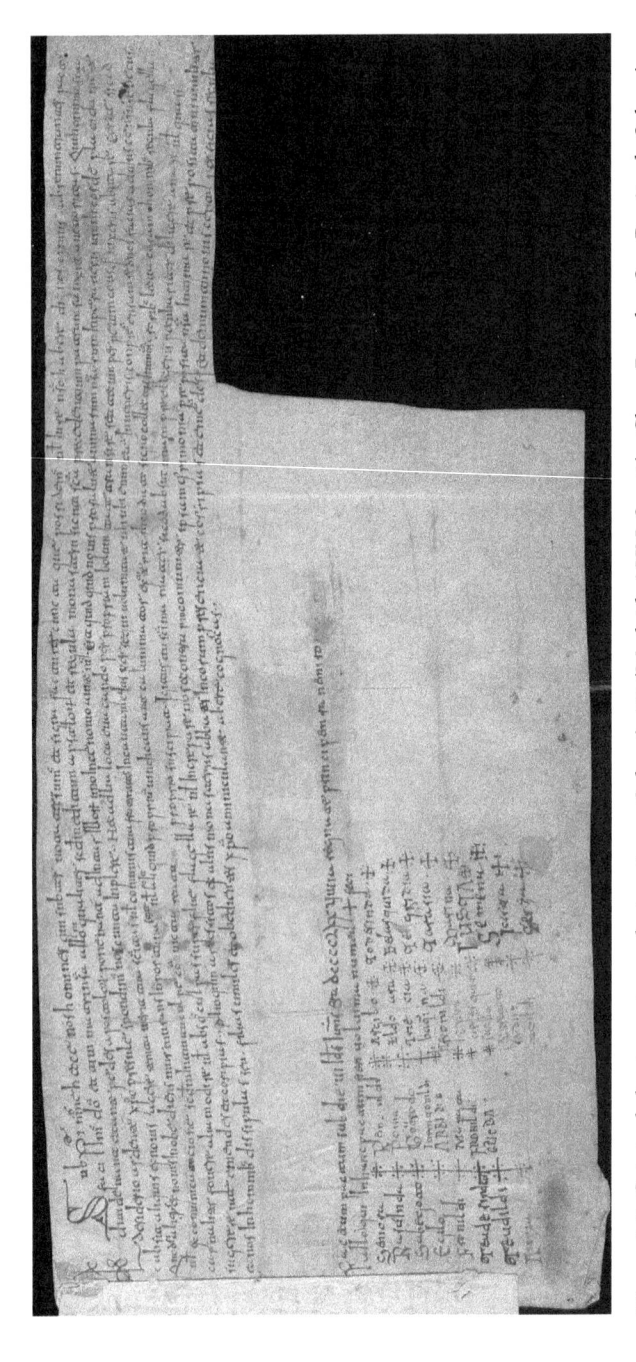

**Figure 2.1** Original charter, autograph signatures: *Sahagún* 79 (Madrid, AHN, Sección Clero, Regular, San Benito de Sahagún, carp. 873, no. 6: Ministerio de Cultura y Deporte. Archivo Histórico Nacional. CLERO-SECULAR_REGULAR,Car.873,N.6)

every such instance of minimal participation in writing straightforwardly reflects an inability to do so.[6] Returning to Sahagún, a remaining 15 original charters conjure an interesting contradiction: the scribe is responsible for all the subscriptions, but as if to mimic a lower level of proficiency has deliberately shifted to a distinct 'signature hand' to write them, in one example even simulating a crude *feci* ('I have made [a cross or sign]') beside the name of each granter.[7] Particularly telling is a donation to Piasca from 945 where the confirmations of the witnesses have been written out by the scribe at a slight tilt relative to the main text, characteristic of 'signature hand', while on the reverse side of the parchment are what seem to be autograph signatures of the same (see Figures 2.2–3).[8]

The phenomenon suggests that personal validation, in spite of its overall rarity, was a general expectation, but responsibility for the act had been shifted to the scribe. Perhaps this first took place to accommodate those unable to intervene directly in the text themselves, before it then gradually became normal, even preferred practice on account of the greater facility of the scribe, as we can see in the improved versions on the front of the Piasca charter. Both the palaeography and the rhetoric of the text seek to veil this more complex reality of what a 'signed charter' entailed: as Osorio Díaz claims in his testament to Sahagún of 986, *pagina stilo signamus* (we sign the page with a pen), or Alfonso V in a sale and donation of 1012, *manu mea stilo* (with a pen by my hand).[9] Charters claim to us that they have been ratified *sigillatim* (individually), signed *per singula capita* (one by one, by head count); granters can be introduced as *qui subscripta vel signa facturis sum* (I who am going to make subscriptions or signs), or *qui subter notari vel signaturi facti sumus* (we who have been recorded and are going to have signed below), priming us to process as personal efforts the corresponding names, monograms, crosses, or other signs which follow.[10] Yet when we look closer, we find something else entirely.

Not all granters affix signs to their charters: especially when husbands and wives act in tandem (even if kings and queens), or parents and children, or abbots and monks, there can often be more names than signs in the confirmation. In 950, for example, Abbaz and Iaquinti, together with their wives, made a sale to San Cipriano del Condado, but only the two men are

---

[6] Youtie, 'Pétaus', 127–43; Youtie, 'Literacy', 239–61.
[7] *Sahagún* 3; cf. 4–5, 39, 52, 78, 153–4, 228, 242, 311, 379, 407, 426.      [8] *Sahagún* 96.
[9] *Sahagún* 330; *Otero* 90; cf. *Celanova* 91; *Sobrado* 1.49.
[10] *Albelda* 19; *León* 628; *Astorga* 77; *Santillana* 3; cf. *Liébana* 24; *Santillana* 10; *Samos* 44; *Celanova* 1–2, 4; *Lorvão* 24; Bádenas Población, 'Representaciones', 335–54.

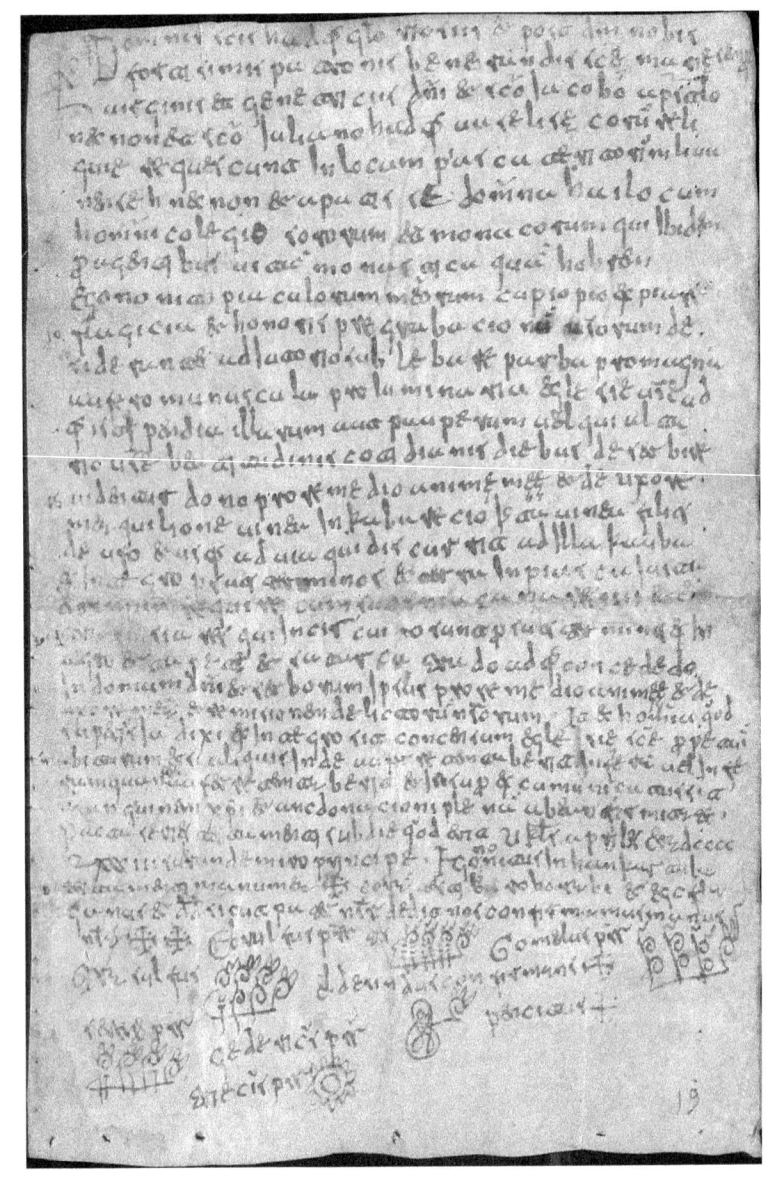

**Figure 2.2**  Original charter, 'signature hand': *Sahagún* 96 (Madrid, AHN, Sección Clero, Regular, San Benito de Sahagún, carp. 873, no. 10: Ministerio de Cultura y Deporte. Archivo Histórico Nacional. CLERO-SECULAR_REGULAR,Car.873,N.10)

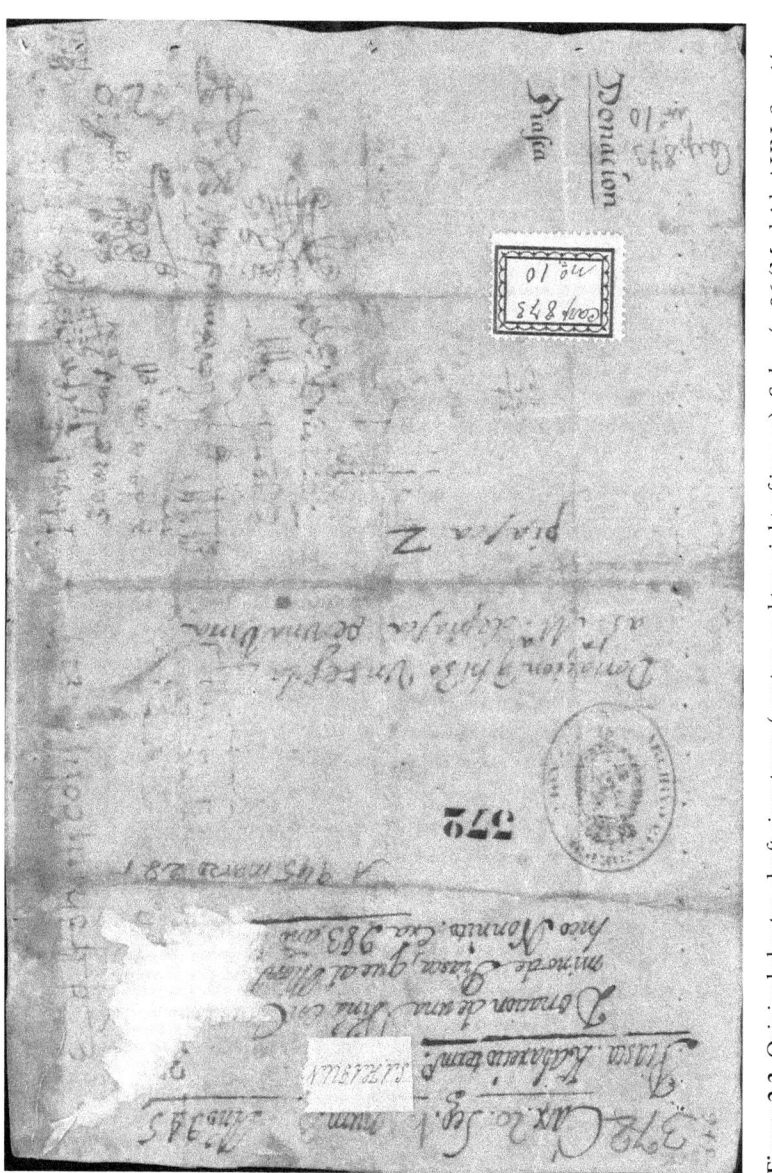

**Figure 2.3**  Original charter, draft signatures (see top and top right of image): *Sahagún* 96 (Madrid, AHN, Sección Clero, Regular, San Benito de Sahagún, carp. 873, no. 10, dorso: Ministerio de Cultura y Deporte. Archivo Histórico Nacional. CLERO-SECULAR_REGULAR,Car.873,N.10).

listed as subscribers, with just one sign between them; similarly, when Columba and her six children sold land to San Pedro de Eslonza in 963, she alone is identified as a subscriber, yet alongside four signs.[11] The temptation here is to draw inferences as to the scope of literacy in society: that men were more able to write than women, or adults more than children, that men or adults were primary participants in charters, women or children secondary.[12] All seemingly reasonable propositions, but the evidence is unclear. In 988, two married couples sold a pair of vineyards to Velasco and his wife Leda: not only are there four names with just three signs in the confirmation, but they have all been made by one hand, and with a common crossbar.[13] Who should we deduce is literate or illiterate? The passage from signs to signatories is further complicated when the former outnumber the latter, such as the sale by Hazan and Alvalide to the monastery of Abellar in 990, to which three marks of confirmation are affixed.[14] Did one of them or someone else make the third? Why? How can we use it as evidence without being sure? On some occasions, extra signs may well reflect intervention by other parties: in a sale by Salvatus and Framildi in 1031, for instance, Toda, the mother of Salvatus, puts in a sudden appearance in the confirmation, and yet we still have four signs for three names.[15] Recipients could decide to subscribe their own charters; mostly an explanation proves elusive.[16]

The same problematic applies to witnesses. We read that they are *pro roborem subter adnotantium* (recorded below for confirmation); when we look, we duly find that *sunt firmes* (there are confirmations), even autograph subscriptions like those of Bishop Oveco of León, an abbot, and two others at the foot of the testament of Diego Muñoz and his wife Tegridia in 940.[17] But can we always be certain? Where a name stands out in script or formula from the rest of the confirmation, is it a solitary autograph or a discreet identifier of the scribe?[18] What about when we encounter a set of four witnesses, all with signs written by a single hand, and another set of eight

---

[11] *León* 221; *Eslonza* 28; *cf. León* 205, 226–7, 235, 237, 284, 449, 460, 502, 526, 534, 537, 609, 612, 685, 760; *Eslonza* 20; *Otero* 20, 46, 77, 82, 117, 123, 135, 139, 165–6, 169, 180, 182; *Sahagún* 400; *Covarrubias* 2–3; *Ourense* 1.

[12] Riesco Terrero, 'Diplomática', 445–57; García Medina, 'Signos', 85–94.

[13] *León* 523.

[14] *León* 542; *cf.* 345, 519, 664, 678, 712, 739, 766; *Coruña* 8; *Coimbra* 72; *PMH* 214, 243, 268.

[15] *León* 895; *cf.* 267, *Otero* 14; *San Vicente* 18; *Albelda* 8; *Celanova* 92.

[16] See *e.g. León* 168, 176, 185, 642.

[17] *Celanova* 23; *San Juan* 35; *Entrepeñas* 1; *cf. San Vicente* 18.

[18] See *e.g. Otero* 52; *Eslonza* 22; *San Vicente* 5; *Liébana* 4; *Celanova* 4, 7; *Coimbra* 514; *Guimarães* 53, A2.

witnesses with only two signs written by a second hand, in a charter from 988, or 12 subscriptions, the first four and the last eight by different hands, in a document from 951?[19] Who has signed on behalf of which witnesses and why? Comparing names with signs once again counsels caution when determining who could confirm for themselves. Not all witnesses affix signs of confirmation, but in no obvious pattern: in a sale to Munio Flaínez and his wife Froyleva from 961, there are no marks beside any of the eight names, whereas in another sale of 1023 a priest is the only witness with a sign, yet in a third from 949 the priest is the only confirmer without one.[20] What conclusions can we draw about status and ability to write even a simple cross in subscription? Witnessing a royal diploma of 912 is a quartet of names, untitled and unqualified, with four signs and a trio of bishops with only two signs, but does this tell us that the laity, counterintuitively, were more able in this regard than the higher clergy?[21] In a donation of 1020, the *primiclerus*, senior cathedral official amongst the clergy present, is one of four witnesses of the 16 listed not to make a sign.[22] Or take the series of originals from Eslonza: sometimes there are fewer signs than names for the ecclesiastical witnesses, sometimes for the lay witnesses, more often for both of them.[23] Across the corpus of originals, indeed, there are consistently more names than signs in confirmation.[24]

Can we say only that some were able to put a cross next to their name and others were not? Bound to be true, so far as it goes, but the evidence can bring us a little farther. Mascito and Odo, making a donation to Eslonza in 929, handed their charter over to witnesses *rogitas* (invited) to confirm it: what follows in the first witness column is four blank fields, each of them lined up with the word *confirmans* and a sign, and a fifth space beside the title *presbiter* and a sign, while there are additional blanks in two of the other four columns (see Figure 2.4).[25] The simplest inference is that the scribe had expected at least five more witnesses, including a priest, than ended up materialising, and had prepared the text accordingly, or conceivably that the five or more witnesses had left by time the scribe wrote out the text, and as such were not listed with the ones who stayed on. Nor is this case an anomaly: 15 of the originals from

<hr />

[19] *Otero* 29; *Oviedo* 25.    [20] *Otero* 12, 162, 8; *cf.* 87, 105, 110.    [21] *Eslonza* 1; *cf.* 2.
[22] *Oviedo* 43; Pérez Rodríguez, '*Primiclerus*', 77–101.
[23] See *e.g. Eslonza* 5–6, 8–9, 11, 14, 21, 24, 26, 31, 33.
[24] See *e.g. León* 600; *Sahagún* 250, 407; *Oviedo* 1, 12, 33, 40–1; *Valpuesta* 45; *Coruña* 10, 19; *Mondoñedo* 6; *VDJ* 4–5; *Ourense* 3; *Samos* S3; *ChLA* 114, 32; *PMH* 16.
[25] *Eslonza* 10; *cf. León* 4; *Ramiro II* 5.

**Figure 2.4** Original charter, empty brackets: *Eslonza* 10 (Madrid, AHN, Sección Clero, Regular, San Pedro de Eslonza, carp. 957, no. 13: Ministerio de Cultura y Deporte. Archivo Histórico Nacional. CLERO-SECULAR_REGULAR,Car.957,N.13)

Sahagún, or almost 20% of the total, have empty brackets, unused place-holders for additional witnesses.[26] Ordinary if not ubiquitous, this may account for the two erased witnesses with only incomplete signs in a charter of 974, for example, and many or most of the cases where signs outnumber names.[27] Indeed, when taken together with the infrequency of autograph names and signs, the subscription sector of the charter comes into new focus as something other than it seems: less a set of signatures by parties and witnesses than a roll call, a sort of attendance register kept by the scribe but variously made to look like individual work to fit expectations. And even when the textual framing recognised some intermediacy, this fiction remained: Abbess Momadonna, in her testament of 1006, *testes ad roborandum conscripsi* (wrote out the witnesses for confirmation), while in a charter of sale to Valpuesta from 935, the witness list ends with the name of Abbot Severo, *in cuius manus rovoraberunt* (by whose hand they confirmed), a common formula applied to parties and witnesses in documents from this archive and others mainly in the east.[28] Twelve witnesses in a late tenth-century dispute *scribserunt conditiones sacramentorum per manum saioni* (wrote out the terms of the oath by the hand of the bailiff), whereas the *innocens* (neutral party) and two participating bishops affixed signs *per manus meas*.[29] Emphasis varied, but while few really confirmed 'by their own hands' or those of others than the scribe, the rhetoric of the text insisted on it.

The complexity of the relationship between the parties to a charter and its scribe can be appreciated most readily in the use of monograms or elaborate personal *signa* in place of crosses or simple marks for subscriptions.[30] Like other rulers across the early medieval West, the kings of Asturias-León confirmed their own diplomas and private charters with intricate symbols based on the letters of their names, since at least the earliest surviving originals of Silo and Ordoño I in 775 and 860.[31] Every monogram for an Alfonso or a Ramiro, in other words, is formed of the

---

[26] *Sahagún* 80, 125, 164, 170, 221, 228, 251, 264, 266, 269–70, 302, 316–17, 426; Sáez Sánchez, 'Crismones', 439–42; Cabezas Fontanilla, '*Invocatio*', 62–9.

[27] *Otero* 19; cf. *Covarrubias* 14; *San Juan* 55.

[28] *San Millán* 696, 316; *Valpuesta* 14; cf. 16, 19, 33, 44, 49; *San Millán* 359; *Oña* 6, 10; *Cardeña* 295; *Celanova* 244.

[29] *Sobrado* 1.109.

[30] Casado de Otaola, 'Representaciones', 39–56; Sáez, 'Signo', 339–63; Sánchez Prieto, 'Poder', 101–15.

[31] *León* 1–2; *ChLA* 114, 11–12; Floriano Llorente, 'Documentos', 171–4; Ruiz Asencio, 'Escritura, monogramas', 1, 274–95; cf. Garipzanov, *Language*, 157–202; Garipzanov, *Signs*, 199–205, 255–72.

same elements, a message of dynastic continuity; as the work of the scribe, a commission of the king executed by proxy (beyond perhaps a line or two), it is also a reference to all other written acts under his name and those of his predecessors.[32] As such the monogram can further be read as an emblem of royal authority in general, and indeed the legislative *Fuero de León* of 1017 provided that anyone who should break this *sigillum* (here a figurative sign, made by hand or ring—the pendant seal comes later) should pay 100 *solidi* plus the value of what he had stolen, as if he had broken oath with the king.[33] Original royal diplomas before the later tenth century are rare, and reconstructing prior practice from single-sheet and cartulary copies which could be projecting a tradition back in time risks circularity, but we have originals with monograms of García I, Ordoño II, Fruela II, Alfonso IV, Ramiro II, and Ordoño III, alone or in company with queens or princes.[34] Thereafter we are on much firmer ground: Vermudo II, Alfonso V, and Vermudo III all arranged for their monograms to be affixed to diplomas surviving in the original, both their own grants and in contemporary or posterior confirmation of those made by others.[35] The kings of Navarra present rather more of a problem, owing to the prevalence of forgery amongst their diplomas; it is not until the reign of Sancho III that the practice can be attested, and then in only a single example.[36]

As in the Carolingian world, but more broadly still, monograms were also employed at other levels of society.[37] From the latter half of the tenth century especially, the bishops of León appear in charters with their *sigillum* as granters, recipients, witnesses, and participants in disputes, though much of the evidence comes from imitations in cartulary copies.[38] They acted furthermore as confirmers of charters concerning parties and properties in the diocese, especially religious houses in the environs of the city, where their

---

[32] Mendo Carmona, 'Signos', 77–101; Pacheco Sampedro and Sotelo Martín, ' "Signum" ', 2, 419–38.

[33] *Oviedo* 42; Canellas López, 'Sigilografía', 49–58; Menéndez Pidal, 'Sellos', 245–82; Menéndez Pidal, *Sellos*, 101–93; *cf. LV* 7.5.1–2.

[34] *Eslonza* 1–2, 5; *Sahagún* 22; *Eslonza* 6, 9; *Ramiro II* 63; *León* 298.

[35] Vermudo II: *León* 530, 541, 548–9; *Otero* 30; *San Pelayo* 1. Alfonso V: *León* 581, 588, 707–8, 741, 754, 748, 760, 767, 770, 788, 806; *Otero* 90, 101, 124; *Braga* 22; *Lugo* 58. Vermudo III: *León* 708, *Otero* 196.

[36] *Albelda* 32; *cf. San Juan* 16.

[37] Riesco Terrero, 'Diplomática', 457–69; Ostolaza, 'Validación', 453–62; Sáez and García Medina, 'Signos', 207–18; Ruiz Asencio, 'Escritura, monogramas', 1, 296–312; *cf.* Garipzanov, *Signs*, 205–16, 255–72.

[38] *León* 220; *cf.* 521, 530, 539, 541, 548, 571, 574, 611, 623, 629, 658, 677, 707–8, 736–7, 741, 746, 803, 806; *Sahagún* 402; *Otero* 90, 124; *Eslonza* 9.

monograms stand for their regional authority.[39] In comparison the habit is scarcely attested in the west or east, but since there are far fewer surviving originals, it may be wise to reserve judgement as to the localism of the phenomenon.[40] At one step down, abbots had their roles in the documentation, not only as parties but also as witnesses, attested by monograms. Again these are Leonese in the main, but the practice may differ: Abbot Pedro affixed the *sigillum* of his monastery of San Pelayo de Cerrato to a testament of 934 on behalf of his congregation and their future ownership of the donated property, implying that it was corporate as much as personal.[41] Priests from León made some use of monograms too, primarily as witnesses, but also on occasion when acting as recipients.[42] And while deacons could likewise have personal devices of their names, the examples are found primarily in royal diplomas and include Petrus Kendulfiz, the scribe and future bishop of Astorga.[43] Then again, when 11 religious made a 'charter of unity' to an Asturian monastery in 976, three of them had monograms affixed, forming part of a small set of humbler and more obscure members of the clergy who used their own such signs.[44]

The employment of monograms had a degree of corresponding purchase amongst the men and women of the laity, so far as one can judge, but primarily those from the upper strata of society. In a minority of cases they apply to untitled granters or witnesses to unexceptional transactions, but most are in royal diplomas, for counts, judges, 'majordomos', and their ilk.[45] Once described as the *proceres palatii* and *onestissimi laici* (nobility of the palace and most distinguished laymen) of Alfonso IV, they participated regularly in documentation by virtue of proximity to the court.[46] The most common users of monograms, however, are the scribes themselves. Some of those with high profiles, like Cidi and Sampiro, have left more than a dozen

---

[39] *León* 514, 587, 617, 618B, 627, 630, 635, 659, 700–701, 703, 706, 710, 732, 748, 767, 788, 796; *Otero* 2, 30, 101; *Eslonza* 1–3, 5, 10.

[40] See *Alfonso V* 4; cf. *San Juan* 44.

[41] *San Isidro* 6; cf. *León* 7, 531, 544, 549, 640, 788; *Sahagún* 384; *Eslonza* 6, 9; *Covarrubias* 2; *Alfonso V* 4.

[42] *León* 527; *Otero* 186; *Eslonza* 31; cf. *León* 88, 138, 531, 666, 708, 732, 736, 767; *Valladolid* 3; *Otero* 11; *Eslonza* 1–2, 5–6; *Valpuesta* 3.

[43] *León* 865; cf. 442, 549, 736; *Otero* 30; *Eslonza* 1–2, 6; *Lugo* 58; Ruiz Asencio, 'Escritura, monogramas', 1, 298–303; Castro Correa, 'Pedro', 103–32.

[44] *Otero* 20; cf. *León* 439, 454, 489, 512, 531, 535, 582, 587, 857.

[45] *León* 531, 694; *Otero* 19; cf. *León* 530, 548–9, 587, 729, 837; *Sahagún* 407; *Valladolid* 3; *Otero* 196; *Eslonza* 1–2, 5–6, 8; *Celanova* 302; *Alfonso V* 4; *Valpuesta* 3; *Covarrubias* 7; Ruiz Asencio, 'Escritura, monogramas', 1, 296–8, 310–12.

[46] *Eslonza* 9; Estepa Díez, *Estructura*, 154.

examples, others such as Vivi and Fulgentius nearly as many.[47] Three to five instances survive for another ten scribes, while a further 103 are uniquely documented.[48] As a sign of professional competence, many scribes played with text in their monograms, incorporating into the design a system of letter correspondences called 'Visigothic cryptographic' to hide the reading of their name from all but the initiated.[49] Yet, looking across the full range of its uses, the monogram is the seal of early medieval Iberia: synecdoche for that sector of society which, without needing to be personally literate, dealt ordinarily and often with the written word.[50] Though our sense of its scope is limited by the concentration of surviving originals in the centre, socially the monogram had a wide compass, identifying royalty, clergy, and laity alike. To have one known to a scribe, or to arrange for one to be designed by a scribe, marks a reality, or the expectation, of regular recourse to documentation, even a pride in doing so, a desire to stand out from others with rudimentary crosses. It carried a certain 'literate status' or cachet: to have one meant association with those who habitually engaged in written modes of transaction, even though, like the charter itself and its apparatus of confirmation, it was in the first place the work of the scribe, the architect of this textual society.

## Scribes

If we start our search for the scribe by looking for granters or recipients who wrote for themselves, we quickly run up against the same limits and contradictions as govern the study of subscriptions. Take the most famous testament from the period, drawn up by San Rosendo in 977: he calls it *olografum* ('holograph'), and as it is preserved only in a cartulary copy and a scribe is not named in the text, there is no proof to the contrary.[51] In the same vein, Gotina Núñez opens her testament to Sahagún of 1025 with the words *hunc textum nostrum seriem paginali stilo contexens* (composing this our series of

---

[47]   Cidi: *Otero* 67–71, 121, 125, 127, 140, 165, 172, 174, 194; Sampiro: *León* 541, 549–50, 594, 669, 707–9, 730, 748, 754, 767; *Sahagún* 404; Vivi: *León* 647, 854, 856, 866–8, 870, 877–8; Fulgentius: *León* 621, 661, 666, 700, 710, 731, 746, 804.

[48]   (1) *Otero* 75–6, 105, 183, 189; (2) 110, 117–20; (3) *León* 777, 803, 857, 860, 893; (4) 608, 618, 658, 827; *Sahagún* 427; (5) *León* 558, 604, 617, 698; (6) *Otero* 37, 90–91, 175; (7) 177, 191–3; (8) *León* 556, 561–2, 605; (9) *Valpuesta* 37, 40, 45; (10) *Otero* 151, 164, 176.

[49]   Galende Díaz, 'Elementos', 173–83.

[50]   Riesco Terrero, 'Diplomática', 417–45, 469–93; Clanchy, *Memory*, 309–18.

[51]   *Celanova* 185; Díaz y Díaz, 'Testamento', 55–8; Sánchez Collado, 'Aproximación', 567–86.

text with the pen of the page), just as a bishop of Pamplona asserts that he *exaravi* (noted down) two royal diplomas of which he was beneficiary in 1018 and 1031.[52] Other cases are more ambiguous: when Iohannes *confessus* confirmed his testament to San Vicente de León with the words *a me exaratum* (noted down by me) in 1028, was he referring to the charter or his own subscription?[53] How indeed are we to read any such statement of authorship when Alfonso II declares in 812 that he has *contulit conscribsit firmavit* (granted, written out, confirmed) his testament *stilo conscribtionis nostre* (by the pen of our composition), and yet at its conclusion Iustus is named as scribe?[54] Some recipients may have copied out their own charters. In a sale from 984 to Vita *ebreo* (the Jew) and his wife Vita, the scribe is identified as Vitas, plausibly one of those two, while another to Lalano *presbiter* in 1001 was written by a certain Lalano *presbiter*, and in the Liébana we find the priest Iohannes apparently writing up two sales to himself in 1001.[55] Given the rarity of the name, could the Argirigu who made a sale to Celanova alongside his wife and children in 954 be its copyist Argirigo *presbiter* too?[56] In 991 the judge Braolio heard a case of battery and seems to have written up the *plazum* (for *placitum*) of resolution.[57] Of course, it could all be one great onomastic coincidence, but at least there are two charters addressed to the notary Sampiro from 1013 which are written in his own recognisable Visigothic cursive.[58]

While such first-hand literacy can be glimpsed, for members of the clergy and scribes especially, second-hand composition of charters is the norm. What most frustrates the search for the scribes responsible is that they do not always identify themselves: Sampiro may have written those two charters for himself, but he nowhere says so, just as Onorio *presbiter* names himself as writer of a document dated to 28 August 1017, yet on 18 May 1017 leaves only his monogram.[59] In fact, a scribe is identified in only 1,676 (41%) of the charters (see Figure 2.5). There is a definite regional pattern here: in the centre, with the fewest forgeries and the most originals, a much higher incidence than in the west or the east (except Portugal and Arlanza respectively). Scribes, unexpectedly, are named the most often in lay charters, the least often in ecclesiastical charters,

[52] *Sahagún* 415; *Pamplona* 9, 11; *cf. Valpuesta* 6; *San Juan* 8; *Coruña* 4.
[53] *León* 847; *cf. Liébana* 57; *Albelda* 22; *Pombeiro* 1.    [54] *Oviedo* 2–3; *cf. Coruña* 110.
[55] *León* 495; *Otero* 51; *Liébana* 78, 80; *cf. León* 687; *Otero* 3, 19; Puentes Romay, 'Caracterización', 2, 679–86.
[56] *Celanova* 106.    [57] *Otero* 31; *cf. León* 677.    [58] *León* 715, 717.
[59] *Otero* 109–10.

| | Scribe | | Overall | |
|---|---|---|---|---|
| | # | % | # | % |
| Total | 1676 | 41 | 4095 | 100 |
| **Region** | | | | |
| West | 404 | 24 | 1284 | 31 |
| Centre | 1120 | 67 | 2088 | 51 |
| East | 152 | 9 | 723 | 18 |
| **Personnel** | | | | |
| Royal | 221 | 13 | 522 | 13 |
| Comital | 31 | 2 | 71 | 2 |
| Ecclesiastical | 970 | 58 | 2710 | 66 |
| Lay | 449 | 27 | 769 | 19 |
| **Typology** | | | | |
| Donation | 920 | 55 | 2212 | 54 |
| Sale | 625 | 37 | 1469 | 36 |
| Other | 130 | 8 | 411 | 10 |
| **Complexity** | | | | |
| Simple | 1109 | 66 | 2797 | 68 |
| Complex | 565 | 34 | 1292 | 32 |
| **Palaeography** | | | | |
| Original | 490 | 29 | 888 | 22 |
| Copy | 147 | 9 | 261 | 6 |
| Cartulary | 914 | 55 | 2438 | 60 |
| Other | 124 | 7 | 507 | 12 |
| **Diplomatic** | | | | |
| Authentic | 1517 | 91 | 3781 | 92 |
| Suspicious | 10 | 1 | 24 | 1 |
| Interpolated | 29 | 2 | 57 | 1 |
| Falsified | 118 | 7 | 227 | 6 |

**Figure 2.5** Named Scribes

while neither typology nor complexity has a noticeable correlation with the distribution. The rate of scribal identification rises along the diplomatic scale from authentic to false, and we may take naming a scribe to have been a common component of forgery; conversely, it wanes along the palaeographic scale from original to late summary, and was evidently a feature frequently dropped in the course of transmission. Even amongst originals, however, a scribe is recorded in just over one out of every two charters: if we had more, the notable inconsistency of the practice would still impede our enquiry.

What can be said about scribes from this subset of the charters? In their subscriptions they made regular, though far from constant, use of titles: from these, all scribes seem to have been members of the clergy, or more accurately, none is demonstrably one of the laity.[60] How we evaluate that absence of evidence depends on our assumptions about access to education; the charters themselves offer no objection to at least some untitled scribes being laymen, and while church and cloister were doubtless the majority context for scribal activity throughout our period, we should resist making any categorical judgements.[61] The titles most commonly used are *presbiter* and *diaconus* (priest and deacon), which almost all titled scribes adopted at some point. Less so are various other clerical and monastic labels, such as *clericus, confessor, confessus, conversus, frater, monachus, sacerdos*; rarer still are *episcopus, abba, praepositus* (an 'estates manager' of sorts), tending to be employed only in transactions involving senior ecclesiastics.[62] More functional terms for writer—*exarator, notarius, scriba, scriptor*—have an intermittent presence, sometimes substituting for or combining with religious epithets, but they are also applied to scribes whose careers are confined to forgeries, such as Gomessanus, Possidonius, Umbertus, or Velasco.[63] Rarest of all are professional identifiers, *grammaticus* or *iudex* or *magister* (grammarian, judge, teacher), which convey a sense of what else these shadowy figures may have done.[64] The one classic distinction of no significance here is that between 'private' scribe and 'public' notary: over 22 appearances, Fulgentius calls himself a *notarius* only once, roughly two-thirds of the way through his 'career', without any obvious explanation or implications for his status or role in what was a pre-notarial society.[65]

Beyond a few titles, scribes have left us precious little evidence for building a picture of their identities. Scribal colophons to documents mainly take the form of brief, impersonal prayers or requests for prayers, unlike those in literary manuscripts which can be longer and more expressive of the craft of

---

[60] Mendo Carmona, *Escritura*, 385–92; Mendo Carmona, 'Escribas', 27–32; Riesco Terrero, 'Diplomática', 365–70; Zabalza Duque, *Colección*, 90–1; Fernández Flórez, 'Documentos', 2, 115–16; *cf.* Mundó, 'Statut', 21–8; González González, 'Cultura', 196–200.

[61] Fernández Flórez, 'Escribir', 17–67.

[62] Andrade Cernadas, 'Aproximación', 279–92.

[63] Riesco Terrero, 'Diplomática', 370–5; Álvarez Maurín, 'Léxico', 2, 523–8; Fernández Flórez, 'Documentos', 106–10, 118–22.

[64] Jeannin, 'Greffier', 119–31.

[65] Canellas López, 'Notariado', 1, 105–6; Mendo Carmona, 'Consideraciones', 11–23; Riesco Terrero, 'Notariado', 137–46; Davies, *Acts*, 99; *cf.* Everett, 'Scribes', 42–55; Zimmermann, *Écrire*, 1, 138–74.

writing and the practice of reading.[66] One exception comes in a donation from 1022 written by Citi *presbiter*, writer of 17 other surviving charters: a second hand added the greeting *ego Fortes ppresbiter saluto vobis domno Citi ppresbiter* (I, Fortes the priest, greet you, lord Citi the priest), and appeal *multum et per multum memento nostri* (remember us well, indeed very well).[67] Perhaps a student to his master? Not much to go on. Scribes of charters could of course be copyists of books, and we meet Vigila of Albelda and Florentius of Valeránica in the documentation, both creators of famous manuscripts.[68] Some of their signatures accordingly draw from the vocabulary of codicology: Florentius employs the verb *depinxit*, for illumination, in a donation of 937 to San Andrés de Boada, while the writers of a series of charters from Arlanza prefer *titulavit*, for rubrication.[69] There is no obvious difference in formulation between these and others in the same collection where the scribes opt for *exaravit*, originally denoting writing on wax tablets.[70] Florentius may have been referring to the drawing of his elaborate 'castle-shaped' monogram, or perhaps this is simply romanticising the drudgery of drafting with words of artistry; writers emphasised different aspects of the process, and practice varied.[71]

Scribal confirmations underline a range of actions which the work could entail. Some draw attention to the specific type of writing, whether *notas fecit* (he made [these] notes) in a notice or inventory from 924, or *iterum notavit* (he transcribed or copied it out for the second time).[72] Others focus on the writing up as a totality, as in one *testamentum a me conscriptum* (testament composed by me), or broken down to its most basic unit: *hanc cartam scribi et per alfabetum divisi* (I wrote this charter and distributed it letter by letter).[73] At the conclusion of a long charter from 929 confirming the foundation of a monastery we encounter Petrus, *qui hoc testamentum dictando percucurri* (who ran through this testament by dictation), but if so, who dictated and who wrote?[74] Aloytus *diaconus et notarius* stated in a

[66]   Díaz Salvado, 'Colofones', 361–78; *cf.* Sanz Fuentes, 'Tiempo', 48–56; Brown, 'Remember', 262–78; Brown, 'Scratching', 199–214; and now Brown, *Remember*.

[67]   *Otero* 152; *cf. Lugo* 10.

[68]   Williams, 'Contribution', 232–5; Pérez de Urbel, 'Monasterio', 2, 71–90; Fernández Flórez, 'Calígrafo-miniaturista', 162–80; García Molinos, 'Florencio', 259–64, 381–414; *cf.* Fernández Flórez, 'Escribir, en León-Castilla', 158–61; Fernández Flórez, 'Escribas', 169–99.

[69]   *Arlanza* 14; *cf.* 6, 8, 13, 23–4.

[70]   *Arlanza* 5, 25–6; *cf. León* 520; *Otero* 188; *Eslonza* 33; *Valpuesta* 27.

[71]   Escalona, Velázquez Soriano, and Juárez Benítez, 'Identification', 274; *cf.* Díaz y Díaz, 'Cultura altomedieval', 1, 218–40.

[72]   *Vermudo III* 2; *PMH* 27.        [73]   *Eslonza* 1; *San Juan* 13; *cf. Celanova* 111.

[74]   *Eslonza* 9.

donation to Celanova of 941 that he *scribens dictavi*, repeating a year later *dictavi et scribsi*, but do both mean that he 'took dictation', or that dictation was synonymous with writing?[75] When Bishop Oveco of León endowed San Juan de Vega de Monasterio in 950, the abbot confirmed, *ubi presens fui* (being present in person), the text as *bene dictata per manus* (well dictated through the hands) of the scribe Adulfus *diaconus*.[76] Plausibly this 'through' could mean that the recipient of the transaction explained its terms to the writer as he cast it into shape. Simply put, dictation was part of the act of writing: Ledantinus *presbiter* and Sempronia *testamentum nostrum condidi scrivendum dictavi* (dictated our testament to be set down in writing) in 951, but the work of writing it up fell to Ermegildus Menendus *presbiter qui unc scripsit*, as he signs off.[77]

Scribes could also specify various roles in the transaction itself, emphasising overall their intimate involvement in how it played out. There is more than 'present and accounted for' even in a simple signature such as Romanus *presbiter qui interfuit* (who took part in it).[78] In a royal diploma of 955 we find Menzius *presbiter et notarius scribsit et pro testis*, acting dually as writer and witness, or as elsewhere that year expressed more simply, *excripsit et ic preses fuit* (he wrote and was present here).[79] Scribes highlighted the act of witnessing, like Egilanem *sacerdos* who *quod vidi manu propria notuit* (transcribed what he saw by his own hand), or of auditing, like Simplicius *diaconus* who wrote down *quod audivi et vidi* (what he heard and saw).[80] There is something faintly defensive about Urno *presbiter qui hanc carta rogitus non presumtus scripsit* (who wrote this charter by request, not presumption), perhaps an insurance policy of sorts, to stress that he was no busybody but working on commission.[81] Invitation was evidently key: Vermudo *scripsit per mandatum de* (wrote at the order of) the signatories of a monastic pact in 1009, and the granters of a donation in 850 stipulated that *rogabimus fratrem Galindonem qui pro nobis scriptor accessit* (we invited brother Galindo who attended on our behalf as the writer).[82] More than a relationship, a partnership between party and scribe was being delineated, a claim to status such as Sampiro made when titling himself *notarius* or even

---

[75] *Celanova* 65, 72.   [76] *León* 220; *cf. Celanova* 198.
[77] *Oviedo* 25; Álvarez Maurín, 'Léxico', 528–30; Davies, *Acts*, 99–101.
[78] *Astorga* 180; *cf.* 225; *San Millán* 147.
[79] *Celanova* 110; *Sahagún* 366; *cf. Arlanza* 10; *Celanova* 3; *Guimarães* 68, A6.
[80] *Celanova* 304; *Sobrado* 1.34; *cf. Celanova* 326.
[81] *Huesca* 12; *cf. León* 11; *Oviedo* 28; *Huesca* 8.   [82] *Santillana* 20; *San Juan* 5.

more grandly *maiordomus regis*.[83] With some self-congratulation Bishop Sancho of Pamplona wrote *sub prefati regis imperio pulsus et culmine fretus* (driven by the command of the aforesaid king and reliant on His Highness [Sancho III]); on another occasion Bishop Jimeno was present at a transaction *quia ille fecit scribere istam cartam suo notario* (because he made his own notary write that charter), lending out his aide.[84]

How then to interpret those cases of more than one scribe being credited in a charter? Some are the legacy of later acts of confirmation, or reflect the process of transcription into a cartulary as we have seen at Sahagún.[85] But we also encounter brother Munnio *iudex et notuit* (a judge who transcribed) alongside Sampiro in a charter not written in his recognisable hand, Ascarius *presbiter notuit in Pravia* (in Asturias) beside Sampiro *quasi presbiter et notarium regis*, two names both followed by *qui et notuit*, and even Fulgentius *notuit* identified alone on an original definitely not his distinctive work.[86] These are all royal diplomas: perhaps we have a senior scribe like Sampiro supervising an apprentice doing the work, or someone on site like Ascarius or performing another office like Munnio. There must have been practical arrangements for division of labour; where one *exaravit* and one *scribsit* or *notuit*, maybe the former produced a rough draft, the latter the final version.[87] In some cases the verbs describe distinct functions, such as *scripsit* and *titulavit*, *scripsit* and *pinxit*, or *exaravit* and *pernotavit*, which match with drafting versus finalising, especially for charters with a pronounced visual element to their presentation.[88] An interpolated testament to Antealtares of 932 seems to have had three scribes who *scripsi*, *notuit*, and *exasserit*, involving (if it can be trusted) successive stages of preparing, drafting, and revising.[89] Yet collaboration is rarely attested in practice, at least in documentary writing: in one Portuguese charter of sale from 1024, there is detectable alternation between two hands or styles, throughout the text, which suggests that the Alovitus *qui exaravit* and Gutiere *qui notuit* jointly identified as scribes worked together, one perhaps revising or modifying the prepared document at some stage in the transaction (see Figure 2.6).[90] In a donation by Audisenda to San Salvador de Matallana in 989, there is a palaeographically simpler change of hands halfway through the text, but

[83]  *León* 594, 599.
[84]  *Pamplona* 11; *San Juan* 34; cf. *Albelda* 29, 32; *San Juan* 41; *Huesca* 7; *Pamplona* 4.
[85]  *Otero* 196; *Sahagún* 308, 328; *Coruña* 110, 132; cf. 77, 127.
[86]  *León* 541; *San Pelayo* 1; *León* 530, 788; cf. 45; *Carracedo* 1.
[87]  *León* 754; *Celanova* 242; *PMH* 254.        [88]  *León* 712; *San Isidro* 7; *Sahagún* 426.
[89]  *Coruña* 33.
[90]  *PMH* 254; cf. Fernández Flórez and Herrero de la Fuente, 'Copistas', 105–30.

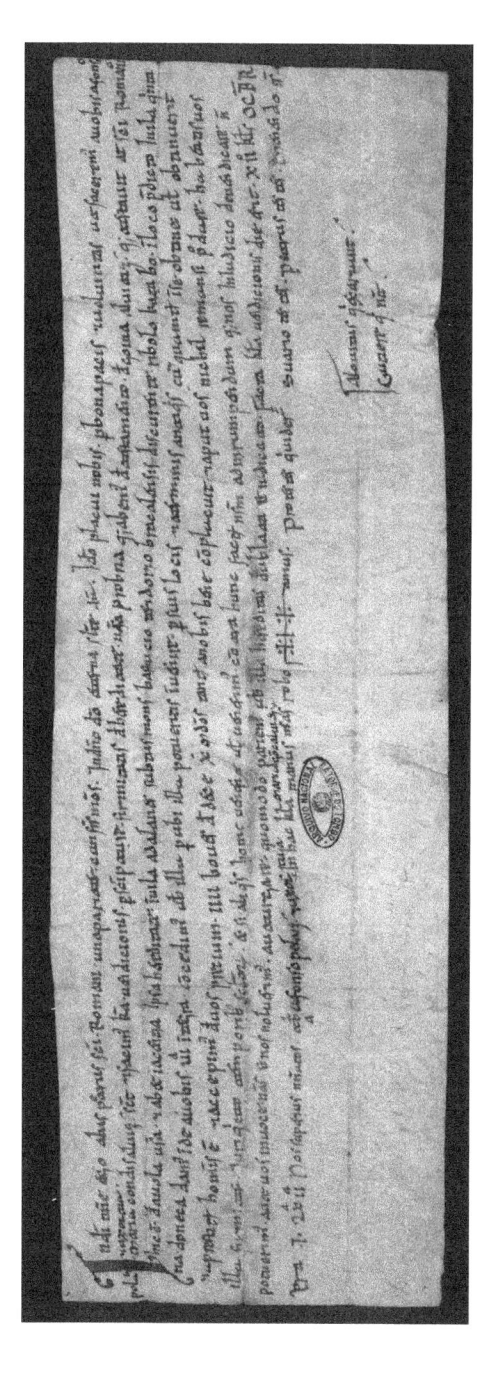

**Figure 2.6** Original charter, product of scribal collaboration: *PMH* 254 (Lisbon, ANTT, Ordem de São Bento, Mosteiro de São João Baptista de Pendorada, mç. 1, no. 5 (PT/TT/MSJBP/004/0001): Imagem cedida pelo ANTT)

interestingly Bellite *fratre* is named as the only scribe, while in a testament from 1006 two lines towards the middle are by a second hand.[91] All other examples are confined to changes of hand amidst subscription lists, or else the addition by second hands of later stages of a transaction.[92] As Recemirus *presbiter* wrote on a donation of 918, he both *incoavit* and *consumavit* (started and finished) it: scribes, in the final phase of composition, worked alone, and they took pride in their work.[93]

## Employers

We can approach the identity of scribes from another angle by considering who hired their services. Our list of 1,676 charters which identify a writer is the starting point, but in 649 cases (39%) the name is unique, encountered just once, drastically curtailing what can be said about its bearer. Fortunately, the name on each of the remaining 1,027 charters appears more than once in the corpus, and these instances can be grouped to construct scribal profiles (see Appendix 6).[94] Grouping is not without difficulty: multiple scribes may be disguised by identical names, one scribe may be concealed by variant spellings of the same name, and the minority of surviving originals means that palaeography cannot resolve all such ambiguities. Any attempt to control runs a risk of predetermining the results, as a history of the strangely named can demonstrate. If we were tempted to set 30 years—a generation—as a working limit for a scribal career, to bracket similar names by chronology, Sampiro would caution us against it, writing his first diploma in 977 and making a last donation in 1042. Both dates are secure; he must have started young, or been something of a Methuselah.[95] But is he typical, unusual, or unique? If we were to demarcate a local sphere of operations for a scribe in order to discriminate amongst similar names across different collections, how would we allow for Arias *presbiter et confeso exarator filius Telloni* ('Arias the priest, confessor, and writer, son of Tello'), who produced charters at Oviedo and Sahagún, or Petrus Kendulfiz *diaconus*, who wrote diplomas at Lugo and Otero?[96] Where the documents came to rest is of course another matter from where they were written, but in most cases we

---

[91]  *León* 531, 664; Ruiz Asencio, 'Trabajo', 1, 115–18.
[92]  *Oviedo* 25–6; *Otero* 29, 137, 162.    [93]  *Celanova* 13.
[94]  González González, 'Cultura', 200–10, 231–5.    [95]  *Documentación*, 661–6.
[96]  *San Vicente* 16; *Sahagún* 268; *Lugo* 58; *Otero* 196; Ruiz Asencio, 'Escritura, monogramas', 1, 298–303; Castro Correa, 'Pedro', esp. 109–12.

cannot know for certain since the text gives us no location: to assume regionalised scribal practice is to impose it. Sampiro also cautions against using similar parties or types of parties from one transaction to another as an index of scribal identity: archetype of the royal notary he may be, yet a quarter of his charters from before 1031 involve non-royal actors.[97] If we presume rigid chronology, geography, or social milieu in our method, that is only what we shall discover. There is little alternative but to categorise on some such bases, however, and so I have tried to isolate scribes by attending to ranges of dates and sites which seem reasonable enough, with reference to the persons and institutions acting as parties and witnesses to the transactions. The result is a tolerable degree of security, nothing more; and since a scribe may identify himself in one charter but not the next, the 'total' for any scribe likely understates his output. But it is a place to start.

Scribes may be divided into five basic categories by the identities of their employers, spanning all the strata of society. At the top, there are royal scribes: the best known by far is Sampiro, notary, chronicler, bishop of Astorga, who wrote 17 charters in the late tenth and early eleventh centuries, mostly but not exclusively for Vermudo II and his successors.[98] We find him named in two versions of the same diploma of 991 clearly written by different persons, a more functional precept in a business hand, a more formal privilege recognisably by the man himself.[99] There were multiple scribes writing for the king, but Sampiro seems to have been senior amongst them. He also participated in some of these transactions, acting as *saio* in a dispute before Alfonso V in 1008 and recording the settlement.[100] He moved in the royal entourage, and we meet him in company of the king on visits to Sahagún in 1012 and 1018, writing the diplomas which resulted; his first known charter is for the same monastery, and may hint at his otherwise unknown background, though a *villa* named Sampir is recorded in Galicia.[101] Sampiro earned a tidy sum from his career, as Vermudo II and Alfonso V made gifts of land to *sacerdoti et famulanti nostro* (our priest and servant), *fidelem et notarius meus* (my faithful [servant] and notary), in 998 and 1023.[102] Fulgentius *presbiter* also accompanied Alfonso V to Congosto for an *agnitio vel placito* (acknowledgement and agreement) in 1017, and to Sobrado two weeks later for a confirmation of a charter from 966.[103] But

---

[97] *León* 669, 709, 715, 717.
[98] Pérez de Urbel, *Sampiro*, 11–125; Morala Rodríguez, 'Grafías', 1, 620–2.
[99] *León* 549–50.     [100] *León* 669.
[101] *León* 707; *Sahagún* 404, 287; *cf. Celanova* 53, 183, 334–5, 374; *Santiago* 91.
[102] *León* 581, 802.     [103] *Alfonso V* vii; *Sobrado* 1.6.

he is harder to pigeonhole: of the 22 documents which he wrote from 995 to 1030, the majority are for the clergy, and only three of them royal diplomas.[104] Royal scribes did not serve kings alone, and it is anachronistic to speak institutionally of a royal chancellery; more accurately, there were simply those who sometimes wrote royal diplomas, some more often than not.[105]

Episcopal scribes are in comparison poorly attested. The only clear case is Florentius *presbiter*, who wrote four charters for the see of Mondoñedo from 911 to 922, but on closer inspection these include two (well-informed) forgeries.[106] Ababdella *presbiter*, who drafted a sale at a church of San Martín in 943, is identified elsewhere as *cellarario* (overseer of stores) for Bishop Oveco of León.[107] As a rule, when we look at the bishops of León, they employed the same writers as worked for Leonese monasteries. The monastic scribe is the best attested in the corpus, no doubt in part an artefact of its composition, but also reflecting a wide range of service. We can reconstruct some scriptoria in detail: from Santillana del Mar between 980 and 1030, for instance, there are 33 charters, 26 bearing the names of four scribes (Cissilani, Ermegildo, Iohannes, Petrus) who wrote solely for that institution, so far as we can see. This isolation in Cantabria is exceptional, however, and monastic scribes normally wrote for other parties as well, at least periodically, supplying their writing skills far beyond the walls of the monastery. Ordonius *presbiter*, for example, wrote not only for Santiago de León in the early eleventh century, but also for Abellar, San Miguel de León, and a brother and sister making a sale to a priest in 1019, while Ferro *presbiter* drafted a lay transaction in 955 before acting on behalf of Sahagún and Santiago de Cellariolo until 967.[108] Adulfus *diaconus* Gendoni seems to have been a roving Leonese 'scribe-at-large', responsible during the 920s for diplomas to Abellar, Sahagún, Valdevimbre, even Compostela, and if it should be the same figure (these are mainly cartulary copies and he seldom uses his patronymic, if that is what 'Gendoni' is), charters to monasteries and the see of Santa María de León from 943 onwards.[109]

Why did a monastery employ a particular scribe? Adulfus appears to have had some kind of joint property ownership with Abellar as of 929, which might explain it, but he had also bought land around the city of León

---

[104]   *León* 737, 788, 871.
[105]   Collins, 'Literacy', 124–5; Ruiz Asencio, 'Escritura, monogramas', 1, 268–71; Davies, *Acts*, 93–5; cf. *Ramiro II*, 524–9; *Documentación*, 217–33.
[106]   *Braga* 19; *VDJ* 3; *Mondoñedo* 3, 5.          [107]   *León* 162, 167; cf. *Astorga* 192.
[108]   *León* 764; *Sahagún* 366; cf. *León* 125.
[109]   Fernández Flórez, 'Documentos', 110–15, 116–18, 135.

by 939, and it could equally be a matter of simple proximity.[110] Some monastic scribes may have been in house, fitting the famous image of the busy scriptorium of San Salvador de Tábara in 970, where two monks, Senior and Emeterius, sit writing, while in a separate room to the right a third is cutting parchment (see Figure 2.7).[111] Albine *presbiter* wrote up a pair of testaments to San Salvador de Matallana at the monastery itself in 1026, while Ansedeus *presbiter*, who documented a gift to San Martín de Turieno in 963, is included in the address as one of its brothers.[112] Similarly, Egila and Orbanus pop up as witnesses to, even granters of charters to Sahagún besides acting as its scribes; Veremudus, who recorded a sale for it in 949, operated as its purchasing agent on three other occasions in the same year.[113] Sometimes, we can see an entire career unfold at a single institution: Citaius *presbiter* writes for Abellar in 952, then accepts its *patrocinium* (patronage) in 955, witnesses the granting of a testament to it that year, acts for it in a sale of 968, and has become abbot by 972, while the scribe Vivi *presbiter* appears to be abbot of Valdevimbre by the early eleventh century.[114] In Galicia, similarly, Aloytus *diaconus* prepared charters for Celanova over more than two decades, and rose to the rank of *praepositus* by 954.[115] But this is not necessarily the only, nor the most common, working model. Baroncellus *presbiter* wrote primarily for Santos Justo y Pastor during the 950s, yet in a sale to the monastery in 952 he appeared as a witness from Santa Marina, confirmed another sale to Valdevimbre a few months before, and acted as scribe for Abellar, possibly, in 954.[116] We need to allow for a variety of experiences, and for the further possibility that monks moved house for employment, however much all normative rules frowned on going out into the world with its temptations.[117] Not every monastic scribe had a fixed monastic base, any more than all scribes were monks; as kings for their diplomas, monasteries called on whoever was closest to hand to write their charters as needed.

[110]  *León* 84, 134.

[111]  See O'Neill (ed.), *Art*, 155–6; Brown, 'Thinking', 358–62.

[112]  *León* 832–3; *Liébana* 67; *cf. León* 600; *Sahagún* 310.

[113]  *Sahagún* 17, 15; 42, 48, 53; 117; *cf.* 115–16, 118.

[114]  *León* 256, 288, 293, 408, 417; *cf.* 210, 219; Álvarez Álvarez, 'Monasterio', 1, 52; Morala Rodríguez, 'Grafías', 1, 622–4; Fernández Flórez, 'Documentos', 132–3; González González, 'Cultura', 215–20.

[115]  *Celanova* 104; *cf. Sobrado* 1.64; *Lorvão* 52.      [116]  *León* 254, 247, 265.

[117]  See *e.g.* Leander of Seville, *Regula*, 31, Isidore of Seville, *Regula*, 24, Fructuosus of Braga, *Regula*, 22, *Regula monastica communis*, 20, ed. Campos Ruiz and Roca Meliá, *Padres*; Caner, *Monks*, 1–18; Dietz, *Monks*, 69–105, 155–88.

**Figure 2.7** Bell tower and scriptorium of the monastery of San Salvador de Tábara (Beato de Tábara, Madrid, AHN, Códices, L.1097, fol. 171v: Ministerio de Cultura y Deporte. Archivo Histórico Nacional. CODICES,L.1097)

The aristocratic or household scribe comes into view in those relatively rare instances of a lay archive surviving in quantity.[118] This is the case at Otero, where in the early eleventh century Cidi *presbiter* and Citi *presbiter*, near homonyms but separate scribes, wrote at least 17 and 18 charters respectively, all but two and five for Count Pedro Flaínez, in whose employ the latter also acted as judicial agent on two occasions. Since almost every one is preserved in the original, we can build up palaeographic, diplomatic, and linguistic profiles for both scribes.[119] The other archival aristocrat, Count Fruela Muñoz, relied more variously and less regularly on Christoforus, Eterus, Onorio, and Sescuto to write his charters, on five, five, six, and seven occasions.[120] By way of comparison and control, in the roughly 70 Otero charters which do not correspond to one of the two counts or their families, Sescuto alone appears with any regularity (twice).[121] The ecclesiastical vocation of these scribes is further testimony to clerical provision of literate services to wider society; the consistency with which they serve single employers, by no means absolute but greater than for monastic scribes serving monasteries, suggests that they either lived in the aristocratic household or worked in the aristocratic retinue. But how this employment worked in practice was more complicated than a simple 'job for life' scheme. We find Addaulfus *presbiter*, for example, writing charters for the Galician aristocrats Hermegildo and Paterna in 943 and 945, before spending the next 30 years of his scribal career acting for Sobrado, their own foundation, while Ansedeus *presbiter*, who served San Martín de Turieno, also wrote for relations of its abbot Opila, a couple named Savarico and Vistrilli.[122] Scribes do not fit discrete categories; the balance of their scribal service reflects whom they knew and how they knew them.

In all these cases proximity, geographical as well as social, will have been a factor in forming the working relationship; many royal, episcopal, monastic, and aristocratic scribes will also have been 'urban scribes', based in the major towns of Asturias-León and Navarra, and enjoying some measure of social status as a result of their activities.[123] The most elusive scribes, but surely the most common, are their counterparts, those who

---

[118] See González González, 'Cultura', 210–15.

[119] *Otero* 73, 149; *cf.* 174; Puentes Romay, 'Notario', 519–36; Herrero de la Fuente and Fernández Flórez, 'Cidi', 1, 651–88; Puentes Romay, 'Notarios', 235–46; Fernández Flórez, 'Documentos', 124–6; Davies, *Acts*, 95–6; *cf.* Zabalza Duque, *Colección*, 91–4.

[120] Puentes Romay, 'Documentos', 769–80.     [121] *Otero* 156, 159.

[122] *Sobrado* 1.10, 1.12; *cf.* 1.1, 1.13, 1.17; *Liébana* 64; *cf.* 60, 63, 67.

[123] González González, 'Cultura', 193–235.

operated at the level of village society.[124] The education of the local clergy was a perennial problem for the early medieval Church, but when the documentation is dense priests do emerge writing charters on behalf of others in their communities alongside their duties of pastoral care; however, these are best defined as 'local' rather than 'parish' priests, largely autonomous in the absence of administrative structures which emerged only in the high Middle Ages.[125] One such figure is Stephanus *presbiter*, a Leonese scribe who wrote two charters of exchange between members of the laity in 926 and 928, both involving property in Marialba where he himself acquired land by exchange in 926 and 943.[126] He also acted as scribe for a series of transactions in or around Marialba and the monastery of Abellar between 942 and 954, including an exchange by Fortunio and his wife Speciosa in 950 and a sale by their sons Felix and Fruela four years later; that he was not just a monastic agent passing through is implied by the donation of 951 which he wrote up in the local church of Santa María in Marialba, presumably his base.[127] Hints of other village scribes appear everywhere, if only hints due to a scarcity of evidence: Migael *presbiter* recorded a sale of land in the *conventum eglesie* (local church) at Vega de San Adrián in 1000, while Servandus *presbiter* twice wrote for his neighbour Salamona in 1005, one of a number of similar cases in León, Sahagún, Otero, and Celanova.[128] When a witness to one transaction reappears in another with similar parties as the writer, we may also conjecture that we have found a local scribe, such as Ermoigius in the earliest Piasca charters of Argemundo and his wife Recoire from 857 and 861, or when a judge like Braolio *presbiter* in Valdoré both hears disputes and writes up ordinary transactions.[129] Gundemarius *notarius* was doubtless a village scribe, recording a gift of property *in villa Peraria* on site in 916, and the same applies to Aloytus *diaconus de Mendunito* in 936; we have already met Nepotianus, planter of a vineyard in Rabal, who wrote up a sale there in 961, while an aside in a charter of 1001, *ubi ego modo Fredenando abitavi* (where I, Fredenando, have lately taken up residence),

---

[124] See Cromwell, *Recording*, esp. 22–66, 156–92.

[125] Davies, 'Parishes', 379–97; Davies, 'Local Priests in Northern Iberia', 125–44; Pérez, 'Clérigos', 547–74; Zeller *et al.*, *Neighbours*, 143–8; *cf.* Hamilton, 'Educating', 83–113.

[126] *León* 69, 78, 70, 161.

[127] *León* 209, 282, 236; *cf.* 150, 178, 319; Martínez Peñín, 'Orígenes', 103–36; Davies, 'Local Priests', 29–43; Martín Viso, 'Worlds', 261–7.

[128] *León* 593; 645–6; *cf.* 644, 647, 673, 757; *Sahagún* 47, 54, 92, 399, 416; *Otero* 158; *Celanova* 286.

[129] *Sahagún* 1–3; *Otero* 19, 26, 31, 34, 43; *cf.* 13–16, 33.

tells us that the witness Fredenando was also its scribe—the question is, did he relocate for work?[130]

Royal, episcopal, monastic, and aristocratic scribes could carve out mobile careers for themselves, writing on behalf of employers with interests in various places, against the more stationary background of urban and village scribes called on as and when business required it, establishing local names for themselves in the process. By virtue of this network, we can be sure that literacy—or perhaps better a 'service provider' of writing and reading—was always within reach.[131] But if the careers of local scribes were defined by a greater variety of actors and a lesser variety of (territorial) interests, we should nevertheless resist conceiving of each one as enjoying a limited monopoly. Parties could employ scribes consistently, but equally on *ad hoc* terms: Menicio and his wife Avola made six successive purchases of land in Villa de Monna from 894 to 914, and to this end engaged the services of Fruela *presbiter* and Zezus *presbiter* once each, Severus *presbiter* twice, while the remaining two charters lack scribal names.[132] Nuño Sarracinez and his wife Gudigeva, in contrast, engaged Maternus three times between 960 and 972, during the same period opting for Petrus in a donation of 962.[133] Once again, personal relationships came into play: a family might share a scribe, like Munio Flaínez and his wife Froileuva or the relations of San Rosendo.[134] But the most important implication of dense availability of scribes is the potential for competition amongst them, and the shifting balance in the documentation between occasional and more consistent scribal service points us towards a key development in documentary practice across the tenth century.

⸱ If we track the rate at which scribes are named in the charters, we can see a twofold rise from 911 to 1031. This is not simply a reflection of greater survival of originals, but our first indicator of a process of consolidation under way in the scribal profession (see Figure 2.8). What is the underlying change? If we divide our corpus of scribes into three broad categories of regularity, as writers of one, two to four, and five or more surviving charters (subject to the same errors as other questions of scribal identity), there is a clear turning point (see Figure 2.9).

[130]  *Celanova* 12, 52, 128, 141, 249.
[131]  Orme, *Children*, 240.      [132]  *León* 9, 14, 25–6, 32–3; *cf.* 13.
[133]  *León* 353; *cf.* 331, 335, 420.
[134]  *Otero* 6; *Sahagún* 107–8, 124, 189, 205; *e.g. Celanova* 28, 64.

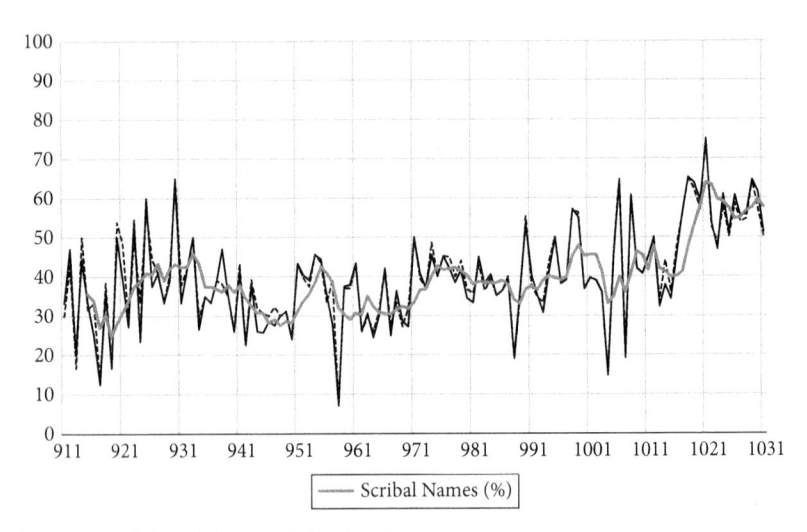

**Figure 2.8** Named Scribes (911–1031)

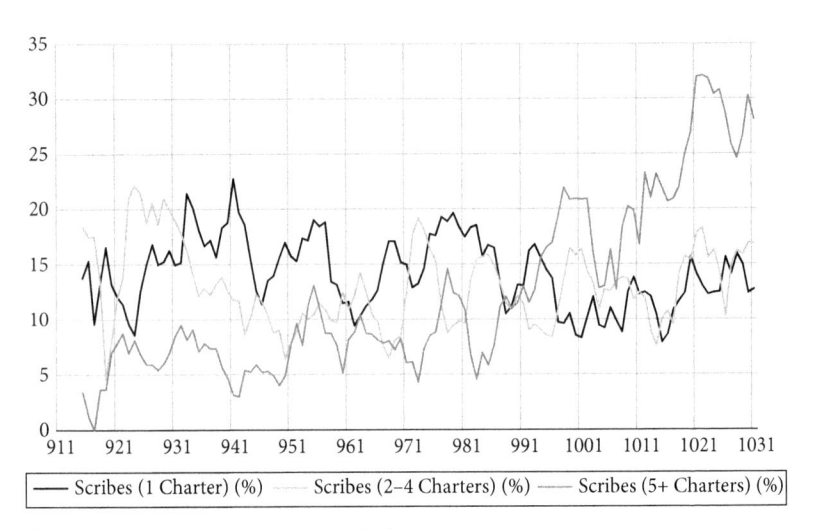

**Figure 2.9** Scribal Careers (911–1031)

Beginning around 970 or 980, it becomes steadily more common for any given scribe to have written other surviving charters, such that by 1031 almost a third of our charters are the work of scribes with five or more others to their name. What does it mean? There was a network of scribes encompassing king and peasant and everyone in between, but the foundations of this society of second-hand interaction with documentation were slowly shifting. Over time, even as the number of charters preserved increases, we can perceive a transition from occasional to something more like career scribes as the norm, and this in turn brought revolutionary changes in how the employers of those scribes took advantage of the written word.

## Methods

Scribes were the primary agents of text, but what did the production of text entail? We have seen that barely a generation stands between the Muslim conquest and the first surviving documents from early medieval Iberia; we are dealing not with a new written culture, but the continuance of an old one. Allowing for much variation and individuality, the language of the charters is fundamentally formulaic, and a connection with the collection of models known as the 'Visigothic formulary' has long been recognised, and amply illustrated.[135] The persistence of this language is striking, in that while the *formulae* seem to have been prepared in the 610s and compiled at some point thereafter in the seventh century, they refer back to late Roman models and beyond.[136] The consequent time warp leaps off the parchment: in a Valpuesta charter of 894 quoting the *Lex Aquilia* of 286 BC (!), or Galician charters purporting to grant manumission from slavery by the words *licentiam tribuo civium Romanorum consequi privilegium* (I allow freedom to obtain the status of Roman citizens), even dowry deeds which describe the wife as *dulcissime* (sweetest) and present her with ten *pueros* and *puellas* (boys and girls) each, repeating the Visigothic text verbatim.[137] Some editors have proposed restoring 'corrupt' charters with reference to the appropriate formula, and one does see their point.[138] Documents can emerge from the 'formulary' almost unaltered, especially the *condiciones sacramentorum* (terms of the oaths) sworn in court cases; use of such formulaic language

---

[135] See *FV*; Codoñer, 'Léxico', 141–9; García-Gallo, 'Documentos', esp. 393–4; Pérez González, 'Formulismo', 117–39; Fernández Flórez, *Elaboración*, 68–78; Fernández Flórez, 'Génesis', 89–117; Calleja-Puerta, 'Ecos', 45–63; *cf.* Zimmermann, *Écrire*, 1, 246–84; Zimmermann, 'Acte', 203–6.

[136] Bastardas Parera, 'Latín', 270–2; Petit, 'Práctica', 184–9; Córcoles Olaitz, 'Origin', 201–8; Córcoles Olaitz, *Formulae*.

[137] See *e.g. Valpuesta* 6 (*FV* 1, 6–7, 20); *Samos* 127, 44, *Celanova* 76 (*FV* 2–6); *Sobrado* 1.119, *Celanova* 24 (*FV* 20, 23); Martínez Díez, 'Instituciones', 104–7; Collins, 'Literacy', 117; Isla Frez, *Sociedad*, 203–14; Córcoles Olaitz, 'Manumission', 339–49.

[138] *León* 5; *Montes* 7–13; see *FV* 8.

structures both the practice and presentation of dispute settlement.[139] At other times, the resonance is more limited, as in the formula for dating by regnal year, *anno feliciter glorie regni nostri* (in year [X], happily, of the reign of Our Glory), reproduced *in toto* in a diploma of Alfonso III from 905, whereas elsewhere it is reduced to the *feliciter* found also across the early medieval West.[140]

The charters speak the language of the 'Visigothic formulary', but did scribes draw on it when writing them? The objections to this hypothesis are twofold. First, of the 45 *formulae* which comprise the collection, many are a poor fit for the corpus in terms of typology, while most are introductory or concluding passages instead of complete documents; given that the 'models' also include a lengthy verse presentation of a wedding gift, the *formulae* seem more likely to have been compiled out of literary interest rather than for practical use by a working notary or scribe. Secondly, there is minimal indication that any such book of *formulae* was in consistent circulation during our period. Aside from sundry fragments, just this one survives for Asturias-León and Navarra, in an early modern copy made for the historian Ambrosio de Morales (d. 1591) from a lost medieval manuscript compiled by Pelayo of Oviedo, the noted forger, possibly in furtherance of his schemes (for example, its *anno feliciter* dating formula is found in some of his contrivances).[141] In contrast, we have a contemporary formulary from Catalunya, produced in the tenth century at the monastery of Ripoll, and many more can be reconstructed for the Carolingian world.[142] This is not to say that the Visigothic *formulae* or other sets like it could not have been to hand at moments and in contexts where we find their language cited with some density, perhaps for literary flourish, such as at Valpuesta around 900 or at Oviedo in the 950s, but what makes better sense of the whole corpus is a less static, more flexible working method whereby scribes drew on older charters as models for newer ones.[143] If we return to regnal dating and take

---

[139] *FV* 39; Fernández Flórez, *Elaboración*, 108–15; Tarozzi, 'Spunti', 917–29; Marques, 'Language', 128–64.

[140] *FV* 1, 7, 20, 25, 39; *León* 18, 753; *Sahagún* 9; *Eslonza* 5; *San Isidro* 1, 7; *Vega* 1; *Albelda* 3; *Santiago* 11, 26; *Celanova* 9, 72; *cf. Sahagún* 68, 87; *Liébana* 13; Martínez Díez, *Colección* 14; *Samos* 33; *Celanova* 95; Díaz y Díaz, 'Titulaciones', 140–1.

[141] Collins, 'Ambrosio, Pelayo', esp. 618, 621–2, 626–7; Collins, 'Ambrosio, *Codex*', 49–69; see *e.g. Oviedo* 16–17; Robinson, *Manuscripts*, 71–3; Vives, 'Oracional', 25.

[142] Zimmermann, 'Formulaire', 25–86; Zimmermann, 'Vie', 337–58; *cf.* Rio, 'Charters', 8–20; Rio, *Practice*, 9–40.

[143] Fernández Flórez, *Elaboración*, 78–81; Collins, 'Ambrosio, *Codex*'; *cf.* Everett, 'Scribes', 63–73.

| | Reign | | Overall | |
|---|---|---|---|---|
| | # | % | # | % |
| Total | 1351 | 33 | 4095 | 100 |
| Region | | | | |
| West | 56 | 4 | 1284 | 31 |
| Centre | 780 | 58 | 2088 | 51 |
| East | 515 | 38 | 723 | 18 |
| Personnel | | | | |
| Royal | 87 | 6 | 522 | 13 |
| Comital | 41 | 3 | 71 | 2 |
| Ecclesiastical | 992 | 73 | 2710 | 66 |
| Lay | 229 | 17 | 769 | 19 |
| Typology | | | | |
| Donation | 766 | 57 | 2212 | 54 |
| Sale | 496 | 37 | 1469 | 36 |
| Other | 89 | 7 | 411 | 10 |
| Complexity | | | | |
| Simple | 1023 | 76 | 2797 | 68 |
| Complex | 328 | 24 | 1292 | 32 |
| Palaeography | | | | |
| Original | 296 | 22 | 888 | 22 |
| Copy | 78 | 6 | 261 | 6 |
| Cartulary | 867 | 64 | 2438 | 60 |
| Other | 110 | 8 | 507 | 12 |
| Diplomatic | | | | |
| Authentic | 1252 | 93 | 3781 | 92 |
| Suspicious | 10 | 1 | 24 | 1 |
| Interpolated | 16 | 1 | 57 | 1 |
| Falsified | 71 | 5 | 227 | 6 |

**Figure 2.10** Regnal Dating

stock of the practice in the round, we can see this method in operation. Some 1,351 (33%) charters are dated by reign (see Figure 2.10).[144] From the numbers, it is obvious that the practice was profoundly regionalised: almost absent from the west, more common in the centre, surprising

[144] *León*, 1, 406–8, 2, 368–70; *Ramiro II*, 683–97; Rodríguez Fernández, *Ordoño III*, 315–23; *Documentación*, 487–614; *cf.* Davies, 'Incidence', 217–32.

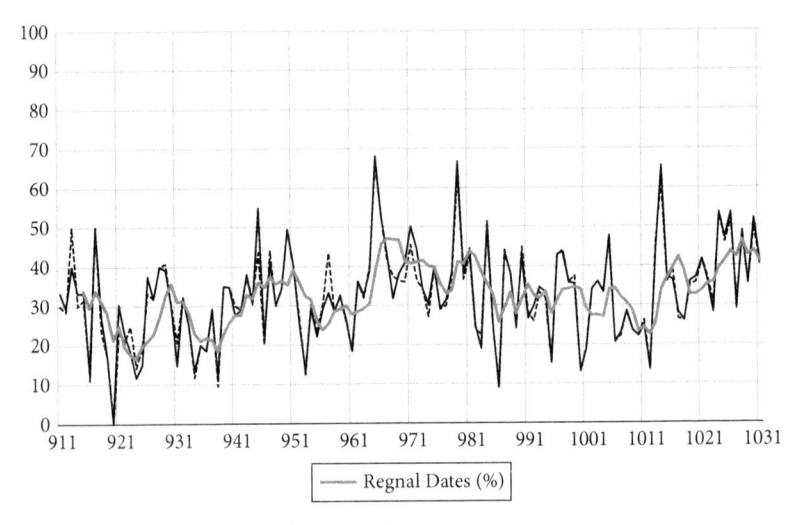

**Figure 2.11** Regnal Dating (911–1031)

in the east, where the Navarrese kings can be obscured by forgeries.[145] Above all, scribes around León followed the basic pattern of dating by regnal year, customising it in a wide variety of forms.[146] This best fits them doing as their predecessors had done, and consistently so across the period (see Figure 2.11).

Finer details of how scribes worked with earlier charters as models begin to emerge if we look at those dated by reign, rather than regnal year. In the formulaic language which they used, Leonese scribes were alone in situating the king in the *civis* [*sic*] *vel sedis* (city and see) of León during the late tenth century and the early eleventh.[147] Others like Mirele *presbiter*, who ranged farther afield, put him *in sede patris sui* (on the throne of his father) or variants.[148] At the level of an individual monastery, charters from Sahagún uniquely register the years since the return of Sancho I from al-Andalus in 960, while documents from Cantabria, by the scribe Ermoigius particularly, have the king *sedente in Asturias* (sitting in Asturias) during the ninth century, idiosyncratically continue to situate him there in the tenth, and

[145] Cabezas Fontanilla and Ávila Seoane, 'Oficina', 73–8.

[146] See *e.g. León* 38, 247, 482; *Astorga* 8; *cf. León* 41–3, 73, 75–6, 93, 256, 401, 865; *Sahagún* 101, 245, 250; *Astorga* 71; *Eslonza* 1–2, 9; *Liébana* 22; *Valpuesta* 3; *Santiago* 18; *Samos* 93; *Sobrado* 1.8, 1.64; *Celanova* 91; *San Esteban* 1.

[147] *León* 543; *cf.* 551, 622, 628, 640, 645–6, 714, 723.

[148] *León* 652, 657; *cf.* 478, 653, 675, 687, 729, 755, 828B, 885; *Sahagún* 267, 270; *Otero* 170.

recognise the 'reign' of Alfonso Froilaz, hardly acknowledged anywhere outside of Galicia.[149] Cardeña offers the clearest evidence, however, that the regionalism of regnal dating is related to modelling new charters on old ones: the earliest documents from the reign of Alfonso III situate his reign in Oviedo, but the scribes of the monastery failed, or declined, to take due notice of the move to León after his death in 910, and carried on dating charters by the king in Oviedo until 976.[150] The simplest explanation is that they were working from an 'Asturian model': either literally or in the sense that each copied the work of his predecessor, perpetuating the practice of the former era. Sporadic cases of such 'Oviedo anachronism' at Arlanza, San Millán, Valpuesta, and even Celanova, where Ramiro II is once placed *in sedem regum Ovethao* (on the throne of kings in Oviedo), could respond to chance use of similar model charters.[151]

These varieties of regnal dating point to scribes drafting charters with reference to a range of exemplars in circulation within regions, cities, localities, monastic scriptoria, over the short or long term. The same model also fits those dating clauses which state the sitting bishop alongside the reigning king. In 915, the scribe Velasconi *presbiter* dated a sale to the reign of Ordoño II in León as well as to the episcopacy of Bishop Cixila in the see of Santa María the Virgin.[152] For several decades this remained an outlier, until it was picked up as a model in 952 and definitively from 964, thereafter coming to be a nearly ubiquitous element of dating clauses in Leonese charters.[153] It can be seen too at Sahagún from 945/6 and Otero from 949, and came into fashion at both in the early eleventh century.[154] At times the bishop is cited alone, at times with phrases such as *civis vel sedis* which play with language normally reserved for the king.[155] Of course, this is evidence for the history of the episcopacy of León, but it is also testimony to scribal method: the anomalous appearance of the Leonese episcopal dating formula in two charters from the Liébana in 962 demonstrates that scribes periodically took up new models from old charters.[156] And much the same process can be seen in Astorga: a charter of 936 dated by the reign of

[149] *Sahagún* 164, 175–6, 1–4; *Liébana* 20, 24, 32; *Puerto* 2–3; Carriedo Tejedo, 'Familia gallega', 109–54.

[150] *Cardeña* 102, 61–2; cf. e.g. 11, 169; Martínez Díez, *Condado*, 1, 225–62; Escalona, 'Name', 74–102.

[151] *Arlanza* 14–15, 17; *San Millán* 689; *Valpuesta* 32; *Celanova* 72.

[152] *León* 37.

[153] See *e.g. León* 247, 372, 374, 376; Pérez, 'Monasterios', 95–124.

[154] *Sahagún* 100; *Otero* 7–8.     [155] *León* 202, 554, 592; *Sahagún* 30; cf. *Astorga* 254, 259.

[156] *Liébana* 64–5.

Ramiro II in León and Genadio, by the grace of God, bishop of Astorga, adopted as a regular formula from the late tenth century onwards.[157]

Yet the use of model charters is more than simply a matter of regionalism and a linear diffusion. The only way to account for the complexities of commonalities across the corpus is to make allowance for a greater degree of interregional circulation of charters—as models for other charters—and a greater role for scribal choice, the vagaries of fashion, in selecting from amongst the available options to create new charters. Regonalism and indeed localism reflect and result from mobility of written material and autonomy in scribal activity, balanced by the tendency of scribes to do as their predecessors had done and their neighbours were doing.[158] As such, when we try to identify regional phrases in the documentation, we tend to find that they are not exclusive to one area, only more common. Take the inclusion of *petras mobiles vel inmobiles* (moveable and immoveable stones) in appurtenance clauses: quite *de rigeur* in Galicia and Portugal, where Sandinus *presbiter* favoured it.[159] And yet it is also found twice in León and twice in Astorga, including in a donation by Sampiro, who could have run across the formula in the course of his travels as royal scribe.[160] Similarly dispersed is the use of the words *karrale qui discurrit ubique* (by the road to everywhere) in boundary clauses, attested occasionally in León and Otero during the early eleventh century, once again in the output of Sampiro, but also farther afield generations earlier, at Cardeña from the mid-tenth century.[161] Writers and writing circulated in ways which exceed any model of a localised world, and did so creatively: a Leonese appurtenance clause of 959 ends with *usque minima petra* (down to the smallest stone), expressing the totality of testamentary transfer, and this formulation was later taken up at Astorga, but a Leonese scribe in 961 preferred *usque ad modica gallina* (down to the humble hen), and his rephrasing gained traction at other points north and east.[162]

At the same time, individual preferences and the happenstance of models available to hand both contribute to a personalising of language from one

[157] *Astorga* 135; Cavero Domínguez, 'Organización', 67–101.
[158] Davies, *Windows*, 95–120; Davies, 'Regions', 305–23.
[159] *Coimbra* 135, 204, 207, 527, 156; *cf. Sobrado* 1.76; *Celanova* 37; *Coruña* 50; *Pombeiro* 1; *PMH* 6; Varela Sieiro, 'Petras', 211–18; Marques, *Representação*, 324–5.
[160] *León* 779; *cf.* 779; *Astorga* 20, 17.
[161] *León* 687; *cf.* 709; *Otero* 129, 139; *Cardeña* 49, 205.
[162] *León* 313; *cf. Astorga* 145, 202, 207, 264; *León* 346; *cf. Sahagún* 266, 275; *Liébana* 76; *Valpuesta* 45; Pérez González, 'Fórmula', 525–38.

document to the next.[163] In 950 and 951, the scribe Iohannes *presbiter* developed a fondness for recording the hour of the day in charters of sale; in the late tenth century and the early eleventh, the *ira regis* (royal wrath) is invoked in sanction clauses at three Leonese religious communities.[164] Each scribe had a few peculiar habits of his own: Iulianus *presbiter* called Alfonso V the *parvulus* (infant) first in León, then in Galicia, in the dating clauses of testaments to Santos Justo y Pastor, while Gudesteus *presbiter* identified Bishop Servando as *catedra continens* (holding the chair) of the see of Santa María in the transactions which he wrote up for Cidi Domínguez in 1031.[165] Two testaments to Santos Justo y Pastor are so similar in preamble, Scriptural allusion, and sanction that they must share a single scribe, even though Ennego *presbiter* is named in only the first one; the same can be said of another pair to Santiago de León.[166] Turns of phrase flit in and out of fashion: when Sampiro wrote his first charter in 977, describing how the devil had made Rapinatus and his wife Celedonia *ebriati a vino* (intoxicated on wine), was this his own original choice of words?[167] Or was he following Sahagún house style, since two priests had taken care to clarify in their testament to the monastery in 959 that they were acting *sine ebrietas vino* (without intoxication on wine)?[168] And is it pure random chance that Anagildus *presbiter* later on thought to specify in the preamble to a sale between members of the laity in Braga in 1026 that it was done *non per vinum vel metum* (not through wine or fear), or has Roman law on acts done *per vim vel metum* ('through force or fear') been somewhat lost in transmission?[169]

Like phrasing associated with a particular region, house style is better thought of not as a distinctive, exclusive set of taught practices, but as a matter of drawing more often than the norm on some elements of the common pool of models.[170] We meet the formula *et dicunt homnis populi fiat fiat* (and all the people say, 'Let it be! Let it be!'), adapted from the Book of Judith, in a donation to San Salvador de Matallana from 997, and while it is characteristic of its documentation in the late tenth century and early eleventh, it is by no means unique to it.[171] The alchemy of formulaic and more

[163] Díaz y Díaz, 'Cultivo', 79–81.
[164] *León* 226, 237, 574, 696, 703; cf. Saraiva, 'Data', 104, 127.
[165] *León* 615, 619, 648; 882, 884; cf. 132, 135; 172–4; *PMH* 14, 16.
[166] *León* 490, 493; cf. 413, 425.    [167] *Sahagún* 287.    [168] *Sahagún* 170.
[169] *Braga* 76; Pérez González, 'Bebidas', 61–77; Carriedo Tejedo, 'Viñedo', 145–52; see Frier (ed.), *Codex*, 2.19.4.
[170] Davies, *Acts*, 91–3; cf. González González, 'Cultura', 221–5.
[171] *León* 575; Judith 13:26, 15:12; cf. *León* 582, 631, 656, 765, 794–5, 812, 832, 836, 837, 1982 bis.

idiosyncratic wording combining in charters which express originality can be seen when we have a sufficient density. At San Martín de Turieno, a run of self-donations from 946 to 950 address future holders of the *paginola* (little page) in the confirmation clause, conjure the spectre of the tribunal of the Lord in the sanction, label themselves *roboratio* (reinforcement) in the dating clause, and recognise the reign of Ramiro in León, amongst other individual features.[172] In 951, however, a scribe working in the same scriptorium named Teodarius *presbiter* devised his own formula, professing the inability of the granter to raise his or her eyes up to Mount Olympus, and introduced it into the current model for self-donations.[173] Superseding its predecessor, his revised model can be tracked in use, by his colleagues too, for more than a decade.[174] Testaments, meanwhile, had a different template: in 946, one Catila Thodarius, perhaps the same scribe, wrote up a charter invoking the fear felt by the donor of the Day of Judgement in the preamble, the prospect of *temporale iudicia* (secular judgements) by king, bishop, or count in the sanction, and the reigning king, typically in León, in the dating clause.[175] For long after, into the eleventh century, all of these features continued to be included by scribes writing testaments for the monastery.[176]

There were always models to hand, and more than one which served; scribes had only to choose amongst them, or decide to innovate. Circumstances could compel change: take the scribe of two charters of sale to Lorvão from 1016/17, a generation after the reincorporation of the region into al-Andalus, who adapted the 'Spanish era' and Latin calendar of a standard dating clause to read Hijra 407 and *mense ragab* (the month of Rajab) instead, in deference to a new reality.[177] Could the two seemingly Muslim vendors, selling to a Christian monastery, have made a special request, or given instructions to do so? But these are outliers; normally a prior charter provided model enough, even in defiance of the passage of time. One charter of sale presents such an anomaly, in that it is dated to both the year 987 and the reign in León of Ramiro III, who died in 985. The original survives: conceivably the scribe had a charter from a couple years earlier in front of him to use as a model, and copied in the anachronistic name without thinking.[178] Another charter records Abbess Felicia Monnoia making a gift to Santiago de León in 970 of properties which she had mostly received by donation in 917, and

---

[172] *Liébana* 51–3.     [173] *Liébana* 54; Rucquoi, 'Peregrinos', 45.
[174] *Liébana* 55, 58, 70, 71.     [175] *Liébana* 50.     [176] *Liébana* 56, 60, 67, 77.
[177] *Lorvão* 9–10; *cf.* 15; Aillet, 'Chrétiens', 44–7; Martín Escudero, 'Calendario', 221–47.
[178] *León* 519.

the texts of the two transactions turn out to be nearly identical. The scribe of the one must have had the other before him, perhaps at first for just the details, then ultimately to save time for the entire composition.[179] These two examples capture the *ad hoc* variety of scribal practice, its reliance not on books of models but the charters to hand for writing up the business of the day.

## Processes

The use of earlier exemplars to produce new charters may explain why the process of writing itself, joining content to form, has otherwise left so little physical trace. And for this reason, while the questions of when and how scribes drew up documents may seem obvious, answers are far from certain. But we can reconstruct the basic stages.[180] According to a note at the conclusion of the testament of Bishop Diego of Oviedo from 967, it was written *in die prevegilio* and confirmed *in die Pasca Domini* (respectively on the day before and on Easter itself), which supports our conjecture, on the basis of the presence of more than one scribe in a text, of multiple phases of composition, of preparation and finalisation.[181] Insight into the first stage of writing comes from the reverse of another testament to Eslonza in 954, a rare set of notes by its scribe recording the names of the granter and eight witnesses (see Figure 2.12).[182] One can imagine jotting down the key details of the transaction—parties, properties, prices (if applicable), witnesses—before slotting these into a charter based on an earlier template, then registering the witnesses who remained for its final confirmation. But can we prove it? In the archive of Sahagún are four documents, three to the monastery and one to Iscam and his wife Filauria, which contain not single transactions set out with the usual clauses and *formulae*, but a series of bare minutes: granter, recipient, property, price, date, and little more.[183] The span of time covered by the transactions in a given document ranges over anywhere from one year to nine, and for the lay couple there is even a collective confirmation, putatively signed by all granters and witnesses as usual. Plausibly the documents

[179] *León* 412; *cf.* 42.
[180] *Documentación*, 217–19; Zabalza Duque, *Colección*, 86–90; Ruiz Asencio, 'Trabajo', 94–100; Kosto, 'Practices', 279–80; *cf.* Zimmermann, *Écrire*, 1, 113–35.
[181] *Oviedo* 27.    [182] *Eslonza* 26; *cf. León* 772; *Sahagún* 179; *Lugo* 37; *PMH* 244.
[183] *Sahagún* 94; *cf.* 34, 36, 297.

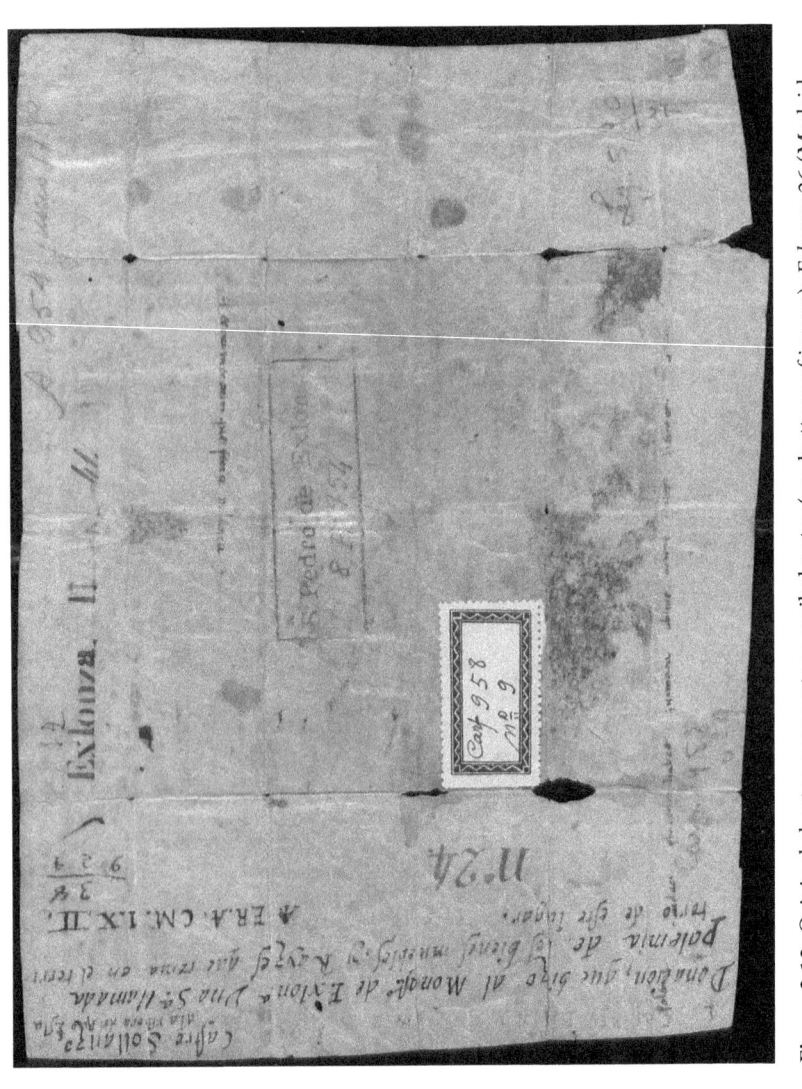

**Figure 2.12**  Original charter, preparatory scribal notes (see bottom of image): *Eslonza* 26 (Madrid, AHN, Sección Clero, Regular, San Pedro de Eslonza, carp. 958, no. 9, dorso: Ministerio de Cultura y Deporte, Archivo Histórico Nacional, CLERO-SECULAR_REGULAR,Car.958,N.9)

began as notes taken for individual transactions, which were never written up as charters, but later transcribed into series.

In this light, more minutes may survive than at first seems to be the case. An unusual text from Sahagún offers an unformatted description of a body of water, a channel, and a hill or mountain all belonging to the monastery: it could be some sort of inventory, but a diploma of Ordoño III from 951 donates the same properties, suggesting that it could instead be a set of notes for use in drafting the boundary clause of the formal charter.[184] And indeed, one has to wonder whether the many transactions recorded in summary form for San Millán could be similar such minutes, rather than inventories compiled during the creation of its cartulary.[185] Typically the entries are comprised of granter, recipient, property, price, and date, though not always even so much, but some do contain elements of charters, a stray confirmation here or sanction clause there, which bring them far closer to extracts from documents.[186] In this they parallel inventories from Celanova and Lorvão where a few of the charters extracted or cited survive, or the entries call themselves charters.[187] But equally, aggregated proto-charters can be found scattered across archives as diverse as Coruña and Valpuesta, along with irregularly drafted texts unsusceptible to standard diplomatic classification which bear headings such as *noticia* or *notum*.[188] These include skeletal transactions and circumstantial narratives which could likewise be working notes made by scribes for use in preparing legal records.

Once minutes had been taken, the next step was to draft a charter. The mechanics of writing are one question: the model text must at times have been rendered from memory, to judge from imperfect versions of standard clauses and phrases which nonetheless retain some of their constituent elements, but at other times copied directly from an exemplar, resulting in errors typical of transcription such as duplicating or skipping lines of text.[189] Where then did our minutes fit into this writing process? One option is that the scribe inserted the details into a template prepared in advance by either method, which finds some limited support. Taking the 84 originals from Sahagún, there are three fairly clear cases of 'template writing': where the

---

[184] *Sahagún* 1170; *cf.* 132.
[185] See *e.g. San Millán* 523, 371, 382, 378, 544, 384; Escalona, 'Cartularios', 141–9; Davies and Peterson, 'Management', esp. 49–53.
[186] See *e.g. San Millán* 421, 627.        [187] *Celanova* 285, 309, 315, 328, 338; *Lorvão* 32.
[188] *Coruña* 55; *Valpuesta* 47; *Huesca* 4, 8; *cf. León* 668; *Astorga* 133, 260; *Liébana* 72–4; *Floriano* 157; *Leire* 8; *San Juan* 45.
[189] Ruiz Asencio, 'Trabajo', 90–100.

granter was written in after the balance of the text, where the price was inserted, or where at least one witness was added.[190] And in a lay charter of sale from Portugal in 995 the scribe even left a sizeable blank space to fill in the price but never actually did so (see Figure 2.13).[191] Otherwise, if we allow for imperfections in the parchment surface and the consequences of fading, staining, and folding since, what impresses is the prevalence of 'continuous writing', charters written from start to finish integrally. Occasionally a detail belies this impression. In two cases from 986 and 987, the same scribe left a space for the king in the dating clause but never filled it in: the first still has its blank, while another scribe came along later and wrote Vermudo II into the second.[192] There are cases from León and Otero in which subscriptions of granters, witnesses, even scribes are in a perceptibly different tint of ink or hand from the charter itself; in one the date too is distinct from the main body, suggesting another variety of preparing the text at least partly in advance.[193] Creating a charter could be divorced from its contents, yet the regularity of 'continuous writing' counters that this was the exception.

While a charter may have been written before or after the transaction which it records, the addition of supplements to the text suggests on the contrary that the transaction was often ongoing when its charter was being written. In 874, for example, the scribe of a donation by Bishop Fronimio to the see of León added ten cows to the gift, but separately from the rest of the enumerated property, after the sanction and dating clauses; in another Leonese charter of 942, the scribe Freda inserted the price received by the last of the four vendors on the bottom left of the parchment, after he had written his own name.[194] Such supplements to the property or price, even the introduction of a countergift, out of proper place are in fact fairly frequent in charters from the centre and west.[195] Other recurrent additions include limiting conditions, as in the *ratione servata* (proviso) to a donation of 983 that the wife of the donor should have two months after his death to hand over the property, and further specifications, as in spelling out the time-shares in a mill sold in 970 per party and down to the hour.[196] These

[190]  *Sahagún* 241, 135, 134; cf. 251, 268, 275.    [191]  *PMH* 175.
[192]  *Sahagún* 334–5; cf. *Escalada* 1.    [193]  *León* 107; cf. 10, 25, 35, 65, 73, 416; *Otero* 118.
[194]  *León* 6, 158; cf. *Otero* 53, 82, 106.
[195]  *León* 224, 288, 296–7, 483; *Sahagún* 75, 78, 92; *Samos* 104, S1; *Celanova* 65, 141, 178, 228, 381; *Coimbra* 454; *Lorvão* 5; *PMH* 267; cf. *Sahagún* 253, 370.
[196]  *Guimarães* 68, A6; cf. *Sahagún* 352; *San Juan* 35, 44; *Huesca* 9; *Celanova* 104; *Guimarães* 67; *PMH* 164; *Coimbra* 211; *Concejo* 1; cf. *Santillana* 14; *Sobrado* 1.43, 1.38; *Celanova* 222, 351, 363; *Mondoñedo* 6.

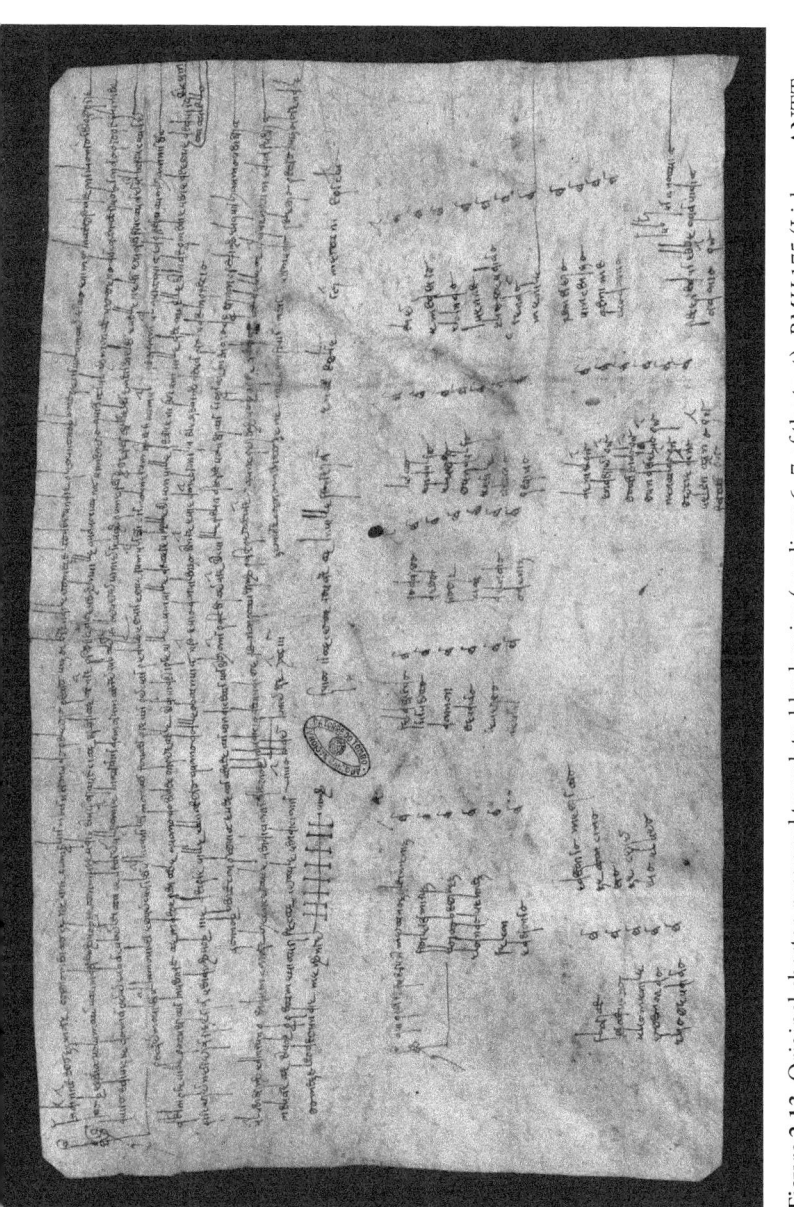

**Figure 2.13** Original charter, prepared template, blank price (see lines 6–7 of the text): *PMH* 175 (Lisbon, ANTT, Ordem de São Bento, Mosteiro de São João Baptista de Pendorada, mç. 1, no. 2 (PT/TT/MSJBP/004/0001/02): Imagem cedida pelo ANTT)

both appear amidst the subscriptions, and one can imagine negotiations continuing as the scribes were at work. Nor is it scribal incompetence, or the oversight of later copyists: when Sampiro, who hardly lacked experience, wrote up a sale for himself in 1013, he added five *solidi* to the price after the sanction, dating, and confirmation clauses, presumably once the final terms had been agreed.[197] Far from a mutual ignorance or momentary contact, transaction and documentation had an organic and recursive relationship, proceeding in tandem and in feedback.

The writing process could also be drawn out. In three cases from Otero, further hands intervened subsequent to the writing of the main text: to add more property, to specify it with greater detail, and to substitute the price paid for what the scribe had anticipated.[198] Similarly, in 961, *offertionem* (compensation) for defaulting on a judicial fine was tacked on *deorsum* (below) the *cartam que sursum resonat de donatione* (charter of donation which is recorded above), serving as a reminder that transaction could play out over days, while the writing up kept pace alongside it.[199] Equally it could spill over into subsequent undertakings: when the family of San Rosendo made a *collmellum divisionis* dividing up their patrimony in 934, they consented, after the confirmation and dating, to a secondary exchange between Adosinda and Ermesinda, before subscribing the charter.[200] One combination sale and donation to Viliulfu and his wife Ezilu in 968 seems to have been transformed over the course of its transcription: after the subscriptions, a new scribe began a formula for price, not even mentioned until this point, but then left it blank and recorded instead a series of additions to the donation *per ista karta* (by that charter), finally dating it once again and listing more witnesses.[201] An organic and evolving relationship between document and transaction is underlined by countergift in confirmation of the charter itself, rather than the deal which it records. The two oxen worth 30 silver *solidi* and a *lenzo* (linen cloth) of 50 cubits which Pelayo Vermúdez received from his wife Godina *ad confirmanda cartula* (to confirm the charter) in 1011 or the vineyard and moveables which Xemena received from Beira *presbiter* in 1005 *ad investimentum carta* (for completion of the

---

[197] *León* 717.    [198] *Otero* 162, 152, 137.
[199] *Sobrado* 1.46; cf. 1.45; *San Isidro* 15–6.
[200] *Celanova* 40; cf. *Sahagún* 400; *Leire* 22; *Sobrado* 1.1, 1.115–16; *Celanova* 43, 322; *San Clodio* 1.
[201] *PMH* 98.

charter) tie text and transaction tightly together.[202] Configured on occasion even as the price of a sale completing its written record, these documentary countergifts seem to say that transaction confirmed charter just as charter confirmed transaction.[203]

## Presentations

Another approach to the writing process is by way of how the scribe of a charter made use of parchment. The question is simply put but challenging to answer: was a charter written primarily to be read or laid out mainly to be displayed?[204] Returning to the Sahagún corpus, I have attempted to divide the 84 originals into charters for reading, consisting only of running text, and charters for displaying, with a clear eye to visual consumption. Some charters, royal diplomas especially, are obviously meant to be impressive, such as a grant of jurisdiction by Alfonso III to the monastery in 904, where the subscriptions and monograms of the king and his sons, at almost three times the size of the text, dominate the parchment (see Figure 2.14).[205] And yet, even here, the text itself is laid out with minimal adornment, simply and cleanly for reading; it is impossible to make such a division systematically. Of course, this is not to say that layout did not matter: the writers of 59 of the originals (70%) have taken pains, however minimal, to highlight certain areas of the main text, such as the date or the name of a king, or to distinguish it from the subscription area, by altering script size or line spacing, distributing names into columns, or using arresting signs. As in one typical lay sale from Portugal in 936 where the scribe wrote the witnesses in a different pen and ink, no viewer could fail to notice that it was duly confirmed, and in this sense most charters are for display (see Figure 2.15).[206]

The other 25 originals (30%) feature continuous script, and minimal alteration of layout or use of signs, for a less apparent, though not always absent, differentiation of main text and subscriptions.[207] Most of these charters are simple sales, straightforward in content and so to be dashed off with equal

---

[202] *Sahagún* 397; *León* 654; cf. 707; *Sahagún* 19; *Otero* 55; *San Vicente* 29; *Benevívere* 1; *Pamplona* 4; *Tumbo Viejo* 16; *Santiago* 62; *Samos* 171; *Celanova* 291; *PMH* 14; Martínez Díez, 'Terminología', 238–40; Sánchez González de Herrero, 'Usos', 256–7.

[203] See e.g. *Sahagún* 412; *Astorga* 254.    [204] Sáez, 'Documentos', 899–916.

[205] *Sahagún* 6.    [206] *PMH* 41.

[207] *Sahagún* 1–5, 134–6, 148, 160, 180, 200, 204–5, 207, 211, 258, 285, 288, 306, 310, 353, 397, 400, 427.

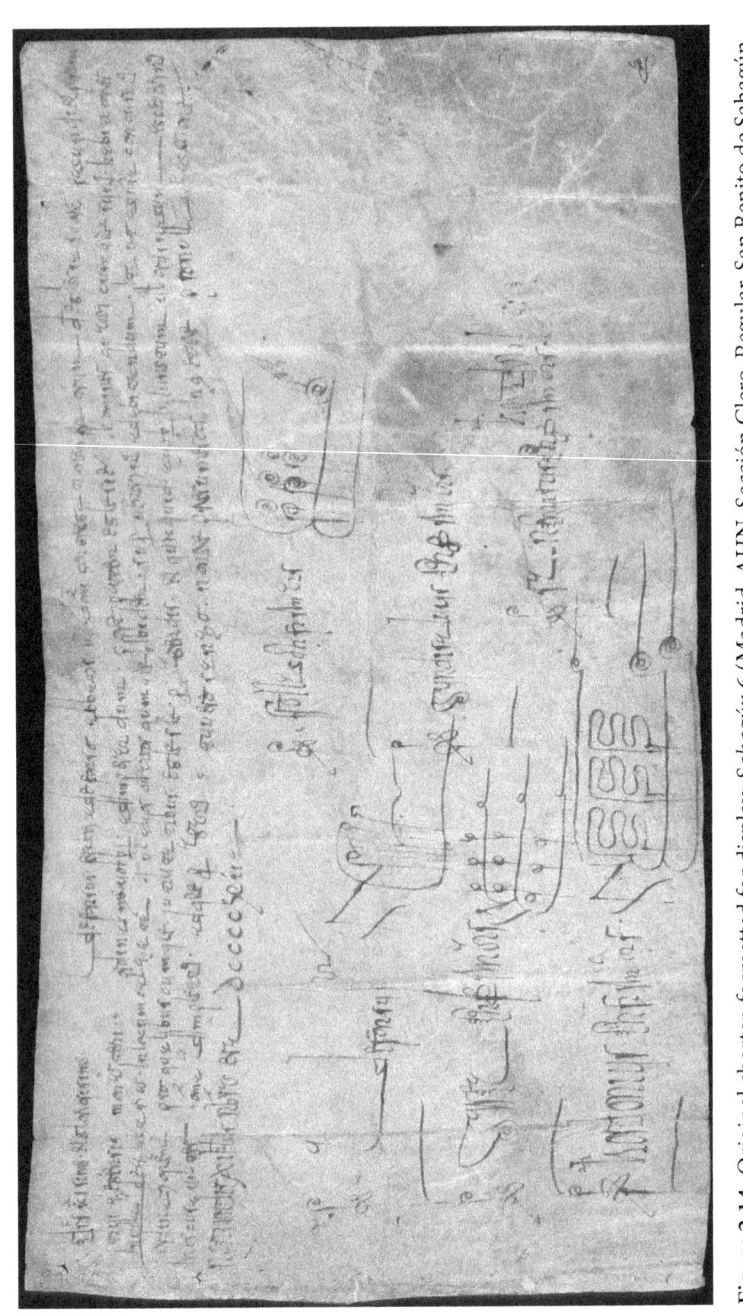

**Figure 2.14**  Original charter, formatted for display: *Sahagún* 6 (Madrid, AHN, Sección Clero, Regular, San Benito de Sahagún, carp. 872, no. 6: Ministerio de Cultura y Deporte. Archivo Histórico Nacional. CLERO-SECULAR_REGULAR,Car.872,N.6).

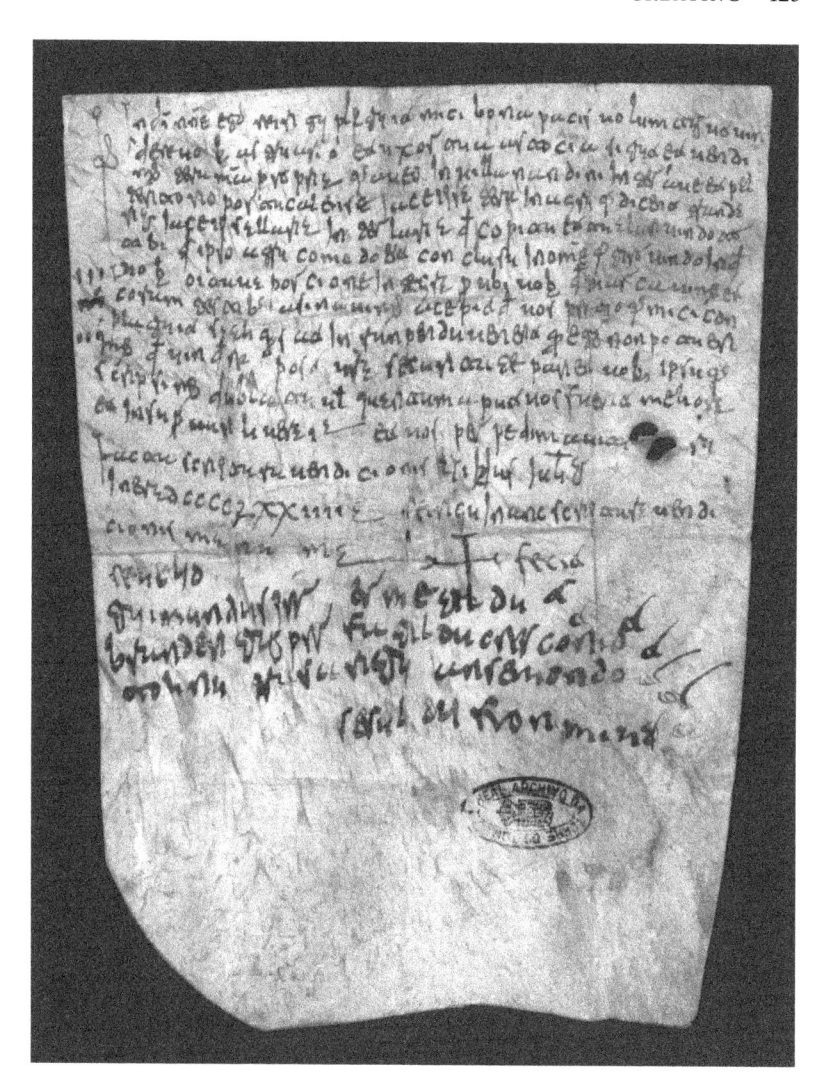

**Figure 2.15** Original charter, main text distinct from witness section: *PMH* 41 (Lisbon, ANTT, Cónegos Regulares de Santo Agostinho, Mosteiro do Salvador de Moreira, mç. 1, no. 5 (PT/TT/MSM/A/M01): Imagem cedida pelo ANTT)

dispatch, while nine are lay transactions; beyond that there is little relating them.[208] Even in a characteristic sale to Sahagún from 955, however, while the text runs continuously, plainly meant for reading, the date is spaced out slightly more, a bracket marks out granters and confirmers, and the summary reference to *alios plures* (many other witnesses) is set off at the lower right, all of which catch and guide the eye (see Figure 2.16).[209] Overall the norm must have been to make charters suitable for both reading and show.[210] The use of Visigothic cursive script is standard regardless of other elements of format, though on occasion semi-cursive and 'rounded' scripts more typical of codices are found.[211] Selection of parchment typically shows an effort to choose a piece of roughly appropriate dimensions in advance, or to cut the end product down to size, but even so practised a scribe as Fulgentius nods, snipping off a witness while trimming a charter.[212] Parchment dimensions and shape vary so widely overall that availability must have been a constraint, and while few palimpsests have been identified, opistographs are commonly encountered: these could also be a product of poor planning, or a result of the transaction unfolding at greater length than anticipated, since it is the final sectors of the charter text, from the date or subscriptions, which normally run onto the reverse.[213]

Parchment choice turns out in many cases to have entailed prior coordination, and this can help us better to understand the relationship between the parties and the scribe, as well as revealing one aspect of archival practice. In 979, for example, when Revel paid off a judicial debt by selling a vineyard to the bishop of León, the scribe Gamar *presbiter* used the reverse of the same parchment for the *placitum firmitatis* (agreement of confirmation) made the same day to guarantee the sale.[214] And when Vermudo III gave property to Munio in reward for his service in 1030, the scribe Fulgentius promptly took advantage of the reverse side to write the charter by which Munio then 're-gifted' that property amongst his wife and children.[215] There is a clear effort here to keep related but distinct documents

<hr />

[208] *Sahagún* 1–5, 205, 207, 211, 397.      [209] *Sahagún* 148.

[210] Alfonso, 'Formato', 210–16; Davies, *Windows*, 65–94.

[211] Ruiz Asencio, 'Escritura visigótica', 93–118; Herrero de la Fuente, 'Producir', 89–129; Alturo i Perucho, 'Script', 143–84.

[212] *León* 711; Ruiz Asencio, 'Trabajo', 104–5.

[213] Guerra, *Diplomas*, 83–100; see *e.g. ChLA* 114, 27–8 (a palimpsest); and *León* 53, 468, 742; *Otero* 25, 34, 45, 86, 90, 159; *San Vicente* 30; Fernández Flórez, 'Escribir, en León-Castilla', 153–7; Herrero de la Fuente and Fernández Flórez, 'Cidi', 685–7; Ruiz Asencio, 'Trabajo', 101–2, 105–6.

[214] *León* 463–4; *cf.* 476–7, 739; *Otero* 38–9, 125, 150–1, 188–9; *PMH* 6–7, 167.

[215] *León* 871; *cf. Oña* 3–4; *Coruña* 135–6; *Sobrado* 1.115–16.

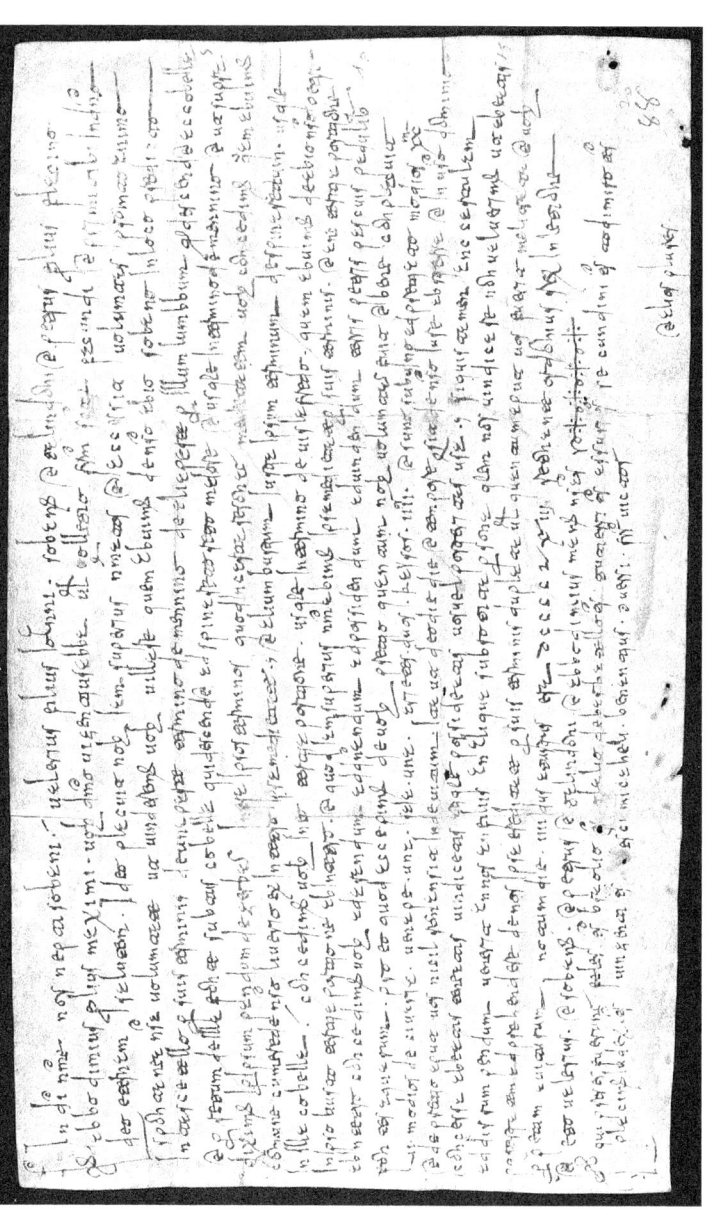

**Figure 2.16** Original charter, formatted for reading: *Sahagún* 148 (Madrid, AHN, Sección Clero, Regular, San Benito de Sahagún, carp. 874, no. 5: Ministerio de Cultura y Deporte. Archivo Histórico Nacional. CLERO-SECULAR_REGULAR,Car.874,N.5)

together in the same place for ease of reference, and at least some of the many perceptible but illegible fragments of further texts in the lower quadrants or on the reverse sides of originals must follow this pattern.[216] Behind such 'parchment organisation' lies intelligent cooperation between granter and scribe, as well as between recipient and scribe. In one case, the local scribe Durabilis *presbiter*, seemingly in collaboration with another writer, documented two sales of land in Villobera to Abellar three months apart in 939 using the front side of the same parchment, just as Vistremiro, party to a charter of exchange in 909, had a sale in which he was purchaser recorded on its reverse side four years later.[217] Two sales to Leda, meanwhile, are on the same side of one parchment, but in opposing directions (elsewhere we find dividing lines); dated a year and a half apart and in distinct tints of ink, they are by the same hand, returning to write again (see Figure 2.17).[218]

The practice of parchment organisation is one facet of the formation of archives, and in some cases we even see individual parchments becoming miniature archives. Over a week in 943, the scribe Fredenandus wrote a trio of sales to Vincimalo *presbiter* on the reverse side of a parchment, while Vivi *presbiter* did likewise on behalf of Cidi Domínguez and his wife Oria for a *plazo* and four sales over two weeks from 24 April to 8 May 1030 (see Figure 2.18).[219] In contrast, over a year, from October 978 to October 979, seven sales to Munnio *presbiter* of property around Villa de Montane were recorded on one parchment by various contemporary hands: here the recipient or scribe could have selected the writing medium (see Figure 2.19).[220] In all these cases, instant archives: multiple transactions with the same recipient set down in one place, transactions not only on the same day as might be expected, but also distanced in time. Whether all these charters are strictly originals in the sense of having been drawn up at the moment of those transactions misses the point.[221] Four charters of sale to Sahagún from 965 which are written on one parchment are clearly the work of the same moment in spite of spanning half a month in real time, and they are in

---

[216] See *e.g. León* 156, 227, 262, 345, 576; *Sahagún* 330; *Otero* 75, 102; Ruiz Asencio, 'Trabajo', 105–10.

[217] *León* 132, 135, 23, 31; *cf.* 316, 323; *Sahagún* 203–4; *Otero* 106–7; *Coruña* 51–2; Davies, 'Local Priests', 35–41.

[218] *León* 519, 523; *cf. Sahagún* 153–4, 226–7; *Otero* 40–1, 64–5, 79–80, 138–9.

[219] *León* 172–4; 864, 866–8, 870.

[220] *León* 457–9, 465, 467, 471–2; *cf.* 637, 656, 668; *Sahagún* 134–6; *Otero* 94–6; *Coruña* 78–80; Ruiz Asencio, 'Trabajo', 102–4, 110–15.

[221] Escalona, 'Cartularios', 135–41.

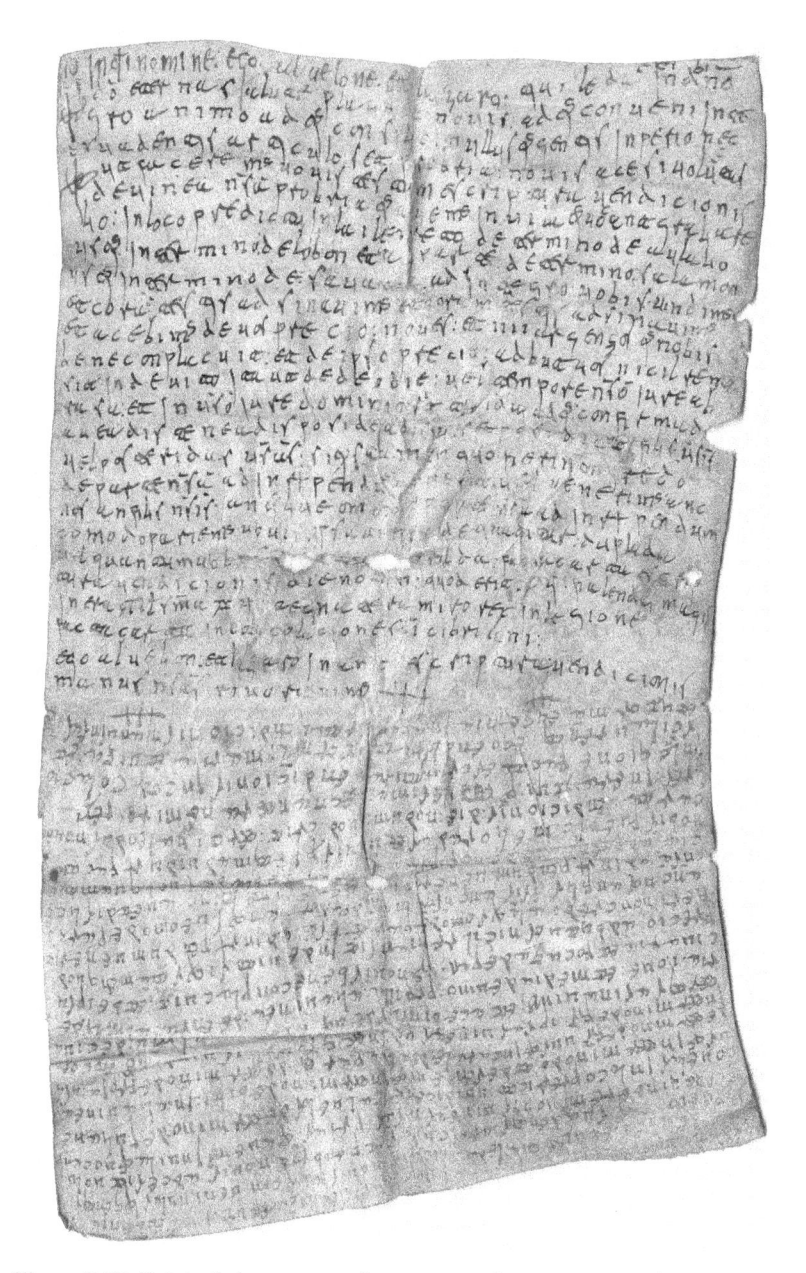

**Figure 2.17** Original charters, two documents written on one parchment: *León* 519, 523 (León, Archivo Catedralicio, Pergaminos, no. 146A–B)

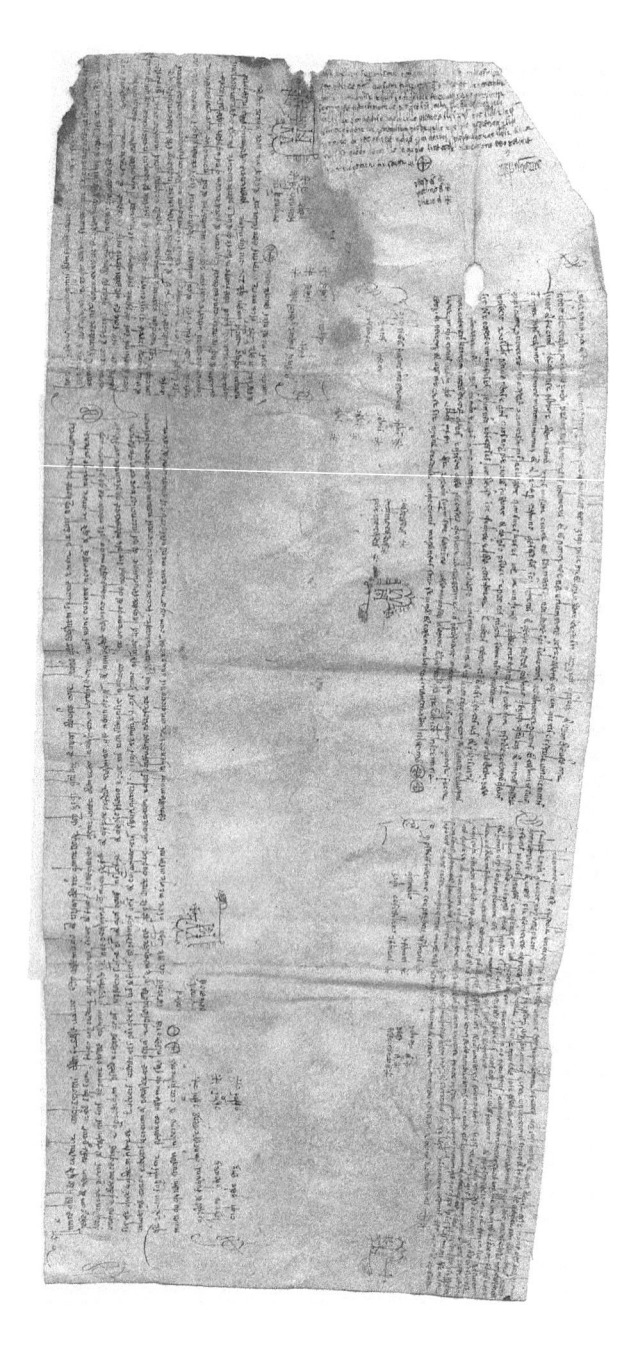

**Figure 2.18** Original 'miniature archive', single scribe: *León* 864, 866–8, 870 (León, Archivo Catedralicio, Pergaminos, nos 152–153A–E)

**Figure 2.19** Original 'miniature archive', multiple scribes: *León* 457–9, 465, 467, 471–2 (León, Archivo Catedralicio, Pergaminos, no. 7255)

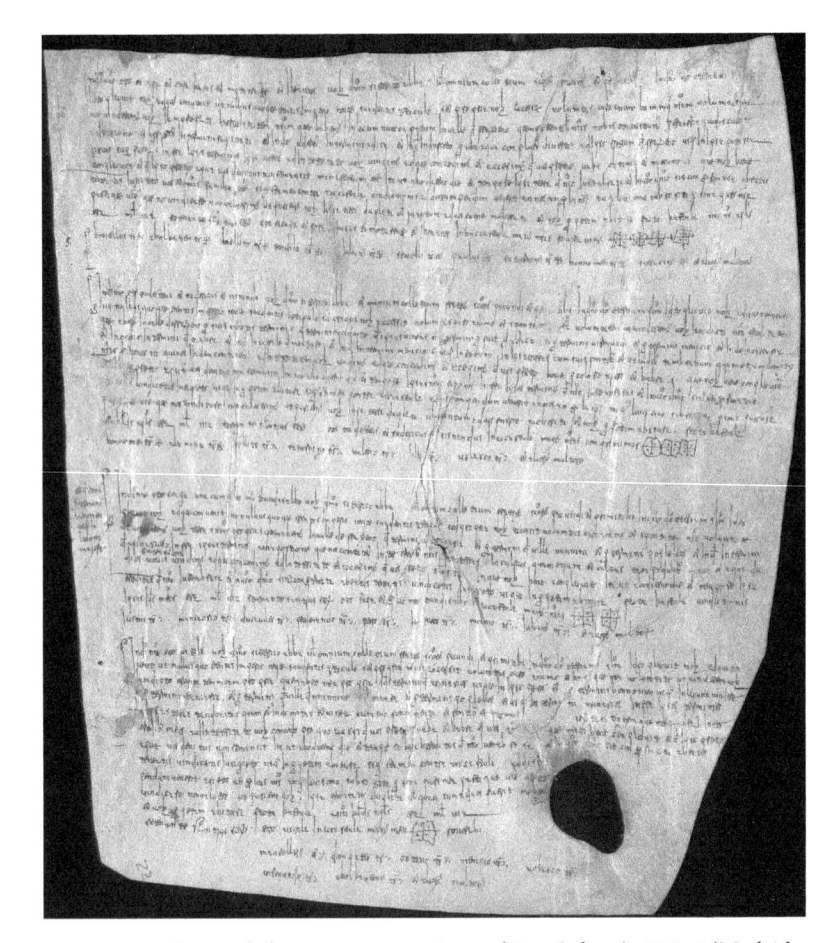

**Figure 2.20** Original charter, retrospective archive: *Sahagún* 233–6 (Madrid, AHN, Sección Clero, Regular, San Benito de Sahagún, carp. 875, no. 13: Ministerio de Cultura y Deporte. Archivo Histórico Nacional. CLERO-SECULAR_REGULAR,Car.875,N.13)

any case out of chronological order when reading from top to bottom, but all concern property located in Valdefresno (see Figure 2.20).[222] As transaction followed on transaction, the advantage of assembling them will have become steadily more obvious. Similarly, there has been debate over the originality of a parchment from the cathedral archive of

---

[222] *Sahagún* 233–6.

Lugo containing two *placita* to Bishop Gladila and a confession to his benefit, spanning 15 May to 5 June 861 and fruit of a judicial process; the latter
may in fact have been written first, the former two then added in the blank
space underneath, at a few strokes becoming an archive in miniature presenting a full accounting of the case.[223]

Who took the lead in parchment choice? As the Munnio *presbiter* sales of
978 to 979 have highlighted, we cannot assume that it was primarily the
scribe, acting as a kind of local archivist, and the reuse of parchment for
related but temporally more remote charters offers further caution. Take the
case of Seovanus *presbiter*, who gave his property to the church of San
Martín de Noanca in 895: beginning on the lower left front side of the same
parchment, and running onto the reverse, is a *placitum* from 960 guaranteeing transfer of San Martín to a monastery of Santa María.[224] When it came
time to write up this latter charter, therefore, the church must have rum-
maged in its archive and dug out the original parchment from 65 years
before, handing it over to the scribe for the new transaction. Parties and
scribes often agreed in advance the most appropriate site for a text. When
the recipient is a Church institution, the archival connection is obvious, but
when a member of the laity it can be harder to determine: a parchment
from Otero bears a dispute of 946 in benefit of Flacino and a sale made in
1022 to Count Pedro Flaínez, which could be linked via family archives, if
they are related as the names suggest.[225] Does some unstated relationship
bind together a sale of 883 to Kartemiro with two more to Fruela and his
wife Eleuva in 933 and 952, all on the same parchment, all by different
scribes, or is the whole a later copy?[226] In some cases the continuity must lie
in persons, in others in the property itself changing hands with its title
deeds, in still others with both factors; what it betrays is an awareness of,
and a concern for, the written history of land and its owners. In a remarkable case involving the Asturian monastery of Gordón, we even find
Florentina returning to the parchment of a dispute settled in 953 to confirm
it on behalf of Cogina, a party to the original text, in 981.[227] Reuse could be
for unrelated purposes, most notably the *nodicia de kesos* (list of cheeses
paid out), written around 980 on the reverse of a testament to Santos Justo y
Pastor dating back to 959, but there may be linkages of property, lineages of

---

[223] *ChLA* 114, 22A-C; *Floriano* 73–5; Davies, *Windows*, 126–32.
[224] *León* 10, 330.    [225] *Otero* 4, 155.
[226] *PMH* 10, 38, 64; cf. *Sahagún* 242, 304–5; *Otero* 21, 26, 43; *PMH* 30, 43, 48.
[227] *Oviedo* 26; cf. *Liébana* 24; *Sobrado* 1.107; Collins, 'Law', 500–1; Davies, *Windows*, 1–5, 146–9.

parties, or modalities of use even here, concealed by time, which those who knew sought to solidify by presenting one particular parchment to the waiting scribe.[228]

The writing process could also span more than one parchment, in generating multiple originals for various parties and audiences. The fact that complementary versions of a charter were made is partly obscured by the anomalous palaeographic label of 'contemporary copy', and was probably a matter of course.[229] Reminiscent of the classic chirograph, or a split tally stick, the *Becerro Gótico* of Sahagún contains an identical exchange made between Alfonso III and Sarrazino, Falconi, and Dulquito in 909 twice over, with the order of parties reversed, but only slight variations in formulation from one copy to the next attributable perhaps to the scribe of the cartulary.[230] Two texts of an exchange between six laymen and Bishop Cixila of Abellar in 925, similarly, are transmitted by the *Tumbo* of León, but in this case cast as a pair of reciprocal donations.[231] Sometimes the signs are less obvious: the cartulary of San Millán includes a handful of sales framed as purchases, opposite to the 'normal' formulation, which could be the other side of a twofold record, while the testament of Gundulfus as preserved in the cartulary of Celanova is confirmed by only San Rosendo out of its many recipients, implying that the source text was his personal copy.[232] This reality of multiple copies is embedded in the language of exchange, which owing to its nature is the transaction most explicit about it. In 961, for example, Abbess María and two religious *facimus kartulas comutationis* (made charters—not a charter—of exchange) with Abellar, a practice deemed *sicut mos esse solet* (as is usually the custom) by a Portuguese charter of 959, while still more evocatively three religious from a house of San Vicente in Galicia made *scripturas contramutationis unus ad alios* (documents of exchange: one [each] for the others) with Bishop Sisnando, Hermegildo, and Sobrado in 964.[233] But the same can be seen too for sales, such as one made *carta ad cartam* (charter for charter) in the Liébana in 915, or another *per scriptis firmitatis* (by documents of confirmation) in León in 1030, and

---

[228] *León* 313, 480; *cf.* 593, 597; 643, 750; *Sahagún* 261; *Otero* 53–4; *Coruña* 112, 120.

[229] See *e.g. León* 58, 316, 323; *Escalada* 1; *Oña* 8, 17; Fernández Flórez, 'Fondo', 130–2.

[230] *Sahagún* 9–10; Lowe, 'Literacy', 161–204.

[231] *León* 66–7; *cf.* 244–5; *San Millán* 382; *Oña* 10–11.

[232] *San Millán* 16, 498, 382, 538; *Celanova* 23.

[233] *León* 340; *Guimarães* 54; *Sobrado* 1.121; *cf. León* 386; *Santiago* 63; *Sobrado* 1.97, 1.9; *Celanova* 84, 315.

maybe for a donation, by three religious to San Salvador de Matallana in 989, which also survives granted by just one in a personal copy.[234]

Multiple versions could take different forms for different audiences. Vermudo II, in a diploma of 999 for Assur Sarraciniz and Elvira, *ipsa scriptura nobis confirmabit* (confirmed that document to us), but then *alia nobis manu propria roborabit* (affirmed another to us with his own hand) as well.[235] What this signifies may be illustrated by a donation which the same king made to Bishop Savarigo of León in 991 and survives in two originals: one of these is a precept, conveying in spare text ownership of two *villas* and jurisdiction over the inhabitants, the other is a rhetorically expansive donation in remedy of the royal soul.[236] And while both are signed by Sampiro *presbiter* as scribe, the first is written in rapid Visigothic cursive, a 'business hand' not his own, the second in the characteristic fine script of the royal notary himself, reminding us of the complexity of scribal operations as well as scribal outputs. In some cases we could be looking at a draft and a good copy, like the two foundation charters of Covarrubias written by the same scribe in 978, differing only in brevity.[237] But in others we indisputably have 'proper' redactions, such as the testaments of Iulianus *presbiter* from 954, one tersely donating all his property to Santos Justo y Pastor, one colourfully narrating his trials and tribulations in quest of a suitable beneficiary.[238] We should imagine different versions for different contexts, practical enforcement of ownership, say, versus liturgical or historical celebration of an act of generosity—like a gift receipt versus a birthday card—to appreciate the multiplicity built into the writing and rewriting of any given charter.

Revisiting a document presented a further opportunity to revise its text, in a sign that the writing process could be ongoing and flexible as much as discrete and fixed. In 990, when sisters of San Lorenzo made an *unatem* (joint donation) to San Salvador de Matallana of half their property in Alija de la Ribera, they changed their minds that same day to make another, this time of all their property; though the first charter was later overwritten, both survive.[239] At greater remove, the bishop of Astorga seems to have returned in 1021 to elaborate on his gift of a year before to the monastery of San Dictino.[240] Such cases where the second charter offers a larger gift, describes it in greater detail, or characterises parties more precisely tell us

---

[234] *Liébana* 20; *León* 869; 529, 531; *cf.* 539, 545; 725–7; *Sahagún* 29–30, 32; *Cardeña* 54; *PMH* 167, 271; *Coimbra* 518.
[235] *León* 587.    [236] *León* 549–50; *cf.* 588–9; Collins, 'Documents', 31–2.
[237] *Covarrubias* 7–8.    [238] *León* 278–9.    [239] *León* 534–5, 575.
[240] *Astorga* 230.

that return to the charter was regular, reconsideration of its formulations recurrent.[241] When we are at the mercy of cartularies or later copies, however, it is difficult to know how much to read from multiple versions with apparently trivial discrepancies. Sales to Iuzef and his wife Iusta in 1021 and 1026 are each preserved in a pair of copies: in the second of both, Iuzef is identified as *ebreo* (Jewish), the property located with greater precision, and the price revised downwards by half a *solidus*, to name only the most prominent differences.[242] But does this simply represent the vagaries of transcription or illuminate a highly plastic transactional and documentary process, recurring on itself in light of negotiation, in search of specificity, in the interest of finer phraseology, in need of more imposing witnesses, or for some other elusive motivation? We should be wary of ascribing multiplicity to error, and ground ourselves in a flexible process. As the scribe pivoted between his model and the moment, he situated and customised composition to the needs and advantage of the parties, resulting in a background to the writing of each charter as flexible and variable as the transaction itself.

## Contexts

Taken together, documentation and transaction were a complex and recursive process, but should they be taken together? Can we marshall our scribes, parties, and witnesses, at the same time and the same place, and demonstrate that documentation and transaction were an integral process? In theory, this scarcely needs proving: clauses such as *ordinamus vobis eam possidere per hanc cartulam testationis nostre* (we direct you to take possession of it through this charter of our bequest), or indeed *quod supra scriptum est sic vobis ad integro firmamus possidere perpetualiter* (what is written above we thus confirm to you in its entirety to own in perpetuity), identify the charter with the transfer of property.[243] To put it in traditional terms, it is dispositive rather than evidentiary. Rhetoric, of course, need not be reality, but it is borne out here in charters which document incomplete transactions, framing and thereby helping to conclude them. Far from retrospections on business conducted orally, if anything these texts anticipated and set it in motion, just as we have seen the scribe at work while terms were still under

---

[241] See *e.g. León* 437, 479, 618, 818, 826, 832–3; *Cardeña* 207, 89; *San Millán* 313, 697, 97, 717, 315, 701.
[242] *León* 774, 828.          [243] *León* 548, 619.

negotiation. The sale made by Godiosa and her son Seniore to Goinu around 960–73 is one of many where the statement of price is limited to a noncommittal *accepi de precio que michi bene conplacuit* (I have received in or of the price what has pleased me well).[244] In all other respects the charter is final—confirmed, witnessed, even signed by the scribe—and as such it defines the scope of or sets parameters for the final negotiations outstanding.

We find signs of incompleteness in both originals and cartulary copies, so that faults of transcription cannot explain it away. Take a sale to the scribe Sampiro which he wrote up for himself in 1013: he stated the currency of the price as *solidos*, but left a blank space for the amount.[245] The text was an organic part of this transaction too, where all that remained to be agreed was price; aside from property under sale, the scope or the parameter which it set was the unit of the price, constraining the settlement of the transaction within certain terms. Comparable cases include a sale in 936 for a *vacca colore ruvea et alio pretio que mici bene conplacuit* (a red cow and another price which has pleased me well), partly determined and partly undetermined; a sale in 1009 for *alia terra quantum a nobis bene conplacuit* (another plot of land such as has pleased me well), defining the category of the price, not its amount; and a sale in 929 for a *saia* (tunic) and *alio pretio sub uno modios VII quod sus pretius dedit* (another price, in total seven *modios* which he has given as the price), stating the amount but not determining its components.[246] Even when the price was realised in the text, however, we should not assume that this was the end of it. In another sale made by Agildo and Gualamiru to Cresconius in 1007, the two vendors have subscribed it, but Agildo, who is supposed to receive four *modios* in price, adds a plaintive note, *abeo heu adhuc proinde ipsam kartam ad roborare* (I have—alas!—still to confirm the charter in this regard), suggesting that payment of the price was still up in the air, and that a document could both frame and add pressure to the implementation of a transaction.[247] How long this intermediate stage could ultimately last is underlined by an exchange (formulated as a sale) between Count Pedro Fláinez and Fruela Sendínez made on 15 February 1029. On the same parchment is a *placitum* of 8 December in which the *fidesiunsores* (guarantors) of the count

---

[244] *León* 421; *cf.* 573, 768; *Sahagún* 94; *Astorga* 62; *Coruña* 62; *Sobrado* 1.73, 1.95, 1.49; *Celanova* 19, 122, 237, 293; *PMH* 38, 41, 72, 80, 90, 98, 105; *Guimarães* 14; *Coimbra* 530.

[245] *León* 715; *cf. Sobrado* 1.83.

[246] *León* 111, 684; *San Vicente* 6; *cf. León* 156; *Sahagún* 53, 56; *Otero* 69, 72; *Coruña* 45; *Sobrado* 1.81, 1.67, 1.79, 1.27, 1.12; *Celanova* 22, 145; *PMH* 102; *Floriano* 163.

[247] *Celanova* 306; *cf.* 307; *León* 167, 182; *Liébana* 47.

undertake to hand over his land if he should default, while in a second *placitum* confirmed that day, though written on another parchment, a second set of *fidesiunsores* for Fruela Sendínez and his family vow to give their land to the count on his return to Valdoré.[248] Almost ten months after the original document set this sale or exchange in motion, it was still being worked out through further documents.

If texts were written 'live', and acted to engender and frame transactions, how did the writing of the charter reflect the process which it recorded? Some texts purport to offer a one-to-one relationship to reality, transcribing direct speech and in theory putting the scribe in the middle of the action, making notes. There are first-person utterances in testamentary acts and dispute settlements: requests, arguments, pleas, agreements.[249] But caution is needed before taking them to be *viva voce* records. In 990, we read, Pelagius Zuleiman *frater* asked Queen Tarasia, his *domina* (mistress), for permission to make a testament, and in reply, we hear, the queen said, *placuit mihi ut testare facias illum tu Zuleiman frater omnia quod mihi petisti* (it has pleased me that you should make a bequest of everything which you have asked of me), a formal statement of authorisation, seemingly spoken words copied down verbatim.[250] Alfonso V too was petitioned by Bishop Nuño of León to confirm a *kastellum* or *kastrum* (a 'castle' or fortified site) in 1012, and responded, *faciam quod postulatis mici* (I shall do what you have requested of me), yet two months later, when petitioned by Teodemirus *frater* of Santiago de León for the return of a *villa*, he echoed himself exactly, if more expansively, *ego faciam et adinpleam at domum Sancti Iacobi quod mihi postulatis* (I shall do and fulfil for the house of Santiago what you have requested of me).[251] The scribe of both diplomas was Sampiro, and what we are reading is not real but 'scribal speech', a rhetorical strategy of authentication by a pretence of quotation, like the 'personal' but often stereotyped postscripts added to papal, episcopal, and other early medieval letters.[252] This is not to deny any connection between written and real words: *condiciones sacramentorum* were standardised in content, according to the 'Visigothic formulary', but the prescribed words were combined with the particularities of a given dispute and sworn as the oath (or so we are told),

---

[248] *Otero* 188–90.
[249] See *e.g. León* 754, 856; *Sahagún* 340, 386, 404; *Benevívere* 1; *San Juan* 32; *Sobrado* 1.48; *Celanova* 88, 236; Davies, *Windows*, 121–45; Carvajal Castro, 'Politics', esp. 30–41, 44–6.
[250] *León* 543; *cf.* 560.       [251] *León* 707–8.
[252] Mathisen, 'Subscriptions', 243–51; Moreau, 'Notes', 235–62.

in an interplay between written and spoken language.[253] What we cannot do is use direct speech in charters to prove that they were transcriptions or even simplifications rather than formulaic representations.

At first glance it can also look like some dispute settlements were documented 'live' by the scribe, written up in the form of a series of texts describing stages of the process, each confirmed independently as if a discrete document.[254] The record of a dispute in 915 consists of four 'sub-charters': first an undertaking by Velasco, arguing on behalf of the monastery of Valdevimbre, to present witnesses supporting its version of the ownership history of a stretch of the Bernesga River, set out very much as an opening argument. In the following text, the witnesses testify to that effect, rehearsing the story in full; in the next text they swear an oath on the same testimony, recapitulating it again; and in the last, their adversary Munnio finally capitulates, which constitutes the 'settlement' proper.[255] The repetition hints at the originally separate composition of each text, though they are now amalgamated into one in the *Tumbo* of León, and the range of forms in which such documentation survives is sufficiently varied for us to think that it is not simply a shared fiction.[256] In 1022, a case of abduction unfolded over another four 'sub-charters' written on one parchment: first a *manifesto* (a statement of confession) to the accusation by Eneco, then a *placitum* to consult the Visigothic law code, followed by the text of the relevant law in full, and lastly a *placitum* in which Fruela Muñoz offered him a contract of service by way of compromise settlement.[257] The scribe has signed the first three texts and the fourth, dating them to 21 and 23 June respectively; the stages may differ from our first case, but the record reads as another judicial process playing out.

The constituents of these texts are not mere rhetorical exercises in authentication, for examples of stray procedural documentation survive outside of amalgamated form: *manifesta* with an attached *placitum* or sale, *condiciones sacramentorum*, an isolated settlement, a list of property at issue in a case of theft.[258] Sometimes it clearly mattered that the intricacies of the competing claims be set down stage by stage, whereas in others the resultant transaction seems to have been more important, hence those charters—recurrent in

---

[253] See *e.g. Sobrado* 1.109.
[254] Collins, 'Law', 498–506; Collins, 'Visigothic Law', 87–90, 94–5; Alfonso, 'Formato', 201–9; Davies, 'Language', 241–52; Davies, 'Records', 53–75.
[255] *León* 34.
[256] See *e.g. Otero* 116, 125; *Liébana* 66; *Valladolid* 3; Davies, *Windows*, 35–64.
[257] *Otero* 150–1.     [258] See *e.g. Otero* 38–9, 147–8; *Valpuesta* 10; *Puerto* 1–2; *Otero* 114.

Celanova, Otero, and Sobrado—which take the form of a brief judicial background followed by the payment of an agreed penalty or fee, subordinating narrative to outcome.[259] We should think again of scribes customising presentation according to different functions and audiences. At the same time, in the executions of testaments or the 'property history' narratives behind many transactions and disputes, we catch sight of prior stages which may not have been written down, or meet with parties or witnesses who cannot be made to fit the date, implying retrospective documenting of earlier transactions or 'charters after the fact'.[260] Occasionally this appears to have been a flurry of such texts at the last minute to go along with a new transaction.[261] In 1027, a *kartula perfiliacionis vel vendicionis* (charter of formal adoption and sale) was explicit about what it was doing: the *villa* in question had been purchased during the lifetime of Amuna, wife of Fruela Muñoz, but *non ubiarunt de illa carta facere* (they had not made a charter of it) back then, and now they were making up for this after her death, with her present spectrally beside her husband.[262] Some documentation was evidently not contemporaneous with the transaction which it records, but the question is whether, given the multiple versions ordinarily written up of donations, sales, and disputes, it is right to consider such charters anachronistic.

And indeed, not all disputes fit the structure of 'live' serial documentation, suggesting two different modes of recording settlements. In one case from Celanova in 987, the first part of the charter narrates the whole process from start to finish, while four subsequent texts read like the procedural papers generated in its course: a formal confession, a *placitum* to consult the law, an undertaking to bring witnesses, and a final *placitum* to hand over the property.[263] What we have, in other words, is a synthesis with supporting materials. When the bishop of Astorga and Munio Fernández locked horns before Alfonso V in 1008, the *saio* was Sampiro *presbiter*, and his text of the proceedings applies the same method. Though recording much purportedly direct speech and naming some of the typical documentary stages along the way, he works through them without a break: the *series condiciones* (sequence of terms) sworn by Munio and two others, or

---

[259] *Celanova* 126, 160, 195, 311, 332; *Otero* 31, 109, 168; *Sobrado* 1.75, 1.54, 1.29, 1.21, 1.23, 1.31, 1.103.
[260] See *e.g. León* 28, 118, 863; *Sahagún* 337; *Samos* 29, 7; *Celanova* 219; *Lorvão* 17, 15; *Guimarães* 60.
[261] *Sahagún* 145–7, 272–3.      [262] *Otero* 179.      [263] *Celanova* 200.

the final *difinitionem et cartam securitatem* (settlement and charter of guarantee).[264] This 'end product' charter is the more common type, and highly variable in format.[265] It implies rationalisation after the fact of however the dispute had been recorded in progress, and settlements introduced by words such as *notum facimus concilio* (we make note [of it] in council) or labelled *seriem brevem* (short schedule) may be acknowledging this fact, and recognising the summarisation and simplification which it must have entailed.[266]

If we return to documents written in the 'procedural' rather than 'synthetic' style with this in mind, we can see a more subtle situation than is at first apparent. The great (in length) dispute from 953 over the Asturian monastery of Gordón appears to consist of seven separate texts, depending on how one demarcates them: the opening statement of arguments ending in a *placitum* to produce witnesses, the rehearsal of their testimony, *conditiones sagramentorum* sworn by these witnesses leading to the settlement, and three *placita*, to present the witnesses, accept the settlement, and hand over the property, plus a confirmation added on in 981. Yet a cursory glance at the parchment belies this presentation: the first six documents have clearly all been written at the same time by a single hand, the first three *en bloc*, the second three in a column on the lower right side, positioned below the names of the witnesses to the ordeal as if to suggest that these procedural *placita* are offered as similarly supporting testimony. The document is nonetheless formally an original, in that the subscriptions include autographs or at least have been written by more than one hand.[267] In a sense, there should be no surprises here: disputes written up both procedurally and synthetically attest internally to taking place over days, months, even years, exactly as with other transactions, and some reckoning of the paperwork would have been necessary after all that time.[268] This settlement is therefore both an original charter and not, the 'end product' of a longer process which witnesses confirmed at its end, and which continued to accrue additions thereafter in later confirmation.

---

[264] *León* 669.

[265] See *e.g. León* 191; *Sahagún* 406; *Castañeda* 1; *San Vicente* 29; *Liébana* 62; *San Millán* 390; *San Juan* 13; *Celanova* 260; *Alfonso V* vii; *Sobrado* 1.129; *Samos* 126; *Coimbra* 212.

[266] *Celanova* 223; *Sobrado* 1.109; *cf. Castañeda* 3; *Santillana* 31; *Samos* 35; *Santiago* 59.

[267] *Oviedo* 26; Rodríguez Fernández, *Ordoño*, 171–8; Collins, 'Law', 498–501; Davies, *Windows*, 1–5, 146–51.

[268] See *e.g. León* 128, 192; *Sobrado* 1.132; *Guimarães* 24; *cf.* Bowman, *Landmarks*, 194–210.

## Affirmations

The writing of a charter can be thought of as a moment, or a series of moments, which occurred in the course of a transaction. It might fall anywhere from start to finish and beyond, but when we consider it in the context of the witnessing process, contemporaneity between its content and composition comes to the fore as the overriding norm. Confirmation involved not only granters and at times recipients, but also of course witnesses, and an expectation of their presence is embedded in the formulation of the text. This might be expressed simply as those who were present in 926 or as witnesses who were present *ibidem* (right there) and confirmed in 945; there were those who were present here in 997 and who were present there in 1020.[269] *Formulae* might accompany individual names in witness subscriptions, such as *ubi preses fuit* (where he was present) in 951 or *ic preses fui* (I was present here) in 957, or a more emphatic Arias Muniz, who was present, saw, and confirmed in 988.[270] But why were they present? In lengthier *formulae* this tends to be made more explicit, whether *in istam rovorationis cartam* (for that charter of confirmation) in 984, or *testibus qui ibidem presens fuerunt tradimus ad rovorandum* (we gave [the charter] to the witnesses who were present there to confirm it) in 899 and many other instances, or simply the *testibus a me rogatis* (witnesses invited by me) in 942.[271] And what did they do? In the first place they watched, though what is often unspecified: the witnesses *quos viderunt* (who saw) in 961, or who were present and saw in 1016, or who even were present and *ista kartula roborare viderunt* (saw this charter confirmed) in 1010.[272] They both listened and watched—*et audierunt et viderunt*—like those on hand in 1025.[273]

While we naturally associate witnesses with the final confirmation of the charter, they may have been present from as early as the point of its inception in an expression of intent. In 937 the last will of Mater was set down in writing and executed, but she had declared it from her deathbed some time before, in the presence of seven people named in the testament.[274] At a more middling stage, ten witnesses met at a church of San Lorenzo *ad terra consinanda et terminos postos* (to delimit the land and its limits) for a sale in 930, and this formula is a very common feature of boundary clauses; in 952,

---

[269] *León* 71; *Cardeña* 23; *Otero* 43, 129.   [270] *León* 240; *Eslonza* 27; *Coruña* 102.
[271] *Sobrado* 1.64; *Cardeña* 102, 19.   [272] *Celanova* 144; *Sobrado* 1.9; *Otero* 83.
[273] *Coimbra* 203.
[274] *León* 118; cf. *San Vicente* 18; *San Millán* 696, 316; *San Juan* 41; *Samos* 29.

the process involved putting up *karacteres fitos* (fixed devices), and Quinderedus *presbiter* linked his subscription to a testament of 816 to the establishment of limits for the property concerned.[275] Boundaries were always potential flash points, and multiple disputes feature the dispatch of *previsores* (inspectors) who *previderent* them: in the records of such acts, called *previsiones*, they tend to subscribe with *quod previdi* (what I have inspected).[276] But sometimes the language is ambiguous. The 20 witnesses present when four defeated parties to a dispute *adsignarunt* (set limits? handed over?) a *serna* (common land) in 946 may have observed the same process, since *adsignabimus* appears in a boundary clause of 1024, or they may have watched over the formal transfer of ownership, to judge by the use of *signavimus* in a confirmation clause from 944; indeed, one witness to an exchange in 948 confirmed *pro quod dare vidi villam* (because I saw [you] give it over).[277] Witnesses could equally be present to certify or even set the price: five silver *solidi* were *in pondere pesatos coram multitudine* (weighed before a crowd) in 1010, while 14 people *ipsa villa apreciaverunt* (priced the property?) in 999.[278] And there was no use for a private oath, hence *iuravimus coram testibus* (we swore before witnesses) in 954, nor to undergoing the ordeal without onlookers, hence the listing of those who were present *ad iuramentum* (at the oath) as well as those who were present *quando innocens ingressus est ad pena kaldaria* (when the neutral third party entered into the ordeal of hot water) in a dispute of 953.[279]

The confirmatory oath is situated directly before the sanction clause, and 211 charters (5% of the corpus) state that one has been taken, spread evenly over the period (see Figure 2.21). An oath can be expressed as a simple statement by the granter, *quod et iurationem confirmo* (which I also confirm by oath) as in 918, or *coniuratione vero confirmo* (I confirm in truth by oath) as in 1030, or in a range of other forms such as transaction *super iuramentum* (on oath), *per scripto et per cruce* (in writing and by the cross?), and pronounced *cum omni voce*

[275] *León* 88; *Celanova* 96; *Floriano* 25; cf. *León* 91; *Sahagún* 264; *Otero* 83; *Eslonza* 19; *Cardeña* 197; *Samos* 115, 199; *Sobrado* 1.67; *Celanova* 16; *PMH* 24; Martínez Sopena, 'Palabras', 133–54; Pérez Rodríguez, 'Descripción', 253–313.

[276] See e.g. *Coruña* 65, 107; *Celanova* 86; *Sobrado* 1.122; *Lorvão* 30; *Braga* 19.

[277] *León* 191, 810, 188; *Celanova* 83; cf. *León* 519; *Samos* 7; *Celanova* 5; Martín Viso, 'Commons', 376–9; Gómez Gómez and Martín Viso, 'Rationes', 372–8.

[278] *León* 688; *Celanova* 238; cf. 265; *Lugo* 56; Mateu y Llopis, 'Notas', 63–8; Davies, 'Sale', 165–70.

[279] *San Isidro* 10; *Oviedo* 26; cf. *León* 697; *Coruña* 95.

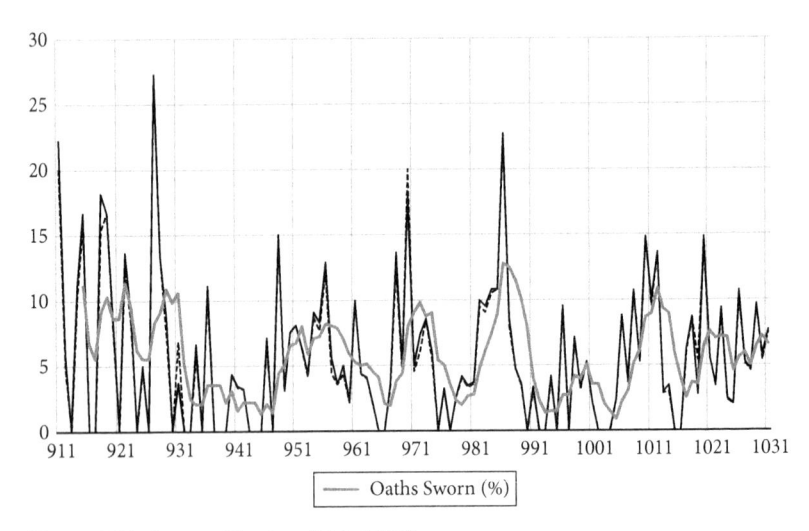

**Figure 2.21**  Sworn Charters (911–1031)

*nostra* (with our whole voice).[280] When its content is outlined, it can straightforwardly invoke God or the holy sacraments, or echo Visigothic models as an *adiuratione* ('adjuration') *per Deum et divina omnia que sunt sancta* (by God and all divine things which are holy).[281] One could take a *coniuracionem* ('oath', but with an added sense of acting in company) on *Deum celi et thronum glorie eius* (the God of heaven and the throne of His glory), or else His kingdom.[282] Or the *eiuratione* (swearing) could be based on the Trinity, called on plainly, or as the divine *nomen* or *numen* (name or essence), or associated to the *regnum Catholicorum* (kingdom of Catholics), while *Trinitatem* is on occasion by a quirk of copying or visual memory replaced with a similar word, whether *aeternitatem, maiestatem,* or *serenitatem* (eternity, majesty, or peace).[283] But there was plenty of scope too for

---

[280]  Canellas López, *Diplomática*, 270 (221); *FV* 39; *León* 47, 860; *Sahagún* 266; *Otero* 188; *Samos* 94; *cf. León* 270; *Sahagún* 56; *Otero* 26; *Astorga* 143; *San Isidro* 10; *Eslonza* 8; *Oviedo* 25; *Liébana* 5; *Valpuesta* 3; *San Millán* 531; *San Juan* 14; *Coruña* 21; *Celanova* 159; *Lorvão* 47.

[281]  *León* 756, 333; *Arlanza* 21; *Huesca* 3; *Celanova* 1; *Santiago* 54; *cf. León* 66, 147; *Sahagún* 212; *Benevívere,* 1; *Liébana* 14; *Samos* 127; *Celanova* 90.

[282]  *León* 567; *cf.* 594; *Arlanza* 11; *Valpuesta* 21; *Santiago* 32; *Samos* 119; *Coruña* 19; *Sobrado* 1.43; *Celanova* 50; *Guimarães* 62, A4.

[283]  *León* 296, *Sahagún* 145–7, *Astorga* 145, *Arouca* 51, *PMH* 146; *León* 520, *Sahagún* 284, *Samos* 93, *Celanova* 18, *Pombeiro* 2, *Lorvão* 73; *Astorga* 11, *Montes* 2, *Covarrubias* 1, *Guimarães* 68, A6; *cf. Samos* 128, 99; *Huesca* 6.

scribal ingenuity in crafting a more bespoke statement, and the oath will often have been a highlight of the theatre of the charter.[284]

Subscription was simply the final stage of the transaction which witnesses attended. When Iulianus *presbiter* made his testament to Santos Justo y Pastor in 954, he confirmed it at home *in conspectu de* (in the sight of) a series of relations and non-relations *qui veniebant me visitandum* (who were coming to visit me), while Garvissus, in the course of a dispute in 958, came to Sahagún with *frater* Vistremiro and *in presentia* (in the presence) of the abbot and *praepositus* confirmed *placita* to appear before the bishop in León.[285] Across the entire corpus of documentation the attendance and involvement of witnesses is axiomatic: a charter *tradita et roborata* (handed over and confirmed) before them in 979, those who were present *quando ipsa cartula rovoravit isti sunt* (grammatically mysterious, but something to do with confirming the charter) in 943.[286] When granters *manus proprie sygnum inpressimus* (affixed a sign by hand), typically it was *coram testes ad roborandum* (before witnesses in confirmation), as in 947, *coram multitudine* (before a crowd), as in 984, or *cunctis videntibus* (as everyone was looking on), as in 993, even though this more often than not meant watching the scribes affix signs on their behalf.[287] Perhaps for that reason the scribes of Otero favoured a formula without definite agency for the act: *qui preses fuererunt et ista karta roborare viderunt* (who were present and saw the charter confirmed).[288] In other cases the emphasis is more general, on witnessing the writing of the charter as a whole: *facta hac scriptura a nobis et roborata simul cum tistibus* (this document made by us and confirmed jointly with the witnesses) in 922, or before the prince, bishops, and orthodox men in 902, or—*ut tunc mos erat* (as was then the custom)—*coram idoneis testibus Smaelitis* (before appropriate Ishmaelite witnesses), around 1018.[289] In one unusually precise description, Ambrosio *presbitero et notarius* drafted a diploma *in casa dominica in Lionia* (in the lord's house in Lionia—from context, clearly not León) *ante nostro domno simul cum illo*

---

[284] See *e.g. Otero* 84; *Eslonza* 5; *Montes* 7; *San Pelayo* 1; *Cardeña* 87; *Valpuesta* 6; *Samos* 210; *Sobrado* 1.3; *Celanova* 85; *Coruña* 135; *Lorvão* 66.

[285] *León* 278; *Sahagún* 159; *cf. León* 293; *Sahagún* 283.          [286] *León* 470; *Sobrado* 1.10.

[287] *Cardeña* 347; *León* 498; *Santiago* 57; *cf. León* 37; *Sahagún* 4; *Otero* 1; *Eslonza* 14; *Astorga* 77; *San Isidro* 9; *Castañeda* 7; *San Vicente* 17; *San Pelayo* 1; *Santillana* 3; *Liébana* 4; *Puerto* 5; *Valladolid* 3; *Valpuesta* 9; *San Millán* 313, 697; *Covarrubias* 11; *Cardeña* 297; *Arlanza* 2; *Oña* 16; *Concejo* 1; *Aguilar* 2; *San Juan* 49; *Pamplona* 4; *Celanova* 25; *Coruña* 61; *Samos* 144; *Lorvão* 50; *Arouca* 51.

[288] *Otero* 24; *cf.* 27, 42, 48–9, 51, 53–6, 58, 66–71, 73.

[289] *Sahagún* 29; *Samos* 33; *Lorvão* 15; *cf. León* 824; *Covarrubias* 15; *San Juan* 13; *Sobrado* 1.3; *PMH* 167.

*comite* (before our lord together with the count) in 956.[290] Both the witnesses present when *isto mercato* (that business) was done in 1005 and the granter who declared *conparavi illum montem coram testibus* (I purchased that mountain before witnesses) in 971 understood that a transaction was a collective context.[291] Not every witness was present for every stage, not even the last and most important, but every stage was witnessed, and those acts of participation were embodied in the text of the charter.

## Settings

The image of that charter of 956 being witnessed in a public context of dignitaries yet written in the private context of home reminds us of the twofold setting of text: the communal situation and the physical location of writing. Where did transaction and documentation take place? The answer is surprisingly varied, and points us towards a twofold conclusion in turn, that the act of writing could be encountered anywhere, but the whereabouts of writing did not in itself matter. Since literacy has so often been linked to pressure from above, let us begin at the top.[292] During the Asturian period, it is strikingly difficult to find evidence of Oviedo, the hall of the mountain king, as a setting for the conduct of written affairs.[293] Authenticity is part of the problem, and genuine diplomas locating themselves in the royal capital are confined to the donation of Abellar to its monks by Alfonso III in 905 and a dispute between the bishops of Coimbra and Iria heard first at Oviedo, then at Santiago *ad Archis* in 906, albeit not before the king explicitly; the grant *ad populando* which Ordoño I ostensibly made there in 854 may date from the early eleventh century.[294] Indeed, there is just as much evidence for Oviedo in the Leonese period, including a dispute heard in the *aulam regiam* (royal hall) before Ramiro II in 942, and a confirmation of confiscated property to Munio Muñoz by Alfonso V in 1012, written up at the *sedis Ovetao* (see or seat of Oviedo).[295] But beyond another case held at San

---

[290]  *León* 295.

[291]  *León* 649; *Sahagún* 264; cf. *León* 513; *Sahagún* 33; *Astorga* 10; *Liébana* 45; *San Millán* 535; *Valpuesta* 28; *Cardeña* 98; *Albelda* 5; *Leire* 3; *Pamplona* 11; *Coruña* 21; *Samos* 175; *Celanova* 326.

[292]  Remolina Seivane, 'Oviedo', 229–42.

[293]  Lacarra, 'Panorama', 59–63; Sánchez-Albornoz, '"Palatium"', 5–104; Sánchez-Albornoz, 'Sede', 75–86.

[294]  *León* 18; *Coimbra* 354–6; *Otero* 1; Almeida, 'Documento', 97–107; Fernández Flórez, 'Purello', 179.

[295]  *Oviedo* 24, 41.

Vicente de Oviedo before judges of the king in 1028, there is little reason to see the former base of the kingdom as a major centre for writing or the diffusion of writing.[296]

In contrast, the new capital at León is better attested, and seems to have developed a more important role as a context for documentation over time.[297] Alfonso III himself made an exchange in 909 while *commorantes in civitate Legionensi* (staying in the city of León), even though he was still *residentes troni solium in sede Oveto* (occupying the seat of the throne in Oviedo), while the bishop of Lugo sought out Ramiro II at León in the mid-tenth century for approval to take the monastery of Carboeiro under his protection.[298] Precisely enough to help reconstruct the contemporary urban topography, Ramiro III with his aunt Elvira and mother Tarasia made a donation to Sobrado *in civitate Legionense in recluso Sancti Iohannis iuxta Portam Comitis et monasterium puellarum* (in the city of León, in the convent of San Juan, next to the Puerta del Conde and the girls' monastery) in 968.[299] But it is often by inference that we can locate the Leonese kings here, by 'the palace' standing in for 'the city', and this implicit contextualisation is another sign of its growing establishment as a setting for written transactions. With *cunctis senioribus et magnatis palacia* (all the palatine lords and grandees) in attendance, Ordoño II had confirmed the testament of Iulianus *archipresbiter* back in 912, but this applies mainly to later kings: Alfonso V granting a diploma with seven *monacorum palacii* (monks of the palace) amongst the witnesses in 1002, or Vermudo III in the company of *omnem togam palatii* (all the nobility of the palace) in 1030.[300] Of course, business purely local to the city was recorded there, like the testament of Bishop Cixila to Abellar, which he granted at León in 927; and the affairs of those based or present in León could be transacted there too, like the gift by Jimena to Sobrado in 984, written up *hec in sede Legionensi* (here in the Leonese seat).[301] But we encounter the capital far more often in royal contexts.

The most prominent of these contexts is the documentation of justice in León, at both the palace and the episcopal church. Some disputes simply state the fact of having been held in the city, *in presencia iudicum magnatorumque Legionensium* (before the judges and lords of León) as in 941, or the

[296]  *San Vicente* 29; cf. *Samos* 35; *Coruña* 113.
[297]  Represa, 'Evolución', 244–55; Estepa Díez, *Estructura*, 113–24; Carvajal Castro, 'Construcción'; see Sánchez-Albornoz, *Ciudad*; González González, *Bastiones*.
[298]  *Sahagún* 9; *Coruña* 114; cf. *San Isidro* 1; *Eslonza* 5.          [299]  *Sobrado* 1.107.
[300]  *Astorga* 10; *León* 623, 871; cf. *Samos* S2, 2, 39; *Sahagún* 328; *Otero* 30; *Astorga* 171.
[301]  *León* 75; *Sobrado* 1.64; cf. *León* 849, 895; *Sahagún* 284.

intention of being held there, when Ramiro II returned from Galicia as in 946.[302] But the royal palace emerges in the late tenth century as a venue reserved for the settlement of disputes in cases where the stakes were highest. In 998, for instance, Vermudo II made an example of Gonzalo Vermúdez, the captured rebel, before *omnes magnati adque fideles palatii nostri* (all the aristocrats and faithful of our palace), handing over his property to Sampiro, and Alfonso V confirmed his donation in the same context in 1020.[303] All kinds of appeals reached the king here, but they tended to involve important parties or have wider implications: Sahagún vindicating a *villa* from a vexatious litigant in 1013, a curious case of family property come into Jewish ownership in 1015, a homicide prosecuted by law in 1020, or back in 952 the court and the *magnatorum palatii regis* (nobles of the king's palace) evicting Osorio Gutiérrez from a monastery and transferring it to the see of Astorga.[304] The other key urban centre for documentation, the episcopal church, grew up in tandem from 915, when a dispute pitting the monastery of Valdevimbre against Monio and his brothers was arranged by *placitum* to be heard before unspecified judges in León, and settled by an oath on the altar of Santa María.[305] There was greater variety of cases here than at the palace: the wretched Iulianus *presbiter* appealed to the bishop at the cathedral portico in 954, asking him to void his testament to a nunnery which had turned out to be a brothel, while in 1021 two Leonese monasteries vied before the king for ownership of the site where one was founded, settling with the bishop at his church in 1029.[306] But it may in time have overtaken the palace as a 'textual site', for when Alfonso V promulgated the *Fuero de León* in 1017, he did so in the company of bishops, abbots, and *optimates* (best men) in the see of Santa María.[307]

Prior to this act of legislation, there is little evidence that the Christian kingdoms and counties of early medieval Iberia were or even aspired to be highly centralised polities, much less bureaucratic states, and capitals have a comparatively minor presence in the corpus. The others—Pamplona, Nájera, and Viguera in Navarra, Burgos in Castilla—are scarcely attested as

[302]  *León* 144, 192; *cf.* 187, 243; *Oviedo* 8.
[303]  *León* 581; *cf.* 741, 748; Sánchez-Albornoz, *Ciudad*, 75–112.
[304]  *Sahagún* 401; *León* 737, 772; *Astorga* 71; *cf. León* 508, 708; *Samos* 40, S9; *Celanova* 263; *Coimbra* 81.
[305]  *León* 34; Estepa Díez, *Estructura*, 199–202; Linehan, 'León', 411–33.
[306]  *León* 278, 777; *cf.* 707, 779; *Sahagún* 159; *Otero* 153.
[307]  *Oviedo* 42; *cf. Celanova* 302.

centres of documentation, discounting forged charters.[308] Yet this also reflects the itinerant nature of contemporary kingship. In 952, the parties to a court case signed a *placitum* in the presence of Ordoño III at Simancas, undertaking to appear before the king upon his return to León, or if he were running late to present themselves to the bishop instead, nicely illustrating the twin axes of the city. In the event he did prove tardy, and the disputants had to track down the bishop at San Feliz de Torío, just north of León, where he was *sedente* (visiting?) with his clergy and where he heard the case.[309] Allowing for quite a significant difference in scale and intensity, the system was not unlike it had been in the Roman Empire of old, and remained in the Carolingian Empire: rulers travelled in pursuit of government, and government travelled in pursuit of rulers, who issued diplomas in response to petitions from wherever they reached them.[310] For citizens to obtain royal justice involved a lot of hot pursuit, and the charters are just forthcoming enough about where they were written up to reconstruct a partial outline, no doubt representing only a fraction of the movements of these itinerant kings (see Figure 2.22).[311] Santiago de Compostela was clearly a key destination for kings, but other less obvious places including Zamora, Palacios de la Valduerna (where Alfonso V built a residence), and Pravia also emerge as secondary centres for issuing royal diplomas.[312] The better informed we are, however, the more obscure locations appear, and so we follow Vermudo II and Alfonso V presiding over judicial assemblies at a series of remote or unknown villages and hamlets in Galicia especially, such as Larín and the 'spa towns' of Laias and Molgas (see Figure 2.23).[313] The movements of the kings of Navarra and the counts of Castilla are more rarely recorded, at least in genuine texts: the closest we come is a famed charter by which the monks of Monte Laturce entered the monastery of Albelda in 950, confirmed during a commemorative ceremony for Sancho Garcés I at Resa on the Ebro River, site of a fortified tower and where he

---

[308] *San Millán* 50, 96, 556; *Albelda* 29; *Cardeña* 98; *San Juan* 49; Gambra Gutiérrez, '"Palatium"', 1, 11–64.

[309] *León* 256.   [310] Millar, *Emperor*, esp. 15–57, 203–72; McKitterick, 'King', 145–69.

[311] Cabezas Fontanilla and Ávila Seoane, 'Oficina', 78–83.

[312] González y Fernández Valles, 'Pravia', 87–104; Rubio Pérez, 'Valduerna', 18–20; Fernández Conde and Santos del Valle, 'Corte', 866–81; Martín Viso, *Fragmentos*; Carvajal Castro, *Máscara*, 262–8, 291–2.

[313] Andrade Cernadas, 'Villas', 18–35; Andrade Cernadas, 'Baños', 13–30.

| Alfonso III (866–910) | | |
|---|---|---|
| Santiago de Compostela | 862 | *Santiago* 3 |
| Castillo de Tudela | 895 | *Astorga* 8 |
| Santiago de Compostela | 899/900 | *Santiago* 18 |
| Zamora | 907 | *Celanova* 9 |
| **García I (910–14)** | | |
| San Pedro de Eslonza | 912 | *Eslonza* 1–2 |
| **Ordoño II (910/14–24)** | | |
| Lugo | 910 | *Tumbo Viejo* 80 |
| *Aliobrio* (Lobrigos?) | 911 | *Braga* 19 |
| Zamora | 915 | *Santiago* 26 |
| *Baronceli* (Verín) | 921 | *San Esteban* 1 |
| Lózara (Samos) | 922 | *Samos* 35 |
| Crestuma | 922 | *Coimbra* 81 |
| **Fruela II (910/24–5)** | | |
| Santiago de Compostela | 924 | *Santiago* 38 |
| **Sancho Ordóñez (925/26–9)** | | |
| Santiago de Compostela | 927 | *Santiago* 51 |
| **Alfonso IV (925/26–31)** | | |
| San Adrián de Boñar | 929 | *Eslonza* 9 |
| Villafría | 931 | *Cardeña* 197 |
| **Ramiro II (931–51)** | | |
| Viseu | 926 | *Guimarães* 9 |
| San Isidro de Dueñas | 935 | *San Isidro* 7 |
| Astorga | 937 | *Astorga* 48 |
| Zamora | 940 | *Castañeda* 2 |
| **Ordoño III (951–6)** | | |
| Santiago de Compostela? | 951 | *Sahagún* 132 |
| Simancas | 952 | *León* 256 |
| *Lionia* | 956 | *León* 295 |
| **Sancho I (956–8, 959–66)** | | |
| Larín | 960 | *Samos* 126 |
| **Ramiro III (966–84)** | | |
| Numantia (Zamora) | 976 | *Sahagún* 284 |
| **Vermudo II (984–99)** | | |
| Larín | 985 | *Coruña* 95 |
| Santiago de Compostela | 985 | *Celanova* 195 |
| *Luna* | 993 | *Celanova* 218 |
| Laias | 995 | *Celanova* 223 |
| Astorga | 995 | *Tumbo Viejo* 141 |
| Pravia | 996 | *San Pelayo* 1 |
| Rábade | 997 | *Tumbo Viejo* 135 |
| Santiago de Compostela | 999 | *Santiago* 58 |

| Alfonso V (999–1028) | | |
|---|---|---|
| Laias | 1002 | *Celanova* 263 |
| *Villa Plana* | 1005 | *Celanova* 292 |
| Gomariz | 1007 | *Celanova* 302 |
| Palacios de la Valduerna | 1008 | *León* 669 |
| Pravia | 1010 | *Alfonso V* 8 |
| Baños de Molgas | 1012 | *Celanova* 331 |
| Sahagún | 1012 | *León* 707 |
| Palacios de la Valduerna | 1014 | *Astorga* 212 |
| São Miguel das Caldas de Vizela | 1014 | *Guimarães* 46 |
| Congosto | 1017 | *Alfonso V* vii |
| Sobrado dos Monxes | 1017 | *Sobrado* 1.6 |
| Sobrado dos Monxes | 1017 | *Sobrado* 1.107 |
| *Rapati* | 1017 | *Tumbo Viejo* 136 |
| Lugo | 1017 | *Tumbo Viejo* 136 |
| Sahagún | 1018 | *Sahagún* 404 |
| *Veiga* | 1019 | *Sahagún* 406 |
| São Miguel das Caldas de Vizela | 1025 | *Alfonso V* x |
| *Faukis* (Tougues?) | 1025 | *Alfonso V* x |
| Braga | 1025 | *Alfonso V* x |
| Cea | 1026 | *León* 829 |

**Figure 2.22** Royal Movements

seems to have been buried on his death in 925.[314] They will have been itinerant too; decentralisation of writing was the norm, and a 'capital' was only one source amongst many for diplomas.

When we turn to private charters, the picture is even more disparate. Bald indicators of location have a random character: a lay sale of an unidentified Leonese field in 967 was recorded *in illa scola* (at a school, apparently in Oviedo) by Migahel *presbiter*, perhaps an urban priest, while two tenth-century donations to Sahagún were written up at Santiago and Castro de Nuño, places with no stated relation to the properties involved.[315] In Portugal, one sale from 994 was set down, charmingly, *in mazinata sub illa nocaria* (in the orchard under the walnut tree), others *in villa Abozamates* or *in villa Ferrarios*, both very local contexts.[316] Disputes were held at similarly diverse sites: Count García Gómez and one Zahbascorta ven Abolhauz sat in judgement at Villalpando in 998 to hear a case involving Sahagún, some 70 kilometres away, while a *placitum* of 1014 promised payment to

[314] *Albelda* 19; García Turza, *Prudencio* 1; cf. *Albelda* 15–16, 20, 28; *San Millán* 221, 181; *San Juan* 14, 56; Ubieto Arteta, 'Panteón', 267–78.
[315] *León* 404; *Sahagún* 132, 279; cf. *Benevívere* 1; González González, 'Cultura', 221.
[316] *PMH* 172; *Lorvão* 33; *PMH* 175.

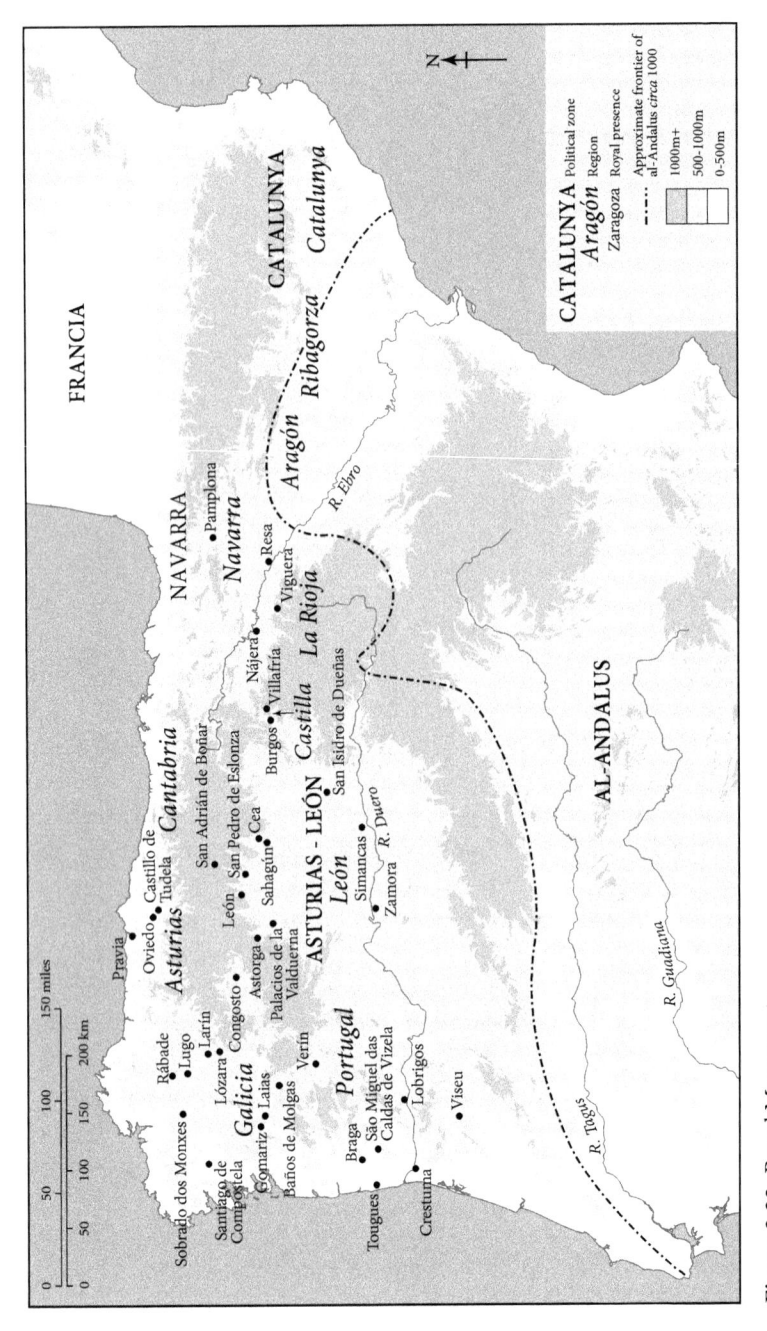

**Figure 2.23** Royal Movements

Count Pedro Flaínez in his *mandacione* (jurisdiction), and parties out west appeared before lay and ecclesiastical judges at Pezobre and Gondomar, both barely villages.[317] But most locations for written transaction fall into one of four categories: at a church, at the property involved, or with either granter or recipient. In 930, for example, the witnesses of a sale to Felis *presbiter* and his family came together to delimit the property *ante* (in front of) the church of San Lorenzo.[318] Sales in 940 to Mavia Indura *presbiter* and in 943 to Flazino and his wife Eogenia, meanwhile, happened before witnesses *in conventum eclesie* (in the church) of Santa Cecilia and in the *eglessie* of San Martín, just as Alfonso V presided over the restoration of San Esteban de Ribas de Sil at the monastery of Celanova in 1007.[319] Doubtless linked to the ecclesiastical status of many if not most scribes, the church was a major gathering place for the writing of charters; these are only three of many instances, especially prevalent around León.[320] At times we can even see that it was the local church specifically, as when Leocadia gave land in Marialba to Abellar in 951, our village scribe Stephanus *presbiter* wrote it up *in conventu* of Santa María.[321]

Churches recur as venues for disputes, and with their connection to divine power they lent an element of the supernatural (or theatrical) to the settlements. Many stops on the royal itinerary were churches: after Vermudo II returned to León from Galicia, where he had taken refuge during noble revolt, he heard a case *in covento eglesie* (in the church) of San Salvador in 993.[322] There were hearings *in aula* (the basilica?) of San Martín at Villazahid (Villacid) in 1013, and at San Martín de Turieno in 962, while in the west parties met with judges at San Cristóbal *ad Malage* in 987, and in another case first at Guilhabreu, the property at issue, then at Santa María *de Villa Mediana* in 1011.[323] In these obscure churches we must be glimpsing something of the sites of local authority, but the choice was also functional: not only was the scribe typically a cleric, but the *condiciones sacramentorum*, the terms of the oath, was also held and sworn over the text of the Gospels and relics of the saints at the altar.[324] At Burgos in 972, before Count García

---

[317] *Sahagún* 356; *Otero* 99; *Sobrado* 1.132; *Coimbra* 203; *cf. León* 452; *Sahagún* 417; *Coimbra* 193; Estepa Díez, 'Poder', 285–328.

[318] *León* 88.        [319] *León* 137, 162; *Rocas* 1.

[320] See *e.g. León* 253, 262, 342, 398, 460, 536; *Sahagún* 174, 275, 334, 341, 353, 407; *Astorga* 61; *Castañeda* 9; *San Vicente* 11; *San Juan* 34, 48; *Coruña* 94; *Samos* 102; *Coimbra* 139.

[321] *León* 236; *cf.* 513, 593, 686; *Sahagún* 428; *Otero* 88–9.        [322] *León* 559.

[323] *Sahagún* 400; *Liébana* 66; *Celanova* 200; *PMH* 216; *cf. Sahagún* 424; *Otero* 4; *Sobrado* 1.134; *Coimbra* 212.

[324] See *e.g. León* 34, 192; *Castañeda* 1; *Oviedo* 26; *Puerto* 2; *Valpuesta* 10–11.

Fernández, two parties took an oath in a church of Santa Lucía *in vanitate* (failing the test), while two disputes from San Millán were settled by oaths in Santa María de Siete Finiestras in 936 and 940, and a case involving the bishoprics of Lugo and Iria in the late tenth century by the *conditiones* sworn on the *sacrosanto altario* (most holy altar) of San Julián.[325] The intimidation factor should not be underestimated. In the face-off between San Rosendo and Bishop Sisnando in 961, the disputants agreed to take *sacramentum* (oath) at the tomb of Santiago himself in Compostela, but there the partisans of Rosendo withdrew, refusing to swear lest they lie, and left those of Sisnando to do so instead.[326] Many a dispute ends at just this stage, a sure sign of the workings of God's authority in His churches.

The other venues for written transaction are altogether more pragmatic, and witness how intimately writing was embedded in the community of its users. We have already seen a scribe recording a donation on site at the property concerned when Ordoño III made a gift of the *villa* of Lionia to San Martín de Fonte de Febro in 956, just as Alfonso IV was at Villafría in person when he confirmed it to Cardeña in 931.[327] But the same happens in private charters too: Iuliano and Ilduara bequeathed land in Melgar to Sahagún in 978, and the testament was drafted *hic in Melgare* (here in Melgar), just south of the monastery.[328] Similarly, the pact made by the sisters of Villagonzalo Pedernales was drawn up at the eponymous *villa vocitata de Gundissalbo Telliz* (villa named after Gonzalo Téllez) in 947, and Blasco Garciez sold a house in Salinas to Albelda with *tota villa testificante* (the whole town witnessing) in 947.[329] Some disputes were also settled on site, such as between Munio Gutiérrez and Christoforus *presbiter* in 992, where the parties and judges *coniuncti sunt in ipsa casa* (assembled in that house), a contested church of Santa María in the territory of Présaras.[330] But it was boundary disputes where the records were most often made on site. The *previsores* (inspectors) set out, like the *homines bonos qui solent antiquitum conprovare* (good men who are accustomed to verify age-old arrangements) at Dume in 911, travelled *ad locum* (to the place), met up at the *arcas* (stones) marking the limits, like at Alcainça and Vila Cova in 936, and

---

[325] *Cardeña* 98; *San Millán* 390–1; *Sobrado* 1.109; *cf. San Millán* 221, 181; *Coruña* 95; *Celanova* 362.

[326] *Santiago* 42; *cf. Celanova* 260, 292; *Guimarães* 24, 51.

[327] *León* 295; *Cardeña* 197.        [328] *Sahagún* 294; *cf.* Carvajal Castro, 'Castros', 11–29.

[329] *Cardeña* 115; *Albelda* 14; *cf. Pamplona* 2; *Celanova* 12; *Guimarães* 67; *Coimbra* 135.

[330] *Sobrado* 1.130; *cf. Otero* 31, 43; *Pamplona* 10; *Coruña* 59; *Coimbra* 202; *PMH* 268; Bermúdez Beloso, 'Presares', 98, 103.

followed their course on horse or on foot.[331] Just as we see elsewhere in early medieval Europe, the text of perambulations typically features an intrusive shift from third- to first-person narration, for as one scribe claimed in 950, *scribere studuimus* (we endeavoured to write up) the boundaries *in ipso loco* (on the very spot), an instant passage from memory to written record.[332] Boundaries should furthermore be understood to encompass any kind of delimitation, be it to draw a line between the inhabitants of Abeancos and Cornado, as in 1007, or to allocate family property, as when Mumadona and her children made a *culmellus divisionis* ('column of division', also used of perambulations) in Guimarães, site of her future monastic foundation, in 950.[333] Just as boundary clauses tediously enumerated as well as delimited the appurtenances of each plot of land to hammer home the rights which were being transferred, by bringing the text to the land and perambulating it parties made certain where ownership began and ended.[334]

The writing process seldom took place at the location of the granter, and only in the case of the clergy. In 1006, for instance, Totadomna and Auria of San Miguel Arcángel de León made *apices testamenti* (the letters of a testament) to Abellar, which Gómez *presbiter* wrote *subtus* (under, around, within) their church, while three religious of a monastery of San Vicente in Besoxo, the congregation confirming, exchanged land with Sobrado in 964.[335] The charter was far more commonly written at the site of its recipient: although it was in his own house that Iulianus *presbiter* sent for the witnesses of his last wishes in 954, he had first been to two monasteries in his ill-starred quest to make a testament.[336] Intriguingly, when Severus and his wife Recesinda granted a *scriptura profiliationis ac donationis* (document of formal adoption and donation) to Gundefredo in 905, one witness signed *dum essere pausati in domo istius Gundefredi* (having stopped at the home of that same Gundefredo), seemingly a visitor drafted into service, while Sampiro records in 1018 putting his donation to Santiago de León onto its *sancrosancto altario* after confirmation *coram multitudine fideli ecclesiae* (before the faithful multitude of the church).[337] Since the charter typically

[331] *Braga* 19; *Lorvão* 36; *cf. San Juan* 7, 12, 14, 18; *Samos* 46; *Celanova* 62, 94; *Coimbra* 118; *Arouca* 84.
[332] *Celanova* 86; Collins, 'Visigothic Law', 101–3; Pastor, *Resistencias*, 78–80; Davies, *Acts*, 200–1; Morala Rodríguez, 'Léxico', 1, 412–17; *cf.* Keynes, 'Councils', 66–7.
[333] *Santiago* 59; *Guimarães* A1; *cf. Santiago* 23.
[334] Miceli, 'Formulismo', 39–42; *cf.* Zimmermann, *Écrire*, 1, 208–17.
[335] *León* 660; *Sobrado* 1.121; *cf. Sahagún* 78; *Astorga* 48; *Santillana* 41; *Celanova* 44; *PMH* 157.
[336] *León* 278.
[337] *San Vicente* 3; *León* 756; *cf.* 803.

stayed together with the land, changing hands from old recipient to new, conducting transaction at the destination of both text and property was only logical, and we can identify documents destined for all the great Leonese monasteries being drawn up there: before San Salvador at Matallana, or inside the *collegium* of San Cipriano at Valdesaz, or Alfonso V, during a dispute in 1025, commanding that a testament for San Vicente de León be prepared in the monastery itself.[338]

Where we know the location of a transaction, the site of the beneficiary is in fact the most common by far, and this applies across the corpus. It can be expressed with the words *in loco sacrosancto altario vestro* or *ad locum vestrum* (on your most holy altar, at your place), in documents drawn up to found, consecrate, endow, or confirm a religious institution, when signing a monastic pact or entering a monastery, making or affirming a donation or testament, even in a sale by Argerigo and Adosinda to Evenando *presbiter* written with *nos totos tres in tua casa* (all three of us at your house).[339] There are numerous charters addressed to Sahagún and composed there in the *aula* of Santos Facundo y Primitivo, featuring the visit by Alfonso V with Sampiro in tow in 1018, as well as to subsidiary houses such as San Andrés in a Villa Motarrafi, where a sale was recorded in 979.[340] An exception to the singular direction of travel being to the Church is the visit paid by the brothers of Eslonza to Oveccus ibem Telliz in 988, seeking funds for reconstruction after 'Saracens' had razed it, but extraordinary times called for extraordinary measures.[341] Writing before the recipient was particularly common in Galicia: of course, Santiago was a frequent stop for kings and their agents, and hosted both a council presided over by the future Alfonso III in 862 and the great *exquisitio* (inquest) held before Alfonso V in 1019, though there is some question as to its authenticity.[342] Charters to Samos were often made in its *congregatio*, and Sobrado welcomed Alfonso V on 18 April 1017 to confirm two of its charters in the *cimiterio* (the cemetery? or simply the monastery?), just as its patrons Hermegildo and Paterna triumphed in court cases heard there in 951 and 952, rather rigging the game by

[338] *León* 529, 761, 822; *cf.* 490, 509, 547, 566, 590, 648.
[339] *Eslonza* 1–2, 9; *Coimbra* 155; *cf. San Isidro* 7; *San Vicente* 18; *Liébana* 24; *Santillana* 9–10; Martínez Díez, *Colección* 14, *Albelda* 15–6; *Arlanza* 9; *Valpuesta* 35; *San Juan* 14; *Coruña* 63; *Mondoñedo* 6; *Lorvão* 41.
[340] *Sahagún* 164, 404, 301; *cf.* 175–6, 190, 258, 285, 289, 303, 317, 429.
[341] *Sahagún* 340; *cf.* 314; Isla, 'Warfare', 241.
[342] *Santiago* 3, 61; *cf.* 1–2, 18, 38, 51, 40; Díaz Salvado, *Falsos*, 67–8, 210–11, 646, 717–18.

playing before a friendly crowd.[343] Many a text was likewise written up on the very *pallam altaris* (altarcloth) of Celanova, notably the testament of San Rosendo in 977, while the monastery hosted the congregations of two other houses for a charter signing in 993.[344] And similarly to Sobrado, a series of judicial proceedings turning out in its favour were conducted at Celanova between 1007 and 1012; churches not only acted as centres for writing, but also capitalised on this role to defend and advance their own interests.[345]

## Communities

When the varied locations for transaction and documentation are taken together, they form a picture of parties, participants, witnesses, and scribes constantly on the move, on their way from church to church and site to site, heading to and fro doing business and recording it in writing, everywhere and anywhere. Yet this variety suggests that location as such was not the primary consideration, and indeed the charter is more insistent on the fact of a collective context, wherever it may have been, for the transaction being documented.[346] Witnessing, of course, was the most basic manifestation of this, but there was also a specialised terminology of 'councils' and 'gatherings' for the collectivities from which charters emerged with the key endorsement of select members of society. Traditionally, in legal-institutional historiography, the *concilium* has been traced back to the Visigothic *conventus publicus vicinorum* (literally, 'public assembly of neighbours'), though it actually appears only once in a law on reporting stray animals, and tracked forward to the *concejo* of medieval Iberia.[347] More recently it has become the focus of a debate over the consolidation and development of village communities in the tenth century especially, and the stratification or feudalisation of power.[348] Terms and practices varied, however, and there

---

[343] *Samos* 175, 44, 239, 178, 151, 157, 64, 82, 76, 19, 69; *Sobrado* 1.6, 1.107, 1.31, 1.103; *cf.* 1.2, 1.7, 1.36, 1.8, 1.38, 1.126.

[344] *Celanova* 242, 185, 219; *cf.* 9, 95, 192, 215, 231, 261, 265, 298, 319, 322, 332, 371.

[345] *Celanova* 308, 312, 315, 331.

[346] Zeller, 'Charters', 27–37; Davies, *Windows*, 204–31.

[347] *LV* 8.5.6; Hinojosa, 'Origen', 5–70; Carlé, *Concejo*, 9–42; Sánchez-Albornoz, *Regimen*, 161–97; García de Valdeavellano, *Curso*, 533–54; Sánchez-Arcilla Bernal, 'Derecho', 295–306.

[348] Barbero and Vigil, *Formación*, 354–80; Martínez Sopena, *Tierra*, 505–8; Estepa Díez, 'Formación', 191–5; García de Cortázar, 'Formas', 11–44; *cf.* Peña Pérez, 'Comunidades', 331–58; Davies, 'Lordship', 31–2.

remains much work to be done on who was involved in such meetings, where they met, how often, and for what purposes, and how they enabled and channelled other local and supra-local social and political structures and arrangements.[349]

The tenth century is the formative period for the *concilium*. One of the first mentions of its existence comes in a grant of water for irrigation by Bishop Cixila on behalf of Abellar in 925, enacted *coram concilio et plures testibus*, and when he made further arrangements for water usage in 932, the charter was again drawn up before the council and many witnesses.[350] But what was it?[351] At least we can say from this context that it was some kind of witnessing body, in essence a group of people, and it appears without qualification or localisation—such as *ceteri concilius* (the rest of the council) and similar formulations—in subscriptions across the corpus of documentation, most of all from León.[352] It could be anchored in place, with a physical location or 'territoriality' proximate to the property in transaction: when Domnatia sold part of her vineyard in Valdesogo to her son Halile *presbiter* in 966, the eight witnesses were joined by *alios pluris concilio* (many others from the council) of Santa Eufemia, while another sale of property on the Cea River was set down in both the council of Palazuelo and the council of Cea in 1003, possibly overlapping spheres of interest.[353] When Riquilu handed houses in the marketplace of León to his benefactor Havive Alvinizi in 1029, the transaction appears to have been carried out *in coro concilio* (before the council) of the entire city rather than one of its neighbourhoods.[354] At other times it was simply the local church providing a focal point for assembly, like the *omne concilium cenobitarum fratrum Albaildensium* (whole council of Albeldan brother monks) who turned out to witness a monastic pact in 983.[355] But it could also have a legal identity, owning property in the locality: the testament drawn up by Riquilo for Abellar in 955 includes a *regum qui discurrit ad ortos et linares de Sancta Maria Alba concilio* (watercourse flowing to the gardens and fields of flax of

---

[349] Davies, *Acts*, 201–7; Davies, *Windows*, 213–17; Carvajal Castro, 'Meetings', 186–207; Escalona, 'Meetings', 216–37; Carvajal Castro, 'Action', 281–99.

[350] *León* 67, 94; *cf.* 66.      [351] *Léxico*, *s.v.* 'concego'.

[352] *León* 145; *cf.* 416; *Sahagún* 40; *Otero* 1; *Astorga* 254; *Liébana* 71; *Albelda* 16; *Samos* S2; *Celanova* 242; *Santiago* 21; *Coruña* 96; *Coimbra* 144.

[353] *León* 396; *Sahagún* 382; *cf. León* 515, 586, 607, 807; *Sahagún* 268, 399–400; *Astorga* 103; *Albelda* 8; *San Juan* 49; *Sobrado* 1.64; *Celanova* 188; Larrea, 'Invisibilidad', 169–207; Escalona, 'Aproximación', 273–93; Escalona, 'Territorialidad', 55–82.

[354] *León* 849 *cf.* 643; Estepa Díez, *Estructura*, 197–9, 455–9.

[355] *Albelda* 28; *cf. León* 482; *Sahagún* 428; *Sobrado* 1.4; *Samos* 178; *Celanova* 371; Martínez Sopena, 'Reforma', 347–61.

the council of [Santa] Marialba).[356] It even acted as a party in a grant of water usage to the council of Villabáscones in 956, and in a *fuero* confirmed by Fernán González to the council of Barrio in 955.[357]

In terms of who attended the council and what they did, the latter is easier to be sure of than the former. Certainly there is some mileage in thinking of its membership as the local élite: the council of Santa Eulalia consisted of *multorum bonorum hominum* (more than a few good men) in 983, and the council of San Salvador of *filios bonorum* (the well born) in 1024, in both cases the *boni homines* or key community players familiar from charters across early medieval Iberia and beyond, many of whom turn out to be members of the clergy.[358] But the development of councils across the tenth century is also an aspect of the 'growth' of literacy in wider society. Take the *alii multorum filii benenatorum qui erant in concilio de Vimaranes* (many other sons of the well born in the council of Guimarães), who may first appear in 986 (or 1036).[359] Though this body appears three decades after the founding of the monastery, the circumstances in which it emerged are obscure; since it then takes part in both monastic and non-monastic affairs, its creation should not automatically be tied to the Church.[360] Councils proliferate as communal contexts for the writing process, and in parallel to three other trends which we have so far observed: the increase of documentation, greater lay participation in it, and the consolidation of the scribal profession. When Vita Riquilo was lying on her deathbed in 1030, she summoned abbot, clergy, and family, and ordered *in concilio* that a document of her possessions should be written, just as Gisvado and his wife Leoviva founded San Adrián de Boñar in 929 by the sanction of the assembled *sanctissimum* (most holy) council, drawing its first abbot from that company.[361] The point is that it contributed to the decisions which lie behind the documentation: Jimeno and Adosinda outlined to Ordoño III *et omni concilio* (and the whole council) the conditions of a donation to San Rosendo and Celanova in 951, asking for oversight.[362] The payment in 1016 of a sale price *que nobis et vobis et omni concilio bene complacuit* (which well pleased us and you and the whole council) is a phrase much favoured at Celanova,

---

[356] *León* 293.  [357] *Cardeña* 54; *San Millán* 535; *cf. Nájera* 4.

[358] *León* 492, 812; *cf.* 634, 654, 691, 769, 771, 832–3, 836–7; Corral, 'Lugares'.

[359] *PMH* 152; *cf. Guimarães* 27.

[360] See *e.g. Guimarães* 58, 39, 61; Merêa, 'Concelho', 49–69; Sousa Soares, 'Notas', 71–92.

[361] *León* 873; *Eslonza* 9.

[362] *Celanova* 91; *cf. Astorga* 65; *Eslonza* 24; *Castañeda* 2; *Benevívere* 1; *Cardeña* 353; *Santiago* 3–4; *Samos* 58; *Coruña* 132; *Celanova* 174.

underlining its approbatory role as the communal context of transaction, the site of the decisions which *facimus cum omni concilio* (we make with the whole council).[363]

The greatest imperative for approbation arose in the settlement of disputes, and this is where we see councils playing a prominent role in fashioning consensus. Nemorellus *presbiter* and Valdevimbre, for example, argued their respective rights to some mills before magnates of León in 941: *omni concilio iudicum discernentes iusticia* (with the whole council of judges distinguishing a just resolution), the priest prevailed and a prior settlement made *in conspectu concilii* (in the sight of the council) of Ordoño II and his bishops and judges was confirmed, resulting in Valdevimbre abandoning its claim in writing.[364] Mention of a council is often a sign of the implementation of royal justice, whether the palace nobility of the *fideli concilio regni nostri* (loyal council of our kingdom) assisting Vermudo II in chastening one rebel in 998, or the dispute between Rodrigo Románez and Jimena Jiménez settled in council before Queen Elvira and her judges in 1001; indeed, it was a *collecto concilio* (assembled council) which elevated Alfonso V to the throne in 999.[365] Councils were party and witness to every aspect of judgement: authorising the seizure of property, appointing judges, hearing claims, considering evidence and law, receiving oaths, making or confirming decisions, negotiating settlements, and overseeing implementation.[366] But the same functions were also performed by non-royal councils with local memberships of bishops, abbots, monks, priests, deacons, counts, *iudices, boni homines* (judges, good men) performing the same functions. At Otero especially, they arranged the move from formal judgement *ad atiba* (to negotiation), to reach a compromise, and at various times they scheduled court dates, imprisoned offenders, valued damages, selected witnesses, mandated oaths, oversaw ordeals, or heard confessions.[367] All in some sense were members of the élite, though in what sense can be difficult to specify; even the seemingly ecumenical *omni concilio de Vurgientium civitate* (whole council of the city of Burgos), staffed by *multorum bonorum*

---

[363] *Celanova* 342, 353; cf. 338–9, 341.     [364] *León* 144; cf. 34.
[365] *León* 581; *Samos* S10; *Lugo*, 2, 591–4; *Celanova* 302.
[366] See *e.g. León* 508; *Sahagún* 284; *Otero* 90; *Astorga* 5; *Oviedo* 8; *San Millán* 221; *Pamplona* 10; *Santiago* 46; *Samos* 126; *Sobrado* 1.131; *Coruña* 59; *Celanova* 223; *Rocas* 1; *Coimbra* 81.
[367] *Otero* 4, 43, 149; cf. *León* 184; *Sahagún* 101; *Otero* 38; *Oviedo* 26; *Santillana* 31; *Arlanza* 18; *Albelda* 27; *Coruña* 50; *Samos* 112; *Sobrado* 1.109; *Celanova* 52; *Guimarães* 66; cf. Sánchez Badiola, *Territorio*, 1, 459.

*ominum a minimo usque ad maximo* (many good men from least to greatest), probably on reflection means from youngest to eldest.[368]

And yet, these recurrent references to judicial councils seldom specify a location. The point was evidently less to situate the settlement spatially than contextually: the equivalent of saying 'in court', flagging the presence of authority, collectivity, proper procedure. Charters emerged from councils, and looked to a future in councils: a standard feature of the sanction clause is an undertaking by the granter to *vindicare, auctorigare, sanare,* or *firmare* (reclaim, vouchsafe, restore, or confirm) the property—or the charter of the property—*in concilio,* for the recipient, *prout decet* (as is right), threatening 'see you in court' to potential violators.[369] The document was to retain force *in omni concilio* (in every council), or the penalty had to be paid *in quaqumque iuditio et fideli concilio* (in any judicial action and faithful council).[370] In the terms of the *Fuero de León* in 1017, if anyone should infringe what had been granted to the Church by testament, that testament should be brought to the council for investigation.[371] The communal focus is both omnipresent and underdetermined, even more so in the principal synonym for council, *collatio* ('gathering'). The term has a Visigothic and Roman prehistory encompassing all forms of comparison and combination, including the bringing together of property for redistribution, but the *kartula perfiliationis* (charter of formal adoption) made by Aveiza and his wife Egelo to Nuño Sarracinez and his wife Gudigeva in 960 is emblematic: the witness list ends *et aliorum de collacione* (and others of the 'collation').[372] Again it could have territoriality, to judge by a sale in 965 of land *in conlationis villa* (in the *villa* of the gathering) of Villacalbiel, and it overlapped with *concilio,* since the transaction was written up in the council of San Esteban; another sale took place at the *collatione* of San Juan in 972.[373] It could also denote a church, as a donation to Valdevimbre in 1022 was recorded *in collatione* (in the assembly) of Santa María itself, or a congregation, as the *collacionem de sancto*

[368] *Cardeña* 98; Oliva, 'Roma', 32–8.

[369] *León* 29, 499, 613; *Celanova* 371; *León* 647; García de Valdeavellano, 'Escodriñamiento', 2, 236–324; Davies, *Windows,* 107–8.

[370] *Celanova* 224; *León* 581; *cf.* 52; *Sahagún* 120; *Otero* 37; *Oviedo* 32; *San Vicente* 30; *Santillana* 25; *Oña* 4; *Santiago* 4; *Samos* S10; *Celanova* 109; *Arouca* 1.

[371] *Oviedo* 42.

[372] *León* 331; *cf.* 420, 742, 791; Martínez Díez, *Colección* 37; *Du Cange,* 'collatio'; *Blaise, s.v.* 'collatio'; *Niermeyer, s.v.* 'collatio'; *Léxico, s.v.* 'collacione'.

[373] *León* 391, 418; *cf.* 485; *Astorga* 121; *Otero* 106–7; *Cardeña* 56; Gutiérrez González, 'Páramo', 85–8.

*Iusto qui presentes fuerunt* (those who were present at the gathering) of San Justo in 981.[374]

There is a third term, *conventus*, which can occasionally stand for an assembly, as in a donation to Sahagún confirmed at that of Cisneros in 986, but normally it is employed together with *ecclesia* to denote, like *collegium*, the corporate entity or community of a given church or monastery.[375] If there is a distinction to be drawn between the words *concilium* and *collatio*, council is predominantly the usage in the west and centre, 'collation' in the centre and east. Both express collectivity, and collective action. Consider a sale made of a vineyard *in collationem* (in the gathering) of San Juan Apóstol y Evangelista in 979: its boundaries were delimited *in facie de omnis de collatione* (in the presence of all, or the men, of the assembly) of San Juan and of San Pelayo de Capezutos.[376] When the gathering acts as a party its double signification with place is as a coming together there, like the *omni collacio* of Melgar which took part in a donation of 932, or the gift made by Tellu *presbiter* in 951 to Valpuesta *et tota collatione qui ibi sunt in ipsa regula* (and the whole congregation who were there in that rule or monastery).[377] But the term could also take in that sense of a collective decision on which charters are predicated: when Alfonso III issued a precept to Bishop Sisnando of Iria in 880, it was according to what had been determined *in concilio per collationem* (in council by the gathering), just as the abbesses Aeylo and Goysenda made their testament in 993 *deliberata collatione et prefinito consilio* (once the gathering was resolved and the course of action had been defined).[378] From here it is a small step to go seek settlement of a dispute with the words *pervenimus inde ad collationem* (we come to assembly for it) before *omni concilio* as in 959, *in colacione iudicum* (at a meeting of judges) as in 946, or to be negotiated *per colacione de omines bonos ad atiba* (by the gathering of good men for compromise) as in 1019.[379]

Parties, witnesses, and scribes assembled for written transaction sufficiently often that it was not always registered explicitly, and a singular focus on terminology can distract from this fact. Some parchments are records of 'business fairs' more than discrete transactions, like the original from 1005 which contains three sales by four couples to Maurele Velázquez and his

[374]  *León* 796, 484; *cf.* 253, 491, 493; *Coruña* 10; *Valpuesta* 45.
[375]  *Sahagún* 334; Pick, 'Nephews', 60–61; Carvajal Castro, 'Meetings', 191.
[376]  *León* 468; *cf.* 402; *Sahagún* 335; *Astorga* 35; *Otero* 83.
[377]  *Sahagún* 44; *Valpuesta* 32; *cf. León* 128; *Valpuesta* 46; *Santillana* 1, 10; *Guimarães* 68, A6.
[378]  *Santiago* 8; *Celanova* 219.
[379]  *León* 312; *Otero* 4, 116; *cf. León* 577, 597; *Cardeña* 69.

wife Gudina, or the ten self-donations to Piasca made on one day in 957; some inventories from Celanova and San Millán could stem from such occasions.[380] Parchments with multiple transactions sharing the same recipients are instant archives, as witnessed by one with a joint dorsal note summarising both, and indeed some involving adjacent properties even reflect an archival mindset of geographical organisation, such as when Baldemiru and Placidia, selling to Valdevimbre on 29 February 952, cross-referenced their land as neighbouring that bought by the monastery from each other.[381] We also catch sight of assembly when we have multiple parchments recording charters of the same date. On 20 February 950, a husband and wife and another woman with five children made sales to Iulianus *presbiter*, witnessed by two distinct groups of people, whereas on 26 February 1026, two scribes, Ermegildo and Iohannes, wrote up donations to Santillana del Mar first by Citi Petriz, then by three daughters of Romano and Argylo.[382] Sharing witnesses was more common, however, and the scribe Ranulfus *presbiter* stuck around on 1 July 930 for the second transaction documented by Etylmirus *presbiter* for San Pedro de Montes.[383] The scribe could be 'hired for the day': Iulianus *confessor* recorded two gifts made by Ramiro III to Sahagún on 11 May 971, while Florentius *scriba* illuminated both the restoration of San Andrés de Boada and the confirmation of Santa María de Cárdaba to Arlanza for Fernán González on 1 March 937.[384] And there are numerous cases of 'charter days', like market days, when three, four, or even more transactions were recorded, all to the same recipients, but only some with the same witnesses or written by one scribe.[385]

Clearly the writing process involved planning ahead, picking days to gather together parties, witnesses, and scribes, but we have to imagine a surplus for each text, a larger of pool of those milling about, waiting their turn. From what little we know about when exactly the act took place, it could be on any day and at any time: one sale to Agube and his wife Auria

---

[380] *León* 652, 657; *Sahagún* 153; *Celanova* 338; *San Millán* 421; cf. *León* 689; *Sahagún* 299; *Astorga* 260; *Santillana* 3; *Valpuesta* 49; *San Millán* 382; *Cardeña* 363; *Coruña* 93; *Celanova* 310.
[381] *León* 563–4; cf. *Sahagún* 226–7; *León* 246–7; cf. *Sahagún* 272–3; *Celanova* 148–9, 205–6.
[382] *León* 211–12; *Santillana* 37–8.
[383] *Montes* 11–12; cf. *León* 254–5; *Sahagún* 40–1; *Otero* 156–7; *Astorga* 90–1; *Eslonza* 1–2; *Castañeda* 3–4; *Liébana* 50–1; *Cardeña* 276, 125; *San Millán* 557, 307, 435; *Santiago* 46–7; *Sobrado* 1.24, 1.29; *Celanova* 114–15; *Lorvão* 60, 29.
[384] *Sahagún* 261–2; *Arlanza* 14–15; cf. *León* 708–9; *Otero* 160–1; *Astorga* 225–6; *Santillana* 26–7, 35–6; *Arlanza* 23–4.
[385] See e.g. *León* 371–4, 457–9, 874–7, 891–3; *Sahagún* 145–7, 229–32, 324–6; *Otero* 59–61, 67–9, 94–7, 137–9, 172–4; *Astorga* 14–16; *Sobrado* 1.91–3; *Celanova* 130–3, 135–7, 253–9, 305–7; *Coimbra* 354–6.

in 950 was documented on a Sunday at *ora III* (terce, or nine o'clock in the morning), another in 951 on a Saturday at *ora erad quasi vesperum* (around vespers, the late afternoon or early evening), and both were the work of the same local scribe.[386] Reflecting that range of possibility, even when transactions took place at the same site the witnesses are not always identical, such as two testaments granted on 9 December 1022 to San Salvador de Matallana before the council of San Salvador and witnessed by two entirely different groups, though some overlap is normal.[387] On 27 April 1030, indeed, Vivi *presbiter* wrote up a sale by Vermudo and his wife Donna Nova to Cidi Domínguez and his wife Oria before six witnesses, then a second by Zidi Pelagiz and his wife Tarasia to the same on that parchment, the only new witness being Vermudo himself, in a change of roles.[388] This act of bringing people together must be what underlies the formation of councils and 'collations' as legal entities and actors in their own right: once they had met often enough, their members were no longer being 'brought together', but meeting at established points of assembly. The writing for which they were meeting was a community affair, and that communal quality is the essence of witnessing. Witnesses are ubiquitous in the documentation, absent from just four original royal diplomas and 50 private charters, or 1% of the corpus. All the royal cases are precepts, the 'business end' of the diploma, while 13 of the 50 others are lists, hardly calling for witnessing, or contracts of some sort where the mutuality might have rendered them superfluous, leaving 37 unwitnessed charters; some are incomplete, and others share witnesses with documents on the same parchment.[389] The point is the constancy of witnessing, and therefore the constancy of collectivity. In contrast to the few without any witness, some 389 or a tenth of the charters refer to 'many others' present for some or all of the transaction: *alius plures qui ic non sunt* (many others who are not here) in 940, or *aliorum multorum que non sunt scripti* (many others who have not been written down) in 1013.[390] The list of people who assembled for writing is a long one, but even so only a partial record of reality.

---

[386]   *León* 226, 237; Davies, 'Local Priests', 36.

[387]   *León* 794–5; cf. *Sahagún* 175–6; *Otero* 106–7; *Santillana* 9–10; *Albelda* 15–16.

[388]   *León* 866–7; cf. 800–1; *Sahagún* 16, 361, 29–30, 234–5; *Otero* 64–5, 111–12, 118–19, 131–2, 189–90, 191–2.

[389]   *León* 18, 149, 300, 500; 480, 668, *Otero* 22, *Coruña* 136, *Coimbra* 118; *León* 477, 677, *Otero* 38–9, 150, *Coruña* 9, *Floriano* 73, 75; *Sahagún* 306, *Otero* 40–1, *León* 364–6.

[390]   *León* 139; *Sahagún* 400.

## Individuals

Those present for the confirmation of charters identified the role which they played as *confirmans* or *testis*, acting as confirmer or witness. The former tend to be listed ahead of the latter, but the distinction between the two labels is not clear, since for every instance where it may signal some status difference, another gives this the lie.[391] Many such seemingly obvious categories of role, indeed, can dissolve on closer inspection, including the difference between granters and both confirmers and witnesses. Rebelle signs but his wife Maosavara confirms in 965, just as Ordoño III signs but his queen Urraca confirms in 954; a bishop of Segovia signs but eight kindred witness in 960, just as Valencia signs but eight of her nine children witness in 950, while the donor Dompater appears in the witness list of his own donation from 961.[392] Traditionally, witnesses have been studied from the perspective of prosopography, which in practice means using the subset bearing titles—royal, comital, ecclesiastical, aristocratic—as evidence for the composition and movements of courts, aristocratic networks, or the identities of local élites.[393] The upper echelons of society do of course feature in witness lists, and these are regularly, though not uniformly, organised by order of rank or status, but that could stand for anything from the rituals of transaction to the habits of scribes and later copyists.[394] What fraction of society more broadly took part in charters as witnesses? Or put another way, what sort of person made a witness? General descriptors are limited: *homines bonos, filii bonorum hominum, viros veridicos*, good men, sons of good men, truthful men, *idoneis testibus*, apt or able witnesses, including the *idoneis testibus Smaelitis* whom we have already met, *laycos* or laymen, *clericis et laicis*, clergy and laity, and the noble *barones* and *infanconibus* of suspect diplomas.[395] But were only the better sort meant to witness? If we try to categorise witnesses more imaginatively than by status alone, there quickly emerges a picture of diverse and often unexpected varieties of social participation in the witnessing of written transaction.

---

[391]  See *e.g. León* 432, 68.
[392]  *León* 388, 280, 333, 216, 337.
[393]  See *e.g.* Pérez de Urbel, *Historia*, 3, 1389–1432; Pérez de Urbel, *Sancho*, 455–66; *Ramiro II*, 513–24; Rodríguez Fernández, *Ordoño*, 194–240; Rodríguez Fernández, *Sancho*, 125–33, 185–90.
[394]  Roach, 'Rites', 182–203.
[395]  *León* 634; *Lorvão* 17; *Cardeña* 107; *Lorvão* 60, 15; *cf. Oviedo* 42; *Coruña* 58; *Nájera* 4; *Huesca* 5; *Santillana* 8; Alvarado Planas, 'Orígenes', 439–59; González González, 'Status', 331–54.

Witnesses could be identified by geographical origin, converging from near or far on the location of the charter. In one exchange involving land in Marialba from 965, the witness Corasce is called *de Sancta Maria Alva*, evidently local, while a sale of property beneath the city wall of León in 974 features a witness from the neighbourhood of Puerta del Obispo.[396] They could come from a religious institution party to the transaction, such as a *soror de casa* (sister of the house) attending a testament to Santiago de León in 1028, or a *frater de Domnos Sanctos* (brother of Sahagún, the 'holy lords' in question being Santos Facundo y Primitivo) at a sale to that monastery in 997, just as San Miguel de Támara brought its own *testimonias* to a donation in 968.[397] But other witnesses originate from places which were not so directly involved, like the exchange of vineyards on Monte Aurio in 942 with one witness from Cea, or the donation of another vineyard in Marialba attended by one from Monasteriolo.[398] They could even come from a considerable distance: one from Burgos at a sale to Piasca, some 150 km away, in 959, or two from Pamplona at a donation to Sahagún, remarkably 320 km away, in 962; and what should we make of the *episcopus de Grecia* (bishop from Greece) sitting in on a testament to San Salvador de Oviedo in 1012?[399] The clergy are more obviously mobile, moving within a radius of their home base, like the priest of Sahagún at a donation to Santos Justo y Pastor (50 km) in 980, or the abbot of Sahagún at Cea (12 km) in 1026 for restoration of property to Santa María de León; the bishop of Ourense attended a testament to Celanova (25 km) in 962, stating that the monastery was in his own diocese.[400] We regularly see groups of bishops from sees hither and yon at royal undertakings and others of high status.[401]

But lay men and women travelled to witness transactions too. If we recall the colourful testament of Iulianus *presbiter* from 954, it was ultimately

---

[396] *León* 386; *Sahagún* 278; *cf. León* 148; *Sahagún* 160; *Liébana* 28; *Cardeña* 198; *Albelda* 21; *San Millán* 240; *Celanova* 302.

[397] *León* 848; *Sahagún* 354; *Cardeña* 239; *cf. Sahagún* 340, 359; *San Millán* 138; *Nájera* 4; *Mondoñedo* 6.

[398] *León* 153, 264; *cf.* 243; *Sahagún* 91; *Astorga* 28; *Eslonza* 17; *San Vicente* 16; *Cardeña* 308; *Covarrubias* 6; *Valpuesta* 33; *San Millán* 689; *Irache* 3; *Pamplona* 9; *Huesca* 8; *Sobrado* 1.43; *Celanova* 59; *PMH* 161.

[399] *Liébana* 57; *Sahagún* 196; *Oviedo* 41; *cf. Samos* S5; Rucquoi, 'Peregrinos', 45–6.

[400] *León* 479, 829; *Celanova* 154; *cf. León* 167; *Sahagún* 68; *Astorga* 49; *Castañeda* 11; *Floriano* 12; *Oviedo* 33; *Liébana* 39; *Oña* 2; *Valpuesta* 32; *Irache* 1; *Samos* 126, 248; *Sobrado* 1.3; *Celanova* 100; *Mondoñedo* 7; *Guimarães* 53, A2.

[401] See *e.g. Sahagún* 93; *Vega* 1; *Eslonza* 1–2; *Oviedo* 2–3; *Coruña* 96; *Santiago* 13; *Samos* 34; *Sobrado* 1.129; *Celanova* 47; *Lorvão* 3; *Coimbra* 56; Recuero Astray, 'Relaciones', 77–84; García de Cortázar, 'Reyes', 1, 201–63.

confirmed in sight of the crowd of family visiting him.[402] The most remarkable charters in this regard are those listing witnesses from multiple locations, such as an exchange of land in Valdemorilla and Matella (uncertain) made in 952 before not only a group from Matella itself, but also a person from Villaseca, or a gift of property in Rioseco to Abellar in 943 witnessed by a party of six from Villobera and one each from Covellas and Villacete.[403] The documentation of Sahagún has a particular line in enumerating witnesses by *villa* of origin, up to seven on two occasions, while a donation to Eslonza in 946 lists witnesses from nine different sites.[404] Normally they stay relatively local, but lay witnesses could also travel some distance, like the two from Guimarães and León who were at a testament to Celanova in 1000, or the three from León, Simancas, and Córdoba who were on hand for a donation to Abellar in the mid-tenth century.[405] Collectively, as with the clergy, these are signs of how every text is a confluence of actors, and transaction must have entailed preparation, inviting parties, scribes, and witnesses both nearby and remote.

Transaction had ramifications at the higher levels of élites and estates, but it was first an event with implications for the 'small worlds' of local communities.[406] We can see this in the presence as witnesses of the immediate neighbours of the property under donation or sale, such as *ipsos vicinos qui sunt presens* (the neighbours who are present) at a sale to Buezo de Bureba in 950.[407] More specifically, persons and places cited in boundary clauses reappear in witness lists with some regularity. The witnesses Baltario and Ferrocinti were neighbours of the land sold in Valdesogo in 939, as was Vigila *presbiter* of Revendeca in 966, while Arias Dagaredi could well correspond to the *villa* of Dagaredi where the *salinas* (salt-pans) for sale in 929 were to be found; a certain Aiub makes a sudden appearance confirming alongside the granters of a charter in 947, perhaps because they were selling property *iusta kastro* (next to the fortification) which bears the same

[402] *León* 278; cf. *Sahagún* 302; *San Vicente* 3.      [403] *León* 244, 175.

[404] *Sahagún* 87, 364; *Eslonza* 21; cf. *León* 118; *Sahagún* 18; *Eslonza* 23–4; *Otero* 9; *San Vicente* 3, 19; *Liébana* 31; *San Millán* 512; *Pamplona* 2; *San Juan* 35; *Covarrubias* 15; *Celanova* 238; *Lorvão* 24; Davies, 'Local Priests in Northern Iberia', 128.

[405] *Celanova* 242; *León* 276; cf. 147; *Sahagún* 310; *Astorga* 8; *Montes* 11; *Eslonza* 18; *Puerto* 2; *Valpuesta* 44; *Cardeña* 112; *San Millán* 54; *San Juan* 18; *Leire* 9; *Celanova* 142; *Rocas* 1; *Guimarães* 1A, A3.

[406] Martín Viso, 'Worlds', 255–79.

[407] *Valpuesta* 28; cf. *Albelda* 14; *Leire* 8; Zeller et al., *Neighbours*, 181–221.

name.[408] Still more explicitly, amongst the witnesses given provenances in a sale of land at the *villa* of Aspera in 978 is one Valeyrus *qui ibidem abitabit* (who dwelt there), and the laconic language of boundary clauses and subscriptions must conceal the presence of many such immediate neighbours.[409] In the event of a dispute over the transaction, their recognition of its legitimacy mattered as much as that of previous owners, the other local constituency which we encounter in charters. In 909, a sale of lands formerly belonging to Petro and Arias was witnessed by Petro and Arias themselves, just as another sale of a vineyard *quem nos abemus de patre nostro Baldreo* (which we have from our father Baldreo) featured Baldreo as witness in 1024; a sale of property which the mother of the granters had obtained by a charter from Anagildo even took place before Anagildo in 1012.[410] The object was to get all those with a claim to ownership on board with it changing hands, thereby producing a written history for use in the event of any contention.

In this connexion, one final if metaphorical category of 'local' witness is the relation, easy to find and presumably more common than the evidence allows us to state. Immediately the testament made by Mumadona in 959 comes to mind, which all six of her children signed off, given that much of their property was passing to the monastery of Guimarães.[411] In some cases, relationships are declared, such as Mihael *presbiter* and Laurenze, *iermani* (brothers) of Fructuoso, who witnessed a sale by the selfsame Fructuoso *presbiter* in 1028, but they are more often implied by a patronymic: granter Vigila Verobiz and confirmer Sendino Verobiz in 974, granter Pedro Flaínez and witnesses Munio and Fernando Flaínez in 1002, or Ioacino and Gaudinas iben Ioacino in 998, though latter may also be one of the granters.[412] In a case from 976, we have Vela Vermúdez and Vermudo Velaz as granter and recipient together with their respective sons Nuño Velaz and Fernando Vermúdez as confirmer and witness, but this is exceptional; the form and use of such patronymics was only beginning to be standardised in the tenth century, and remained irregular and intermittent into the high

---

[408] *León* 133; *Valpuesta* 37; *PMH* 35; *León* 197; *cf.* 214; *Sahagún* 81; *Otero* 3; *Eslonza* 14; *Cardeña* 137; *Valpuesta* 42; *San Millán* 315, 701; *Santiago* 45; *Sobrado* 2.46; *Celanova* 92; *PMH* 57.

[409] *San Vicente* 19.

[410] *Cardeña* 62; *Otero* 164; *Junqueira* 2; *cf. León* 340; *Sahagún* 279; *Eslonza* 21; *Cardeña* 268; *Sobrado* 1.94; *Celanova* 53; *Coimbra* 208.

[411] *Guimarães* 1A, A3.

[412] *Otero* 186; *Sahagún* 277; *Otero* 62; *Lorvão* 37; *cf. León* 322; *Sahagún* 196; *Astorga* 103; *Eslonza* 9; *Liébana* 21; *Santillana* 15; *Albelda* 14; *Valpuesta* 28; *San Millán* 32; *San Juan* 40; *Leire* 14; *Coruña* 50; *Celanova* 22, 188; *Samos* 214; *Sobrado* 1.115, 1.35; *Mondoñedo* 7; *ChLA* 114, 32.

Middle Ages.[413] In 'bringing the family', however, the parties to a transaction were not alone. There are a father and son amongst the witnesses in 930, and three married couples, one with a sister too, in 937, while we have a husband, wife, and their three children in 959, and four individuals with the patronymic Ruderici in 945.[414] Granters involved their families to ensure that they signed off on a transaction with lasting implications for them, and when witnesses brought their own relations it served to perpetuate the memory of the act into subsequent generations.

Another way to approach the question of what sort of person made a witness is to ask whether the composition of the witness list exceeds in any respect those whom we expect to be there. Beginning with the most obvious, the scribe is present and accounted for: we have next to nothing in terms of personal information on writers, but Felix Cromaciz *et notarius* witnessed a testament to San Salvador de Oviedo in 976, and to judge by his unusual Greek patronymic he must have been the son of an earlier granter named Cromacius Melliniz, an aristocrat of the notary corps.[415] Sampiro regularly appears as witness in royal and socially elevated documents, especially if written by his seeming protégé Petrus.[416] The same is true of Fulgentius, who even witnessed a donation by Sampiro in 1018, though caution is needed, since in 1013 he is called witness but the charter is written in his hand.[417] The testament made by Sarracino Ariani before Alfonso V in 1018 is a special case: witnessed by Sampiro as well as Fulgentius, written by Petrus and another illegible name, it gives the distinct impression of a scribal 'old boys' network' acting as witnesses for each other.[418] More broadly, notaries are common witnesses across the corpus; as to why, it was presumably for such literate expertise that Bishop Indisclo hired Argimirus *notarius* as his *assertor* (representative) in a dispute of 878.[419]

---

[413] *Sahagún* 283; Boullón Agrelo, 'Cronoloxía', 449–75; Boullón Agrelo, *Antroponimia*, 26–54; see Martínez Sopena (ed.), *Antroponimia*, for the most thorough comparative treatment of naming systems.

[414] *León* 85, 118, 313; *Cardeña* 288; *cf. León* 322; *Sahagún* 46; *Otero* 26; *Eslonza* 15; *Liébana* 11; *Puerto* 2; *Arlanza* 16–17; *Cardeña* 19; *Albelda* 8; *San Millán* 526; *San Juan* 18; *Sobrado* 1.43; *Ourense* 3; *Celanova* 38; *Lorvão* 61.

[415] *Oviedo* 30; *cf.* 29; *Otero* 30; Becker, *Namenbuch*, 334.

[416] *León* 565, 594, 749, 763, 777, 855, 862, 865, 880; *Sobrado* 1.109; *Coruña* 95; *Samos* S1; *Lugo*, 2, 555–65.

[417] *León* 756, 711; *cf.* 733, 752, 776, 803, 815–16; *Sobrado* 1.49, 1.17, 1.115, 1.39, 1.42; *Coruña* 110.

[418] *León* 754.

[419] *Astorga* 5; see *e.g. León* 7; *Sahagún* 22; *Otero* 113; *Oviedo* 8; *Liébana* 38; *Arlanza* 20; *Valpuesta* 18; *Coruña* 72; *Santiago* 13–14; *Sobrado* 1.23; *Celanova* 64; *Lorvão* 3; *Lorvão* 12; as a proper name *León* 408; *Celanova* 2, 34, 115; *PMH* 89, 102, 149.

The term *magister* naturally suggests itself as a second class of presumptively literate witness, even if it had a wider range of meanings in Late Antiquity and the early Middle Ages more akin to 'master' generally than 'schoolteacher' specifically, and could extend to skilled artisans and craftsmen.[420] Amidst the palace monks who witnessed a precept of Alfonso V and Elvira in 1000 is a *magister* Ascarius *presbiter*, in the context of the king's minority (he was about six years old) probably a royal tutor, like the Fruela Hamitiz *magister regis* who witnessed the testament drawn up for Bishop Sisnando in 983.[421] Bishop Salomon, in a testament of 937, calls Bishop Genadio his *magister*, noting that Bishop Fortis was another *discipulum* (follower), which again suggests an educational use.[422] What little we know of education in early medieval Iberia has an ecclesiastical context in the church or cloister, and this background may explain the seeming preponderance of the clergy amongst our scribes.[423] Cresconius *confessus*, the roving *praepositus* of Celanova, records in a testament of 1010 how he raised his nephews, and *emerit litteris in scola* (gained letters for them in school) by engaging meritorious *magistros*, much as San Rosendo had done for him when he was an child oblate.[424] The *majordomo* Ansur, moving in royal circles, describes in his own testament of 976 placing both of his sons in the care of the abbot of Sahagún no less so that *vere confessorum literas docuisent* (they might learn the letters of confessors rightly), revealing where literacy was expected; Genitrigus enjoined his kin in 947 to *litteras didicerit* (learn their letters) if they were to retain a stake in his foundation of San Salvador de Flavelo.[425] Accordingly, we encounter Sampiro identified in a witness list as *scola regis* ('school of the king') in 1012, and at Celanova in 1002 the abbot, all the brothers, priests, *laicos*, and a *turba puerorum degentibus in scola et in capitulo* (crowd of boys spending time in the school and in chapter), while a fire at San Pedro de Rocas in 1007, caused by the negligence of the boys who were in school learning their letters, destroyed the *firmitates et scripturas* (confirmations and documents) of the monastery.[426] Maybe our old friend

---

[420]  Conant, 'Literacy', 223–4; see *e.g. Tumbo Viejo* 111.    [421]  *León* 599; *Samos* 156.

[422]  *Astorga* 48; *cf. Lorvão* 45.

[423]  Collins, 'Literacy', 131–2; Guijarro, 'Masters', 220–9; Carriedo Tejedo, 'Libros', 44–55; Sánchez Prieto, 'Aprender', 3–34; Andrade Cernadas, 'Edades', 123–36; *cf.* Petrucci, 'Literacy', 96–8; Alturo Perucho, 'Sistema', 42–5; Everett, 'Scribes', 63–4.

[424]  *Celanova* 318, 321; Orlandis, 'Notas', 165; Carzolio de Rossi, 'Cresconio', 277–9; Andrade Cernadas, 'Vida', 303–5; *cf.* Jong, *Image*, esp. 126–32, 232–45.

[425]  *Sahagún* 284; *Samos* 226; *cf. Celanova* 326; *Coruña* 113.

[426]  *León* 709; *Celanova* 261; *Rocas* 1; *cf. San Juan* 12, 56; Rucquoi, 'Ordres', 309–14.

Petrus *gramaticus*, who witnessed a donation in 928, taught at one such centre of learning in the environs of León.[427]

Masters appear often as witnesses, especially in charters from Celanova and Portugal, as well as in background roles like a *magister* Ascarigus (the Ascarius above?), from whom Sampiro had received a *villa* by charter, or *magister* Recemundo, neighbour of a property of Vacariça; on occasion they act as granter or recipient in a transaction.[428] At least some were managers or middle men, to judge by the wine which the monks of Santa Cruz had to render to Celanova *per manum de magister Busiano et Lalli* (through the agency of master Busiano and Lalli).[429] They could also be scribes: one sale to Unisco and her son Oseredo in 1018 is even witnessed by two *magistri*, Cidi and Sandinus, and written up by (the latter?) *magister* Sandinus.[430] Perhaps masters might best be defined as having public careers in written affairs, including dispute settlement, such as the *magister* Santius *confessus et iudex*, a judge attached to the monastery church of Mixós.[431] In Portugal, *magister* Evenando, *qui illam terram mandabat* (who governed [or held the commission for] that land), is amply attested in the early eleventh century, as judge and confirmer of a dispute in 1004, witnessing a gift by Unisco and her son Oseredo in 1021, and defending Cresconius *per ingenium* (through his skill) as an *assertor* in a dispute of 1025, each time with other masters.[432] The closest comparison, indeed, may be to the *iudex*, who both presided at disputes involving written evidence and the law and crops up often as a witness, especially in León.[433] Like masters, judges could be ecclesiastics, since the title is periodically paired with abbot, priest, or *frater*.[434] They could also hold secular office, like Count Suario Gundemáriz in 992 or Iustus *iudice rex* (royal judge?) in 1029, and some had a regional base too like (the same?) Iustus *iudice Legionum* (judge of León) in 1011; one Eyto Furtuniz, *qui iudigabit et omnia per verifice ordine exaravit* (who judged and recorded everything in a

---

[427] *León* 76.

[428] *León* 756; *Coimbra* 118; cf. *León* 700; *San Juan* 41; *San Millán* 138; *Celanova* 154, 160, 290, 325, 372, 382; *Lugo* 57; *Mondoñedo* 6; *Coimbra* 81, 147; *Guimarães* 55; *Lorvão* 6, 37; as granters or recipients *Astorga* 77; *Celanova* 352; *Irache* 2; *Pamplona* 9, 11.

[429] *Celanova* 272; cf. *Floriano* 43.

[430] *Coimbra* 156; cf. *Celanova* 375, 381; *Lourenzá* 9.      [431] *Celanova* 362.

[432] *Coimbra* 212, 142, 203; cf. *León* 559; *San Juan* 14; *Celanova* 261; *Guimarães* 66; Rucquoi, 'Compostela', 514–15.

[433] See e.g. *León* 34; *Sahagún* 33; *Otero* 21; *Montes* 5; *Eslonza* 9; *Valpuesta* 7; *Albelda* 12; *Irache* 2; *Coruña* 95; *Celanova* 51; *Sobrado* 1.132; *Alfonso V* 4; or as maiorinus *León* 689; *Cardeña* 6; *Arouca* 2; *Coimbra* 147; *Samos* S1, S9.

[434] *Albelda* 29, *San Millán* 54, 50, *Sobrado* 1.129; *León* 478–9, *Sobrado* 1.43; *Samos* S1; *Lugo*, 2, 555–65.

truthful sequence), acted as scribe alongside Martinus Vermudiz *presbiter* in 1025.[435] And in the same line, the *saio* (court bailiff) similarly, though more rarely, witnessed charters, such as Gonzalvo Beilaz, identified as the *saio* of Salinas, in a donation granted in 988.[436]

What if we turn our expectation of literate witnesses on its head? The audience of the charter extended past the important and predictable to society at large; the point was as much that anyone could and should witness as that a particular person or class had to witness, still less someone in whom literacy might assuredly be presumed. Otherwise, why round up four *homines de tributa*, men obliged to pay rent or dues, and eight *fugitivos* in 1002, or Menendo *latron* (the bandit) in 1011?[437] Why have a *servuo* (slave or serf) witness the testament in 984 which transferred him along with the *villa* where he lived unless some larger social consensus was at stake?[438] What about recruiting rueful failure Diego, *qui vult esse episcopus et non est* (who wants to be a bishop and is not), to witness the restoration diploma for San Vicenzo de Pombeiro in 997?[439] We should not expect or require first-hand literacy of these witnesses for them to have participated in the confirmation of charters. Take tradesmen—*aurifice, ferrario, cisor,* goldsmith, blacksmith, stonecutter or woodcutter—whom we encounter respectively on five, seven, and four occasions.[440] Or those in humbler occupations: a *molinario* (miller) is to be found six times confirming Leonese documents, and we variously encounter a *verducario, sartor, pellicularius, tinturario, sellero, techarius* or *teliario, carpentario, karrario,* and even a *ballestario* (verger, tailor, tanner, dyer, leatherworker, weaver, carpenter, cartwright, and engineer).[441] And those working in the fields, as *oveliarius, ortolano, harrarius, stabularius, iugarii, vigarii, peguriarius* (a shepherd, gardener, ploughman, stablekeeper, oxherds and horse-drivers, a herdsman), or the *coquinarius* (cook), others *de quoquina* (from the kitchen), right the way

---

[435]   *Sobrado* 1.130; *León* 849, 700; *Braga* 22; cf. *San Millán* 181.
[436]   *San Millán* 411; cf. *Sahagún* 162, 164; *San Vicente* 29; *Liébana* 66; *Valpuesta* 33; *San Millán* 181; *Arlanza* 17; *Cardeña* 210; *Sobrado* 1.129, 1.132; *Celanova* 261.
[437]   *Celanova* 264, 324.        [438]   *Lorvão* 48; cf. *León* 7.
[439]   *Pombeiro* 3; cf. *Carracedo* 1.
[440]   *León* 241, *Otero* 108, *Celanova* 28, 63–4; *León* 148, 496, 664, *San Vicente* 22, *Liébana* 69, *Celanova* 136, 232; *Liébana* 39, *León* 223, *San Vicente* 12, *Liébana* 41; Pérez González, 'Oficios', 111–25.
[441]   *León* 243, 254, 267, 272, 350, 645; cf. *San Vicente* 15, 22; *León* 230, 405, 533; *Liébana* 18; *León* 272, 157, 293; *Albelda* 7; *Covarrubias* 12; Clavería Nadal, 'Léxico', 1, 531–61; Clavería Nadal and Torruella i Boix, 'Historia', 67–114; Maas-Chauveau, 'Nombres', 83–116.

down to the unassuming *pescador* (fisherman).[442] Perhaps the surest sign that we must rescale our conception of witnessing comes from the 'paid witnesses': when Albaro *frater* sold a vineyard to Munnio Asurizi in 966, the scribe Didaco Munniozi made a note not transcribed by later cartulary copyists of the *arenzata* (measure of wine) *que veberont ipsas testes* (which those witnesses drank).[443] The act of witnessing was about rallying community around text; a broader social participation meant a deeper dissemination into society.

## Audible Texts

Each charter was a convergence point, where witnesses from a broad range of origins came together at an equally broad range of sites, watched and listened to successive stages of transaction, and internalised the salient details into communal memory.[444] But how did these witnesses engage with text? What was the interface between written transaction and attending community? Confirmation of a charter relied on two oral processes: for witnesses, hearing the granters swear their oaths was a prelude to listening to the text itself read out loud. This was a basic part of the subscription process, and some 522 (13%) of the charters mention being read in that context, at a rate which though fluctuating holds steady over the period (see Figure 2.24). Donadeus confirmed his sale in 894 with the typical words *relegendo audivi* (I heard it from rereading), while Abbot Indulfo said of his testament in 980, *coran legenter audivi* (I heard it read in person), and a series of parties asserted of their transaction in 979, *audivimus legere* (we heard it read).[445] Sancho García and Urraca heard their own privilege, *sicut hic scriptum est* (just as it is written here), around 1012.[446] The emphasis might be on the act of listening: as Ilduara put it in 925, *presenti adfui et propriis auribus audivi* (I was present for and heard it with my own ears).[447] Or the action might be expressed as a quality of the document itself, as in a *scriptum* (writing) of Arvildi and his son Diaco *a nobis factum et auditum* (made and heard by us) in 1024, or as Rapinate professed in 1027, *ista carta scripta*

---

[442] *León* 267, 272, 156, 288; *Sahagún* 410; *León* 183, 322, 289, 314, 327, 404; *Albelda* 10; Ayala Martínez, 'Yuguero', 17–46; Andrade Cernadas, 'Refectorio', 51–2; Davies, 'Gardens', 345.
[443] *Valpuesta* 37; cf. 36.
[444] Geary, 'Land', 169–84; Kosto, 'Reasons', 143–6; Jarrett, 'Ceremony', 275–95.
[445] *León* 9; *Santillana* 9; *Sahagún* 299.
[446] *San Millán* 535.      [447] *Celanova* 23; cf. *Albelda* 19.

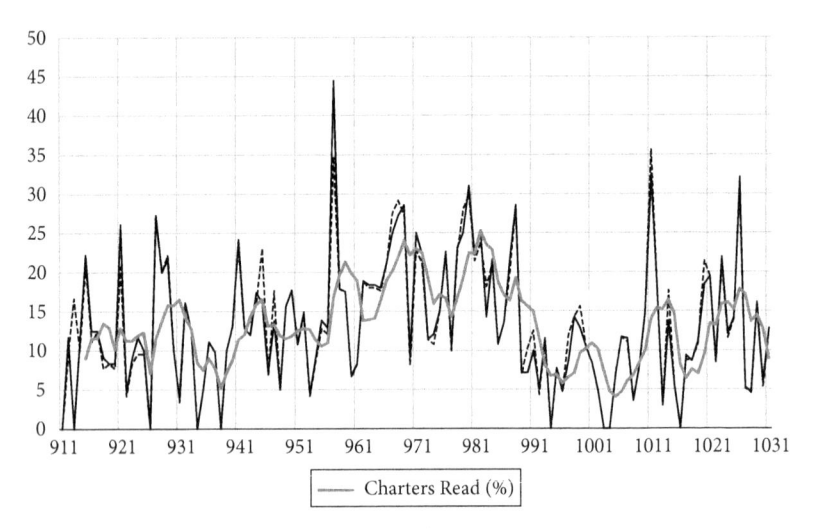

**Figure 2.24**  Reading Charters (911–1031)

*et cognita legente audivi* (I heard that charter, written and understood from reading).[448] But it was done for the benefit of the granters as well as other parties and witnesses, a communal activity reaching all those who were there. Consider the words of a testament of 1024, *scitote qui hec lecturi estis et audituri* (know you who will read and hear this), or another testament of 936 prefacing the business of the charter *ut auditus sequitur* (as 'the listening' follows).[449] The expectation was of general dissemination, and the sanction of a donation in 1005 accordingly warns any who *verba legerit ut legentem audivit* (have read the words or heard the reading) not to trespass on it, while a confirmation of 948 hopes that *pax sit legentibus bel audientibus* (peace should be upon those reading or hearing it).[450] We should credit the ubiquity, so notable in the Liébana and Castilla, of documents read aloud for their witnesses to hear.[451] In 950, when Egilo and Goto handed their charter of donation to the witnesses for confirmation, those named *legendo audierunt et sic rovoraverunt* (heard it from reading and therefore confirmed it).[452]

[448] *Sahagún* 412; *Covarrubias* 14.      [449] *Albelda* 32; *Celanova* 52.
[450] *Astorga* 131; *San Juan* 18; cf. *Floriano* 185.
[451] See e.g. *León* 315; *Sahagún* 52; *Astorga* 140; *Montes* 8; *Otero* 83; *Eslonza* 7; *Benevívere* 1; *Oviedo* 29; *Santillana* 3; *Liébana* 44; *Cardeña* 17; *Irache* 2; *Covarrubias* 1; *Arlanza* 1; *Oña* 3; *Valpuesta* 14; *San Millán* 696, 316; *Silos* 2; *Puerto* 2; *Pamplona* 2; *Concejo* 1; *Aguilar* 2; *Samos* 248; *Celanova* 79.
[452] *Cardeña* 49; cf. *León* 723, 800–1; *Cardeña* 46.

There is some indication that the alternative to hearing a charter was to read it oneself, but all is not quite what it seems. The words of Roderigo *diagunus* in 787 are straightforward enough, *religendo me cognovi* (I know from my own reading), as are those of Countess Tota in 1031, *legendo cognovi et satis michi complacui* (I know from reading and am well pleased in myself).[453] Agione *frater* was more emphatic in 944 about his *religiendum* (rereading), and Beatus *presbiter* in 889 signed *que fieri volui et relegendum* (what I wished done and [know from] rereading).[454] Yet note, as with hearing, the reliance on an impersonal gerund: 'I know from reading' or 'I know from the reading'. Categorical first-person statements are rarer by far, and scarcely representative. Monnio *episcopo* said in 937, *primitus legi et confirmavit* (I read it first and confirmed), and Mumadona Dias in 959, *in prompti loco testamento legimus* (we read the testament immediately), but both are high-status granters.[455] In fact, references to documents being 'read' are too common to mean first-hand reading; they are as ubiquitous as those to documents being 'heard'. At Cardeña they are in alternating usage, whereas in the west 'reading' is far more frequent than 'hearing', as if what we are seeing is two different preferences, scribal and regional, for a single phenomenon.[456] Are we looking at the same or glimpsing real distinctions in literacy when Gutier confirms his testament in 925, *secundum quod relegendo certissime cognovi* (according to what I know most certainly from rereading), where his wife Ilduara says only that she has heard it?[457] When Gotina Núñez determines her own testament for herself in 1025, *singillatim per ordinem recitatum*, what does this mean in practice? Read aloud one by one and in order: but by or to each party and witness?[458]

The language of confirmation is evidence of a collapsing distinction between text and speech. What is the message of Ansur confirming everything *que abuiit lingua sua per notitia* (which his tongue had listed in writing) in his testament of 976, or Sancho Ordóñez 'hearing from rereading' the testaments of his ancestors in 927, or Gómez Díaz and his wife Ostrocia exchanging property *cum foro exlecto* (with its privileges either determined or read aloud) in 1011?[459] Simply put, *sit verbum nostrum auditum* (let our

[453]  *Floriano* 12; *Sahagún* 428; González Paz, 'Rodrigo', 1, 445–50; Godoy, 'Escribientes', 85–91.
[454]  *Coimbra* 526; *Celanova* 7; cf. *Astorga* 129.
[455]  *San Millán* 525; *Guimarães* 1A, A3; cf. *León* 824.
[456]  See e.g. *León* 37; *Sahagún* 4; *Astorga* 2; *Otero* 7; *Eslonza* 8; *San Isidro* 12; *Montes* 9; *Oviedo* 25; *San Vicente* 3; *Liébana* 13; *Cardeña* 102; *Albelda* 15; *Covarrubias* 12; *Arlanza* 3; *Leire* 9; *Valpuesta* 19; *Coruña* 94; *Celanova* 1; *Samos* 7; *Sobrado* 1.18; *Guimarães* 16.
[457]  *Celanova* 23; cf. *León* 8, 57, 88, 146.      [458]  *Sahagún* 415; cf. *Lourenzá* 185.
[459]  *Sahagún* 284; *Santiago* 51; *Oña* 10; cf. 17; Torrens Álvarez et al., *Documentación*, 20–8.

word be heard), as Bishop Jimeno wrote or said in 1020; this conjunction of oral and written existed in recitation, declamation, proclamation of the charter.[460] But by whom? Perhaps one of the parties, where possible: as Fafila *confessor* said of his testament, *ore meo nuntiavi* (I announced it with my own mouth), in 952, and in that same year, when Velasco lost his dispute with Abellar, *ex ore suo proprio prefatus est* (he uttered from his very own mouth) the terms of the sanction clause.[461] Perhaps by a stand-in, where necessary: Sigericus *presbiter et primiclerus annuntiavit* (pronounced) a testament written by David *presbiter* for Bishop Diego in 967, while the donation of Eldoara and her children from 864 provides that, if anyone should break it, *ste testamentus ei legatur* (let the testament be read to him).[462] Or is there more to such statements? Iohannes *sacer* tells us of his testament, *scribere mandavi et lingua mea legi* (I ordered it written and read it with my tongue), in 968.[463] He could mean that he read out what the scribe had written for him, or his words could be in line with the 15 parties who made gifts to San Mamés de Obarenes in 1009: after hearing their charter from rereading, they labelled it *hanc dicta vel scripta* (the spoken or written).[464] Reading was hearing, and the writer of the charter its speaker.

Early medieval Iberia was a society organised for literacy at one remove, by means of the scribe. Consider the responsibility vested in this figure: to write the charter and record all those involved in and present for it, and to disseminate knowledge of it, in the absence of any other obvious agent, by reading it aloud to the assembled multitude. Here the language of the text and the relationship of scribe and audience to it comes into focus, a late, vulgar, or even 'notarial' Latin inextricable from early Romance; while tenth- and eleventh-century glossing activities at San Millán have been taken to signal the emergence of Old Spanish, they reveal lexical variety, but no awareness of two distinct languages.[465] For the writers of the charters, who had first learned to read, orthography was separate from phonology.[466] In their myriad divergences from standard Classical Latin, the charters were comprehensible rather than representations of barbarism or incapacity, but Roger Wright's lesson for the historian of literacy is that any adaptation from text to speech was simpler than we might think. The scribe speaking his writing adjusted it from the more conservative written word to an

---

[460]  *Astorga* 230.      [461]  *Celanova* 95; *León* 256.      [462]  *Oviedo* 27; *Valpuesta* 3.
[463]  *Castañeda* 9.      [464]  *San Millán* 421; cf. *Oviedo* 35.
[465]  Emiliano, 'Latin', 233–47; Wright, *Study*, 211–42; Emiliano, 'Models', 17–57; Dworkin, *Guide*, 3–16; cf. Puentes Romay, 'Aproximación', 483–9.
[466]  Wright, *Ibero-Romance*, esp. 165–208.

evolving spoken word. The challenge came not from vocabulary, syntax, or phonetics, but certain aspects of grammar such as nominal morphology; nonetheless, the scribe could manage even these by reading in a 'comprehensive manner', or 'sympathetically'.[467] The prevailing layout of *scripta continua*, the minimal or inconsistent spacing of words and syllables, reflects the living language of the literate, and suggests a phonographic more than logographic reading which would have lent itself to active 'conversion' or glossing by the scribe for the illiterate.[468] At the same time, it would have called for some *praelectio* or preparatory study, with an eye to identifying areas needing register translation appropriate to the audience, and archaisms or legalese requiring careful pronunciation or explanation. But then Isidore of Seville had expected nothing less of his *lector*, and elsewhere we meet this professional 'reader' acting as scribe.[469] For listeners, text would have been 'read as Romance', 'felt as Latin'.[470] When one first heard a charter, much of it likely sounded old-fashioned or idiosyncratically 'notarial', but only that first time; the constant cycling of text back into speech kept written and spoken registers in touch.[471]

The entire process of composition, comprehension, and confirmation points to a social integration of the charter: in planning ahead, coordinating assembly, inviting a broad range of witnesses, all through the involvement of the scribe, we see a society with seemingly limited primary literacy relying on writing, a society of secondary literacy with a documentary habit, fully expectant of access by proxy to the written word.[472] What is the most important factor to take forward from here? The tenth century saw a consolidation of the agents and contexts of documentation, a trending towards a scribal profession and the nascent institutionalisation of gatherings for written affairs, but the central figure in all this remained the scribe as mediator between the written and the world. What were the consequences of stabilising the personnel of writing? The ability to write conferred power in a world with little of it but reliant on it.[473] Scribes had a service to market, in

---

[467] Wright, *Early Ibero-Romance*, 167; Wright, 'Gontigius', 1, 407–20; Wright, 'Writing', 1, 273–92; Wright, 'Scribes', 71–83; Wright, 'Difusión', 117–30; *cf.* Blake, 'Squeezing', 1–14; Wright, 'Reading', 505–16; Wright, 'Léxico', 133–49.

[468] Finbow, 'Latin', 521–31; Finbow, 'Conventions', 159–85.

[469] Isidore of Seville, *De ecclesiasticis officiis*, ed. Lawson, *Officiis*, 2.11; Banniard, 'Lecteur', 112–44; Denecker, 'Accent', 138–48; *cf.* Ganz and Goffart, 'Charters', 917.

[470] Pensado, 'Latin', 201.

[471] Álvarez Maurín, 'Registro', 23–41; Álvarez Maurín, 'Formulismo', 419–31; Pérez González, 'Latín medieval', esp. 86–98; Barrett, 'Conservatism'; *cf.* Menéndez Pidal, *Orígenes*, esp. 454–60.

[472] Moore, 'Hand', 18–32.

[473] Davies, 'Local Priests', 41–3.

return for payment, protection, preferment from patrons; in royal employ, Sampiro climbed from deacon to bishop.[474] And yet we increasingly find, in every locale, multiple 'literate providers' for kings, bishops, monasteries, churches, and lay men and women of every social stratum—multiple providers becoming more practised and professional with time. As they grew more numerous, competition for patronage must have grown accordingly, leaving scribes and their employers in a balance of power. What could a scribe offer to distinguish himself from his competitors? He could tilt the scales of supply and demand in his favour by offering higher levels of literate expertise. What we shall see is the growing incidence of charters citing other texts over the tenth century, in parallel with the consolidation in the scribal profession. Scribes—at least some scribes—were not only writers and readers binding society and text together, simple providers of skills, but also advisers, counsellors, interpreters of the written sources of authority and power. The dynamic of literacy over time in early medieval Iberia is this: a growing and intensifying organisation of society around the central and intermediary figure of the scribe.

---

[474] Garín, 'Economía', 238–42; *cf.* Hartmann, *Scribes*, esp. 111–39.

# 3
# Retaining

The creation and confirmation of a charter marked the beginning of a long afterlife of continuing use, and grasping this ongoing relevance of text requires understanding both why and how it worked in practice. The language of the charter is expectant of an active future, in that the sole purpose of its sanction clause is to deter any who might seek to disrupt the terms of the transaction: the permanence of the arrangements which it put in place was safeguarded carefully, and often with direct reference to the document recording them. In parallel to these precautions, the endurance of the charter itself was not simply assumed, but ensured through various forms of endorsement, preservation, and organisation which taken together constitute the archival mindset and habits of early medieval Iberia.[1] One common means of bringing the charter forward in time was to renew its confirmation, whether by affixing further signs to it after the fact, generally the monograms of kings or bishops, or by creating new charters, even writing them on occasion in free space left on the original parchment. Such interactions with text reflect how it remained a participant in the relationships evolving around it, and presume a dynamic circulation of documentation in society. There were functioning archives, in other words, but in whose hands?[2] The cities and towns of the Roman world had *gesta municipalia*, civic registers of property ownership and transaction, which the state used in taxation and the citizenry looked to for security; in the western provinces, elements of the institution survived the Empire in different forms, especially the tradition of public validation of documentation.[3] The normative sources for Visigothic Iberia certainly presume a range of archives both public and private, but the 'slate texts' of the northern Meseta, which account for essentially all the evidence on the ground, are equivocal on the question of control.[4] Should we think of 'stone archives' in the hands of local

---

[1] Chastang, 'Écrire', 135–56.    [2] Brown *et al.* (eds), *Culture*, 1–16, 363–76.
[3] Brown, '*Gesta*', 345–75; Barbier, *Archives*, esp. 135–64.
[4] Everett, 'Documents', 82–93.

*Text and Textuality in Early Medieval Iberia: The Written and The World, 711–1031*. Graham Barrett,
Oxford University Press. © Graham Barrett 2023. DOI: 10.1093/oso/9780192895370.003.0004

élites, who wielded the written word as intermediaries between the king-dom and the peasantry?[5] And did early medieval Iberia inherit this legacy?[6]

The clearest way forward is to 'follow the parchment' wherever it leads us. When any given charter was drawn up, the beneficiary typically received both that record of transaction and prior written titles of that property; repeated over time, this process formed and combined and recombined archives. The scope of archival practice appears ever more ecclesiastical as a plurality of western European land passed through donation and sale into Church ownership, just as the singular focus on land of the charters which the Church preserved makes the nature of property rights seem self-evident.[7] But if we step back to the first stage in the process, the initial handover, we see signs that parties of all types—institutions and individuals, the clergy and the laity—maintained and curated archives, and not always with land tenure foremost in mind. The dorsal notes found on the reverse side of many originals, summarising key details to facilitate identification and consultation, point to organisational habits and awareness of a need for access spanning society.[8] Charters were not written and then forgotten, or husbanded by the powerful; they were kept at the ready for use as needed. References in documents from the ninth and tenth centuries also imply efforts at storage with a greater degree of security or in better, more access-ible order by preparing copies and compiling extracts, leading up to the confection of the oldest surviving Iberian cartularies in the later eleventh century. Yet these advanced expressions of medieval archiving, at least as they have been preserved, were the work of the agents of churches and mon-asteries. Far from alone, but more than other actors, they had realised how to use the written word to shape the contours of historical memory as well as organise the management of property, and applied themselves to this end.[9]

## Extension

The active and engaged future which awaited transaction and its written record can be found embedded and expressed in the language of the

[5] Martín Viso, 'Tributación', 263–90; Martín Viso, 'Slates', 145–68; Martín Viso, 'Huellas', 285–314.
[6] Romero Tallafigo, 'Concepto', 3–11.
[7] Wood, 'Entrusting', 37–73; Innes, 'Practices', 247–66; cf. García-Gallo, 'Bienes', 351–87.
[8] Erhart, 'Charters', 27–39.
[9] Geary, 'Gestion', 13–26; Declercq, 'Originals', 147–70; Bouchard, 'Cartularies', 22–32; Agúndez San Miguel, 'Tumbo', 17–47; cf. Kosto, 'Liber', 1–22.

sanction, one of the concluding clauses of the charter. In transferring the property concerned into the hands of its new owner, the text typically expressed the hope that it remain as such *iure quieto* (essentially, in undisturbed or unchallenged right of ownership) henceforth.[10] In understanding human frailty, however, the charter also made provision for the contrary eventuality being realised. This takes the form of a tripartite condition set immediately before the date and subscriptions: the protasis envisions a range of potential violators and violations of the terms specified in the main text, while the apodosis defines a range of consequent spiritual and secular punishments.[11] The goal was not only to ensure that a donation or sale stayed intact, but also that its documentation remained inviolate. When the *infante* García made a gift to Abellar in 909, for instance, the target of the various attached penalties was anyone who should attempt to infringe the charter itself, rather than the transaction, while in a testament to Valpuesta of 864, the same sanction included an instruction to read out its text to the transgressor, so that he or she grasp the full enormity of the crime.[12] The monks at Eslonza seem to have been especially worried that the permanence of their documents might be endangered, and half of their charters deploy this tactic: a quarter penalise anyone who should infringe the decree, testament, or document, another quarter any who would disrupt it.[13] To enhance the efficacy of such sanctions, it was common practice to identify the typology of the charter precisely, so that anyone who should break the document of exchange drawn up at Ourense in 888 was obliged to pay the penalty, as was anyone who upset the *placitum* (agreement) reached at León in 930, while the judges of a dispute heard by Vermudo II at Rábade near Lugo in 997 ordered that the *agnitioni* (record) of its resolution be *exhiberi* (shown) to anyone who would seek to overturn it.[14] The donation to Sahagún from 983 which provides against interference with the deed, *pictacium* (bill), testament, and charter of *perfiliatio* (legal adoption) is extreme, but only just.[15] The sanction clause of another confirmation by Vermudo II from 999, suggestively, cites both itself and the *priorem testamentum* (earlier testament) renewed through it.[16] Charters extended in time indefinitely, and

---

[10] *Lexicon, s.v.* 'quietus'; García-Gallo, 'Bienes', 369–78; Campos, '"Quietus"', 105–7; *cf.* Balzaretti, *Lands*, 269–70, n. 250.

[11] Mattoso, 'Sanctio', 397–428; Domínguez, 'Fórmulas', 475–80; Meyer-Hermann, 'Cambio', 245–89; Carvajal Castro, 'Sanctions', 151–60; *cf.* Kosto, *Agreements*, 121–4.

[12] *León* 24; *Valpuesta* 3; *cf. Sahagún* 429; *Cardeña* 35.

[13] *Eslonza* 1–2, 10, 14–15, 25, 31; 11–12, 16, 19, 22, 26, 32.

[14] *Ourense* 1; *León* 85; *Tumbo Viejo* 135; *cf.* Cabezas Fontanilla and Ávila Seoane, 'Oficina', 64–6.

[15] *Sahagún* 316; *cf. León* 116, 409, 674; *Valpuesta* 34; *Samos* 115, 199; *Ourense* 4; *Guimarães* A1.

[16] *Coruña* 113.

when Egeredus and Rosula, offering a gift to Samos in 960, prayed that no one tamper with their testament and what was noted in its contents, they spoke on behalf of all parties to documents.[17]

The written record mattered, and it had to be defended actively. Clearly the possibility of future dispute focussing on the text was in the mind of the scribe who drafted a donation to Celanova in 995 and added after the penalty that the charter should have perpetual validity in every council and for all time, just as at the end of a sale to Bishop Oveco of León in 939 the vendor Lopo Royo committed himself to vindicating *hanc scriptura* (this document).[18] With the *placitum* particularly, the contract will provide that the parties, in the event of breaking it, must pay a set monetary fine, or even enter into 'slavery' per one case in 985.[19] As sanction clauses anticipated, text might be taken to court, mutilated, or maliciously altered.[20] Payment of one talent of gold *post parti testamenti* (on behalf of the testament) as required by a charter of 882 from Portugal is evocative, but few other sanctions mention any targeted measures.[21] By and large text could look after itself, and one of the two penal applications foreseen for it was to oppose future counterclaims. Typically a sanction expects the granter to vindicate or defend the property against any judicial action, and lays out the penalties for failing to do so: Santo Toribio has a distinctive variant on this condition calling for vindication or defence by means of the charter explicitly, sometimes envisioning the granter taking action alone (after retrieving the charter, or using his or her own copy?), sometimes with the recipient.[22] There is a constant assumption of lasting relevance for written title to property, even when a sale made to Bagaudano and Faquilona in 916 conjures complementary scenarios of the granter Liberius and the text itself proving inadequate in the face of challenge.[23] The corollary of this foreseen future was of course the use of a charter for initiating a claim against others. Fronili undertook in 1029 not to make trouble by any agency or with any charters earlier or later in date, and as Flaviano and Ranimiro promised Oseredo Tructesindiz in their *placitum* of 1016, they would cause no more difficulties, by themselves, via *potestates* (powerful allies), with *scripturas*, or through any action.[24] Such sanctions foreshadow

---

[17] *Samos* 248; cf. *León* 47; *Montes* 4.    [18] *Celanova* 224; *León* 130.
[19] *PMH* 144; cf. *León* 597; *Sahagún* 424; *Valladolid* 3; *Paço de Sousa* 121.
[20] *Ourense* 3; *Sahagún* 336, 391.    [21] *ChLA* 114, 31; cf. *Arouca* 2.
[22] *Liébana* 14, 26, 79; 27, 35; 57, 68.    [23] *Liébana* 23.
[24] *Sahagún* 424; *Coimbra* 202; cf. *León* 887; *Paço de Sousa* 142; Sánchez-Albornoz, 'Imperantes', 352–73.

the reuse of documents in court, and for that they had to be retained and prepared for life long after the moment of their creation.

## Confirmation

The first sign that charters did carry on in active use can be found on the parchments themselves as well as their copies, many of which bear a simple statement or signature added later in validation, support, or renewal. This practice of confirmation has attracted little in the way of dedicated study, primarily in royal diplomas or during the later Middle Ages, but it is central to the afterlife of text in early medieval Iberian society more broadly.[25] It is attested in at least 149 documents or 4% of the corpus, but few notices of confirmation are dated, while most can be dated only approximately based on what is known of the careers of their authors (where they are identifiable). These difficulties are compounded by the comparatively small number of originals, which deprives us of the materials to distinguish between contemporary and posterior subscriptions. The true incidence could therefore be much greater (see Figure 3.1). As a phenomenon, confirmation is mainly represented in the west and centre, and especially in the archives of Samos, Santiago, Eslonza, and Oviedo; this reflects the fact that it features in royal diplomas and ecclesiastical charters, above all those recording donations by kings to monasteries and churches, which are major constituents of the collections. Statistically there are only a few more confirmations on originals than on single-sheet copies because they are a common component of forgeries, ideally suited to endowing texts with spurious written histories. The majority of confirmers after the fact were kings, but members of both the clergy and the laity had an important role too as recipients of confirmations and even authors of their own. Most of the diplomas and charters confirmed are from between the accession of Alfonso III and the death of Ordoño II. This is the formative age of Asturias-León, to which many ecclesiastical foundations traced, or wished to trace, their origins and written histories (see Figure 3.2).

What purpose did confirmation serve? Typically a notice consists of a name, maybe a title, next to *confirmans* or a cognate verb: the simplest explanation is that it was a renewal of the personal relationship established by the

---

[25] Marín Martínez, 'Confirmación', 3, 583–93; Sánchez Belda, 'Notas', 85–116; *cf.* Sanz Fuentes, 'Confirmación', 341–67; Pardo Rodríguez, 'Confirmación', 247–76.

| | Notices | | Overall | |
|---|---|---|---|---|
| | # | % | # | % |
| Total | 149 | 4 | 4095 | 100 |
| Region | | | | |
| West | 78 | 52 | 1284 | 31 |
| Centre | 63 | 42 | 2088 | 51 |
| East | 8 | 5 | 723 | 18 |
| Personnel | | | | |
| Royal | 80 | 54 | 522 | 13 |
| Comital | 2 | 1 | 71 | 2 |
| Ecclesiastical | 64 | 43 | 2710 | 66 |
| Lay | 3 | 2 | 769 | 19 |
| Typology | | | | |
| Donation | 120 | 81 | 2212 | 54 |
| Sale | 8 | 5 | 1469 | 36 |
| Other | 21 | 14 | 411 | 10 |
| Complexity | | | | |
| Simple | 75 | 50 | 2797 | 68 |
| Complex | 74 | 50 | 1292 | 32 |
| Palaeography | | | | |
| Original | 28 | 19 | 888 | 22 |
| Copy | 25 | 17 | 261 | 6 |
| Cartulary | 81 | 54 | 2438 | 60 |
| Other | 15 | 10 | 507 | 12 |
| Diplomatic | | | | |
| Authentic | 123 | 83 | 3781 | 92 |
| Suspicious | 0 | 0 | 24 | 1 |
| Interpolated | 7 | 5 | 57 | 1 |
| Falsified | 19 | 13 | 227 | 6 |

**Figure 3.1** Notices of Confirmation

original act. In juridical terms, at least according to Visigothic law, a charter was revocable, but there is no evidence to suggest that any need to renew its legal force was a spur to action.[26] Beginning with royal diplomas, the most often confirmed, it is essential to draw a clear line (to the degree possible) between confirmations contemporaneous with the transaction and those

---

[26] Sánchez-Albornoz, 'Documentos', 152; Sánchez Belda, 'Notas', 85–90, 115–16; Sánchez-Albornoz, *Orígenes*, 157–90.

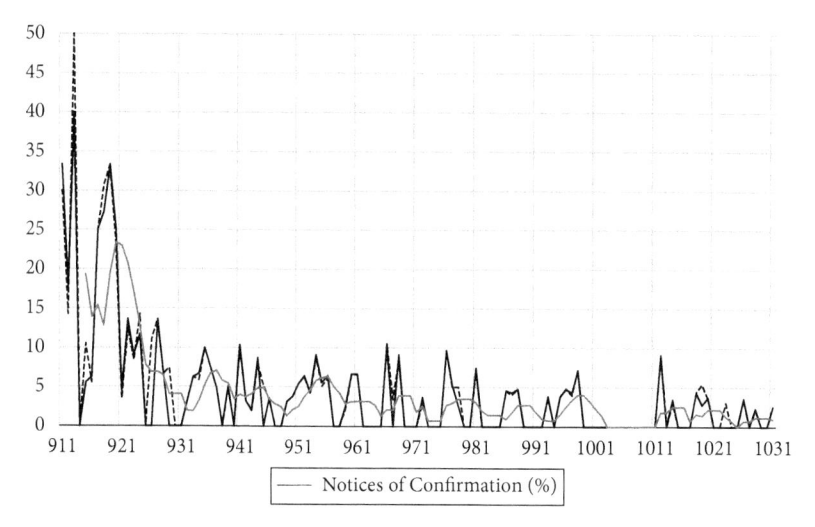

**Figure 3.2** Notices of Confirmation (911–1031)

posterior to it.[27] Every king from Alfonso II onwards (except the short-lived García I) confirmed diplomas issued by his predecessors. The chief practitioners were Ramiro II, Ordoño III, Sancho I, Vermudo II, and Alfonso V: the last three sat on decidedly precarious thrones, and one purpose of confirming must have been to build or rebuild networks of support. Some diplomas have been confirmed once only, others multiple times over. The earliest preserved in the original with a single confirmation is a gift by Ordoño I to Bishop Fronimio of León from 860, which Alfonso III confirmed with a curt *Adefonsus confirmans* and a *signum* beneath the name of his father.[28] It can serve as a model for both technique and timescale: granter and confirmer are normally within one generation. Vermudo III confirmed a testament granted by Alfonso V to Santiago de León in 1012 as *rex prolis Adefonsi* (king and son of Alfonso), affixing his monogram, while Ordoño II affirmed both grants made by his brother García I to the monastery of Eslonza in 912, and Vermudo II did the same for the donation by his uncle Sancho I to Lorvão dating from 966.[29]

---

[27] *León*, 1, 399–405, 2, 362–7; Rodríguez Fernández, *Ramiro*, 667–9; Rodríguez Fernández, *Ordoño*, 305–11; *Alfonso V*, 253–62; Rodríguez Fernández, *Sancho*, 203–5, 209–10; *Documentación*, 83–8, 417–50.

[28] *León* 2; *ChLA* 114, 12; *cf.* Millares Carlo and Ruiz Asencio, *Tratado*, 2, 109.

[29] *León* 708; *Eslonza* 1–2; *Lorvão* 5; *cf. León* 45, 48; *San Isidro* 3, 7; *Pamplona* 9; *Santiago* 17, 29, 33, 44; *Samos* 38, 2; *Celanova* 69, 198, 218; *Lorvão* 41; *Braga* 19.

The notices of confirmation themselves tend to the laconic, but the odd brief formula highlights that it was mainly the dynastic relationship being emphasised by the act. One gift from Ordoño I to Vincentio *presbiter* and Audofredo in 857 includes a statement added later by Alfonso III to the effect that he confirmed it just as his father had done.[30] While most are simple names, some were witnessed by a member or members of the royal family, usually the queen or another close relative: a diploma of Ordoño II from 920 was affirmed by Alfonso IV together with the future Ramiro II, a second of García I from 913 confirmed by Ramiro II and his wife Urraca, while a testament of Ordoño III dating to 954 was attested by Sancho I in the company of two members of his court instead.[31] But documents could evidently remain both of relevance and in circulation well beyond a single generation. One diploma of Ramiro II to Celanova from 949 bears a confirmation by his grandson Vermudo II, dating from at least 36 years later, and another made by Ramiro II to Abellar in 934 bears attestations by Alfonso V and his trusty Sampiro, added almost a century thereafter.[32] For these embattled confirmer kings, the message of a longer-term continuity, belonging to a line of kings stretching far back into the past, would have resonated as they joined their names in the same written space.

In a similar vein, royal diplomas with multiple confirmations not only bear witness to text remaining current over significant spans of time, but also transformed into a medium by which kings articulated dynasty itself. The earliest example is the renowned diploma of Silo from 775, confirmed by Alfonso II and, running over onto the reverse side of the parchment, the full gamut of his successors: Ramiro I, Ordoño I, and Alfonso III, the last a century later if not more.[33] The rather obscure Galician religious community originally favoured with this grant plainly took steps to reaffirm it with each new reign, and acceding to their request was equally clearly part of the performance of Asturian kingship. Alfonso II mounted the throne by a distant relationship to his predecessor, and may have welcomed or even sought here an opportunity to fashion a link to the past, while those who followed his example were joining themselves to his own legacy. The point is less that the descendants of Silo's beneficiaries conferred legitimacy on the new king, though they did implicitly offer him recognition, than that the parchment

[30]  *Samos* 1; cf. *Castañeda* 4; *Ramiro II* 42.
[31]  *León* 51; *Eslonza* 3; *León* 270; cf. *Otero* 196; *San Isidro* 1; *Santiago* 92.
[32]  *Celanova* 85; *León* 101; cf. *Santiago* 38; *Guimarães* 10.
[33]  *León* 1; *ChLA* 114, 11.

of the charter was a space for performing rulership to the ruled.[34] Many royal diplomas from the Leonese period too were confirmed by multiple kings, if not always in consecutive reigns: a gift by the *infante* Ramiro to Valdevimbre from 918 has attestations by Fruela II, Alfonso IV, Sancho I, and Alfonso V, a documentary afterlife spanning nearly a century and witnessing a continuing, albeit discontinuous, dynastic tradition of patronage.[35] Yet parchment could also be an arena for rivalries to play out, and the tumultuous contest of Sancho I and Ordoño IV led both to affix their names, as had Ordoño III before them, to the record of a dispute heard before Ramiro II in 950 and settled in favour of Celanova.[36] On a grant by Ordoño III himself to the monastery of Pardomino from 954, we find not only later confirmations by Sancho I with two bishops and his sister, and Ordoño IV with his wife, but also by Vermudo II, Alfonso V, and even Fernando I a century after the fact (see Figure 3.3).[37] Just as Sancho I, Ramiro III, and Vermudo II tried with a donation by Ordoño III to Santiago from 952, there is an effort here to forge and reforge links with important institutions.[38]

Confirmation had benefits for both parties, but did the initiative for the act come from granter or beneficiary? At the end of a diploma of Ramiro III to Sobrado from 968 there is a note that Alfonso V came to the monastery on 18 April 1017 and confirmed it by hand with his *signum* beside the sign made by his father Vermudo II before him. No ordinary day but the *die cenalis Domini* (day of the Lord's Supper), the timing was surely deliberate, chosen to provide a grandly ceremonial setting.[39] One could imagine such an embattled king in search of allegiances actively seeking out texts to join their living histories, but the evidence cannot take us quite so far. Some coordination at least with Sobrado would have been politic, and we have an example from Guimarães of a confirmation for which beneficiary initiative is stated, yet it looks to the later era of Alfonso VI for the addition of his *roborem* (support).[40] Seldom is it demonstrable one way or the other, still less a case of canny clerical beneficiaries pulling the levers of power to their sole benefit.[41] Take a diploma of Alfonso III to a priest from 875, already signed by Ordoño II and Fruela II: the three bishops who joined Ramiro II

---

[34] Pacheco Sampedro, 'Diploma', 149–67; *cf.* Pacheco Sampedro, 'Arqueología', 2, 59–77; Pacheco Sampedro, 'Tradición', 2, 776–88; Koziol, *Politics*, esp. 17–62, 97–118.

[35] *León* 47; *cf. Santiago* 21, 55; *Celanova* 44, 77, 123.

[36] *Celanova* 86.    [37] *León* 280.    [38] *Santiago* 43.

[39] *Sobrado* 1.107; *cf. Celanova* 9.    [40] *Guimarães* 46.

[41] Sánchez Belda, 'Notas', 111–13; *Documentación*, 83.

**Figure 3.3**  Original charter, posterior notices of confirmation: *León* 280 (León, Archivo Catedralicio, Pergaminos, no. 892)

to confirm it could have been resident at his court, which might suggest an audience granted on a request for confirmation by the descendants of its original beneficiary.[42] The abbot, deacons, priest, notary, and others who joined Sancho I to confirm an exchange made between Ordoño III and San Martín de Fonte de Febro in 956, later confirmed by Ordoño IV and Vermudo II, could be read as denizens of that monastery, which might suggest that the new granter visited for the purpose of confirmation.[43] On the whole, the evidence is equivocal. For beneficiaries, the charter retained its validity, but relationships called for renewal in writing with the passage of time; for kings, itinerancy offered an opportunity and a context for inscription into the actions and networks of their predecessors. Both parties shared an interest in confirming the text.

Royal confirmations can also be found on private charters, but generally by one king only rather than a series. The earliest example is a sale made by a certain Quiza Gonteriquiz to Cakaril, Gondemaro, and Fonsino in 788, much debated as to dating, originality, and even authenticity. The anachronistic appearance of Silus *rex*, the deceased king Silo (774–83), as a confirmer does raise a red flag (and note too that he bears no such title, nor any title at all, in the one diploma in his name), but could be resolved if we imagine a simple error in the date; the attestation by Ramiro I (842–50) poses no problem, and is remarkable on a lay transaction involving only seven cows. If Silo had been involved in guaranteeing or otherwise arranging the sale, he could be present *post mortem* like the ghostly granters we have seen in testaments carried out by executors. As for Ramiro I, unless these were long-lived cows, the sale cannot have been the object of affirmation; descendants of the purchasers were renewing their royal contacts for use in future networking and name-dropping. But the diploma may instead be a confirmation copy issued by Ramiro I, which could account for its anomalies.[44] The practice seems to have been rare: there is only one other confirmed lay charter, a sale by Zahadon and four others to Gondemiro and his wife Susanna from 933 possessing atypical features of its own, not least an anomalous price of 210 *solidos toletanos* (Toledo dirhams?). The land, in the vicinity of Coimbra, had originally been obtained by exchange with Ordoño II, and this sale was witnessed by Ramiro II (unless it was later confirmed by Ramiro III); at the end of the century

[42] *León* 7.  [43] *León* 295; cf. 38, 41; *San Isidro* 8; *San Pelayo* 1.
[44] *Coruña* 1; Lucas Álvarez, 'Paleografía', 444; Sáez and Sáez, 'Diploma', 78–82; cf. *León* 1; *ChLA* 114, 11; Souto Cabo, '"Charte"', esp. 240–5.

Vermudo II added his sign, renewing the 'royal associations' of the property and perhaps thereby enhancing its value.[45] Most single notices, however, appear on ecclesiastical charters, normally donations to monasteries or churches. The habit is documented in earnest from Ordoño II, and its principal exponents were Ramiro II, Sancho I, and Vermudo II, three of the five most regular confirmers of royal diplomas.[46] The rule of one generation applies in the main, as in a donation of Egeredus and Rosula to Samos from 960 which Ramiro III (966–84) confirmed.[47] But there are exceptions in the minority of witnessed confirmations, such as when Ramiro II, two bishops, a *dux*, and a *comes* confirmed a charter of endowment made by Godesteus *presbiter* for a Galician church in 854, nearly a century earlier; and a few disputes involving the Church have royal confirmations spanning a longer time than usual.[48]

The primary purpose of kings confirming private charters was therefore to renew links between the crown and religious institutions, and it is solely on donations to such institutions that we find multiple royal confirmations. Often this occurred within a narrow timeframe: the second testament of Bishop Sisnando to Sobrado, made in 966, was confirmed by Vermudo II *pro memoria* (for his memory), then by his son Alfonso V, who in confirming records how he travelled to the monastery with his notary Fulgentius for that purpose specifically in 1017, on the same day as he reaffirmed another of its diplomas.[49] We have already seen how Sancho I and Ordoño IV affixed their signs to major private endowments for Celanova from 942 and 951 in their struggle for its allegiance and support, and this is emblematic of the dynamic of confirmation.[50] But it is difficult to be certain of cases where the kings involved were more remote from each other: a donation made by Visclafredus *sacerdos et abba* to the monastery of Rosende from 874 seems to have been confirmed later by Ordoño II (or III), Ramiro II (or III), and Vermudo II (or III), but the date is in error for around 951 and these may instead be contemporary confirmations.[51] Similarly, a testament bequeathed by Gundesindus and three others to Lorvão in 919 was confirmed successively by Ordoño II (or III), Ramiro II (or III), Sancho I, and Vermudo II

[45] *Lorvão* 7; Chalmeta, 'Précisions', 316.   [46] *Documentación*, 451–85.
[47] *Samos* 248; cf. *León* 278, 709; *Eslonza* 7; *San Isidro* 10; *San Juan* 9; *Samos* 210, 23; *Sobrado* 1.2; *Celanova* 174; *Lorvão* 19, 46, 29.
[48] *Samos* 99; cf. *León* 75, 93, 333, *Samos* 61, 27; *León* 191, *Oviedo* 26, *Santiago* 42.
[49] *Sobrado* 1.6.
[50] *Celanova* 72, 91; cf. *León* 220; *Celanova* 53, 185; *Lorvão* 61; *Coimbra* 56.
[51] *Samos* S1; *Lugo*, 2, 555–65; cf. *San Isidro* 15; *Arlanza* 5.

(or III), across at least 60 years, but it is clearly a copy and has raised concerns as to its authenticity.[52] Nonetheless, the written word in its afterlife provided a canvas for composing narratives of succession and legitimacy, and such notices do at least chime with the evidence of diplomas and charters confirmed singly that text stayed in active circulation for as long as both granters and beneficiaries could benefit from it.

Confirmation of earlier documents with names, titles, and *signa* was also undertaken by ecclesiastics and the laity, but how often in comparison with kings is unclear. No obvious chronological pattern is perceptible in the six identifiable charters confirmed after the fact by bishops: a donation by Abbot Cipriano to Santiago de León from 944 bears the confirmation of Velasco of León from 20 to 30 years later, whereas the testament made by Bishop Ranulfo to San Pedro de Montes in 892 was attested by Fortis of Astorga in the 920s, then by Gonzalo in the late tenth century.[53] Three of the other four instances are dubious, but the last is suggestive, a charter recording the restoration of San Antolín in Güimir by Abbot Diego in 1026. Bishop Pedro of Astorga consecrated the basilica in 1030, and confirmed the earlier document in the company of eight priests and a dozen others; some such ceremonial could be the context for most or all of these episcopal acts.[54] For non-royal confirmations in general, family was in many cases the connection, and after the inventory and testament drawn up by Abbot Offiloni and companions for Samos in 872, we read that Visterla *diaconus* confirmed the document in accordance with what his forebears had done.[55] The donation by Terenzanus *presbiter* to Abellar from 960 has a codicil to the effect that, after his death, *gens* (relations) from Valdesogo and the brothers of the monastery witnessed its validation and confirmation, while the testament of the religious woman Velasquita to Santa María de Mezonzo from 988 records Teobaldus visiting later to confirm his mother's pious act.[56] One exceptional case is a dispute of 995 which describes how Citi Lucidi had forced Senta to surrender all his property by *cartula conscripta* (a charter written up), then fled with rebels to Portugal; a royal council voided that document and Senta left his lands to Samos, but per a postscript the villain came back, confessed, and confirmed the testament before witnesses.[57] There is a belief here in the charter as a living record, to be updated as

---

[52] *PMH* 22; Azevedo, 'Mosteiro', 184, 190–1, 200; Fernández Catón, 'Documentación', 2, 478–83 (4).
[53] *León* 180; *Montes* 2.      [54] *Samos* 7; cf. *Coruña* 12, 27; *Diócesis* 1.
[55] *Samos* 5.      [56] *León* 329; *Celanova* 203; cf. *León* 338.
[57] *Samos* S9; *Lugo*, 2, 585–90.

circumstances changed, and if we knew episcopal histories and lay identities like the reigns of kings no doubt more such confirmations would emerge. But we can conclude that all took active part in the afterlife of documents, in which granters, beneficiaries, family, and followers renewed their relations through text.

## Augmentation

Charters gave rise to further charters, and another sign that they continued in use past the first moment of writing is the range of additional texts which confirmation generated. The most basic means of confirming a charter was by issuing a new one to say so, and if the reign of Alfonso VII (1126–57) is its 'golden age', the practice is well attested in the early medieval period.[58] In 998, a council presided over by Vermudo II confiscated property from rebels and handed it over to the notary Sampiro; on 13 July 1020, according to a statement at the end of the diploma, Alfonso V confirmed it before the *armiger regis* (royal armsbearer), two monks of the palace, and others in León. Since from top to bottom, notice of confirmation included, it is written by one hand in a Visigothic cursive script characteristic of Alfonsine diplomas, it is clearly a notarial transcription, and indeed it informs us that many witnesses to the original have not been recorded in this copy.[59] There are sufficient cases from the tenth century to the early eleventh for us to conclude that confirmation through transcription developed as a habit in these years, multiplying documentation with time, though they are partly unacknowledged. The donation and sale by Eugenius *diaconus* to Abellar from 923 is a 'contemporary copy' in the eyes of its editor: the later attestation which it bears by Alfonso IV and a bishop could be the context for its production.[60] The diploma made by Ordoño III to the religious community of Pardomino in 954 has been confirmed repeatedly, by Vermudo II and Alfonso V amongst others, but all in the same script as the scribe of the main text, an odd coincidence unless it is a copy prepared at the time of the latest intervention.[61] Further 'confirmation copies' can be detected even where palaeographic analysis of an original is impossible. The donation made by Felix *presbiter* to San Miguel Arcángel de León in 1021 has an

---

[58]  Sánchez Belda, 'Notas', 92–3; see *e.g. San Esteban* 1.
[59]  *León* 581; Carriedo Tejedo, 'Diploma', 71–2; Carriedo Tejedo, 'Documentos', 155–203.
[60]  *León* 58.      [61]  *León* 280; *cf. VDJ* 2.

additional clause dated to 1029, recording that the granter reaffirmed his gift and presented more liturgical objects and books; only the witnesses to this second act are listed, suggesting that those to the first were not copied over into its confirmation, which has in turn been transmitted to us via cartulary.[62] The document whereby Gutier and Ilduara restored Santa María de Loyo in 927 now includes a later family confirmation and donation in memory of Gutier after his death; this could be an interpolation as its editor supposes, yet beneath four names of contemporary and later kings is a note that bishops and others may be found *in carta vetera* (in the old charter), a comment of the cartulary copyist, perhaps, or possibly a giveaway sign of another 'confirmation copy'.[63]

Further testimony to the ongoing accessibility of text comes from an alternative mode of making a charter of confirmation, by writing it directly onto the original parchment instead of in a new copy. When in 986 sundry relations confirmed the donation made a decade earlier by Adrianus and Leokadia to a monastery of Santa Marina, they chose to situate the record of it in the blank space next to the columns of witnesses to that act, while the Gordón dispute of 953 bears an endorsement by Florentina, a relative of one of the defeated parties, added onto the lower left of the parchment in 981.[64] Beyond the ability to consult and complement prior written acts, this presupposes ongoing awareness of their existence and provisions, that texts were common knowledge. The first known *fuero*, a set of rights and responsibilities granted by Count Munio Núñez to Brañosera in 824, was confirmed three times in succession by the counts of Castilla—Gonzalo Fernández in 912, Fernán González in 968, and Sancho García in 998—each with the formula that he saw this charter and confirms it. Much about the form and content of this document is debated, but all four components are transmitted together in one copy by an early modern archivist, supposedly from an eleventh-century source, which could indicate that they were originally to be found on the same parchment.[65] Comparable to this is a donation by Riquilo to Abellar from 955, preserved in a cartulary copy but with the text of a confirmation in the presence of three brothers on 11 February 965 at its conclusion.[66] Another donation made by Vermudo to Valpuesta in 957–58 also describes how Proclina

[62] *León* 777; cf. *Celanova* 25; *Huesca* 10; *Vega* 2.      [63] *Celanova* 29; cf. *Pamplona* 10.
[64] *Otero* 21, 26; cf. *León* 10, 330; Davies, *Windows*, 1–5, 146–7.
[65] *Arlanza* 1; García-Gallo, 'Carta', 1–11; Martínez Díez, 'Fuero', 31–47, 59–65; see now Baró Pazos, *Fueros*, 61–8; Ruiz Asencio *et al.*, *Fuero*.
[66] *León* 293, 385.

and Anderazo, after the death of their brother, went to the church and confirmed the transaction a year later, affixing signs to it in the presence of the original witnesses: they even received an honorarium for their trouble, suggesting one strategy by which beneficiaries anxious for extra security might go about getting it.[67] Some such confirmations also involved new transactions, and in the course of Aloytus giving a gift to his wife Paterna in 965 a document was added to the lower right of the parchment relating how one of the confirmers had met with *previsores* (inspectors) to apportion the land; further subscriptions were then written around it.[68]

Standard practice for confirming a charter was by means of a subsequent but separate document, a charter of confirmation in the strict sense. Creation involved consulting one text to create another, and this act accounts for 124 charters or 3% of the corpus (see Figure 3.4). The type is most concentrated at Santiago and Samos in the west, at Oviedo in the centre, and at San Juan, Arlanza, Albelda, and Oña in the east. These collections contain notable numbers of royal and comital diplomas, but also forgeries, both features associated with confirmations; authentic originals are rare. The earliest example comes from 811, while distribution over the Leonese period is even, with no trend indicating innovation or falling out of use (see Figure 3.5). One precious account of 1020 walks through the confirmation process step by step. Fernando Flaínez, brother of Pedro Flaínez from the Otero charters, had founded the monastery of San Martín de Pereda with his wife Elvira, and after a time petitioned Alfonso V to confirm their endowment of it; this he agreed to do in return for a horse with saddle and harness. Donating more property to their foundation, they then recognised the king's confirmation in an *agnitio et confirmatio testamenti* (attestation of a testament), in the presence of sundry relatives and the bishop of León. All gathered together at the *castello* of Aguilar del Esla, they listened as the documentation was read aloud, and affixed signs 'once again' to this new charter.[69] They had seemingly witnessed the original too, in a process extending over multiple texts.

Yet these figures understate the regularity of documentary confirmation, because of a frequent mismatch between what a charter calls itself and what

---

[67] *Valpuesta* 35; cf. *Albelda* 20, 25; *Sobrado* 1.107.
[68] *Coruña* 71; cf. 29; *Sobrado* 1.115–16; *San Isidro* 15–16; *Astorga* 10, 14–16.
[69] *Benevívere* 1; Martínez Sopena, 'Relaciones', 79–81.

| | Charters | | Overall | |
|---|---|---|---|---|
| | # | % | # | % |
| Total | 124 | 3 | 4095 | 100 |
| Citing Charters | | | | |
| Total | 60 | 48 | 620 | 15 |
| Region | | | | |
| West | 47 | 38 | 1284 | 31 |
| Centre | 31 | 25 | 2088 | 51 |
| East | 46 | 37 | 723 | 18 |
| Personnel | | | | |
| Royal | 77 | 62 | 522 | 13 |
| Comital | 10 | 8 | 71 | 2 |
| Ecclesiastical | 32 | 26 | 2710 | 66 |
| Lay | 3 | 2 | 769 | 19 |
| Complexity | | | | |
| Simple | 0 | 0 | 2797 | 68 |
| Complex | 124 | 100 | 1292 | 32 |
| Palaeography | | | | |
| Original | 6 | 5 | 888 | 22 |
| Copy | 19 | 15 | 261 | 6 |
| Cartulary | 76 | 61 | 2438 | 60 |
| Other | 23 | 19 | 507 | 12 |
| Diplomatic | | | | |
| Authentic | 78 | 63 | 3781 | 92 |
| Suspicious | 3 | 2 | 24 | 1 |
| Interpolated | 7 | 6 | 57 | 1 |
| Falsified | 36 | 29 | 227 | 6 |

**Figure 3.4** Charters of Confirmation

it actually does.[70] Sometimes there is complete consistency. In 945, for example, Bishop Oveco of León issued a *scriptura agnitionis et confirmationis* (document of recognition and confirmation) to Sahagún: brothers of the monastery had brought him a charter of *perfiliatio* and a testament, still surviving, from the *infante* Ramiro, and he confirmed them.[71] Similar terminology is used in the account of a great *exquisitio* (inquest) held at

[70] Martín López, 'Léxico', 142–3.
[71] *Sahagún* 101 (see 12–13); *cf.* 404 (6); *Liébana* 75 (58); *Cardeña* 37.2 (37.1); *Valpuesta* 6; *Celanova* 30.

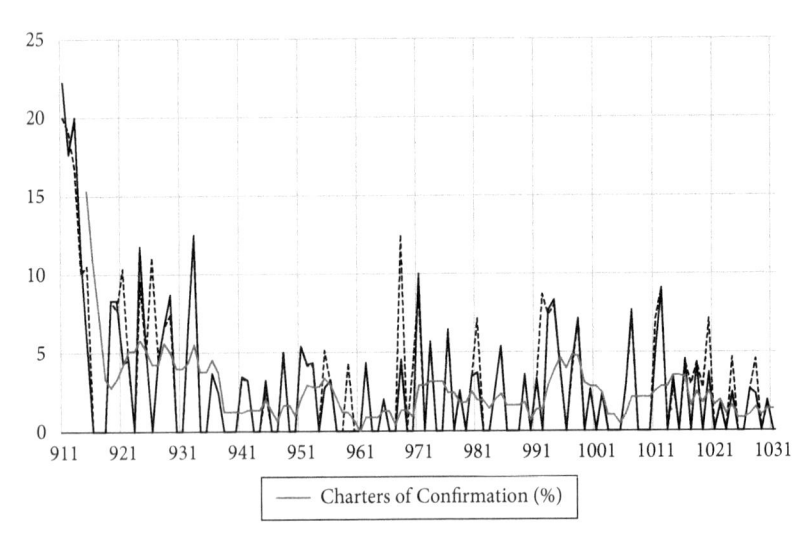

**Figure 3.5** Charters of Confirmation (911–1031)

Santiago before Alfonso V in 1019, which took oaths from a host of *seniori-bus prioribus* (elders?) of the see before reaffirming eight of its royal diplomas, from Alfonso II down to Vermudo II.[72] But in many cases, a charter not labelled as such turns out to be a confirmation. Take the *kartula dona-tionis vel comutationis* (charter of donation or exchange) made by Verisimo and Salvatore to Bellite *presbiter* in 999, which in fact confirms a *perfiliatio* by their mother in return for some property, or a *seriens testamenti* (sequence of testament) granted by Vermudo II to San Andrés de Pardomino in 985, which concedes tax or rents from the Esla basin per the testament of his predecessors to that monastery.[73] Senioldus even saw the *testamentum conscriptum* (written testament) of Didacus and Argilo held in the hands of Abbot Albaro of Santillana in 962, and nonetheless called the document confirming it a simple testament.[74] Subtle distinctions may be at work behind the scenes: in the first case the beneficiary seems in effect to have purchased a confirmation, which implies real value to having extra documentation. But regardless of how they were presented and described, these acts reaffirmed prior charters, renewing and extending relationships through text.

---

[72] *Santiago* 61.
[73] *León* 585, 506; *cf.* 40; *Sahagún* 26 (24); *San Isidro* 3; *Albelda* 29 (8); *Sobrado* 1.108; *Celanova* 110.
[74] *Santillana* 5.

One final form of confirmation took place in the context of dispute settlement, where confirming a charter may even have been the object of going to court. Boundaries were often at stake, and Vermudo II recounts in a diploma to Samos from 993 how his predecessors had made testaments to the monastery demarcating its lands which malicious men had infringed, forcing him to dispatch agents to retrace the limits, while litigation between the *villa* of Santa María de Verín and its neighbours in 950 twice required involvement by officials, first royal then local, to establish its bounds with landmarks, and a charter issued the next year records *previsores* inspecting and confirming this perimeter.[75] Another dispute between Sahagún and relatives of Liubila *presbiter* over the disposition of his testament was in contrast resolved by producing and confirming the original text, and the narrative concludes that the *fedus novum* (new contract) was made precisely in order to bring *scandalum* (discord) to an end *per hunc scriptum* (through this document).[76] Like at a *Scheinprozess* or mock trial, argumentation is noticeably absent or irrelevant, controversy as to the facts superficial or non-existent, raising the possibility that the victorious parties here, in the first case at least if not all three, were in reality testing their written title, proving it in the full sense of *probatio* to deny the defeated parties any avenue to future appeal.[77] Charters were by definition permanent, but one could never be too careful. Iohannes and his wife Flamula explained in 941 how they had made a testament to Bishop Cixila and Abellar, but Melic *presbiter* had seduced them into recalling and voiding it and making a new one to him; after realising the error of their ways, they had decided to reconfirm their original act.[78] The premise for most court cases involving written evidence was violation of it by a third party, and the typical outcome was its restoration. In 1012, when Teodemirus of Santiago de León appealed to Alfonso V to restore a *villa* which his monastery held by testament but had wrongly been taken under royal administration, the king agreed without demur and issued a fresh charter of the property.[79] Some of these cases will have been 'real', others going through the motions, but that was the point. Confirmation provided an opportunity for reinforcing the relationships of persons and property which the documentation recorded. Doing so in the context of dispute, where if not always the purpose it was invariably an

---

[75] *Celanova* 88, 94; *Samos* 40; *cf.* 46.     [76] *Sahagún* 276; *cf.* 183.
[77] Collins, 'Law', 496–8; but see Kano, 'Procès', 329–53; Murray, 'Trial', 297–327.
[78] *León* 147.     [79] *León* 708; *cf.* 707.

outcome, offered a greater audience and higher social pressure to build consensus around the written word as it was cycled into the next stage of its afterlife.

## Preservation

In the language of expectation and the practice of confirmation, the charter remained in active circulation long after it was written, and this depended on organised safekeeping. At the present stage of its transmission history, the corpus of documentation is divided amongst 28 major and many more minor supporting archival collections. By rearranging the charters by their original beneficiaries, however, we can partly reconstruct the much greater range of archives which existed in early medieval Iberia—or rather that fraction selected for survival in the winnowing of years (see Appendix 7). The Church still bulks large: nearly three quarters of the charters as preserved for us were in the first instance addressed to a religious institution. We have three or more texts for 109 different monasteries or churches, fully half of them located in the centre, the other half in the west or the east. Some of these were very substantial houses indeed, and 20 or more documents survive from 29 such institutional archives. Celanova in Galicia has the largest, as recipient of 280 charters (not to be confused with the 383 charters which make up its published early medieval corpus), closely trailed by 260 for Sahagún in León (to be distinguished from the 432 in its modern edition). Over time, as we have seen, the larger houses absorbed many of the smaller original collections and are now containers for them, though in some Leonese cases, like the 180 charters for Abellar, it was the episcopal see which incorporated them into its archive. The overall predominance of monasteries and churches reflects the decisions which they made in their role as stewards of the corpus down to the nineteenth century, but the remaining charters, nearly a quarter of the total, have individuals—both ecclesiastical and lay—as their initial beneficiaries. This is our first sign that personal archiving was common practice in the early Middle Ages too.[80]

The identifiable personal archives are concentrated in the centre, where we are not so reliant on the cartularies of monasteries and churches for transmission of texts. Regrettably, there is nothing comparable to the

---

[80] Kosto, 'Practices', 269–81.

extraordinary *rotulae* of Benasque and Ballabriga, which document the business affairs of the twice-widowed Sancha in the Ribagorza valleys during the first half of the eleventh century, and hint at a surviving matriarchal organisation of local society.[81] These consist respectively of 70 and 27 original charters sewn together in two rolls, though whether the arrangement was the work of Sancha and her agents or a product of when the properties concerned passed into the ownership of the monastery of Obarra is difficult to determine.[82] What we do have is a roster of 34 individual ecclesiastical beneficiaries with multiple documents surviving in their name, such as 13 charters addressed to Melic, priest-at-large in the mid-tenth century in the environs of Sahagún, or ten to the Leonese priest Munnio from the 970s.[83] In all probability, more such archives are implicit in institutional collections, because this total, unexpectedly, is far smaller than the 95 lay archives, accounting for over four times as many documents and including numerous quite sizeable dossiers belonging to the élite.[84] There are ten aristocratic couples, many of whom we have met, each represented by at least 11 charters, most notably the 59 for Pedro Fláinez and his wife Bronildi, and the 53 for Fruela Muñoz and his wife Amuna: both were based around Otero de las Dueñas and remained active well after the cut-off date of our study, their descendants going on to found that monastery.[85] Other major archives include Hermegildo and his wife Paterna in Galicia, whose monastic foundation of Sobrado held 45 of their charters.[86] There are 14 documents for Bagaudano and his wife Faquilona, local élites of the Liébana, which passed via their son Abbot Opila into the hands of what became Santo Toribio.[87] And the same applies to Gutier and Ilduara, whose archive of 15 charters entered the family monastery of Celanova, joining the documentation of their son San Rosendo, its abbot and bishop.[88] In all these cases, earlier lay archives were carried over into later ecclesiastical foundations.[89] For some, however, the precise channels whereby the papers have survived are not obvious. Munio Fernández and his wife Elvira, for instance, made at least

---

[81] Galtier Martí, *Ribagorza*, 148–53; Collins, *Caliphs*, 215–16; Tomás-Faci, *Montañas*, esp. 82–8; *cf. Sobrarbe* 4–11.

[82] Martín Duque, *Obarra*, xv–xxv; Tomás-Faci, 'Construcción', 92–4.

[83] Carbajo Serrano, *Monasterio*, 165–7; Casado Quintanilla, 'Melic', 48–9; *cf.* Fernández Flórez, 'Documentos', 110–15.

[84] Calleja-Puerta, 'Archivos', 9–36; Calleja-Puerta, 'Sources', 105–16; Pérez, 'Posibilidades', 1–12.

[85] García Leal, 'Archivo', 121–8; García Leal, 'Condes', esp. 7–19, 64–70.

[86] Pallares Méndez, *Monasterio*, 29–43, 71–6; Portela and Pallares, 'Elementos', 17–32.

[87] Pontieri, 'Familia', 119–29; Loring García, 'Nobleza', 93–100; Portass, *World*, 66–96.

[88] García Álvarez, 'Gutier', 119–53; Díaz y Díaz, 'Rosendo', 73–84; Portass, *World*, 133–52.

[89] Blasco, 'Monasterio', 13–26.

one gift of their property to a religious house, and their 21 charters have been preserved in the collections of Leonese monasteries and churches, but others such as Fruela Velaz and his wife Jimena, with eight charters to their name from León and Sahagún, are relative transients in the historical record, known solely through those texts.[90] Frustratingly, this last category is the most common, and can be augmented by the remaining 12% of the corpus comprised of charters addressed to miscellaneous beneficiaries, uniquely attested. What it nevertheless serves to demonstrate is that, beyond ecclesiastical institutions, plenty of individuals received documents and held onto them carefully for future use.

Even without this highly schematic and preliminary reconstruction of contemporary archives, the charters themselves hint at their existence and operation at the individual level. One document from 1008 records a dispute over ownership of a *villa* being decided against Bishop Jimeno of Astorga, and in favour of Munio Fernández, through an oath in support of written evidence. It is quite exceptionally rare for the Church to lose out to a member of the laity in a settlement, at least as we have them: since only the victor had a reason to hold onto this text, it must originally have formed part of his own papers.[91] Another charter from 1019 describes how Alfonso V confiscated property from two homicides and presented it to Cidi Domneliz; the account of the more formal judicial proceedings held a year later is stitched to the same parchment, conceivably an archival unity dating back to when both texts were kept together by their lay beneficiary.[92] What happened next will have varied with happenstance or circumstance. In 1008, for example, Martino made a sale to Xemena and Fernando *frater*: the rubric in the cartulary labels it a charter of San Juan de Corniero, and the two appear in a subsequent transaction alongside a Michael, *frater* of San Juan, which implies that they were monastic agents whose individual archive was incorporated at some stage into their house.[93] Such cases are illuminating, but the most consistent sign of a personal collection remains the survival of a series of charters with beneficiaries of identical (or similar) name, properties in the same area (or close by), and proximate dates. To name just two, Ederonio Alvitiz and his wife Crastina made six purchases of land in the *villa* of Custóias over the first decade of

---

[90] *León* 701; Torre Sevilla-Quiñones de León, 'Munio', 149–72; *cf.* Rodríguez Fernández, 'Notas', 2, 145–53.
[91] *León* 669; *cf. Astorga* 212; *Paço de Sousa* 142; Durany Castrillo and Rodríguez González, 'Obispado', 191–201.
[92] *León* 760, 772.     [93] *Sahagún* 393–4.

the eleventh century, while Advocatus and his wife Leovilli twice did likewise in the middle of the tenth.[94] They are the 'middling sort', the small proprietors otherwise unknown, who had need of and held onto written records the same as the great monasteries, churches, and élites did with theirs.[95] We cannot lose sight of them simply because they are hard to see.

## Consolidation

How were these institutional and individual archives formed? The process was set in motion by the transactions which charters themselves record: once the text had been written up, it was delivered into the safekeeping of its beneficiary. In his bequest of 1018 to Santiago de León, the notary Sampiro describes how he confirmed the testament before a multitude of the faithful, then placed it onto the altar of the monastery, not unlike when Bishop Reccared, confirming the endowment of Piasca by Theoda and Aragonti in 930, consecrated the charter which had been brought to the church in his very presence.[96] In 995, the pious widow Faquilo could not make the journey to deliver her charter donating a monastery to Vermudo II in person on account of her age and infirmity; instead it was drawn up in Bárzana (Asturias) before several bishops who then delivered it to the king at Astorga for completion.[97] Whether by the granter or some agent, physical handover of parchment is explicitly attested as a matter of course.[98] But many of these notices also take a step farther to state its transfer to the recipient for preservation in an archive. Velasco *presbiter* is illustrative, declaring in a donation to the abbot of Congosto from 950 that *reponimus* (we set down) the document *in arcis* (in the chests or boxes).[99] This formula is characteristic of charters from Buezo de Bureba, delivered to the church and stored in its archives, just as a Gundesalvus, on the far side of the Peninsula, says that he placed his testament to the monastery of Guimarães in the *thesauris* (treasuries) of the basilica in 983.[100] Some documentation from the west even identifies the beneficiary, suggestively, as the actual archive: Elarinus and

[94] *Coimbra* 518, 523, 204, 207, 529, 527; 530, 205.     [95] Portass, 'Sort', 111.
[96] *León* 756; *Sahagún* 39; *cf. Lugo* 8, 34; *Tumbo Viejo* 111.
[97] *Tumbo Viejo* 141; Carriedo Tejedo, 'Nacimiento', 149–50.
[98] See *e.g. Sahagún* 101, 164; *Albelda* 19; *Samos* 248; *Sobrado* 1.52; *Celanova* 154; *Coimbra* 139; Rodríguez-Escalona, 'Gestos', 804–5.
[99] *Covarrubias* 1.
[100] *Valpuesta* 22–3, 26–7; *Guimarães* 68, A6; *cf. Sobrado* 1.43; *Lugo* 28; *Pallares* 1.

Gundilo, in a charter to Samos from 931, donated half their property *in archivis vestris* (into your archives) with permanent effect, thereby equating the maintenance of the transaction in effect with the ongoing preservation of its written record.[101]

Narrative accounts of consulting charters not only confirm this picture of beneficiary archiving, but also reveal the accessibility of archived text. In 1026, the bishop of León told of *perexquirens* (investigating) the charters and testaments of his see on assuming office and discovering that a *villa* belonging to it had been seized by an outlaw count during the recent period of unrest; he successfully appealed to the king for restoration.[102] The majority of cases come from Santiago, whose bishops were careful custodians of their documentation. Sancho Ordóñez visited in 927 and Bishop Hermegildo read out loud the testaments of his ancestors *recondita in tesauris Apostoli* (put away in the treasuries of the Apostle) for his confirmation, while Ramiro II, on inquiring in 934 what his ancestors had given to Compostela, was shown testaments dating back to the reign of Alfonso II, and added one of his own.[103] The *exquisitio* held there in 1019 had the purpose of confirming eight royal diplomas by oath, and noted that all documentation of the episcopal patrimony was kept in its archive.[104] The effort had already proved worth it in a dispute with a local lord over division of property amongst intermarried dependants in 999, when Bishop Pedro was able to argue before Vermudo II that the relevant testaments, confirmed in the treasury of Santiago, must not be voided.[105] Conflict at court was the principal spur to consulting such holdings, and when the same bishop confronted Bishop Pelayo of Lugo in the late tenth century, the latter claimed for *familia vel plebs* (dependants) of Sobrado by presenting *noticias per nomina eorum* (lists of their names) which he found *in scriniis vel thesaurum* (in the cases or treasury) of his episcopal church.[106] His successor tried the same tack, albeit more speculatively, in 1025, undertaking to furnish *scripturas veredigas* (truthful documents), if he could locate them in the treasury, in support of reclaiming *servos* (slaves?) alienated from the see.[107] But crucially for disputing, it was not only the beneficiary who remembered the whereabouts of the archived text: when Iohannes and his wife Flamula

---

101  *Samos* 119; *cf. Sobrado* 1.33; *Coimbra* 454; Henriet, 'Lettre', 164.
102  *León* 829; *cf.* Ruiz Asencio, 'Obispos', 181–210.     103  *Santiago* 51, 40.
104  *Santiago* 61.     105  *Santiago* 58.
106  *Sobrado* 1.109; *cf.* Carzolio, 'Reflexiones', 36–43.
107  *Braga* 22; Díaz de Bustamante, 'Pastores', 435–48.

decided to void their testament to Abellar in 941, they arranged for it to be returned from the monastery, where it evidently remained accessible to both granter and recipient.[108]

Archives formed at a secondary level, in that when the charter of a transaction passed into the hands of the beneficiary, it tended to be accompanied by past charters relevant to the property involved, as consolidation of ownership entailed the merging of documentation. The records of gift or sale regularly describe joint transfer of both land and charter, such as in 921 when Taion donated to Sahagún property given him by Ordoño II, stating that its boundaries were those in the text which the king had made for him and he now handed to the monastery, or in 833 when Galindo Aznárez I of Aragón gifted land to Siresa with *mea ipsa scriptura* (my very own document), stipulating that its appurtenances and limits were *sicut textus scripture ipse continetur* (just as the text of the document itself contains).[109] The practice is particularly common in the west, and at times uses language encompassing the whole written history of that property. This could be land handed over with *omnibus suis scriptis* (all its documents), as in a donation concerning Samos in 1009, or with *pactos atque testamentos et cartas* (pacts and testaments and charters), as in the background to an exchange involving Santiago in 955; the endowment of Rosende included men in the patronage of Visclamondus with the charters in their possession, while Giloyra, granting a testament to Celanova in 962, confirmed it with *quantum cartas quas in manu fratrum ponimus* (as many charters as we place in the hands of the brothers).[110] But more specific terminology suggests that real papers were in mind. When priests of the Galician monastery of San Andrés donated it to Celanova in 1002, they handed in its documents and *firmitates* (confirmations), notably the founding testament which Abbot Salamirus had made of the site where it was built.[111] Tructesindo Guimiriz clearly had a full chain of title deeds before him when defending his property against Ruderigo Froilaz at court in 1011. He related how Davi and his wife Animie had acquired it through a written *anutione* (recognition), then sold it along with that text to Scemena *per cartula venditionis* (by charter of sale); she in turn had bestowed the property and both documents on her

[108] *León* 147.
[109] *Sahagún* 24, 19; *Huesca* 3; *cf. León* 746; *Sahagún* 273; *Oviedo* 8.
[110] *Samos* 64; *Sobrado* 1.110; *Lugo*, 2, 555–65; *Celanova* 154; *cf. Samos* 61, 98; *Celanova* 192; *Lorvão* 22.
[111] *Celanova* 261; *cf. Samos* 227; *Sobrado* 1.134; *Celanova* 263; *Guimarães* 1A, A3; *Coimbra* 134.

children, and they had finally made a charter of donation of it and all its many records to him.[112]

This phenomenon of 'land and text' must be the cause of a semantic slippage whereby possession of one or the other became interchangeable. Take the donation made by Sampiro to Santiago de León in 1018, which records how he purchased from Ascarigus *magister* both a *villa* and the charter by which he had acquired it from Vermudo II, then also received another charter of confirmation from Queen Elvira after she had briefly seized it: the verb of buying governs both objects.[113] Similarly, when Elena gave property to her cousin Bello in 962, she noted that her father Vigilane had sold it to another cousin by a charter which she herself had then bought from him.[114] Near death, Valasco came to Guimarães in 1022 and handed Abbot Honoricus a document by which he had been granted a church for his lifetime, requesting that it be reconfirmed to his grandson on like terms; both records, of this transaction as well as of the original grant, are copied consecutively in the monastic cartulary, demonstrating that the earlier charter was in fact transferred to the new owner.[115] Presumably because it was utterly routine, however, this process of passage was often left implicit or understood. Ansur and his wife María made a testament to Sahagún in 963 of a meadow which they had purchased from Tota: the charter of sale documenting the earlier transaction in 961 is now in the collection of the monastery, called up from their own lay archive and handed over at that moment.[116] This dynamic repeated over the centuries, and we need to imagine further the wholesale transfer of individual into institutional archives in comparable contexts. Jimena and her son Gonzalo, for example, made two donations to Sahagún late in the tenth century, including estates inherited from her parents Munio Flaínez and Froileuva, and the monastic archive now has 20 of their charters too.[117] Vistrilli did likewise to San Martín de Turieno in 951, which explains how it came to have three documents of her parents Munio and Gulatrudia as well.[118] Such transfers reflect the ongoing relevance of the written record, the need to have the full textual history of a property to hand, but they have also over time condensed this multiplicity of archives into a handful, diminishing and disguising the archival habit of early medieval Iberia.

---

[112] *PMH* 216.    [113] *León* 756.
[114] *Sahagún* 206; cf. *Samos* 64, 82; *Sobrado* 1.130; *Celanova* 44.    [115] *Guimarães* 61, 60.
[116] *Sahagún* 215, 194; cf. 245, 216; Kosto, 'Practices', 273–4, 279.
[117] *Sahagún* 328, 345; Carvajal Castro, 'Sociedad', 114–15.    [118] *Liébana* 54; 19–20, 38.

Charters could alternatively or additionally be archived with third parties, but there is little evidence that this was to the detriment or exclusion of their beneficiaries. The exception to the rule comes in a dispute from 952, in which Velasco claimed to have documentation at the *recluso* (cloister) of an *infante* or prince contradicting what the monastery of Abellar had offered in evidence, but when he and Abbot Severo went looking for it they found nothing.[119] In 960, the disposition of the estate of Melic *presbiter* entailed another hunt for his testament, and the executors tracked down a *notitia* (draft) in the hands of Adulfum *frater*, apparently on a wax tablet; this charter, however, shows signs of tampering.[120] The walls separating 'the Church' from the world around it were not so high, given that the laity maintained close ties of *familiaritas* with monasteries and churches, founding, entering, owning, and bequeathing them in furtherance of family proprietorial strategy.[121] Both texts, if they ever existed, could have been filed intentionally as backup copies in 'friendly' houses. An unusual narrative from Samos dated to 944 conjures just such a repository whence lost diplomas could be restored as needed. During his restoration of the monastery, Berila sent two brothers to petition Fruela II and Bishop Oveco of León for a *cartario* (cartulary) stored in the *thesauro* of San Salvador de Oviedo, the cathedral treasury, and containing copies of lost *firmitates* (confirmations); the request was approved, and some 59 *kartas* (charters) to the house were recovered, amongst them testaments from as far back as the reign of Alfonso II.[122] This archive at the old royal capital seems to have played a 'public' role in preserving the written record, and Samos was not the only monastery to make use of the facility. Gutier and Eloitus indicate in a document of 932 that their ancestor Aloitus, who founded Santa María de Cambre, had *omnes ipsas scripturas testamenti vel benefacti* (all the documents of testament or gift) filed at Oviedo for protection and preservation; when the monks managed to lose many of those, their father paid 500 silver *solidi* to Alfonso III, who *reduxit* (re-sent) them, and they ultimately passed together with the church itself into the stewardship of Antealtares.[123] It is hard to resist comparison to a modern state archive, from which one obtains notarised copies of important documents for a fee. The *Chronicle* of Sampiro, after all,

---

[119] *León* 256.

[120] *Sahagún* 183; Casado Quintanilla, 'Melic', 48, n. 1.

[121] Orlandis, '"Familiaritas"', esp. 195–227; Orlandis, 'Monasterios familiares', 18–46; Orlandis, 'Laicos', 95–104; Pérez, 'Control', 799–822; *cf.* Fernández, 'Property', esp. 519–24; Díaz Martínez, 'Familia', 33–58; Brouillard, 'Family', 1–46.

[122] *Samos* 35; Calleja-Puerta, 'Catedral', 4, 180–5.      [123] *Coruña* 33.

mentions an otherwise unknown monastic foundation charter granted by Ramiro II in about 946, which suggests that its author, perhaps in his role as royal scribe, may have had access to the archives where copies of diplomas were stored.[124]

Yet royal acts of restoration more normally granted fresh written title in response to such petitions, rather than drawing on supplementary copies, which indicates that they were fairly limited in scope. The context for what the law calls *reparatio scripturae* (replacement of a document) was loss, theft, or destruction, and it has a modest incidence, less formalised than in Catalunya and Francia.[125] Theodenandus *archipresbiter* unburdened himself at length in 902 about how the priests of his family foundation of San Esteban de Calvor had mislaid its endowment charter through negligence, vice, and corruption: he notified Alfonso III and the court, and the king ordered that *pictacium hunc testamenti dotis simulque donationis* (this little sheet of testament of dowry and likewise of donation) should be written, itemising and confirming the monastic patrimony.[126] An inventory drawn up by Ordoño II to restore Samos in 922 uses identical vocabulary to explain how the documents of the monastery *deperierunt* (perished) before this renewal; it could represent a standard formula for archival loss, though the latter text could also have been forged or manipulated on the basis of the former.[127]

The king does seem to have been first port of call in such situations. Bishop Pedro of Lugo delivered a *subiessionem* (appeal) to Alfonso V in 1027, complaining that Vermudo II had made a testament granting authority over Mera to the episcopal see, but hostile or malign parties had lifted it from the *scriniis et tesauris* (archives) of his church, and he duly received a confirmation in memory of the original act of piety.[128] The restoration charter of San Pedro de Rocas from 1007 sets a wider compass, recounting its foundation under the patronage of Alfonso III and how all his successors down to Vermudo II had confirmed his testament to it, before describing the great conflagration which had destroyed its *firmitates et scripturas*. By this petition Alfonso V was moved to issue an *agnitio* (recognition) of the

---

[124] *Chronicle of Sampiro*, ed. Estévez Sola, *Chronica*, 25.6; *cf.* Pérez de Urbel, *Sampiro*, 329–30 (24); *San Isidoro* 1.
[125] Rius Serra, 'Reparatio', 246–53; Brown, 'Documents', 344–54; Ruiz Asencio, 'Obispos', 181–210; *cf.* Zimmermann, *Écrire*, 1, 71–80; Bowman, *Landmarks*, 151–63; Salrach, 'Valor', 309–30; Salrach, 'Recreación', 219–32; Salrach, *Justícia*, 185–211.
[126] *Samos* 33.      [127] *Samos* S2; D'Emilio, 'Charter', 281–342.
[128] *Lugo* 58.

history, property, and documentation of the monastery.[129] In a sense, these are miniature house histories, each telling its own story of royal favour past and present, but lost charters could also on occasion be restored by non-royal actors. When the sons of Argilo learned from their mother that the testament which she and her husband Aloitus had granted to Santa María de Cinis was now missing from its *tesauro* through priestly negligence, they made a new donation reaffirming the old one in 915, just as, when rampaging Northmen *concremaverunt ipsasque scripturas* (burnt to a crisp the documents) of Santa Eulalia de Curtis, the bishop of Santiago, Pedro de Mezonzo, stepped in as a descendant of its founder to narrate its history, list its estates, and re-found it for the soul of his father in 995.[130] No doubt there is a degree of rhetorical *tabula rasa* here, clearing the slate to start over, but given the almost limitless scope for beneficiary manipulation, granters who had their own archives to consult in these situations would have been much better placed to guard against the record being rewritten in its restoration.

## Organisation

This active afterlife of the charter called for more than careful safekeeping. Archives kept without order or system could be places of loss as much as preservation.[131] Organisation was needed to ensure that a charter remained readily accessible for consultation, and the form which this took in early medieval Iberia was the dorsal note, a summary of the text written on the reverse side of its parchment. Occupying the scant space left free once a charter had been folded for storage, these notes were simple reference aids, brief and to the point, normally no more than a few words in length. Over the centuries, subsequent strata were added as the text changed hands, was filed and re-filed, and became an object of study. Traditionally, however, they have been ignored as evidence, even by editors; only relatively recently has the value of the 'humble' dorsal note, and of the reverse side of the parchment generally, for the handling and transmission of charters begun to be appreciated.[132] Of major published collections with significant numbers of originals, León, Otero, Eslonza, San Vicente de Oviedo (to 1000), A Coruña, and Lugo all now have at least some degree of identification and

[129] *Rocas* 1.  [130] *Coruña* 21, 110; García Álvarez, *Pedro*, 143–58, 305–9.
[131] Barrett and Woudhuysen, 'Assembling', 47–8.
[132] Bono, *Archivos*, 18; López Villalba, 'Normas', 298; Suárez González, 'Memoria', 77.

transcription of the dorsal notes, though editorial criteria and presentation vary.[133] I have supplemented these by examining the two main outstanding blocs of originals from Sahagún and Portugal. For the present discussion I am only concerned with those dorsal notes contemporary with the writing of the charter, but it is far from a straightforward determination to make. The brevity of the text, and the typically poorer condition of the reverse of the parchment, which faced outward after folding, together caution us to allow a substantial margin for error; some will turn out in time to date from a generation or two later, if not more, and many are hidden from sight by overwriting or the adhesion of backing papers. Defined and framed as such, there are dorsal notes on 290 (33%) of the 888 originals in the corpus (see Figure 3.6), but this is simply a first pass at identifying and summarising the traces of archival practice.

From the overall numbers a few crucial points emerge. While dorsal notes appear somewhat less often at Otero than in the other collections, it

| | Notes | | Original | |
|---|---|---|---|---|
| | # | % | # | % |
| Total | 290 | 33 | 888 | 22 |
| **Region** | | | | |
| West | 72 | 25 | 210 | 24 |
| Centre | 213 | 73 | 658 | 74 |
| East | 5 | 2 | 20 | 2 |
| **Personnel** | | | | |
| Royal | 25 | 9 | 62 | 7 |
| Comital | 0 | 0 | 3 | 0 |
| Ecclesiastical | 170 | 59 | 449 | 51 |
| Lay | 94 | 32 | 369 | 42 |
| **Typology** | | | | |
| Donation | 125 | 43 | 367 | 41 |
| Sale | 152 | 52 | 444 | 50 |
| Other | 13 | 4 | 76 | 9 |
| **Complexity** | | | | |
| Simple | 205 | 71 | 587 | 66 |
| Complex | 85 | 29 | 300 | 34 |

**Figure 3.6** Dorsal Notes

[133] For San Vicente de Oviedo, see García Arias and Miranda Duque, *Documentos*, 19–95.

is because they are somewhat more typical of royal and ecclesiastical charters, and the rate for lay charters is by no means insignificant even so. The laity, in other words, had their own carefully curated archives too. In typology, the occurrence on donations *post mortem* stands out as abnormally high: these documents by definition had longer-term implications, and needed to be to hand when the moment came to put their terms into effect. For chronology, the sample size is too small to extract a consistent trendline, but the incidence regularly tops 30–40%, and the practice was continuous (see Figure 3.7). When charters with contemporary dorsal notes are divided by beneficiary into ecclesiastical and lay archives, then subdivided by broad social category into episcopal, monastic, clerical, aristocratic, and peasant (or non-aristocratic) collections, what also becomes apparent is the application of similar sorting and labelling strategies across every level of society. Allowing for institutional and individual particularities, different types of actors nonetheless organised their charters in comparable ways to ensure that they remained accessible for use.[134]

Basing what follows on the Leonese corpus, for its size and security of identification and transcription, only one episcopal archive is represented

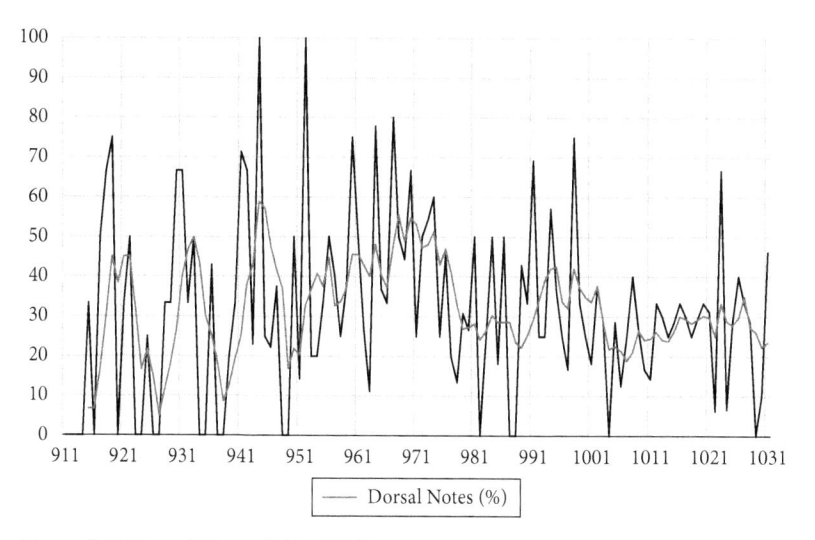

**Figure 3.7** Dorsal Notes (911–1031)

---

[134] Mendo Carmona, *Escritura*, 1, 122–38; *cf.* Balzaretti, *Lands*, 60–2.

in a significant number of originals, but it is sufficient to give us a clear sense of the archival practices of a great cathedral see. The dorsal notes on the charters of Santa María de León consistently identify the location of the property involved in the transaction, implying a geographical arrangement of the documentation in the archive. This will have supported management of the estates, and since our cartularies almost all have the same internal logic, at least partly, they too appear to reflect the disposition of the source materials.[135] Alongside geography, a plurality of dorsal notes also state the typology of the document and name the granter, such as a parchment with a charter from 960 labelled 'the testament of Bishop Ilderedo of the *villa* of San Claudio Araduey', or another bearing a pair of texts from 979 summarised jointly as 'the charter of Revel, Godesteo, and Duraviles of the *villa* of Mahudes'.[136] Slightly less common are notices limited to location: a donation from 860, for example, is described quite fully as 'concerning the *villa* of Usso in Asturias, San Martín in Asturias, and Sauceta', while a second from 999 is more concisely catalogued 'the *castello* of San Salvador'.[137] There are other combinations of geographical whereabouts with various additional details, including granter, document, and transaction type, but rarely, and some are simply fragmentary, as the writing on the hair side of the parchment is worn or degraded.[138] One exceptional case records only typology and granter, designating a donation of 928 as 'the testament which Fronimio Olemundi made', but then he was bishop of León, and the property was in his see, so this notice has taken much as read.[139] Dates are altogether absent from the dorsal notes; they might have pointed to a more historical arrangement of the holdings. Episcopal archives seem instead to have been organised pragmatically, primarily by geography, anticipating that the charters would be used in the administration of property over the long term: physical location is the one point of reference with no date of expiry.

Monastic archives account for the most surviving dorsal notes, and they reflect largely the same set of practices. Again a plurality name the granter and state the document type and place, briefly but indicatively: a bequest to Eslonza from 936 is summarised as 'the testament of Muza son of Armentarius of Cañones', providing a lineage for the granter beyond what is given in the text while omitting the second *villa* involved in the transaction.[140] Evidently

---

[135]   Kosto, 'Practices', 269–71.
[136]   *León* 333, 463–4; *cf.* 108, 130, 217, 549; Carriedo Tejedo, 'Obispos', 47–78.
[137]   *León* 2, 588; *cf.* 550, 707.       [138]   See *e.g. León* 111, 548, 145.
[139]   *León* 76.       [140]   *Eslonza* 12.

the personal relationship could matter as much as or more than the location, and indeed, though property is generally localised quite specifically and precisely, in at least one case it is baldly described as 'land', irreconcilable with archival organisation based purely on geography.[141] Occasionally the standard data are also complemented by the beneficiary name, such as in a dorsal note of unusual length for a donation to Santiago de León from 1015: 'the charter of testament which Bishop Jimeno and Gotina *confessa* granted of the *villa* of San Pelayo in El Bierzo on the Oza to Abbot Todemiro Muza'.[142] The apparent need to name the beneficiary could suggest third-party archiving, and there is no reason to exclude the possibility entirely, but given that the text followed the property from recipient to recipient, it is equally likely to anticipate a future in which both would change hands. Variation is the norm, and transaction substitutes at times for document type, such as a parchment of 923 from Abellar described as 'the sale and donation of Eugenius *diaconus* of lands and *bustos* in Covellas', while at other times both attributes are missing.[143] Location is the one most broadly shared feature, and the dorsal notes on the charters of Eslonza habitually mention either documentary typology and the property involved or property alone, such as a donation of 918 labelled 'the testament of the land of Fonte de Sabucco', or a sale from 946 summarised simply as 'of Lampreana', the territory where all the many properties concerned in the transaction are situated.[144]

Like episcopal archives, monastic collections of charters were arranged by geography, but a secondary level of organisation based on the granter is apparent. In one sense this is the best evidence for beneficiary archiving, since such an arrangement speaks to the relationships between parties engendered by transaction. An individual or personal filing system is no less viable than geographical organisation, but would have required more regular updating, since names are less enduring than places as points of reference; monasteries did periodically draw up rosters of their dependants, facilitating operation on personal terms within localities, as in the collection of rents or dues, and this is not so different. Dorsal notes based on the granter name lack any statement of location, and most often identify both granter and typology, such as a sale to Santiago de Cellariolo from 931

---

[141] *León* 586; *cf.* 18, 41, 227, 383, 547, 628, 889.
[142] *León* 736; *cf.* 93; Mariño-Veiras, 'Religiosas', 1, 137–8.
[143] *León* 58; *Lorvão* 37; *cf. León* 98, 267, 401; *Eslonza* 17.
[144] *Eslonza* 5, 21; 24, *León* 89, 229; *Eslonza* 27, 29, *León* 817; Granja Alonso, 'Dominio', 1–18.

designated 'the charter of Stefano', omitting the second vendor, his wife Fackina; with greater precision, a donation made by a son acting as testamentary executor for his father to a monastery of San Martín y San Sebastián in 1001 is summarised as 'the testament of Sesgudo on behalf of Fruela'.[145] As we have seen in dorsal notes based on geography, transaction can substitute for document type, and a parchment of Santiago de León from 1015 has only 'Arbidio' and 'exchange' on the reverse, direct and to the point.[146] Periodic inclusion of the beneficiary alongside the granter is again ambiguous: a donation of 999 labelled 'Sarraciniz to the brothers of Valdecésar', or another from 917, 'the testament of San Cristóbal Antealtares from Bishop Fronimio'.[147] Still other summaries note the beneficiary institution alone, or pair it with the transaction or document type.[148] Is it more likely that some monasteries kept their documents elsewhere, off-site, or that the properties in question had changed hands again by the time the dorsal notes were written? One sale of 990 is called 'the charter of Doña Imilo of Refoyo': in the text itself she is the beneficiary, acting as purchaser and bearing the title of abbess, so this archival summary could date from a later moment when she gave her possessions (with their documentation) to her monastery.[149] The timing of dorsal notes must be a factor in their content, and since ownership history remained relevant in case of dispute, monastic archives may have preserved this in their notes.

The charters of individual clerics are more seldom preserved in blocs of originals with dorsal notes, but from what we can see they too were organised by the same twofold logic of geography and personal name. Standard practice was to list granter, typology, and place, and one sale to Servandus *presbiter* from 1023 does so in uncharacteristic detail, describing itself as 'the charter of the vineyard of Ariolfo of Villavente', noting the property boundaries on all four sides, and naming his daughter Mater, who figures in the underlying dispute.[150] It could be an example of preparatory notes for drafting the text, but given the background of conflict it could alternatively be a case of the real possibility of future contention making it advisable for fuller information to be available at first glance. The variations, including substitution of transaction, omission of granter, and citation of location alone, are all otherwise familiar, and argue for comparability of practice.[151]

[145]   *León* 90, 600; *cf.* 221, 732; *Eslonza* 26; *Otero* 21; *Vega* 3.
[146]   *León* 739; *cf. Eslonza* 14.      [147]   *León* 587, 43; *cf.* 295.
[148]   *León* 298, *Mondoñedo* 6; *León* 538; *Otero* 20.
[149]   *León* 537.      [150]   *León* 799.
[151]   *León* 7, 212, 468, 814, 825; *cf. Otero* 186; *León* 83; 563–4, 593.

The clergy of Otero, however, arranged their archives consistently by personal name: a sale made to Braolio *presbiter* in 964 is labelled 'the charter of Gogina', the vendor, while another from that year between the same parties has a slightly fuller 'charter of sale of Gogina', whereas two others name the beneficiary.[152] Again perhaps different systems for different purposes or in different contexts. The seemingly contemporary dorsal note on a sale made by a lay couple to Felis *presbiter* in 930 refers instead to 'the *villa* of the bishop', unaccounted for in this transaction; conceivably he was the priest in later life, or a later recipient of the property involved who gave it to his own see in turn.[153]

The laity, both aristocrats and peasants, were no less involved than ecclesiastics in the world of documentation, and accordingly had just as much need to organise their archives for use. The strategies which they employed to do so are comparable, the major difference being that they relied on the personal system more often than geographical organisation: this might tell us that individual relationships formed within a lifetime were crucial to the creation and maintenance of lay patrimonies. Aristocratic archives begin, of course, with the Flaínez and Muñoz families, and in the dorsal notes for their charters we typically find the document or transaction typology, the name of the granter, and the location of the property all recorded. The summary of a judicial payment made to Flaíno Muñoz in 993, for instance, describes it as 'the charter of Mater of Villar', and the parchment even has its own binding strip to hold fast its 13 foldings and leave only this brief text visible; a sale to Cidi Domínguez and his wife Oria from 1031, meanwhile, is labelled with rather greater precision 'the charter of Stevane of land in Coreses at the spring'.[154] For the collections of other Leonese aristocrats, however, archival notices commonly mention location alone, or alongside typology, as in a donation to Munio Fernández from 989 with the isolated toponym of 'Taural' on its reverse side, or a sale to Fruela Velaz from 962 called 'the charter of Valdevimbre'.[155] It is therefore not the case that the lay élite never looked to the longer term in organising their archives by the topography of their estates, but Pedro Flaínez and Fruela Muñoz, as well as a handful of others, normally thought in terms of persons, usually together with the type of documentary arrangement which they had entered into

---

[152] *Otero* 15, 14; *cf.* 49; *León* 161.      [153] *León* 88; *cf.* 398.
[154] *Otero* 34; *León* 883; *cf. Otero* 12, 31, 75, 118, 129, 135, 164; *León* 305, 378, 560, 612, 760, 882, 895; Fernández Catón, 'Fondo Rodríguez', 489–50 (4), figs 4–5.
[155] *León* 530, 352; 315, 655, 669; 562, 741, *Otero* 90; *León* 3, *Otero* 11.

with each. As such, a *perfiliatio* of Pedro Flaínez from 1001 is catalogued as 'the charter of Cidi and Nadalia', a donation in lieu of a judicial debt to Fruela Muñoz in 1022 as 'the charter of Aragonti', while a parchment with two sales to Jimena Muñoz from 1003 has a composite note, 'the charter of Maxito and Monio', name-checking the two vendors at once.[156] Transaction could occasionally be substituted, such as a charter to Menicio and his wife Avola from 898 labelled 'the sale of Donadeus', but this was scarcely needed given that most recorded business amongst the laity took the form of sale.[157] Rarely was the beneficiary name added; aristocratic archives were held in house.[158]

Peasants who have left no more than a few modest charters under their name had the same need as lay aristocrats to preserve them arranged for consultation, and the dorsal notes on their surviving originals take similar forms. The free peasantry provided the backbone for traditional scholarship on the *Reconquista* and 'repopulation', but one need not take so robust a view of their independence to recognise the agency of small proprietors in the documentary record.[159] Most such archival notices locate the property involved, as in a sale to Flaynus and his wife Bronildi from 941 described as 'the charter which Ermegildos made of a vineyard in Torre': granter, document type, and geographical whereabouts are all given here, though the first or the first and second were also regularly omitted.[160] The sample size is small, and any generalisation must be made with caution, but many of these summaries are really quite full, adding in the name of the beneficiary, at times substituting type of transaction for document. One charter of 908 with a decidedly archaising granter, for example, is catalogued as 'the sale of Splendonius of land in Viego which he sold to Fredesinde'.[161] Does this mean that it was archived with a third party, or labelled at a later stage of ownership? There are references to the beneficiary but not the granter, which may date to when the property next changed hands and record its history; a sale to Agube and his wife Auria in 950 is described as 'the charter of Oteros del Rey to San Julián', once again introducing a party not named in the text.[162] But the personal system is also very much in evidence, fitting

---

[156] *Otero* 55, 142, 64–5; *cf.* 37, 58, 74, 124, 134, 141, 179; *León* 780, 839.
[157] *León* 13; *cf.* 25, 324; *Otero* 32.      [158] *Otero* 176; *León* 719.
[159] Sánchez-Albornoz, 'Propietarios', 178–201; García García, 'Propietarios', 33–53; Davies, 'Peasants', 368–78; *cf.* Bonnassie, *Catalogne*, 1, 224–36, 307–43.
[160] *León* 143; *cf.* 194, 223, 711, *Otero* 61, *Ourense* 4; *León* 391, 616, 652; *León* 234, *Carrizo* 1.
[161] *León* 21; *cf.* 35, 404, 429; Kremer, 'Antroponimia', 14–15.
[162] *León* 226; *cf.* 12, 158, 476.

better with beneficiary archiving: a sale to Vegila and his wife Arilo from 1009 is summarised in familiar terms as 'the charter of Dominico and Infante', jointly vendors in that lay transaction.[163] Whatever fraction survives, peasants had their own collections of documents, sufficient in size and importance that they sought to keep them manageable. How they did so was by means common to early medieval Iberian society as a whole, regularly calling on a scribe to add a summary to a given charter. Whether organised for the short term by personal name or for the long term by geographical location, whether written on the day or in retrospect, whether stored in house or held by some third party, the object was for it to remain readily accessible for present or future use.

## Portable Texts

Early medieval Iberian society largely shared a common archival culture, but against that background some monasteries and other élites began to develop one further mechanism of documentary stewardship, assembling and transcribing their charters into cartularies. The first references to the existence of such manuscript compilations date to the mid-tenth century and come from or concern Galicia and Portugal.[164] Though we now only glimpse the results in outline, this evolution seems to parallel the practice of confirmation through making a new copy of a text. We have already considered the narrative of 944 which describes a codex kept at Oviedo containing copies of diplomas granted to Samos: as far as one can tell, these were copies *in extenso*, a kind of royal backup cartulary from which the monastic archive could be restored.[165] Other citations from the orbit of Samos provide minimal detail or context. In 976, for example, Sunilani *confessus* made a gift including the site of San Salvador along with its appurtenances and *cartarios* to his son Vermudo *presbiter* of Santiago de Barbadelo; in 1009, similarly, Abbot Vermudo gave property and books to the same house, dependent on Samos, noting a *liber cum nostrum renovum*, or ledger of loans, if that is what the last word means.[166] Are these just another way of

---

[163] *Otero* 78; *cf. León* 82, 297, 579, 886, 894; *Otero* 5; *Ourense* 1.

[164] Sáez, 'Origen', 12–13; Sáez, 'Códices', 833–4; Carriedo Tejedo, 'Libros', 62–7; Sánchez Díez, 'Estudios', 254–5.

[165] *Samos* 35.

[166] *Samos* 61, 64; *cf. Celanova* 321; García de Valdeavellano, 'Renovo', 408–30; Carzolio de Rossi, 'Constitución', 23; Godoy, 'Riqueza', 3–6.

saying 'the property and its papers'? Seemingly not: Ramiro II gave a *villa* to the monastery of Castrelo in 947 only after *revolvimus carturarios nostros* (we reviewed our cartularies) and confirmed that it was in the royal gift, while Flamula specified in her testament to Guimarães of 960 that all her *cartarios* were kept at Salzeta, perhaps held in the hands of a third party, and should be brought from there to the monastery.[167] This term is clearly explicated, however, in the bequest of Abbot Randulfus from 994, where he set out what he had acquired *per nostras kartas* (by our charters) as recorded *in ipso nostro kartario* (in that cartulary of ours).[168] Evidently a compilation of charters in some form, full or partial, is intended, and other personal cartularies appear in the adventures of Odoíno as recounted in 982 and in the testament of Cresconius from 1010, both in the sphere of Celanova.[169]

These passing references imply that compiling documents into a book or volume was common practice for both institutions and individuals in Galicia and Portugal. Frustratingly, the only surviving cartularies which could plausibly date from the early Middle Ages are the brief, likely abortive projects from Buezo de Bureba and San Martín de Cercito, transmitting a handful of texts each, and later folded into the archives of Valpuesta and San Juan. This is true, at least, of 'proper' cartularies with full transcriptions of charters, but what we do have are archival indices of securely early medieval date. One from Otero made in 976 is headed, 'inventory which Fernando Vermúdez and Elvira made of charters of the *villa* of Natahoyo', and summarises the salient details: 'the charter of Donnon of the apple-tree in Ramma by the house of Negelle', and so on for eight more.[170] The resemblance to the formulation of dorsal notes is plain to see, and it is reasonable to think that they evolved directly from these ready-made extracts or résumés of texts, as if registers of dorsal notes.[171] They are not clustered in any one region: another from Lorvão also made in 976 provides a précis of eight testaments granted to the monastery on a single day, and amalgamates the granters and witnesses into a composite confirmation clause in which they affix their signs onto the *cartas testamentorum* (charters of testaments).[172] But can we be sure of an archival intention? As we have seen, in the case of Sahagún especially, some texts in this and cognate formats could instead be series of preparatory minutes for documents, or gatherings of notes on

[167] *Lugo* 15; *Guimarães* 3; Carriedo Tejedo, 'Libros', 69–71.   [168] *Paço de Sousa* 132.

[169] *Celanova* 191, 321; Carzolio de Rossi, 'Cresconio', 277–9; *cf. Piasca* A4.

[170] *Otero* 22; Prieto Prieto, 'Fernando', 197–213; Kosto, 'Practices', 274–6; Calleja-Puerta, 'Conservación', 225–6.

[171] Escalona, 'Cartularios', 135–41.   [172] *Lorvão* 32.

transactions never written up formally. The list of 12 sales to Iscam and his wife Filauria from 945 to 954, for instance, consists of simple statements, 'Teuda sells half an enclosure for 20 silvers' and so forth, with a synthetic confirmation.[173] An archival register is distinguished by some indication, at the outset or in its entries, that it derives from existing documentation. One such index from 971 is entitled, 'notice or inventory of the *villas* and properties recorded in the testaments of Sobrado and donated by Hermegildo and Paterna as well as their descendants', while another document from around 1011, though termed only a '*nodicia* of the property and vineyards of Santiago de León', makes note in its final entry of 'the charter which Arvidio made'.[174]

This mode of abridging and systematising documentation was employed at Celanova more than anywhere else. The monastery has left us the largest archive from early medieval Iberia, and the key figure in its development was Cresconius *praepositus*, who in the course of his activity as purchasing agent compiled registers to manage the paperwork of his many acquisitions.[175] The most archival or 'cartularyesque' is a series of seven summaries of sales with a single amalgamated confirmation which dates the transactions to 1001 and locates the property involved in the territory of Sorga: again they might be preparatory notes were it not for the concluding statement that the inventory had been written and *translatum* (transcribed) from charters in 1005.[176] Another undated 'inventory which Cresconius *praepositus* made of many parts or sources' is comprised of 43 short statements, variously simple notices, extracts from extant documents, and transcriptions of whole texts; since 25 entries mention a charter, a textual origin for the entirety seems likely.[177] The range and extent of this register exceeds the norm, however, and most inventories put together by Cresconius are declaredly limited by region, or on occasion by party. One from 1005, for instance, is labelled 'inventory of all the properties which Cresconius *frater* bought or acquired *pro pretio digno* (for the just price) in the *villa* of Moreira', near Celanova, while another lacking any date is described at the end as 'concerning the lands recorded in the charters of Alvito and his wife

[173] *Sahagún* 94; Mínguez, 'Ordenación', 1035–7; Kosto, 'Practices', 279–80; *cf. Huesca* 4; *Celanova* 184.

[174] *Sobrado* 1.112; *León* 704; Kosto, 'Practices', 270–1; *cf. Astorga* 224; *Samos* 24; *Coruña* 55 (54), 56, 68.

[175] Carzolio de Rossi, 'Cresconio', 242–79; Portass, *World*, 161–3.

[176] *Celanova* 299, 253–9.

[177] *Celanova* 315 (216), 273, 293.

Nunillo, also located in Moreira.[178] And where Cresconius led, other agents of the monastery followed with their own registers: Abbot Aloitus, who listed in composite form 13 purchases of vineyards made in Bobadela in 1013, or Vermuduz Eroptiz, who wrote a *noticia de testamento* (testamentary list) in 1026 of the men of Santa María de Verín.[179] When the *Tumbo* was finally assembled in the twelfth century, it was not an innovation but an extension of the effort which Celanova had made to safeguard and rationalise its archive, and as we shall see this early mastery of its records enabled the monastery to deploy written evidence effectively at court.

The afterlife of the charter in early medieval Iberia was both enduring and active, and the archives in miniature created at Celanova show us one way in which it was sustained and managed. Yet in a real sense all archives were miniature: with some variation of practice, the parchment of the average charter, once written, was typically folded over until reduced to the size of a (thick) business card, leaving exposed a surface area just large enough for a concise dorsal note.[180] The parchment of one lay charter from Portugal of 1021 was already only the size of an index card, the text filling up the front side and running over onto the reverse, but it was nonetheless folded four by five times, resulting in a 'closed' charter the size of a postage stamp. In this small area, the scribe wrote the name of the granter in one of the two squares of parchment left visible, while in the other a roughly contemporary hand identified the property involved, allowing for multiple organisational modes of archiving the charter (see Figure 3.8).[181] Minimised dimensions maximised portability: in consequence, we need to picture an archive as closer to a wallet than even a folder or a box, much less a bookcase or a library—ready to exchange, simple to rearrange. And preservation by means of such organised archives, when taken together with the expectation latent in sanction clauses and the practice of confirmation through notices and new charters, reveals recognition of the ongoing value of documentation. Common to all three facets of this second life is a concern to maintain the permanence of the arrangements set down in writing, which mandated continual, careful reengagement, whether in the obligations assumed by the granter in the sanction, the names added by new parties to old parchments, or the sorting and resorting of charters in constant

[178] *Celanova* 290; 289 (243), 266–7, 286, 288; *cf.* 293, 296–8, 309, 327–8.
[179] *Celanova* 338, 368; *cf.* 285, 382.
[180] Mendo Carmona, *Escritura*, 1, 133–6; *cf.* Fernández Catón, 'Fondo Carrizo', 209.
[181] *PMH* 250.

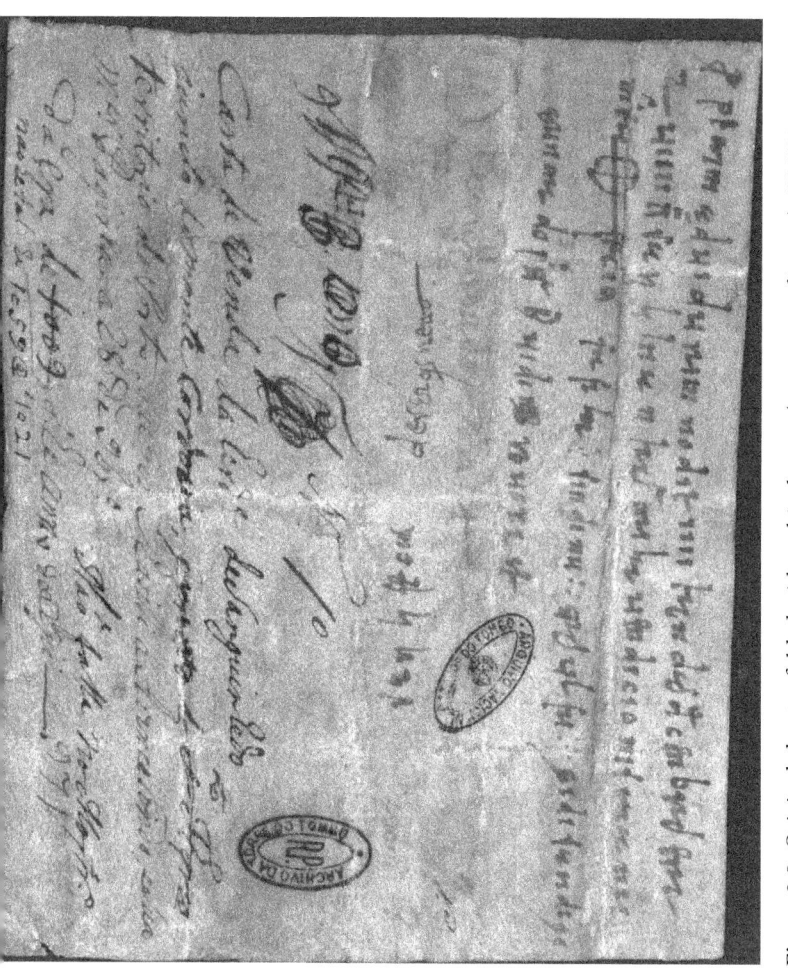

**Figure 3.8** Original charter, folded with archival notes (see centre of image): *PMH* 250 (Lisbon, ANTT, Ordem de São Bento, Mosteiro de São João Baptista de Pendorada, mç. 1, no. 4 (PT/TT/MSJBP/004/0001), dorso: Imagem cedida pelo ANTT)

movement from original to subsequent beneficiaries. But it is this dynamic circulation more than anything else which characterises the charter after the fact, underlying the transmission history of the corpus and making possible the prevalence with which, as we shall also see, charters cite other charters. Above all, there is the keen attention paid by every user of documents to those documents, from kings and bishops via monasteries and clerics to aristocrats and peasants: organising their collections by place or person, looking forward to reuse and redeployment, in archival procedures which can still be reconstructed from dorsal notes, guides to their safekeeping. Yet in practices of confirmation and preservation, two innovations of the mid-tenth century changed the balance of this shared archival culture. As kings issued confirmation copies of prior diplomas, as the clergy distilled documentation into summary form and monasteries curated cartularies, they gained greater control of the afterlife of texts, realising more fully their potential power as tools or weapons to be wielded in their own interests.

# PART II

# THE NETWORK

Then those who feared the Lord talked with each other, and the Lord listened and heard. A scroll of remembrance was written in his presence concerning those who feared the Lord and honoured his name. 'On the day when I act,' says the Lord Almighty, 'they will be my treasured possession. I will spare them, just as a father has compassion and spares his son who serves him. And you will again see the distinction between the righteous and the wicked, between those who serve God and those who do not.

Malachi 3:16–18

# 4

# Proving

The charter is more than a written record of transaction: it is a point of intersection in a network of texts which encompasses other charters, secular and canon law, Holy Scripture, and monastic rules. The charter, in other words, is not a singularity but an intertextuality, and its combination of sources establishes its full meaning. The question of why one should write a charter is not quite the same as what to do with it once written: documents assert and defend title to property, but how did one realise those claims in real terms?[1] Part of the answer is the interconnectedness of the corpus through mutual citation, which proves that charters mattered in the world around them; they speak not in statements but as conversations, they live not for moments but in continuities. It has been argued of early medieval Italy that written evidence, if wielded skilfully at court and in broader processes of dispute and settlement, could secure property rights, extend the scope of ownership, and impose authority on others, and that this in turn encouraged monasteries and churches to master their organisation and use via scribes.[2] Writing was a tool not only for resolving disputes but also, and crucially, for determining the form of their records, which overwrite competing histories to construct a narrative of settled, documented proprietorship.[3] In early medieval Iberia, we have encountered this first element of the network of texts within which the charter is embedded in the practice of confirmation, but that is a limited case of charters citing other charters. Available and in circulation through habits of archiving and retrieval, charters situated themselves in the context of other charters to establish ownership histories for property, and to provide points of reference for resolving disputes. By tracking how texts located themselves textually, in the background as a working framework and in the foreground as evidence, we can

---

[1] Everett, *Literacy*, 197–234; Costambeys, *Power*, 19–48.
[2] Balzaretti, 'Monastery', 1–18; Bougard, 'Justice', 1, 133–76; Costambeys, 'Disputes and Courts', 265–89; Costambeys, 'Disputes and Documents', 125–54.
[3] Davies and Fouracre (eds), *Settlement*, 207–14; Brown, *Seizure*, 124–39, 166–85; Brown, 'Charters', 226–48; *cf.* Carvajal Castro, 'Politics', 21–46; Jarrett, 'Story', 123–42.

*Text and Textuality in Early Medieval Iberia: The Written and The World, 711–1031.* Graham Barrett, Oxford University Press. © Graham Barrett 2023. DOI: 10.1093/oso/9780192895370.003.0005

delineate a trend of charters promoting their own use over time, redefining the past and future of property as written history.

As a point of departure for assessing this phenomenon, I have recorded every instance of charters citing other charters, whether or not the cited text survives or can be identified, by marking the terms which they employ for themselves. These range from the general, *carta* or *testamentum* (charter or testament), to the very specific, *colmellum divisionis* or *titulum dotis* (column of division or title of dowry), though the actuality of each reference will bear closer scrutiny. Overall, we find documentary citations in 620 (15%) of the charters (see Figure 4.1).

| | Citations | | Overall | |
|---|---|---|---|---|
| | # | % | # | % |
| Total | 620 | 15 | 4095 | 100 |
| Region | | | | |
| West | 355 | 57 | 1284 | 31 |
| Centre | 239 | 39 | 2088 | 51 |
| East | 26 | 4 | 723 | 18 |
| Personnel | | | | |
| Royal | 132 | 21 | 522 | 13 |
| Comital | 5 | 1 | 71 | 2 |
| Ecclesiastical | 404 | 65 | 2710 | 66 |
| Lay | 79 | 13 | 769 | 19 |
| Typology | | | | |
| Donation | 342 | 55 | 2212 | 54 |
| Sale | 99 | 16 | 1469 | 36 |
| Other | 179 | 29 | 411 | 10 |
| Complexity | | | | |
| Simple | 199 | 32 | 2797 | 68 |
| Complex | 421 | 68 | 1292 | 32 |
| Palaeography | | | | |
| Original | 133 | 21 | 888 | 22 |
| Copy | 62 | 10 | 261 | 6 |
| Cartulary | 384 | 62 | 2438 | 60 |
| Other | 41 | 7 | 507 | 12 |
| Diplomatic | | | | |
| Authentic | 557 | 90 | 3781 | 92 |
| Suspicious | 2 | 0 | 24 | 1 |
| Interpolated | 19 | 3 | 57 | 1 |
| Falsified | 42 | 7 | 227 | 6 |

**Figure 4.1**  Charters Citing Charters

There is a pronounced regional variation to the practice, which is significantly more common in the west, at Samos, Santiago, and Celanova, than in the centre, excepting Oviedo, while in the east it is almost non-existent.[4] Royal diplomas cite other documents by far the most often, reflecting the tendency of kings to build on the acts of their predecessors; both ecclesiastical and lay charters do the same, however, if less frequently. In terms of typology, confirmations, disputes, and archival inventories are prominent as sites of citation, whereas of donations and sales it is those with more complex formulations. Forgeries habitually mention other charters in their armature of verisimilitude, while such references are regularly absent from late copies and extracts; otherwise, neither authenticity nor transmission seems to be an important factor in reconstructing the practice. If effectively confined to the west and the centre, documentary citation was widespread in the written world of early medieval Iberia, and growing more so. Across the Leonese period, the incidence rises from under 10% to over 20%, coming to be a regular feature of the corpus, and giving us some sense of what may be lost (see Figure 4.2).[5]

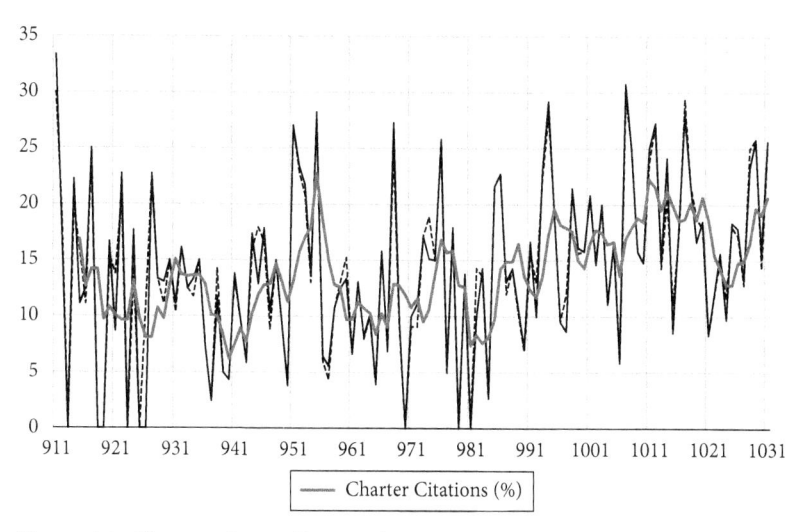

**Figure 4.2**  Charters Citing Charters (911–1031)

---

[4]  García de Cortázar and Agúndez San Miguel, 'Memoria', 3, 263–4.
[5]  *Documentación*, 379–415; *cf.* Sierra Macarrón, 'Producción', 110–13.

# Reference

The question is so obvious it has seldom been asked: why do charters cite each other? The safest ground on which to proceed is with the minority of cases where the cited charter is extant, so that we can first establish if and when such citation is rhetorical or real. References in charters to other charters are classifiable by their function into four types, each presenting a distinct facet of the afterlife of text: in confirmation, to document the means of acquisition of property, for further information, or as justification for a transaction. Citing a prior charter in confirmation is the most straightforward, and we have already considered this as evidence of the continued applicability and accessibility of documentation beyond the immediate context of its creation. There are paradigmatic examples from Sahagún: when Adileubus sold certain property to Melic *presbiter* in 940, he also confirmed a charter of *perfiliatio* (adoption) which he had made to the same eight years earlier, while Infante, newly widowed in 956, confirmed the testament which her husband Foracasas had made to the monastery the year before.[6] The original transaction, in the first case, is complemented by another between the same parties.[7] In the second, the scope of the original transaction is extended by a third party entering into its terms, often a close relative as here, but also an outside or higher authority, like a bishop or king; the modes of citation are prevalent at León, Samos, and Santiago, and overlapping.[8] Confirmation brought past charters forward in time, to updated or new social configurations, and the citation refers to the relationships as much as the transactions which they document, defending and extending them to the present and beyond. This is especially apparent in more formal contexts, such as when Bishop Oveco of León convened a *magnato concilio* (a sort of 'council of barons') in 945 to confirm a testament granted to Sahagún by the *infante* Ramiro three decades earlier, together with other charters pertaining to the same property which do not survive; in the great *restauracio* or refoundation of 1018, the monastery hosted the court of Alfonso V, who listened as the abbot read aloud a testament, then more than a century old, made by his ancestor Alfonso III, and reinstated it

---

[6] *Sahagún* 75 (*Sahagún* 45); 150 (144).
[7] *León* 290 (184); 506 (280, 41); 798 (759); *Santiago* 4 (3, 1–2); 8 (4, 1).
[8] *Otero* 26 (21); *Coruña* 21 (12); *Sobrado* 1.6 (1.2); *Arlanza* 1D (1A–C); *cf. Sahagún* 265 (162); *Santiago* 39 (1); *Samos* 37 (36); S2 (3, 36).

against some *scurrones* (clowns) who had invaded the property involved.[9] In both cases relationships were renewed via the medium of revisiting prior documentation, a practice particularly common in the west.[10]

These confirmations cite the fact of another text, while others quote content, pointing to specific provisions or drawing terminology from the earlier transaction. When in 932, for example, Ramiro II confirmed the endowment of Samos, he observed that his father Ordoño II had granted the monastery a diploma expelling a *scortum* (prostitute, or illicit wife?) with other unchaste inmates and ordaining a new congregation of brothers in their place: Sancho I confirmed this in 962, and recorded how his father Ramiro II had directed the inhabitants of the surrounding mile and a half to render it *opus fiscale* (tribute).[11] In 862, the future Alfonso III held a council at Santiago and issued a confirmation of a charter from four years before, a grant of all *villas* and their inhabitants within six miles; later kings repeated the terms defined by Ordoño II in a diploma from 911, that they should pay *censum* (rent) to the see as *homines ingenui* (free tenants).[12] Such citations do more than bring prior charters forward in time: they demonstrate close rereading, situating a new transaction in detailed recollection of its written predecessor. Again this appears to have been a principally western practice, which Samos and Santiago above all deployed to safeguard and expand their patrimonial jurisdictions.

## Documenting

The most important function for documentary citation was to provide evidence of how property had been acquired, which served both to establish the right of the granter to dispose of it and to ground that disposition in its written history. When David and his wife Margarita gave a vineyard to Abellar in 921, for example, they recorded the fact that they had bought it by means of a charter of *comparatio* (purchase) from four named persons nine years earlier, while Citaius *presbiter*, on entering the same monastery

---

[9] *Sahagún* 101 (12–13); 404 (6, 7–8); Fernández Flórez, *Elaboración*, 89–92; Alfonso, 'Rhetoric', 55–8.

[10] See *e.g. Santiago* 8 (4); *Samos* 33 (137); *Celanova* 94 (88); *Braga* 19 (*VDJ* 2); *Guimarães* 61 (60); *Cardeña* 37.2 (37.1).

[11] *Samos* 34 (S2, 37, 1, 3, 41, 36); 39 (46, 38, 36); *cf.* 2 (34, 46, 38, 36).

[12] *Santiago* 3 (2); 35 (21, 1–4); 38 (21, 1–4); 41 (38, 34–5, 21, 1–4); *cf.* 21 (4); *Coruña* 20 (19); López Sabatel, 'Apuntes', 222–3.

in 955, gave it property in Covellas which he and his sister Filauria had purchased by charter five years previously. In each case, citing charter and cited charter both survive, the latter clearly having been handed over with the former for safekeeping in the archive of Abellar.[13] This habit of citing proof of the means of acquisition was common to all sectors of society, royalty and laity, but foremost amongst the clergy.[14] And as with confirmations, some citations are more detailed than others. In 952, for instance, Hermegildo sold property to Santos Justo y Pastor which Ramiro II had seized from the killers of his nephew Odoario Díaz and given to him by written ordinance in return for his faithful service: this case sets out the circumstances of the original transaction which made the new one possible.[15] In 1030, comparably, Bishop Servando of León donated *corte propria obtima* (his best farm or other working estate, probably walled) to the abbess of San Vicente, which Flamula had deeded him by testament, in memory of her sister, on condition that he leave it after his death to a religious institution of his choosing. In this case, the prior terms or conditions are related, legitimising disposal of the property ahead of schedule (with permission from Flamula), while commemorating both her, whose pious bequest the bishop was fulfilling, and her sister, in whose memory it had originally been made.[16] Such detailed citation seems to have been practised mainly by the great monasteries and aristocrats, perhaps those most aware of potential litigation.[17] But it shares with the simpler forms of referencing a consciousness that a transaction might be just the most recent in a documented chain. Each of these acts of recognition argued that the history of property was properly written.

This was the primary reason to cite, and indeed most documentary citations where the cited charter is lost record the means of acquisition in comparable terms. Sarrazino Silez and his wife Sacia sold a *villa* to Fafila Fernández and his wife Adosinda in 1002, for example, which they had obtained by diploma from Ramiro III; in considerably greater detail, Valerio and Dominico, with their wives and children, tell us how they sold property to Furakasas and his wife Korexia in 1014 once belonging to an Olalio,

---

[13] *León* 57 (29); 288 (219); Carbajo Serrano, *Monasterio*, 111–26.

[14] See *e.g. Sahagún* 293 (144, 150); *León* 753 (730); *Samos* 5 (1, 3), *Guimarães* 67 (A1), *Coimbra* 109 (143–4).

[15] *León* 253 (123).

[16] *León* 862 (857); *cf. Lexicon, s.v.* 'corte', 2, 4; Varela Sieiro, *Léxico*, 60–5; García Cacho, 'Memoria', 1–21.

[17] See *e.g. León* 596 (541); *Sahagún* 24 (19), 245 (216); *Celanova* 246 (223).

which Vermudo II had confiscated and given by charter to Vellite, who then sold it to Dominico.[18] Establishing a 'parchment trail' is one context where personal archives were brought to bear, such as when Bishop Fruela cited three donation charters, from Queen Elvira, Abbot Cixila, and Betotti, in his testament to the see of León in 1002, or when Assur Sarraciniz and his wife Elvira, making the legitimating purpose of the practice explicit in another donation from 999, declared that they had vindicated their owner-ship of the properties in question before Vermudo II with the charters of purchase of his parents Sarracino Munioniz and Sarracena.[19] Further paral-lel cases can be found across the centre, in Asturias, Cantabria, and León.[20] Yet over half of all identifiable instances come from the west, rapidly emer-ging as the most densely textual region, especially from Sobrado, Samos, and Celanova. Here citation of single charters is the norm, and we can fol-low behind Hermegildo and Paterna as they acquire properties obtained in turn *per scripturam*, building up their estates by purchase from ordinary laymen who themselves made use of documents.[21] But denser citation of multiple charters is also visibly more frequent in the west, especially in the documentation of kings, bishops, and aristocrats; to record the means of acquisition, these references typically specify a charter, type of transaction, and parties to it, even payment of a price.[22] More detailed references to the particulars of prior transactions such as circumstances and conditions are comparatively rare across all the regions, though again the most common in the west.[23] Overall the regularity of the practice demonstrates not only an awareness of the written history of property, but also an interest in harness-ing its potential advantages.

These advantages came to bear most fully in court, but we also see a con-sciousness of the web of documentation in which land and ownership were enmeshed implicit in references to other charters for further information. At the beginning of the eleventh century, Amico and his wife Columba paid a judicial fine by giving half a meadow to Cresconius *praepositus*, and

---

[18] *León* 614, 724.    [19] *León* 629, 587; *cf.* 703, 865.

[20] See *e.g. Oviedo* 8; *San Vicente* 12; *Liébana* 7; *Santillana* 23; *Sahagún* 206; *Otero* 56; *Astorga* 53; *San Isidro* 7; *Eslonza* 21.

[21] *Sobrado* 1.25, 1.14, 1.129, 1.12, 1.63; Sierra Macarrón, 'Tipologías', 1029–30; Portass, *World*, esp. 141–9; *cf. Santiago* 16; *Samos* 93; *Sobrado* 1.1; *Celanova* 53; *Coruña* 50; *Ourense* 1; *Oseira* 1; *Guimarães* A1.

[22] See *e.g. Santiago* 23; *Samos* 217; *Sobrado* 1.110; *Coruña* 110; *Celanova* 57; *Guimarães* 1A, A3, 54; *Coimbra* 124.

[23] See *e.g. León* 703, 432; *San Vicente* 29; *Samos* 58; *Sobrado* 1.42, 1.39; *Samos* 198, *Sobrado* 1.43, 1.115, *Lorvão* 37; *León* 432, *Sahagún* 200, 386, *San Vicente* 16, *Coruña* 29, *Santiago* 63, *Guimarães* 60; *Junqueira* 2; *León* 865, *Liébana* 38.

specified that it was beside a *quinione* (plot of land) belonging to Lovesindo, who had made a charter of it already to Celanova.[24] This citation flags a related but distinct transaction, with a different granter; in other cases, the granter of both texts is the same, like in a confirmation.[25] In a sense, it is footnoting, or referencing relevant transactions extant in writing: if the object was to provide full context for each charter, the outcome was the progressive construction of interconnections amongst charters. And the more this was practised, the more each user of a text was incentivised to have in hand, or at least to have access to, every other pertinent text. Some references, indeed, are for critical details which would have had to be checked at some point in the cited charter. In 1029, for example, three *fideiussores* (sureties) made a *placitum* (agreement) on behalf of Fruela Sendínez, undertaking to hand over a certain price to Pedro Flaínez once he returned to Valdoré, but for the actual amount they refer to the charter of sale which had been written up ten months earlier. Still more remarkably, for the boundaries of the property under sale they cite the original grant of it by Ordoño I to Purello, perhaps a distant ancestor of the vendor, in 854, though the copy which we have of this seems to be an early eleventh-century version.[26] It was more normal to cite properties or appurtenances less integral to the transaction: the second testament of Bishop Sisnando to Sobrado, made in 966, waves at all the moveables listed in his first one which would take too long to enumerate here, assuming the direct and ongoing accessibility of that text for reference as needed.[27]

Where we do not have the cited charter, most cases of citing other charters of related transactions or with further information once again come from the west, in a familiar pattern, but two Leonese examples are nonetheless illustrative. In 954, when Iulianus *presbiter* made a testament to Santos Justo y Pastor, he related the fiascos of his two previous attempts to do so, recording how he had been obliged to have both documents voided by episcopal council as the beneficiary houses were rocked by scandal, while Brandila gave to Abellar in 942 half of the property which he held by purchase from his mother-in-law Marie and by inheritance from his wife, on condition that he continue to work it in his lifetime together with the other

---

[24] *Celanova* 315 (310); *cf.* 297 (296).

[25] See *e.g. Santiago* 44 (1–4), *Samos* 44 (36); *San Isidro* 16 (15), *Sahagún* 345 (342, 328), *León* 772 (760), *Guimarães* 1B, A5 (1A, A3).

[26] *Otero* 190 (188, 1); Pérez, 'Parentesco', 84–5; Fernández Flórez, 'Purello', 175–9.

[27] *Sobrado* 1.6 (1.2); *cf.* 1.46 (1.45); *Guimarães* 68, A6 (50).

half which Marie had granted by charter to the monastery.[28] What these citations are doing is noting the written bases for any exceptions, limitations, or additions applicable to the current transaction. Indeed, in the noted, and probably interpolated, testament of Bishop Rosendo of Mondoñedo from 867, he confirmed that, while he bequeathed his *servos* and *ancillas* (male and female slaves, servants, or dependants of some kind) to the patronage of the brothers of a monastery in Almerezo, he had also legally freed them *per alia scripta* (by other documents) and even granted them property by another testament.[29] The goal must have been to prepare by flagging evidence which would be needed should a future challenge arise. In this respect, a sale made in 930 by Sarracinus and his wife Lela to Felis *presbiter* of land inherited from his father Terencius is explicit that its limits are where the charter of inheritance confirms: if they ever had to be proven, the relevant text would have to be available for consultation.[30]

Citing a prior charter as justification for a current transaction brings us full circle back to confirmation. As have already seen, when Sancho Ordóñez visited Santiago de Compostela in 927, he heard Bishop Hermegildo read aloud the testaments made by his predecessors, and duly confirmed them. According to the diploma, Fruela II had previously come there to pray, and the bishop had shown him these testaments as encouragement, but he declined to imitate their example, and instead alienated properties bestowed by them, violating the very sanction clauses which Sancho Ordóñez now reviewed.[31] The former king had in fact made a number of donations to the see, and the latter was here creating a *leyenda negra* around his rival, but he was also making an implicit point that the legacy of past written acts should shape present choices; many subsequent Leonese rulers accordingly grounded their generosity to Santiago in recollections of what their ancestors had done by document, motivated perhaps by similar beneficiary representations.[32] At a less exalted level, a dispute between the family of Alvarus and Abellar over land in Covellas was settled when the former

[28] *León* 278, 150; cf. *Otero* 21, 27, *Oviedo* 8, 43, *Liébana* 75, *Coruña* 71, 96, *Santiago* 21, *Samos* 144, 95, 23, *Celanova* 218, 309, *Guimarães* 15, 66, *PMH* 172, 197; *Sahagún* 30, *Otero* 181, *Sobrado* 1.59, 1.64, *Celanova* 105, 315; Davies, *Acts*, 79–80.

[29] *Coruña* 4; *Sobrado* 1.52; Sánchez-Albornoz, 'Libertos', 9–45; cf. *Sahagún* 416; *Santiago* 32; *Samos* 203; *Celanova* 199, 316, 373; *Lorvão* 13.

[30] *León* 88; cf. 189, 492, *Sahagún* 161, *Coruña* 58, *Samos* 136, *Sobrado* 1.6, *Celanova* 174; *León* 340, *Oña* 17, *Huesca* 3, *Coimbra* 72; *Otero* 76, *Astorga* 226, *Oviedo* 8, *Sobrado* 1.9, *Celanova* 8, 121.

[31] *Santiago* 51 (22, 1–4); cf. 36–8.

[32] *Santiago* 25 (15, 12); 40 (1–4); 43–4 (1–4); cf. *Samos* 100 (39); Sáez, 'Notas', esp. 35–46, 80–2; Isla Frez, 'Nombres', 19, 24–31.

sold it to the latter in 941, and eight months later Argemir cited this charter of sale while selling his own share, bought from his brother Alvarus, back to the monastery.[33] Of cases where the charter cited in explanation for a new transaction does not survive, access and knowledge are similarly the preconditions, such as for a sale by Ermoriquo and his wife Rosaldi to Pedro Flaínez from 1003, carried out in lieu of a charter of *perfiliatio* which they had made to him of one-third of their property.[34] Evidently it remained to hand and relevant, and in all these ways the written record acted, by means of recurrent reference in bare outline or in great detail, to legitimise, contextualise, and rationalise; in its continued circulation it stimulated and structured subsequent actions.

## Emphasising

Charters could also cite other charters in more general terms, but the question in such cases is whether it was purely rhetorical, drawing on the authority of text where none existed. Take the example of Vermudo II confirming the property of San Vicenzo de Pombeiro in 997 by reference to its *scripturas veteres et novas* (documents old and new), or that of Ramiro III restoring to Sobrado the *comitatos* ('counties', jurisdictions) which its founders had held *per commissorios* (by appointments) in 968, though this diploma bears some signs of tampering, or indeed of the same ten years later reaffirming its tenure of the *mandationes* (commissions) recorded in its *pactos et testamentos* (pacts and testaments).[35] Based on what we have so far seen, in many cases these must be real citations, and yet specificity does not appear to be the goal: they look instead to the fact of documentation and the legitimacy which that bestowed. This is clear in a donation and confirmation issued by Sancho III and Queen Muniadona to Albelda in 1024, declaring that, as he had given his pledge in other donations and transfers, so did he here, just as Alfonso V, after the fire at San Pedro de Rocas, had reaffirmed all the *firmitates et scripturas* (confirmations and documents) granted by his ancestors dating back to Alfonso III in his own diploma of 1007.[36] General citations on the acquisition of property played the same role, pointing less to a specific title deed than to the existence of title deeds

---

[33] *León* 148 (141).     [34] *Otero* 66; *cf. Astorga* 190; *Coruña* 53, 110; *PMH* 115, 255.
[35] *Pombeiro* 3; *Sobrado* 1.107–8; *cf. Benevívere* 1; *Coruña* 114; *Celanova* 110; *Samos* 39.
[36] *Albelda* 32; *Rocas* 1; Rodríguez Lajusticia, 'Presencia', 734–46.

in order to emphasise the right of disposition by the granter. Alvarus and Abraham, deacons, made a charter of sale to Bishop Velasco of León in 967, of a *villa* purchased from various vendors by *ceteris scripturis* (those other documents), as if saying a documentary *et cetera*.[37] The overall pattern is for the charters cited to belong to the granter or a relative and to record the purchase of what was now the object of a pious donation, indicating that religious houses especially wanted at least the suggestion of a written history for their benefactions.[38]

These 'textual expectations' are most apparent in the west, where Celanova, Sobrado, and Samos are prominent in the evidence with general citations of prior transactions ranging from donation to sale or exchange and inheritance through *colmellos* or *scripturas divisionis* (columns or documents of division).[39] Particular to Galicia and Portugal, moreover, is a habit of underlining the written quality of past acquisition, by using phrases like *sicut exaratum est* (as it is written) rather than referring to a text as such, or noting the fact of previous texts and prior granters, by using formulas like *per cartas et auctores proprios* (with charters and their authors).[40] On occasion former owners can be identified in such otherwise general citations: in an exceptional example from León, the testament of Bishop Fruela from 1002 enumerates properties obtained *per cartas emptionis seu placita iuditiorum* (by charters of purchase and agreements of judgements) from Bellito Gallego and Iusto of Santibáñez.[41] Here the vague expression of a written history has been solidified with participants in it, but that is atypical. The overriding thrust of these forms is best encapsulated in the endowment of the monastery of San Antolín in 1027 by Abbot Diego, who donated all his *villas* and lands which he had bought for a price and recorded in his *cartulas*, as their former owners had consigned them to him before witnesses.[42] The price had been paid and possession transferred publicly; in other words, all the elements of a charter of sale were present. The property

---

[37] *León* 403.

[38] See *e.g. León* 265, 405, 462, 611, 655, 754, *Sahagún* 145–7, 330, 345, *Otero* 185, *Castañeda* 6, 11, *Astorga* 263, *Oviedo* 41; *León* 180, 600, *Sahagún* 111, *San Vicente* 25.

[39] See *e.g. Samos* 158, 217, 61, 202, 58, 19, 69, 95, *Sobrado* 1.45, 1.13, 1.42, *Coruña* 116, *Celanova* 57, 81, 99, 154, 188, 199, 202, 215, 326, *Pombeiro* 2, *Coimbra* 81, 197, 142, *Paço de Sousa* 132, *Guimarães* 7, *PMH* 214, *Junqueira* 2; *Samos* 111, *Sobrado* 1.16, 1.9, 1.134, *Celanova* 84, 192, 290, 338, *Coimbra* 527, *Guimarães* 22; *Samos* 23, *Sobrado* 1.6, *Coruña* 135, *Celanova* 304, *Guimarães* 1A, A3.

[40] See *e.g. Santiago* 90, *Sobrado* 1.110, *Celanova* 229, 318; *Samos* 32, *Celanova* 97.

[41] *León* 629; *cf. Sahagún* 125; *Otero* 11; *Guimarães* 58.          [42] *Samos* 7.

had its proper written history, answering every possible question, so why go into any further detail here?

Where these citations state specific parties but at the same time use the plural for the texts and remain vague as to contents, they convey a similarly general message. When Placia sold her fifth, held from her husband Illalli, to Vimara *presbiter* in 932, she observed that her children had already made charters to him, while Sesmiro *frater* gave a third of his property to Bishop Rosendo and Celanova in 962 but reserved the remainder for his wife and children, to whom he had earlier made charters.[43] Waving at a wider written context, it is as if they say, 'see the family papers', warding off challengers with rhetoric of textuality. The same mode is attested for supporting documentation of appurtenances and boundaries: Egeredus and Rosula gave their monastery of San Mateo to Samos in 960, for example, with everything belonging to it as recorded in its *scriptis veteris et teneris* (documents old and recent), and Vermudo II transferred men into the service of Pico Sacro in 987 within the limits set in the *testamenta et agniciones* (testaments and settlements) of the monastery.[44] One sometimes wonders at the purpose: to give the impression of a written foundation where it was absent, or if it was extant to leave the recipients, all religious institutions or individuals, room for manoeuvre to refine the auxiliary texts as necessary? In this light imprecision need not always have constituted a disadvantage. And the practice is part of how such citation promoted itself: the more charters cited other charters, the more interconnected all charters became, and the more conspicuously a charter without citation, or property without charters, lacked this written context.

While common, charters citing other charters make up only a fifth of the corpus, and some consideration of the many charters which do not is in order. At times, the absence of a documentary citation is misleading. In 954, for example, Ordoño III explicitly confirmed the endowment of Pardomino, but also, implicitly, an earlier written confirmation by Ordoño II in 917: the same passage of Scripture is quoted in both diplomas, which also specify that its boundaries should be just as the abbots Fredamundus and Maximus obtained them.[45] Clearly the scribe had the prior text before him and drew

---

[43] *Celanova* 37, 155; cf. 308; *Coimbra* 155; *Santillana* 22; García de Valdeavellano, 'Cuota', 153–5, 165.

[44] *Samos* 248; *Santiago* 55; cf. *Samos* 2, 100, 151, 76, S1, *Sobrado* 1.42, *Celanova* 37, 98, 154, 199, *Guimarães* 7, *Coimbra* 197, *Sahagún* 308; *Samos* 2, 61, 82, *Sobrado* 1.134, *Oviedo* 25, *San Vicente* 29.

[45] *León* 280 (41); cf. 102 (40); *Sahagún* 342 (328); Álvarez Maurín, 'Estudio', 95–104.

on it in drafting its successor; if both were read out at the same time, the sense of continuity would have been unmistakeable. Similarly, when Constancius *confessor* made a donation to Abellar in 944 including land gained by exchange with Bera, probably the namesake of Villobera, the scribe appears to have been looking at not only the charter of this transaction of 923, but some other (written?) source whence he added in additional information, *inter alia* identifying Bera as a monk of Valmadrigal.[46] Detecting 'silent citation' is a challenge in so large a corpus of documentation, and with so many cited sources doubtless lost, but simple non-citation of a known charter is easy enough to spot. In 985, for instance, Sancho Garcés II confirmed the donation of a *villa* to Pampaneto made by his father García Sánchez I, but did not mention the diploma of 941 recording this gift, while Alvito and his wife Nunillo in 1005 sold one-quarter of a vineyard to Cresconius *praepositus* in addition to the three-quarters which they had sold him already, without indicating that they had made a charter of that very sale four months before.[47] Even the most preliminary survey is sufficient to find that non-citation of other charters spans early medieval Iberia regionally, socially, and across the four fields of confirmation, means of acquisition, further information, and justification where we have seen citation practised with surviving documents.[48]

Why not cite a charter? In those transactions involving parties with known archives of their own, such as Hermegildo and Paterna, it must reflect deliberate choice, rather than some accident of being unable to access the text. When confirming their endowment of Sobrado in 952, they did not cite their supporting documentation even as they passed it to the monastery, in the archive of which it has been preserved.[49] More subjective are the many instances where a charter cites no written record yet describes prior transactions in such number or detail that, notwithstanding the potential of memory, a text seems essential, especially when it comes to specifying means of acquisition. Vitalis *confessor* gave nine properties to

---

[46] *León* 187 (59); *cf. Santiago* 18 (15); Martínez Sopena and Carbajo Serrano, 'Notas', 113–25.

[47] *Albelda* 29 (8); *Celanova* 288 (286); *cf. León* 233 (232); Olcoz Yanguas, 'Pampaneto', 232–6.

[48] See *e.g. Sahagún* 26 (24, 19), 290 (286), 406 (391), 422 (333), *Castañeda* 4 (2), *Montes* 5 (2), *Liébana* 75 (58), *San Juan* 30 (25), *Celanova* 186 (110), 298 (296–7), *Santiago*  2 (1), 17 (1–2), 39 (1), *Coruña* 16 (15), *Lorvão* 1 (19), 58 (57); *León* 617 (557), *Sahagún* 215 (194), 284 (272–3), 322 (78), 333 (332), *Astorga*  8 (7), 84 (71), *Cardeña* 54 (37.1), *Oña* 12 (10), *Celanova* 210 (206), *Santiago* 29 (30), *PMH* 16 (14), *Lorvão* 4 (7), 34 (36), *Arouca* 2 (1), *Guimarães* 67 (50), 68, A6 (50); *Sahagún* 11 (9–10), 217 (208), 279 (145), *Celanova*  222 (206), *Coimbra* 135 (126); *Santiago* 64 (52–4, 56), *Samos*  178 (115, 199).

[49] *Sobrado* 1.1; *cf.* 1.2; *Celanova* 40, 72; *Sahagún* 306.

Sahagún in 970, for example, in each case naming from whom he had purchased it and for what price; Fredesindo *confrater* and his family, donating lands to Eslonza in 950, narrated their ownership history from acquisition by his grandparents to the delimitation of their boundaries at a council held by the son of Alfonso III.[50] Given that documentation was routinely handed over whenever property changed hands, explicit reference to it was not strictly necessary from the point of view of the beneficiary, though perhaps it was read aloud in some cases of confirmation. If the practice is to be understood as optional, this in turn has two implications: first that the citation rate must underestimate the frequency of consulting charters, and secondly that those who made note as they did so were drawing attention to it. In the world of our texts, basing a positive statement on documentation was not obligatory, but seemed in some circumstances to confer advantage, and the explanation for this can be found in the function of charters in settling disputes.

## Evidence

Take any transaction, and it likely did not generate just one document but occasioned the creation and consultation of a wide array of procedural texts. In addition to the drafts and versions which we have encountered in considering the craft of the scribe, 'parchmentwork' produced in the course of writing a charter includes permission slips, provisional wills, lists of property, and correspondence, each less a discrete operation than a brief pause in a longer textual journey. When Fruela planned to sell to Imilo the *villa* which he held in service from Queen Tarasia in 994, for instance, the purchaser required him to produce a charter from his mistress granting *mandato* (permission), and use of such slips appears to have been normal, logically, when disposing of property over which another party had a claim through lordship, familial ties, or tenure.[51] Provisional wills, analogously, commission a testamentary executor, typically a relation or the beneficiary, to act on behalf of the granter, and we have already met Vita, on her

---

[50]  *Sahagún* 258; *Eslonza* 24; *cf. León* 543, 679, 691, 709, 815, *Astorga* 151, *Santillana* 6, 37, *Oviedo* 40, *Albelda* 17, *Irache* 2, *Leire* 14, *Celanova* 122, *Santiago* 65, *San Clodio* 1, *ChLA* 114, 32; *León* 736, *Sahagún* 175, 255, 402, *Otero* 32, *Astorga* 230, *Liébana* 57, *Coruña* 99, *Celanova* 30, 65, 68, 108, 158, 216, 233, 238, 262, 342, *Santiago* 47, *Lorvão* 5, *Coimbra* 517, 121.

[51]  *León* 560; *cf.* 543, 862, 895; *Samos* 132; Grassotti, '"Dominus"', 656–62; Fernández Conde and Torrente Fernández, 'Orígenes', 187–94.

deathbed in 1030, summoning the abbot of San Miguel de León to inventory her estate, selecting agents from her *gens* (family?), and directing them *de suo ore* (orally) and in writing to donate it on her behalf to the monastery, as they duly carried out after her death.[52] Inventories also featured frequently in the writing process: Serenianus *presbiter* gave Bishop Rosendo and Celanova, amongst other possessions, the *libertos* (freedmen) belonging to his family named *in noticia* in 947, and there was evidently an attachment to this charter, likely on the reverse side of the original parchment, a working register of dependants or one drawn up for this transaction.[53] From such a density of intermediary and supplementary texts, it was a short step to deploying written evidence routinely at trial, and indeed, the business of going to court was itself, in the wording of a diploma of Alfonso III to Santiago from 866, expected to be initiated *per nuncium et scriptum* (by oral and written notification).[54] This is altogether apt for what turns out to have been a deeply textual process of dispute and settlement.

## Parchmentwork

Like engaging in transaction, settling disputes generated texts: agreements, affidavits, and written oaths facilitated reaching a resolution.[55] To take the most common, the purpose of some *placita* (agreements) was to bind the parties to the next stage of settlement, whether this was to give testimony, offer evidence, take an oath, undergo the ordeal, or consult the law. In 878, the advocates of Varoncelus and Bishop Indisclo of Astorga were required by judges to *conscribere roborare et firmare* (write, sign, and confirm) a *placitum* to produce witnesses in support of their claims when the king next came to León, while Hermegildo made a *plazum*, a variant spelling, in 991 to send a representative on an arranged date to undertake the ordeal of hot water on his behalf.[56] Such agreements were not always kept, of course,

---

[52] *León* 873; *cf.* 830; *Sahagún* 284; *San Juan* 10; *Sobrado* 1.6; *Lorvão* 33; García-Gallo, 'Testamento', esp. 471–97; Taylor, 'Publication', 767–80.

[53] *Celanova* 81; *cf. Sobrado* 1.132; *Samos* 151, 82; *Guimarães* 22; Pallares Méndez, *Monasterio*, 13; Carzolio de Rossi, 'Reflexiones', 36–43.

[54] *Santiago* 4; *cf.* 8; *Samos* 35.

[55] Collins, 'Law', 498–506; Collins, 'Visigothic Law', 87–90; Davies, *Windows*, esp. 35–55, 279–83.

[56] *Astorga* 5; *Otero* 31; López Ortiz, 'Proceso', 207–8; Quintana Prieto, 'Obispado', 165–7, 172–9, 193–4; Davies, *Windows*, 211–12; *cf. Santillana* 31, *Santiago* 24, *Sobrado* 1.129–30, 1.132, *Celanova* 260, *Braga* 22, *Guimarães* 24, *Coimbra* 212, 202, *PMH* 216, *Arouca* 84; *Cardeña* 210, *Sobrado* 1.134, *Guimarães* 51; *Coruña* 95, *Puerto* 1; *Celanova* 345.

but defaulting on one could provide a route to resolution, as in the dispute which played out between Sahagún and the family of Vigila from June to August in 958: both parties signed a *placitum* to present themselves and their evidence before the king and bishop of León, but only Vistremiro *frater* showed up, and so, after waiting three days past the agreed date, the judges decided in favour of his monastery.[57] At the settlement stage, the terms of a compromise could also be secured by written agreement: in 1014, at the end of a convoluted contretemps, Mitto Todegildiz and his partisans reached an accord, promising to restore the contested *villa* to Guimarães within three days.[58] Promises made in writing were binding, and if these conditions were infringed, further litigation ensued. The rebel Conanzo and family, held by Vermudo II and released on a *placitum* to remain peaceable, found on resuming their villainy all their property forfeit on the grounds that *mentiti sunt ipsum placitum*—they had lied to or deceived the text.[59]

The other key procedural text is the affidavit, which comes under a range of different titles but all with the function of recording testimony at one or another stage of dispute. They are often cited in charters where the defeated party is obliged to make compensation, as part of the process of accepting liability. Cidi *presbiter* and his mother Goda made a *manifestum* (confession) before judge, *saio* (bailiff), and *homines bonos* (good men) in 1021, admitting that they had usurped a *villa* from Mumadona, a religious, and agreeing to sell her a court in return.[60] When Lupi and his wife Elo sold a vineyard to Fruela Velaz and his wife Jimena in 963, in contrast, they were paying for damages to person of 30 *solidi* and to property of 60 *solidi*, as enumerated *in noticia* (in a schedule), which reads less like a confession than some statement or assessment of charges, perhaps written in the margin of the parchment.[61] Both confessions and charges could evidently be 'filed' by defendants and appellants in the course of disputes, since Mater confirmed a *manifesto*, recorded *in noticia*, in 993 concerning items of clothing which she had stolen from Zislla; in consequence of her guilt, she

---

[57] *Sahagún* 159; Prieto Prieto, 'Sahagún', 493–4; Collins, 'Law', 502–3; *cf. Otero* 109; *Sobrado* 1.29, 1.21; *Celanova* 223; *Guimarães* 8; Wood, 'Disputes', 10–14; Fouracre, ' "Placita" ', 33–4.

[58] *Guimarães* 51; Prieto Morera, 'Proceso', 479–81; *cf. León* 777; *Otero* 4, 147, 195; *Samos* 44; *Sobrado* 1.31, 1.103, 1.132; *Celanova* 315, 331; *Alfonso V* 7; *Guimarães* 24.

[59] *León* 541; Pérez, 'Insumisión', 368; *cf. Sahagún* 427; *Otero* 56–7; *Santiago* 57; *Sobrado* 1.130; *Celanova* 326, 345, 360, 382; *Coimbra* 212.

[60] *León* 779; Martínez Díez, 'Instituciones', 164–6; Corral and Pérez Rodríguez, 'Fines', 178; *cf. León* 378; *Otero* 148, 151, 187; *Floriano* 75; *Sobrado* 1.54, 1.21, 1.31.

[61] *León* 360; Davies, *Windows*, 47; Carvajal Castro, 'Houses', 82, 90–3; *cf. Sahagún* 261; *Sobrado* 1.31.

made a charter of half of her property to Flaíno Muñoz and his wife Iusta.[62] The terminology can be difficult to pin down, and varies from scribe to scribe, including outliers like a *documentum petitionis* (notice of appeal) from Samos and an *indiculum testimonii* (written deposition) at Celanova.[63] But all these texts emerged organically from the settlement process and are cited in the more streamlined accounts made after the fact. Gontrigo represented Pedro Flaínez on a date set by *placitum* in 1019, arguing that Zidi Andrias had taken property from him, as documented in a *noticia*, and given it to a third party: the parties then made a *placitum* to inquire as to relevant law, and after this accusation was repeated at the next stage of the process, Zidi Andrias made a *placitum* confessing that he had done what was stated in the *manifestum*, and a final *pactum* (agreed resolution) brought the whole affair to a conclusion.[64] Six texts in total, in addition to the narrative; settling disputes was a documentary undertaking every step of the way.

Even oaths relied on the written word. The *condiciones sacramentorum* is a particular type of procedural text with soundly late Roman and Visigothic legal and documentary pedigree, which records the 'terms of oaths' to be sworn. In early medieval Iberia, this was normally an oath taken by parties or witnesses during a court case, though in Catalunya it was also used in the context of testamentary publication; invoking the Gospels, saints, and other spiritual authorities, setting out testimony, and stating penalties for perjury, it was placed on a Bible or altar, according to its own narrative, and the oath-takers recited its contents while touching it with their hands.[65] When Celanova made a complaint before the court of Alfonso V in 1001, accusing a certain Adefonsus of usurping its property, the judges asked both parties to produce witnesses, and selected ten to swear the *seriem conditionum* (list of terms) on behalf of the monastery, as well as a neutral third party to endure the ordeal of hot water, but on the day Adefonsus yielded outside the church where the rituals were to occur.[66] And significantly, the party who was not appointed to take an oath interacted with its text nonetheless. Once Lovesindo Abenazar and Guimarães had elaborated their competing claims

---

[62] *Otero* 34.  [63] *Samos* S10; *Lugo*, 2, 591–4; *Celanova* 52; *cf.* 260.
[64] *Otero* 116; Prieto Prieto, 'Otero', 640–2; *cf. Castañeda* 1; *Oña* 3; *Celanova* 292; *Arouca* 84.
[65] *FV* 39–40; *LV* 2.1.23, 2.1.25, 2.2.5, 12.3.15; Canellas López, *Diplomática*, 57–8; Velázquez, 'Elementos', 563–4; Alvarado Planas, *Problema*, 156–71; Marques, 'Language', 140–2; *cf.* Benito i Monclús, Kosto, and Taylor, 'Approaches', 48–59; Blidstein, 'Swearing', 53–72; Matthews, 'Boundaries', 284–305.
[66] *Celanova* 260; *cf. Otero* 31.

in 999, each offered five witnesses before the *saio*, agreed by *plazo* to go *pro ad lege* (for the law) to the count and judges, and compared their respective evidence, before agreeing in another *plazo* that the witnesses for the monastery should swear. Yet here again Lovesindo capitulated, and was abruptly ejected from the church; he then confirmed in the hands of the *saio* the monastic *conditione* or the written statement of the oath taken by the victorious Guimarães, receiving a payment *in conpagina* (in compensatory settlement).[67]

These references matter because they point to real procedural documents in use. The final syntheses of settlements, as we have seen, not only cited *placita* but also incorporated them as attachments. The narrative section of a dispute from 978, for example, gives way to two written agreements by Magito, one to return land which he had taken from Sahagún, the other to exchange it for property elsewhere, probably reflecting a compromise arranged after the fact.[68] There are a few *placita* surviving as standalone texts, such as that between Abbot Montanus and Cissela *presbiter* in 927, promising the *saio* to appear before the judges on the next feast-day of San Bartolomé with their witnesses for the oath, and their similarity serves to confirm the representativeness of those incorporated into the 'end product'.[69] The same too can be said of original affidavits. Emlo admitted in 1022 that he had, as charged, convinced Todildi *ancilla* to steal grain from her master Fruela Muñoz, shortly before Eneco confessed that he and his mother had tried to abduct Midona Vita from the household of Fruela Muñoz again, both texts preserved in and cited by the procedural documentation of the settlements.[70] And standalone records of oaths provide us the very text which once rested on the altar. Four witnesses swore on behalf of Abbot Tello in 911, invoking the Trinity, the four Gospels, and the relics of San Millán in the basilica dedicated to him at Gabinea (unidentified, somewhere in Orduña): they knew first-hand that one of two priests had given himself and his property to the monastery and received lease of land in return, leading both respondent priests to confess as much.[71] When Bishop Pelayo of Lugo and Bishop Pedro of Santiago, the latter acting for

---

[67]  *Guimarães* 24; Davies, 'Judges', 194–5; *cf. Guimarães* 51.

[68]  *Valladolid* 3; Prieto Prieto, 'Sahagún', 503–4; Ruiz Albi, 'Hallazgo', 143–6; *cf. Oviedo* 26; *Otero* 38–9, 116, 150–1; *Liébana* 66; *Floriano* 73–5; *Celanova* 200; *PMH* 167.

[69]  *Puerto* 3; *cf. PMH* 144; *Coimbra* 193.

[70]  *Otero* 147 (148); 150 (151); Astarita, 'Prácticas', 48–9; *cf. Otero* 38 (39), 125; *Cardeña* 210; *Puerto* 1; *Celanova* 200.

[71]  *Valpuesta* 10; López Mata, *Geografía*, 69; Collins, 'Visigothic Law', 94–5; Carvajal Castro, 'Houses', 86–7; *cf. Valpuesta* 11, 33; *Puerto* 2; Humfress, 'Judging', 155–8.

Sobrado, argued over ownership of some men later in the tenth century, two each from nine *villas* in the locality were chosen for the *conditiones sacramentorum* at the hand of the *saio*. Holding these terms, now incorporated into a holistic account of the case, they swore by the Patriarchs and Apostles, amongst others, on the altar of San Julián that they were legally free and owed only *vectilia et tributa* (rental payment) to the monastery.[72] Whether an agreement, an affidavit, or a written oath, procedural documentation was not some fossilised Visigothic formula, but the means by which each successive stage of the settlement was negotiated, and the raw material from which the scribe fashioned a final treatment to secure it.

## Litigation

In this context of documentary disputing, written evidence played a fundamental role in advancing and defending claims to property. Possession of a supporting charter could lead simply and straightforwardly to a successful outcome at court, but in most cases success was achieved through complementary oral modes of proof, a combination of inquests, testimony, oaths, and ordeals which saw text introduced, evaluated, and confirmed or destroyed.[73] Only a minority of settlements involve written evidence, and within this subset the narrative of the record is at pains to minimise actual dispute: what we typically find is one party producing a text, the other conceding with little to no fight. Some cases are functionally indistinguishable from confirmation charters. Bishop Savarigo of León reminded Vermudo II in a *querimonia* (complaint) of 985 that his forebears, as recorded in prior diplomas, had granted *villas* to the see which Gómez Díaz and his magnate cronies had seized by force, and the king promptly restored possession.[74] Elsewhere the respondent yielded immediately, as Lellitus and Lillus did in 885, admitting that they had received a church of San Andrés from a bishop attached to San Martín de Turieno which its founders left to the monastery via testaments, but had given it away six years later. Crucially, they

---

[72] *Sobrado* 1.109; Prieto Morera, 'Proceso', 476–8; Davies, *Windows*, 243–5; Davies, 'Language', 241–4; *cf. Castañeda* 1.

[73] Martínez Díez, 'Instituciones', 162–3; Collins, 'Law', 495–6; Collins, 'Visigothic Law', 86–7; Martínez Díez, 'Terminología', 256–7; *cf.* Heidecker, 'Communication', 101–26; Bowman, *Landmarks*, 141–7; Kosto, *Agreements*, 134–57; Heidecker, 'Charters', 39–53.

[74] *León* 508; *cf. Sahagún* 183 (167–8); *Castañeda* 3; *Coruña* 128 (73); *Santiago* 58; *Samos* 239; *Celanova* 263, 302; Fernández Flórez, 'Documentos', 110–15.

concluded, they lacked any means of contradicting the charge, such that the whole account serves to validate the written evidence.[75] Disputes might even be cast bluntly as violations of charters, clear-cut cases requiring compensation. In 997, for instance, Belito and Kalendo accepted that they had cultivated land owned in testament by Santa Marina de Viñayo, overturning their document with its penal clause of 500 *solidi*. This text and the cited testament of 976 are written on the same parchment, and they duly restored its provisions, reiterating its penalty in direct quotation, though they do not seem to have paid it.[76] Collectively such examples recall the practice of *ostensio cartae* (exhibition of a charter), the fictive disputes attested in early medieval Italy, but the timespan between the original text and the formal confirmation is much longer here, suggesting that more is going on behind the scenes.[77] In many cases the losing party barely registers; whatever argument and compromise actually took place *en route* to resolution, the victor, it seems likely, has arranged for the final record to be simplified, presenting the validity of the written title in splendid isolation.

There are only two potential instances of a party in sole possession of documentation not emerging from court victorious, and they tend to confirm the presumption of superiority for written evidence over other forms of claim. In 1009, a disagreement arose between Nina Meirelez, Ioannes *presbiter*, and others over the monastery of Valdearcos and its patrimony, but they made a pact, granting it for life to Ioannes on condition that after his death it should pass to the mother house of Abellar. Later on, both main parties asked the abbot of the latter to return the testament, and the cell stood empty until a new brother was sent; then the abbot confirmed the document, restoring a fifth of the property to Valdearcos and reserving the rest for Abellar after Nina and his wife Cida had died.[78] The story is convoluted and obscure, but the point is that, while earlier charters of agreement and testament were overturned, it was the parties to them who decided to do so in order to make new arrangements, reflecting evolving circumstances of vocation and life. The dispute which arose between Furtunius Ermiariz and Gutier *diaconus* in 1027 marks something of a contrast. Furtunius

[75] *Liébana* 17; Loring García, *Cantabria*, 235–41; Collins, 'Visigothic Law', 94; Portass, *World*, 64–5; *cf. León* 829; *Sahagún* 159; *Cardeña* 275 (297); *Celanova* 195 (113); *Tumbo Viejo* 136.

[76] *Otero* 43 (21); Carvajal Castro, 'Sanctions', 163–4; Carvajal Castro and Escalona, 'Value', 43–4; *cf. León* 379, 624; *Valladolid* 3; *Celanova* 126, 270, 308; *PMH* 163; *Guimarães* 66.

[77] Wickham, 'Disputes', 117–18; Brunsch, 'Authority', 277–87.

[78] *León* 677; Carbajo Serrano, *Monasterio*, 71, 80, 95; Arias y Alonso, 'Notas', 1, 89.

asserted that his father, *per suas cartas* (by his charters), had bought himself a certain *villa*, but Gutier replied that he had taken it from him in payment of a debt: the judges decided on behalf of Gutier, who went on to make an exchange with Furtunius by way of settlement.[79] Here the victor proved his claim without written proof, but the original deed was not at issue; the dispute concerned the history of the *villa* subsequent to that text, and for this neither party offered documentation.

The advantage of a charter for defending a claim is underlined by scenarios in which that written evidence was itself the object of dispute. Even if the goal was simply to deny the advantage to the holder, without it surely no effort would have been made to obtain or retain the text. We have already read part of the Samos chronicle of 944, which relates how Berila, when commissioned to restore the monastery, sent two brothers to acquire copies of its lost *firmitates* (confirmations) from the royal archive in Oviedo, and they returned from Fruela II with a *cartario* (cartulary) of 59 charters. After Berila had departed on pilgrimage, however, Bishop Ero of Lugo usurped control of Samos and seized its cartulary, forcing the brother in charge to appeal to Sancho Ordóñez to restore it to him.[80] The centrality of documentation to claims of ownership also underlies a codicil added to a diploma of 968 by which Ramiro III had granted various *comitatos* to Abbot Pedro of Sobrado: 40 years later Bishop Pelayo of Lugo explained that Gutier Osoriz had stolen this document from the monastery and given it to him, but the good Munia had apprised him of the situation and he now returned one of the counties to its control, along with the text.[81] Munio Gutiérrez told a similar story in 992, that his father had owned a church in Galicia, with the testaments of its founders, and had leased it to Viliulfus on terms of service, but that he and his brother Christoforus *presbiter* had then conspired with others to pilfer and conceal the documents. When Viliulfus made a deathbed confession, they were discovered in the hands of Christoforus, and he was obliged to sign a *placitum* to retain the church on the same terms as before. Later, however, he claimed anew that Viliulfus had been granted it outright and that he himself had held the stolen testaments for 30 years, but he was charged with breaking his agreement and finally lost to Munio in court.[82] Since charters did not simply confer ownership on any new holder

[79] *Sobrado* 1.134.
[80] *Samos* 35; Sá Bravo, *Monacato*, 1, 446–60; Freire Camaniel, *Monacato*, 2, 886–92; Rucquoi, 'Peregrinos', 55.
[81] *Sobrado* 1.107.     [82] *Sobrado* 1.130.

like bearer bonds, the motive for such thefts must have been preventive, a calculation that if their beneficiaries were denied them, they would occupy a weaker position when defending their claims.

It is worth noting that the world of written evidence also extended beyond parchment charters to stone boundary markers, by which the landscape could be read like a text. These are especially prominent in Galicia and Portugal, and in many cases astonishingly long lived, dating back as far as the Iron Age and still *in situ* today.[83] As with more traditional forms of documentation, reading the shapes, patterns, images, or writing on such markers, or even the presence of earthworks or inscribed trees, could help to resolve disagreement over the limits between properties, and the Visigothic law code made provision for this, giving great weight to their antiquity and immobility, at least since the Roman period.[84] In 911, as we have seen, Bishop Savarigo of Mondoñedo made a *sugessionem* (petition) to Ordoño Adefonsiz for the see of São Martinho de Dume, producing the testament which Alfonso III had granted to his predecessor Bishop Rosendo and requesting *previsores* (inspectors) to go and perambulate it, a procedure described and indeed implemented in Visigothic secular and canon law as a way of creating consensus.[85] Accordingly, bishops, abbots, priests, and *homines bonos* who were accustomed to *antiquitum comprovare* (verify the age-old arrangements) climbed atop a hill or mountain between the bishopric and the *villa* of Infias, evidently the point of conflict, and found there a stone marked with a *caracterem* (device) of San Vicente, a term defined in the Visigothic code as a *decuria* or 'X', and another engraved with a cross.[86] Thence they traced the perimeter along a course of *petras fictas* (fixed stones) erected *ab antico* (since Antiquity, or by an ancient?), including one *petra scripta* (written stone) inscribed quite definitely with the word *terminum* (boundary), and a second identifiable with Santa Eulalia. At least one of these stones corresponds with the reconstructed cadastral map of the country north of Braga; as they walked, the inspectors were literally reading a Roman centuriated landscape.[87]

---

[83]   Ferro Couselo, *Petroglifos*, esp. 13–45; García Quintela and Seoane-Veiga, 'Vida', 243–66; Vázquez Martínez, Rodríguez Rellán, and Fábregas Valcarce, 'Petroglifos', 61–83; *cf.* Santos Estévez, *Petroglifos*.

[84]   *LV* 10.3; Bermejo Barrera and Romaní Martínez, 'Cojuración', 560–95.

[85]   *Braga* 19; *LV* 10.3.4–5; II Seville 2; López Ortiz, 'Proceso', 211–12, 218–19; Ferro Couselo, *Petroglifos*, 198–9; García Álvarez, 'Ordoño', 219, 232–4; *cf.* Bowman, *Landmarks*, 192–7.

[86]   *LV* 8.6.1, 10.3.3.       [87]   Carvalho, 'Marcadores', esp. 158–62.

On the ground, milestones, boundary markers, funerary stelae, and other decorated or inscribed stones from the imperial period are also particularly concentrated in the northwest of Iberia. They are a physical manifestation of that denser textuality of Galicia and Portugal, and such stones may be found in boundary clauses of charters throughout the region, serving the function of delimiting space.[88] This might take the form of property given to San Martiño Pinario in 912 and *cautata per petras erectas et scriptas* (bounded by the stones which were set up and inscribed), or land paid in fine to Celanova in 952 and marked out to witnesses by its *karacteres fitos* (fixed devices), or estates gifted to Lorvão in 974 and delimited *per arcas antiquas et per petras sicilatas* (by ancient markers and by figured stones).[89] The inscription need not have been textual, as in two Leonese examples: Sarracinus and his wife Lela sold to Felis *presbiter* and his wife Elduara in 930 property bounded by crosses which his father had set up for him, while Martino and his wife Semena sold trees to Dominico and his wife Matre in 1002, some of them with *suas signas vel notas per suis terminis* (their signs or marks along their borders).[90] Boundary markers could be written with simple shapes or signs, or complex designs, animals, or figures, and as such they could be read like the monograms and signs on charters, where necessary as evidence in disputes.[91] As the foregoing two cases also indicate, they were not limited to the west or prehistory, but formed part of a general, ongoing struggle for control over writing the landscape.[92] In Valdoré in 946, a fragmentary charter recounts a dispute which involved the destruction of two *limides verdes* ('green boundaries', or hedges) and the illicit relocation of two *moliones pedrinios* (boundary stones or cairns), while Donum and others shifted *arcas petrinias* (stone markers) on mountains owned by Pedro Flaínez, and had to pay him in penalty property demarcated by *moliones petrinius* (boundary stones) of its own in 1022.[93] As with other written evidence, stone texts were advantageous in dispute, but they had to be accepted in order to be effective. In 950, a disagreement over

---

[88]  Rodríguez Colmenero, Ferrer Sierra, and Álvarez Asorey, *Miliarios*, esp. 52–7; Schattner, 'Imagen', 349–81.

[89]  *Coruña* 15; *Celanova* 96; *Coimbra* 2; *cf. Montes* 7; *San Pelayo* 1; *Coruña* 76, 96; *Celanova* 90; *VDJ* 2; *San Esteban* 1; Martinón-Torres, 'Megalitos', 97–100.

[90]  *León* 88, 613; *cf. Otero* 120; *Astorga* 5; *Sobrado* 1.43; *Coruña* 19; *Guimarães* 68, A6.

[91]  Ferro Couselo, *Petroglifos*, 173–90; Vázquez Varela, 'Petroglifos', 43–51; Correa Arias, 'Petroglifos', esp. 25–53; Monteagudo García, 'Sistematización', 57–72.

[92]  Fernández Ibáñez and Lamalfa Díaz, 'Manifestaciones', 257–67; Mallo Viesca, 'Grabados', 17–53.

[93]  *Otero* 4, 149; *cf.* 121; *León* 191; D. Kremer, '(R)espigando', 27–8.

borders between the inhabitants of Santa María de Verín and several neigh-bouring *villas* required the *maiores natu* (elders or better born?) of Baronceli (Verín) to trace the boundaries by perambulation, following distinctive signs such as a *petram ferro sculptam quasi laco* (stone carved out by an iron tool resembling a basin), but they had to do it all again in 951 for the settlement to stick.[94]

Turning back from stone to parchment, settlement took on a particular character when both parties possessed written evidence. Sometimes this turned out to be a specious claim, but where true it called for careful com-parison of the documentation. In the case of Arborius and María, they made a simple commendation of themselves to Abellar, donating all their lands to the monastery in 927, but two decades later, after both had died, Velasco seized that property, claiming to hold it by an earlier *kartulam firmitatis* (charter of confirmation). According to an extensive account of the dispute from 952, the parties then appealed to Ordoño III, and signed a *placitum* to appear before him in León with their respective documents, including the trump card of Abellar, a written agreement by Velasco pledg-ing his lifetime service to Arborius and María. As it transpired, they met at a council chaired by the bishop of León, where the abbot of Abellar produced both the testament and the *placitum*, but Velasco brought only the feeble excuse that his charter was elsewhere, prompting both parties to go in search of it. When they had found nothing and returned to court, the narra-tive states, interestingly, that they consulted the law *tanquam si* (just as if) the document had actually been brought to the council: even if an earlier testament had been made, they found, the granter had the right to change his mind, and as such the later arrangement should stand.[95] In other cases, failure to produce spelled an instant defeat, but here Velasco appears to have capitalised on the willingness of the court to take his pretence of having a charter and his 'inability' to find it in good faith.[96] There was a procedure in place to handle contradictory written claims, clearly, and the court decided that the potential of documentary proof was sufficient to justify going through the motions.

[94] *Celanova* 88, 94; Ferro Couselo, *Petroglifos*, esp. 200–2; cf. *Samos* 40; *Coruña* 65; *Celanova* 62, 86; *Lorvão* 36; Pallares Méndez and Portela Silva, 'Lugar', 65–7; Davies, *Windows*, 210–12, 221–2.

[95] *León* 72, 256; Sánchez-Albornoz, ' "Juicio" ', 383–6; Orlandis, 'Monasterios dúplices', 85–6; Rodríguez Fernández, *Ordoño*, 164–7; Carbajo Serrano, *Monasterio*, 70, 94–6, 194.

[96] *Cardeña* 210; *San Millán* 80; cf. Collins, 'Visigothic Law', 92–3; Bowman, *Landmarks*, 151–64.

If both parties not only claimed but also produced valid written evidence, compromise became necessary, reflecting their competing legitimacies. Felix *presbiter* built the monastery of San Miguel Arcángel on land which Columba had given to him by testament in memory of her parents, but in 1021 the abbot of Celanova hauled him before Alfonso V and alleged that Bishop Sisnando of Santiago had drawn up a document granting the same property to his own monastery. Felix heard this text read aloud, and soon came to an arrangement with the abbot, set down in a *placitum*, that within a fixed time he should build a house in León to exchange for that document, with a *cautum agnitionis* (stipulation of settlement) that Celanova trouble him no more.[97] Much is left unexplained, but the narrative accepts the validity of both written grants, and the workaround settlement carefully avoids compromising either one. In a similar though possibly interpolated case of 1025, the bishop of Lugo sought the restoration of some *servos ecclesie*, and argued at the court of Alfonso V that his predecessors all the way back to the (legendary?) Odoario in the eighth century had until recent civil strife held them through *colmellos* and *scripturas firmitatis*, which he promised to retrieve from the archive. In reply, the advocate of the 'Church slaves', backed by San Salvador de Oviedo, countered that their ancestors had come to the area as *ingenuos* (freemen) by mandate of Alfonso III and settled abandoned *villas*, which Alfonso V had lately granted them by diploma. Both parties made a *placitum* to marshal witnesses, then another to consult the law, before the judges investigated their testimony by comparing it with the *scripturas vetustas anterioras et posterioras* (olden documents, both earlier and later). But when it came time to swear an oath at a church just outside of Braga, the *servos ecclesie* relented, accepted the truth of the records supplied by Lugo, and agreed to return into service.[98] Despite the stark difference in status between these parties, the presence of text still commanded respect, though the outcome was capitulation by the weaker party. Yet there must once again be more going on beneath the surface: could Alfonso V have granted diplomas to both parties? The narrative refuses to confront this possibility, and leaves the conflicting documentation behind unresolved, moving on swiftly to the resolution.

---

[97] *León* 777; *Alfonso V*, 142–5; Carriedo Tejedo, 'Fraudes', 43–62; *cf. Sahagún* 277.
[98] *Braga* 22; Sousa Soares, 'Testemunho', 151–60; Pastor Díaz de Garayo, 'Uso', 86–94; *cf.* D'Emilio, 'Legend', 50; Calleja-Puerta, 'Delimitación', 39–57.

## Integration

In the Braga case, in other words, close attention was paid to written evidence, yet the path to resolution opened only through appeal to a higher authority. While text was central to disputing, it seldom provided the sole basis for settlement: oral and ritual processes served to integrate the proffered documentation into the participating community and create consensus around an outcome.[99] Building on what we have seen of boundaries, one means of doing so was to confirm a charter through inquest.[100] In 931, the monks of San Julián de Ruiforco had to defend their ownership of two *villas* granted to the monastery by diplomas of Alfonso III, García I, and Ordoño II, whose denizens claimed to hold them independently *de presura* (a charged and controversial term: most simply 'by seizure', but from a wide range of potential conditions and encompassing both 'top-down' and 'ground-up' initiative).[101] Alfonso IV and his court paid a personal visit to hear testimony, then set the limits for the landholdings of the respective parties according to what the documents recorded as well as what the *vetustiores* (elders) reported.[102] Peace was restored by bringing written and oral evidence into contact, possibly competition, though if so the concise narrative has smoothed over it. Other situations called for more demonstrative intervention. Ramiro II was obliged to send two *missi* (agents) to Samos in 933 to demarcate the *millas*, the mile and half surrounding the monastery which represented its jurisdictional boundaries, as granted by the testaments of Alfonso II and later kings. Inhabitants of two neighbouring *villas* had infringed these diplomas, usurping property within the specified limits, but the royal agents 'crushed their arrogance': intervening directly in the landscape, they erected *archas* (stone boundary markers) to make explicit the monastic domain, and these became a reference for future generations.[103]

More common than inquest was for modes of proof to collide at trial, where having a written basis for a claim ensured the upper hand. An unusual text of 974 from Sahagún, while possibly interpolated, is evocative

---

[99] Geary, 'Oblivion', 111–22; Davies, *Windows*, 204–31; Martínez Llorente, 'Justicia', 13–43.
[100] Cerdá Ruiz-Funes, 'Pesquisa', esp. 490–501.
[101] Wiener, *Commentary*, 77–108; Domínguez Guilarte, 'Notas', 287–324; Concha Martínez, ' "Presura" ', 382–460; Benavides Monje, 'Presura', 1, 255–62; *cf.* Chandler, 'Court', 19–44; Jarrett, 'Settling', 320–42.
[102] *León* 89; Collins, 'Visigothic Law', 88; Davies, *Acts*, 200–1; Andrade Cernadas, 'Voz', 13–19.
[103] *Samos* 46; López Alsina, 'Millas', 159–87; López Salas, 'Papel', esp. 20–2; López Salas, 'Decoding', 49–55; *cf. Sobrado* 1.129; *Celanova* 86; *Lorvão* 36.

of how this played out. Liubila *presbiter* had donated two churches by charter to Abbot Gonzalo, and when he became bishop of León, he left them by testament to his old monastery. After his death, however, a certain Taion, brother of Liubila, appealed to the court of Ramiro III, and argued in public oral testimony that he should have inherited the churches, but the monks produced both documents and their abbot verified that the second of them, the testament, had been made in his sight. This settled the matter, as the court resolved that Sahagún should have its ownership confirmed in writing.[104] And yet, the supporting statement by the abbot, emphasising personal witness, demonstrates how written evidence and spoken testimony had a complementary relationship. Even when they were in contradiction, indeed, both had to be reckoned in the settlement. In one of the rare surviving cases where the ecclesiastical party to a dispute was not entirely victorious, Didaco Luboniz and his family made a complaint against Froilo and San Vicente de León in 1025, alleging in council before the bishop of Astorga that they had bought half of a *villa* for a just price from Ecta Fernández and his brother. But Froilo countered that the king had granted the same *villa* by charter to her late husband for 'population', and after his death had ordered a testament to be made of it to that monastery, where he was interred. For his part, if Didaco had a charter, he made no mention of it; even so, the presiding bishop, though confirming the *villa* itself in the possession of San Vicente, determined that he should have half the surrounding land lest he lose the whole price which he had paid.[105] Forging lasting consensus was a balancing act, and called for respecting the value of speech while recognising the validity of writing.

Just as reading aloud was the medium through which text had to pass for a transaction to be accepted beyond the parchment and pen of the scribe, a charter was ordinarily read into a dispute in the company of oral testimony. Visigothic law recognised its importance as a part of the process, but also worried about perjury, especially falsehood in contradiction of written evidence.[106] Davi and his wife Animie, according to a tangled narrative of 1011, had obtained property by means of an *actio* (deed), then sold it on to Scemena *per cartula venditionis* (by a charter of sale), handing her the earlier text; she left the land and documents to her children, who made a

[104] *Sahagún* 276; Prieto Prieto, 'Sahagún', 498–500; Mínguez Fernández, *Dominio*, 73–4; Davies, *Acts*, 40–1; *cf.* Mínguez, 'Justicia', 1, 491–548; Bowman, *Landmarks*, 165–82.
[105] *León* 822; García Cacho, 'Memoria', 13–14, 17–18; *cf. Sahagún* 401 (333).
[106] *LV* 2.1.25, 2.4; Alejandre García, 'Delito', esp. 30–42, 63–70; Bowman, 'Infamy', 97–102; Dumézil, 'Crime', 27–42; Iglesias Rábade, 'Testimonio', 71–9.

charter of it to Tructesindo Guimiriz with all its titles. After 35 years had passed, however, Ruderigo Froilaz claimed that it was his property because Asperigo, a *serbo* (slave, literally, but clearly a more complex reality) of his grandfather, had acquired it by yet another charter of sale. He was unable to produce the text in court, and so the parties made a *placitum* to reappear in three days, each with five witnesses knowledgeable about the property; judges selected those of Tructesindo as *quales plus melioras*, in some sense better, and reconfirmed the lengthy parchment trail with their aid.[107] This role of 'text-helper' was normally played by those identified as *auctores*, in context a granter, witness, or even a scribe to a past charter at issue, in the case of the granter fulfilling the standard obligation of the sanction clause to *auctorigare* (guarantee or vindicate, variously spelled) the transaction in future. The classic example is Nemorellus *presbiter* and Abbot Balderedus of Valdevimbre, who both laid claim to certain mills in 941, meeting at trial in León before royal judges: the former produced his charters of sale and their *auctores*, the original vendors, *transeuntibus* (going back) twenty years, the latter brought the same, but dating back only four years. The *auctores* of Nemorellus testified to a dispute two decades before between the prior generation, judged in favour of their parents against the parents of the *auctores* acting for the abbot at a council of Ordoño II. The record of this settlement survives, and the judges, confirming it on behalf of Nemorellus, quoted details from it, tying testimony together with text.[108]

When parties to prior documentation were called upon to confirm what they testified, they did so in the first instance by oath, one of two key rituals which functioned to reinforce written argumentation in disputes. In 946, for example, Berulfo *presbiter* sought to prove his ownership of a church of San Esteban against the counterclaim of Matheo by introducing his testament and its *auctores*, Gualamiro and Flaíno *presbiter*. In familiar language, they stated that they saw, heard, and were present as witnesses when sons of Godesteo iben Mazaref had made charters of that church to Berulfo and Sisebuto *diaconus*, as attested by surviving texts, and swore *condiciones sacramentorum* to this effect, included in the composite record of the settlement.[109] But more generally an oath was taken by one of the main parties in a dispute to break the impasse once arguments had been made and evidence

[107]  *PMH* 216; *cf. Coimbra* 202; *Celanova* 331.
[108]  *León* 144 (34); García de Valdeavellano, 'Escodriñamiento', 274; Davies, *Windows*, 221; Carvajal Castro, 'Sanctions', 168; Martín Viso, 'Authority', 124; *cf. León* 724; *Samos* 126 (127); *Liébana* 66; *Arouca* 84; Barthe Porcel, 'Vindigare', 1, 117–22; Clavería Nadal, 'Latín', 116–24.
[109]  *León* 192 (176, 186); Davies, 'Records', 58–63.

had been adduced.[110] Bishop Jimeno of Astorga asserted in 1008 that his sister Velasquita had made a charter of a *villa* to Munio Fernández against her will, but he countered that he had bought it from her for a price of 250 *solidi*, and presented the charter recording the transaction. The charge was difficult to prove or disprove, since it concerned the circumstances behind the sale rather than the sale as such; the judges thus directed Munio and two associates to confirm his text and testimony *per sacrum iuramentum* (by sacred oath), and they duly swore *per series condiciones* (by a list of terms), achieving a rare outright victory by a layman over an ecclesiastic.[111] By similar means Guimarães was even able to defend itself against royal incursion, when Vermudo II made an attempt on its patrimony. According to a later charter of 1014, the abbot and brothers brought their *testamentos et scripturas* to court and took an oath on them by order of the king, forcing him to back down and issue a confirmation. Unfortunately, *inique et maliciantes* (evildoers) convinced Alfonso V that these documents were not *verificos* (truthful), but the redoubtable monks came before him too, read out their texts, and swore another oath by terms attached to the record.[112] Handled in the right way, with all due process, this pairing of written and ritual authority was an effective means of telling truth to power, and getting away with it.

Oaths were a matter not only for parties and *auctores*, but also other actors commonly called *iuratores* (oath-takers), who gave their word on behalf of written evidence. The precise identity of these persons is not always clear, perhaps partisans or dependants of the appellant or respondent, but they were knowledgeable about the matter, or at least willing to take a side publicly. In 998, when Vela Velaz usurped a *villa* which Sahagún held by testament from the *majordomo* Ansur, the abbot appeared before the rebel allies Count García Gómez and Zahbascorta ven Abolhauz, offering requested but unidentified oath-takers in support of his claim, just as Abbot Indulfo of Santillana brought two *iuratores* before the judges in 1006 to swear that his monastery held land *per pactu vel testamentu* from Didaco Albariz, and had only loaned it to Guntesalbo in usufruct.[113] In the latter case, the *iuratores* are described as *omines bonos*, men of good social standing in the community, and the importance of these secondary participants

[110] Prieto Morera, 'Proceso', 471–4; Davies, *Windows*, 28–9; *cf.* Kosto, *Agreements*, 143–57.
[111] *León* 669; *Alfonso V*, 70–1; *cf. León* 410 (298), 695.
[112] *Guimarães* 46; Alfonso, 'Rhetoric', 80–1; *cf. San Millán* 181; *León* 724; *Lugo* 54.
[113] *Sahagún* 356 (284, 272); *Santillana* 19; *cf. Santiago* 59; *Coruña* 95.

in disputing lies in how often the oath constituted a breaking point where one party conceded, opening the way to settlement. We can see it play out at a momentous trial of 961, when two powerful bishops fought over *piscarias* (fishing sites or rights) in Posmarcos. Rosendo of Mondoñedo argued that his mother Ilduara had held a quarter share, while Sisnando of Santiago countered that his predecessor had been given them *ingenuas* (freely, or in full?) by a diploma of Ramiro II. Meeting at Guimarães, both presented *homines bonos veridicos* (good and truthful men) to confirm their claims, but the partisans of Rosendo withdrew, fearing to utter falsehood under oath. Those assembled then ordered the agents of Sisnando to enter the tomb of Santiago and swear over his body that since the date recorded in the diploma no share of the *piscarias* had ever belonged to anyone except him, and possession was thereby confirmed.[114] The authority of the holy and the legitimacy of the text here acted in concert, deterring as well as resolving contention, at least as presented by the victors to posterity. The *Fuero de León* canonised this relationship in 1017 when it provided that, if the Church held any property without a charter, its *cultores* (worshippers) could affirm their ownership by oath, as guarantor of truth.[115]

The second rite of confirmation for written evidence was the ordeal, linked in context to oath-taking but involving separate personnel. When a party cited a charter in a claim and offered supporting witness testimony, another individual could on occasion be invited to take the 'test of the cauldron' to provide further substantiation. Originating though not described in late Visigothic law, the ordeal served to put the text to the test of divine judgement by way of an intermediary; it was necessitated by either intransigence on the part of the disputants or the failure of the habitual modes of proof, by writing and speech, to result in settlement.[116] In 953, for example, Pedro *frater* argued that Victinus had granted him by *placitum* vacant land worth 100 *solidi* in order for him to build a monastery there, but had taken back the property by force after he had built it, with much else besides. Thirty witnesses testified under oath to his allegations, before an *innocens*, a neutral third party named Fernando, swore to the same terms and then underwent the *pena kaldaria*, the ordeal of plunging his hand into a

[114] *Santiago* 42; Collins, 'Visigothic Law', 93–4; Carrillo Boutureira, 'Actividad', 109, 112; *cf.* *Cardeña* 98; *Celanova* 292; *Braga* 22; *Guimarães* 24; Varela Sieiro, *Léxico*, 342–6.
[115] *Oviedo* 42.
[116] *LV* 6.1.3; Collins, 'Law', 503–4; Collins, 'Visigothic Law', 87; Alvarado Planas, 'Ordalías', 507–617; García López, *Estudios*, 513–54; Alvarado Planas, *Problema*, 179–90; *cf.* Iglesia Ferreirós, 'Proceso', esp. 65–198; Bartlett, *Trial*, 4–33; Bowman, *Landmarks*, 119–40.

cauldron of hot water, held there by a *fidelis* (partisan) of each party, and reappearing three days later to show it off *limpidus* (unmarked).[117] Similarly, when bishops Pelayo of Lugo and Pedro of Santiago were locked in their great dispute of the later tenth century, Pelayo claimed that the men at issue were dependants of his see, recorded in the lists kept in its archive, while Pedro countered that they were granted by Ordoño III to Sobrado *per testamentum*. The inquest did not succeed in resolving matters, and so witnesses swore an oath on behalf of the monastery, and the parties nominated *fideles* to lead one Salamirus *presbiter* through the ordeal.[118]

The Sobrado case explains the process in some detail. It was held at a church of Santa Eulalia on the Narla River, probably identifiable with Santalla de Madelos, before more than 50 witnesses: *ego innocens*, speaking in the first person, reached into the cauldron of *calida aqua* (hot water, even boiling), grasped some *lapides igneos* (literally, 'burning stones') with his hands, and cast them *foras*, presumably out and onto the ground. Returning to the council three or four days later *sub sigillo fidelium* (under the custody of the agents), he exhibited his *illesus vel limpidus* (unbroken and unblemished) skin. At this stage, the *innocens*, two *fideles*, and the *saio* confirmed a *placitum* of the successful ordeal, and Pelayo yielded at last, leaving Sobrado victorious.[119] Surely only divine intervention could permit one to emerge from such a testing unscathed, and belief in the ritual provided a way out from a stalemate of conflicting written evidence and oral testimony on both sides. But as with the oath, the hocus pocus had heft too as a deterrent: the liturgical exorcism of the hot water which preceded the ordeal will only have intensified the presence of supernatural authority which could provoke default by a party.[120] Such was the case in the early eleventh century, when Alfonso usurped land which Abbot Salamirus had given in testament to Celanova, with all relevant charters and *firmitates*. He denied the charge before Alfonso V and court, but the monastery produced 356 witnesses (!) to his meagre ten; of the former crowd, Vimara, the monastic advocate, sent ten to swear the *seriem conditionum*, as well as an *innocentem* to undergo the *pena caldaria*. Emphatically outnumbered and outgunned, Alfonso was prompted to confess and return the property, duly deterred by the prospect

---

[117] *Oviedo* 26; Davies, *Windows*, 29, 136–9; *cf. Pino* 2.

[118] *Sobrado* 1.109; Davies, *Windows*, 243–5; Davies, 'Language', 241–4; *cf. Santiago* 24.

[119] Pérez de Urbel, *Sampiro*, 65–9; García Álvarez, *Pedro*, 69–72, 161–4, 309–12; Ares, 'Roimil', 243–8; *cf.* Prieto Morera, 'Proceso', 476–8.

[120] Villaamil y Castro, *Uso*, 11–12, 31–5; Alturo *et al.*, *Liber*, 251–5, 793–7; Rodenbusch, 'Framing', 6–7; *cf.* Barthélemy, 'Présence', 191–214.

of heavenly wrath from pursuing the matter further.[121] The message of these rituals is that written evidence was not simply the end of a dispute, but a stage in the choreography of settlement. It was neither required nor ubiquitous, and indeed the same four procedures used to confirm it—inquests, testimony, oaths, ordeals—were equally effective as modes of proof if text was absent. Yet written evidence clearly conferred advantage, and here the losing party was on the back foot from the moment the monastery mentioned its charters.

## Manipulation

Recognition of the potential of text is latent in the misuse of charters, which like their theft reveals a desire for documentation by the owners, or would-be owners, of property. The category encompasses two strategies for establishing false claims on written foundations, but the difference is really one of degree: false transfer by charter, whereby a text created outside of valid conditions was employed to alienate stolen property, and transfer by false charter, in other words outright forgery of a text for commission of a theft.[122] We have already met with examples of the first, which is a logical extension of the value accorded to property having a written history. In 1002, the bishop of León narrated in a testament how a certain *dux*, during the previous episcopacy, had seized and alienated land from the see *per scriptura testamenti* (by a document of testament), but he, after his election, had petitioned Vermudo II to restore it.[123] Such trickery was most common in the west, and a charter from Celanova of 927 can be read as representative. Abbot Quintila had endowed Santa María de Loyo in writing, but then his successor violated the rights of his descendants, handing it by text to Countess Hermesinda; when her son Count Gutier came to Sancho Ordóñez and Alfonso IV with *testamento pristino* (the original testament) and *extremam kartam* (the latest charter), however, the council set to reviewing them and ultimately made provision for its restoration.[124] At Samos, there

---

[121] *Celanova* 260–1; Davies, *Windows*, 211–12, 244; cf. *Castañeda* 1; *Alfonso V* vii; White, 'Proposing', 89–123.

[122] Goffart, *Forgeries*, esp. 2–6, 191–239; McKitterick (ed.), *Uses*, 325–6; Koziol, *Politics*, 315–99; Roach, *Forgery*, 1–20; cf. Linehan, 'Forgeries', 1, 643–74; Díaz Salvado, *Falsos*, 5–41.

[123] *León* 629; Ser Quijano, 'Renta', 72; cf. *Sahagún* 424; *Astorga* 13.

[124] *Celanova* 29; Sáez, 'Notas', 82–6; cf. *Santiago* 35; *Sobrado* 1.48; *Ourense* 3, *Celanova* 312; *Coimbra* 134.

are three cases of persuasion or force, including that involving Abbess Fernanda, who reported in 1011 how Onega had convinced her with honeyed words to transfer by testament the monastery of San Pelayo de Piñeira, founded by her parents.[125] In 995, after Senta had been compelled by Citi Lucidi to make a *cartula conscripta* (written charter) contrary to his *volumptas* (will), he turned to Vermudo II, and the king investigated and invalidated the extorted text.[126]

Such schemers evidently calculated that having a document in hand could be a ticket to acceptance of their actions, even if in these cases their plans failed to come off. But as the Visigothic law code recognised, outright forgery was a far more serious business, because it threatened to compromise the integrity of the written word itself.[127] In his testament of 863 to Trubia, an Asturian church, Bishop Gladila of Braga noted a complaint by its *cultores* that his nephew had created a *cartam falsariam* (false charter) for himself of land which Gladila had in fact given to them, and he rejected this *scriptum* as a fabrication.[128] The threat was real and not to be taken lightly: in 944, the brothers of San Salvador de Loberuela accused one of their own named Conantius of evicting them by *cartas falsarias*, and were only able to prove that these had been forged by consulting the monastic pact which he himself had made on entering into the monastery.[129] Guarding against that possibility required not only careful comparison of conflicting charters, but also authentication, and a dispute settlement of 1014 describes the procedure. The brothers of Guimarães objected to Countess Tutadomna that Ordonho Sentariz had usurped a *villa*, thereby violating the testaments by which their founder Mumadona and their abbots had held it, and so she directed both parties to make a *plazum* to appear in due course with all their documents. The judges listened as these were read out, then *adtestarunt* (set side by side, or compared) the date recorded in the texts brought by Ordonho with that in the texts produced by the abbot. Finding the latter to be earlier and the former later, inconsistent, and therefore false, they concluded that Ordonho must have substituted them for the genuine charters, ordered his texts annulled and burned, and endorsed those of the monastery. At this point, however, Ordonho argued in an obscure passage that the charters of

[125] *Samos* 76.
[126] *Samos* S9; *Lugo*, 2, 585–90; *cf. Samos* 82; García de Cortázar, 'Memoria', 95.
[127] *LV* 7.5; Alejandre García, 'Estudio', esp. 136–55; Marlasca Martínez, 'Regulación', 221–33.
[128] *Oviedo* 8; Fernández Conde and Fernández Fernández, 'Abades', 69–78.
[129] *Oña* 3; Torrens Álvarez *et al.*, *Documentación*, 8–10; Collins, 'Law', 508; Santos Salazar, 'Ruling', 141–2; *cf. Sobrado* 1.131–2; *Santillana* 31; *León* 887.

Guimarães did not refer to the correct *villa*, and alleged that his relatives, Todegildo and Guntina, had given it to him in writing; the monastery claimed to hold it by gift from Count Gonzalo, to whom Mitto, son of Todegildo, had transferred it *per cartulam firmitatis*. Sensationally, Mitto Todegildiz declined to *auctorgare* any such document for Guimarães, as the sanction clause would have obliged him to do, forcing the monastic advocate, at the direction of the judges, to find other *auctores* in Tegio Gundesindiz and Emila *presbiter*, respectively a witness and the scribe of the charter in question, to swear to its validity along with three others. But before they did so, Mitto relented and admitted his lie, presumably having been put up to it by his father.[130]

The manifold machinations of the adversaries of Guimarães were confuted by careful investigation of the documentation, complemented with testimony from parties to its creation. But the most important act here is the destruction of the false charters produced by Ordonho Sentariz, a judicial command which is common to such cases. When a dispute erupted in 945 between Stefanus *frater* of Valeránica and Ariolfus *presbiter* over property sold to the latter in 914, the former presented a charter of transfer, the latter a charter of purchase now copied together with the record of settlement. Four abbots at Cardeña *exquierunt* (investigated) these documents: once they had determined that of Stefanus to be *falsaria* and that of Ariolfus to be *valida* (authentic), they ordered the *frater* to cast his forgery into the fire before them.[131] In a similar case, Salamirus *presbiter* and Vivili Truitesendiz both laid claim to a church in 1015; the judges accepted the documentation of Vivili, finding it to be earlier in date, whereas they *crebaverunt* (broke up) the charters of Salamirus, which were later.[132] In one sense, this was simply a precaution, designed to eliminate potential contradiction and suppress recurrence of contention.[133] But destruction was also the fate of texts which had proven unreliable through misuse: Repparatus and his wife Trasvinda had made a charter of *perfiliatio* to Adericus and Sesina, but the recipients used it to seize all of their property, and so in 936, once the granters had retaken it with help from Celanova, they destroyed

[130] *Guimarães* 51; Prieto Morera, 'Proceso', 479–81; Alvarado Planas, 'Problema', 130–1; *cf.* Marlasca Martínez, 'Requisitos', 563–84; Bowman, *Landmarks*, 147–51.
[131] *Cardeña* 69; Escalona Monge, 'Lucha', 216–17; Santos Salazar, 'Ruling', 141–2.
[132] *Paço de Sousa* 142; Carriedo Tejedo, 'Libros', 60–1; Marques, 'Language', 148; *cf.* Azevedo 2.
[133] Sennis, 'Documents', 156–9.

the failed document in court, denying it any future *roborem* (force).[134] According to a much-told story from the end of the eleventh century, when Alfonso VI was seeking to replace the Mozarabic rite with the Roman liturgy, he presided at Burgos over a trial by combat between two knights to decide the issue, and his champion was defeated: much to his ire, a second attempt, whereby one book of each office was cast into fire, had the same result, as the 'Toledan' rite leapt from the flames unharmed while the 'Gallican' service was consumed.[135] This may draw liberally on dramatic licence in defence of a liturgical nativism, but it speaks to the same mentality which treasured trust in text, and suggests that disputing, with all its associated procedures and rituals, had taken up the burden of the *gesta municipalia*, to provide a forum for authentication of documentation and sustain belief in it.[136] At the same time, it points to a hierarchy of authorities by which archives and their contents, however curated, ultimately played by the rules of the law and yielded to its standards of admissibility.[137] With such power resident in written proof, it was imperative to ensure that it stood for an acceptable and accepted truth.

## Textual Mentalities

There is nothing quite so dramatic and satisfying here as the Carolingian former slave clutching his charter of manumission as a safeguard of freedom. There the freedman came to be known as a *cartularius*, a 'charter man', from the text which guaranteed his new status.[138] But as we have seen, writing could within limits be a means of speaking truth to power and getting away with it, and remained so into the later Middle Ages.[139] The centrality of text to the history and context of property is reflected in a vocabulary of transfer by charter almost unique to Iberia, originating in the early medieval period. The verb *incartare* is a compound of the prefix *in-* with the noun *carta*, as if 'to en-charter': it means to consign ownership of property in writing, and its use is attested across the corpus and throughout Iberia

---

[134] *Celanova* 52; *cf. Guimarães* 24.
[135] David, *Études*, 391–405; Hitchcock, 'Rito', 19–41; Hitchcock, *Mozarabs*, 126–7.
[136] Bougard, 'Écrit', 299–314; Mostert, 'Forgery', 37–59.
[137] See Maskarinec, 'Archives', 331–65.
[138] Mordek, 'Texte', 458–9; Nelson, 'Literacy', 262–3, 296; Devroey, 'Men', 10–11.
[139] Ríos Rodríguez, 'Valor', 151–71.

from the tenth century to the thirteenth.[140] The word is employed in reference to means of acquisition and to related transactions, but examples of the first are more numerous, occurring in León and especially Galicia and Portugal. One of the earliest instances is a fragmentary charter of 932, which records Gunterogia giving certain properties to Carboeiro, including what a party now illegible says *incartavi* ('I have en-chartered') to her; in 945, similarly, Sisimiro sold a *villa* to Hermegildo and Paterna which he held *incartatum* ('en-chartered') from Annisco.[141] It is possible to push this linguistic innovation even earlier, depending on the interpretation of *quartavit* and *quartaverunt* in a complex dispute over a *piscaria* at San Martín de Castañeda in 927.[142] The timing is in any case notable, since it parallels two other developments which we have traced in the tenth century, the career scribe and the local council, revealing a third facet to the growing written arrangements and written expectations in society.

From the mid-tenth century onwards, the vocabulary sees regular use in donations, lay transactions, and a handful of disputes. When Vermudo and his wife Onega donated property to Santiago de Barbadelo in 1031, it included a quarter of a *villa* which a monk named Gaton had *incartavit* to them and a third of another acquired by the same means, while Adosinda in 964 made an exchange involving two *villas* which she and her deceased husband Ramiro held *incartata* from Ordoño III.[143] The verb is used to reference the charter of a related transaction in cases mainly from the west, such as when Edronios sold an agent of Bishop Rosendo land bordering on the property of Ascarigo, *que iam tibi est incartata* (which has already been en-chartered to you), in the mid-tenth century, or the widower Donazano gave all his property to his two children in 1001, excepting what he *incartavit* to Gonzalo.[144] The lengthy testament of Mumadona Dias from 959 includes much land which many a previous owner *incartavit* to her, but also a *villa* obtained *per incartatione*, a verbal noun for 'transfer by charter' thought to

[140] See *e.g. Léxico, s.v.* 'encartare'; *Lexicon, s.v.* 'incarto'; *cf. Du Cange, s.v.* 'incartare'; *Blaise, s.v.* 'incarto'; *Niermeyer, s.v.* 'inchartare'.

[141] *Coruña* 34; *Sobrado* 1.12.

[142] *Castañeda* 1; Pastor, *Resistencias*, 56–73; Anta Lorenzo, 'Monasterio', 40–3, 49–50.

[143] *Samos* 74; *Guimarães* 50; *cf. Sahagún* 285, 308, 328, 342, *Sobrado* 1.6, *Samos* 23, 19, 69, *Celanova* 210, *Lugo* 23, *Tumbo Viejo* 102, *Guimarães* 67, *Coimbra* 191; *León* 741, 753, *Lugo* 30, *Guimarães* A1; *Sobrado* 1.110, 1.134, *Samos* 64.

[144] *Celanova* 184; *Coimbra* 522; *cf. Celanova* 222, 289, 297, 315; *Coimbra* 187; *PMH* 149; *León* 376.

be a coinage of the eleventh century.[145] Some documents even refer to themselves by this terminology: *inkarto* ('I en-charter'), says Auria in a text of 1003, a court to Munio Fernández in payment of a judicial fine, meaning the transfer effected by that text.[146] And there may yet be other verbs for written transaction, *pactare* from *pactum* or *implacare* from *placitum*, both 'to agree in writing', further enshrining the functions of charters in the language for them.[147] The obvious comparison is with England, where 'book-land' (*bocland*) could be disposed of by its owner freely, as opposed to 'folk-land' (*folcland*) which was subject to obligations. In essence, property covered by a charter was guaranteed alienability, hence the attraction of the laity to acquiring written title.[148] But here what stands out is the banality of the usage, a lack of special status for 'en-chartered land', the simple association of transaction with text.

Charters in early medieval Iberia were the surest defence in cases of dispute, and this belief in the written record is what granted it steadily increasing purchase in society, broadly greater use over time reflecting recognition of its efficacy. The moment one person obtained written title to property, all those neighbouring it came under the pressure of self-interest to do so urgently, as we proposed in the case of Rabal: otherwise defeat could almost certainly be expected if ever a disagreement arose. In this fashion, charters were self-promoting: they situated themselves in a network of other charters, bearing witness to the ongoing relevance of each one beyond its creation, and serving to identify additional means of defence in court. As charters cited other charters to confirm themselves, to establish a background of textual transactions, to flag other relevant records, and to supply further pertinent information, they constructed a network of interconnections, and created a written world in which parchment was power, each text opening onto others. They defined ownership of property as possession of written title. As documentary evidence was brought to bear in settling disputes, it was not simply for display, like the waving of a totem, but was integrated through testimony, oaths, and ordeals into the participating community even as it was put to the test. Written evidence was substance, not show, and in serial attempts to steal it, extract it by force, or even forge

---

[145] *Guimarães* 1A, A3; *cf. Sobrado* 1.46; *Lugo* 23, 30; *Tumbo Viejo* 102; see *e.g. Léxico, s.v.* 'incartacione'; *Lexicon, s.v.* 'incartatio'; *Niermeyer, s.v.* 'inchartatio'; Andrade Cernadas, 'Fuentes', 45; Reis, 'Diogo', 180.

[146] *León* 632; *cf. Celanova* 31, 264, 334.   [147] *Celanova* 357; *Guimarães* 36.

[148] Kelly, 'Society', 44–5; Ryan, 'Problem', 19–32.

it, we perceive widespread acceptance of and desire to capitalise on its potential. In each victory for the text in court, and with firm action taken against incidences of false documentation, its social status rose; in this circularity, use of charters led to use of charters, respect for charters built up respect for charters. Those who could acquire written title to property put themselves at decided advantage, as those who did not would soon come to realise and regret.

# 5

# Framing

Charters cited other charters routinely and effectively, but a second component of the network of texts in which they positioned themselves is written law, as deployed and debated in the records of transactions and disputes. The practice is complex and multi-layered, and it can offer a rounded answer to the basic question of what law actually did in the early Middle Ages, whether legislation was primarily symbolic or had real bearing on the world around it.[1] In the corpus of documentation, some citations of legal precepts and provisions recur so often as to be formulaic: invoked in the preamble or corroboration to confirm the legality of the act, or in the sanction clause to assess or assign the penalty for interfering with it, law is a crucial element of the legitimising rhetoric of the text. But at a deeper level, there are many citations which are unique or too extensive or adapted in wording to be template, and imply first-hand engagement with law, at some stage; here the weight of legislation—on inheritance, property, procedures, and penalties—made itself keenly felt, providing not so much a determinant of as a foundation for transaction and dispute. Written law enjoyed an acceptance of its framework for social relations both general and flexible, yet it was also an aspect of power, and the kings and counts of León above all realised its potential to be a tool of lordship, wielding it against renegades, rivals, rogues, and roués in furtherance of their own interests. The degree to which these normative sources have been internalised can be measured by silent citation, where the phrasing or force of relevant legislation has shaped the text and the process. Law had become the language of custom and habit, and it was spoken most fluently by the scribe.

What was law in early medieval Iberia? It came from a code known variously as *Lex Visigothorum* ('Law of the Visigoths') or *Liber iudiciorum* ('Book of judgements'), enacted in 654 by the Visigothic king Reccesuinth (649/53–72), and later revised and reissued in 681 by Erwig (680–7). One of the most ambitious compilations from the post-Roman kingdoms of the

---

[1] Wormald, 'Legislation', esp. 18–37; Wormald, 'Law', 26–8, 35–8; Lambert, *Law*, esp. 111–59; *cf.* Reuter, *Germany*, 3–4.

*Text and Textuality in Early Medieval Iberia: The Written and The World, 711–1031.* Graham Barrett, Oxford University Press. © Graham Barrett 2023. DOI: 10.1093/oso/9780192895370.003.0006

West, it is comprised of 12 books, treating legal philosophy and procedure, family and relationships, business affairs and crime, theft and damage to person and property, ties of obligation and dependence, divisions of space and time, doctors, traders, and in conclusion an extraordinary series of anti-Semitic legislation designed to limit, and ultimately eliminate, the presence of Jews in the kingdom.[2] The code presents itself as a uniform codified bloc, but this screens an ideology of good and bad kingship and orthodox rule, reflected in the assignment of credit for the authorship of laws to certain kings only; in reality it was the iterative product of case law, as Visigothic rulers issued judgements on matters brought before them.[3] Study of the text, however, is by definition post-Visigothic: the oldest surviving copy dates to the early eighth century (Vatican City, Biblioteca Apostolica Vaticana, Reg. lat. 1024). And indeed, by necessity, study of the text in practice is post-Visigothic too; the code is deeply textual, based on the conduct of business in writing, but documentary sources prior to the Muslim conquest of 711 are few.[4] The kingdom of Asturias-León, by the ninth century if not before, carefully cultivated an identity of continuity, perceptible in ongoing use of Visigothic monastic rules and Visigothic liturgy, which its kings promoted by issuing no secular or canon law of their own, instead simply observing the normative monuments of their putative predecessors. The point is underlined by the brief regnal list prefixed to contemporary copies of the code, noting rulers who legislated; though varying in form, it normally has no break from the fifth century to the eleventh, conjuring a seamless dynastic succession from the Visigothic to the Asturian and Leonese kings.[5] More than any other text, the code defined the cultural inheritance of the kingdom, where the legitimacy of kingship itself was expressed in continuity of law.[6]

It is no revelation to say that the Visigothic code had an active afterlife in the early to high Middle Ages. This has been the subject of much valuable scholarship, especially for the Catalan counties, where there was broad engagement with what some charters call 'our laws': both vague allusions to

---

[2] See *LV*; García López, *Estudios*, 207–590, for emended editions of late sixth- and early seventh-century legislation; transl. Scott, *Code*; Bellès i Sallent *et al.*, *Llibre*; Ramis Barceló and Ramis Serra, *Libro*; *cf.* Álvarez Cora, 'Naturaleza', 11–117; Koon and Wood, 'Unity', 793–808.

[3] King, *Law*, 1–51; Martin, '*Liber*', 17–34; Kelly, *Isidore*, 175–208.

[4] Marlasca Martínez, 'Actos', 87–113; *cf.* Petit, 'Negotiis'.

[5] *Chronica regum Visigothorum*, ed. *LV*, 457–61; García-Moreno, 'Ejemplar', 5–14; Bautista, 'Historiografía', 118–41; Isla Frez, 'Construcción', 33–44; Barrett, 'Hispania', 90–2.

[6] Otero, 'Códice', 557–68; Iglesia Ferreirós, 'Derecho', 124–31; Deswarte, *Destruction*, 191–5; Reeves, *Visions*, 153–94; *cf.* Álvarez Cora, 'Noción', 1–38; Pacheco Caballero, 'Reyes', 165–206.

and precise citations of laws, with more or less intentional rewritings of their text, or rather of a subset of laws within the code, a culture in which 'Visigothic law', not the Visigothic code as such, was alive and known.⁷ It was consulted intensively as well as extensively, however, and became an object of study, glossing, and revision in the tenth and especially the eleventh century, culminating in 1011 with the preparation of a *Liber iudicum popularis* ('Book of judges for the people'), a handbook for lay judges including an edition of the code, by Bonhom of Barcelona, himself a working judge and jurist.⁸ For the kingdoms of Asturias-León and Navarra, in contrast, there is something of a consensus that the eighth and ninth centuries saw a hiatus in the Visigothic legal tradition, until its renewal by 'Mozarabic' immigration or royal initiative during the tenth century.⁹ Thereafter scholars have observed a general recognition and implementation of the Visigothic code, and the specific citation of a discrete number of Visigothic laws, in approximately one hundred records of transaction and dispute.¹⁰ Yet debate continues around the presence in practice of what seem to be evolutions, departures, and innovations from usages in the code, at least as viewed from a strictly legalist perspective, such as extrajudicial suretyship and processual oaths.¹¹ And the location of legal knowledge and expertise, amongst the clergy or the laity, remains an open question.¹²

An admirable starting point, but the full range of legal citations in the corpus still has not been properly reckoned. The editions themselves can be an obstacle, or offer no help: few register even explicit citations of law, let

---

⁷ Zimmermann, 'Usage', 233–81; Iglesia Ferreirós, 'Creación', esp. 125–252, 284–8, 406–17; Salrach, 'Prácticas', esp. 1011–24; Zimmermann, *Écrire*, 2, 922–48; Salrach i Marès *et al.*, *Justícia*, 1057–67; *cf.* Rius Serra, 'Derecho', 65–80; Abadal y Vinyals, *Comtes*, 229–30; Lalinde Abadía, 'Pactos', 135–71; Kienast, 'Pervivencia', 265–95.

⁸ Alturo *et al.*, *Liber*, esp. 67–117, 167–219; García López, *Estudios*, 41–118; Bowman, *Landmarks*, 33–55, 84–99.

⁹ Martínez Díez, 'Instituciones', 135; Coronas González, 'Derecho', 73–95; Martínez Díez, 'Fueros', 289–91; Sánchez-Arcilla Bernal, 'Derecho', 226–36; Prieto Prieto, 'Potestad', 533; Coronas González, 'Orden', 13–28; Coronas González (ed.), *Fueros*, 16–27; *cf.* Gibert, 'Enseñanza', 35–6.

¹⁰ Collins, 'Law', 489–512; Plettenberg, *Fortleben*, esp. 132–63; García López, *Estudios*, 119–54; Rodiño Caramés, '*Lex*', 9–52; González Díez, 'Decir', 30–53; Martínez Sopena, 'Uso', 97–114; *cf.* Alvarado Planas, *Problema*, 216–30; Alvarado Planas, 'Conclusiones', 109–27.

¹¹ García-Gallo, 'Carácter', esp. 597–640; Sánchez-Albornoz, 'Tradición', 114–31; Isla Frez, 'Pervivencia', 75–86; *cf.* Orlandis, 'Prenda', esp. 104–83.

¹² Martínez Sopena, 'Justicia', 239–55; Davies, *Windows*, 26–7, 138–9, 160–4, 205–11, 236–59.

| | Citations | | Overall | |
|---|---|---|---|---|
| | # | % | # | % |
| Total | 464 | 11 | 4095 | 100 |
| Region | | | | |
| West | 225 | 48 | 1284 | 31 |
| Centre | 208 | 45 | 2088 | 51 |
| East | 31 | 7 | 723 | 18 |
| Personnel | | | | |
| Royal | 91 | 20 | 522 | 13 |
| Comital | 6 | 1 | 71 | 2 |
| Ecclesiastical | 258 | 56 | 2710 | 66 |
| Lay | 108 | 23 | 769 | 19 |
| Typology | | | | |
| Donation | 308 | 66 | 2212 | 54 |
| Sale | 55 | 12 | 1469 | 36 |
| Other | 101 | 22 | 411 | 10 |
| Complexity | | | | |
| Simple | 126 | 27 | 2797 | 68 |
| Complex | 338 | 73 | 1292 | 32 |
| Palaeography | | | | |
| Original | 124 | 27 | 888 | 22 |
| Copy | 31 | 7 | 261 | 6 |
| Cartulary | 277 | 60 | 2438 | 60 |
| Other | 32 | 7 | 507 | 12 |
| Diplomatic | | | | |
| Authentic | 423 | 91 | 3781 | 92 |
| Suspicious | 1 | 0 | 24 | 1 |
| Interpolated | 8 | 2 | 57 | 1 |
| Falsified | 32 | 7 | 227 | 6 |

**Figure 5.1** Charters Citing Law

alone implicit allusions.[13] As a preliminary effort, I have myself identified direct or indirect references in 464 (11%) of the charters (see Figure 5.1). Proportionately, Visigothic law is considerably more common in Galicia and Portugal than in Asturias and León, dramatically more so than in

---

[13] See *León*, 1, 411; *Coimbra*, 973–4; Plettenberg, *Fortleben*, 129–31; Rodiño Caramés, 'Lex', 47–9.

Castilla and La Rioja.[14] The later medieval legend of Fernán González casting off the Leonese yoke by rounding up all copies of the *Libro Judgo* for a book-burning at Burgos may be just that, part of a tradition of sovereign Castilian lawgivers and legislation created in retrospect, but it does reflect this decreasing level of legal 'textuality' from west to east which we can observe in the early medieval documentation.[15] Citation is predominantly a royal and lay act, in complex donations, confirmations, dispute settlements, and *placita* (agreements). Authenticity does not seem an important factor, but the occurrence is proportionately higher in originals than other forms of transmission, indicating that its frequency, varieties, and implications may have been even greater than we can perceive in what survives. In spite of the scant material from the Asturian period, the earliest plausibly genuine references to the law actually date from the second half of the eighth to the first half of the ninth century, pointing to unbroken continuity of practice from the Visigothic era, instead of a caesura and revival.[16] Over time, however, legal citation did become more frequent, rising fourfold in incidence across the Leonese period, and as we shall see, the granting of the *Fuero de León* in 1017, when the king returned to legislate, caps off this increasingly authoritative connection of charters with written law (see Figure 5.2).

## Rhetoric

The rhetoric of the charter was self-authenticating, aiming to legitimise the transaction which it recorded, and it drew on a range of written sources—a network of texts—to enhance the authority of its own text. Law was undoubtedly the most potent of them, but in this aspect of the corpus we are confronting a culture, as in the Catalan counties, where 'Visigothic law' as much as the Visigothic code properly speaking was in play. Here we meet for the first time the resonant and revealing clause *sicut lex docet*, also *sicut lex gotica docet* and variations on the same theme of 'as Visigothic law teaches', which animates so much of the documentation and has occasioned

---

[14] Collins, 'Visigothic Law', 97–104; Laffón Álvarez, 'Arenga', 149–50; Pastor Díaz de Garayo, *Castilla*, 186–95; Martínez Llorente, 'Aplicación', 56–93; María Castro, 'Aspectos', 134–9; Bowman, 'Galicia', 343–60.

[15] See Alvarado Planas and Oliva Manso, *Fueros*, 'Fazañas', 615–16; Pastor Díaz de Garayo, *Castilla*, 189–95; McGlynn, 'Laws', 93–100.

[16] *Tumbo Viejo* 110; *San Vicente* 1; *Samos* 36; *Celanova* 1; *Sobrado* 1.34.

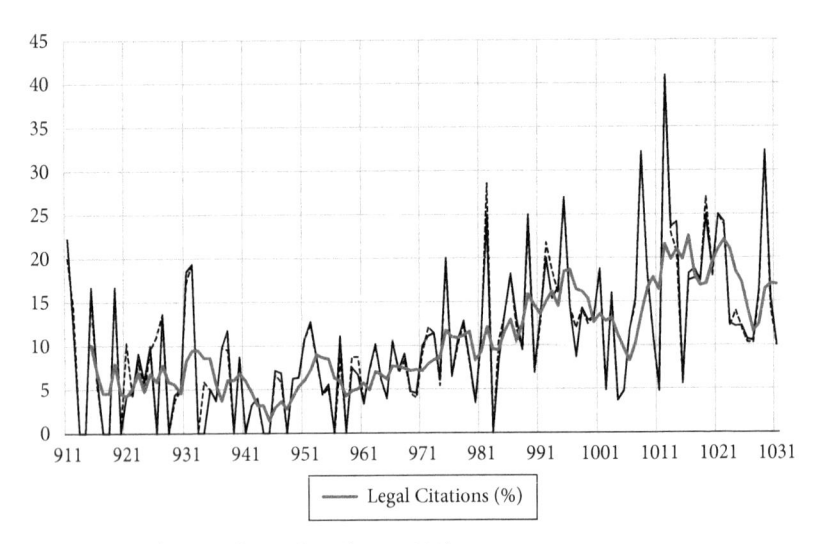

**Figure 5.2**   Charters Citing Law (911–1031)

so much comment. How are we to interpret the actuality of this seemingly straightforward marker of legal citation? The language is formulaic, and questions have been raised about how often real references to the law lie behind it, and indeed whether in some of its earlier instances it might be a sign of inauthenticity.[17] What balance, moreover, should we strike between formulaic and pragmatic implementation of law on the basis of such evidence: were scribes and their working models points of access to the code, chains of transmission for its text, or did they instead simulate and displace it?[18] There is no gain from contending all or none; some citations were real and others rhetorical, though the ratio is more in favour of the former than is often allowed.[19] The interest lies in the function of legal rhetoric, and a survey of the most formulaic invocations of law, found in the preamble, corroboration, and sanction clauses, reveals a textual strategy.[20] These recurrent references conjure the code: they build on its authority and, since not all try to be specific, on that of written law more generally, to ground the documentation of transaction on a firmly legalistic foundation.

---

[17]  García Toraño, 'Remisión'; cf. Kano, 'Loi', 126–36.
[18]  Wormald, *Making*, 70–92; Oulion, *Scribes*, 21–4, 402–4; Marques, 'Language', 128–34, 158–60.
[19]  Pérez-Prendes y Muñoz de Arraco, 'Frialdad', 346–52.
[20]  Collins, 'Law', 494–5; Martínez Díez, 'Fueros', 291; Rodiño Caramés, 'Lex', 21–4.

## Legalities

Rhetorical citation of law in the preamble affirms the legality of the transaction or the charter itself. 'Great is the title of donation', as many a text opens, 'in which none can intrude upon the act of liberality nor cast it beyond the law': emerging from the Visigothic *formulae*, the language looks back beyond the Visigoths to Roman legislation.[21] Surely, therefore, this is classic legalese, mindless repetition of a formulaic exordium already antiquated before the fall of the Visigothic kingdom? But how then should we interpret a charter of Flamula to her sister Clixovara from 963, preserved in the archive of Celanova, which adds to this formula that, according to the *lex gotica*, a donation should have force just as a sale?[22] The provision is in fact a verbatim quotation from the Visigothic code, or nearly: the original law governs exchange, and the scribe has substituted in the pertinent transaction.[23] Behind the formulaic mumbo jumbo, in other words, is a legal consciousness, a capacity to think legally and with legal sources. The same can be seen in monastic documentation from Portugal, which often references *instituta sententia* (established opinion) or the *lex quod gloriosi principes nostri constituerunt* (law which our glorious kings have instituted) in company with illustrious and orthodox men, that everyone should have licence to transfer their property to family as well as others with permanent force; this is the substance, rather than the language, of Visigothic law on donation, evocative of the legislative authority of the kings.[24] Uniquely, a charter of Lucedus to Nuvidio and his wife Sunildi from 865 paraphrases a law on the validity of sale when evidenced by a written record with the concise statement *licet ordo venditionis legem obtineat* (it is right for the arrangement of sale to maintain the law).[25] Other preambles focus on highlighting the legal force of the charter itself, as at Guimarães, where the 'great is the title of donation' formula has *scripture firmitatis* (document of confirmation) added in twice, linking it explicitly to the validity of law.[26] Asking whether such citations are 'real' misses the point of their rhetorical nature and purpose, to bind the charter and the law together, yet they do show the

---

[21] *FV* 30; Laffón Álvarez, 'Arenga', 147–57, 211–25; Davies, *Acts*, 104–5; *cf. León* 719, 730, 871; *Sahagún* 318; *Astorga* 17; *Arlanza* 14; *PMH* 174, 197, 214.

[22] *Celanova* 158; Davies, 'Gift', 228; *cf. Coimbra* 366, 527.     [23] *LV* 5.4.1.

[24] *Coimbra* 111, 2, 126, 121; *Lorvão* 2, 68; *LV* 5.2.6; Rodiño Caramés, 'Lex', 17.

[25] *Sobrado* 1.58; *LV* 5.4.3; Bastier, 'Vente', 572–83; Córcoles Olaitz, 'Contrato', 309–30; *cf.* Hammer, 'Sales', esp. 49–63.

[26] *Guimarães* 20, 66; *cf.* Rubio, 'Transmisión', 351–71.

capacity of scribes to work creatively with legal text. Allusion to the code can also be subtler and more sophisticated: three separate sales, from Sobrado, Sahagún, and Arlanza, open with a disclaimer that, in a transaction between buyer and seller, there should be *firmitas scripture* (the confirmation of a document), lest any *repetitio* (recall) take place.[27] Citing no law, the formula combines legislation on sales, which gain *firmitatem* when effected *per scripturam*, and donations, which should never be *repetantur* (demanded back).[28]

The same diversity of composition and engagement with the law can be seen in legal citations in the corroboration clause. Some formulas are taken verbatim from the code, such as one which we have seen in modified form in the preamble: an exchange between Fortunio and his wife Speciosa and Abbot Severo of Abellar in 950 says that, *sicut lex docet*, exchange should be as valid as sale.[29] Another charter of Sarrazino Arias and his wife Froilo features a different but equally word-for-word reference to the *lex gotica*, that sale by document should have full force; in a third, 'donation' is substituted into the same clause.[30] One cannot always be sure how specifically such pointers would have been received and interpreted. Sometimes the vagueness seems studied: peculiar to pious donations and testaments is an obscure nod to *leges pacificas vel testacio testatoris* (peaceable laws and the testamentary act of the testator), by which the granter affirms the text and it gains force.[31] This may refer to the permanence of ecclesiastical donation under Visigothic law, or just to law in general.[32] Once legal authority had been invoked, the language and substance of the reference could evidently be tailored to the occasion. Standard scribal practice was creative engagement with the legal text, adapting it to the present context for maximum effect. In this light we might revisit the simultaneously more anachronistic and evocative words of a donation by Bishop Fredulfo to Valpuesta from 894, citing the *Lex Aquilia* which grants firmness to all documents.[33] This archaism, though a corrupt fossil of the 'Visigothic formulary', could also be a deliberately Romanising choice, a potent reminder of the ancient and enduring origins and authority of written records.[34]

---

[27]  *Sobrado* 1.34; *Sahagún* 179; *Arlanza* 13; Bastier, 'Vente', 574; *cf. Otero* 176.
[28]  *LV* 5.4.3, 5.2.6–7.        [29]  *León* 209; *LV* 5.4.1.        [30]  *León* 751, 713; *LV* 5.4.3.
[31]  *León* 93, 115, 399, 683, 796; *Santiago* 31.
[32]  *LV* 5.1.1; Rodiño Caramés, 'Lex', 21, 28–9; Agúndez San Miguel, 'Memoria', 884–5; Isla Frez, 'Pervivencia', 78.
[33]  *Valpuesta* 6.
[34]  *FV* 1, 6–7; Levy, *Vulgarrecht*, esp. 328; Collins, 'Literacy', 117; Martínez Llorente, 'Aplicación', 65–6; Córcoles Olaitz, 'Manumission', 342–4; Vogel, *Kontinuitäten*, 93–6.

The rhetorically legitimising function performed by these acts of citation is reflected in a distinctive terminology which grants the charter itself legal quality.[35] We encounter it in *placita* (written agreements) generated during transactions and disputes, especially at Otero. Fernando Braolizi and his wife Tegridia acknowledged in a *pena placita per iscriptum certu ligavile firmitatis* (penalty agreed by a settled legally binding document of confirmation) to Pedro Flaínez in 1021 that they had defrauded him of *iudicatos* or judicial fees owed to him, while *fidesiunsores* (sureties) for Pedro Flaínez undertook in another *placitum per scriptum certum ligavilem firmitatis* to pay an agreed price to Fruela Sendínez in 1029.[36] The range of cases from León and particularly the west include the *ligali placitum* (legal agreement) made by Nazari and his wife Emiso to Donani Zalamizi in 985, promising to present themselves for judgement, and the record of a settlement between Rodrigo Románez and Jimena Jiménez in 1001, which notes that they had signed a *ligavile* to give testimony under oath.[37] The question is whether the force is 'binding' or properly 'legal': this descriptor is applied to the *placitum* only, a binding agreement typically, if not exclusively, linked to resolving a dispute, but since that regularly involved consulting Visigothic law, the sense may be twofold. The intermediate stage of the settlement process, when the parties checked with the code, had a special turn of phrase of its own. After making arguments, disputants could agree as a next step to go *pro ad lege*, such as Oseredo Tructesindiz, his wife Unisco, and Godesteo, who made a *placitum ad legem* (agreement for law) in 1004, returning in three days *pro ire ad legem* (to go to law).[38] The meaning is quite clear in the *placitum per scriptura ligavile* made by Didago and Enego in 1022, whereby they agreed to go *ad lege* with their parties and proofs, reappearing before the judges three days after *cum lege de libro iudicum* (with the law of the book of judges) to do as the law ordained.[39] Cida Aion simply went *ad librum* (to the book) in 994, an oft-cited case which has been taken to stand for a whole culture of judgement by written law.[40]

---

[35] Martín López, 'Léxico', 137–8, 142–3.

[36] *Otero* 136, 189; *cf.* 99, 125, 150, 159, 190; Sánchez González de Herrero, 'Campesinado', 1, 524–6; Corral and Pérez Rodríguez, 'Fines', 180–2.

[37] *PMH* 144; *Samos* S10; *Lugo*, 2, 591–4; *cf. Valladolid* 3, *Oseira* 1, *Braga* 22; *León* 798, *Samos* 64, *Celanova* 199–200, *Guimarães* 66.

[38] *Coimbra* 212; Wireback, 'Origins', 548–52; García López, *Estudios*, 131–5.

[39] *Otero* 150.

[40] *León* 561; Sánchez-Albornoz, ' "Juicio" ', 383–4, 386–7; Sánchez-Arcilla Bernal, 'Administración', 46–8; Díaz y Díaz, 'Ensayo', 1, 287–305; *cf. León* 597; *Celanova* 200; *Lugo* 22; *Braga* 22; *Guimarães* 24; *Coimbra* 193, 203.

## Penalties

Formulaic legal citation is most common in the sanction clause, where it supports the assessment or assignment of a penalty for violating the terms of the charter. There was much law to draw on here, as the Visigothic code recognises the sanction as a diplomatic unit, and prescribes appropriate punishment for all manner of crimes, from treason down to heresy, as well as the fee payable to the judge hearing the case.[41] Certain sanctions take explicit notice: in the testament of Elvira and Ramiro III to Celanova from 968, any violator is required *per canonicam et godigam sententiam* (by canonical and Gothic provision) to pay the monastery *quod lex imperaverit* (what the law has commanded), while a settlement reached in favour of Celanova in 1007 appoints the king and judge as recipients of *quantum lex godica et veritas ordinaverit pariare* (as much as the Gothic law and truth has ordered to be paid) if a dispute should arise again.[42] The generic term for secular penalties is *damna legum* (the damages of the laws), borrowing from Visigothic legal vocabulary: a donation made by Bishop Teodisclo to Sahagún in 969 enumerates spiritual sanctions and *insuper damna legum*— mundane fines as well.[43] Royal diplomas to Samos especially tend to label these as temporal in nature, while specifying that the violator is constrained and compelled to pay; according to a testament to Celanova from 973, he is *temporali lege quoactus* (compelled by temporal law) to do so, or under the authority of king or judge in a text of 999.[44] One donation by Ansemirus *presbiter* to San Pedro de Montes in 923, however, calls for restoration of all alienated ecclesiastical land *ut legis est exinde sententia* (as is the opinion of the law in the matter), reflecting not the code but the 'Visigothic formulary'.[45] There is a sense once again of invoking 'the law' as much as any particular law to deter those who would trespass against what the charter records.

Legal citations in the sanction clause provided a basis or reason for setting the penalty at a certain amount. In doing so, they drew on a wide range of multipliers and figures in the Visigothic code, even when the monetary units and values no longer had any literal meaning in the early Middle Ages,

---

[41]   *LV* 2.1.26, 2.5.5, 2.5.17–18, 3.1.4, 5.4.8; Carvajal Castro, 'Sanctions', 160–71.
[42]   *Celanova* 171, 302; *cf. Rocas* 1; *Crasto* 27.
[43]   *Sahagún* 253; *LV* 2.1.11, 2.1.29, 3.5.2, 3.5.6, 12.2.3; Rodiño Caramés, 'Lex', 46; *cf. Astorga* 10; *Samos* 33, *Santiago* 21.
[44]   *Celanova* 175, 236; *cf. Samos* 34, 2, 39, 40, 177, S2.
[45]   *Montes* 7; *FV* 8; Córcoles Olaitz, 'Origin', 213.

but served rather as an index of the social status of the parties and transactions involved.[46] Some sanctions simply demand equivalent recompense, as required by law for forcible seizure of landed property.[47] In this line, a donation by Aroza to Santiago de León in 982 orders violators, *ex proprie lege* (by the law itself), to restore as much as they have tried to steal, while in 993 a diploma of Vermudo II to the monastery of Laroá mandates them to repay, by the *lex gotica*, as much as they have attempted to molest.[48] There is no such legal provision as the *auri talentum unum* (one gold talent) which a gift by Bishop Pelayo and others to Celanova from 978 establishes as the damages of the laws, but the same one-for-one principle could be present in creative reworking by a scribe with a parable of Jesus in mind.[49] The standard penalty in the code is twofold, prescribed for the theft or destruction of property belonging to another.[50] By the testament of Virio and family to Castañeda in 965, a violator must repay twice the donated mill *pro dampno legum*, while in 982 the donation by Ramiro and Vermudo, priest and confessor, of themselves and their property to Arlanza sets a double penalty, *sicut lex mandat* (as the law requires).[51] Wording varies with scribal practice, and so the testament of Abbot Astrulfo from 842 speaks of doing penance at the gate of the church, compelled by the laws or judges, for twice what was stolen, while a grant by Ordoño II to the monastery of Triacastela in 919 adjures the offender under the *leges puplicas* (public laws) to render twofold what he has dared to defraud.[52] Showing a deeper knowledge of the code, this recompense was on occasion further enhanced, as in the confirmation of Alfonso II to Samos from 811, which establishes *per legis ordinem* (by order of the law) that he who contravenes it should offer double satisfaction and receive 100 lashes, ubiquitous in Visigothic law as the sentence for corporal punishment.[53] And in a kind of equivalence, the sanction of the pact of Zuleiman *conversus* and others with Castañeda from 953 tells violators to

---

[46] Mateu y Llopis, 'Cláusulas', 579–93; Carvajal Castro and Escalona, 'Value', 23–49; *cf.* Orlandis, 'Concepto', 139–46; Orlandis, 'Consecuencias', 158–63; Bowman, *Landmarks*, 192–4.

[47] *LV* 8.1.2; Marlasca Martínez, 'Aspectos', 206–13; *cf. LV* 7.2.17, 7.3.1, 7.3.4, 8.3.2–3, 8.3.11–12, 8.4.1–3, 8.4.7, 8.4.13, 8.4.21, 8.4.31.

[48] *León* 486; *Celanova* 218; *cf. Sobrado* 1.1.

[49] *Celanova* 188; Matthew 25:14–30; *cf. Samos* 217; Matthew 18:23–35; Revelation 16:21.

[50] *LV* 8.1.5; García de Valdeavellano, 'Conceptos', 211–51; Córcoles Olaitz, *Hurto*; *cf. LV* 7.4.4, 8.1.7, 8.3.5.

[51] *Castañeda* 8; *Arlanza* 23; *cf. León* 781; *Astorga* 71; *Arlanza* 26; *Celanova* 357; *PMH* 119; *Crasto* 27.

[52] *Celanova* 1; *Santiago* 31; *cf. Celanova* 207.

[53] *Samos* 36; *LV* 8.1.4, 8.1.10–12, 8.2.1–2, 8.3.6, 8.3.14–15, 8.4.15, 8.4.24, 8.4.26, 8.4.29–31, 8.5.3, 8.6.3, *et passim*; *cf. Castañeda* 3.

pay two pounds of gold or twice the property *pro dampna legum*, while a grant by Vermudo II to San Pelayo de Oviedo in 996 demands the two talents of gold alone, *sicut lex codicet disnuciat et kanonica censura confirmat* (as the Gothic law pronounces and canonical censure confirms).[54] While the talent had not been in current use for some time, two and twice both had definite legal connotations.[55]

Fewer sanction clauses setting higher penalties also cite the law, but these too can be traced to injunctions found in the code. Several Leonese cases present twofold and threefold compensation as alternatives, in accordance with Visigothic legislation on seizure of property which could not be legally obtained: a donation by Vermudo II to Munio Fernández from 989 enjoins violators to restore double or triple, *secumdum gotica lex sanxit autoritas* (according to what the authority of the Gothic law has ordained).[56] This sense of a legal connotation to a particular number may also explain the sanction of the dedication charter of Cozuelos from 1011, which sets a fine of three pounds of gold, *sic ayt in lex* (so it says in the law), payable to the count of Castilla.[57] In the west, with its denser textuality, sanctions frequently mandate a fourfold penalty, as required by law for specific crimes like damaging enclosures.[58] The testament of Ordoño II restoring San Esteban de Ribas de Sil in 921 called for the offender to repay fourfold as the *leges pacificas precipiunt* (peace-making laws instruct), while a *perfiliatio* (formal adoption) by Fruela Lederiguz of Munia Tegiz in 985 demands a double or quadruple fine, according to what the law teaches; Lorvão used the in-house formula of fourfold penalty for those humbled by the *damna legum*.[59] Interestingly, though the Visigothic code has no fivefold penalty, it charges five *solidi* for offences against appurtenances such as trees, fences, and livestock, and by the same equivalence which made twofold compensation two talents of gold, a gift by Vermudo II to Celanova in 986 directs a transgressor, under *gotdigam legem*, to cough up five talents of gold.[60] At a still higher level, in a charter between Aloytus and his wife Paterna from 965, the sanction stipulates a fine for the *damna legum secularii* of 500 *solidi* paid to 'the fisc', plus two- or threefold recompense: another legally resonant

---

[54] *Castañeda* 5; *San Pelayo* 1; Fernández Conde and Torrente Fernández, 'Orígenes', 191–4; *cf. Samos* 32, 181.

[55] Poiares, 'Nomenclatura', 19–21, 26–7.

[56] *LV* 8.1.7; *León* 530; *cf. LV* 2.5.8; *León* 89, 891.     [57] *Cozuelos* 5.

[58] *LV* 8.3.7; *cf. LV* 7.2.18, 8.1.9, 8.1.12.

[59] *San Esteban* 1; *PMH* 146; *cf. Lorvão* 4, 12, 34.

[60] *LV* 8.3.1, 8.3.6, 8.3.14, 8.4.8, 8.4.29, 8.6.2; *Celanova* 198; *cf. LV* 7.2.22, 7.4.1, 8.1.6; *Samos* 100.

figure, set in the tables of compensation as the maximum applicable for physical injury, it represents the 'value' of the social élite, and situates the transaction in that milieu.[61] Who exactly determined this or any other value to be found in a sanction clause is a far broader question, but in terms of its framing much of the practice reviewed here must reflect scribes 'thinking with the law', whereby the penalty rose in predictable, familiar steps deriving at some stage from the code. And indeed, a special circumstance could have called for checking its text. By a unique monastic pact of 871, those who return to secular life forfeit both all their property and *omnem vocem causandi pro ipsa legis mundane* (any right to bring a legal action under the secular law itself), citing key legislation on *infamia*, loss of the legal right to testify.[62] To counter a special threat, a special deterrent was deployed.

The second sort of legal citation in the sanction clause, assigning rather than assessing the penalty, is far less precise as a rule. In general, Visigothic law awards the fine for a crime to the injured party or, if a slave, to the owner, and this principle may at some level underpin one very common formula, requiring the violator to pay the penalty to the beneficiary or else to whom the law has given it.[63] At an even greater stretch, the wording in a donation of 871 is to whomever *pro futuris* (in future generations?) the law has given it, which could, with some squinting, be a reference to inheritance legislation.[64] But most such citations simply direct the penalty to its legal recipient without further detail, enhancing enforcement of the sanction by conjuring the spectre of the law.[65] In certain late Leonese documents, however, including two royal diplomas and private charters written by royal scribes (Sampiro, Fulgentius, Petrus), the king has been inserted into this otherwise generic formula: the testament of Munio Rodríguez and his wife Razel to San Miguel de León in 1012, for instance, assigns the fine to the king or to whom the law has given it.[66] In the code, the king is only compensated in cases with direct effect on him such as treason and heresy, whereas this modified formula promotes his greater potential benefit, and rhetorically parallels royal and legal authority as partners. This may be part of an increasingly 'royal outlook' amongst Leonese scribes, perceptible in

---

[61] *Coruña* 71; *LV* 6.1.2, 8.4.16; *cf. Sahagún* 33; Carvajal Castro and Escalona, 'Value', 39–44.
[62] *Celanova* 4; *LV* 2.4.1; Marlasca Martínez, 'Supuestos', 247–51; Fernández, 'Witnesses', esp. 509–21.
[63] *León* 8; *cf. León* 84, *Astorga* 171; Petit, 'Crimen', 215–38.    [64] *Celanova* 3; *LV* 4.2.
[65] See *e.g. León* 882, 570, 649; *Sahagún* 129, 220, 262, 427; *Celanova* 181, 231.
[66] *León* 709; *cf.* 748, 788; 710, 715, 717, 732, 756, 855, 857, 860, 862, 880; 514, 635, 681, 736, 826.

the testament of Fernando Núñez to San Miguel de León from 1021, where the violator repays twofold per the *sacrum canonem et lex godice* (sacred canon and Gothic law), and two talents of gold to the king or to whom the *speculatorem legem* (examining law) has given it.[67] Of course, this same textual strategy could be used to promote other authorities, and one record of a council in 995 from Celanova substitutes (the local?) judge for king, while a donation to Covarrubias from 950 adds in the count.[68] In all these ways, Visigothic law has a constant presence in the language of transaction and contention: even if much is formulaic, it witnesses a high degree of consciousness of the code, an omnipresent legal hinterland, on the part of the scribes who drafted these documents. But it also betokens a taste and facility for legally resonant rhetoric, the discourse of a world in which using text meant going to the book, and this framework of written law finds its counterpart in concrete cases of consulting the code in practice.

## Practice

The longer and less glancing references to Visigothic law more obviously originate in encounters with its text, be they first- or second-hand or at yet greater remove. The legislation cited can be grouped under four headings, on inheritance, property, procedures, and penalties, each offering a basis for working through the transaction or other matter at hand by providing a complex of operational parameters for implementation and subject to pragmatic negotiation. Some laws recur so often as to suggest a formulary or copy in common circulation, but others are unique to the context. Taking inheritance law as paradigmatic, one of the basic principles of the Visigothic code is enunciated in a law of Chindasuinth (642–53), apparently abrogating one by Euric (466–84), and known by its incipit *Dum inlicita* ('While anything illegal'): that parents, lest they disinherit their children, may dispose freely of no more than a fifth of their property, the rest being reserved for the family.[69] It followed that only those without children should have completely free disposition, and this right is cited in charters of testament

---

[67] *LV* 2.1.8, 12.2.12, 12.2.18, 12.3.2–5, 12.3.8, 12.3.11, 12.3.17, 12.3.19, 12.3.22; *León* 781; Rodiño Caramés, 'Lex', 40–1, 46.

[68] *Benevívere* 1; *Celanova* 223; *Covarrubias* 1; cf. *Astorga* 111, 230; *Sahagún* 167; Escalona, 'Name', 91–100.

[69] *LV* 4.5.1; Velázquez Soriano, 'Herencia', 209–54; Velázquez, 'Relations', 225–70; Létinier, 'Enigma', 367–88.

across the west with great frequency.[70] When Unisco and her son Osoredo decided in about 1027 to make a testament of all their property to the monastery of Leça, they stated that Oseredo was *sterelis absque liberis* (barren without children), and so their act had the support of Book IV, Chapter II, Sentence XIX of the *libro iudicum* (using the numbering of the Erwig recension), before quoting the law *in extenso* from the first word of its title to the final word of its body.[71] Such precise referencing is not unique: Ermengro made a donation to the same two and their monastery of Vermoim in 1014, noting that how *invenimus* (we found) in Book IV, Title II, Sentence XIX that he who does not leave child, grandchildren, or great-grandchildren has the licence to do what he wishes with his property, an extract from the opening of the law.[72] The scribe of the testament made by Iquilo to Santa Baia in 973 may have mistaken the reference as XVIII, but even so he evidently knew the text, partly extracting and partly paraphrasing it in the preamble to declare somewhat differently that every freeborn man or woman who does not leave son or daughter has licence to do as he wishes with his property.[73] Further citations are still more reworked, such as a testament by three religious to Celanova from 972, which begins with their decision to make it because the *gotorum sanxit auctoritas* (the authority of the Goths) has ordained that *homini filios non abenti de re sua quod voluerit faciat* (the man having no children may do what he wishes with his property).[74] This conveys the tenor of the law through vocabulary derived from or synonymous with its text, and was likely made from memory; even a donation to the monastery of Carracedo from 994 which misattributes the law to Scripture follows its language closely.[75] Scribes were clearly knowledgeable of and confident about relevant legislation, and while the citation might seem formulaic in its repetition, they customised it in use.

## Families

This is only one instance of inheritance law in practice, which more broadly provided norms for handling transactions and disputes involving family and patrimony.[76] By limiting free disposition for all but the childless, the

---

[70] *LV* 4.2.20; García Toraño, 'Ejecución', 293–316; Collins, 'Law', 508; Davies, *Acts*, 66–80; *cf.* Bastier, 'Testament', 373–417.

[71] *Coimbra* 147.      [72] *Coimbra* 197.      [73] *Mondoñedo* 6.

[74] *Celanova* 174; *cf.* 242, 321; *Samos* 164; *Mondoñedo* 1.      [75] *Carracedo* 2.

[76] White, 'Inheritances', 55–103.

Visigothic code effectively prioritised children in legal succession, and this seems to be the explanation for the curious institution of *perfiliatio* ('son-ification'), by which a donor would formally adopt a beneficiary as heir for the purpose of bequeathing property. Though attested in the *Lex Romana Visigothorum* ('Roman law of the Visigoths') of 506, it is documented only from the early Middle Ages, when these limits imposed by the law gave rise to a new social arrangement to work around them.[77] In an early case, Licerius and his wife Faquilo made a *perfiliatio* to Adeit in 875, for him to inherit like one of their sons, just as the law teaches.[78] In contrast, Repparatus and his wife Trasvinda, in a testament to Celanova of 936, record how, being childless, they put all their property in the hands of their *suprinos* (nephews) by charter of *perfiliatio*, but they were treated scurvily and changed their minds, leaving it to the monastery as they were wholly entitled to do, *secundum gotorum iubet auctoritas* (according to what the authority of the Goths commands).[79] Gift by those with and without children was framed by inheritance law; understanding this brings the *perfiliatio* into focus as legal fiction in the full sense of the term, a ruse sustained by the laity to permit bequest of more than one-fifth of family property to outsiders. The alternative may be implied in a donation by Abbot Vermudo from 1009: a fragmentary curse of his *familia* or household for their arrogance, *sicut liber goticus docet*, hints that he is disinheriting his own family, and the *Dum inlicita* laid down the offences which could justify such action.[80]

From the point of view of the Church, what mattered was that Visigothic law, with its strictures on inheritance, constrained donors with children to pious donations of a fifth of the family patrimony. Influenced by Augustinian teachings on charity, this is known as 'the fifth of free disposition', and it appears with regularity in donations and testaments.[81] In 1009, for instance, Iusta left *sua quinta* ('her fifth') to Santos Justo y Pastor, *sicut lex gotica disnunciat et canonica censura confirmat* (as Gothic law pronounces and canonical judgement affirms), while the testament of Bishop Pelayo to Celanova in 982 notes that his father had given him a fifth as monastic

[77] *LV* 4.2.2; Otero Varela, *Estudios*, 100–20; García de Valdeavellano, 'Comunidad', 9–40; Otero, 'Realidad', 1143–9; Ruiz Pino, *Vertiente*, 252–64.
[78] *Liébana* 14.    [79] *Celanova* 52.    [80] *Samos* 64.
[81] *LV* 4.5.1; García de Valdeavellano, 'Cuota', esp. 137–57; Maldonado y Fernández del Torco, *Herencias*, 36–7; Infantes Florido, 'Agustín', 89–112; Martínez Díez, 'Instituciones', 107–23; Arvizu y Galarraga, *Disposición*, 155–62; Davies, *Acts*, 72–5; *cf.* García Toraño, 'Notas', 83–90.

stipend, *sicut lex gotica docet et sanctorum canones iubentur* (as Gothic law teaches and the canons of the Holy Fathers command), because he could do with it as he saw fit, paraphrasing the cited provision.[82] Acts of giving feature this fifth to the degree that it was internalised as the *quinta* or *quintana*, a unit of land and land exploitation, as if 'law-land' in parallel to the 'charter-land' which we have already encountered, and proudly enduring today on the label of many a bottle of fine Portuguese wine.[83] But as the occasion required, a wider range of inheritance law could also be referenced. Imiloni made a donation to Sahagún in 961 for the memory of her late husband and family, including goods vindicated, *secundum gotica lege*, from her son Vincentio: the implicit citation is clarified by the testament of Mumadona Dias from 959, which justifies her disposition of the property of her son Nuño, dead of fever, by the law authorising the estates of a deceased child with no surviving offspring to return to the possession of his parents.[84] In contrast, when Cresconius made an exchange with Quinto and his wife Tructesinda in 997, he received property which the law had given to the latter in inheritance on the death of her mother, as the Visigoths had legislated in great detail.[85]

For the marital unit, the same laws offered an elaborate regulatory framework, and so married couples often asserted legal rights in disposing of their property, amongst themselves or with others. When Aloytus gave his wife Paterna a third of his property in 965, he declared it *licitum* (permitted) because *lex goddiga docet* (the Gothic law teaches), in Book V, Title II, on donations, that if a husband donates anything to his wife beyond the dowry, the act should have full validity according to his wishes, summarising legislation while switching the active and passive parties.[86] In the testament of Hermegildo and his wife Eldonza to Samos in 978, he begins by stating that, as they have no children, *sicut lex gotica docet* in Book IV, Title II, Sentence XIX, he may do with his property as he wishes, a verbatim extract. But he goes on to refer to Book V, Title II, Sentence IV, as above, in condensed form, excising the irrelevant and redundant, while distilling the essentials with vocabulary borrowed from the text; clearly the work of a scribe in full command of the law, this prefaces a disclaimer that wife has made husband

---

[82] *León* 681; *Celanova* 190.
[83] Davies, *Acts*, 76–9; Marques, *Representação*, 240–3; *cf.* Álvarez Maurín, *Diplomática*, 210; *Lexicon, s.v.* 'quinta'.
[84] *Sahagún* 190; *Guimarães* 1A, A3; *LV* 4.2.18; *cf. Sobrado* 1.122; *LV* 4.2.19.
[85] *Celanova* 234; *LV* 4.2.2, 4.2.9–10, 4.2.14, 4.2.17.      [86] *Coruña* 71; *LV* 5.2.4.

a charter by which he may dispose fully of their joint possessions.[87] Indeed, property within marriage had a comprehensive legal regime, and Ildras, in a donation to Lorvão from 952, explicitly exempted the portion of his wife, *quod lex continet*, meaning either the dowry under her control or her right to inherit equally with their offspring after his death.[88]

In a legal sense, the institutional Church was an undying family, and in this regard the inalienability of its property was a key principle. The Visigothic code dedicates an entire title of four emphatic laws to the subject, endeavouring to draw a line between the endowments of monasteries and churches and the estates of individual ecclesiastics.[89] As we have seen, when the bishop of León made a testament to his see in 1002, he lamented that one *ignorans sacros canones et lex gotica* (ignorant of the sacred canons and Gothic law) had appropriated some of its possessions and given them away, while the abbot of Santa Lucía contended in 952 that Osorio Gutiérrez taking control of the monastery was what *lex non continet nec sancta regida docet* (the law does not allow nor the holy rule teach).[90] Confirmation clauses pick up on this concern over secular intrusion, stipulating in a donation by Muzara and Zamora to the church of Lordosa in 882, for example, that the property be reserved for those pursuing the holy life or distribution to the poor, *sicut lex et canonica sententia docet* (just as the law and canonical opinion teach), to be alienated under no condition, or in the testament of Abbot Donnani and Letula to a monastery of São Martinho in 924 limiting ownership to those in monastic orders, *ut canonica sentencia docet et lex logica (sic) ordinat*.[91] Oveco Orbitaz and his wife Olimpia even wrote in 1028 that relatives had purchased a *populatione* (settlement) from Sahagún, but now they, on realising that it belonged to the brothers, returned it in gift: *sicut constitutum est in lege gotica* (just as it has been established in Gothic law), no one should dare to buy, sell, or lessen ecclesiastical property, a pithy summary of the pertinent law.[92] While joint citation of canon law is often the case, its general quality is noticeable, 'the canons' rather than 'that canon'; the Visigothic code is the source for the specific provisions being mobilised.

Whether transcribing or 'treating' the law, scribes used their working knowledge of it to underpin the transactions of a wide variety of royal,

---

[87] *Samos* 132.
[88] *Lorvão* 66; *LV* 3.1.5, 4.2.14, 4.2.16; *cf. Celanova* 12; Bermejo Castrillo, *Parentesco*.
[89] *LV* 5.1.1–4; Martínez Díez, *Patrimonio*; Roca, 'Distinción', 1–16.
[90] *León* 629; *Astorga* 71; *cf.* Davies, 'Competition', 125–38.
[91] *ChLA* 114, 31; *Coimbra* 514; *cf. Coruña* 101.　　[92] *Sahagún* 422; *LV* 5.1.3.

ecclesiastical, and lay actors, stamping their arrangements with an imprimatur of legitimacy. The function of such pragmatic citation was not only to validate the outcome of the charter, however, but also to authorise the terms of reference and the procedures involved. When Alfonso V rewarded Sampiro with a gift of land in 1023, he stated that it now belonged to him to bequeath to whomever he should wish, since any donation in the name of the prince, *sicut lex docet*, should remain irrevocably in the right of the beneficiary, summarising the legislation on royal donation.[93] Meanwhile, in 1012, he had issued a confirmation to Sahagún with licence to rule *mandationibus* (commissions or jurisdictions) with or without the royal *saio* (bailiff), just as *lex sancta vobis auctorigat* (the holy law authorises you), and indeed, if we check our code we find that this official could legally exercise authority only over his appointed district.[94] And when Alfonso V restored San Pedro de Rocas in 1007, he located the motivation for his own and prior royal confirmations of the original foundation by Alfonso III in a law that children and grandchildren must not infringe but rather make all due effort to confirm what their parents had granted by document.[95] At a humbler level, Veila *presbiter* began his charter to Iusta of 860 by recalling how *lex gotorum canet* (the law of the Goths tells us) that a donation made before witnesses cannot be claimed back, but the beneficiary should confirm it *per scriptura at per testes* (by a document and by witnesses), and the gift will have full validity thereafter.[96] Condensing a formidably complex law, this treatment retains all the essentials, its wording drawn largely from the text.[97]

Bequest and inheritance consistently generated such recourse to law. The *personarii* (representatives) who acted on behalf of Iustesenda in her testament to Santiago de León of 1001 confirmed that they were present when she expressed her last will, *secundum continet lex gotica*, fulfilling a legal requirement for testamentary executors.[98] And Bishop Rosendo reportedly decided, in company and with the counsel of his brothers at Celanova, to compose a *testamentum olografum* (autograph testament) in 977, *ex legali precepto* (by legal precept), though this was to be done only in the absence of witnesses, and the reference may simply be rhetorical reinforcement of the text with legal verbiage.[99] But when Assur and his wife Elvira gave a *villa* to the churches of Valdecésar in 999, they declared that, with the delivery of the countergift, this transaction was in compliance with Book V, Title II of the *lex gotica*, which confers validity on written transfer or gift of land, just as brothers of San Martín de Turieno sold property to Munio and his wife Gulatrudia in 915 under the *lex gothica* and *lex canonum* (law of the canons), in accordance with legislation on the sale of ecclesiastical estates and sale by charter.[100] In both cases, the parties were scrupulously acting by law, and a still more striking instance of this is the division of the patrimony of Munio Fernández and Elvira amongst their children by drawing *sortes codicas* or 'Gothic lots' and recording the results in a *colmellum divisionis*, that curious 'column of division': adjudging the settlement just and legitimate, the document seems to implement a process carried over from the fifth-century *Code* of Euric for apportioning land between Goths and Romans, much debated in the historiography.[101] Such an obscure, anachronistic citation must presume an act of checking the code for this transaction particularly; the estate was, after all, unusually rich, and called for a special process hallowed by legal antiquity to forestall the real possibility of present and future contention.

## Findings

Procedural citation was even more common in disputes, where the code provided the guide for judicial intervention and the evaluation of evidence. We have already observed the written agreements signed by adversaries at court undertaking to 'go to the law' or 'go to the book', and the Visigothic code mandates that its rulings be the sole point of reference for all resolutions and settlements.[102] This is implicit in the *placitum* of 987 between the inhabitants of Zacoys and the monastery of Celanova not only to go *pro ad lege*, but also to accept what it directed them to do and thereby reach a legal settlement.[103] The code is quite specific about how this should unfold, requiring the judge first to hear witness testimony, then to inspect the documentation, which should take priority as evidence, and finally at his

---

[100] *León* 587; *LV* 5.2.6; *Liébana* 20; *LV* 5.1.3, 5.4.3; *cf. León* 798; *Celanova* 246; González Díez, 'Reflexiones', 188.

[101] *León* 743; *LV* 10.2.1; García-Gallo, 'Notas', 40–63; Goffart, *Barbarians*, 103–26.

[102] *LV* 2.1.2–3, 2.1.10–11, 2.1.13–14; Collins, 'Visigothic Law', 88–90; Plettenberg, *Fortleben*, 44–58.

[103] *Celanova* 200; *cf.* 344–5; *Guimarães* 24.

discretion to oblige the parties to swear oaths.[104] Careful following of the guidelines can clearly be seen in a case involving Palla and San Martiño Pinario in 985. The judges ordered both parties, *pulsator* (plaintiff) and *responsor* (defendant), to present 12 witnesses, then selected the monastic dozen, *per auctoricentiam regem et legis goddice* (by authority of the king and Gothic law), to confirm the testaments and *firmitates* of Pinario; lastly, they had the witnesses take oath at San Miguel de Barbadelo, following 'the three easy steps to judgement' as outlined in law.[105] Further engagement with the detail emerges from a sale by Count Pedro Flaínez and his wife Bronildi to Fruela Sendínez and his wife Rosla Geta in 1029, where the object is property in Sobrepeña, including *iudicatos* (land received in judicial fine) *per mea veritate et per legem* (by my truth and by the law), the remuneration of judges which legally came from fees paid by the defeated party.[106] And note a case from 1028: a prior judgement regarding Munia was overturned because the code did not authorise it to stand for one as young in age, and so she petitioned once again, presumably now grown up.[107] No one under 14 years old could appear in court; though cited after the fact, the law still served to right a wrong.[108]

Records of dispute are frequently frustrating, glossing over much of what we wish to know, not least how exactly the judges above decided on the party to take the oath, but this is in keeping with the tenor of the law, which leaves much left unstated, outside its strict scope. Legislation on handling evidence is cited less often, but more precisely, and conveys how the procedural guidelines of the code took form in practice. The most revealing case involves the see of Lugo in 1025 reclaiming those persons who had become *extranei* (alienated) from its service.[109] The episcopal *assertor* (champion) Tardenato argued in the presence of Alfonso V and his judges that Bishop Odoario had 'repopulated' the region with their ancestors, *ex pleve familie servorum suorum* (out of people from the household of his own slaves), and that since then the bishops had held them under *colmellos* and *scripturas firmitatis*, until the recent spot of bother. The first legal checkpoint comes when he undertook to furnish the documentation and *testimonias*

[104] *LV* 2.1.23, 2.1.25; Merêa, 'Nota', 1163–8; Piquer Marí, 'Justicia', 269–75.
[105] *Coruña* 95; Andrade Cernadas, 'Villas', 29–30; *cf. Guimarães* 24; *Celanova* 362; *San Millán* 391.
[106] *Otero* 188; *LV* 2.1.26.      [107] *San Vicente* 29.
[108] *LV* 2.4.12; Osaba García, 'Impacto', 343–66.
[109] *Braga* 22; Fernández Flórez, 'Documentos', 137–9; Pastor Díaz de Garayo, 'Uso', 86–9; *cf. Lugo* 12; Sommar, 'Servi', 70–6.

(witnesses) to swear to his assertion and undergo the ordeal, if the *lex godiga* should order it, nodding to legislation on judicial process and trial by hot water.[110] Vermudo *presbiter* countered that the respondents were *ingenuos* (freemen), first sent there by Alfonso III, and claimed to have written evidence to this effect. Both parties then agreed by *placitum* to produce 30 *testimonias* each, though in the event only 29 came to speak for the episcopal *scripturas* and 26 in rebuttal, after which they agreed another *placitum* to 'go to the law' and do as it said. This is our second checkpoint, where the judges *previdimus* (determined) those *testimonias* of the appellant to be *idoneas meliores et pluriores* (qualified, better, and greater in number): the terminology here is deliberate, citing Book V, Title VII, Sentence VIII to the effect that, in a dispute over the status of a freeman or slave, the testimony of those *meliores adque pluriores* should be taken, but how that finding is to be made is left to the 'perception' of the judge.[111] Next they cited the law on general procedure (adding an extra digit to its title in error), followed by Book II, Title IV, Sentence V, that every witness must testify in person, truthfully and only to what he knows first-hand.[112] The legal foundation is sound, and quoted verbatim with slight morphological variants, but indeterminate as far as reaching a verdict is concerned. The judges proceeded to compare the testimony of the chosen witnesses with the *scripturas vetustas anteriores et posterioras* (olden documents, both earlier and later) of Lugo, further terminology taken from the laws on forgery.[113] Finally, they had the parties agree one last *placitum* just as the *lex godiga* ordains, for Tardenato to bring his *testimonias* to swear an oath in Braga, but here the men conceded, and were duly restored to episcopal service.

In practice, the Visigothic code offered a resource of authority and legitimacy not for determining what decision to reach but for setting parameters to reach it rightly. If resolution was ultimately achieved outside the book, the consensus needed for its enforcement rested on a perception that the process leading to it had been according to the book.[114] Take the dispute between Velasco Hanniz and Abellar in 952. Both parties claimed to have supporting written evidence, but Velasco tried on the old wheeze of being unable to find it, so they appealed *ad librum* as if he had, and agreed to do what 'the book' mandated.[115] The settlement quotes the familiar Book IV,

---

[110] *LV* 6.1.3.      [111] *LV* 5.7.8; Merêa, 'Gaveta', 173–5; *cf.* Bowman, 'Infamy', 108–15.
[112] *LV* 2.1.23, 2.4.5.      [113] *LV* 7.5.7–8.      [114] White, 'Settlement', 281–308.
[115] *León* 256; Sánchez-Albornoz, ' "Juicio" ', 383–6; Gibert, 'Enseñanza', 36–7; Martínez Díez, 'Fueros', 292–6; Sánchez-Arcilla Bernal, 'Derecho', 275–7; Prieto Morera, 'Proceso', 403–24, 444–7, 482–3, 486–7.

Title II, Chapter XIX, that the childless may dispose freely of their estate, before citing Book V, Title II, Chapter VI on donation in writing: this states that a testament should take precedence over an earlier document where either it or the property has not been delivered, and that a donor may alter a gift at any point in life if it does not take effect until death.[116] Both citations are literal extracts from the code—the second omitting an irrelevant passage on stolen testaments—and the presiding bishop confirmed Abellar in possession of the property. So far, so final, yet this proved an intermediate stage in the process, because a compromise settlement was then arranged. The same laws were at work in 974 when Taion argued to Ramiro III that Sahagún had taken the property of Liubila, his *frater*, denying him his inheritance.[117] One of the monks riposted that the latter had left it by testament to Bishop Gonzalo, who had donated it to them by charter more than 31 years before, and Sahagún was therefore confirmed in ownership, *secundum lex sancta precepit* (according to what the holy law instructed), seemingly a simple case of the code compelling a conclusion. Yet there is an additional legal principle here in the thirty-year rule, effectively a statute of limitations on the right of appeal; the timing is awfully convenient, and the monastery could have delayed trial to run out the clock, scheming behind the scenes to work the rules in its favour.[118] Visigothic law was a reliable friend to the written record, and when Senta asserted to Vermudo II in 995 that he had been compelled to confirm a *cartula conscripta* (written charter) to Citi Lucidi, he was able to cancel it, as *per veram scientiam canonica et lex gotica* (by the true knowledge of canon and Gothic law), all documents made unwillingly or invalidly have no force.[119]

Separate from and normally subsequent to the establishment of 'right and wrong' in a dispute, the process of settlement also drew from the code to set a penalty for the perpetrator of a crime, echoing the practice of legal citation in sanction clauses. We find the twofold fine *passim*. In 1025, for example, Losidio and his wife Aleza admitted imprisoning dependants of Vela Vermúdez and seizing their property; guilt established, *invenimus in lege* (we found in the law) that one who usurps the property of another without supporting judgement must double it, and sold him a *villa* in compensation.[120] Negotiation was central to the process, and when Daildo and family

---

[116] *LV* 4.2.20, 5.2.6; Merêa, 'Revogabilidade', 1, 173–98.
[117] *Sahagún* 276; Prieto Prieto, 'Sahagún', 498–500.     [118] *LV* 10.2.3.
[119] *Samos* S9; *Lugo*, 2, 585–90; *LV* 5.2.1; Carriedo Tejedo, 'Libros', 60–1.
[120] *Sahagún* 417; *LV* 8.1.5; *cf. León* 559.

were ordered to *componere per lege* (compensate by law) twice what they had taken from Celanova in 1012 but lacked the wherewithal, they arranged labour service in place of it.[121] Similarly, after the erstwhile patrons of Santa María de Ribeira had despoiled it, descendants of the founders appealed to Alfonso V and Menendo González for judges, *sicut lex gotica docet*, to discern the truth in 1005: first they *dederunt inter eos libris* (gave out the books amongst them) and requested sworn testimony from the appellants to justify twofold restoration on top of a monetary fine, then reached another settlement confirmed by the king, *lex gotica cogemte* (Gothic law compelling them).[122] Less often documented are those higher legal penalties, but Duano Teodac did confess to Ero Salidec in 1030 that he had stolen, *inter alia*, his cow, and *lex codorum auctoricava* (the law of the Goths enjoined him) to repay nine cows and endure 40 lashes; ninefold compensation is prescribed for generic theft or killing of animals, and the lashes derive from separate legislation on confinement of cattle without cause—ultimately he made a gift to settle both obligations.[123] The highest multiplier applied is elevenfold, in documents of Pedro Flaínez, such as when Serbodei and his wife Madre sold him half a *villa* in 1018 for a dozen oxen and cattle. As the text explains, judgement had gone against them *per lege et veritate* (by law and truth): Book VIII, Title I, Chapter V, the last off by one digit again, provides that he who incites another to theft, destroying land or livestock, should restore 11 times what was lost, and they handed over their land instead.[124] Yet his counterpart in the Otero archive, Fruela Muñoz, seems to have been oblivious to this, as Emlo repaid him just twofold in 1022, in accordance with the *lex godica*, for convincing his *ancilla* (slave or servant girl) to steal cereals from his house, then helping her to hide them.[125] It paid to have legal expertise at hand, for the leverage which it could lend in such negotiations.

The parameters of settlement were established by law, as penal citation functioned to frame the resolution, while the actual terms of settlement were negotiated extra-legally, in the literal sense of the word. We can see this in cases of assault: the Visigothic code, in common with other post-Roman law, had a tariff for physical injury, and—unusually—it is attested in practice.[126] Each bruise was five *solidi*, and when Massoria and her husband

---

[121]   *Celanova* 332.      [122]   *Celanova* 292.
[123]   *LV* 7.2.13–14, 7.2.23; *León* 872; *cf. LV* 8.4.11; *PMH* 210; King, *Law*, 251–8.
[124]   *LV* 8.1.6; *Otero* 133; *cf.* 116.      [125]   *Otero* 147; *cf.* 148; *LV* 8.1.10.
[126]   *LV* 6.4.1; Oliver, *Body*, 247–62; Iglesia Rábade, 'Penas', 123–47.

Tidon confessed to assaulting Cidi, dependant of Count Pelayo Muñoz and his wife Sancha, in 1029, they said that they had bruised him to a value of 280 *solidi* (56 punches?), which the law ordered them to pay; the next year, Enegus and his wife Arbidio, whose son had left bruises on Flagino and Marino worth 30 *solidi*, handed over six *solidi* to them and half a vineyard to Fruela Muñoz and his wife Gunterodo in *vestro iudicato* (judicial fees), *quomodo lex mandasse* (as the law had required), having negotiated this means of amends.[127] In the majority of cases, however, the tariff is applied without any legal citation. Todemiro admitted in 964 that he had stabbed Albaro *frater* in the arm, causing it to wither, while on the road from Sahagún to Melgar, and in compensation made a testament of land to the monastery, but normally the penalty is first calculated monetarily, as provided in the code, before conversion into property.[128] In 991, for example, Fredino and his wife Leobina gave Flaíno Muñoz and his wife Iusta various goods for the *plagam* (wound), valued at ten *solidi*, inflicted by their son Hermegildo on Sesgudo, and in 1008, another Fredino sold Pedro Flaínez and his wife Bronildi a *villa* for the *livores* (bruises), judged at 100 *solidi*, which he had made on Vicenti, liable for causing injuries of his own.[129] Both terms for physical harm are drawn from the law, but in both cases the fine went not to the injured party, as prescribed, but to the count prosecuting. Algastre gave land to Fruela Muñoz and his wife Amuna in 1012 because he had confined María in her home, an act which features specifically in the tariff, and *lancavit* (struck) her, causing bruising of 30 *solidi*, while Lupi confessed in 963 to causing *cedes* (damages) of 30 *solidi* too at the house of Helyas and Sabildi, *presbiter* and *seror* (cultivator?), and setting it on fire, for 60 *solidi*, a calculation conceivably made by the legal schedule set for arson.[130]

Such cases at least understand the concept of a fixed rate specific to a type of harm, but others more partially and simply reflect acceptance of a penalty determined legally, by the book, like proof by 'the papers'. Fernando Vermúdez and his wife Eldensenda sold part of a *villa* to Fruela Muñoz and his wife Amuna in 1021, which Aita Cotinizi had stolen and the law *autorkavit* (authorised) them to receive, but took no notice of the ninefold fine legislated for theft, while a donation by the monk Ysydoro recorded in an inventory of

[127] *León* 851; *Otero* 193; Corral and Pérez Rodríguez, 'Fines', 179–80.
[128] *Sahagún* 218; *LV* 6.4.3.      [129] *Otero* 31, 75–6; *cf.* 107; *Sobrado* 1.103.
[130] *Otero* 163; *León* 360; Carvajal Castro, 'Houses', 82, 90–3; *cf. LV* 8.2.1; Orlandis, 'Paz', 108–13, 143–50; *Celanova* 160.

Cresconius and given for what the *lex gotica* ordered him to pay for a stolen horse, likewise mentions no law setting the amount for this crime.[131] Cresconius received a further payment from Aloyto and his children in 1007 for the theft of two *quiniones* (plots of land): the judges enquired *pro lex cotica* and decided to repossess one and double the other, but it is not stated that either comes from the legislation on unjust seizure.[132] Legal knowledge will have varied, yet specificity or precision may not always have been the point. Provisions against concealment of theft could lie behind an exchange of 932, involving a vineyard received in fine from Turibius: the text, however, only reports that the law fined him for hiding his brother, who had stolen three oxen.[133] In the dispute of 992 between Munio Gutiérrez and Christoforus *presbiter*, the latter was judged for the crime of stealing testaments from the former, *secundum legem goticam docebat et canonicam sententiam ordinabat* with no further detail.[134] Neither citation states any legal penalty; the purpose was rather to show that a penalty should be paid than to settle what penalty was paid.

The mechanics and dynamics of negotiation which brought disputes from this point to settlement are complex matters in their own right, but for now it is important to note that they were framed by written law. When Olidi and his wife Gota handed Cresconius half of a *villa* in 1001, it was to settle his debt *in iudicatu* for being an *indicatore falso* (false informer): he could not afford what the *lex cottica* demanded, and made this offer instead.[135] Citing the law was to deliver an opening bid in a bargaining process; the higher the start, the more profitable the finish for the beneficiary. We can see it at work in the judgement of Aita Randemiriz and Anserigo Lovegildiz in 1020: as they had conspired to murder Albitto Ennegoz, royal *saiones* (bailiffs) seized them and their property, pending a ruling. Alfonso V, accordingly, consulted Book VI, Title V, Sentence XII of the *lex godiga*, which requires that, if a freeman should kill another by common counsel, the conspirators be condemned to death.[136] He directed them by law to compensate Cidi Domneliz, whom he nominated as beneficiary, and bargaining ensued, whereby the offenders arranged through *rogatores* (go-betweens) to negotiate a compromise, surrendering a *villa* inherited from their parents.

---

[131] *Otero* 131; *Celanova* 315; *cf. LV* 8.4.1; *Otero* 132, 195.
[132] *Celanova* 308; Carriedo Tejedo, 'Viñedo', 127–8; *cf. LV* 8.1.2, 8.1.5; *Celanova* 315; *Cañizares* 65.
[133] *Liébana* 41; *cf. LV* 8.1.10; *Celanova* 312.       [134] *Sobrado* 1.130; *cf. LV* 7.5.5.
[135] *Celanova* 248; *LV* 7.1.1, 7.1.5; *cf. Celanova* 249.       [136] *León* 772; *LV* 6.5.12.

This is related after the fact; the year before, the king had granted half of that *villa* to Cidi, leaving the other half as the royal cut.[137] Like procedural laws, legal penalties were a framework, boundaries for seeking settlement, which incentivised further citation each time they were deployed. Offer death, settle for land.[138]

## Advantage

In rhetorical and pragmatic citation, the Visigothic code was always present, whether accessed through models, memory, or consultation, enjoying and exercising a broad authority to frame what was right. In the full scope of transactions and disputes, it guided and shaped how action was taken and set the terms by which outcomes were reached, defining truth and justice in its own image.[139] There was great potential latent in the law, waiting only for some to realise and exploit at the expense of others. We have seen already one context where Pedro Fláinez took advantage, and Fruela Muñoz failed; it was a question of means. How could the code be mastered? We began by observing an overall trend in the documentation, a rising rate of legal citation over time, which calls for exploration and explanation. Royal diplomas of the late tenth century onwards are more remarkable for their deployment of law to justify seizure of property from rebels and homicides, while aristocratic charters of the same period begin to employ it to legitimise profitable interference in prosecutions of adultery and other crimes. It was the kings and counts of León who grasped the opportunity for 'legal profit', as they made the Visigothic code a tool of lordship, wielding its provisions against rebels and adulterers to reap not inconsiderable benefits. Yet how did they do it? The answer lies in those who spoke this language most fluently, as the same decades saw scribes become not only technicians of writing, but also advisers on written authorities, experts on law. And as those who employed them realised the potential gain, they passed a milestone in the progress of power.[140]

---

[137]   *León* 760; Corral and Pérez Rodríguez, 'Fines', 176–9.
[138]   Lorenzo-Rodríguez, 'Usos', 8–20.
[139]   Alfonso, 'Rhetoric', 78–85; Davies, 'Judges', 193–203.
[140]   Alfonso, 'Litigios', 917–55; Casado de Otaola, 'Cultura', 46–7, 53–5; Davies, 'Lordship', 23–6; Davies, *Windows*, 181–203; *cf.* Bowman, *Landmarks*, 211–28; Mínguez, 'Pervivencia', esp. 15–52; Calleja-Puerta, 'Señores', 19–57.

## Treason

The Visigothic kings saw enemies everywhere, and were obsessed with treason. The basic law was enacted by Chindasuinth in the second year of his reign (643–44), prescribing death or disfigurement and full confiscation of property for even the ghost of an intention to betray king, people, or homeland, though this was later modified by his son Reccesuinth or in the production of the Erwig recension to repeal execution and blinding as punishments.[141] For the kings of Asturias-León, treason law proved a powerful ally against rebellious subjects, in Galicia especially, with the pressure which its severity applied to a settlement for land.[142] We catch our first glimpse of it in the late ninth century, when Alfonso III granted three diplomas to Santiago of property confiscated by law from traitors against his rule. In the earliest, from 886, he handed over possessions formerly belonging to Hermegildo and his wife Yberia, who had rebelled and lost them *per legum decreta et nostre sinodis instituta* (by the decrees of the laws and the teachings of our synod).[143] The citation is general, imprecise, and on three more occasions the king made no mention of the law at all, but simply gave away the properties of faithless subjects. Here he seems to have relied implicitly on his legal right to do so, as when in 895 he made an exchange of a *villa* owned by Vitizane *infideli* (the unfaithful), who lost it for his *culpam* (offence); according to a retrospection of 1007, this vexatious *dux* rebelled for seven years, until Count Hermegildo Gutiérrez delivered him to Oviedo, and all his land was seized and redistributed.[144] Silent lurks the Visigothic code: behind these all is a presumption, without direct legal citation, that traitors forfeited their possessions to the crown.

Yet few successors of Alfonso III adopted the same tactics, until the end of the tenth century. Ramiro II gave three *villas* of Gonzalo Muñoz, rebel aristocrat, to San Cristóbal de Vega in 946, while Ordoño III donated a district to San Rosendo which *suprini* (cousins) had lost on account of

---

[141] *LV* 2.1.8; Lear, 'Law', 1–12; Iglesia Ferreirós, *Historia*, 21–81; Díaz, 'Confiscations', 93–112; Gallegos Vázquez, 'Delito', 35–60.

[142] Grassotti, 'Ira', 5–135; Iglesia Ferreirós, *Historia*, 83–146, 269–85; Rodiño Caramés, 'Lex', 26–8; Pérez, 'Insumisión', 371–5; Lorenzo-Rodríguez, 'Culpa', 127–41; *cf.* Orlandis, 'Concepto', 125–36, 187–92; Orlandis, 'Consecuencias', 133–9; García González, 'Traición', 323–8, 337–4; Baliñas, *Defensores*; Pino Abad, *Pena*.

[143] *Santiago* 13; 15, 18; Martínez Díez, 'Instituciones', 134–6; Prieto Prieto, 'Potestad', 530–3; González Díez, 'Monarquía', 2, 204–22.

[144] *Santiago* 16; *Celanova* 302; Alfonso, 'Rhetoric', 58–63; *cf. Santiago* 5, 12; Sánchez Badiola, 'Terminología', 2, 688.

*execrabili infidelitate* (abominably disloyalty) in 955, and Ramiro III made a bequest to the see of León in 981 of property impounded for similar betrayal of the king.[145] The same legal background, no doubt, but still implicit. The citation first becomes explicit in documentation from the reign of Vermudo II, when royal authority had reached a nadir as he battled magnate insurgency and Umayyad incursion. The chronicler Sampiro, who had begun his career as a notary under this king, was conscious of a shift in practice, recording that *leges a Banbano principe conditas firmavit, canones aperire iussit* ('he confirmed laws established by King Wamba [672–80] and ordered canons disclosed').[146] The attribution is notable: some Visigothic legislation bears Wamba's name, and identifying him here presupposes a fair knowledge of the code in currency.[147] More to the point, this sense of legal—and canonical—restoration or *renovatio* perceived in the imaginary of contemporaries tallies with the activity which we find in the diplomas, for Vermudo II cited treason law more than any other king.[148]

The earliest case vindicating Sampiro comes from 994, when he gave Celanova a *villa* which Suario Gundemáriz had usurped *extra mea iussione vel voluntate* (without my order or assent), before rising in revolt. After God had restored the king, all property of this rebel was his to do with as he pleased, *sicut canones sancti et lex gotica de talibus ordinat et iudicat* (as the holy canons and Gothic law provide and judge in such matters).[149] Despite being the work of Sampiro himself, the diploma does not draw directly on the text of the relevant legislation, but a year later, when an Erus Fofiz was discovered to have joined the insurgency, fleeing the royal presence to camp with the villains, his possessions were seized pursuant to *canonem et lex gotica* (the canon and Gothic law) on those who evilly disobey the king: here an unnamed scribe has paraphrased its opening words.[150] The joint citation of both secular and canon law in these cases is noticeable, and suggests an awareness that the Visigothic statute on treason had been reinforced by subsequent councils of the seventh-century Church in its compact to support the crown.[151] The two authorities were intended to be

---

[145] *Vega* 2; *Celanova* 110; *León* 482.
[146] *Chronicle of Sampiro*, ed. Estévez Sola, *Chronica*, 25.10; Pérez de Urbel, *Sampiro*, 11–125; Collins, 'Law', 509; Rodríguez Fernández, 'Monarquía', 356–67.
[147] *LV* 4.5.6–7, 6.5.21, 9.2.8; Isla Frez, 'Monarquía', 53–4.
[148] Orlandis, 'Huellas', 644–58; Orlandis, 'Pervivencia', 125–36; Ruiz Asencio, 'Rebeliones', 233–4; Sánchez-Albornoz, *Orígenes*, 66–71; Isla Frez, *Realezas*, 65–71; Martínez Sopena, 'Reyes', 132–40; Martínez Sopena, 'Herederos', 87–8.
[149] *Celanova* 221.    [150] *Celanova* 223.
[151] Collins, 'Law', 503; Linehan, *History*, 22–50.

complementary, and Vermudo II drew on them as such, underlining this in a donation to Celanova from 996 of lands taken *per auctoritatem catolice legis decretum* (by authorisation of the decrees of Catholic law).[152] Osorio Díaz had joined the 'Saracens' *adversus gentem et patriam nostram* (against our people and country), two-thirds of the secular trinity of *princeps, gens, patria* which echoes through the pronouncements of the Visigothic Church and crown.[153] He had been expelled and lost all his possessions, for it is only *idiote homines et imperiti qui nesciunt legis principum decreta quasi reprehendunt* (oblivious and uneducated men who know nothing of the law—like they reject the decrees of kings), and ignorance had no validity as a legal defence.[154]

By deploying these twinned bodies of law, a ruler could not only regain his position in material terms, impoverishing his enemies and enriching faithful supporters, but also reassert his legitimacy on a more symbolic level via the grand spectacle of consulting and announcing its provisions. Vermudo II held one such council in 998, as recorded by a chancery copy from 1020, to denounce *filii perdictionis* (sons of perdition) who had sought out Muslim allies and overthrown his reign for an interval: *ut ceteris de hac opinione in exemplo fiat* (to be done by way of an example to others of this persuasion), he disposed of all the property of one of the captured conspirators, Gonzalo Vermúdez, by authority of *quiquid in sacratissimum canonem et godicam legem invenitur de revellionibus uel contradictoribus regis sive de fagultatibus eorum, sicut in libro secundo et in eius titulis constitutum vel exaratum a prioribus sanctis patribus scriptus ecce decernitur* (what is found in the most sacred canon and Gothic law on rebellions and opponents of the king and their belongings, as is declared to be instituted and inscribed in Book II and its titles, written by the Holy Fathers of old).[155] The beneficiary was none other than Sampiro, who also received another *villa* seized *per legem sanctam* (by holy law). Such public acts had resonance. Osorio Iohanni, in a donation to Celanova from 1001, took care to relate how our friend Erus Fofiz had scorned the service owed his king in accord with the *canones et liber iudicum* (canons and book of judges), and Vermudo II had taken his lands *per auctoritatem legis* (by authorisation of the law) and *canonica et iuditialis sententia* (canonical and judicial opinion), giving one part of them to Osorio Iohanni.[156] Similarly, his son and successor

[152]  *Celanova* 229.      [153]  Sirantoine, *Imperator*, 81–122, esp. n. 92.      [154]  *LV* 2.1.3.
[155]  *León* 581; Carriedo Tejedo, 'Diploma', 72–7; cf. *Fernando I* 31.
[156]  *Celanova* 246; cf. *León* 724.

Alfonso V (999–1028), meditating on his father's reign in 1012, recounted how Ablabel and his wife Gunterodo had agitated against him, joining Count García Fernández of Castilla: the king seated himself before his court, and *facta est questio per omnem volumine legis* (an enquiry was made through the whole volume of the law), like the Day of Judgement come early. The diploma, surviving in the original, proceeds to quote extracts of treason law nearly verbatim, on the fugitive or insolent against prince, people, or *patria*, establishing how the book sentences the goods of the 'nefarious transgressor' to belong wholly to the king, for him to give away with permanent effect.[157] The omissions and discrepancies are minor, while the whole clearly reflects the Erwig recension, mobilised effectively. When Alfonso V gave this sequestered property to Munio Muñoz on Easter Sunday at Oviedo, he participated in the self-fashioning narrative of authority and legitimacy articulated by his father before him, and gained the same advantage over his rebellious subjects.[158] By the same token, each property took on a 'legal history' as it passed from rebel to king and king to faithful subject.

Yet there was more than one way to cite the law, and in other contemporary cases of treason and confiscation the code justified and enabled royal action purely through language, silent or implicit citation discreetly endowing the diplomatic text with words of power. The earliest instance of all from the reign of Vermudo II falls under this heading: he explained in 990 that a certain Conanzo had begun spreading rumours of his death while he was in Galicia and had raised uproar around León; returning and arresting the rogue, the king extracted a promise by *placitum* that he would offer no further opposition, or forfeit his possessions. As such, when Conanzo, *ex infidelitate*, resumed his life of villainy, all property of this *nefarie transgressoris* passed by charter to the king, and he was quite free to give it to whomsoever he wished.[159] Surviving in the original, the diploma is signed by Munnio *frater* and *iudex*, a notary, but it also bears the monogram of Sampiro. We may detect his hand in the narrative, which reflects not only the terms of treason law but also its text; even without a citation, the 'nefarious transgressor' or 'so heinous offender', one of its more memorably baroque terms, leaps straight off the parchment. In other words, Visigothic legislation frames both the action and its presentation, and diplomas into and through the reign of Alfonso V report rebellions by and confiscations from other rogues in the same discursive mode, quietly predicating the legitimacy of

---

[157] *Otero* 90.     [158] Carvajal Castro, *Máscara*, 273–82.     [159] *León* 541.

appropriation on the law.[160] Even his mother Queen Velasquita, widow of the late king, seized land from the rebel Felix Agelazi after he had resourcefully fled royal wrath by Viking barque.[161] It was simply part of the mentality of royal documentation, and this may explain a curious outlier from 906, preserved in a later imitative and interpolated copy, which describes how Alfonso III, after putting down a Galician insurrection, announced at Lugo his right, *in legali sentencia* (under sentence of law), to seize all the property of his enemies and bestow it on anyone of his choice. Citing the *liber iudicialis* (judicial book) at Book II, Title II (this should be I), Sentence VI, on those who scorn royal command, the quoted text comes from another related law, but the scribe made this more familiar reference out of habit.[162]

The immediate successors of Vermudo II faced equal unrest in their reigns, and they followed his lead in deploying Visigothic law to meet the challenge.[163] Alfonso V granted a donation in 1023, once again to Sampiro, of property formerly owned by Eicta Fosatiz, who had betrayed his king, joining with Count Sancho García of Castilla in rebellion, and so lost his lands to the crown, as *lex abtorigat* (the law authorises).[164] The scribe Viliulfus may have offered a rather vague citation of 'Book II and its titles', but in what follows he demonstrates thorough internalisation of treason law, that nefarious criminals who deceive and oppose the prince, people, and *patria* should be wholly at his disposal, with their possessions, drawing recognisably on the language of three discrete passages from its text to fashion his summary. On a similar occasion four years before, Alfonso V had given estates taken from his enemies Cotina Fernández and Fernando Peláez to his loyal Pedro Fláinez, and in the written record, we find the *lex godicat* cited chapter and verse, as Book II, Title I, Chapter VI, on those who abandon, deceive, or are insolent to prince, people, or *patria*.[165] The notary Veila evidently knew his law, expanding on the title and distilling, if overly concisely, the treatment of penal slavery and exile with keywords from the text. When reiterating the royal privilege of seizing and disposing of the property of the rebel, he has also clarified that privilege, complementing its use of the passive with a statement of agency to eliminate ambiguity.

---

[160] See *e.g. León* 719, 741; *Astorga* 230 (B); *Santiago* 90, 63; *Alfonso V* S; *Tumbo Viejo* 15.

[161] *San Vicente* 30; Sánchez Candeira, 'Reina', 479–80, 502–4.      [162] *VDJ* 1; *LV* 2.1.33.

[163] *Alfonso V*, 135–7; Isla, 'Warfare', 233–46; Martínez Sopena, 'Reyes', 141–50; *cf.* Fernández del Pozo, 'Alfonso', 85–106.

[164] *León* 802; *cf.* 748; Carvajal Castro, *Máscara*, 132–6.

[165] *Otero* 124; Prieto Prieto, 'Otero', 644–6; Salazar Acha, 'Conde', 87–98; Martínez Sopena, 'Reyes y nobles', 1, 165–8, 192–6.

The latest case, from the reign of Vermudo III, takes the practice a step farther by grounding treason law in other related legislation. The colourful narrative of 1029 retails how Ovecus and his wife Adosinda refused to do *servitium* for properties which they held *ad operandum* (in contract of labour), or to acknowledge the new king when he demanded their return, and barricaded themselves in the fortified *castro* of Aguilar in Galicia, looking to Count Rodrigo Románez as their new patron and protector.[166] The king intervened to take back a church of San Salvador in Maceda in the midst of the warzone and hand it to Bishop Pedro of Lugo, confirming a gift made by his father: the diploma cites not only Book II, Title I, Sentence VI, by which all possessions of the nefarious transgressor should be wholly at the disposal of the prince, but also Book V, Title II, Sentence II, which provides against vacating royal donations without any fault by the beneficiary.[167] The scribe handled both laws the same way, running the title together with the main provision: for royal donations, the pertinent text came from the end of the statute, while for treason, from the middle, twofold legal cover for confirmation and appropriation.

One final aside of interest is that the compensation for homicide often ended up in the hands of the king as well, rather than with an immediate relation. In the case of Odoario Díaz, murdered by men from Matella, he turns out to have been the nephew of Ramiro II, but in the main no connection between king and victim is declared.[168] Ramiro III, for example, claimed the right to dispose of the property of Salbator and Mahamuthi for their killing of Abgizza in 975.[169] How can we explain this? If we consult the Visigothic code, we find a provision that, where the family of the victim decline to take action, a third party may prosecute a homicide and thereby receive the compensation.[170] In 943, accordingly, Ramiro II gave away the lands confiscated from Patre and family because he had committed homicide and many other evils besides, and so been exiled *a patria* (from the country): the punishment suggests that the king had adopted the expedient of assimilating homicide to treason, for which exile was a standard policy, to add further legal justification to his seizure of property.[171] Alfonso V seems to have done likewise in 1016, when Fromarico Sendiniz killed two men *in regionem nostrum* (in our realm), then fled to seek refuge with

---

[166] *Tumbo Viejo* 16; *Vermudo III* 3; *cf.* Ser Quijano, 'Renta', 64–70.    [167] *LV* 5.2.2.
[168] *León* 123, 253; Carvajal Castro, 'Houses', 94–7; *cf. León* 567, 605, 788; *Sobrado* 1.117.
[169] *León* 442.
[170] *LV* 6.5.14–15; King, *Law*, 259–64; *cf.* Orlandis, 'Consecuencias', 88–104.
[171] *Sahagún* 84.

Sancho García of Castilla; pardoned and entrusted with a *realengo* (royal domain) in León, he pillaged it instead, violating the virgin daughters of *viris idoneis* or men of substance, a crime penalised harshly by adultery law, and killing two more, before being obliged to restore his patrimony to the king.[172] One victim, however, was a royal dependant, and the king could also have been acting as he did in 1022, when he exchanged a *villa* seized from Cipriano Vimaraci for the murder of Salla, his servant, since as lord he was entitled by homicide law to compensation.[173] But in all these cases, as in the many instances of bringing traitors to book, the code was the most reliable ally of royal power. By citing and rewriting the law, drawing on and demonstrating its authority, to re-establish their position in both material and symbolic terms, the rulers of Asturias-León were better able to confront the many challengers amongst their sometime subjects, emerging enriched and affirmed.

## Adultery

The kingdom over which these rulers presided was less an administrative entity than a political sphere for cooperation and, more often, competition amongst various élites and their fluid relationships, groupings, and networks.[174] When kings cited treason law, it contributed to consolidating power in royal hands, but the lay aristocracy of León also used legal citation as a tool of lordship from the late tenth century, and the benefits accruing to them intensified the existing tensions between counts and the crown.[175] The specific arena of their intervention was in the settlement of disputes involving crimes of a sexual nature, or the range of offences which the code and the documents tend to encompass under the broad, often misleading label of 'adultery'.[176] The most important of many laws on this subject mandate that an adulterous wife, her lover, and their property should be delivered into the power of the wronged husband for disposal, making exception for possessions of legitimate children; and, on those who may bring charges, that if the king or any royal agent is forced to act where the family has failed

---

[172]  *León* 741; *LV* 3.3.1; Carriedo Tejedo, 'Merino', 59–68.       [173]  *Santiago* 63.
[174]  Portass, *World*, 98–101; Carvajal Castro, 'Monarchy', 232–48.
[175]  *Alfonso V*, 147–51; Martínez Sopena, *Tierra*, 327–67; Martínez Sopena, 'Reyes', 125–7; Martínez Sopena, 'Justicia', 239–55; Davies, *Acts*, 143–9, 181–5.
[176]  Lorenzo-Rodríguez, 'Denuncias', esp. 107–11, 119–24; Lorenzo-Rodríguez, 'Violaciones', 309–12; *cf.* Tyszka, 'Violence', 12–13.

to so, he should receive a stipend for his public-spirited efforts.[177] In early medieval Iberia, this 'third-party rule' offered a profitable way in for those such as counts defining themselves as delegates of the king, whatever the reality of the comital office, while the 'delivery clause' was an important source of new slaves, or in practice a resource for commuting penal slavery into profit.[178] The payment made by Froylo to Barilli in 954 after being caught *in flagrante* with her husband is a rare instance of compensation paid to the offended party.[179] But the classic example is the case of Cida Aion, who made a charter to Count Munio Fernández and his wife Elvira in 994 handing over all her property except that of her husband, belonging to her children. She had been caught committing adultery with Pedro, *meo cumpatre et marido alieno* (my godfather, husband to another woman), and when they had gone 'to the book', its verdict was that she be enslaved; in lieu of this penalty, she surrendered her land.[180] Using the legal definition of adultery as a 'public' crime meriting a 'public' response, Munio insinuated himself into a private dispute, then traded slavery for settlement, pocketing the profit. There is an awareness here of the potential of written law, and an imaginative extension of its rules for personal enrichment, founded on a generalised acceptance of its applicability.

The most active in taking advantage of Visigothic adultery law were the two counts so richly documented in the Otero archive, Pedro Flaínez and Fruela Muñoz, who capitalised on a broad range of legal precepts on sex and marriage in their respective spheres of operation or 'jurisdictions' in Valdoré and Viñayo, just north of León. This contributed significantly to the both of them, and their networks, amassing substantial landholdings, and becoming important players both locally and on the royal stage.[181] In 1006, for instance, Iusta made a charter of all her property to Pedro Flaínez and his wife Bronildi because she had committed *avulterio sine lege* (adultery without the law) with Martino, husband of her sister: their relationship is stated to underline the gravity of the offence, by categorising it as adulterous

---

[177] *LV* 3.4.1–3, 3.4.12–13; Álvarez Cora, 'Derecho', 1–52; Osaba García, *Adulterio*; Torrent Ruiz, 'Represión', 7–74; Torrent Ruiz, 'Protección', 725–54; Quesada Morillas, *Delito*, 117–72.
[178] Rio, 'Enslavement', 79–107; Rio, *Slavery*, 42–74; *cf.* Portass, *World*, 102–7, 186–90; Davies, 'Counts', 143–68.
[179] *Lugo* 22.
[180] *León* 561; Sánchez-Albornoz, '"Juicio"', 287–91; Orlandis, 'Consecuencias', 150–7; Davies, *Acts*, 184–5; Díaz de Bustamante, 'Imágenes', 2, 185; González González, 'Esclavitud', esp. 177–83, 194.
[181] Prieto Prieto, 'Fruela', 20–3, 30–4; Sánchez-Albornoz, *Regimen*, 44–57; Estepa Díez, 'Poder', esp. 288–96, 314–23; García Leal, 'Condes', 24–63, 71–103; González Jiménez, 'Moralidad', 2, 289–98; García Leal, 'Sistema', 311–28; Carvajal Castro, 'Sociedad', esp. 118–29.

and incestuous in legal terms, and so to command a higher compensation.[182] For his part, Fernando not only engaged in adultery with another Iusta, wife of his brother, in 1020, but also put away his own partner without the marital *dos* or *arras*, the dowry and pledge which as we shall see belonged to her by law, and was obliged to cede all his property to Pedro Flaínez and Bronildi.[183] Two years later, however, a rather more elaborate domestic drama unfolded when Fruela Muñoz accused Eneco and his mother and brother of attempting to kidnap Midona Vita, a *cubileira* (domestic maid) and one of his own dependants, reporting that he had pursued and captured this bandit family *cum voce de rapto* (with the cry of abduction). Once Eneco had confessed, the parties made a *placitum* to go *ad lege* and return after three days *cum lege de libro iudicum* (with the law of the book of judges) to do as it ordered: they duly found in Book III, Title III, Sentence II (correctly I) that if a freeman should forcibly abduct a virgin or widow, and she be rescued prior to intercourse, he must yield half of his property to her, but if there has been intercourse, marriage is forbidden, and he must be delivered to her with all of his property, sustaining 200 lashes and losing his liberty.[184] This is quoted nearly verbatim from the cited law, yet when it came time to settle, Midona Vita expressed a desire not to be separated from Eneco as the *lex godiga* mandated, suggesting that events may not have been exactly as narrated; nevertheless, constrained by the law, they made a *placitum* to do lifetime service together to Fruela Muñoz and his wife Amuna.[185] The 'true story', of course, is unrecoverable, but the count could have opposed a union originally, and, after catching them in the attempt to circumvent him, rolled out the law as a prelude to setting it aside for his benefit.[186] This same strategic use of legal citation as an opening gambit in the bargaining process is explicit in a case from 1027, when Auria, *secundum lex non docet* (as the law does not teach), became pregnant from fornication with her *primo congermano* (first cousin). She was brought before Fruela Muñoz and ordered to be whipped, *sicut lex continet* (as the law provides), but then her mother and sister stepped in, offering land instead of the scourge.[187] Incest is once again flagged to confirm the gravity of the offence, while the threatened lashing is part of the punishment prescribed

---

[182] *Otero* 71; *LV* 3.5.5.     [183] *Otero* 125; *LV* 3.6.1.
[184] *Otero* 150; *LV* 3.3.1; *cf.* Orlandis, 'Consecuencias', 147–9.
[185] *Otero* 151; Rio, *Slavery*, 64–5.
[186] Lorenzo-Rodríguez, 'Denuncias', 123–4; *cf.* Quesada Morillas, *Delito*, 195–7.
[187] *Otero* 177; Carvajal Castro, 'Sanctions', 159.

by the same 'third-party rule' which led the count to intervene; both were traded in for wealth.

These means of action were theoretically open to anyone with some 'public' standing, but others beyond the Otero circle appear to have been slower off the mark in taking on cases of adultery, or at least they are less well documented. In 1012, the bailiffs of Alfonso V and Count Rodrigo Ordóñez *calumniaverunt* (accused) Daildo and family of raping the daughter of Gunderigo Dadilaz. The dispute was heard at the monastery, and when they could not pay what *hordinabit nobis lex gotica* (Gothic law commanded us), the abbot of Celanova stepped in to pay the *rausum* (rape penalty) for them, and they agreed to work two *villas* on behalf of the monastery.[188] Often the legal citation is only implicit, such as when Letasia confessed in 858 that *commiscui me in adulterio* (I mixed myself up in adultery) with Ataulfo, a 'slave' of Hermegildo: the wording is quite peculiar to Visigothic adultery law, including legislation on freeborn women and slaves specifically, but the charge was set aside to reach settlement, and the pair only ended up with a twofold fine, payable to the lord, for having made off with four of his cows and, heroically, 60 of his cheeses.[189] How this might work is illustrated by the charter which Abita made to Iusta in 1028, for 'mixing herself up in adultery' with Fronimio, *marido alieno* and *compatre de mi filios* (husband to another, godfather of my children; she was *matrina* or godmother to his daughter). Compensation was negotiated by the mediation of *omnes bonos* (good men), surprisingly to include the inheritance of her children, but given all the links between the parties they could have been illegitimate, legally disqualifying them from exemption.[190] In a rare Castilian case, Zite Pinniolez acknowledged in 979 that, despite having a dowried and pledged wife, he had 'mixed himself up' and fornicated first with Gota, then with Zitiella, his *nuera* (daughter-in-law), impregnating her with a son: the peculiar turn of phrase and the twin components of a legal marriage contract serve to establish his liability, and he delivered all his property to Urraca of Covarrubias.[191] Neither she nor Iusta above had any stated standing, but intervened by the same 'concerned citizen' statute as the counts.

---

[188]   *Celanova* 332; Pérez González, 'Néologismes', 134; Lorenzo-Rodríguez, 'Denuncias', 107–11.

[189]   *Sobrado* 1.75; *LV* 3.2.2, 3.4.8, 3.4.15; Díaz de Bustamante, 'Imágenes', 180–1; Díaz y Díaz, 'Vida', 1, 563–70; Portela Silva, 'Rey', 220–1; Díaz de Bustamante, 'Violence', 454–5; *cf.* Adams, *Vocabulary*, 180–1.

[190]   *León* 846; Martínez Sopena, 'Justicia', 255–60.

[191]   *Covarrubias* 11; *LV* 3.1.3, 3.1.5, 3.1.9; *cf. Oña* 23.

Whether mobilised explicitly or implicitly, Visigothic law provided a framework for third parties of ambition and awareness to take profitable action on adultery, and with this in mind we can identify a wider range of cases initiated or diverted by elements of the Leonese aristocracy.[192] When unnamed persons *levantarunt crimine* (raised a charge) against Aurelio in 1024 that he had 'mixed himself up' with the wife of Arkaio, he was cleared, but because Fruela Muñoz had acted as his *adiutatore* (advocate), Aurelio gave him land *in ofercione* (as an offering or payment): here the experience of the count in prosecuting adultery served the defence, just as much to his own profit.[193] Experience brought expertise, and when Fredino and his wife Leobina made a charter of their land to Count Flaíno Muñoz in 992, the account relates that it was for their son Argemiro, who went in the *ora nocturna* (night-time hour) to the house of Lecinia, a relative in the third grade, and took her virginity by force.[194] The legal principles embedded in this narrative are multiple, and would have placed the count in a very strong bargaining position: nocturnal crime meant a heftier fine, adultery in the parental home was punished by death, their relations made it incest, and her virginity doubled the penalty.[195] But how did these activist lords get involved in the first place? Estevano granted property to Pedro Flaínez and his wife Bronildi in 1028 for likewise 'mixing himself up in adultery' with Belita, wife of Belito; granter and beneficiary, according to the record, were neighbours, and the perpetrator had the misfortune to live within the effective reach of the count who brought the charges.[196] One wonders, reading a charter of 1003, whereby a *mulier* (wife) named Auria gave property to Count Munio Fernández and his wife Elvira for the act of fornication which she had perpetrated with Nuño, a married *textore* (weaver).[197] Why was no explanation of any kind offered? Had the comital right to demand payment here become internalised?

These efforts at self-enrichment, however, were not entirely unopposed. In a famous case from 1012, two *potestates* (powerful men) from Nave de Albura came to Count Sancho García at Término to protest that Beila Ovecoz of Palencia had turned up with two *merinos*, judicial officers of some sort, and sought to exact *omicidium* (a homicide fee). Customarily, they objected, their *villa* did not pay either this or *fornicio* (the adultery fee),

[192]  Astarita, 'Prácticas', 41–4.     [193]  *Otero* 168; *cf.* 133, 166.
[194]  *Otero* 33; Díaz de Bustamante, 'Imágenes', 184–5.
[195]  *LV* 3.3.1, 3.4.5, 3.5.1, 4.1.3, 7.2.16; *cf.* Orlandis, 'Concepto', 156–64.
[196]  *Otero* 187; *cf.* 38.     [197]  *León* 632; *cf.* 671.

nor did the *saio* or bailiff of the king have right of entry. In response, the count directed the two *potestates* to take oath *cum suo scripto quod habebant de suo foro* (with their document which they had of their custom), and once they had done so in the church of Santa Ágata, he confirmed it before witnesses. Thus defended by its local élite on the basis of written evidence, the *fuero* of Nave de Albura was a privilege of exemption from paying the count of Castilla precisely the fines for homicide and adultery which lords had come to exact by authority of Visigothic law; the *saio* too was reminded that he was legally bound to operate only where appointed.[198] Trying again that same year, Beila Ovecoz and his henchmen sought the homicide fee from Berbeia and Barrio, but four villagers (including one of the *potestates*) swore similarly before Sancho García at Término that they were exempt from *homicidio*, *fornicio*, and *calda* or the ordeal of hot water prescribed by law. The count again confirmed their privilege, *sicut hic scriptum est* (just as it is written here), incorporating into the record as transmitted by the cartulary of San Millán a somewhat dubious diploma of 955, whereby men from these two villages as well as San Zadornil testified to their *fuero* before Fernán González.[199] Successful defiance of lordly imposition, though implicitly recognising the right of the count to exact or exempt; if the fine for adultery was part of this dynamic, its 'public' prosecution had become normalised.

Compared with these representatives of the lay élite, the clergy exploited written law more episodically, and mainly in the west with its denser textual culture. Bishop Fruela made a gift to Santiago de León in 1006 of property confiscated by *lex et kanonum* (law and canon) from Gonzalo *frater*, who had become involved with a 'daughter of perdition', forfeited all of his property, and fled the diocese: the relevant law, with its supporting canon, enjoins bishops to punish adulterous clerics under their jurisdiction with confinement and penance, but here it justified exaction of a more tangible penalty.[200] The hapless Iulianus *presbiter* seems to have been surrounded by adulterers, as he describes in his testament of 954. When he was visiting the monastery of Valdesaz, its abbot elected to patronise a prostitute in León, got caught with her in public, and was obliged to pay 200 *solidi* to the *pressores* (movers and shakers?) and *potestates* of the city; when he moved on to

[198] *San Millán* 181; Martínez Díez, *Fueros*, 14–18; Pastor, *Resistencias*, 40–3; Álvarez Borge, *Poder*, 27–51; Casado de Otaola, 'Cultura', 54–5; Martínez Martínez, 'Notas', 247–64; Sánchez González de Herrero, 'Campesinado', 520–4; Martín Prieto, 'Elementos', 26–7.

[199] *San Millán* 535; Pastor Díaz de Garayo, *Castilla*, 195–9; Peña Bocos, 'Aldea', 69–96; Martín Viso, 'Poder', 533–52; Santos Salazar, 'Privilegios', 51–81.

[200] *León* 658; *LV* 3.4.18; VIII Toledo 5; *cf. Astorga* 371.

another monastery of a certain Froilo, its sisters turned out to be pregnant or sexually involved, and their families showed up to kill some and disperse the others.[201] Both episodes in the narrative are framed by the categories of the code, which singles out public prostitution for condemnation, though prescribing a punishment of 300 lashes for the woman alone, and requires relations to take action against adulterers in the family.[202]

Sometimes it is not clear that the prosecution of ecclesiastical sex crime was itself ecclesiastical: Cisilu gave Ermiario and Semena half his property in 949, for the *culpa* of his daughter Baselesa, who had perpetrated (*penetravi* [*sic*]) adultery with the monk Nausti, but nothing is said of anyone bringing charges against him.[203] When Gontoi and family gave half of their property to Vimara Kagitiz in 1022, however, it was because their son Alamiro had committed adultery with *nostra sobrina et sua congermana prima*, his or their niece and first cousin, breaking her chastity in their own home. Once the case had been settled with his help, Vimara undertook to defend them against future charges for the crime, with *defensionem* and *moderationem* (protection and guidance), *consilio* and *benefactoria* (advice and service), the last a term and an example much discussed in the context of feudal relations.[204] Whatever the identity of Vimara (likely an agent for Celanova, where the text was preserved), this 'defence contract' expects other third parties to initiate prosecution for the adultery, capitalising on the legal right to act, and turns that expectation into a tool of lordship and profit; to underline the gravity of the deed and ratchet up the pressure, the text thickly contextualises the crime in the law, as incest, virginity, and the home setting are all culpable categories.[205] Celanova showed a marked enthusiasm in this field of 'adultery advocacy', such as when Gigulfo ceded a fifth of his property to the monks in 989, seeking pardon for sinning in *contubernio* (cohabitation) with his *conmatre* (godmother), or when Tusto handed over half of his own for incest with his granddaughter, who had turned to the monastery for redress.[206] But other members of the clergy also had a business in this line, and Argerigo and Adosinda gave Evenando *presbiter* half their property in 1008, because *fabulastis* (you have spoken) on her behalf

[201] *León* 278; *cf.* 279; Linehan, *Ladies.*
[202] *LV* 3.4.17, 3.4.13; Osaba García, 'Imagen', 658–66.      [203] *PMH* 58.
[204] *Celanova* 353; Sánchez-Albornoz, 'Behetrías', 1, 71–3, 86–7; Díaz de Bustamante, 'Imágenes', 184; Martínez García, 'Pactos', 333–43; Graça, 'Prácticas', 40–6; *cf.* Estepa Díez, *Behetrías*, 1, 13–27; Estepa Díez, 'Hombres', 113–40; Gilsdorf, *Favor*, esp. 24–41.
[205] *LV* 3.3.1, 3.4.5, 3.5.1, 4.1.4.
[206] *Celanova* 205, 315; Díaz de Bustamante, 'Imágenes', 182; *cf. Celanova* 206, 313.

for betraying her husband in sin and owing him *mercem* (reward).[207] Sex and the law spelled profit.

Yet the practice of prosecuting adultery with reference to the Visigothic code was the pursuit of the laity above all, and particularly the Leonese aristocratic networks of the Flaínez and Muñoz families. Fruela Muñoz was amongst the most active in this regard, and there is a certain symmetry in the fact that his father Munio Fernández not only took similar advantage of the legislation, but was also one of the rebels against whom Alfonso V sought to reassert his authority through citation of treason law, following the lead of his own father. Kings and counts both understood the potential of written law to legitimise their actions, and thereby to defend or enhance their positions and patrimonies: they exploited the same code in pursuit of divergent interests, constantly checking and always accepting it as a source—the source—for the rules of the game of power. But how, and why? The outline of an answer emerges from a startling statistical corollary: the rate of legal citation and the incidence of career scribes take off together in the decade of the 970s, and thereafter rise steadily in near tandem (see Figure 5.3). Consider that the majority of references to treason and adultery law are in the last quarter of the tenth century into the early eleventh, and that all the

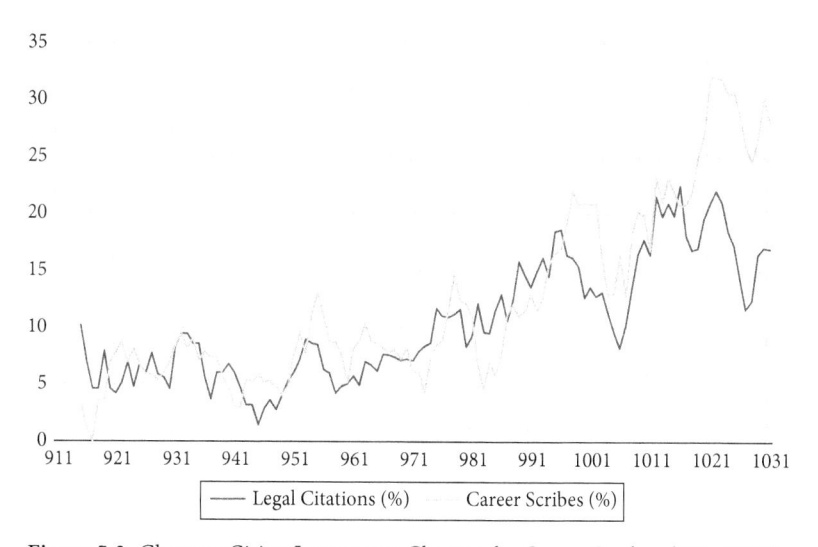

**Figure 5.3** Charters Citing Law versus Charters by Career Scribes (911–1031)

---

[207] *Coimbra* 155; *cf. León* 799; *Sahagún* 427.

big names amongst the 'career' class of notaries and scribes can be found at work in the diplomas and charters citing them. Notice the presence of Sampiro as beneficiary of several royal confiscations by treason law, and the role played in comital prosecutions of adultery by those who employed Cidi, Citi, and other career scribes in the Otero archive. It was a compact: as first steps towards a scribal profession were taken, legal expertise spread, as the writer of a record became more often one of a few practised hands, written law was deployed more densely and creatively. Scribes set the terms of transaction and dispute in the framework of the code, and made themselves indispensable as the experts in its text. Marketing their services to royalty, aristocracy, clergy, and the laity alike, they promised employers a weapon to delegitimise rebels and penalise adulterers, and in both cases to make them pay, innovations in 'literate lordship' which had ready acceptance waiting in a society long and deeply accustomed to living by the rules of written law.

## Silence

If the scribe doubled as an expert in the law, we need to rethink the forms which legal citation might take. The depth of contact between the clergy and the Bible led them to 'write Scripturally', processing the world around them through the holy book, and scribes, through their regular engagement with the Visigothic law code, came likewise to 'write legally'. They were 'literate interpreters', whose internalisation of a textual framework for thought, speech, expression, and action shaped the behaviour of their communities, and if we read the charters with sufficient sensitivity, we can realise that more than just those on treason and adultery are animated by laws, cited in silence, reflecting the passage of the code into customary practice. By silent citation, what was done and how it was done were legally constrained in matters of inheritance, property, procedures, and penalties, identical in remit to explicit citation. As we have seen, Visigothic law includes complex regulations for succession, and many donors, for example, predicated the pious donation of all their property on their lack of children, pointing discreetly, by their perception of a need to justify themselves, towards the familiar legislation that only the childless may dispose of their possessions freely.[208] Lurking in the background of the arrangements being made, this

---

[208]   *LV* 4.2.20.

legal awareness seems to have been especially acute, as ever, in the west. Elarinus and Gundilo gave all their property to Samos in 931 because they had reached old age without any children, while Ansur and Eieuva in 951 endowed a church in Arouca because God had not willed that they have children to inherit their estate.[209]

For those with children, the 'fifth of free disposition' is equally often implied. Donors simply had to allow for the law, limiting their donation accordingly, and testamentary proviso clauses take the presence or absence of children into account as a matter of course.[210] Married without children, Rodrigo and Elvira made a charter in 959, lest they die intestate, arranging that the one who outlived the other should inherit all of their property: after both were dead, it would pass to Sobrado, but if they did have children, only a fifth would be given in charity.[211] This may also recognise that, without a charter, full transfer between husband and wife would be legal solely if there were no relations within seven degrees; conversely, descendants of the founders of San Pedro de Laroá in 909 claimed full rights to dispose of the monastery on the grounds that their parents had in fact died intestate.[212] Children could only be disinherited if they were guilty of a crime, which accounts for the convoluted complaint lodged in 1029 by Fronili against her father, accusing him of seeking to make a charter to his wife of a third of his property and thereby excluding his daughter without fault on her part, though she ended up losing her appeal.[213] In 978, similarly, Abgamira had to swear an oath that one Tota was not his son, as had been claimed, before he could freely leave his lands to Albelda.[214] And indeed, Ramiro III was deemed to have acted *indecenter* (unbecomingly) for appropriating the estate of Sarracinus after he had been taken captive to Córdoba, even though he left no relative to inherit it; the king is absent from the order of succession to the maximum degree, and Vermudo II in 986 donated it to Santiago on behalf of the unfortunate man.[215]

The intersection of property with the marriage contract is another area where charters quietly abide by the terms of Visigothic law. Letitia observed in a testament to Abellar from 927 that her parents had united her to her

---

[209] *Samos* 119; *Arouca* 2; *cf. Samos* 227; *Celanova* 23, 119; *PMH* 16; *Lorvão* 27; *León* 73; *Astorga* 169.

[210] *LV* 4.5.1.

[211] *Sobrado* 1.4; *cf. León* 528, 718, 855; *Sahagún* 335; *Oviedo* 29; *Samos* 175.

[212] *Celanova* 10; *LV* 4.2.2, 4.2.11.      [213] *LV* 4.5.1; *Sahagún* 424.

[214] *Albelda* 27; Santos Salazar, 'Ruling', 136–7; *cf. LV* 4.5.4.

[215] *Santiago* 45, 52; *LV* 4.2; *cf. León* 788.

husband *per rectum hordine* (in the right order), and when Donazano asserted in a charter of 1001 that he and his wife Leodesinda had been joined together for many years *per dotalis ordinis* (by the order of the dowry), he was pointing to the legislation which defines it.[216] By law marriage required a betrothal surety or pledge, termed an *arras*, and the dowry or morning gift, the *dos*.[217] In 1019, using the precise terminology of the code, Sendina donated to Santillana houses which her husband had given her as *mea dote vel in meas arras*; Eldesenda lamented in 962 how she had married Zulaiman without *dote* or *arras* and he *damnabit* (did damage) to her property, but fortunately Godesteo Menéndez and Ledegundia restored it, and she gave them a portion in gratitude.[218] The Visigothic code and formulary both set the *dos* at a tenth of the goods of the husband, plus ten boys, ten girls, and 20 horses, and these all appear in the *dotis titulum* (title of dowry) of Sisnando to his wife Eldontia from 887 as well as that of Oliti to his wife Adosinda from 946: in the first case, the 20 dependants are even named, taking us beyond the realm of an ossified formula.[219] And if law defined the terms of marital legitimacy, it stands to reason that it should have regulated divorce. Gontrode reported in 1013 that her husband had dismissed her to the religious life in order to remarry, and so she exchanged a *villa* for one which he had given her *pro nuptiis* (for their nuptials), since divorce was permitted if the woman entered a monastery, and a woman who divorced legitimately retained whatever she had received in marriage.[220] The testament of Christoforo and Gunterodo to Ardón made similar provision in 1012 that if the wife should outlive the husband and remain *in continencia* (celibate), she could hold onto all the property of their union, but only her portion if she remarried, precisely according to marital law.[221] In the same line, Sahagún sold off properties in 1006 donated to it by Gunterode, which Vermudo II had seized after her husband died childless but half of which she had regained by arguing that she had acquired them with him; the appeal was a success, bearing out the legal principle that husband and wife have equal claim over what they accumulate in their married life.[222]

---

[216] *León* 73; *Coimbra* 522; González Paz, 'Repensando', 17–50.

[217] *LV* 3.1.3, 3.1.5, 3.1.9; Merêa, 'Dote', 1, 59–77; Otero Varela, 'Arras', 189–97; Otero, '"Liber"', 545–55; Marcela Mantel, 'Problema', 63–72.

[218] *Santillana* 23; *León* 355.

[219] *Sobrado* 1.119; *PMH* 56; *cf. Celanova* 24; Martínez Díez, 'Instituciones', 104–7.

[220] *Samos* 198; *LV* 3.6.2.    [221] *León* 706; *LV* 4.2.14.

[222] *Sahagún* 386; *LV* 4.2.16.

When is a parallel between prescription and practice merely coincidence? In 975, the monasteries of Sahagún and Abellar reached an agreement to share evenly the building of a *presam* (weir or dam) on the Porma River, an arrangement notable for its compatibility with Visigothic legislation, which limits diversion of rivers to half the total flow per party: could this represent the internalisation of a legal 'principle of halves'?[223] For certainty, there should ideally be intertextualities, and cases of explicit citation as a control. With procedural law, for instance, judges in 972 chose the 15 witnesses produced by Gudesteo Muniz on behalf of Arouca over the ten brought by Adaulfu because the former were *pluriores* and *meliores*. We have already encountered 'many' and 'better', language from the guidelines for evidence in a dispute over the status of a slave, and the situation and outcome here both reflect its terms.[224] The descriptive title of *condiciones sacramentorum*, the written oath sworn by witnesses, also reflects Visigothic legal terminology, exemplified in a model incorporated into the code to be taken by (forcibly) converted Jews and kept in episcopal archives.[225] There is another model amongst the Visigothic *formulae*, but the examples preserved or cited in charters, comparable amongst themselves, feature elements common to both sources, such as invoking the four Gospels as guarantors of sincerity, and fit neither exactly.[226] The code called for the judge to take sworn statements from parties, calling the written record of them *condiciones*, and in this sense, the vocabulary of dispute itself had a legislative register, while following legal norms.[227]

Sensitivity and imagination are needed to appreciate how 'legal' a charter might have felt, and how many connections to law those who read or heard one might have realised, with all their implications. In this regard, there are signs that legislation on destruction of property served to inform the thinking behind its ownership. In a dispute from 978 involving Sahagún, the monastic *mandator* (representative) argued on behalf of a tenant brother that he had held a mountain possession *in suos scriptos* (in his documents) for over 30 years before Magito ploughed it 'presumptuously', this term *presumtive* present in pertinent laws against cutting down trees or claiming

---

[223] *León* 437; *LV* 8.4.29; Pérez Rodríguez, 'Agua', 91–3, 98; Sandoval Parra, 'Leyes', 209–26.

[224] *Arouca* 84; *LV* 5.7.8; *cf. PMH* 216.

[225] *LV* 12.3.15, 12.3.28; Juster, 'Condition', 273–4; Linder, *Jews*, 311–17, 330–2.

[226] *FV* 39; *cf. León* 34, 192, *Castañeda* 1, *Oviedo* 26, *Puerto* 2, *Valpuesta* 10–11, *Alfonso V* 15; *León* 669, *Otero* 31, *Sobrado* 1.109, *Celanova* 260, *Guimarães* 24, 51.

[227] *LV* 2.1.23, 2.1.25.

land within the boundaries of other estates.[228] And when Abbot Salito founded and endowed Hiniestra in 947, a clause was added by Fernán González that one who chopped down trees on its land should be fined, or if during the night tossed *ad carcerem ad partem comitis* (into the comital jail), reflecting the harsher penal regime for crime committed after dark.[229] Donum and others made recompense Pedro Flaínez in 1022 for felling trees on his mountain, creating a clearing, and shifting the *arcas petrinias* (boundary stones), damage totalled at 300 *solidi*, but is it significant that each offence is covered by law?[230] Think about the testament of Fredesindo and family to Eslonza from 950: it included *bustos* (pastureland, normally with stables), and on the reverse side of the parchment two laws on injury or death suffered by livestock in the charge of another have been written out in their entirety, as if they applied to the ownership of such property.[231] Pastures and stables may seem straightforward, but they clearly had some legal resonance; the testament contains no explicit citation, nor any obvious implicit citation, yet someone (the hand is different) read relevant law in its contents, and copied that onto the back. For context, or as a precaution? These *bustos* could be sites of litigation exactly as envisioned by the code: Vegilio and his wife Gunterodo gave a vineyard to Fruela Vimarédiz and his wife Adosinda in 995 as payment for the sheep, geese, and pigs injured while entrusted by Fruela to Vegilio.[232] Other cases deal more generally with damage to property and reparations, but one from 1022 may point to a particular law against wrecking gardens, and another from 1008 to the legal punishment for destruction by fire.[233]

## Numbers

The most frequent silent citation, again especially in the west, concerns the extent of tenure beyond which possession became incontestable. The Visigothic code provides that no case can be brought more than 30 years after its cause, a statute of limitations effectively recognising any arrangement

[228] *Valladolid* 3; *LV* 8.3.1, 10.3.4; Marlasca Martínez, 'Tala', 553–60.
[229] *San Millán* 377; *LV* 7.2.16, 7.2.23; Díez Herrera, 'Organización', 153.
[230] *Otero* 149; *LV* 10.1.13, 10.3.2; *cf. Otero* 121.
[231] *Eslonza* 24; *LV* 5.5.1–2; Moralejo Álvarez, 'Arco(s)', 219–38; *cf.* Fernández Conde, 'Ganadería', 139–58; Fernández Mier, López Gómez, and González Álvarez, 'Prácticas', esp. 191–7.
[232] *Otero* 40.
[233] *Otero* 128; *Celanova* 311; *LV* 7.2.17, 8.2.1, 8.3.2; *cf. Celanova* 80; *Lorvão* 37; *LV* 10.1.11.

or situation upon the expiry of the term: this 'thirty-year rule', inherited from late Roman law by way of the *Code* of Euric, played an important role in the documentation of land ownership in early medieval Iberia, as it did across western Europe.[234] Often it simply served to affirm the right of disposal. Ermesenda Díaz stated in a donation to Samos in 1011, for example, that she and her husband had owned the property for over 30 years, while Gunterigo and Osorio, deacon and priest, agreed to divide their inheritance with Bishop Rosendo in 955, because he had held *pars nostra* (our share) for over 30 years and therefore had a legitimate claim.[235] In disputes, it was part of the discourse of argument, such as when Velasco argued in 915 that the monastery of Valdevimbre had owned a weir or dam and mill for 30 years, until Monnio had diverted their water only three months earlier; the latter was forced to admit his misconduct after witness testimony delivered under oath.[236] As this case also demonstrates, the rule worked hand in hand with other forms of proof, and that included written title. Using the precise legal term *tricennium* to refer to the period, Didacus *presbiter* asserted on behalf of San Martiño Pinario in 985 that the monastery had owned two contested *livertos* (freedmen) as well as their ancestors *per tenpus et tricinos per escripturas et testamentos vetustus* (for a time and for 30 years by old documents and testaments), and emerged victorious.[237] In 992, however, when Christoforus *presbiter* and his brother stole the testaments of a church and claimed rightful ownership after holding them 'in theft' for 30 years, they were unsuccessful: it did not automatically override other evidence.[238]

The rule was amongst the most thoroughly internalised precepts drawn from the code, and parties played number games at court with the term of years. Sobrado argued in 1001 that Lucido Quiriaci had contrived to sneak into the monastery and substitute *scripturas invalidas* (invalid documents) for one part of a *villa*, but no need to worry: only 20 years before.[239] In 927, witnesses for Castañeda testified that Evorico had invaded a *villa* and *piscaria* or area of fishing rights, yet since the *auctores* (in this context, the former owners) had *quartaverunt* or 'chartered' them to the monastery within the preceding 30 years, Castañeda retained its rights; in the face of further litigation in 952, the monastery changed tack, now claiming that it had held the properties uncontested for 36 years, unobtrusively adding a decade to

<hr />

[234] *LV* 10.2.3–4, 10.2.6; Levy, *Law*, 176–94; Petit, *Iustitia*, 413–21; Esders, 'Verjährungstitel', 57–86; *cf.* Bowman, *Landmarks*, 47–51.
[235] *Samos* 94; *Celanova* 113.   [236] *León* 34; *cf. Coimbra* 212; *Lugo* 24.
[237] *Coruña* 95; *cf. Sobrado* 1.129.   [238] *Sobrado* 1.130.   [239] *Sobrado* 1.132.

the time elapsed between the two cases, pushing it past the magic number.[240] Still more emphatically, when Lupella identified Muzurri and others as his *servi* (slaves) in 912, the reply came that his *casada* (dependants) had in point of fact been *ingenua* (free) for more than 90 years, and they held onto their freedom even when sons of Lupella purported to have been 'served' by them within the previous 30 years, a notable though not unique instance of the weaker party winning out, albeit helped along by royal oversight.[241] Visigothic law also sets a fifty-year time limit for appealing divisions of property and definitions of status, and this moved Tarasia to manumit *liberti* (freedmen, but seemingly slaves) of over 50 years' standing in 1000, after relatives had made a *scripturam falsitatis* (forged document) attempting to seize some of them.[242] In 999, meanwhile, Lovesindo Abenazar alleged that men of Sautello were not dependants of Guimarães because they had held their own property for 50 years, but he was defeated by the monastery producing written evidence to the contrary; Guimarães and Ordonho Sentariz both brought charters to their dispute in 1014, and the monastic document dating back 50 years duly prevailed.[243] Remarkably, the two timeframes are even cited in the same case: in rebutting a claim by the bishop of Lugo, the bishop of Santiago maintained that the men in question had been granted by Ordoño III to Sobrado for these 30 years, and marshalled supporting witnesses who swore to know nothing to the contrary, either first-hand or from their *prioribus* (predecessors) going back 50 years.[244] The numbers game reached its logical conclusion when Gontigio *presbiter* defended his ownership of a church in 991 by means of written title and by claiming to have held it undisturbed for 80 years, handily the sum of the two statutes of limitations.[245] In some or all these cases, there may have been no code to hand or in mind, only a shared legal inheritance, but its text has been internalised to shape an entire social understanding of proprietorship and the passage of time.

## Customs

Charters 'speak legally' because that came naturally to their writers, and by doing so they transmitted norms originating in writing into more general

---

[240] *Castañeda* 1, 3; Anta Lorenzo, 'Monasterio', 40–3, 49–51.
[241] *Santiago* 24; *cf.* Carvajal Castro, 'Resistencias', 13–33.
[242] *LV* 10.2.1–2, 10.2.5, 10.2.7; *Sobrado* 1.131.     [243] *Guimarães* 24, 51; *cf. Santiago* 59.
[244] *Sobrado* 1.109; Prieto Morera, 'Proceso', 476–8; *cf. Puerto* 2.
[245] *PMH* 163; Wright, 'Scribes', 74–6.

awareness. Silent citation is an advanced stage in this process, wherein conceiving of transactions and disputes, defining and debating the decisions involved, had come to be shaped profoundly by the law, such that reference to it became habitual practice, or the literacy of custom. Of course, the code is only one source for and part of the broader category of 'norms' brought to bear in transaction and dispute, and this is the basic sense of *consuetudo* and its synonyms: the established, accepted, and useful.[246] When the charters cite 'custom', therefore, they have in mind not some ancient alternative authority fundamentally opposed to the written, but a variety of such traditions, and not unlike how Roman law can lie behind 'customs' codified in post-Roman law, many of these are deeply entangled in text.[247] Indeed, when charters apply customary terminology to documentation, they show that text itself had become habit. Silus Lucidi *confessor* recalled in 960 how Abbess Elaguntia had founded a monastery and made a testament of endowment, *ut mos fidelium extat* (as is the custom of the faithful), while Didacus and his wife Ildoncia in 959 identified Gunteroda as the prior owner of a property which they had acquired, *sicut mos esse solet* (as is usually the custom), by preparing charters of exchange for each other.[248] And even more revealingly, in contrast to Catalunya where the names given to the Visigothic code tend to be quite obviously 'legal' (Gothic law, worldly law, secular law), here 'custom' could also point to a particular written act of legislation.[249] Far from uncovering a hidden source of rules and regulations or the vulgarisation or corruption of law, this type of citation testifies to the internalisation of norms from the code.[250] According to the *agnitio* (confirmation) of San Pedro de Rocas from 1007, its founder Gemondus discovered the site when preparing for the customary aristocratic *venatum* (hunt), but the same document describes the attestation of the original founding diploma of Alfonso III by his successors as customary by the *lex gotica* and *gotorum libri* (books of the Goths).[251] The cited 'custom' turns

---

[246] Brown, 'Use', 15–40; Cañón Dunner, 'Prácticas', 37–60.

[247] *Sobrado* 1.106, 1.107; *Celanova* 85; *Santiago* 58–9; *San Millán* 535; *Celanova* 215, 52; *Guimarães* 68, A6; Petit, 'Consuetudo', 209–52; Alvarado Planas, *Problema*, 15–103; cf. Barnwell, 'Emperors', 6–29; Humfress, 'Law', 23–47; Kleffens, *Law*, 122–3, is amusing.

[248] *Sobrado* 1.122; *Guimarães* 54; Kosto, 'Practices', 259–60; cf. *Guimarães* A1; *Lorvão* 15.

[249] Iglesia Ferreirós, 'Creación', 416–17; Salrach i Marès *et al.*, *Justícia*, 1057; cf. Rodiño Caramés, 'Lex', 46.

[250] Martínez Díez, 'Fueros', 286–8; Casado de Otaola, 'Escribir', 141–8; Miceli, 'Derecho', 9–27; Miceli, *Derecho*, esp. 27–138; Álvarez Cora, 'Interrelación', 49–75; cf. García-Gallo, 'Consideración', 409–23.

[251] *Rocas* 1.

out to be a law which we have already seen in practice, that sons should confirm the charters of their fathers.[252]

In other cases, customary citation is a mode of silent citation, referring to some of the more common laws and legal principles. We can see this immediately in the prescription of a twofold penalty, *qualiter est consuetudo* (in the manner which is customary), in the sanction clause of a Castilian sale from 950, or the arrangement to share water from the Torío River in equal halves, as per custom, carried out in 925: both practices may have become normal, but they derived from legislation.[253] When Rapinatus and his wife Celedonia admitted in 977 that they had drunkenly broken down the doors of a deaconry of Sahagún and murdered a brother within, they accepted that an agent of Ramiro III had seized their property *ut consuetudo est secundum quod veritas docet per canonica sententia* (as is customary according to what truth teaches through canonical opinion), silently citing homicide law and including canon law too in the realm of custom.[254] Theodenandus *archipresbiter* went still further in 902, recounting how prior priests of San Esteban de Calvor had, amongst their many crimes, failed to make a written pact in compliance with the custom of all monks and clergy, even though *instituta est canonum* (it is the teaching of the canons) and *sanctorum norma docet apostolorum* (the rule of the holy Apostles teaches it); he also quoted Scripture to found this 'pactual tradition' on additional textual authority.[255] Custom becoming law is a sign of law becoming custom: the code, whether all or any of its silent citations would have been recognised and appreciated in general, had come to frame transactions and disputes to the point that it no longer needed, or possibly even involved, conscious explicit invocation. Visigothic law was simply the right way, and many likely never realised the degree to which they lived in the world of its text.

## Practical Texts

Alfonso V, that embattled king, is an unlikely father to early medieval Iberian law, yet in 1017 he issued the *Fuero de León*, the first act of legislation since the fall of the Visigothic kingdom three centuries before. None of his

---

[252] *LV* 2.5.4.
[253] *Cardeña* 67; *Sahagún* 33; *LV* 8.1.5, 8.4.29; *cf. Santiago* 35; *Guimarães* 1A, A3; Pastor, *Resistencias*, 97–100.
[254] *Sahagún* 287; *LV* 6.5.14–15; *cf. Sahagún* 183.
[255] *Samos* 33; D'Emilio, 'Charter', 304–13; *cf. Celanova* 263.

predecessors had made new law; all had retained and respected the law of their forebears, to secure the legitimacy which continuity conferred. What Alfonso V attempted, beset by enemies, was to reset the relationship of crown to code from passive to active, to reassert royal control through legislative initiative, and to restore a measure of 'public' power to the regulation of transaction and dispute in his kingdom.[256] The text which he promulgated in council with bishops, abbots, and *optimates* or the high nobility at Santa María de León is nevertheless mediated through the ongoing relevance of that code, and the two fairly compatible versions of the *Fuero* surviving in the cartularies of Oviedo and Braga confirm, supplement, and revise its provisions.[257] In some cases, there is a clear shift in the balance amongst the key actors: where Visigothic law had stated an order of priority placing the affairs of the king first, the *Fuero* amended this to put the Church and servants of God up front, followed by royalty, aristocracy, and the people, and in later centuries appealing to 'the book' became identified with a sector of the west front of the cathedral of León adorned with an iconography of justice.[258] But this new regime still spoke the old language of power.[259] The schedule of penalties and payments owes much to quantities common to the code, while even a seeming departure such as the dismissal of the thirty-year rule where it harms Church possession echoes an exception already made by Wamba.[260] Less a revolution than an act of transmission; the written framework of judicial practice remained Visigothic law.

Of course, much took place beyond the parchment. Who really settled a dispute? The process involved two groups who have received most of the scholarly attention. Judges may not all have been kings, counts, and courts, royal or comital delegates, or bishops and senior clergy, but they clearly had standing, as we have seen, to exercise some procedural direction. At the same time, it is difficult to find evidence of 'summary justice' being handed down by such actors; the norm was rather a collective form of judgement, a 'public' system of shared acceptance of Visigothic law, frequently involving

[256] Otero, 'Códice', 568–73; Pérez-Prendes y Muñoz de Arraco, 'Potestad', 502–17, 527–45; Prieto Prieto, 'Potestad', 552–8; Rodríguez Fernández, 'Monarquía', 385–92; Isla Frez, *Realezas*, 110–18; Isla Frez, 'Proyecto', 172–5; Díaz-Plaza Casal, 'Recuperación', 143–60.

[257] García-Gallo, 'Fuero', esp. 150–3; Martínez Díez, 'Tradición', 117–39, 155–72; Fernández Conde and García Arias, 'Forum', 207–33; Coronas González (ed.), *Fueros*, 35–91; cf. García y García, 'Concilios', 385–6; López Alsina, 'Reyes', 1, 95–8.

[258] *LV* 2.1.4; *Oviedo* 42; Sánchez-Arcilla Bernal, 'Administración', 46–8; Cavero Domínguez, Fernández González, and Galván Freile, 'Imágenes'; cf. Martínez Llorente (ed.), *Milenario*.

[259] Zimmermann, 'Tutelle', 27–56.

[260] *LV* 4.5.6; Martínez Díez, 'Fueros', 296–308; Sánchez-Arcilla Bernal, 'Derecho', 236–74; Álvarez Cora, 'Derecho penal', 217–33; Alvarado Planas, 'Pervivencia', 141–52.

agents of a very local kind and emanating from wider elements of the community.[261] In this regard, the *boni homines* (good men) were manifestly important figures, and we have witnessed them intervening to barter down the severity of a legal penalty or ensure enforcement of a verdict: here no doubt the weight of the 'better sort' made itself felt. Reaching a resolution will in many cases have provided an opening for local élites to articulate their standing and authority, or an opportunity to forge partnerships with supra-local actors and promote themselves at the expense of others, though they could equally capitalise on their implication in the locality to frustrate their betters by pursuing an autonomous agenda of their own.[262] But for our purposes it matters less who judged and who mediated than who knew the law, since it constituted the baseline for proceedings. However familiar it was to society at large, and to those most active in dispute and settlement, scribes spoke the code with the greatest fluency, and as the 'guardians of legal tradition' they were points of access to the law and its norms, advisers or quasi-lawyers to those who made the most use of it.[263] If coincidence of names can count for certainty, Braolio *presbiter* acted as both scribe and judge in Valdoré at least once, and there must be more cases, now obscured, of priest, scribe, and judge in one person, with outsize influence over local affairs.[264]

What did the law look like to these legal experts? Based on what scribes cited in their charters, a fraction of the whole, yet a substantial fraction all the same, comparable to and in some respects greater than what can be reconstructed for the Catalan counties (see Figure 5.4).[265] This working knowledge of the code concentrated in procedures and penalties, but within the text of each law, it often represented only part of the whole.[266] To take one example, there are three diplomas which cite treason law and survive in the original, and we can compare their legal citations

---

[261] Davies, 'Justice', 43–58; Davies, 'Court', 150–3; Davies, *Windows*, 155–80; Martín Viso, 'Authority', esp. 130–1; Carvajal Castro, *Máscara*, 268–72; Davies, 'Worlds', 396–407; González González, 'Jueces', 1–20; Cañón Dunner, *L'exercice*, 389–465.

[262] Martínez Sopena, 'Justicia', 239–55; Corral, 'Lugares'; Corral and Pérez Rodríguez, 'Fines', esp. 176–80; Davies, 'Homines', 60–72; Godoy, 'Fraudes', 167–94; *cf.* Bowman, *Landmarks*, 185–210.

[263] Innes, *State*, 111–18; *cf.* Collins, 'Law', 506–7, Collins, 'Literacy', 129–31; Rodiño Caramés, 'Lex', 38–43; Bowman, *Landmarks*, 54–5, 236; Brundage, *Origins*, 46–74; Menzinger, 'Profession', 125–9.

[264] *Otero* 31; Davies, 'Local Priests', 33–41; *cf.* Larrea Conde, 'Iglesias', 330–1; Godoy, 'Escribientes', esp. 94–9.

[265] Iglesia Ferreirós, 'Creación', 401–6.

[266] Barrett, 'Text', 46–9.

On the negotiation of legal cases: *LV* 2.1.3–4, 2.1.8, 2.1.11, 2.1.14–5, 2.1.18, 2.1.23, 2.1.25–7, 2.1.29, 2.1.33, 2.2.5, 2.4.1, 2.4.5–8, 2.4.12, 2.5.4–5, 2.5.8, 2.5.12, 2.5.16–8

On marriage protocol: *LV* 3.1.3–5, 3.1.9, 3.2.2, 3.3.1, 3.4.1–3, 3.4.5, 3.4.8, 3.4.12–3, 3.4.15, 3.4.18, 3.5.1–2, 3.5.5–6, 3.6.1–2

On natural origin: *LV* 4.1.3–4, 4.2.2, 4.2.9–11, 4.2.14, 4.2.16–20, 4.5.1, 4.5.4, 4.5.6

On transactions: *LV* 5.1.1–4, 5.2.1–2, 5.2.4, 5.2.6–7, 5.4.1, 5.4.3, 5.4.8, 5.4.13, 5.5.1–2, 5.6.1–4, 5.7.8

On crimes and tortures: *LV* 6.1.2–3, 6.4.1–3, 6.5.12, 6.5.14–5

On thefts and deceptions: *LV* 7.1.1, 7.1.5, 7.2.4, 7.2.7, 7.2.9, 7.2.13–4, 7.2.16–8, 7.2.20, 7.2.22–3, 7.3.1, 7.3.4, 7.4.1, 7.4.4, 7.5.1, 7.5.5

On assaults and damages: *LV* 8.1.2, 8.1.5–7, 8.1.9–10, 8.1.12, 8.2.1, 8.3.1–3, 8.3.5–7, 8.3.11–2, 8.3.14, 8.4.1–3, 8.4.7–8, 8.4.11, 8.4.13, 8.4.16, 8.4.21, 8.4.29, 8.4.31, 8.6.2

On fugitives and those seeking refuge: *LV* 9.2.8–9

On divisions, times of year, and boundaries: *LV* 10.1.11, 10.1.13, 10.2.1–7, 10.3.2, 10.3.4

On removal of repressions and elimination of all heretical sects: *LV* 12.2.3, 12.2.12, 12.2.18, 12.3.2–5, 12.3.8, 12.3.11, 12.3.15, 12.3.17, 12.3.19, 12.3.22, 12.3.28

**Figure 5.4** Laws Cited in Charters

with the code, highlighting all words independent to the charters (see Figure 5.5). In this snapshot of Visigothic treason law in practice around the millennium, the scribal text shows a reasonable degree of fidelity, but it is also very partial, simplified and shorn of detail and context. By a comparable process of retaining only what was essential, case law initially issued *in extenso* became the telegraphic statements of most late antique and early medieval codes.[267] Here the full text of treason law has been winnowed down to a few passages, readily remembered and with one simple message: the property of traitors belongs to the king.

When the kings of Asturias-León had their diplomas equipped with legal citations, the code was a sure ally in the consolidation of power. But it was something of a free agent, and when their counts took action in the same line, the benefits accrued to them, with predictably destabilising results. It is easy to fall back on the truism that writing is power, and the writers the powerful, yet each time a scribe read out a charter citing the law, explicitly or implicitly, legal knowledge came to be more broadly diffused, and future

---

[267] Charles-Edwards, 'Law', 260–87; Humfress, '*Codex*', 241–54.

[*Otero* 90] De is contra principem vel gentem aut padriam refugi **vel** insolentes existunt.

[*Otero* 124] De iis qui contra pricipe gente vel patria refuca aut **mentitus fuerit vel ars fecerit tam compleri quam consiliarit vel** insolenter exsitant.

[*Otero* 124] **Sic** inventus **fuiset** aut efussione aucculorum **at** dekalbatum tamen **aut** exilio **perditurus** dignidate set serbus pricipe factus et sum perpetua sebitutis catena in pricipis potestate retus eterna tenebitur exilio relicacionem obnosius.

[*León* 541] Res tamen uius omnes tam nefarie transgressoris in regis ad intecrum potestate persistat et cui donate fuerint ita perpetim secure posside[at **talis et non traditis**] **nobis**.

[*Otero* 90] [**Et** rem] uius tamen nefarie transgressoris in regis ad integrum potestate persistant et cui donate fuerit ita perpetim secure possideat ut nullus unquam succedencium regnum causam suam et gentis viciaturus ullatenus auferre presumat.

[*Otero* 124] Res tamen **vel** omnes nefarii trascresoriis in regis ad intecrum potestatem persistent et cui donate fuerit **de manu pricipis** ita perpeti securi posidiat ut nulus umquam succedecium recum causam suam egentis viciaturus facia.

[*LV* 2.1.8] De his qui contra principem vel gentem aut patriam refugi sive insulentes existunt.

…horum omnium scelerum vel unius ex his quisque reus inventus, et si nulla mortis ultione plectatur, aut effosionem perferat oculorum, secundum quod in lege hac hucusque fuerat constitutum, decalvatus tamen C flagella suscipiat et sub artiori vel perpetuo erit religandus exilio pene et insuper nullo umquam tempore ad palatini officii reversurus est dignitatem; sed servus principis factus et sub perpetua servitutis catena in principis potestate redactus, eterna tenebitur exilii religatione obnoxius.

Res tamen omnes huius tam nefarii transgressoris in regis ad integrum potestate persistant et cui donate fuerint ita perpetim securus possideat, ut nullus umquam succedentium regum, causam suam et gentis vitiaturus, has ullatenus auferre presumat.

**Figure 5.5** Treason Law in Practice

users of text had a better idea of the written norms at their disposal, a better sense of what to ask of the scribes whom they hired. The source of the expertise behind the rhetorical, pragmatic, and silent citation of law in charters was the same figure responsible for their creation and dissemination, and with the incipient rise of a scribal profession from the late tenth century came a greater use of law by rulers and aristocrats, in a documentary tradition which had long reflected legal principles. A network of scribes operating at every level of society, from royal court to rural village, meant that there was always supply to meet demand in this special service sector. Though the west is where the densest legal culture can be found, it is in the charters now collected at León and Otero that we can identify the greatest concentrations of career scribes, and the most frequent legal citation directly to the benefit of their employers.[268] Kings and counts needed writers for their skills, but they had much to offer in return; the presence of alternative providers would have given rise to fierce competition for patronage. In these scribes marketing their services, we can recognise how Visigothic law came to be more than a framework for transaction and dispute, and supplied the very voice for the ambitious to make their authority known.

---

[268] Estepa Díez, *Estructura*, 240–54; Portela Silva, 'Galicia', 12–41; Álvarez Palenzuela, 'Nobleza', 208–39.

# 6

# Sacred Words

As the documentary practices of the laity centred on the observation and exploitation of Visigothic law, the habits of the clergy revolved correspondingly around Scripture, canon law, and monastic rules. Across early medieval Europe, the Bible in particular cast aspects of transaction in its image: mediated through mass, it inspired and informed a theology of pious gift whereby donation came to represent, if not the purchase price of outright salvation, then the membership fee for the community of those expecting to be saved.[1] In this respect, Iberia was no exception, and acts of giving speak a Scriptural language of charity as the coin of the soul.[2] Words and images from its vast store of principles and parables served both to explain and defend donation in salvific terms, which sanctified in turn the written record itself. Yet to probe this network of texts beyond the Bible is to pose a question less often asked, at least in the context of charters: what did the normative sources of the Church actually do? By way of an answer, it is helpful to revisit what it meant to be part of a 'textual community', and ask a further question: did the men and women whose actions and conceptions those texts inspired and informed constitute one? In loose usage, the term can seem to say simply that they were Christians, even if on the model of secular law their 'literate interpreters' were scribes. As a model, however, the 'textual community' describes a specific social formation, of dissenters from the mainstream who justified their position by reference to text, founded their internal behaviour on it, and crucially formed their solidarity around it, using it to define themselves against external society.[3] In early medieval Iberia, it is an ideal fit for the martyrs of Córdoba, who under charismatic leadership resisted acculturation and conversion to Islam in the middle of the ninth century by taking refuge in literary archaism.[4] In Asturias-León and Navarra, we are dealing not with dissenters but the

---

[1] Jussen, 'Discourses', 173–92; Angenendt, 'Gift', 131–54; Ganz, 'Giving', 18–32; *cf.* Rosenwein, *Neighbor*, 35–48, 109–43.

[2] Davies, 'Buying', 401–16; Davies, *Acts*, esp. 113–34.     [3] Stock, *Implications*, 88–151.

[4] Barrett, 'Hispania', 76–81.

*Text and Textuality in Early Medieval Iberia: The Written and The World, 711–1031*. Graham Barrett, Oxford University Press. © Graham Barrett 2023. DOI: 10.1093/oso/9780192895370.003.0007

mainstream, clergy as well as the laity who interacted with them. The better model is an 'imagined community' organised around a canon (not to be confused with canon law), the canonical text of the Bible, which had ultimate authority.[5]

Yet the documentary practices of the clergy straddled both models. In contrast to Holy Scripture, canon law and monastic rules were established texts handled in a particular way, as scribes refocussed them into a new social and ideological meaning, consistent with the nature of the 'textual community'.[6] Canon law ordered all aspects of Church personnel and property, and by the later Middle Ages every facet of daily life in theory, but before the twelfth century it can be difficult to find in action on the ground outside strictly ecclesiastical affairs and high politics.[7] In our corpus of documentation, the canons remained in the background, supplying general norms and, counter to what we might expect of a world of clerical scribes, reinforcing the foreground of secular law. For monastic rulebooks, in turn, it was that quality of ruling, rather than specific regulations, which mattered most in defining the lives of monks in their monasteries. The point was the fact of text: both sets of normative sources were simplified in use, to mean living by written models, emulating and embodying written standards. But if charters citing the Bible, canon law, and monastic rules in depth and on the surface are the sounds of the clergy speaking amongst themselves in their own special language, what wider significance did these habits have for the members of the laity who did business with them? The network of texts within which the documents are positioned reflects and exemplifies the 'scribal mind'; by delineating its constituents and peculiarities we begin to reconstruct what influence it exercised.[8] The clerical scribes of the charters shared an imagined community of Scripture and emerged from a 'textual community' of canons and rules to write on behalf of others, but for the result of their efforts we need a new term. Collectively, the documentation which they created and communicated transformed its parties, witnesses, and audiences into a 'textual society', defined in their own image by written norms.

---

[5] Lieu, *Identity*, 27–61; Anderson, *Communities*, esp. 67–82.

[6] Niehoff, '*Timaeus*', 161–4.

[7] Halfond, *Archaeology*, 131–58; Bof and Leyser, 'Divorce', 155–80; McKitterick, 'Church', 7–35; *cf.* García y García, 'Derecho canónico', 189–226; García y García, 'Derecho canónico medieval', 704–11; Brundage, *Origins*, 407–65; Rennie, *Law*, 59–86.

[8] Wright, 'Late Latin', 137.

# Scriptures

The Bible contributed a rich array of language, image, and allusion to the legitimising rhetoric of the charter, explaining it, protecting it, infusing it with something of the nature of Scripture, and transforming it into a repository of our sin and salvation. Citations of the Latin Bible are in fact the most recurrent element of the network of texts encompassing the charter, and reflect both the Vulgate and earlier Vetus Latina Hispana translations; the former did not become 'official' until long after our period, and the latter remained in circulation throughout, commonly transmitted in manuscript copies otherwise classifiable as the Vulgate version.[9] In terms of functions, by the inspiration asserted in the preamble and the salvation sought in the exposition, the motivation of transaction was endowed with authoritative spiritual expression, and by the invocation of exemplary punishment in the sanction, the condemnation of any who might violate it was assured. As with the Visigothic code, many common citations could well have been formulaic, but however retrieved, from models or memory, they drew on the Bible and its authority; to be effective, they must have been made comprehensible to listeners. This joining together of charters and Scripture had the effect of sanctifying the written record, and a subset of sanction clauses which deployed Biblical images of judgement 'by the book' only served to intensify that process of identification. The ultimate outcome was an understanding of sin in terms of the written record, as the text of a personal charter by which the sinner was bound to make amends, and of salvation as determined by such documentary evidence. This mentality, as much as a Roman cultural inheritance, is what accounts for the role of text—the value of written title and the respect for written law—in early medieval Iberian society.

While the clergy and the laity both had regular recourse to writing in their daily lives, they spoke distinct dialects of literacy based on the vocabulary of different written sources of authority, as the general features of Scriptural citation make clear. The practice has attracted remarkably little study, perhaps because of its ubiquity, and some editors neither identify nor even mark such references.[10] As a basis for what follows, however, I have

---

[9] Ayuso Marazuela, *Vetus Latina Hispana, I. Prolegómenos*, 313–532; Andrés Sanz, 'Ediciones', 67–80; *cf.* Reinhardt and Santiago-Otero, *Biblioteca*.

[10] Fernández de Viana y Vieites, 'Aproximación', 1, 229–37; *cf. León*, 1, 409–10; *Coimbra*, 969–70; Yáñez Cifuentes, *Monasterio*, 316–17; Pérez González, 'Léxico', 197–228.

flagged and found chapter and verse for 694 charters in the corpus (17%) with citations of the Bible (see Figure 6.1). Proportionately, Scripture is cited slightly more often in the west, slightly less often in the centre and east; at the level of archival collections, much more at Samos, Santiago, Oviedo, Leire, and San Juan, much less at Otero, San Vicente, Albelda, Cardeña, and San Millán. The first series of archives includes the majority of those with notable problems of authenticity, and the practice is more common in interpolated and false charters. Correspondingly, it is most regular in single-sheet copies, so prone to

| | Citations | | Overall | |
|---|---|---|---|---|
| | # | % | # | % |
| Total | 694 | 17 | 4095 | 100 |
| **Region** | | | | |
| West | 256 | 37 | 1284 | 31 |
| Centre | 333 | 48 | 2088 | 51 |
| East | 105 | 15 | 723 | 18 |
| **Personnel** | | | | |
| Royal | 160 | 23 | 522 | 13 |
| Comital | 17 | 2 | 71 | 2 |
| Ecclesiastical | 511 | 74 | 2710 | 66 |
| Lay | 6 | 1 | 769 | 19 |
| **Typology** | | | | |
| Donation | 622 | 90 | 2212 | 54 |
| Sale | 7 | 1 | 1469 | 36 |
| Other | 65 | 9 | 411 | 10 |
| **Complexity** | | | | |
| Simple | 360 | 52 | 2797 | 68 |
| Complex | 334 | 48 | 1292 | 32 |
| **Palaeography** | | | | |
| Original | 118 | 17 | 888 | 22 |
| Copy | 95 | 14 | 261 | 6 |
| Cartulary | 418 | 60 | 2438 | 60 |
| Other | 63 | 9 | 507 | 12 |
| **Diplomatic** | | | | |
| Authentic | 580 | 84 | 3781 | 92 |
| Suspicious | 5 | 1 | 24 | 1 |
| Interpolated | 24 | 3 | 57 | 1 |
| Falsified | 81 | 12 | 227 | 6 |

**Figure 6.1** Charters Citing Scripture

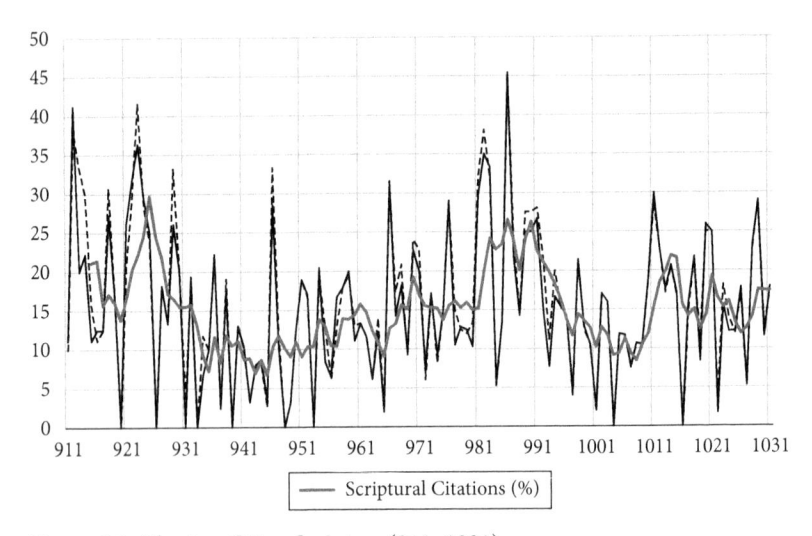

**Figure 6.2**  Charters Citing Scripture (911–1031)

forgery, whereas the lowest incidence overall occurs at Otero, with mainly authentic originals. Of course, this is also predominantly a lay archive: while the rate of citing Scripture is greatest for royal diplomas, much more discursive and elaborate, it is almost zero for lay charters. The Bible supplied the linguistic armature for acts of piety; it can be found in donations (those taking effect *post mortem* especially) and in royal confirmations and monastic pacts, but seldom in any sale. Citing it is distinctively a feature of ecclesiastical documentary practice, and the laity participated in this only insofar as they engaged in written transaction with the clergy, not amongst themselves, even though clerical scribes drafted their charters. Scriptural citation was nonetheless common and continual. Over the Leonese period, when the sample size is sufficient for trends, the incidence fluctuates within a narrow band of 10% to 20%, but tends to stability, closer to the pattern of charters citing other charters and in contrast to legal citation increasing markedly with the passage of time (see Figure 6.2).

## Inspiration

The first function of Biblical citation was to contextualise the transaction. Ordinarily this came in the preamble, site of the most genuine spiritual expression in the charter, and to lend the solemnity of Scripture it might take the form of general invocation, literal quotation, paraphrase, or allusion.[11] The goal was not always exactness or precision, but simply to call on the Bible as a conceptual entity and locate the impetus of an act in its normative field for benefaction.[12] The lessons of the Apostolic *lex omnis et beatus* (law entire and blessed), the *legem santam* (holy law) as preached by the clergy, these are the general Scriptural bases for donation and testament: the text invoked in the broadest terms, as if addressing the reader or listener in verbs of speaking (*dicit, ait*, 'the Bible says') or teaching (*docet*, 'shows...').[13] To take one example, the charter of Aurisindus to Santiago de León from 1011 explains his spur to action as hearing the oracles of divine Scripture, a recurrent phrase pointing to the text as a thing capable of motivating; in this sense, such general invocations become citations.[14] When Galindo Aznárez I gave property to Siresa in 833, he declared up front that *divina admonet Domini scriptura* (the divine Scripture of the Lord advises him), not unlike the monastic pact of 818 which proceeded by edict of the Apostles; preparing an inventory, Abbot Offiloni and companions spoke for all donors when they stated in 872 that *sacrum meminimus evangelium* (we have been mindful of the sacred Gospel).[15] Given the linkage of the two, this could even extend to equating textual inspiration and documentary record, as in a gift of Fruela *presbiter* and two clerics to a monastery of San Juan in 787 thereby placed *sub scripture sancte* (under Holy Scripture).[16] Or more abstractly, when Osorio Díaz donated property to Sahagún in 986, the charter traced a boundary *inde per Sancta Cruce minos LX stadios sicut lex docet* (thence via Santa Cruz less 60 stades, as the law teaches); such a measurement here is meaningless in practical terms, but read with the Gospel of Luke it is the journey from Jerusalem to Emmaus, 'take off 60 stades for the divine law', as if to propitiate the writing of the boundary.[17]

More specific Scriptural citation contributes language for conceptualising, expressing, and legitimising the rationale for acts of giving. The range of passages cited is very wide, but three recur so regularly that they can be understood as the base to which the rest were added, in combinations

---

[11] Laffón Álvarez, 'Arenga', 157–72; García y García, 'Contenidos', 13–62; Benavides Monje, 'Fórmulas', 183–9; Davies, *Acts*, 88–91; Agúndez San Miguel, 'Memoria', 871–4; *cf.* Zimmermann, 'Protocoles', 41–76; Parisse, 'Préambules', esp. 154–5, 156–9.

[12] Álvarez Cora, 'Escrituras', 66–73.

[13] *Samos* 33; *Astorga* 252; *cf. Samos* 128; Velázquez, 'Elementos', 565–6.

[14] *León* 698; *cf.* 445, 512, 617; *Mondoñedo* 7.

[15] *Huesca* 3; *Piasca*, app. 1; *Samos* 5; *cf.* 43, 73; *Valpuesta* 12.

[16] *Sobrado* 2.172; *cf. Samos* 19, 69, S9.

[17] *Sahagún* 331; Luke 24:13; *cf.* Isla Frez, 'Pervivencia', 77.

varying by region and institution, or customised uniquely. The first of these is I Chronicles 29:14, 'Everything comes from you and we have given you only what comes from your hand', common across early medieval Iberia, particularly at Samos, but also in the vicinity of León and Sahagún. When Francius *diaconus* founded a church in 834, he cited the passage generically as his motivation to serve both the Gospel and the dogma of the Prophet (these are frequent stand-ins for any or all of the New and Old Testaments), just as Vermudo and Gudinus, two priests, reported that they had heard the voice of the Lord, paraphrased its text, and donated half of a *villa* to Valdevimbre in 937.[18] In order to broaden or intensify the stated inspiration, cognate verses from both the Old and New Testaments could complement this citation, reproducing or reflecting Numbers, Luke, and Hebrews on offering to the Lord, praising God, and reciprocal charity; the Psalter was especially favoured in the scriptorium of Sahagún.[19] The relevance of I Chronicles 29 is that it narrates the building and endowment of the Temple by King David, and the whole chapter served as a model for donation. In a testament of 1013 to the monks of Parameno, for instance, the Lord's Scripture is cited, 'Lord our God, all this abundance that we have provided for building you a temple for your Holy Name comes from your hand, and all of it belongs to you' (verse 16), while Sarracina, a religious, making a gift in 987, was moved by related words, 'Keep these desires and thoughts in the hearts of your people forever, and keep their hearts loyal to you' (verse 18).[20] The chapter is present in Leonese charters above all, and exceptionally so at Abellar, where scribes combined all three passages in a single document; clearly they were deeply familiar with its language, and made it the house style for donations.[21] In the east, there are no such examples; the fewer surviving from the west combine these verses with others in a distinctive regional tradition.[22]

The second basic citation is Psalm 76:11, 'Make vows to the Lord your God and fulfil them', and it is used more than any other verse as standalone justification for giving. Imiloni Hamita, following the advice of the Psalmist, quoted the text verbatim in a testament granted to Sahagún in 961, but it is

---

[18] *Floriano* 41; *León* 115; *cf.* 93; *Sahagún* 39; *Astorga* 87; *Oviedo* 43; *Samos* 175, 217; *Paço de Sousa* 132.

[19] *Sobrado* 1.106, Numbers 15:3; *Sahagún* 128, Psalms 50:10–12; *Sahagún* 228, Psalms 84:4; *Sahagún* 298, Psalms 137:8; *León* 236, Luke 12:33–4, Hebrews 11:13.

[20] *León* 712, 520; *cf.* 526, 852; 835.    [21] See *e.g. León* 341, 469, 487; 515.

[22] *Sobrado* 1.107, I Chronicles 29:11, Proverbs 15:8, Luke 11:41; *Santiago* 56, I Chronicles 29:11–12, Jeremiah 10:6; *Guimarães* 67, I Chronicles 29:14–15; *León* 621, I Chronicles 29:15.

most characteristic of charters from the west, especially at Samos and Lorvão.[23] And while a broad range of passages was added onto it, we may reduce these to a schema of recurrent pairings with rarer supplements. For example, we find Proverbs 3:9, 'Honour the Lord with your wealth', combined with the Psalm in two charters from Sahagún and another from faraway Sobrado, alongside the further addition of a verse of Deuteronomy and the familiar I Chronicles 29:14.[24] The first and second basic citations, indeed, were often coupled together, notably in preambles from Sahagún and Astorga.[25] At Sahagún, the pairing could in turn be joined again with Proverbs 3:9, evidently a supporting or secondary citation, and supplementary passages.[26] Alternatively, they could be combined with assorted verses of the Old and New Testaments, including I Chronicles 29:18, now coming into focus as another second-order citation, and clusters of excerpts from the Psalms, Isaiah, and Ezekiel on sin and death.[27] In that diffuse distribution of local usages over non-contiguous areas which speaks to the complex circulation of scribes and their models, both patterns occur around León as well as across the west. And there is a further lesson in the donation by Bishop Fruela to Santiago de León in 1006, paraphrasing Deuteronomy and Micah on giving thanks and offerings to the Lord before running Psalm 76:11 together with its parallel, 'Sacrifice thank offerings to God, fulfil your vows to the Most High' (50:14).[28] The habit stands out in Leonese charters, and is suggestive of the organisation of scribal Scriptural memory in chains of cognate verses.

The third and last basic citation is perhaps the most immediately relevant to Christian donation, the simple yet eloquent Luke 6:38, 'Give and it will be given to you'. In documents from León and Portugal, this verse is cited on its own, such as in the preamble to a gift made by Lazaro *presbiter* to a monastery of Algadefe in 1005, introduced by the words *monet enim Dominus*

---

[23] *Sahagún* 190; cf. *León* 491; *Covarrubias* 1; *Valpuesta* 25; *San Juan* 30; *Coruña* 101; *Santiago* 23; *Samos* 93; *Sobrado* 2.172; *Celanova* 3; *Coimbra* 454.

[24] *Sahagún* 130; 192, Deuteronomy 16:16; *Sobrado* 1.3.

[25] See *e.g. Sahagún* 144; *Astorga* 135.

[26] *Sahagún* 165, Psalms 49:7–8; *Sahagún* 164, Deuteronomy 16:16, Psalms 50:12; *Sahagún* 114, Sirach 35:11, I Thessalonians 4:14.

[27] *Sahagún* 219, Psalms 89:28; *Santiago* 35, Sirach 1:4; *Coruña* 94, Jeremiah 13:16; *Sahagún* 381, Psalms 115:17–18, Isaiah 1:18, Ezekiel 18:32; *Coimbra* 147, Genesis 3:15, Job 7:6, Psalms 90:4, Wisdom 7:6; *Celanova* 199, I Chronicles 29:15; *Sahagún* 261, I Chronicles 29:15, Psalms 115:17–18, Isaiah 1:18; *Guimarães* 27, I Chronicles 29:15, 18; *Astorga* 11, *Montes* 2, *Guimarães* 68, A6, I Chronicles 29:18; *Guimarães* 66, Hebrews 11:13.

[28] *León* 658, Deuteronomy 26:11, Micah 6:6; *Samos* 226, Genesis 1:26; *Santiago* 64, Exodus 35:29, Psalms 50:14, II Timothy 2:22; *Celanova* 326, Matthew 16:24.

*dicens* (the Lord speaking advises you).[29] The form is unattested anywhere between the two distant regions, however, as we might expect it to be if it had emanated outward from a point of origin or template. Indeed, like the other basic citations, it was combined with sundry Biblical texts, and in a pattern of local combinations diametrically opposed to a simple model of geographical diffusion. At the disparate houses of Sahagún, Samos, Celanova, and Lorvão, the Evangelist is paired with I Chronicles 29:14. In the donation of Visclafredus *sacerdos et abba* from 874, for instance, the references are attributed respectively to the Lord and David *dicentes* (speaking), as the scribe quoted the former verbatim and lightly adapted the latter; in contrast, in the testament of Repparatus and Trasvinda to Bishop Rosendo in 936, the donors *recte cum propheta clamemus* (may cry out rightly with the Prophet), paraphrasing Luke and citing Chronicles word for word.[30] Comparable geographical disparity applies when the two verses are linked with I Chronicles 29:18, occurring solely in charters of Astorga, Castañeda, and Celanova, even if a donation by Gutinus *frater* to San Salvador de Calvos from 1021 errs in crediting the last citation to *dicens Prophetam* (the Prophet speaking), as it comes from an historical book—or did this label now encompass the Old Testament?[31] At Astorga and León, the verses are once again run into Psalm 50:14, then joined with further citations.[32]

The point is that in the practice of referencing Scripture we see the same selections of book, chapter, and verse made at distinct and diverse sites. To a degree this may be a product of coincidence or the happenstance of mobile scribes and models. More concretely, it reflects a technique of organising and applying this shared textual resource. Scriptural citation may be visualised hierarchically. At the top, the basic citations provided a common language of gift; deployed singly or in combination, these led to an intermediate rank of supporting secondary citations, which acted in turn as way-stations for the final tier of rarer 'tertiary citations'. This hierarchy fits the observed complexity of scribal practice: the three strata of recurrence stand for universal, regional, and individual dimensions in the relationship between standardisation of form and the originality of a scribe. Whereas all writers of charters would have known the basic citations, in other words, they divided according to more local practice when it came to secondary

---

[29]  *Eslonza* 31; cf. *León* 405, 720; *Vega* 1; *Astorga* 145; *Guimarães* 65.
[30]  *Samos* S1; *Lugo*, 2, 555–65; *Celanova* 52; cf. *Sahagún* 22; *Astorga* 84; *Samos* 129; *Celanova* 65; *PMH* 8; *Mondoñedo* 1.
[31]  *Celanova* 350; cf. *Astorga* 32, 35, 121; *Castañeda* 7.
[32]  *León* 539, 545, 689, 697; *León* 554, I Chronicles 29:16; *Astorga* 171, Matthew 7:7.

citations, and each had his own tertiary citations according to personal choice and the particularities of his career, the range of his exposure to sources and exemplars. Regions do of course have peculiarities: at Celanova, the first and second basic citations are combined with other New Testament verses, while at León, the first is cited with others in I Chronicles 29 or else with Matthew 7:7, 'Ask and it will be given to you; seek and you will find; knock and the door will be opened to you'.[33] But as a model for how such a large array of possible gobbets was managed in practice, it explains how a communal stock of borrowed expression played off against regional and individual variation to create a language of gift with multiple dialects, and captures the mental map of the Bible which each scribe brought to work.

In this regard, the complex dynamics of knowledge and choice can operate at the level of a whole book, as the Gospel of Luke is densely cited at Santiago and San Juan, on opposite sides of the Peninsula.[34] Meanwhile, the third basic citation, Luke 6:38, shares company with other common Gospel texts across the corpus, but can also be found in bespoke combinations unique to one context, such as at Coimbra in a dispute settlement over servile status dating to 1025. There are few court cases demonstrably influenced by Scriptural injunctions, but here, on the question of *mancipas* (female slaves) being made *liberas et ingenuas* (free) and given *pecus vel peculiarem nostrum*, the charter adds to this and other verses on generosity Isaiah 58:6, 'Loose the chains of injustice and untie the cords of the yoke, to set the oppressed free and break every yoke'.[35] It is also paired with the cognate Luke 18:22, 'Sell everything you have and give to the poor, and you will have treasure in heaven. Then come, follow me'; but this is more often cited in isolation, as in León and Portugal, while Adosinda *ancilla Christi*, in her testament to Guimarães from 961, admits to being *compunctam divina ammonicione et firmati ex promissione qua dicit* (pierced by divine admonition and fortified by the promise of which it speaks), before quoting its text.[36] It is therefore entirely in keeping with a shared yet individual practice that the three basic citations are combined only once. In their testament to Samos from 958, two religious, Cartamirus and Vidirilli, cited *sigillatim per*

<hr />

[33] *Celanova* 304, Matthew 10:37; *Celanova* 18, Revelation 11:15; *León* 535, 594, 775, I Chronicles 29:16, 18; *León* 489.

[34] See *e.g. San Juan* 48, Luke 19:46; *Santiago* 44, Luke 11:41, Proverbs 15:8; *San Juan* 53, Luke 16:9, Psalms 116:12.

[35] *Coimbra* 203, Psalms 146:4, Isaiah 58:6, Matthew 5:7; Hinojosa, *Documentos*, 15–16 (10); Lange, 'Anmerkungen', 35–7; Marques, 'Rôle', 249, 253; *cf. Sahagún* 77, Matthew 7:7; *Samos* 61, Mark 10:43–4; Esders, 'Use', 55–66; Salrach i Marès *et al., Justícia*, 1055.

[36] *Guimarães* 62, A4, Luke 18:22; *cf. León* 256; *Montes* 3; *León* 696, Luke 6:38, 18:22.

*ordinem recitata* (as recited one by one in order) the words of Scripture which had guided their actions.[37]

Yet the most densely cited Biblical book after the Psalms is not Luke but Matthew by far, and many verses on faith and devotion underpin preambles or expositions, on their own, in sundry combinations, or paired with cognate passages from the Gospels.[38] Donation, as an act of self-denial, could be explained and vindicated by the Christian exhortation of Matthew 16:24, 'Whoever wants to be my disciple must deny themselves and take up their cross and follow me', words which spoke to the founders of a monastery in the Liébana in 918; further support could be found in the Old and New Testaments.[39] The transience of life as incentive to charity is another frequent refrain, as warned of by Matthew 24:42, 'Therefore keep watch, because you do not know on what day your Lord will come', and echoed by passages about generosity and its rewards from the Psalms and the Evangelists.[40] At the opposite end of the spectrum from Matthew, however, many Scriptural verses seem to have been referenced just once or only a few times. Some quotations are immediately relevant to the transaction, such as Deuteronomy 12:6, the *sermocinatione prophetica* (conversation of the Prophet) heard in a donation to San Vicenzo de Pombeiro of 964 on offering, sacrifice, tithes, and gifts.[41] Others, less so: when Hermegildo *diaconus* adapted the exchange between God and Moses in Exodus 3:14–15 ('I am who I am') for the preamble to a nomination of testamentary executors in 936, he was not grounding his actions in Biblical parallel but couching them in Scriptural language of authority.[42] The pairing of rarer verses is notably common in Leonese charters, and certain tandems enjoyed a brief vogue in particular scriptoria. At Santos Justo y Pastor between 983 and 990, for example, three different scribes cited Ezekiel 33:11 and John 12:35 on good

---

[37] *Samos* 127.

[38] See *e.g. León* 627, Matthew 5:12; *León* 651, Matthew 6:21, 24:42; *Otero* 21, Matthew 10:37; *Oña* 17, Matthew 15:37; *Guimarães* 1A, A3, Matthew 22:14; *Celanova* 69, 190, 197, Matthew 25:40; *Samos* 76, Matthew 26:29; *Celanova* 349, Matthew 7:7, 10:9, 10:37–8, Luke 6:38; *Celanova* 196, Matthew 10:32, Luke 14:33; *Valpuesta* 6, Matthew 10:37, 16:24, Luke 18:22.

[39] *Liébana* 24; *cf. Oviedo* 8; *Celanova* 57, Philippians 3:18; *Liébana* 34, Matthew 19:29; *Liébana* 7, Matthew 19:29, Sirach 3:33.

[40] *León* 333; 413, Psalms 49:10; *León* 276, Luke 18:22; *Samos* 64, Matthew 25:11–12, 25:34–6, John 11:26.

[41] *Pombeiro* 2, Deuteronomy 12:6; *cf. Sahagún* 285, Deuteronomy 16:16; *Sahagún* 245, Psalms 137:8; *Celanova* 318, Sirach 1:4; *Sahagún* 330–31, Isaiah 1:18; *Celanova* 76, Isaiah 58:6; *Astorga* 10, *Samos* 33, Acts 4:32; *Lugo* 25, Ecclesiastes 1:4; *Lugo* 34, Psalm 133:1; *Lourenzá* 1-2, Romans 7:18; *PMH* 56, Genesis 2:18.

[42] *León* 109, Exodus 3:14–15; *cf. León* 280, Proverbs 25:2; *Oviedo* 1, Isaiah 58:6; *León* 75, Zechariah 5:7; *Mondoñedo* 6, Romans 13:12–13.

and evil, as *lex canit et dicit* (the law sings and says), in successive charters of donation.[43]

This bears witness to the potential for individuality in documentary composition, and also demonstrates considerable and thorough dissemination of the Bible—scribes knew their Scripture. Yet some citation is so manifold and bespoke that it must have involved first-hand consultation of a complete copy. Such is conspicuously the case at Celanova, the Savile Row of its day: in 942, the charter of endowment from Bishop Rosendo cited at least 25 verses in its preamble, building on the base, as we shall see, of the monastic rule of Fructuosus to rove across the Old and New Testaments.[44] Other major donations to the monastery by figures of high status, including relatives of the founder, to say nothing of the last will and testament of Rosendo himself, offer similar displays; these contexts called for a higher order of Scriptural citation from a senior class of scribe to perform the status of the act as much as explicate it.[45] But class is not everything, and the sole competition for Celanova is from an obscure gift by Eldoara and her children to the church of Tudela in 864, which cites nine verses of Scripture for contextualisation, most of them heavily paraphrased as if dredged up from memory.[46] The individual and the incidental both contributed to constructing the rhetoric of the text.

## Malediction

Just as the preamble to a charter contextualised the transaction in the inspiring words of Scripture, the sanction clause drew from the same to safeguard it, by threatening potential violators with condemnation, punishment, or obliteration at the final examination. Something of this anxiety can

[43] *León* 490, 493, 536.

[44] *Celanova* 72, John 1:1, 5:7, 10:30, 14:9, I Corinthians 13:12, Deuteronomy 4:24, 33:16, I Timothy 1:14, Colossians 2:14, Luke 2:7, 16:9, 18:22, Philippians 2:8, Revelation 14:4, Job 7:20, 16:7, 25:5–6, Psalms 44:23–4, 121:4, 143:2, 144:2, Zephaniah 1:15, Isaiah 34:9, Ezekiel 33:11, Matthew 10:32–3; García de Cortázar and Agúndez San Miguel, 'Memoria', 257–62.

[45] *Celanova* 268, John 10:30, 14:9, Acts 7:49, Luke 12:49, 14:26, 18:22, Matthew 10:37, 16:24, 19:27–9, Sirach 3:33, Psalms 37:27; *cf. Celanova* 53, Psalms 73:28, 76:1–2, 11, 77:11, 141:2, I Chronicles 29:14, Matthew 10:37, 16:17, 24, 25:31–46, Genesis 28:17; *Celanova* 185, Luke 6:38, Matthew 5:3, 10:32, 19:29, 25:40, Job 7:20, I Corinthians 6:10, Mark 10:44; *Celanova* 242, Psalms 19:9, Sirach 1:16, Proverbs 1:7, 9:10, 19:17, Luke 18:22, Matthew 19:29, Mark 10:29–30; *Celanova* 376, Genesis 1:22, 26, 2:18, 23, 34:9, Jeremiah 29:6; Díaz y Díaz, 'Testamento', 72–84; González Lopo, 'Testamento', 217–26.

[46] *Valpuesta* 3, Psalms 50:5, 105:4, Isaiah 56:1, Tobit 13:8, Luke 18:22, I Timothy 6:18, John 13:35, 15:14, Matthew 25:35; Davies, *Acts*, 106–9.

already be seen at the end of the exposition or in the confirmation clause, another key location for Scriptural citation, in the expression of hope for salvation in reward for donation, a sort of gift-exchange with God. From the earliest cases, such as the testament of Alfonso II in 812, absolution of sin by divine judgement and attainment of eternal life and the Kingdom of Heaven are common themes.[47] Biblical passages typically concern entrusting one-self to God, as at León and Lorvão, alluding to II Corinthians 10:18, 'For it is not the one who commends himself who is approved, but the one whom the Lord commends.'[48] Looking to future reward or punishment, repenting evil, and embracing the Christian promise figure as attitudes encouraged by such citation, and a donation made by Bishop Pelayo to Celanova in memory of his father in 982 quotes Philippians 1:21, 'For to me, to live is Christ and to die is gain.'[49] Judgement Day loomed; the verdict to be handed down keeps coming up, especially in the documentation from the centre. Osorio Díaz was simply more graphic than most when he offered a gift to Sahagún in 986 to ensure his reward on the day when the Lord judged the world by fire, while charters of Santo Toribio routinely reference fear of God and of the Last Judgement as motivating factors, right after introducing the names of the donors.[50]

By conjuring a series of vivid Scriptural images of final trial, sanctions weaponise the same anxiety in defence of the charter, and this is truest of León and Sahagún.[51] When Zaton gave himself in 943 to Abbot Severo of Abellar to be led before the tribunal of Jesus Christ, he was echoing a prayer for salvation uttered in confirmations, but also a threat of damnation com-mon in sanction clauses: a favourite formula at San Martín de Turieno promised that any malefactor would have to appear before this tribunal along with the donor.[52] Drawing on the Gospel parable of the sheep and the goats, confirmations often describe salvation as standing on the right of the Son of Man, whereas sanctions frequently define damnation as sharing the lot of the reprobate on His left; both are recurrent usages at Sahagún.[53] Granters everywhere hoped desperately to be found worthy of hearing the

---

[47]  *Oviedo* 2–3; Castro Valdés, 'Notas', esp. 156–62; *cf. Santiago* 46; *Sahagún* 342, 345.

[48]  *León* 576; *Coimbra* 135; *cf. León* 427, Acts 14:23; *Samos* 164, *Aguilar* 2, James 5:16.

[49]  *Celanova* 190; *cf.* 263, Micah 7:11–3, Ephesians 2:11–22, Acts 5:29, I Corinthians 7:20; *Samos* 7, Ezekiel 3:19, 18:32, I Chronicles 29:14–15.

[50]  *Sahagún* 330; *Liébana* 44; *cf.* 50; *León* 701; *Sahagún* 29; *Eslonza* 26; *Sobrado* 1.118; *Covarrubias* 7.

[51]  See *e.g. León* 24; *Sahagún* 175–6; *Eslonza* 9; *Montes* 1; *Santillana* 2; *Cardeña* 41.

[52]  *León* 177; *Liébana* 51–5; *cf. León* 873; *Sahagún* 336; *Liébana* 5; *Celanova* 120.

[53]  Matthew 25:31–46; *Sahagún* 130, 132; *cf. Coruña* 96; *León* 75; *Sahagún* 164–5; *Santiago* 54; García y García, 'Contenidos', 99.

great, sweet, or (at Astorga) mellifluous voice pronouncing the text of Matthew 25:34, 'Then the King will say to those on his right, "Come, you who are blessed by my Father; take your inheritance, the kingdom prepared for you since the creation of the world"'.[54] To be deprived of its comfort was a grave threat, and when the *infante* Ramiro made a donation to Valdevimbre in 918, he vowed that any violator would receive according to his works on that day when all shall listen to this verse.[55] Simple failure to hear it at all features in a few Leonese and Galician sanctions, while some charters from Samos complement this with another Gospel injunction to store up treasure not on earth but in heaven.[56] Nunnu Nunniz and his wife Vida took a step farther in their testament to San Cebrián de Noceda of 1005, asking that any who infringe it behold instead of Matthew 25:34 a terrible voice uttering Matthew 25:41, 'Then he will say to those on his left, "Depart from me, you who are cursed, into the eternal fire prepared for the devil and his angels"', a threat also cited on its own in documents from both west and east.[57] The end of time, as written in Scripture, had great power to justify as well as to defend a charter: as each one was read out, with its impressive, intimidating Biblical citations, all who listened also learned those words which they could expect to hear once more when the promised day finally arrived.

What the sanction clause relied on was cautionary tales to prevent tampering with the charter and its arrangements. Scripture abounds in such exemplary 'judicial' precedents, and here, as across the early medieval West, it constituted the primary source for scribes (and the compilers of formularies) to glean spiritual punishments for those who would transgress the text.[58] Judas Iscariot was the prototypical traitor, and is ubiquitous in the corpus: to take one archive as representative, his comeuppance for betraying Christ the Lord figures in over half of the charters from Eslonza as a deterrent.[59] Yet the ubiquity of references to him, and their rather general

---

[54] See *e.g. León* 543; *Astorga* 111; *Santillana* 8, *Liébana* 76; *Samos* 164; *Celanova* 190; Couzin, *Right*, 3–7.

[55] *León* 47.

[56] *Astorga* 24; *Santiago* 64; *Coruña* 110; *cf. Samos* 180, 190, 103, Matthew 6:19–20, I Chronicles 29:14–15.

[57] *Astorga* 131; *cf.* 241; *Sobrado* 1.126; *Coruña* 54; *San Juan* 5.

[58] Mattoso, 'Sanctio', 407–22; Martín López, 'Cláusulas', 111–18; Díez de Revenga, 'Expresiones', 63–72; García y García, 'Contenidos', 63–84; García y García, 'Imprecaciones', 57–66; Manchón Gómez, 'Tradición', 365–75; Agúndez San Miguel, 'Memoria', 880–7; *cf.* Bowman, *Landmarks*, 56–80, 235–6; Martínez Gázquez et al., 'Fórmulas', 73–96; Gómez Rabal, 'Lengua', 553–63; Lambert, 'Exempla', 45–61; Martínez Gázquez, 'Imprecaciones', 105–21.

[59] *Eslonza* 3, 5, 8–12, 16, 19, 22–3, 25–7, 29, 33; Taylor, 'Curse', 240–3; Martín, 'Utilidad', 81–6; Martínez Martínez, 'Lenguaje', esp. 229–99; *cf.* Perea Yébenes, 'Mención', 235–76.

quality ('share his lot'), suggest that their textual origins lie at some remove; as with generic invocations of Judgement Day, the source is long since internalised. Many other Biblical threats, however, feature less obvious figures, more specifically invoked, whose fates as recorded in that ultimate text served to protect its mundane manifestations. The most often cited are Dathan and Abiram, swallowed alive with their associates and possessions when the ground beneath them split apart and the earth opened its mouth: this punishment is concisely summarised in sanctions throughout the documentation, and also played a role at court in the *condiciones sacramentorum* (terms of the oaths), such as those sworn on disputed testaments of Guimarães in 1014.[60] The citation, in fact, is universal to the early medieval written record, at least in Latin, indicating a late Roman origin; it varies little from one document to the next, a formula copied from a model or prior charter. Occasionally the scribe tacked on their crony Korah, or equated their fate to the Last Judgement, or intriguingly referred to them obliquely, promising the same punitive absorption alive by the land and yet naming no names.[61]

After the fates of Judas, Dathan, and Abiram, another recurrent Scriptural sanction is the threat of *anathema maranatha*. This comes from I Corinthians 16:22, 'If anyone does not love the Lord, let that person be cursed', and is essentially common to the corpus, though in special use at Samos.[62] If it be objected that the content of Biblical citations, particularly this with its fossilised Aramaic vocabulary, must have passed most hearers by as abracadabra, characters and concepts without meaning, do recall that parties to a charter had vested interest in the efficacy of its mechanisms of deterrence, and here indeed an effort to clarify it was made in the text. At Astorga and in Portugal, the words were often followed up with *id est duplici damnatione damnatus* (that is, damned by a double damnation), theologically blunt but quite adequate to get the point across; other charters from Celanova, Astorga, and León preferred 'perdition' or 'confusion' by way of

---

[60] Numbers 16:31–2; *Guimarães* 46; *cf.* Numbers 26:9–10, Deuteronomy 11:6, Psalms 106:17; *León* 27; *Sahagún* 22; *Otero* 21; *Astorga* 11; *Montes* 2; *Oviedo* 2–3; *San Vicente* 20; *Santillana* 6; *Liébana* 5; *Cardeña* 35; *Aguilar* 2; *Arlanza* 2; *Oña* 17; *Valpuesta* 4; *San Juan* 56; *Leire* 9; *Coruña* 29; *Santiago* 25; *Samos* 154; *Sobrado* 1.120; *Celanova* 2–3; *Alfonso V* 15; *Guimarães* 65.

[61] *FV* 39; *LV* 12.3.15; *León* 83; *Sahagún* 418; Beneyto Pérez, 'Fórmulas', 191–7; Beltrán Torreira, 'Reflexiones', 183–94.

[62] See *e.g. León* 176; *Astorga* 8; *Montes* 7–13; *San Isidro* 8–9; *Castañeda* 7; *Otero* 20; *VDJ* 5; *Corniana* 1; *Cardeña* 42; *Silos* 2; *Pamplona* 2; *Samos* 5; *Celanova* 18; *Alfonso V* vii; *Coruña* 94; *ChLA* 114, 31; García y García, 'Contenidos', 93–5; Bougard, 'Jugement', 215–38.

explanation.[63] As ever, house styles jostled with scribal originality: Sobrado opted for the distinctive *abhominatio vel perdictio in adventum Domini* (devastation or destruction on the advent of the Lord) in the charters of donation by Bishop Sisnando, but likened the *anathema maranatha* to hearing Matthew 25:41 in a testament of Gutier Munionis from 1023.[64] One citation of Scripture explained through another is a sure sign of a framing network of texts, and a Portuguese document of 1021 explicated the curse alternatively as 72 maledictions, unattested as a Biblical definition but Biblically resonant in Luke 10:1, 'After this the Lord appointed 72 others and sent them two by two ahead of him to every town and place where he was about to go.'[65] Normally the number is positive or neutral in its associations (languages and nations of the world, translators of the Septuagint), but here the strategy seems to be to link the anathema to another figure charged with power.[66]

These cases are instanced broadly across Iberia, whereas others are characterised by a more regional or even local use. Psalm 128:5–6, for example, holds out hope, 'May the Lord bless you from Zion; may you see the prosperity of Jerusalem all the days of your life. May you live to see your children's children – peace be on Israel'. Many Leonese charters, and a few from Galicia, take the opposite tack in the late tenth century, warning potential offenders that they stand not to see what good things there are in Jerusalem, nor the peace of Israel; the testament of Alfonso II from 812 is exceptional in praying that the king should see them.[67] In a similar vein is II Kings 5:27, '"Naaman's leprosy will cling to you and to your descendants forever." Then Gehazi went from Elisha's presence and his skin was leprous – it had become as white as snow'. The sanction clauses of numerous Leonese documents, and a handful from the east, threaten sharing the fate of that leper, this time in the early tenth century.[68] Here and there, Scriptural sanctions came and went: in the early eleventh century, a favourite was Job 24:18, 'Yet they are foam on the surface of the water; their portion of the land is cursed, so that no one goes to the vineyards', and the Leonese scribe Fulgentius *presbiter*

[63] *Astorga* 11, 32, *PMH* 178; *León* 329, *Astorga* 45, *Castañeda* 4, *Celanova* 350; *León* 574, *Montes* 2, *Astorga* 121, *Eslonza* 6, 9; *cf.* Maxwell, 'Theology', 277–95.

[64] *Sobrado* 1.2, 1.7, 1.5–6, 1.126; *cf. Coimbra* 514; *Oviedo* 42.     [65] *PMH* 249.

[66] Major, 'Number', 7–46.

[67] See *e.g. León* 415; *Santiago* 54; *Coruña* 110; *Celanova* 349; *Vega* 3; *Eslonza* 3; *Otero* 30; *Oviedo* 2–3; García y García, 'Contenidos', 99–100.

[68] See *e.g. León* 5–6; *Astorga* 24; *Montes* 7–12; *Castañeda* 2; *Cardeña* 35, 17; *Arlanza* 3–4; *Santillana* 20; *Corniana* 1.

liked to turn this into a threat.[69] First at Arlanza and Cardeña in the early tenth century, then unexpectedly at Coimbra, Lorvão, and Guimarães from the mid-tenth to the early eleventh, another popular choice was Job 3:8, 'May those who curse days curse that day, those who are ready to rouse Leviathan', and future opponents of the charter were invited to join him in the abyss.[70]

As with fashions, the choices of models are not always what one might expect. Sodom and Gomorrah, perhaps the most obvious case of Biblical vengeance, appear in few authentic charters, highly diffuse in space and time.[71] The less noted Gospel parable of the unfruitful tree is similar in its random distribution, while the sudden deaths of famed wrongdoers Ananias and Sapphira inform just two charters from San Pedro de Siresa and one in León, the drowning of Pharaoh in the Red Sea only a pair of donations to Abellar.[72] If there is a rule at work here, it is variation, and scribal originality lies in mixing and matching with the available options. On the whole, however, there is less of the bespoke in sanctions than in preambles: a testament to Cardeña from 963 with at least ten Scriptural citations (most of them uniquely attested) is the standout, but scarcely seems substantial enough to warrant it.[73] The east is exceptional in that some of its charters name cautionary figures such as Nathanael, Jeroboam, and Jonathan, and boogeymen like Simon Magus and Antichrist, who otherwise rarely feature, as well as other meaningful numbers including the Twelve Apostles and Prophets and the Four Evangelists.[74] The foundation charter of Lourenzá, dating to 969, is similarly unusual in multiplying the standard twofold penalty fourfold to recall the parable of Zacchaeus the tax collector, who after meeting Christ offered to repay anyone he had cheated four times over.[75] But the efficacy of the sanction clause derived precisely from its use of instantly recognisable threats, and few cases, overall, quote less familiar passages: the donation of Abbess Fernanda to Samos in 1011 reached well beyond the norm when it

---

[69] *León* 701, 733, 737, 747, 754, 770, 815, 830, 847.
[70] *Arlanza* 2, 5–6; *Cardeña* 361; *Lorvão* 73; *Coimbra* 56, 126, 121; *Guimarães* 68, A6.
[71] Genesis 19:24–5; *León* 554, 887; *Oña* 17; *San Millán* 358, 535; *Guimarães* 65.
[72] Matthew 3:10, 7:19, 21:19, Mark 11:14, Luke 3:9, *Otero* 30; *Vermudo III* 3; *Coruña* 96; *Oviedo* 43; Acts 5:5, 10, *Huesca* 7, 9, *León* 109; Exodus 14:27–8, 15:1–21, Psalms 136:13–15, *León* 618, 821; Daniel 4:12, *Tumbo Viejo* 15; García y García, 'Contenidos', 101–2.
[73] *Cardeña* 6, I Samuel 4:4–18, 22:9–23, Psalms 52:1–7, Genesis 4:15, Jeremiah 22:19, Deuteronomy 11:6, 28:29, Joshua 6:20, 8:24–5, 10:28–39, 11:14, Ecclesiastes 12:6, Exodus 14:26, Isaiah 14:5.
[74] *Arlanza* 22; *San Millán* 535; *San Juan* 13, 32, 34; cf. *Sahagún* 400; *Guimarães* 7; *Elorrio* 1; García y García, 'Contenidos', 84–92.
[75] *Lourenzá* 1–2, Luke 19:1–10.

raised the spectre of being informed, as in the Gospel parable of the ten virgins, ' "Truly I tell you, I do not know you" '.[76]

Curses and threats are the stuff of sanctions, but from the perspective of textuality the citation of the Book of Moses and the Book of Life in these clauses has special interest. Here an appeal was made to the authority of the written word as exemplified in the Bible to defend the integrity of the written word as instanced in the charter.[77] When Gundisalva made a gift to Abellar in 998, she asked that all maledictions recorded in the Book of Moses befall any who would violate it, alluding to the comprehensive catalogue in Deuteronomy, and this standard formulation is amply attested, chiefly at Samos.[78] But the curse of the Psalmist, 'May they be blotted out of the Book of Life and not be listed with the righteous', was more popular by far, an imprecation distilling and deploying the admonitory power of a recurrent Scriptural image, the written record kept of our sins.[79] In the Leonese charters written by Fulgentius in the early eleventh century especially, transgressors were threatened with the deletion of their names or erasure of their memories from the Book of Life, being unrecorded amongst the just.[80] Bishop Pedro, endowing a church of Santa Eulalia in 995, even prayed to be *conscriptus* ('enrolled') in that text, as if in a sort of census of the saved such as we find in the *libri memoriales* of the Carolingian world.[81] This formula is crucial for the standing of text in early medieval Iberia because appealing to the authority of such books via the authority of the Book gave rise to a sanctified charter, a textual imaginary of salvation.[82] Donors in León, Astorga, Celanova, and Portugal took action *pro abolenda delictorum nostrorum cirografa* (in the hope of erasing the chirograph of our sins), to gain entrance into the heavenly realm of the living.[83] So inspired, in other words, they articulated sin itself in diplomatic terminology, like the

---

[76] *Samos* 76, Matthew 25:12; *cf. Celanova* 1, Deuteronomy 28:20; *Arlanza* 11.

[77] García y García, 'Contenidos', 100–1, 108–9.

[78] *León* 580, Deuteronomy 27:9–26, 28:15–68; *cf. León* 548, 550; *Astorga* 10; *Corniana* 1; *Coruña* 94, 96, 110; *Celanova* 187, 349; *Samos* 33, 127, 141, 158, 102, 175, 44, 115, 199, 104, 76, 198, 180, 190, 103, S2, S9; Sánchez Rodríguez, 'Cláusula', 1, 339–79; Little, 'Morphologie', 43–60.

[79] Psalms 69:28; Campos, ' "Libro" ', 115–47, 249–302; *cf.* Exodus 32:32–3, Psalms 56:8, 139:16, Isaiah 4:3, Daniel 7:10, 12:1, Malachi 3:16, Luke 10:20, Philippians 4:3, Hebrews 12:23, Revelation 3:5, 13:8, 17:8, 20:12, 15, 21:27.

[80] See *e.g. León* 300; *Sahagún* 404; *Astorga* 111; *Oviedo* 29; *Arlanza* 2; *San Millán* 421; *Santiago* 60, 93; *Coruña* 132; *Liébana* 76; *Albelda* 3; *Elorrio* 1; Curtius, *Literature*, 310–15; Rapp, 'Texts', 194–222.

[81] *Coruña* 110; *cf.* Koziol, *Politics*, 269–70, 332–40.

[82] García y García, 'Contenidos', 110–13, 119–28; Casado de Otaola, 'Escribir', 123–8; *cf.* García-Pelayo, *Mitos*, esp. 353–5.

[83] *Celanova* 90; *León* 413; *cf.* 425, 543, 770, 723; *Astorga* 111, 252; *Celanova* 236; *Guimarães* 7; Hahn, 'Letter', 72.

Middle English allegory of the 'charter of Christ', a grant of heaven on condition that man love God and his neighbours.[84] By predicating pious donation and spiritual punishment on Scriptural examples, scribes made charters into selective transmitters of the Bible and its norms, and the result was a parallel passage of Scriptural authority into charters understood as one with that ultimate written record. In such a world, justice could only truly be found in its text.[85]

## Canons

The role played by Scripture as a source of religious regulation for social practice was complemented in a supporting capacity by canon law. There is no single source of canon law in early medieval Iberia, but the *Hispana* is the name given to an assemblage of Greek, North African, Gallic, and Visigothic councils, ranging in date from the earlier fourth century to the end of the seventh. In its oldest form, the compilation is more or less agreed to be the work of Isidore of Seville (d. 636), supplemented by his successors in the Visigothic Church in one or more stages; its afterlife, however, proved both long and changing, and it was epitomised and repackaged over the course of the seventh century and beyond.[86] In terms of 'Iberian content' most relevant to our corpus, the *Hispana* has three main components.[87] One is a series of pre-Visigothic councils from the fourth century onwards: if the synod of Elvira, traditionally dated *ca.* 305–6, is a later literary construct as has been argued, the next earliest is the First Council of Toledo in 400.[88] From the Visigothic period, there is a series of 'national' councils held at Toledo, from the Third in 589 to the Seventeenth in 694 (another was held in approximately 703, but its acts do not survive), and a somewhat miscellaneous series of provincial councils. Collectively, these rulings represent dogma on orthodoxy, the liturgy, the administration of the Church, and its relations with the Visigothic crown, but though there are a few cases of their implementation which have been incorporated into the *Hispana* itself, again

---

[84] Spalding, *Charters*, vii–xii, xxxvi–li; Keen, *Charters*; Steiner, *Culture*, 93–142, 193–228.

[85] Sánchez Domingo, 'Iudicium', 1, 321–30; Petit, *Iustitia*, esp. 443–50; *cf.* Davies, *Windows*, 255–60.

[86] *Hispana*, 1, esp. 257–325, 327–81; Kéry, *Collections*, 57–72.

[87] See *Hispana*, 4–6, for Iberian councils down to XV Toledo; Vives, Marín Martínez, and Martínez Díez, *Concilios*, for the remainder.

[88] Vilella, 'Texts', 210–59; Vilella, 'Collection', 388–424.

its history in practice is essentially post-Visigothic by necessity.[89] Like the Visigothic law code, canon law formed part of the cultural inheritance of the kingdom of Asturias-León especially, and as with the hiatus in royal legislation until the *Fuero de León* of 1017, it was not until the Council of Coyanza in 1055 that conciliar acts properly speaking were promulgated.[90] In the meantime there were sundry royal interventions in canonical matters, not all of unquestioned authenticity as recorded, but nothing comparable to the Catalan counties, where from the last decade of the tenth century 'peace councils' endeavoured to limit Christian bloodshed.[91]

What we have instead is the evidence of the charters, which made reference to Church councils transmitted (to us, not necessarily to them) in the *Hispana* collection. The citation of canon law, however, differs in two respects from what we have observed for charters, secular law, or the Bible. First is the fact that, as we shall see, the practice is far less common, but not because the *Hispana* addresses pertinent issues, such as property ownership, any less than the Visigothic code; it is packed with rulings on managing the estates of religious institutions, yet its penalties tend to be spiritual or expressed as simple prohibition, limiting its potential to be deployed strategically as a tool for the accumulation of property via confiscation. The second point is that canon law is cited almost exclusively in the form of implicit and general allusion, rather than direct and explicit quotation. The charters may be the work of clerical scribes, but it remains difficult to pin down what passage, if any, was intended when their corporate body of regulations seems present. Perhaps as a result, the practice has received cursory treatment in the historiography, confined to brief surveys of canon law found in sanction clauses.[92] The exception is the *sagrera*, the Catalan term (from *sacrarium*) for the area of immunity around monasteries and churches also reserved for the burial of the dead. This developed from canon law on ecclesiastical sanctuary, and has been linked to the 'Peace of God' movement, but the comparable arrangements in the rest of northern Iberia have attracted little attention.[93]

[89] Stocking, *Bishops*, 1–25; Ferreiro, 'Advancing', 27–46; Díaz, 'Concilios', 2, 1095–158; *cf.* Martín-Iglesias, 'Iudicium', 203–31.

[90] García y García, 'Concilios', 356–60; García y García, 'Legislación', 10–20, 30–4; Martínez Díez, 'Tradición', 141–52, 173–83; Sánchez-Arcilla Bernal, 'Derecho', 363–80.

[91] Collins, *Conquest*, 15–19; Martínez Díez, *Legislación*, 73–86; *cf.* Bowman, 'Councils', 99–129; Gergen, 'Peace', 11–27.

[92] Mattoso, 'Sanctio', 408–10, 422–8; García y García, 'Contenidos', 92–102, 110–13; *cf.* Maldonado y Fernández del Torco, 'Líneas', 468–73.

[93] Martín, 'Ensagrerament', 153–82; Farías Zurita, 'Sagrera', 81–123; Farías, Martí, and Catafau, *Sagreres*, 17–35; *cf.* Kennelly, 'Paz', 107–36; Bonnassie, *Catalogne*, 2, 653–6.

Early medieval citations of canon law have never been systematically catalogued, and though I have made a start here, what I have ended up with is really an index of possibilities, because most such references are decidedly—and deliberately—general in nature.[94] With this caveat, canon law is present in some form in 126 (3%) of the charters, performing a range of functions broadly comparable to Visigothic law, including the provision of norms in cases of donation, definition of ownership rights, and authorisation of action in disputes (see Figure 6.3).

| | Citations | | Overall | |
|---|---|---|---|---|
| | # | % | # | % |
| Total | 126 | 3 | 4095 | 100 |
| **Region** | | | | |
| West | 84 | 67 | 1284 | 31 |
| Centre | 37 | 29 | 2088 | 51 |
| East | 5 | 4 | 723 | 18 |
| **Personnel** | | | | |
| Royal | 43 | 34 | 522 | 13 |
| Comital | 0 | 0 | 71 | 2 |
| Ecclesiastical | 83 | 66 | 2710 | 66 |
| Lay | 0 | 0 | 769 | 19 |
| **Typology** | | | | |
| Donation | 98 | 78 | 2212 | 54 |
| Sale | 5 | 4 | 1469 | 36 |
| Other | 23 | 18 | 411 | 10 |
| **Complexity** | | | | |
| Simple | 23 | 18 | 2797 | 68 |
| Complex | 103 | 82 | 1292 | 32 |
| **Palaeography** | | | | |
| Original | 14 | 11 | 888 | 22 |
| Copy | 25 | 20 | 261 | 6 |
| Cartulary | 80 | 63 | 2438 | 60 |
| Other | 7 | 6 | 507 | 12 |
| **Diplomatic** | | | | |
| Authentic | 96 | 76 | 3781 | 92 |
| Suspicious | 1 | 1 | 24 | 1 |
| Interpolated | 8 | 6 | 57 | 1 |
| Falsified | 20 | 16 | 227 | 6 |

**Figure 6.3**  Charters Citing Canons

---

[94] See *León*, 1, 410; Salrach i Marès *et al.*, *Justícia*, 1056–7.

These shared functions are reflected in considerable overlap with legal citation, attested in 59 of the documents bearing signs of canon law (47% of the subset, or 1% overall), and a distinction between the two sets of normative sources does not always seem to have been made.[95] The same regional distribution obtains, however, as for all the other elements of the network of texts, only exaggerated: most common in the west, particularly at Celanova, Samos, Santiago, and in Portugal, far less so in the centre and the east, rare at Sahagún and San Millán, and absent at Otero and Cardeña. As is true of Scripture, canonical citation correlates strongly with inauthenticity, being a frequent feature of later rhetorical enhancement or wholesale invention of documentation, and so with transmission by single-sheet copy; this can be seen in the higher rate for Samos and Santiago, and the lower for Cardeña and Otero. And that points us to a further correlation, with type of personnel: canon law is most often instanced in royal diplomas, specifically those granted to members of the clergy, while for ecclesiastical charters the frequency is greatest in those with only clerical parties. The total lack of canonical citation in lay charters (the bulk of the Otero collection) and in the ordinarily more elaborate comital diplomas could not be more striking; like citing Scripture, it was a distinctively ecclesiastical documentary practice with which the laity came into contact only insofar as they engaged with the clergy. As such, it is present in a clearly delineated subset of transactions: donations, mainly those involving kings and clerics, with complex circumstantial or contextual details or else coming into effect *post mortem*, and confirmations, dispute settlements, and monastic pacts. We virtually never encounter the canons in sales, or lay charters. The earliest reference to canon law comes in an interpolated charter of 745; in the Leonese period, contrasting with the tendency of legal citation to steady increase, the incidence remains stable at under 5%, and often does not register at all (see Figure 6.4).

## Norms

If we ask how this played out in practice, comparison with secular law is instructive. Both code and canons are long, and copies cannot have been commonly available: however, not only is the canonical citation rate much lower, but the range of passages cited is narrower as well. The overall impression can be summed up as a clergy conservative in its usage of the canons, conceivably reflecting a less receptive audience for them, in contrast to a

---

[95] Maldonado y Fernández del Torco, 'Relaciones', esp. 304–81; *cf.* Bowman, *Landmarks*, 52–5.

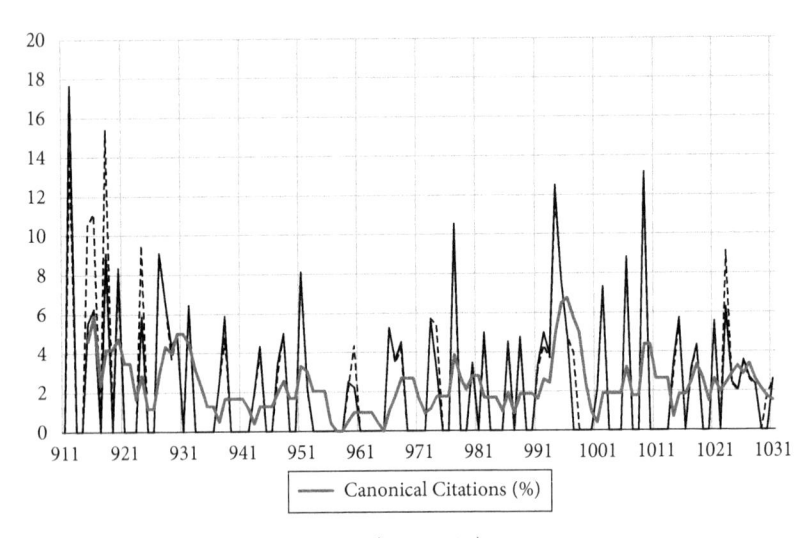

**Figure 6.4**  Charters Citing Canons (911–1031)

laity whose engagement with the Visigothic code was demonstrably deepening. As such, when canon law is cited to define the norms of practice, it is in the broad avenue of 'living canonically' rather than by any particular canon, and confined to monastic contexts. Baltarius *presbiter* donated all of his property to San Miguel de Piñeira in 951, for example, addressing those who would pursue the monastic life there *per regulam et canonicam sententiam secundum iussa patrum priorum* (by the rule and the canonical opinion according to the commands of the Fathers of old), akin to the brothers of Samos who persevered under *normam sanctorum canonum* (the norm of the holy canons).[96] Living canonically may have been broad, but it was still binding: Abbot Salamirus bequeathed San Andrés del Congosto to his heirs *in timore canonicarum* (in fear of the canons), just as Iquilo, before giving to the monastery of Santa Baia, visited it and verified that all was in order *sicut canonum docet* (just as the canon teaches).[97] Endowments and transfers of monastic foundations thus enjoined future occupants to live by the canons, to remain *per regula canonica* (by the canonical rule) in the words of a Portuguese charter from 994.[98] Of course, a donor could have had a specific provision in mind. When Bishop Mauro of León commended churches between the Eo and the Masma to a certain Betotti in the later

[96]  *Samos* 93; 175, 180, 103; *cf.* 7; *Celanova* 199.
[97]  *Celanova* 261; *Mondoñedo* 6.
[98]  *Paço de Sousa* 132; *cf. Floriano* 41; *Montes* 4; *Caaveiro* 220; *Coimbra* 514.

ninth century, he directed the *plebs* to answer to him faithfully in all things, *prout canonicam docet sententiam* (exactly as the canonical sentence teaches); the only conciliar legislation of obvious relevance to such an arrangement concerns taxing religious houses in Galicia.[99] And while another donation by Abbot Indulfo to Guntesalbo framed with the words *ad kanonum vel ad usuris* (on canons and on interest) could be invoking canons on ecclesiastical usury, a flourish *pro forma* is the standard sense of citation, like the generic *pro autoritate canonum* (by the authority of the canons) which wraps up a confirmation to Samos from 966.[100]

The same regulation of religious communities by the shadow rather than the substance of canon law is found in some sanction clauses, but with a twist. More than one threatens the future trespasser with a *canonice sentencie* or *kanonica sentencia* (canonical verdict), and on occasion also prescribes a spiritual penalty such as penance or anathema.[101] More common, however, is the hybrid practice of two charters from Celanova, which declare *per canonicam et godigam sententiam* (by canonical and Gothic provision) that any disruptor must pay *quod lex imperaverit* (what the law has ordered), or repay what they have stolen *ut eis lex canonica ordinaberint* (as canonical law has ordained them).[102] Behind this lies the running together of canon and secular law, grafting the more tangible punishments of the latter onto the largely rhetorical invocation of the former.[103] Take the twofold and threefold fines which we know so well from the Visigothic code: the sanction clause of a donation by Fernando Núñez to San Miguel de León in 1021 mandates that a *disruptor aut intemerator* (violator or defiler) make compensation of twice the *villa* concerned, according to *sacrum canonem et lex godice* (the sacred canon and Gothic law), and pay two gold talents to whomever the *speculatorem legem* (examining law) has awarded them.[104] Consider the testament of the pious Senior to San Paio de Diomondi in 976, which sets a twofold penalty *sicut lex canonica vel romana iubat de rebus ecclesiasticis* (as canon or Roman law orders in regard to Church property), or the donation of Vermudo II to San Pelayo de Oviedo in 996, which establishes the same, *sicut lex codicet disnuciat et kanonica censura confirmat*

---

[99] *León* 16, VII Toledo 4.
[100] *Santillana* 19, Blasco, 'Aproximación', 102–3, Elvira 20, Tarragona 3, II Braga 62; *Coruña* 73; *cf. Alfonso V* 15; León 798; Astorga 10; *Santillana* 3; Coimbra 147; Valpuesta 12.
[101] *Santiago* 14; Mondoñedo 2; Samos 7; Celanova 3.
[102] *Celanova* 171, 91; *cf. San Vicente* 1; Isla Frez, 'Pervivencia', 83.
[103] Humfress, 'Judging', 155–8; *cf.* Bowman, *Landmarks*, 53–4.
[104] *León* 781; *cf. Liébana* 20; Celanova 185.

(as Gothic law pronounces and canonical censure confirms).[105] Is there any such 'canonical censure'? Insofar as the *Hispana* describes anything comparable, it is in the scenario of a rogue bishop who names a relative or favourite to a position of authority at a religious institution for criminal gain, a secular crime punished in secular terms.[106]

The sole case of explicit, specific reference to canon law in a charter, though vexingly fragmented and obscure, serves to confirm this general picture of general citation. Amidst the substantial donation of Abbot Vermudo to Samos in 1009, the donor seemingly pronounces a sanction against his own *familia* (household), haughty and reprobate, *sicut Liber Goticus* [...] *in canone Libro Toletano a capite LXI LXXVII sententia* [...] *ipsa* [...] *Martini*.[107] What could it mean? The Second Council of Braga (not Toledo) was presided over by Bishop Martin, and is also one of only two to have issued so many canons (be it 61 or 77), but no *sententia* under either heading at any council in the entire *Hispana* corresponds with what could plausibly be the context.[108] Nor should the hunt for a correct reference distract from the opening mention of the 'Gothic book'; inasmuch as 'real' canon law is playing a role here, it is supporting and secondary to secular law, safeguarding the donation with the rhetoric of its presence. And no other case of 'supportive citation' factors more significantly into a transaction. Charters from León and Celanova, for example, invoke *lex gotica* and *sanctorum canones* (Gothic law and canons of the Holy Fathers) to define the fifth of free disposition, while one from San Clodio do Ribeiro dating to 928 points to the *canonica sententia* in establishing the tenth required in dowry: but these are purely secular provisions of the Visigothic code to which mention of the canons contributes only nominal support.[109] In contrast, the restoration charter of San Esteban de Calvor in 902 criticises its former custodians for failing to make a monastic pact according to what *instituta est canonum* (is the instruction of the canons), just as three other cases from Sobrado, Celanova, and Samos base communal ownership of property and submission to the abbot on what *canonica docet sententia* (canonical opinion teaches).[110] While canon law does consider these issues in passing, it is only to confirm the precepts of the monastic rules which

---

[105]  *Lugo* 28; *San Pelayo* 1; *cf. Oviedo* 33, *Astorga* 214.     [106]  X Toledo 3.
[107]  *Samos* 64; Carriedo Tejedo, 'Libros', 66–7.     [108]  II Braga 61, 77; *cf.* Elvira 61, 77.
[109]  *León* 681; *Celanova* 190; *San Clodio* 1; *LV* 4.5.1, 3.1.5.
[110]  *Samos* 33; *Sobrado* 1.124; *Celanova* 4; *Samos* 210; *cf. Liébana* 24; Coronas González, 'Orden', 22–4; D'Emilio, 'Charter', 300–1.

are also named by the charters; once more, citation of canons merely adds support.[111]

The *Hispana* was more directly, if rarely, employed to authorise a specific action with respect to property. Bishop Oveco of León, in his testament to San Cipriano del Condado and Santiago de León from 948, is all but unique in quoting the pronouncement of III Toledo 4, 'a bishop may convert one of the churches in his diocese into a monastery', before handing over a church of Santa María for the purpose, as *kanonica instituta sententie doctum* (taught by the opinion of canonical teaching).[112] The councils of the Visigothic Church articulated in detail the contours of the ecclesiastical hierarchy, *inter alia* regulating the ordination and delimiting the spheres of authority of metropolitans and bishops.[113] This seems also to be the concern of the foundation charter of Lourenzá, which uniquely invokes the *canones Esidoris Ispalensis* (canons of Isidore of Seville) to ask the bishops assembled in 969 to grant *discrepcionem*: one usage of that term is in an ordinance delimiting episcopal authority over monasteries.[114] But when the canons are cited in practice, it is for the most part incidentally, such as to affirm the simple fact of dioceses and episcopal appointees in charters from Santiago, or to contextualise the holding of a synod to consult the *sanctas canonicarum sententias* (holy opinions of the canons) in a dispute which involved Celanova in 1002.[115] The testament of Bishop Rosendo from 977 is the exception: *evangelica eruditio instructus necnon et canonum decreta compulsus* (instructed by Gospel learning and driven by the decrees of the canons), the future saint named Manilán to be his successor and made disposition of the property of the monastery, just as IX Toledo 1–2 had exhorted him to do as its founder.[116] More typical is citation of canon law to justify tithing, which gives reason to suspect forgery; the reality of the practice this early is unclear.[117]

The relationship between the citation and content of canon law is closer in those cases concerning the maintenance of ecclesiastical property, but not all of them are authentic. After the death of a bishop, both canonical and secular regulation required that his successor make an inventory of the

---

[111] III Toledo 4; IV Toledo 51; *cf.* Linage Conde, *Orígenes*, 1, 457–90.
[112] *León* 201; Yáñez Cifuentes, *Monasterio*, 143–4.
[113] See *e.g.* I Toledo 12; Tarragona 5; I Braga 6; II Braga 1–10; Narbonne 10; IV Toledo 19; Mérida 4, 6, 8, 11; XII Toledo 3, 6, 8; Poveda Arias, 'Diócesis', 9–24.
[114] *Lourenzá* 1–2; *cf.* IV Toledo 51.     [115] *Santiago* 51; *cf.* 64. *Celanova* 263.
[116] *Celanova* 185.
[117] *Celanova* 10; *Floriano* 6; *cf.* Escalona, 'Organización', 184–7.

property of his church (only if he died intestate, according to the former), lest any of it be lost.[118] This has been hazarded as the origin of cartularies, and indeed, we do read of how Bishop Somna of Ourense *perquireret* (investigated) the patrimony of his see *ut sacros precipuet canones* (as the sacred canons direct) in 900, finding to his dissatisfaction that it was all laid waste, yet this text is commonly agreed to be a later forgery.[119] The same judgement, albeit with less certainty, applies to the record of a dispute over the testament of (the genuine) Melic *presbiter*, which 'quotes' canon law, in fact shamelessly reversing it, to the effect that, if any religious should die without a will, his property is to be divided amongst his nearest relatives rather than retained by his church.[120] The *Hispana*, however, also railed repeatedly against the alienation of ecclesiastical property, with support from Visigothic law, and we find these precepts implemented in genuine charters.[121] In 1002, for example, Bishop Fruela gave to his own see not only *villas* which he had acquired *per auctoritatem canonicam* (by canonical authority), but also those properties pilfered by one *ignorans sacros canones et lex gotica* (ignorant of the sacred canons and Gothic law) and restored by Vermudo II, *sicut sacros canones adtestantur* (just as the sacred canons affirm).[122] In 853, similarly, Ordoño I restored lands which had been alienated from Samos since the death of Abbot Argericus, *pro eo quod sic docent sancti canones* (because the holy canons teach thus), while Ordoño II, in an exchange with Santiago from 920, took care that it was like for like, *secundum canonum decreta* (according to the decrees of the canons).[123] The councils were also obsessed with the sacrament of penance, a last rite subject to continual pronouncements, which bound one over to holy orders until the end.[124] This may explain the colourful experiences of Senta, who took penitential confession when ill and on the verge of death, only to rally unexpectedly; obliged to join the clergy *per doctrina patrum et normam sanctam* (by the teaching of the Fathers and the holy norm), he ended up being scammed out of his property. Ultimately, however, a royal council

---

[118] Tarragona 12; Lleida 16; Valencia 2–3; IX Toledo 9; *LV* 5.1.2; Castillo Maldonado, 'Deceso', 17–25.

[119] *Ourense* 2; Mendo Carmona, 'Tumbos', 172–3.

[120] *Sahagún* 183; *cf.* Valencia 3; IX Toledo 4.

[121] II Toledo 4; Lleida 3; II Braga 14–17; III Toledo 3, 19; II Seville 10; IV Toledo 23; VI Toledo 5, 15; IX Toledo 1, 3–6; XIII Toledo 7; III Zaragoza 3; XVI Toledo 5; *LV* 5.1; *cf.* Addison, 'Property', 175–96.

[122] *León* 629.     [123] *Samos* 41; *Santiago* 29; *cf. Astorga* 173; *Celanova* 1.

[124] I Toledo 2; Girona 9; I Barcelona 6–8; II Braga 82; IV Toledo 54–5; VI Toledo 7–8; XI Toledo 12; XII Toledo 2; XIII Toledo 10; Lozano Sebastián, *Penitencia*.

ruled that, *per veram scientiam canonica et lex gotica* (by the true knowledge of the canonical and Gothic law), a charter made unwillingly or invalidly has no force, drawing on secular and canon law to restore his lands, and protect the property of the Church.[125]

In that last case, one can see further combination of legal authorities, rather than sole reliance on canon law, and this practice is most prominently attested in the familiar arenas of adultery and treason. Clerical chastity was a constant concern of the councils, especially the nightmare scenario of a bishop, priest, or deacon fathering children after ordination, with its potential implications for the ecclesiastical patrimony.[126] When Gonzalo *frater*, deceived by the Enemy, mixed himself up with a woman in 1006, therefore, Bishop Fruela seized all his lands, as the *lex et kanonum* authorised him to do, and donated them to Santiago de León, while the monk himself fled from the diocese.[127] Canon law supplies ample spiritual sanction against adultery, and VIII Toledo 5 charges the bishop to investigate any such crimes within his jurisdiction, but the Visigothic code actually states the material penalty, and so it is cited here as a necessary complement.[128] When Ramiro II restored Samos in 932, however, he first recorded the expulsion of prostitutes and the unchaste, then censured the notion that children born sinfully of the clergy, *quos condempnat canonum* (whom the canon condemns), should have any stake in its estates: instead they should serve it forever, a direct citation of canonical punishment, though coming in a somewhat suspect document.[129] Treason, as we have seen, is another recurrent theme of the *Hispana*, reflecting the peculiar Visigothic compact of Church and crown celebrated at III Toledo, sealed at IV Toledo, and renewed at every major council thereafter.[130] Several charters from Celanova bear witness to Vermudo II seizing the property of rebels in accordance with the *canones sancti et lex gotica*, yet again whereas specific law underpins this action and provides specifics of punishment, the canons cited here tellingly in the plural simply serve as emphatic reminders that

---

[125] *Samos* S9; *Lugo*, 2, 585–90; Carriedo Tejedo, 'Libros', 60–1.
[126] I Toledo 1; IX Toledo 10; *cf.* Elvira 33; I Toledo 3–6; Tarragona 9; Lleida 5–6, 15; Girona 6–8; II Toledo 3; II Braga 27, 30–2, 43–4; III Toledo 5; I Seville 3; Toledo 1; Huesca; II Barcelona 4; Egara; II Seville 4; IV Toledo 20, 42–4; VIII Toledo 4–6; III Braga 4; Fernández Alonso, *Cura*.
[127] *León* 658; *cf. Astorga* 371.
[128] See *e.g.* Elvira 7–10, 12–18, 30–1, 47, 63–70, 78; I Toledo 16–17, 19; II Braga 26, 28, 76, 79–80; III Toledo 10; XII Toledo 8; Hamilton, 'Inquiring', 21–43.
[129] *Samos* 34.
[130] IV Toledo 75; V Toledo 2–5, 7–8; VI Toledo 12, 17–18; VIII Toledo 2; X Toledo 2; XIII Toledo 1–2; XV Toledo; XVI Toledo 10.

betraying the king is both 'against the law' and 'uncanonical'.[131] Alfonso V nodded to both in a confiscation recorded in 1017, and even once titled himself, interestingly, *rector per canonum* (ruler by canon law) in 1009.[132] But in all such usages, canonical citation is really a way of underlining secular law. Think on how in 977, after a drunken home invasion and murder at a deaconry, Gutinus Zelemi sequestered by royal order all the property of the perpetrators, a married couple out of control, *ut consuetudo est secundum quod veritas docet per canonica sententia* (as is the custom in accordance with what the truth teaches by canonical opinion).[133] Canon law confines itself to setting out what 'rectors' should do to prevent subordinates from killing; the 'end citation' is secular homicide law, which justifies penal confiscation, conceivably called canonical to fit the context.[134]

As with cases of silent reliance on the Visigothic code, some charters and transactions have been shaped by the background presence of conciliar legislation, but in keeping with the rest of canonical citation this is comparatively rare. We might detect, for example, a discreet framework of canon law behind a donation made by Alfonso III to Santiago in 869, involving a church needing restoration because negligent monks had lost its lands *illicite* (illegally), or in the preamble to a charter of 988, which offers a lengthy *apologia* for selling off part of the endowment of Eslonza by insisting on the destruction caused by 'Saracen' raids.[135] In both of these cases, the canonical inalienability of ecclesiastical property hovers just out of sight as a principle, while its effect on the narrative of transaction—informing *illicite* and prompting an *apologia*—betrays its almost or nearly presence. By the same silent canons, adulterous clerics could expect the bishop to seize their lands, the justice meted out to the monk Cazeme in 980 for fornicating with a daughter of Albaliti, as well as to the parents of Bitilo in 952 for giving her up *ad adulterio* to Vidramiro *praepositus*.[136] Abbot Saul too may well have turned Santa María de Loyo into a brothel and had to face a reckoning for it, but in none of these instances of the punishment of clerical adultery does canon law figure explicitly, only implicitly in the evident normalisation of canonical provisions.[137] Not that they were always heeded: Taiellus *diaconus* commended his son Revelionem to Riciulfo *presbiter* in

---

[131] *Celanova* 221, 223, 246; Orlandis, 'Huellas', 655–6; Rodiño Caramés, 'Lex', 26–8; Pérez, 'Insumisión', 366, 373–4.

[132] *León* 748, 677.    [133] *Sahagún* 287.    [134] XI Toledo 7; *cf.* II Braga 78.

[135] *Santiago* 6; *Sahagún* 340; *cf.* 386.

[136] *León* 479 C; *Celanova* 96; *cf.* 125, 313; Mariño-Veiras, 'Religiosas', 123–4.

[137] *Celanova* 29; Díaz de Bustamante, 'Imágenes', 182–3; *cf. Samos* 170; *Guimarães* 1A, A3.

889, but the label which he gave him, *quem in peccato meo abui* (whom I had in my sin), may suggest a consciousness of having contravened the councils by fathering him in the first place.[138] Outside these two legal fields, however, silent citation is hard to find, like canonical citation overall: one or two more cases of pulling ecclesiastical rank, maybe, but no excommunication, surprisingly so given its regularity in the *Hispana* as the final spiritual sanction.[139] When a charter of 1021 threatened a curse unto the seventh generation, it reflected no canonical precept but the Visigothic code, which set seven degrees of kinship as the maximum.[140] The difference is one of scale as well as function: canon law, howsoever cited, was secondary and supplementary to secular law.

## Rules

Monastic rules are the third and last ecclesiastical contribution to the network of texts, with narrower use but broader conceptual significance. What we might term 'regular citation' points to one or more of several *regulae* as the written regulations for communal life, and by extension identifies the monastic community itself as a text. This is very much a case of rules in the plural, because the scribes who made such references had in mind a complex of sources with two main constituents: the *corpus regularum* and the *Rule* of Saint Benedict. The former is the name generally given to a series of rules for monks, originating in the seventh century, which tended to be transmitted as a body. Since there is minimal evidence for either the form or the circulation of monastic regulations in Iberia before the tenth century, most of what we can say here is hypothetical, but it may have been assembled initially in the circle of Isidore of Seville, then expanded a generation later under the influence of Fructuosus of Braga (d. 665); both of their rules are included in it, as well as a much wider array of texts such as the handbooks of Augustine and Leander of Seville and eastern material in translation. The components are by no means identical, and speak to notable evolution in monastic practice over time.[141] The Isidorean rule appears to survive in two

---

[138] *Oviedo* 12; Torrente Fernández, 'Relaciones', 50–2, 54–5.
[139] *Astorga* 192; *Samos* 248; *cf.* Sanz Serrano, 'Excomunión', 275–88.
[140] *PMH* 249; *LV* 4.1.7; *cf. Alfonso V* 8.
[141] See Campos Ruiz and Roca Meliá, *Padres*, 21–76, 90–125, 137–62, 172–211, for the monastic rules of Leander, Isidore, and Fructuosus and his followers; transl. Barlow, *Fathers*, 1, 183–228; Godfrey, 'Rule', 8–29; Barlow, *Fathers*, 2, 155–209; Freire Camaniel, 'Liber', 350–8;

recensions, the first reflecting the observance which he laid down in or around 620, the second altered to require much greater disciplinary rigour consonant with the severe brand of Fructuosan monasticism which had come into fashion by the mid-seventh century.[142] Indeed, the peculiar institution of 'pactual' monasticism outlined in the rule of Fructuosus and its derivatives is of key importance to our story. This held that the proper relationship between abbot and monks was based on and maintained by a written and signed agreement which specified reciprocal obligations and pooled their possessions in common; such 'pactual' monasteries were in turn bound into the federal regulatory structure referred to as the *communis conlatio* ('general conference'), headed by the bishop-abbot of Dume.[143] More than any other element of the *corpus regularum*, the literate equivalence in this text influenced the mentality of the corpus of charters. From contracts to communities is the passage which regular citation ultimately represents, and in this transference we can find a model for the textual society of early medieval Iberia, defined by written norms.

The second constituent of regular citation, the *Rule* of Saint Benedict, represents the closest there is to a single norm for monasticism in contemporary western Europe. This too, however, was influenced by and influenced in turn a long run of related texts, and came into its canonical 'Benedictine' form only with the Carolingian monastic reform and the work of Benedict of Aniane (d. 821), compiler of his own *codex regularum*.[144] Insofar as the practice of charters citing monastic rules has been studied, it is as an index of the gradual substitution of the *corpus regularum* indigenous to Iberia by a *Rule* imported from without the Peninsula: this is the arc of the traditional grand narrative of Christian reconquest, early colonisation led by Spanish monks giving way to the arrival of Cluniac reformers under Alfonso VI in the late eleventh century.[145] The background is the situation, by now familiar, that the post-Visigothic kingdoms of the north inherited and perpetuated Visigothic rules and monastic life, producing no normative

---

Velázquez Soriano, 'Reflexiones', 531–67; *cf.* Linage Conde, 'Monacato', 235–59; Dias, 'Idéal', 143–54; Díaz, 'Plurality', 195–212.

[142] Martín, 'Isidorus', 379–86; Díaz, 'Discipline', 107–23; Barrett, 'Librarian', 67.

[143] Bishko, *Monastic History*, §§ I–IV; Linage Conde, *Orígenes*, 1, 291–344; Díaz Martínez, *Formas*, 153–9; Bernaldo, 'Monasticism', 27–63; Díaz Martínez, 'Monasteries', esp. 349–59; Díaz Martínez, 'Regula', esp. 117–19, 130–2; Díaz Martínez, 'Plurality', esp. 197, 200–1, 206–9.

[144] See Vogüé and Neufville, *Règle*, 1–2, for the monastic rule of Benedict; transl. Venarde, *Rule*; Diem, 'Carolingians', 243–61; Diem and Rousseau, 'Rules', 162–94.

[145] Pérez de Urbel, *Monjes*, 2, 253–95, 368–482; Linage Conde, *Orígenes*, 2, 491–768; Bishko, *Frontier History*, § II; Fernández Conde, *Religiosidad*, 297–346; Fernández-Sordo, 'Monasterios', esp. 184–95.

texts of their own, apart from an edition of the *Rule* of Saint Benedict prepared for use at a female monastery in La Rioja during the tenth century.[146] To some extent the east differed: the Catalan counties responded to Carolingian trends in monasticism far earlier, and the great reformer Oliba (d. 1046), abbot of Ripoll and Cuixà, also had close ties to Cluny.[147] In our corpus, some charters cite the *regula sancti Benedicti*, while others invoke the *regula sancta*, their collective name for the Iberian rules; this derives from *sancta communis regula*, the term used by one of the key Fructuosan texts both for itself and for the regional monastic confederations which it promoted.[148] Yet there is in either case an appeal to written authority, and what follows focusses more on the nature and purpose of such appeals than on each text and its content. The dynamic of constancy—ongoing identification by religious communities with their manuals of devotion—matters too, and even as these manuals diversified, the rule as a type came to be synonymous with the monastery itself, the written with the real.

There has only been one tabulation to date of regular citation, and deliberately limited to the Benedictine rule, but reference to this or other monastic rules occurs in 234 (6%) of the charters, more often than canonical citation, less so than Scriptural citation (see Figure 6.5).[149] Atypically, the practice is attested more densely in the west and east than the centre, but this corresponds to where most of the specifically monastic archives are located, except Cardeña where it is almost entirely absent.[150] The apparent correlation, furthermore, between regular citation and interpolation or falsification is an artefact of flawed methodology, since editors have often taken mention of the *Rule* of Saint Benedict at whatever is deemed to be too early a date for its observance as proof of inauthenticity, constructing a circular argument.[151] That said, in the constant medieval updating of texts in transmission, which sits so uncomfortably within diplomatic science, some anachronistic insertion of the Benedictine rule is only to be expected, and indeed regular citation is more common in copies than originals, especially in single-sheet copies. Unsurprisingly, monastic rules are not a feature of charters involving the laity alone, being another distinctive element of ecclesiastical documentary practice, but they did of course

[146] Linage Conde, *Regla*; *cf.* Díaz Martínez, 'Legado', 9–32.
[147] Linage Conde, *Orígenes*, 2, 498–537, 866–86; Codina Giol, 'Oliba', 79–106; Cingolani, 'Oliba', 115–62.
[148] Mattoso, 'Monaquismo', 79–81; Dias, 'Lugar', 231–4.
[149] Linage Conde, *Orígenes*, 3, app. 1A, 513–61; *cf.* Corullón, 'Eremitismo', 27–35.
[150] García y García, 'Legislación', 20–3.
[151] Pastor Díaz de Garayo, 'Testimonios', 365–9; Sanz Fuentes, 'Lenguaje', 126–9, 148–52; *cf.* Linage Conde, *Orígenes*, 2, 559–600.

| | Citations | | Overall | |
|---|---|---|---|---|
| | # | % | # | % |
| Total | 234 | 6 | 4095 | 100 |
| Region | | | | |
| West | 94 | 40 | 1284 | 31 |
| Centre | 89 | 38 | 2088 | 51 |
| East | 51 | 22 | 723 | 18 |
| Personnel | | | | |
| Royal | 51 | 22 | 522 | 13 |
| Comital | 3 | 1 | 71 | 2 |
| Ecclesiastical | 179 | 76 | 2710 | 66 |
| Lay | 0 | 0 | 769 | 19 |
| Typology | | | | |
| Donation | 199 | 85 | 2212 | 54 |
| Sale | 6 | 3 | 1469 | 36 |
| Other | 29 | 12 | 411 | 10 |
| Complexity | | | | |
| Simple | 89 | 38 | 2797 | 68 |
| Complex | 145 | 62 | 1292 | 32 |
| Palaeography | | | | |
| Original | 26 | 11 | 888 | 22 |
| Copy | 39 | 17 | 261 | 6 |
| Cartulary | 147 | 63 | 2438 | 60 |
| Other | 22 | 9 | 507 | 12 |
| Diplomatic | | | | |
| Authentic | 193 | 82 | 3781 | 92 |
| Suspicious | 1 | 0 | 24 | 1 |
| Interpolated | 17 | 7 | 57 | 1 |
| Falsified | 22 | 9 | 227 | 6 |

**Figure 6.5** Charters Citing Rules

confront those interacting with the clergy; they are more prominent in complex donations, and in confirmations and pacts. The earliest instance, naming the *regula sancta*, is in the monastic pact of San Miguel de Pedroso in 759, and the incidence spikes in the reign of Alfonso III and its aftermath, when monasteries and churches were founded amidst the expansion of the realm. The rate is steady thereafter, as with Scripture and canon law, and the absence of any rising trend throws the growth of legal citation into further relief (see Figure 6.6).[152]

---

[152] *San Millán* 301; *cf.* Martínez Díez, 'Monasterio', 27–8.

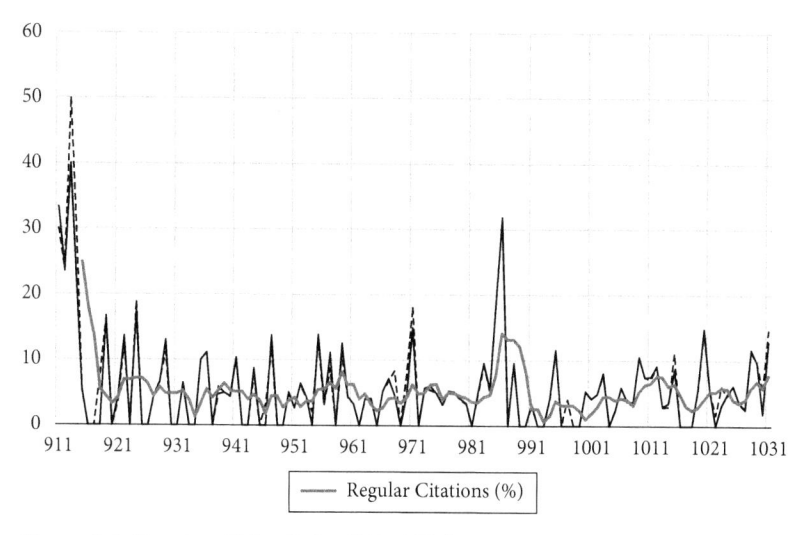

**Figure 6.6** Charters Citing Rules (911–1031)

## Identities

Regular citation was a form of self-identification which set the clergy apart from the laity. Taking the 'holy rule' first, the mode and meaning of invoking it varied by region and institution. Charters of donation to Abellar identify the beneficiaries as the monastery and its brothers living *sub regula sancta* (under the holy rule), stating for the record how communal life was regulated; they do so particularly when the donor was also entering that community, and we glimpse the same house, in an *exaratio* (writing) of 1009, imposing the *recola sancta* on a subject cell.[153] This 'holy rule' was thought of as a monastic constitution: the monks of Santos Justo y Pastor lived the holy life under it, just as other monasteries existed *sub sancta regule norma* or *sub recula patrum* (under the holy norm of the rule, or under the rule of the Fathers).[154] Donations to Sahagún were addressed to its abbot and those under both him and the *regiminis regule sancte* (regime of the holy rule), while monks in Astorga lived under the *regulari monastica* (monastic rule) and the bishop, or in houses *ad regularem iugum sibiecti* and *regularia iussa complentes* (subject to the regular yoke, fulfilling regular commands).[155] When Osorio Gutiérrez occupied a monastery of Santa

---

[153] *León* 288, 677; *cf.* 329, 341, 515.    [154] *León* 432, 295, 674; *cf.* 109; *Liébana* 29.
[155] *Sahagún* 255; *Astorga* 214, 45; *cf. Sahagún* 30.

Lucía in 952, we are told, the *lex non continet nec sancta regida docet* (law does not allow nor the holy rule teach) his act.[156] Even as the terminology for charters establishes an equivalence with rules, therefore, embodied by the *regulae testamenti* (rules of testament) in the name of San Dictino from 986, the granting of a gift to a 'monastery and rule' of San Cipriano in 985 flags a merging of institutions with their regulations.[157] If monastic property was held by those living *comuniter vel regulariter*, communally or regularly, per the words of a testament in the archive of Santillana from 870, and the monastic life meant meditating upon the *reculam monasterii* (rule of the monastery), as formulated by a rare ecclesiastical document of 988 preserved in the Otero archive, it was only the smallest step for a house regulated by a *regula* to become a 'rule' itself.[158]

In the east, regular citation is omnipresent at Valpuesta, and this is where the clearest and most consistent identification of monastery and rule is made. Consider these overlapping and interchangeable usages: Bishop Diego in 929 made a gift of his estate in accordance with the *regula monasterii*, while Tellu *presbiter* joined *tota collatione qui ibi sunt in ipsa regula* (the whole congregation who are there in that rule) in 951, and his son Munnio *presbiter* then confirmed the *regula* which his father had signed in 971.[159] The shift from simple citation to wholesale identification is definite in a charter of 973, whereby Alfonso made a *pacto regule* (pact of rule) to the *regula* of Valpuesta, and everyone in the *regula* affirmed it.[160] Entering a monastery by signing a pact according to a monastic rule, monks came to see themselves and that monastery as one and the same rule.[161] We can perceive this *regula* in its dual form, both object and agent, in two *condiciones sacramentorum* (terms of oaths): witnesses swore in 911 that Analso *presbiter* had been given land from the rule of Valpuesta, and took oath for the rule in 919, whereupon Fenesterius *presbiter* confessed to giving his *atrium* to the abbot or *ad regula sancta* (to the holy rule).[162] The community of the rule as a rule explains and is explained by the *regulantes* ('rule-followers') of Valpuesta, who purchased property in a charter of 975.[163] The full range of 'regular terminology' is found across the east, but most densely here; when gifts to Buezo de Bureba noted that the record had been delivered to the

---

[156]   *Astorga* 71; *cf. Floriano* 41.
[157]   *Astorga* 180, 155; *cf.* 10; *Liébana* 45.
[158]   *Santillana* 1; *Otero* 29; *cf. Santillana* 2; *Otero* 170; *Floriano*, 1, 549–50, 2, 656.
[159]   *Valpuesta* 12, 32, 44; *cf.* 35, 40, 47; Ruiz de Loizaga, *Iglesia*, 123–6.
[160]   *Valpuesta* 45; *cf.* 15, 38, 49.
[161]   Linage Conde, *Orígenes*, 1, 341–4.      [162]   *Valpuesta* 10–11.
[163]   *Valpuesta* 46; *cf.* 13; Carrero Santamaría, 'Vidas', 770–4.

rule and put into the archives of its church, the word gained communal, personal, even physical features.[164]

In the west, regular citation seldom reached this level of intensity. The practice is best represented at Celanova, where the foundational charter of 936 called for the establishment of a house *sub regulari tramite* (on the regular path).[165] The testament of Bishop Rosendo in 977 recorded how it had duly been endowed with everything needed *ad normam regulari* (for the regular norm), and narrated the election of his successor Abbot Manilán *sub regulari iugo* (to the regular yoke); throughout the history of the monastery, citing the rule which governed it is a feature of both its own identity and that of its subject houses.[166] The same is also true of the brothers of Samos, who lived *sub regulari norma*, and those of Sobrado, who *regulariter* pursued the *regulari vita* (regular life), and those too of certain monasteries in Portugal, who served under *regule institutionis eius* and *confesionis normam* (the rule of its teaching, norm of confession).[167] But note the distinction observed between institution and its regulation: the eastern conflation of house and *regula* is absent here except for a donation made by Fruela II to the *sancte regule* of Santiago in 924.[168] Something is different, if only in how explicit this identification was made, but monastic life still meant living by written rules. When Ordoño II visited Portugal in 922, he sent for Bishop Gomado, who had since retired to the monastery of Crestuma, but as he would not *exivit de confessione* (re-enter the world), *secundum regula docet* (exactly as the rule teaches), the king travelled by ship to honour him in person.[169] And the hagiographical life of Froilán, written in the early tenth century, is clear that the monks of his monastic foundations in the west and in León were *sub regulari norma constitutos*.[170]

These references to rules all share a lack of specificity, potentially pointing to any part of the *corpus regularum*, but perhaps deliberately so, since it took different forms in different copies.[171] Citations of the Benedictine rule, in contrast, refer to a discrete source. The earliest incontestably authentic appearance comes in an original diploma of Alfonso III dating to 905, confirming the brothers of Abellar in possession of their monastery, *secundum*

[164] *Valpuesta* 21, 25–6; cf. 9, 17; *Albelda* 15–16, 20; *Cardeña* 200; *Covarrubias* 6; *Oña* 2.
[165] *Celanova* 53; Mattoso, 'Rosendo', 5–27.
[166] *Celanova* 185; cf. 52, 69, 126, 190, 197, 199, 263, 318, 360, *Alfonso V* 7; *Celanova* 3, 95, 196, 292.
[167] *Samos* 217; *Sobrado* 1.6; *Guimarães* 68, A6; cf. *Samos* 104; *Sobrado* 1.2; *Coimbra* 514.
[168] *Santiago* 37.    [169] *Coimbra* 81.
[170] *Vita Froilanis*, ed. Martín, 'Vita', ll. 67–9; Carriedo Tejedo, 'Iter', 76–80.
[171] Mundó, 'Corpora', 2, 477–520; Velázquez Soriano, 'Reflexiones', 532–4.

*regula beati Benedicti precipit* (according to what the rule of the blessed Benedict instructs).[172] The next is another original charter of 929 from Eslonza, which documents the founding of a house in which to lead the monastic life, *secundum docet sancti Benedicti regulam* (according to what the rule of the holy Benedict teaches).[173] From the late tenth century onwards, one can follow the diffusion of the *Rule* in León through citations of institutions and inmates living under or by it: at San Andrés de Pardomino and Santa María de León in 985, Santiago de León in 995, San Cipriano de Valdesaz in 1000, San Vicente de León in 1011, and San Miguel de León in 1012.[174] By far the most references come from Sahagún, but these have been interpreted both arbitrarily and incoherently. Without evident reason, the first genuine mention here is held to be in a testament from Scemena in 985 to the monastery and its servants of God, *qui regulam Benedicti patris meditabant* (who were meditating on the rule of Benedict the father), making the dozen subsequent early medieval citations authentic.[175] The editor of the monastic archive then applied this judgement randomly, deeming some but not all of the 12 prior citations false, even when the property involved is too exiguous and the donors too well attested for that to be likely or credible.[176] Assuming a linear, zero-sum replacement of one rule by the other is in any case flawed. The *corpus regularum*, as its name suggests, was a gathering of rules, and Benedict began to be added into the mix during the tenth century, rather than displacing it wholesale.[177] We should look instead for reasons of personal choice, audience, or monastic fashion to explain why one or the other set of norms was invoked at any given moment.

The evidence for complementarity is staring us in the face. When Bishop Ranulfo of Astorga restored the Fructuosan foundation of San Pedro de Montes in 896, he confirmed the observance of the *regula sancte* even as he appointed San Genadio as abbot under the *regula beati Benedicti*, though this may be later reimagining.[178] In 1006, a donation was made to the brothers of Sahagún under the *Rule*, but they later had cause to gather, *secundum quod sancta regula docet*, to consider the possibility of alienating this gift; by that time, the former may well have come to stand for their

[172] *León* 18; Linage Conde, 'Caminares', 44–8, 61–7; Espirito Santo, 'Benedictinos', 1, 713–16.
[173] *Eslonza* 9; cf. Vivancos, 'Autenticidad', 438, 442.
[174] *León* 506; 507, 770; 568, 592, 617, 658, 698, 803; 594, 775; 697, 723; 709, 777.
[175] *Sahagún* 328; cf. 330–1, 333, 345, 380–1, 386, 407–8, 414, 422, 429.
[176] *Sahagún* 162 (94, 164, 266); cf. 8, 123, 150, 215, 220, 259, 261–2, 299, 321.
[177] Velázquez Soriano, 'Reflexiones', 562–6.
[178] *Montes* 4; *Diócesis* 1; Agúndez San Miguel, 'Tumbo', 28–36.

communal identity, the latter for their monastic practice, but it could equally be a case of citing multiple rules to speak to multiple constituencies under the roof of a single house.[179] Evidently, however, for monks looking back from the 'golden age' of forgery in the high Middle Ages, when full 'Benedictinisation' had long since been enforced, the opposite was true, and a cycle of patently false diplomas from San Millán, San Juan, and Leire recount how Sancho III, acting on the advice of Abbot Oliba, imported Cluniac monks to introduce the *Rule* of Saint Benedict into his realm and thereby restore the cooling ardour of divine work in its monasteries.[180] This disguises a more complex reality of multiple rules coexisting on the ground, and their citation is fundamentally interchangeable in the corpus of documentation.[181] If we look at the numbers, they bear it out: of 220 charters citing monastic rules, some 138 (63%) refer to the *regula sancta*, the other 82 (37%) to the *Rule*, showing no clear trend over time with respect to each other, and certainly no progressive replacement of one by the other—both remained equally in play throughout the period (see Figure 6.7).

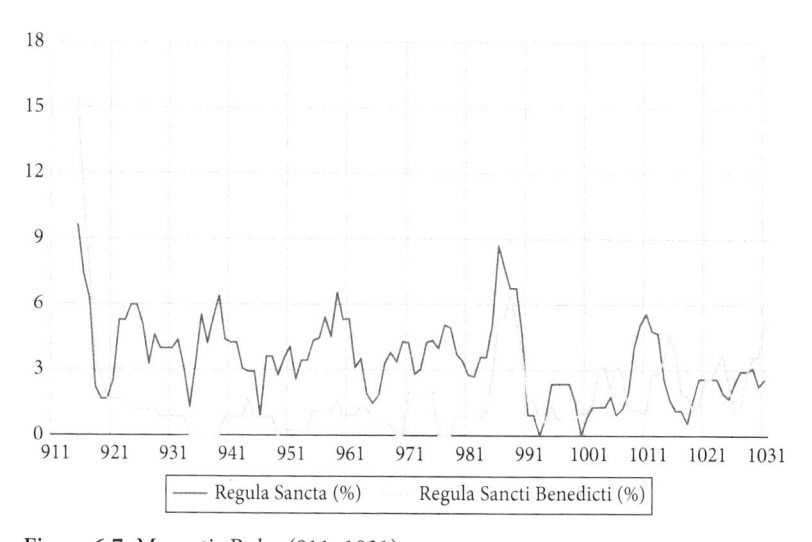

**Figure 6.7** Monastic Rules (911–1031)

[179] *Sahagún* 386; *cf.* Snijders, 'Diversity', 897–930.
[180] Ubieto Arteta, *Millán*, 193–4 (193); *San Juan* 47; *Leire* 17–18, 20; *cf. San Juan* 48; Linage Conde, 'Benedictinización', 57–92.
[181] See *e.g. San Isidro* 1–2; *Astorga* 11; *Entrepeñas* 1; *Oviedo* 41; *Castañeda* 11; *Arlanza* 2–4; *Cardeña* 46; *Silos* 1; *Albelda* 21; *San Millán* 557, 307.

## Contracts

Of these two points of reference for regular citation, however, the *regula sancta* has a contractual dimension which is absent from the *Rule*, and this distinguishing feature underlies the passage from texts to 'textual communities' in early medieval Iberia. Fructuosus of Braga (or follower) began the *Regula monastica communis* with the admonition that no one should establish a monastery without first consulting his congregation and receiving approval from his bishop, in accordance with the canons and the rule (references which are unsubstantiated); he then described who ought to be elected abbot and accepted as monks, before detailing their mutual obligations, making disposition of their possessions, and enumerating the penalties for any infractions. Lest any of the foregoing be mistakenly understood as optional, a model pact helpfully circulated with it, binding both abbot and brothers to these conditions.[182] Visigothic law cast a wide net in its understanding of contract, ranging from sale to servile status, lease to loan, and marriage to medical treatment.[183] In the corpus of charters, it is possible to find rental and labour agreements strictly defined, which have been linked to the consolidation of feudal structures, and more broadly a range of donations and other transactions which, as we have seen, establish an ongoing relationship between the parties.[184] But the monastic pact is the purest example of a contract entered into by signatories, freely or obliged by circumstances, and the 'pactual' monastery was as such the community of the written contract.[185]

The earliest to survive, agreed in the Liébana in 818, can stand for the rest: citing the *regula monasterii*, it lays out the penalties for fraternal misbehaviour and redress for abbatial misconduct, and in a series of appended donations the parties transfer themselves to the new house together with their property.[186] The monastic pact thereby establishes both the real and the 'textual community'. They are especially prevalent in the Liébana: *lectam*

---

[182] See *Regula monastica communis*, 1–5, 18, 20, *Pactum*, ed. Campos Ruiz and Roca Meliá, *Padres*; and also *Consensoria monachorum*, 1, 4, 8–9, ed. Arbesmann and Hümpfner, *Liber*; transl. Barlow, *Fathers*, 2, 217–20; *cf.* Herwegen, *Pactum*, esp. 1–50; Wood, *Church*, 23–4, 147–51.

[183] Álvarez Cora, 'Aproximación', 543–82; López-Rendo Rodríguez, 'Autonomía', esp. 88–93; *cf.* Petit, 'Lex', 5–32; Álvarez Cora, 'Contrato', 309–30.

[184] Sánchez-Albornoz, 'Contratos', 142–79; García de Valdeavellano, '"Renovo"', 408–48; Marlasca Martínez, 'Préstamo', 609–13; *cf.* García de Valdeavellano, 'Prestimonio', 5–122; García-Gallo, 'Hombre', 319–72.

[185] Létinier, 'Pacta', 281–306; *cf.* Létinier, 'Juicios', 467–73.     [186] *Piasca*, app. 1.

*regulam*, the rule being read, they emphasise the authority of the abbot over his monks, citing vague Scriptural and canonical support, to reprove infractions through the harshest measures, and to retain the property of those leaving for secular life, if not to restore them by force to the monastery. All had to sign, and all examples have the crucial clauses on reciprocal responsibility and shared proprietorship.[187] Examples from farther afield are hardly less authoritarian, such as the five priests who bound themselves in 973 or so to the *locellum* (small site) of Fonte Aurea, under an abbot described as *imperator* (commander), and in a relationship characterised as father to son.[188] For every neutral pact, like the several from Cardeña out-lining a sort of collective self-correction led by an abbot who reads and lis-tens to the *maioribus* (elders), another insists that all power and property rested in the institution.[189] When Sonna and his wife Munnina agreed by pact to enter San Cosme y San Damián for a year in 865, it was on condition that, should they disobey the abbot, they would surrender a field and related lands forever.[190] In the west, where similar agreements obtained at Celanova and Samos especially, Bishop Rosendo even followed through on one in 955, enlisting the support of Ramiro II to restore Aseredus to the monastery whence he had fled at diabolical instigation, just as the authorities re-established 'regular order' in Samos from time to time when pacts were felt to be lacking.[191] The monks, after all, had signed up, affixed *scriptura vel signa* or *scripturam vel significati* (their writing or signs), and not only when founding or entering the monastery: *gasalianes* at Orbañanos, a debated term but which looks by etymology to mean 'house-dwellers', renewed their written agreement, first reached under Abbot Guisandus in 870, with his successor Bishop Diego in 900, as if for the next generation.[192] When these and other monks ventured forth from their contractual communities to serve as scribes for the world at large, we can imagine how they brought their 'pactual mentality' with them, modelling how to live by the terms of text, and feeding it back into a society fully at home with doing business in written form.

[187] *Liébana* 56; cf. 1, 6, 24; *Santillana* 10; *Sahagún* 79; Montenegro Valentín, *María*, 22–8; Portass, *World*, 43–8, 57–8.
[188] *Sahagún* 1171.
[189] *Cardeña* 115, 48; Martínez Díez, *Colección* 14; cf. *León* 479; *Sahagún* 257; *Oviedo* 8; *Arlanza* 8–9; *San Millán* 301, 313, 697.
[190] *Valpuesta* 4; cf. 26.
[191] *Celanova* 111; cf. 1–2, 4; *Samos* 5, 33, 210, 43, 35, 7, S1–2; *Sobrado* 1.124; *San Clodio* 1; *Guimarães* 1A, A3.
[192] *Celanova* 1–2; *Valpuesta* 7; cf. *Sobrado* 1.110; Merêa, 'Glossário', 55–64; Marques, *Representação*, 237–40.

## Malleable Texts

The role played by the clergy, as agents and assistants to deals done and documented within the framework not only of other charters and the Visigothic code, but also of the Bible, canon law, and monastic rules, enabled early medieval Iberia to function by text, and in their own image. But what did their mental library look like, and how did they stock its seemingly crowded shelves? Take the most common element of the network of texts, present in the form of Scriptural citation. Collectively scribes had on the order of 200 passages at their disposal (see Figure 6.8). This amounts to 112 verses or sequences of verses from the Old Testament, most notably the Psalms, and 87 from the New Testament, primarily the Gospels and especially Matthew. How did scribes internalise so much of the Bible? Committed Christians were obliged to read their Scriptures daily and deeply, but did they?[193] In part, the contours of citation answer their own question: the Psalter was the basic primer or textbook in clerical education, while manuscripts of the Gospels were in more common circulation than the complete Biblical text.[194] But both could also be accessed through antiphonaries, orationals, and other books of offices, and this is where we need to look. There was a symbiosis between Scriptural text and liturgical practice, visible in the close relationship between the Vetus Latina Hispana and the 'Old Hispanic' or Visigothic-Mozarabic liturgy.[195] Through this distinctive tradition of chant, hymns, readings, and prayers, consolidated by the later seventh century though likely in recognisable form by the end of the sixth, the Bible was made omnipresent by daily perform-ance, cycling through the whole Psalter, for example, in the night services over the course of a week. The tradition was itself created as part of an intel-lectual and cultural project by the Visigothic bishops after the general con-version to Nicene orthodoxy at the Third Council of Toledo in 589. It was meant to educate the clergy, and the wider lay community, in the text of Scripture and its exegesis, and to form identity by teaching doctrine, most noticeably in its Christianised presentation of the Old Testament, which directly informed contemporary anti-Jewish discourses.[196]

---

[193] Andrés Sanz, 'Lectio', 19–39.
[194] Riché, Education, 463–5; Casado de Otaola, 'Escribir', 123–8; Bogaert, 'Bible', 69–92; Riché, 'Apprendre', 54–69; cf. Riché, 'Psautier', 253–6; Rodríguez Martín, 'Salmos', 2, 447–56.
[195] Ayuso Marazuela, Vetus Latina Hispana, V. Salterio, 1, 49–115; Pinell, Liturgia.
[196] Hornby and Ihnat, 'Psalmody', 3–33; Maloy, Songs, esp. 1–18, 42–104; Rojo Carrillo, Text, 114–39; cf. Vitz, 'Liturgy', 20–34; Hornby and Maloy, Music, 1–5; Kurt, 'Piety', 1–37; Urlacher-Becht, 'Doctrine', 403–23.

| Old Testament |
| --- |

Genesis 1:22, 1:26, 2:18, 2:23, 3:15, 4:4, 4:7, 4:15, 14:18–20, 19:24–5, 21:1, 28:17, 34:9.

Exodus 3:14–15, 14:26–8 (*cf.* 15:1–21; Psalms 136:13–15), 35:29.

Numbers 15:3 (*cf.* Leviticus 2:12?), 16:31–2 (*cf.* 26:9–10; Deuteronomy 11:6; Psalms 106:17), 28:2.

Deuteronomy 4:24, 11:6, 12:6, 16:16, 26:11?, 27:9–26, 28:15–68, 32:7, 33:16.

Joshua 6:20, 8:24–5, 10:28–39, 11:14.

I Samuel 2:30, 4:4–18, 22:9–23.

I Kings 8:17–18?

II Kings 5:27.

I Chronicles 29:11–12 (*cf.* II Chronicles 20:6?), 29:14–15, 29:16, 29:18.

Tobit 13:8?

Job 3:8 (*cf.* Psalms 74:13–14; Isaiah 27:1), 7:6, 7:20, 16:7, 24:18, 25:5–6, 34:24.

Psalms 19:9, 22:6, 37:27, 44:23–4?, 45:15–16?, 49:7–8, 49:10, 50:5, 50:10–12, 50:14 (*cf.* 76:11), 50:16–17, 52:1–7, 66:12, 69:28 (*cf.* Exodus 32:32–3), 73:28, 76:1–2, 76:10, 76:11 (*cf.* 50:14), 77:11, 83:13, 84:4, 89:28, 90:4, 97:10, 105:4?, 115:17–18, 116:12, 121:4, 128:5–6, 133:1, 137:8, 141:2, 143:2, 144:2, 146:4.

Proverbs 1:7, 3:9, 9:10, 15:8, 25:2.

Ecclesiastes 1:4, 12:6.

Wisdom 7:6.

Sirach 1:4, 1:16–17, 3:33, 35:11.

Isaiah 1:18, 14:5, 34:9, 56:1?, 58:6.

Jeremiah 10:6, 13:16, 22:19, 29:6.

Lamentations 3:27.

Ezekiel 3:19?, 18:32, 33:11.

Daniel 4:12.

Micah 6:6?, 7:11–13?

Zephaniah 1:15.

Zechariah 5:7, 7:14.

| New Testament |
|---|
| Matthew 3:10 (*cf.* 7:19; Luke 3:9), 5:3, 5:7, 5:12, 5:17, 6:19–20, 6:21, 7:6, 7:7 (*cf.* Luke 11:9), 7:14, 10:9, 10:32–3, 10:37–8 (*cf.* Mark 10:29–30), 11:28, 15:37, 16:17, 16:18–19, 16:24 (*cf.* Luke 9:23; Mark 8:34), 19:17, 19:27–9, 21:19 (*cf.* Mark 11:14), 22:14, 24:42 (*cf.* 25:13; Mark 13:33; Luke 12:40), 25:11, 25:12, 25:21, 25:31–46 (*cf.* 25:23), 26:29? |
| Mark 10:28 (*cf.* Luke 18:28), 10:29–30, 10:43–4 (*cf.* Matthew 20:26–7). |
| Luke 2:7, 6:38, 10:1, 11:41, 12:33–4, 12:49, 14:26, 14:33, 16:9, 18:22 (*cf.* 12:33; Matthew 19:21; Mark 10:21), 19:1–10, 19:46, 22:32. |
| John 1:1, 5:7, 10:30, 11:26, 12:35 (*cf.* Ephesians 5:8), 13:35, 14:9, 15:14–15, 17:4–24?, 18:9? |
| Acts 4:32, 5:1–11, 7:49 (*cf.* Isaiah 66:1), 14:23. |
| Romans 7:18, 10:10, 12:5, 13:12–13. |
| I Corinthians 6:10 (*cf.* II Corinthians 6:10?), 9:27, 10:24 (*cf.* Philippians 2:4), 13:12, 16:22. |
| II Corinthians 9:7, 10:18 (*cf.* 10:12). |
| Ephesians 2:11–12? |
| Philippians 1:21, 2:8, 3:18. |
| Colossians 2:14. |
| I Thessalonians 4:14. |
| I Timothy 1:14 (*cf.* II Timothy 1:14?), 5:14, 6:18? |
| II Timothy 2:22. |
| Titus 1:16. |
| Hebrews 11:13. |
| James 5:16? |
| I Peter 1:18–19. |
| I John 1:17, 5:4. |
| Revelation 2:8–11?, 11:15, 14:4, 21:2. |

**Figure 6.8** Scripture Cited in Charters

As the 'Old Hispanic' liturgy continued in use in the early Middle Ages, so it carried on mediating the experience of Scriptural text in practice. We can model how this may have informed the working knowledge of our scribes in one simple example, the first of the basic citations of the Bible which we encountered in the charters, I Chronicles 29:14, 'Everything comes from you and we have given you only what comes from your hand'. This verse opens *tua sunt omnia* in the standard Vulgate text, whereas in the documentation it reliably begins *tua sunt enim omnia*, a subtle difference matching with the liturgical text of the *Breviarium Gothicum* or 'Gothic breviary' of 1502. Caution is needed here since this edition is a hybrid, a service book of a type originating in the Roman rite, but it is based on manuscripts from the Mozarabic churches of Toledo, and may reflect a service book in that tradition.[197] Similarly, when Sarracina, a religious, made a donation in 987, she was moved by related words from verse 18, 'Keep these desires and thoughts in the hearts of your people forever, and keep their hearts loyal to you', again corresponding to the 'breviary' text rather than the Bible.[198] So far as we can tell, scribes were all ecclesiastics of one sort or another, and a liturgical interface with Scripture would explain how their mentality came to be so deeply imbued in scattered verses, passages, and images, which then richly informed their expression of transaction in writing.[199] It also clarifies how they could, by internalising Biblical language via both indirect and direct channels, come to be guided in thought and behaviour by an authoritative reference text without needing that text to hand.[200] Indeed, not only the wording but also the selection of Biblical passages can offer a clue to the sources through which scribes accessed them, and these extended beyond the liturgy: a number of monastic pacts and donations from the centre and the east quote specific groups of verses, mainly from the Gospels and Acts, which tally with those in the Fructuosan rule, as its template agreement offered both model and resource, a 'Scriptural selection' linking a venerable text and name.[201] So accessed, the authority of the Bible

---

[197] Lorenzana, *Breviarium*, 'Cantica Mozarabica', 64 (87); Ivorra, *Liturgia*, 61–3; Boynton, 'Restoration', esp. 9–10.

[198] *León* 520; Lorenzana, *Breviarium*, 'Cantica Mozarabica', 64 (87); *cf. León* 835.

[199] See García Lobo and Martín López, 'Liturgie', 259–78.

[200] Stock, *Implications*, 88–92.

[201] D'Emilio, 'Charter', 304–13; see *e.g. León* 824, John 10:30, 14:9, Acts 7:49, Luke 18:22; *Sahagún* 257, 402, *Santillana* 9, John 10:30, 14:9, Acts 7:49, Luke 18:22, Matthew 16:24; *Santillana* 1, John 10:30, 14:9, Acts 7:49, Luke 14:26, 18:22, Matthew 10:37, 16:24, Mark 10:29–30; *Arlanza* 8, 21, John 10:30, 14:9, Matthew 10:37, 16:24, 19:28, Mark 10:28; *Santillana* 10, Psalms 66:12, Lamentations 3:27, I Corinthians 10:24, Matthew 7:14, 16:24, 19:17.

as retransmitted by scribes set the terms of religious thought and practice. Bishop Fortis knew this well, and when restoring San Dictino de Astorga in 925, he reflected on words of power, 'If you do what is right, will you not be accepted? But if you do not do what is right, sin is crouching at your door'.[202]

While clerical scribes, by speaking Scripture, promoted documentation to the plane of universal yet individual Christian salvation history, they applied a more internal authorisation and identification to ecclesiastical charters. Canon law was a source of norms for the Church, but less so specific than general ones; the clergy valued a discourse of living canonically, and normalised actions near and far from canonical text in this framing. As such, when we seek to catalogue the canons in the scribal mind, we compile more a set of possibilities (see Figure 6.9). Within the discourse of living canonically, the distance between text and practice was itself a form of mediation, and we can catch glimpses of canon law in the midst of transformation by that use. One of the most important functions of canonical citation was to establish the rights of property or 'immunities' granted to monasteries and churches in Iberia, as across the early medieval West.[203] Like the Catalan *sagrera*, the *dextros ecclesiae* or privileges enjoyed by a given religious institution in Asturias-León and Navarra over its surrounding area developed out of the Tenth Council of Toledo, canon 10, 'On those who seek refuge at a church', which defined a perimeter of 30 *passus* (paces) around the doors, within which a fugitive should have sanctuary; the principle is shared by Visigothic law, but no fixed figure is stated.[204] This normative enclosure took on a physical reality as a privileged burial space, and a visibility in the landscape through markers of the *millas* at Samos and Santiago.[205] But if we look in detail at citation of the canon, we find a transitional state, halfway between past and future conciliar legislation. When Visclafredus *sacerdos et abba* granted the monastery of Rosende in 874 its church, appurtenances, and the 72 *dextros* around it, *sicut lex et veritas docet* (just as law and truth teach), we can recognise the premise of the canon, yet both the area itself and the unit of measurement used for it differ from the source.[206] Another Portuguese

---

[202]  *Astorga* 28, Genesis 4:7; *cf.* Frye, *Words*, esp. 95–125.

[203]  Davies and Fouracre (eds), *Property*, 12–16; Rosenwein, *Space*, esp. 27–73.

[204]  X Toledo 10; *LV* 9.3; Osaba García, 'Deudores', 299–322; Osaba García, 'Realidad', esp. 195–9.

[205]  Bango Torviso, 'Espacio', 94–6; López Alsina, 'Millas', 159–87; López Salas, 'Papel', 19–29; *cf.* Zadora-Rio, 'Making', 9–13; Ripoll and Molist Capella, '*Cura*', 36–40; Alba Bueno and Rodríguez García, 'Muerte', 81–106, is puzzling.

[206]  *Samos* S1; *Lugo*, 2, 555–65.

Elvira 7–10, 12–18, 20, 30–1, 33, 47, 61, 63–70, 77–8.

I Toledo 1–6, 12, 16–17, 19.

Tarragona 3, 5, 9, 12.

Girona 6–9.

II Toledo 3–4.

I Barcelona 6–8.

Lleida 3, 5–6, 15–16.

Valencia 2–3.

I Braga 6.

II Braga cc 1–10, 14–17, 26–8, 30–2, 43–4, 61–2, 76–80, 82.

III Toledo, 3–5, 10, 19.

Narbonne 10.

I Seville 3.

Toledo (597) 1.

Huesca.

II Barcelona 4.

Egara (Terrassa).

II Seville 4, 10.

IV Toledo 19–20, 23, 42–4, 51, 54–5, 75.

V Toledo 2–5, 7–8.

VI Toledo 5, 7–8, 12, 15, 17–18.

VII Toledo 4.

VIII Toledo 2, 4–6.

IX Toledo 1–6, 9–10.

X Toledo 2–3.

Mérida 4, 6, 8, 11.

XI Toledo 7, 12.

III Braga 4.

XII Toledo 2–3, 6.

**Figure 6.9** Canonical Citations

charter of 882 is on the one hand closer, employing the related term *pasales* for *passus* and citing *kanonica sentemtia* (canonical opinion) as well as *lex*; the enclosure, however, is set at 12 for the burial of bodies and 72 for support of the brothers and the poor, a total of 84 echoed in two further testaments from the west using *dextros* instead.[207] When Ordoño I gave a

[207] *ChLA* 114, 31; *Samos* 33; *Coimbra* 123; Ríos Rodríguez, '"Ecclesiae"', 114–15; Marques, *Representação*, 323, 332.

monastery to Bishop Fronimio of León in 860, he included unspecified canonical *dextros* for burying bodies and supporting brothers, but within a generation 12, 72, or 84 had become the standard 'rights'.[208]

As with silent reliance on Visigothic law, certain charters and transactions have been shaped by the background presence of canons, and this is most demonstrable for the *dextros ecclesiae* of the ecclesiastical enclosure. Isidore of Seville had associated *dextra*, 'the right hand', with *dare*, 'to give', in the sense of gift or pledge.[209] And when Agione *frater* in 944 endowed São Martinho de Aldoar with *dextrus* (*sic*) of 12 *passus* for the burial of bodies and support of the brothers, the written record combined canonical terminology (*passus*) with a vocabulary (*dextrus*) and measure (12) which practice had developed and normalised, just as Andreas *clericus* laid out *dextros* of 72 *passos* for Santiago de Toldaos in 849.[210] Alfonso III, indeed, granted a church to Santiago in 893 with 84 *dextris* in all directions, neatly the sum of the two; other references to 82 *pasos* or 60 *passales* could be arithmetical error or subtraction instead of addition.[211] In no case is canon law cited, but a provision emerging from text has been internalised, altered, and implemented. Charters from Samos, Coimbra, Celanova, and Eslonza which note *dextros* or *dextros ecclesie* without further description or specification lack content or force absent awareness, however remote, that the source lay in the *Hispana*.[212] Yet the remoteness is the point: the explanation for these varieties of perimeter is that we are here somewhere between late antique and high medieval canon law. Looking ahead, the Council of Coyanza confirmed the *dextros ecclesiae* in 1055, citing the Visigothic code, though setting them at 30 or 31 *passus*; the next year, the Council of Compostela guaranteed 72 *dextros* around every church, free from lay interference.[213] Early medieval Iberia is on the road from Visigothic source text to its future revised form. What the scribes who cited it were interested in was the assurance, the authority of living canonically, more than a precise figure, and as they drew on the text thus to formulate

---

[208] *León* 2; *cf. Guimarães* 65.

[209] Isidore of Seville, *Etymologiae*, 11 (ed.-transl. Gasti, *Etimologie*), 1.67; *cf.* Franco Júnior, 'Doigts', 418.

[210] *Guimarães* 526; *Samos* 128; *cf.* 99, 226; *PMH* 8; *Arouca* 2.

[211] *Santiago* 14; *Lorvão* 12; *Sahagún* 331; *cf. Samos* 58.

[212] *Samos* 40; *Coimbra* 354–6; *cf. Celanova* 7; *Eslonza* 1–2.

[213] García-Gallo, 'Concilio', esp. 331, 439–44, 459–61, 560–1, 622–9; Martínez Díez, 'Tradición', Coyanza 12; Martínez Díez, 'Concilio', 3/1; *cf. Penitential of Silos*, ed. Körntgen and Bezler, *Paenitentialia*, 11.186; Orlandis, 'Consecuencias', 71–4; García y García, 'Legislación', 23–30, 42–50; Sánchez-Arcilla Bernal, 'Derecho', 367–71, 375–80.

ecclesiastical jurisdiction, the text in turn was transformed over time by its use, and the substance of canon law responded to the evolving practice of property.

We are in a world of malleable texts, somewhere between their 'real' form in the book and as lived and experienced in the world. Clerical scribes understood and expressed gift especially through the terms of their imagined community of Scripture, but Scripture as they had heard it, meditated on it, and prayed with it. Clerical scribes bounded Church patrimonies by the compass of their 'textual community' of canon law, or rather their working idea of what it meant to be canonical; as often as not this was simply a sense, unbounded in its detail to the mooring of text, and therefore susceptible to change. In the same vein, monastic rules were a source for their identity, but in the fact of a rule rather than particularities, as living regularly was what mattered. References to the *regula sancta* or the *regula sancti Benedicti* need not have been to a rule in writing and at hand, nor to one identifiable with any of the rules as we have them; as we see in the practice of eastern monasticism, monasteries will have had their own versions, written or unwritten, but all by those names referring back to the idea of a text as their guide for devotion.[214] And as clerical scribes wrote charters for others, they impressed on them something of their own mentality: through the documentation which they created, they transmitted a network of texts to the parties, witnesses, and audiences. In all these cases, most citations need not have involved any first-hand contact with the Bible, canon law, or monastic rules on the part of the writer; liturgy, memory, other charters would for the most part have sufficed, and help to explain the form in which we encounter many of those texts. But in each case, there was awareness of the texts behind the text, the importance of *being* Scripturally, canonically, regularly. Lay documentary practice was framed first by Visigothic law, but the mentality of textual framing was promoted and valorised by the clerical scribes who doubled as the legal experts in early medieval Iberia. The houses from which they emerged defined themselves by contracts, and the documentary world which they enabled came to define itself by texts—a textual society, governing and governed with reference to written norms, whether or not those who abided by them ever encountered them in their original written forms.

---

[214] Vogüé, *Regards*, 229–57, 275–90; see *e.g.* Binns, *Ascetics*, 171–2; Rousseau, *Pachomius*, 48–53; Layton, *Canons*, esp. 35–49, 77–85.

# Conclusion

## Imaginary Libraries

The written was the world of early medieval Iberia. Few may have been able to read and write, literacy as we know it, yet the extent of textuality was both broad and deep, in the authority conferred on text and the arrangements made to use it. The inheritance of Rome is manifest, in the 'literate expectations' which define the period. The continuity of a culture of documentation and law across conquest by Visigoths and Muslims, in the weak states of the northern Peninsula, must put an end to the reading of literacy against political history which gives us a Middle Ages of darkness and blindness; it calls for a new history.[1] But how broad, and how deep? Looking back, it is tempting to use practical or cultural proxies for a sense of ancient literacy and what came after, but there is no way to measure it with overall statistical accuracy for any premodern society, nor even if there were to be sure how much it counted.[2] Looking ahead, it is easy to get carried away by early modern book culture and imagine that everyone bought, sold, and consumed printed literature, but in the sixteenth and seventeenth centuries Spain was only just nearing and crossing the majority threshold for a basic ability to read or write. Literacy was greater amongst some groups than others, the clergy and nobility, artisans, the Morisco community, men: there were many factors at play, not least the attitude of the Counter-Reformation Church to mass education, and we should not think that the rate travelled solely in one direction.[3] We are somewhere in between, after an empire of literacy, before a republic of letters; reading and writing were surely minority abilities. Yet we are in a society framed by text, and the interest lies in the social and cultural

---

[1] Nelson, 'Ages', 191–201.
[2] Harris, *Literacy*, esp. 285–322; Humphrey (ed.), *Literacy*; Woolf, 'Illiteracy', 31–42.
[3] See *e.g.* Lawrance, 'Spread', 79–94; Tapia, 'Nivel', 481–502; Nalle, 'Literacy', 65–96; Castillo Gómez, *Escrituras*; Dadson, 'Literacy', 1011–37; Cruz and Hernández (eds), *Literacy*; Ares Legaspi, 'Alfabetización', 249–63.

*Text and Textuality in Early Medieval Iberia: The Written and The World, 711–1031.* Graham Barrett, Oxford University Press. © Graham Barrett 2023. DOI: 10.1093/oso/9780192895370.003.0008

ramifications, rather than the numbers. How did literacy reflect its users and how did its users reflect literacy?[4]

From the eighth century to the eleventh, ownership of property expanded to surmount local limits, entering communities which had made do with memory, and thereby incentivised engagement with documentation, especially by the laity. The enabling means followed suit, at one remove: the scribe, who drafted the charter and recorded all those involved in and present at its writing, then recycled its text into the community through a sympathetic public reading. Long before the high medieval notariate, the scribe mediated the document, and as his calling consolidated in the later tenth century, he became more fully a 'literate interpreter'. The charter too, once created and communicated, lived a long and active afterlife of dynamic circulation, made possible by multiple accessible archives, particularly in the hands of the clergy. Written evidence, after all, was the surest defence in case of dispute; charters were self-promoting in their mutual citation as well as practical efficacy in court. But they also functioned to diffuse a second order of knowledge: as each rhetorical, pragmatic, or implied citation of Visigothic law was read aloud by the scribe, how to capitalise on its provisions became better and more widely known, whence kings and counts seized the potential. For the clergy, Scripture, canon law, and monastic rules were the texts behind the text, and as they worked for and engaged in business with lay men and women, they embedded the charter in the story of salvation for all Christians, and modelled the contract to society through their monasteries as microcosms of a written framework. One outcome of this case study is thus to draw a clear distinction between literacy as the ability to read or write and literacy as textuality or the sociocultural meaning of text. The former may have been marginal, yet the latter was profound and growing.

What lends this distinction meaning is the intermediary role of scribes as creators and communicators of the written word, and that in turn makes their stubborn anonymity so much more noteworthy and frustrating. In one sense simple service providers, the meeting point for ecclesiastical and lay communities far from divided or opposed, they were more fully a living structure by which kings, counts, clergy, and the laity arranged to make such intensive use of charters, the channel through which they accessed, internalised, and were guided by so many other texts in their thoughts and actions. From a fundamental expectation of the written word, early medieval Iberian society organised itself around the person of the scribe to

---

[4] Hoggart, *Uses*, esp. 260–82.

compensate for the absence of generalised individual literacy, a cooperative relationship to use and reuse text from which new collectivities, councils and 'collations', arose and consolidated. Via the charter and the scribe, society and social arrangements came increasingly to be influenced by norms originating from a network of texts.

If we pause to take overall stock of this network and gauge the degree to which each document is an intertextuality, 1432 (35%) charters cite one or more of other charters, Visigothic law, the Bible, canons, or monastic rules (see Figure C.1). While textual citation becomes less common from west to centre to east, the practice remains ubiquitous. Most frequent in royal and comital

| | Citations | | Overall | |
|---|---|---|---|---|
| | # | % | # | % |
| Total | 1432 | 35 | 4095 | 100 |
| **Region** | | | | |
| West | 600 | 42 | 1284 | 31 |
| Centre | 659 | 46 | 2088 | 51 |
| East | 173 | 12 | 723 | 18 |
| **Personnel** | | | | |
| Royal | 297 | 21 | 522 | 13 |
| Comital | 25 | 2 | 71 | 2 |
| Ecclesiastical | 950 | 66 | 2710 | 66 |
| Lay | 158 | 11 | 769 | 19 |
| **Typology** | | | | |
| Donation | 1031 | 72 | 2212 | 54 |
| Sale | 155 | 11 | 1469 | 36 |
| Other | 246 | 17 | 411 | 10 |
| **Complexity** | | | | |
| Simple | 631 | 44 | 2797 | 68 |
| Complex | 801 | 56 | 1292 | 32 |
| **Palaeography** | | | | |
| Original | 297 | 21 | 888 | 22 |
| Copy | 152 | 11 | 261 | 6 |
| Cartulary | 863 | 60 | 2438 | 60 |
| Other | 120 | 8 | 507 | 12 |
| **Diplomatic** | | | | |
| Authentic | 1255 | 88 | 3781 | 92 |
| Suspicious | 9 | 1 | 24 | 1 |
| Interpolated | 43 | 3 | 57 | 1 |
| Falsified | 121 | 8 | 227 | 6 |

**Figure C.1** Charters Citing Texts

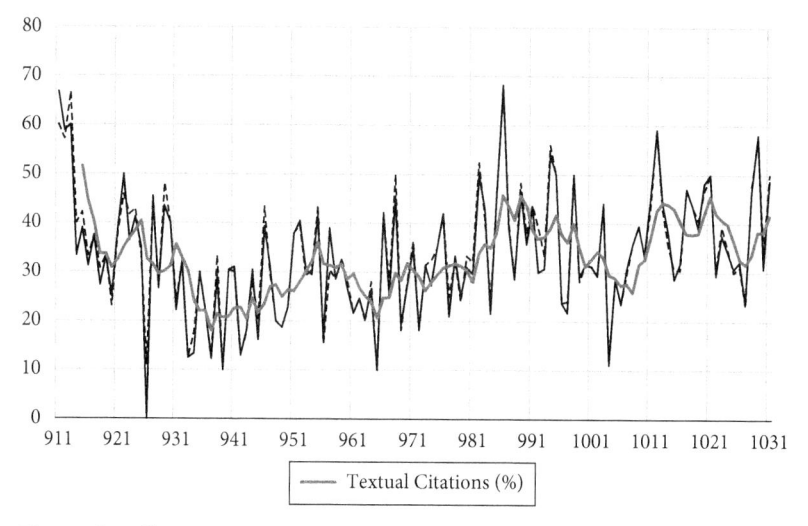

**Figure C.2** Charters Citing Texts (911–1031)

diplomas, it regularly factors in ecclesiastical and lay charters as well. Characteristic of complex transaction records, it is routine even so in documenting donations and miscellaneous other affairs. The stuff of tampering and forgery, it is scarcely less common in genuine charters original to the period. The impression of charters citing other texts is no mirage, nor the limited preserve of any region, social order, or type of business. And indeed, while 'textual citation' is present in between 20% and 50% of charters, broadly steady at 30% to 40%, there is an appreciable rise from the decade of the 970s onwards (see Figure C.2). This growth, as we have seen, is driven mainly by legal citation, but as often as half the time one engaged with a charter, in the role of granter, recipient, participant, witness, or audience, one engaged with a range of texts by way of it. Literacy has no fixed consequences, but plays out via social arrangements, and in early medieval Iberia, by an almost invisible medium, the full range of society made text a fundamental frame of reference for their actions.

## Two Questions

This preliminary treatment of the network of texts only scratches the surface: it is a prompt to look more sensitively for citation of literature in documentation, and more broadly at how documentary and literary discourses spoke to and influenced each other.[5] One charter from Celanova borrows language used by the chronicle cycle of Alfonso III for the churches of the Asturian kings and the construction of Santa Leocadia de Toledo by Sisebut (612–21), borrowed in turn from the *Lives of the Fathers of Mérida* for the building work of its bishop Masona in the late sixth century; an attentive listener would have heard a resonant boundary clause of antiquity, continuity, and legitimacy.[6] But it also raises two critical questions. The greater density of documentary culture in Galicia and Portugal calls for comment, and points to some difference from the centre and east at the level of deep structure. But what is it? The west stands out in one key respect: as soon as it appears in the historical record after 711, and before being incorporated into the Asturian kingdom, Galicia seems to have developed a class of wealthy, powerful magnates, whose cooperation the kings sought in expanding their realm. There is simply no recorded counterpart in the centre, much less the east, to the great families who founded and endowed Sobrado and Celanova in the first half of the tenth century.[7] This may speak to a higher concentration of landholding on a larger scale at an earlier date in the west, a more densely proprietorial society which gave rise to a more densely textual practice of acquiring, holding, claiming, and defending land. Do the inscribed boundary stones which seem to crop up everywhere reflect a more developed and conflictive density of settlement, a world of neighbours cheek by jowl with incentive to more sustained use of the written word? Certainly the open spaces beyond the mountains were not available as a pressure release here, but one could fight it out in court, armed with text. Notwithstanding these contrasts, however, the west and the centre shared the same documentary and textual culture, which could explain why and how Galicia remained part of the Leonese kingdom despite distance and aristocratic dynamism. The network of texts may be some segment of the skeleton, perhaps the whole of it, which gave the kingdom of León coherence, absent a strong court or bureaucracy. The real outlier is Castilla, and the east more generally, initially and increasingly apart until its sudden vaulting to hegemony in the eleventh century. The foundations of power were different there, might more than write; for caliphs in al-Andalus, it was the anxious target of campaign after campaign, where the others and their

---

[5]  Quetglas Nicolau, 'Nota', 313–19; Pérez González, 'Protocolos', 441–9; Zimmermann, 'Charter', 117–44; *cf.* Tock, 'Pères', esp. 414–18.
[6]  *Celanova* 86; *Chronicle of Albelda*, ed. Gil, *Chronica*, 14.24; *Chronicle of Alfonso III*, ed. Gil, *Chronica*, R12, R21, RS26; *Vitas sanctorum patrum Emeretensium*, ed. Maya Sánchez, *Vitas*, 5.3; *cf.* Nieto Alcaide, 'Imagen', 11–34; Dodds, *Architecture*, esp. 47–81; Velázquez, 'Valor', 261–8.
[7]  Portass, 'Quiet', 283–306; Isla, 'Aristocracy', 251–80; *cf.* Carvajal Castro, *Máscara*, 182–95.

charters commanded only the odd raid.[8] They were not wrong; and this may be the starting point for an Iberian history of power relations.[9]

The different presentation of textuality across the regions is one question, but a more basic problem to solve is the means of access to the source texts of the network of texts itself. If charters were readily available thanks to the portability of archives and a growing potential for cartularies, how were scribes able to consult as needed the Visigothic code, the Bible, the *Hispana*, and a panoply of monastic rules, the first three particularly long and unwieldy texts? The liturgy takes us so far as a means of transmission, but no farther; in León, where the law became such an important element of royal and aristocratic power, how was it read? At first glance, the charters offer little help in puzzling out the conundrum which they pose. Citation of books is far less common than of texts, and occurs in only 188 (5%) of the charters (see Figure C.3).[10] These citations are distributed unevenly in space: much more frequent in the west, especially at Samos, as well as at Oviedo and Santillana in the centre and at Valpuesta in the east. Books are mainly found in ecclesiastical charters: in complex transactions, donations, and monastic pacts, though in a few outlying sales. They are an element of interpolated and forged charters, and thus in single-sheet copies, but neither authenticity nor transmission is a key factor in the distribution. The basic problem is that books are not documented often enough, or in the right places, geographically (León?) or socially (the laity?), for 'literary citation' to explain by itself the constant recourse of charters to other texts. The same is true of time, as the citations come mostly in the period 850–930, the age of religious foundation, and lessen thereafter (see Figure C.4).

There has been much useful study of books in early medieval Iberia, but most of it has aimed at reconstructing the libraries of institutions or individuals, or to trace the effects of the 'Mozarabic migration' on literary culture in the north of the Peninsula.[11] Such fixed libraries are important, not least because books jostled together with charters as well as vestments and plate in the treasuries of monasteries and churches.[12] Collections of *liturgica*, Patristics, and to a lesser degree Classics can be inventoried from

[8] Manzano Moreno, *Corte*, 201–34; *cf.* Escalona Monge, 'Comunidades', 85–120; Escalona, 'Stress', 341–67.

[9] Kosto, 'Spain', 157–8; Bianchini, 'Review', 1167–9.

[10] *Floriano*, 1, 570–1, 2, 694–703.

[11] Shailor, 'Scriptorium', 444–73; Pérez de Urbel, 'Cardeña', 217–37; Díaz y Díaz, *Códices*, 149–246; Díaz y Díaz, *Libros*, 53–276; Díaz y Díaz, *Manuscritos*, 63–91, 137–79; Ruiz Asencio, 'Escribas', 151–74; Díaz y Díaz, *Asturias*, 19–30; Yarza Luaces, '*Scriptoria*', 65–88; García Lobo, 'Calígrafos', 2, 19–44; Collins, *Caliphs*, 107–9; *cf.* Faulhaber, *Libros*; Beceiro Pita, *Libros*.

[12] Palazzo, 'Livre', 93–118; Carriedo Tejedo, 'Libros', esp. 36–44, 55–62.

| | Citations | | Overall | |
|---|---|---|---|---|
| | # | % | # | % |
| Total | 188 | 5 | 4095 | 100 |
| **Region** | | | | |
| West | 93 | 49 | 1284 | 31 |
| Centre | 61 | 32 | 2088 | 51 |
| East | 34 | 18 | 723 | 18 |
| **Personnel** | | | | |
| Royal | 17 | 9 | 522 | 13 |
| Comital | 2 | 1 | 71 | 2 |
| Ecclesiastical | 169 | 90 | 2710 | 66 |
| Lay | 0 | 0 | 769 | 19 |
| **Typology** | | | | |
| Donation | 164 | 87 | 2212 | 54 |
| Sale | 7 | 4 | 1469 | 36 |
| Other | 17 | 9 | 411 | 10 |
| **Complexity** | | | | |
| Simple | 95 | 51 | 2797 | 68 |
| Complex | 93 | 49 | 1292 | 32 |
| **Palaeography** | | | | |
| Original | 29 | 15 | 888 | 22 |
| Copy | 30 | 16 | 261 | 6 |
| Cartulary | 114 | 61 | 2438 | 60 |
| Other | 15 | 8 | 507 | 12 |
| **Diplomatic** | | | | |
| Authentic | 160 | 85 | 3781 | 92 |
| Suspicious | 0 | 0 | 24 | 1 |
| Interpolated | 8 | 4 | 57 | 1 |
| Falsified | 19 | 10 | 227 | 6 |

**Figure C.3** Charters Mentioning Books

charters of endowment; they are typically approached from the perspective of the beneficiaries, but the same charters witness the books, liturgical and literary, of their royal, episcopal, ecclesiastical, and lay granters, the collections existing before those assembled by monasteries and churches.[13]

---

[13] Sáez, 'Inventario', 563–8; García Álvarez, 'Libros', 292–329; Sánchez-Albornoz, 'Notas', 273–91; Collins, 'Literacy', 125–7; Linage Conde, 'Caminares', 103–22; Gómez-Moreno, *Iglesias*, 345–53; Sueiro Pena, 'Bibliotecas', 3, 429–45; Davies, 'Local Priests in Northern Iberia', 139–42; Carriedo Tejedo, 'Libros', 33–44; Gouveia, 'Inventário', 167–96; *cf.* Pérez de Urbel and González y Ruiz-Zorrilla, *Liber*, 1, xiii–xxxii; Fábrega Grau, *Pasionario*, 1, 9–15; Zimmermann, *Écrire*, 1, 467–618.

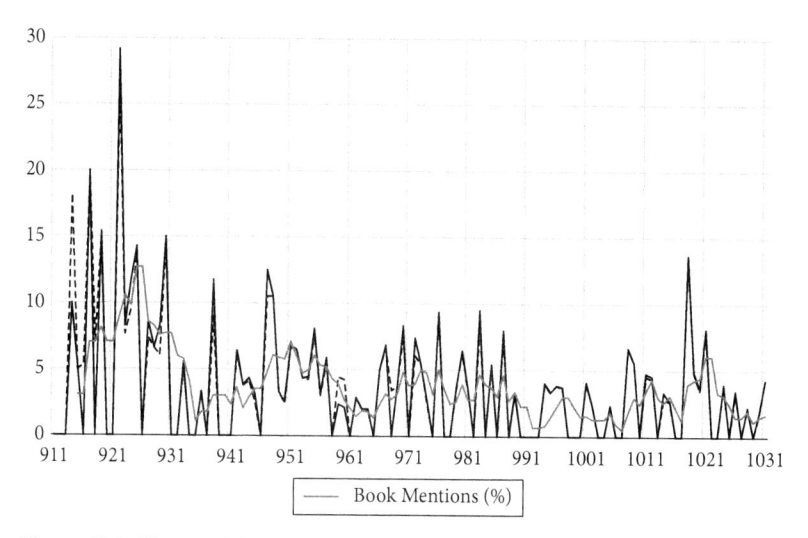

**Figure C.4**  Charters Mentioning Books (911–1031)

Even so, in spite of libraries at all levels of society, the components of the network of texts cited in the charters are rarely catalogued in the corpus of documentation, and this is especially true of the Visigothic code. The manuscripts reflect three broad traditions of use made of the law, in Catalunya, La Rioja, and León and Castilla. Down to the end of the eleventh century there are 20 copies, but 12 belong to the Catalan tradition.[14] The remaining 'occidental' manuscripts include the Codex Albeldensis (or Vigilanus) of 976 and related Codex Aemilianensis of 992–4, famous for their rich illustrative programmes evocative of the Visigothic past, yet they seem to have been produced in the east, in La Rioja or the Pyrenees, where law is cited least often.[15] Three or four charters from Galicia do mention copies in circulation: Beatus *presbiter* gave a *libro iudicum* (book of judges), amongst many others, to San Salvador de Arnoia in 889, the endowment of Celanova by its aristocratic founders in 938 included *libros psalterio I et goticum I* (one Psalter, one Gothic [legal? liturgical?] book), Sisnandus *presbiter* donated a *librum goticum* to Santa María de Barbadelo

[14] Díaz y Díaz, 'Lex', 183–224; García López, 'Tradición', 381–415; García López, *Estudios*, esp. 7–37; Millares Carlo, *Corpus*, 48–9, 193, 247; Collins, *Visigothic Spain*, 223–46; *cf.* Gibert, 'Enseñanza', 39–40.
[15] González Díez, 'Liber', 163–84; Herrero de la Fuente and Fernández Flórez, 'Códice', 117–74; *cf.* Reynolds, 'Civitas', 3, 153–84.

in 967, and the celebrated countess Adosinda Gudestéiz made a rich donation including a *librum iudicum* to San Martiño de Lalín in 1019, taken together hinting at a broader hinterland.[16] But what of León?

The same mismatch of survival and use is appreciable, if less acutely so, for the other texts of the network. We have just six early medieval manuscript copies of the canons: three from La Rioja, including the same two renowned Codices, and three from Sahagún, Celanova, and an unknown scriptorium.[17] To add to this, charters from the west and centre cite a further ten copies, such as in those gifts by Beatus in 889 and Sisnandus in 967, and the restoration undertaken by Abbot Diego, who gave a *canonicum* together with other *libros ecclesiasticos* (ecclesiastical books) to San Antolín in 1026.[18] Somewhat greater than the traces of the code, yet all the more discordant as such with the exiguous rate of canonical versus legal citation in the charters. The evidence for books is substantially out of alignment with the reference made to their contents. Somewhat of a better fit is the documented distribution of monastic rules. We have six early medieval manuscripts of the *corpus regularum*, eight of the Benedictine rule, and in keeping with what we have encountered in practice, there is significant overlap between these groupings: the famous early tenth-century codex linked to Leodegundia, an Asturian princess and Navarrese queen, combines the indigenous rules with an extract from Benedict and much else besides. Both series begin in the ninth century (which really should retire the notion that some 'regular citations' are too early to be genuine), and the majority of them come from the east, where monasteries and rules are most closely associated.[19] And indeed, the rules which we can identify precisely in the documentation fit this picture of mixed practice, if not quite the geographical distribution of citation. When Mumadona Dias endowed Guimarães in 959, she included two *regulas*, a set of the monastic handbooks of Pachomius, Ambrose, Benedict, Isidore, Fructuosus, and Leander, and a similar *libellum* (booklet); expressed more concisely, Bishop Cixila gave Abellar *regularum*

---

[16] *Celanova* 7, 57; *Samos* 91; *Lugo* 55; *cf. León* 75; Gibert, 'Enseñanza', 32–6; Díaz y Díaz, 'Lex', 178–82; Collins, 'Law', 509–10, Collins, 'Literacy', 126, 129; Prieto Prieto, 'Potestad', 544; Castro, 'Aspectos', 135; Casado de Otaola, 'Cultura', 53–4.

[17] Millares Carlo, *Corpus*, 48–51, 139, 157; Martínez Díez, 'Colección', 135–61.

[18] *Celanova* 7; *Samos* 91, 7; *cf.* 43; *Guimarães* 1A, A3; *Bóveda* 2; *Astorga* 12; *Sahagún* 30, 32; *León* 76.

[19] Díaz y Díaz, *Códices*, 89–114; Millares Carlo, *Corpus*, 108; 42, 55, 91, 154, 200; 142, 175, 186, 203, 221, 281, 338; *cf.* Ruiz Asencio, '*Libellus*', 175–200; Varela Rodríguez, 'Autores', 495–504.

*septem in uno corpore* (seven rules bound together) in 927.[20] Certainly there is reason here to imagine greater availability of copies of the key rules, but enough for their presence in the charters acting as substitutes for monasteries themselves?

The transmission history of the Bible in Iberia suggests that we may be coming at the problem from the wrong direction. Nine contemporary copies are preserved, representing the Vulgate and Vetus Latina Hispana versions, and they concentrate in eastern scriptoria.[21] The charters, however, give scant sign of Scripture *in toto*: in the 950s, when Munna drew up her testament to Lorvão *cum una biblioteca*, did she mean with a library or with 'the Library'?[22] The term is listed amongst other books in the endowments of Celanova and Guimarães, and therefore likely denotes the Bible, but it is attested nowhere else.[23] What of its components? Charters cite verses from the Psalms more than from any other Biblical book. We have nine copies of the Psalter, all where identifiable from Castilla or La Rioja, and documents make recurrent and widespread reference to further manuscripts, now lost: a *psalterium perfectum* (complete Psalter) given once again by Sisnandus *presbiter* to Barbadelo in 967, two books of Psalms donated by Emeritus *presbiter* to a monastery of San Cosme y San Damián in 875, and three made over by Fernando Flaínez and Geloira to San Martín de Benevívere in 1020, even seven enumerated in the foundation charter of Lourenzá from 969.[24] When the sainted Bishop Genadio of Astorga endowed his many foundations in 915, he gave each a Psalter, evidently regarding it as a basic part of the monastic library.[25] The example of the Psalms counsels against assuming that our source texts circulated as wholes, and another ten surviving Scriptural codices, in fact, spanning east to west in their provenances, are made up of selections, ranging from single books of the Old or New Testament to the Epistles, and even a complete Bible from

---

[20] *Guimarães* 1A, A3; *León* 75; cf. 42, 412; *Sahagún* 269; *Samos* S2; *Sobrado* 1.2; *Celanova* 95; *Lugo* 55; *Caaveiro* 1.

[21] Millares Carlo, *Corpus*, 30, 33, 80, 96–7, 138, 146, 215, 281.

[22] *Coimbra* 56; cf. *Sahagún* 39; *León* 76; Tischler, ' "Bibliotheca" ', 559–80.

[23] *Celanova* 72; *Guimarães* 1A, A3.

[24] Millares Carlo, *Corpus*, 24, 45, 115, 126, 205–6, 270, 341, 340; *Samos* 91; *Valpuesta* 5; *Benevívere* 1; *Lourenzá* 1–2; cf. *León* 42, 220, 412, *Sahagún* 29–30, 32, 114, *Oviedo* 12, *Samos* 33, 43, 226, 129, 99, *Sobrado* 1.1–2, *Celanova* 7, 57, 95, *Coruña* 19, 110, *Pallares* 2, *Lourenzá* 185, *Melón* 1, *Coimbra* 142, *Valpuesta* 6, Martínez Díez, *Colección* 37, *San Millán* 234, 526; *León* 611, *Samos* 7, *Caaveiro* 1, *Bóveda* 2; *León* 75, 777, *Sahagún* 352, *Santillana* 4, *Celanova* 326; *Samos* 64.

[25] *Astorga* 12; cf. *Samos* S2.

the Psalter onwards.[26] Thinking of these as 'incomplete' texts is to miss the contemporary context, and the point; charters mention such copies of the Pentateuch, Ruth, Chronicles, Tobit, Judith, Esther, Job, and Ezekiel, while Rosendo planned to supplement his own gift of Ezekiel and the Epistles to a monastery of San Vicente in 867 with Job and the Psalms—if he lived to transcribe them.[27] Holy Scripture runs on, and is easier handled in parts.[28] But then so do the Visigothic code and the *Hispana*. What the mismatch between citations and codices tells us is that complete copies of texts cannot have been a precondition for making use of their content. Just as we had to let go of the singularity of text to encompass the full scope of charters built out of citations, we must also rethink texts in light of the dynamic afterlife of charters.

What we need is a more flexible alternative to whole books held in fixed libraries, and we find the first sign of it in a remarkable charter without parallel in the corpus. San Genadio drafted his will in 915, and amongst his other bequests he established a circulating library for the religious communities of Astorga.[29] The text begins by endowing each of his foundations— San Pedro de Montes, San Andrés de Montes, Santiago de Peñalba, and an oratory of Santo Tomás—with a similar, though not identical, set of liturgical books. The first house uniquely received a *canonicum*, the last only a *psalterium*. The voice of Genadio then observes that, as man lives not on bread alone but on the Word from the mouth of God, *caeteros libros quam divinos* (the remaining divine books), a *bibliotecam totam* (whole library or Library), should belong jointly to all brothers in the four foundations, to share amongst themselves and never to alienate. The substantial collection catalogued thereafter includes Scripture, hagiography, theology, treatises by Isidore of Seville, and many other works. In a final codicil he adds that any further oratories built in the mountains should participate in these *specialibus libris*, and so the first lending library of El Bierzo was born.[30] The testament of San Genadio is unique in its details, but it provides a model for thinking about how a limited number of manuscripts of texts might have reached and influenced a much larger audience. The arrangement described may also be reflected in a charter of Samos from 922 which lists both the

[26]   Millares Carlo, *Corpus*, 41, 56, 105, 123, 132, 181, 225, 235, 294, 308.
[27]   *Coruña* 4; cf. *León* 75; *Astorga* 12; *Samos* 33; *Celanova* 72; *Pallares* 2; *Caaveiro* 1; *Lourenzá* 10.
[28]   Petitmengin, 'Bible', 31–53.
[29]   *Astorga* 12; Linage Conde, 'Caminares', 53–7; Gallon, 'Monachisme', 37–75; Álvarez Rodríguez, *Testamento*.
[30]   Carriedo Tejedo, 'Libros', 40–1; Martín Viso, 'Memory', 177–84.

*libros eglesiastes* of the monastery and *libros spirituales* held there and in two dependent houses, dedicated to San Cristóbal and San Juan, possibly even a truncated third.[31] And the same too is implicit in donations of books to churches of San Pedro and San Vicente in 927 and 952, said to be put in the hands or under the regime of Bishop Rosendo, seemingly belonging to subsidiaries of Celanova.[32] Monastic networks could double as common treasuries of the written word.

Beyond these circumstances, if we attune ourselves not to retention but to circulation we can spot both institutional and personal libraries on the move.[33] When the heirs of Indura *presbiter* and Amores donated their church of San Emiliano to Sahagún in 925, they itemised the accompanying books, which included liturgical texts, a *canonicum*, and a Psalter, just as Unisco and her son Oseredo, giving the monastery of Leça to Vacariça in 1021, inventoried in its library a *regula*, a Psalter, and a *passionum de Sancti Asciscli usque Sancto Sebastiano* (a partial Visigothic passionary running from San Acisclo to San Sebastián).[34] Books—even *libros nimis habundanter*, far too many of them—changed hands as their institutional homes changed ownership, the same as charters followed the property which they document. When Taiellus *diaconus* bestowed San Esteban de Elaba on Riciulfo *presbiter* in 889, he explicitly included both liturgical *libros* and *omnes libros ecclesiasticos sive testamenta eclesie* (all the ecclesiastical books and testaments of the church), while Velasco Monnioz and family listed seven liturgical texts amongst the other appurtenances in their gift of a series of *villas* to San Salvador de Boñar in 996, an intriguing case of books in a secular setting.[35] Of course, some mentions of *libros* amidst lands, vineyards, orchards, and the like may be formulaic, and yet there would not be a formula were book transfer not routine enough to call for one.[36]

Libraries were mobile in the same ways as were people and their possessions. Abbot Offiloni and his companions, on restoring the monastery of Samos in 872, enumerated *libros speciales et eclesiasticos* (special and ecclesiastical books) which they had brought with them from Córdoba,

[31] *Samos* S2; *cf.* 129; Sueiro Pena, 'Bibliotecas', 440–1.
[32] *Celanova* 27, 95; *cf. Astorga* 74.
[33] Casado de Otaola, 'Escribir', 128–37; *cf.* Petrucci, 'Literacy', 101–2; Bertelli, 'Production', 41–60.
[34] *Sahagún* 32; *Coimbra* 142; Couceiro, 'Acisclo', 132; *cf. Samos* 99, 91; *Celanova* 7; Martínez Díez, *Colección* 37; *San Millán* 526.
[35] *Sobrado* 1.110; *Oviedo* 12; *Sahagún* 352; *cf. Celanova* 196.
[36] See *e.g. Santillana* 12–13, 18; *Tumbo C* 1.

alongside others which they had found there.[37] Families too took care of their books, and when Fafila *confessor* endowed San Vicente on the Miño in 952, he gave to it his *libros pernominatos* (itemised books), as well as five liturgical codices which had belonged to his brother; Theoda and Aragonti inherited a set of nine liturgical and spiritual texts from their father, and while they may have left them to Piasca, the family retained the right of disposal, and confirmed them in a charter of 930.[38] Perhaps the most common context for glimpsing a personal library in motion is entrance into a monastic *familia*, such as in 1018, when Frissila Annaya delivered himself to Santillana, body and soul, together with property inherited from his parents, *libros* included.[39] Even so, one did not just hand over the books and forget about them. In 917, an abbot gave to Felicia Monnoia *conversa* and the sisters of Santiago de León assorted property, a monastery, a pair of churches, and three books, *antiphonario psalterio et regula* (an antiphonary, a Psalter, and a monastic rule), the standard complement of key texts for a religious house, and when in 970 the long-lived lady, now abbess, made a testament of the same property to that institution, she enumerated the familiar *antiphonario uno psalterio uno et regula*.[40] These were her books, they formed her own collection, and they still retained their special identity after 53 years sitting on the shelves of the library of her monastery.

The background to moving libraries is illuminated by the rare charters in which books are the object of transaction, implying a market economy for the written word.[41] The property given to São João de Ver by Cagido and other priests in 773 (or 902, or 973) was professedly to spend *pro volumine librorum in locis illius ad ecclesie deserviendum* (on the collection of books belonging to the church on site), indicating that land and goods could be translated into the production or acquisition of manuscripts.[42] Indeed, by a charter of 796, certain clerics in the Liébana partly donated and partly sold property in Villeña to Episcopario (a pseudonym?) and his fellow *gasalianes* (house-dwellers), for a price: an ox and a cow with calf, each worth a *solidus* and a *tremis*, and three books, that is, an antiphonary worth three *solidi*, an orational worth two *solidi*, and a *comicu* (lectionary) worth two *solidi*. These

---

[37]  *Samos* 5; *cf.* 43; *Sahagún* 29–30.
[38]  *Celanova* 95; *Sahagún* 39.
[39]  *Santillana* 22; *cf. San Millán* 423; *Covarrubias* 12; *Cardeña* 40; *Arlanza* 22.
[40]  *León* 42, 412; Mariño-Veiras, 'Religiosas', 130; *cf. Lugo* 8.
[41]  Sánchez-Albornoz, 'Precio', 398; Godoy, 'Escribientes', 92–3; *cf.* McKitterick, *Carolingians*, 133–64.
[42]  *Coimbra* 454; *Floriano* 166; Gouveia, 'Inventário', 179, 190; *cf. Coimbra* 129, 161.

books had market value, just like land, and they were specifically confirmed and enumerated in the sanction clause of the document recording their change of ownership.[43] Still more directly, Araspio and his wife and children sold property in Pando to Severus *presbiter* and his *regulantes* (rule-followers) in 929 for a price of two antiphonaries and one ordinal, valued in total at six *solidi*: possibly though by no means necessarily the books were for Munnio *presbiter*, one of the children of the vendor, who was provisioned here at the expense of family land.[44] There are hints in the manuscript evidence that monasteries copied liturgical and other texts for each other; perhaps there are sales contracts awaiting discovery and publication.[45] What is certain is that a market existed for literary material, and that text served as currency in transaction. Those who had need to stock their libraries could do so for a price: there were books available for sale.

What if a library were out of reach, or one lacked a literary inheritance or the means to pay for a copy? Informally, partially, books also circulated piecemeal, in extracts on spare parchment to hand. Here at last we come to León and the law: Fredesindo *confrater*, together with his heirs, brothers, nephews, and *fratres*, made a donation to the monastery of Eslonza in 950 of some *bustos* (pasture), which a son of Alfonso III had demarcated for his ancestors, in order to retire a debt of nine *modii* of wheat in value. Ordinary enough, yet transcribed on the reverse of the original charter is the text of two laws from the Visigothic code (see Figure C.5).[46] As we have already had occasion to consider, the transaction seems related to the legislation, regulating the care of animals on loan; the laws are written by a hand and in a script distinct from the main text of the charter, however, indicating a different context or the involvement of another agent. Whatever the precise circumstances, the clear implication is that, soon after the trans-action had been completed, a scribe jotted down two laws which he considered to be relevant to Eslonza and its affairs. No case study could offer more to resolve how our sources circulated, how they were so widely known: fragmentary libraries were the means of access. At the same time, it gives us a glimpse of possible constraints: the scribe was working with a defective exemplar, and the transcription which he made is missing some text in the middle of each line. Others will have had access to better, more complete texts; the social history of such circulation remains to be written.

[43] *Liébana* 2; Gautier-Dalché, 'Royaume', 81–2.
[44] *Valpuesta* 13; Líbano Zumalacárregui, 'Génesis', 48; *cf. San Millán* 524; *Santillana* 41.
[45] Collins, 'Continuity', 2–5; Hornby and Maloy, *Music*, 7–8.
[46] *Eslonza* 24; *LV* 5.5.1–2; Barrett, 'Text', 52–3.

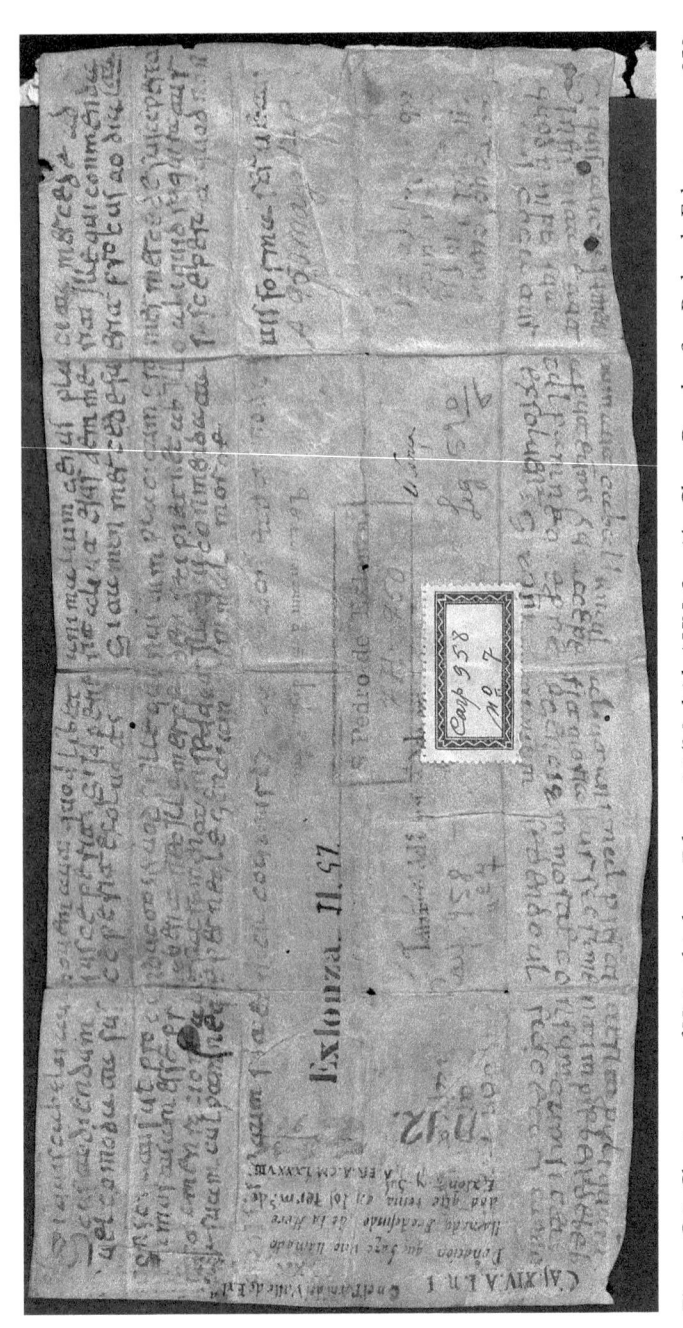

**Figure C.5** Charter copy of Visigothic laws: *Eslonza* 24 (Madrid, AHN, Sección Clero, Regular, San Pedro de Eslonza, carp. 958, no. 7, dorso: Archivo Histórico Nacional. CLERO-SECULAR_REGULAR,Car.958.N.7)

This mode of transmission could stand in too for the glossing activity so common in Catalunya and so absent here in spite of everyday use of the law.[47] And there are more of these fragmentary libraries waiting to be found. On the reverse of a charter from 1007, a sale in consequence of a court case to Pedro Flaínez and his wife, are 25 lines from the *Liber commicus* (lectionary, a neologism, 'companion' or maybe 'arranged, assembled'), a core component of the liturgy, the text of which is laid out in one column with none of the preparation typical for a codex copy.[48] Precisely: this and other partial texts need to be reassessed, not as failures or fragments but as channels to books, while books need to be appreciated for their potential production of such parts.[49] In a society with limited individual literacy, widespread use of the written word was founded on the scribe; in default of universal access to manuscript copies of books, the interconnection of text with text was made possible by the capillary dissemination of their contents in fractions of the whole.

## The Temple of Text

The textual society of early medieval Iberia was built on the foundations of a textual economy, a network of texts in circulation, a written framework for practice always, though not always directly, accessible to its practitioners. Citations of other charters, Visigothic law, Holy Scripture, the canons, and monastic rules constituted the imaginary libraries held in the minds of scribes. But how did they collect them? First by direct consultation: in the stationary libraries of monasteries and churches, possessions of their royal, episcopal, ecclesiastical, and lay patrons. If none were available, it would not be long to wait, for such libraries circulated constantly, changing hands with institutions and individuals as endowments, appurtenances, or the objects of transaction, given incidentally or shared by design in overarching religious structures; these books were aware of their own mobility.[50] Scribes too may have simply remembered their sources from a moment of contact, like the verses of Scripture cited in charters through the intermediary of that liturgy which is omnipresent in the documentary inventories of libraries. Should all this still seem inadequate explanation,

---

[47] Davies, *Windows*, 235–7; *cf.* Alturo *et al.*, *Liber*, 256–70, 635–785.
[48] *Otero* 73; Díaz y Díaz, 'Manuscritos', 77–85; Baldwin, 'Meaning', 439–43.
[49] Perry, 'Sum', 106–26.      [50] Brown, 'Present', 28–40.

recall how they mastered the craft: by copying other charters. Scribes passed on knowledge to other scribes, but charters served as models and resources for further guidance. Charters were conserved, consulted, copied, and circulated as long as they were needed, and thus so too were the fragments of sources which they cited; contact with an actual codex of part or all of a given text could have come as rarely as once every few generations and yet sufficed, while informal copies supplemented both as necessary, when memory and mimesis failed.[51] For some, the Visigothic code must only have existed in charters, as fragments with power. No less for being by such means, scribes could reach out and find a network of texts within easy grasp, to stock the shelves of their imaginary libraries; the advantage in the texts was for their employers to realise, but a textual economy provided the potential.

What was text in early medieval Iberia? For most writers, readers, and listeners, the part was the whole: fragments were the framework. We need to redefine what 'knowing' a text meant in terms recognisable to this world. For some, the fact of charters, law, Scripture, canons, or rules was enough to shape behaviour, and this level of textuality mattered no less then for seeming superficial to us now. For others, scattered passages, sentences, or words from texts seen or heard directly perhaps as rarely as once (if ever), but transcribed or remembered at whatever distance, were the reality of the larger work—to us its real, complete form. This is the textuality of imperfect knowledge: the minority with books and libraries at their disposal enjoyed greater advantage, a fuller armoury of written resources for deployment, but personal access to books was not straightforwardly a limiting factor in the balance of power, so long as texts lived in extracts and citations, in the mind. We confront early medieval books as books, as discrete and integral, and we interpret them as such, but for the majority of their audience, their users, they were only the fragments in use. Books had their hidden knowledge, but they could speak their secrets too.[52] What did the charter, a patchwork of pieces, sound like when the scribe read it aloud? All those layers of borrowed language, quoted and paraphrased, late Roman and Visigothic sources jostling words and spellings of contemporary invention, must collectively have emphasised the reality of its intertextuality, and impressed upon everyone in earshot the breadth and depth of the network animating every stage in its lifecycle.[53]

---

[51] Small, *Tablets*, esp. 47–63, 156–97; Bourgain, 'Circulation', 140–8.
[52] Böse, 'Books', 49–64.
[53] Boscá Codina, 'Voz', 139–75.

**Figure C.6** John receives the Scroll and measures the Temple (Morgan Beatus, New York, NY, Morgan Library, MS M.644, fol. 146r: The Morgan Library & Museum, New York)

Early medieval Iberia was bonded by text, but not as we know it. In the rich tradition of illustrated copies of the commentary on Revelation by Beatus of the Liébana a correlation is embedded which can speak to the nature of this world of the written. The Morgan Beatus, copied in the mid-tenth century, is illustrative: quite unlike the more conventionally formed books of Carolingian and Ottonian illumination, the letters sent to the seven churches of Asia have an odd shape to them, a box with a triangular top, the same as the Book of Life held by Christ in majesty, presiding at Judgement Day. And we see the same form in the Temple of God, which John was told to measure after he had eaten the Scroll of the Word (see Figure C.6).[54] All writing was sacralised, as a portable tabernacle in miniature; once measured, the Temple defined and described the heavenly Jerusalem, and when it descended to earth at the last, the elect would be encompassed by the text, the damned left beyond its margins. Beatus wrote of these final days without being wholly convinced of their imminence, but the imagery inspired by his work was at once a warning and a wellspring of comfort for meeting death in Christian hope, with the shared prospect of God wiping away every tear as all the former things passed away.[55] For Beatus and his illustrators, text on earth was a key to text in heaven; for the kings and counts, the clergy and commoners who had daily recourse to the written word, the charter was a passageway resounding with strange yet familiar and commanding voices, imbued with the same nature, the same purpose as the Book of Life itself. Confronted by a promise of such grace, we might be forgiven for forgetting that only one text was truly lasting and complete:

> Do not think in your spirit or say in your heart that you do not know or do not see that every sin is every day recorded in Heaven in the presence of the Most High. You know now that all your oppression whereby you oppress is written down every day until the day of your judgement.[56]

When the charter of donation prayed for the charter of sin to be erased in salvation, it offered that donor false hope; this law will still be with us and this final text still perfect at the end of time, when all things will be written anew.

---

[54] Revelation 1:11, 10:8–10, 11:1–2, 20:11–15; New York, NY, Morgan Library, MS M.644 (*ca.* 940–5), fols 231v, 83r, 146r; Williams and Shailor, *Apocalypse*; Williams, *Visions*, 69–72, 167–8, 180–1, 202–3; *cf.* Cotter, 'Book', esp. 107–12; Cowling, *Building*, 139–69; Ruiz García, 'Escritura', 71–92; Denoël, 'L'Épiphanie', 15–26.

[55] Palmer, *Apocalypse*, 141–2, 145, 152–4; *cf.* Rosenwein, *Communities*, 57–78.

[56] I Enoch 98:7–8; Frye, *Code*, 135–8.

# Appendices

**Appendix 1** List of Regnal Dates

| Kingdom of Asturias | |
|---|---|
| Pelayo | 718/22–37 |
| Favila | 737–9 |
| Alfonso I | 739–57 |
| Fruela I | 757–68 |
| Aurelio | 768–74 |
| Silo | 774–83 |
| Alfonso II | 783 |
| Mauregato | 783–8/9 |
| Vermudo I | 788/9–91 |
| Alfonso II | 791–842 |
| Nepociano | 842 |
| Ramiro I | 842–50 |
| Ordoño I | 850–66 |
| Alfonso III | 866–910 |

| Kingdom of León | |
|---|---|
| García I | 910–14 |
| Ordoño II | 914–24 |
| Fruela II | 924–5 |
| Alfonso IV | 925–31 |
| Ramiro II | 931–50/1 |
| Ordoño III | 950/1–6 |
| Sancho I | 956–8 |
| Ordoño IV | 958–9 |
| Sancho I | 959–66 |
| Ramiro III | 966–84 |
| Vermudo II | 982/4–99 |
| Alfonso V | 999–1028 |
| Vermudo III | 1028–37 |

| County of Castilla | |
|---|---|
| Fernán González | 931/2–70 |
| García Fernández | 970–95 |
| Sancho García | 995–1017 |
| García Sánchez | 1017–29 |

*Continued*

**Appendix 1** Continued

|  |  |
|---|---|
| **Kingdom of Navarra** | |
| Íñigo Arista | 824–51/2 |
| García Íñiguez | 851/2–82 |
| Fortún Garcés | 882–905 |
| Sancho Garcés I | 905–25 |
| Jimeno Garcés | 925–32/3 |
| García Sánchez I | 925–71 |
| Sancho Garcés II | 971–95 |
| García Sánchez II | 995–1004 |
| Sancho Garcés III | 1004–35 |

**Appendix 2**  Astorga: Concordance of Charters and Corrected Dates

| *Astorga* | Date |
|---|---|
| 2 | 16 May 857 |
| 3 | 28 Oct 877 |
| 4 | Nov 877 |
| 5 | [6 June/10 Nov 878] |
| 6 | 18 Mar 883 |
| 7 | 4 Oct 894 |
| 8 | 2 Feb 895 |
| 9 | 18 Mar 912 |
| 10 | 1 Sept 912 |
| 11 | 28 May 915 |
| 12 | 915 |
| 13 | 8 Jan 916 |
| 14 | 28 Sept 916 |
| 15 | 28 Sept 916 |
| 16 | 28 Sept 916 |
| 18 | 28 Jan 919 |
| 19 | 1 Oct 920 |
| 21 | 17 Sept 921 |
| 22 | 922 |
| 23 | 922 |
| 24 | 4 Jan 923 |
| 25 | 26 June 923 |
| 26 | 25 Feb 924 |
| 27/41 | [18 May 924] |
| 28 | 15 Apr 925 |
| 29 | 1 Aug 925 |
| 31 | 926 |
| 32 | 13 June 927 |
| 33 | 17 Nov 927 |
| 34 | 24 Sept 928 |

| Astorga | Date |
|---|---|
| 35 | 13 June 929 |
| 36 | 14 Jan 931 |
| 37 | 6 June 932 |
| 38 | 18 Oct 933 |
| 43 | 1 Feb 935 |
| 44 | 28 Apr 935 |
| 45 | 12 Dec 935 |
| 135 | [29 Apr 936] |
| 48 | 9 Feb 937 |
| 49 | 1 Aug 937 |
| 51 | 13 Jan 938 |
| 52 | 14 July 938 |
| 53 | 26 Feb 939 |
| 54 | 9 Oct 939 |
| 55 | 11 Apr 940 |
| 56 | 22 Oct 940 |
| 57 | 8 Nov 940 |
| 58 | 1 Jan 943 |
| 59 | 13 Apr 943 |
| 60 | 13 Apr 943 |
| 61 | 21 Jan 944 |
| 62 | 18 Mar 945 |
| 63 | 17 June 945 |
| 64 | 1 Sept 946 |
| 66 | 1 Sept 946 |
| 65 | 5 Sept 946 |
| 67 | 4 Nov 946 |
| 68 | 1 Aug 947 |
| 69 | 20 May 952 |
| 70/71 | 1 Oct 952 |
| 50 | 937–52 |
| 72 | 25 Mar 953 |
| 73 | 953 |
| 74 | 7 Mar 954 |
| 75 | 28 Apr 954 |
| 76 | 22 May 954 |
| 77/47 | [16 Nov 954] |
| 78 | 23 Dec 954 |
| 79 | 22 Jan 955 |
| 80 | 25 Jan 955 |
| 81 | 15 Dec 955 |
| 82 | 1 Apr 956 |
| 83/30/46 | [15 June 956] |
| 84 | 24 Dec 956 |
| 85 | 29 Apr 958 |
| 86 | 4 May 958 |
| 87 | 28 June 959 |

*Continued*

**Appendix 2** Continued

| Astorga | Date |
| --- | --- |
| 88 | 7 Jan 960 |
| 89 | 31 July 960 |
| 90 | 5 Aug 960 |
| 91 | 5 Aug 960 |
| 92/93 | [30 Sept 960] |
| 94 | 1 Nov 960 |
| 95 | 960 |
| 96 | 26 Jan 961 |
| 97 | 12 Feb 962 |
| 98 | 26 Feb 962 |
| 99 | 3 Apr 962 |
| 100 | 9 Apr 962 |
| 101 | 11 Apr 962 |
| 102 | 15 Apr 962 |
| 103 | 14 Oct 962 |
| 104 | 23 Oct 962 |
| 105 | 962 |
| 106 | 23 Jan 963 |
| 107 | 27 Jan 963 |
| 108 | 22 Feb 963 |
| 110 | 17 Mar 963 |
| 111 | 24 June 963 |
| 109 | 1 July 963 |
| 112 | 5 Jan 964 |
| 113 | 22 Feb 964 |
| 114 | 22 Feb 965 |
| 115 | 30 Dec 965 |
| 116 | 1 May 967 |
| 117 | 967 |
| 118 | 30 Apr 969 |
| 119 | 20 June 970 |
| 120 | 24 June 970 |
| 20 | [23 Dec 970] |
| 121 | 15 Feb 971 |
| 122 | 23 Apr 971 |
| 123 | 1 July 971 |
| 124 | 1 Apr 972 |
| 125 | 1 May 972 |
| 126 | 18 Jan 973 |
| 127 | 18 June 973 |
| 128/39 | [17 Jan 974] |
| 40 | [23 Jan 974] |
| 129 | 29 July 974 |
| 130 | 30 Nov 974 |
| 42 | [974] |
| 132/133 | 16 Sept 975 |
| 134 | 18 Dec 975 |

| *Astorga* | Date |
| --- | --- |
| 136 | 2 Aug 977 |
| 137 | 29 Apr 978 |
| 138 | 3 Aug 978 |
| 139 | 28 Oct 979 |
| 140 | 979 |
| 141 | 15 Feb 980 |
| 142 | 3 Apr 980 |
| 143 | 18 May 980 |
| 144 | 30 June 981 |
| 145 | 1 Jan 983 |
| 146–8 | 28 June 983 |
| 149 | 1 July 983 |
| 150 | 19 Mar 984 |
| 152 | 22 June 984 |
| 153 | 25 Nov 984 |
| 154 | 30 Nov 984 |
| 156 | 11 Mar 986 |
| 180 | [3 Dec 986] |
| 157 | 11 Apr 987 |
| 158 | 18 July 987 |
| 159 | 12 Nov 987 |
| 160 | 23 Nov 988 |
| 161 | 12 Feb 989 |
| 162 | 25 July 989 |
| 163 | 19 Jan 990 |
| 164 | 20 Nov 990 |
| 165 | 1 July 991 |
| 166 | 1 Jan 992 |
| 167 | 23 Jan 992 |
| 170 | 1 Apr 992 |
| 171 | 15 May 992 |
| 172 | 19 Nov 992 |
| 173/181 | 12 May 994 |
| 175 | 1 Dec 995 |
| 176 | 24 Feb 996 |
| 177/169 | 29 Mar 996 |
| 178 | 10 May 996 |
| 179 | 1 Sept 996 |
| 182 | 13 Jan 997 |
| 185 | 14 Feb 999 |
| 151 | 8 May 984–99 |
| 186 | 27 Oct 999 |
| 187 | 12 June 1000 |
| 188 | 12 June 1000 |
| 189 | 1 Oct 1000 |
| 190 | 29 Feb 1001 |
| 191 | 1 Mar 1001 |

*Continued*

**Appendix 2** Continued

| Astorga | Date |
|---------|------|
| 194 | 8 Aug 1003 |
| 196 | 28 Mar 1004 |
| 197 | 1 Aug 1005 |
| 131/341 | [15 Sept 1005] |
| 198 | 21 Dec 1005 |
| 199 | 12 May 1006 |
| 200 | 26 June 1006 |
| 201 | 18 Dec 1006 |
| 202 | 13 Feb 1007 |
| 203 | 19 Feb 1007 |
| 204 | 27 Feb 1007 |
| 205 | 1 Aug 1007 |
| 206 | 13 Apr 1009 |
| 207 | 3 Feb 1010 |
| 262 | [28 Nov 1010] |
| 155 | [28 Dec 1010] |
| 208 | 22 May 1011 |
| 209 | 9 June 1012 |
| 210 | 30 Mar 1013 |
| 211 | 25 Nov 1013 |
| 212 | 29 Apr 1014 |
| 213 | 12 Nov 1014 |
| 214 | 22 Jan 1015 |
| 215 | 24 Jan 1015 |
| 216 | 5 Feb 1015 |
| 217 | 17 Apr 1015 |
| 371 | [14 Sept 1014–15] |
| 218 | 12 Oct 1015 |
| 219 | 1 Mar 1016 |
| 220 | 24 Nov 1016 |
| 17 | [8 Jan 1017] |
| 221 | 18 Jan 1017 |
| 222 | 1 Oct 1017 |
| 223 | 19 Dec 1017 |
| 224 | 1017 |
| 225 | 22 Jan 1018 |
| 226 | 22 Jan 1018 |
| 227 | 28 Sept 1019 |
| 228 | 25 Dec 1019 |
| 229 | 1019 |
| 230A | 29 May 1020 |
| 231 | 23 Aug 1020 |
| 230B | 3 June 1021 |
| 232 | 1021 |
| 234 | 26 Dec 1022 |
| 235 | 1022 |
| 192 | [6 Sept 1012–23] |
| 236 | 18 Oct 1023 |

| Astorga | Date |
|---------|------|
| 238 | 24 Aug 1024 |
| 195 | 1003–24 |
| 239 | 1 Feb 1025 |
| 240 | 16 Oct 1025 |
| 241 | 17 Oct 1025 |
| 243 | 28 Dec 1025 |
| 245 | 24 Apr 1026 |
| 247 | 1 Feb 1027 |
| 168 | [15 Feb 1014–27] |
| 248 | 29 Apr 1027 |
| N/A[1] | [24 Sept 1005/1027] |
| 250 | 14 Nov 1027 |
| 251 | 22 Dec 1027 |
| 252/237 | 1027 |
| 253 | 1027 |
| 254 | [22 Jan 1028] |
| 255 | [22 Feb 1026/1028] |
| 256 | 12 Apr 1028 |
| 258 | 31 Oct 1029 |
| 259 | 28 Feb 1030 |
| 260 | 28 Feb 1030 |
| 261 | 25 June 1030 |
| 263 | 19 Jan 1031 |
| 264 | 18 Oct 1031 |

[1] See Durany Castrillo and Rodríguez González, 'Puntualizaciones', 301–2.

**Appendix 3** Celanova: Concordance of Charters and Corrected Dates

| Celanova (continuation from Sáez and Sáez edition) | Date (Andrade Cernadas edition) | Number (Andrade Cernadas edition) | Corrected Date (Fernández de Viana y Vieites review) |
|---|---|---|---|
| 302 | 1 Feb 1007 | 3 | |
| 303 | 15 Feb 1007 | 198 | |
| 304 | 26 Oct 1007 | 301 | |
| 305 | 15 Dec 1007 | 199 | 15 Feb 1007 |
| 306 | 15 Dec 1007 | 200 | 15 Feb 1007 |
| 307 | 15 Dec 1007 | 201 | 15 Feb 1007 |
| 308 | 1007 | 193 | |
| 309 | 1007 | 203 | |
| 310 | 24 Feb 1008 | 335 | 25 Feb 1008 |
| 311 | 22 Oct 1008 | 495 | |
| 312 | 1008 | 194 | |

*Continued*

**Appendix 3** Continued

| *Celanova* (continuation from Sáez and Sáez edition) | Date (Andrade Cernadas edition) | Number (Andrade Cernadas edition) | Corrected Date (Fernández de Viana y Vieites review) |
| --- | --- | --- | --- |
| 313 | 20 July 1009 | 471 | |
| 314 | 28 Dec 1009 | 202 | |
| 315 | 975–1009 | 368 | 1 Oct 975–1009 |
| 316 | 1009 | 195 | |
| 317 | 1009 | 196 | |
| 318 | 3 Feb 1010 | 334 | |
| 319 | 30 Mar 1010 | 427 | |
| 320 | 28 Nov 1010 | 318 | |
| 321 | 1010 | 180 | |
| 322 | 17 Feb 1011 | 491 | |
| 323 | post-17 Feb 1011 | 425 | |
| 324 | 27 Feb 1011 | 333 | 1011 |
| 325 | 4 Aug 1011 | 149 | |
| 326 | 2 Dec 1011 | 276 | |
| 327 | 975–1011 | 197 | |
| 328 | 975–1011 | 205 | |
| 329 | 1011 | 372 | |
| 330 | 23 Feb 1012 | 366 | |
| 331 | 26 Feb 1012 | 548 | 27 Feb 1012 |
| 332 | 13 May 1012 | 572 | 1022 |
| 333 | 26 Jan 1013 | 367 | |
| 334 | 2 Feb 1013 | 473 | |
| 335 | 2 Feb 1013 | 484 | |
| 336 | 26 Feb 1013 | 332 | |
| 337 | 17 Apr 1013 | 371 | |
| 338 | 8 July 1013 | 310 | |
| 339 | 6 Mar 1015 | 387 | |
| 340 | 19 Apr 1015 | 311 | |
| 341 | 23 Feb 1016 | 313 | 24 Feb 1016 |
| 342 | 31 July 1016 | 341 | |
| N/A[2] | 6 Apr 1017 | 552 | 1007/17 |
| 343 | 26 Dec 1017 | 365 | |
| 344 | 1 June 1018 | 363 | |
| 345 | 21 Dec 1018 | 364 | |
| 346 | 18 Jan 1020 | 314 | 1019 |
| 347 | 1 Mar 1020 | 250 | 22 Feb 1012 |
| 348 | 17 Mar 1021 | 362 | |
| 349 | 16 Nov 1021 | 532 | |
| 350 | 7 Dec 1021 | 472 | |
| 351 | 5 Mar 1022 | 321 | 1017 |
| 352 | 8 June 1022 | 521 | |
| 353 | 6 Sept 1022 | 547 | |
| 354 | 18 Dec 1022 | 305 | |

[2] *Alfonso V* vii.

| Celanova (continuation from Sáez and Sáez edition) | Date (Andrade Cernadas edition) | Number (Andrade Cernadas edition) | Corrected Date (Fernández de Viana y Vieites review) |
|---|---|---|---|
| 355 | 1022 | 306 | |
| 356 | 8 Mar 1023 | 486 | |
| 357 | 25 Feb 1024 | 281 | 26 Feb 1024 |
| 358 | 23 Jan 1025 | 308 | |
| 359 | 27 Mar 1025 | 34 | |
| 360 | 20 Apr 1025 | 463 | 19 Apr 1025 |
| 361 | 18 May 1025 | 435 | |
| 362 | 25 June 1025 | 369 | |
| 363 | 1 Sept 1025 | 479 | |
| 364 | 20 Dec 1025 | 358 | |
| 365 | 16 Jan 1026 | 337 | |
| 366 | 17 Jan 1026 | 309 | |
| 367 | 11 July 1026 | 32 | |
| 368 | 1026 | 468 | |
| 369 | 4 Jan 1027 | 574 | |
| 370 | 10 Apr 1027 | 85 | |
| 371 | 25 July 1027 | 434 | 26 July 1027 |
| 372 | 8 Oct 1027 | 319 | |
| 373 | 21 Nov 1027 | 322 | |
| 374 | 1027 | 144 | |
| 375 | 15 Feb 1028 | 339 | |
| 376 | 1 Dec 1029 | 457 | |
| 377 | 15 Dec 1029 | 553 | |
| 378 | 17 Jan 1030 | 10 | |
| 379 | 25 Nov 1030 | 323 | |
| 380 | 8 Mar 1031 | 108 | |
| 381 | 17 Nov 1031 | 55 | |
| 382 | 1031 | 148 | |
| 383 | 1031 | 315 | |

**Appendix 4**  Lugo: Concordance of Editions and Dates of Charters

| # | Lugo | Date | Tumbo Viejo | Date | Cañizares | Date |
|---|---|---|---|---|---|---|
| 1 | 1 | 745 | | | 4 | 745 |
| 2 | | | 2 | 747 | 5 | 747 |
| 3 | | | 110 | 757 | 7 | 757 |
| 4 | 2 | 757–86 | 1 | 760 | 6 | 777? |
| 5 | | | 116 | 787 | 8 | 787 |
| 6 | | | 8 | 832 | 11 | 832 |
| 7 | 3 | 847 | | | 13 | 837 |
| 8 | 4A | 861 | | | | |

*Continued*

**Appendix 4** Continued

| # | Lugo | Date | Tumbo Viejo | Date | Cañizares | Date |
|---|------|------|-------------|------|-----------|------|
| 9 | 4B | 861 | | | | |
| 10 | 4C | 861 | | | | |
| 11 | 5 | 871 | 5 | 841 | 14 | 831/41? |
| 12 | | | 4 | 871 | 20/132 | 831?/71 |
| 13 | 6 | 897 | 57 | 897 | 17 | 897 |
| 14 | 7 | 899 | | | 18 | 899 |
| 15 | | | 13 | 899 | 19 | 899 |
| 16 | 8 | 910 | | | | |
| 17 | | | 80 | 910 | 22 | 910 |
| 18 | | | 9 | 911 | 24 | 915 |
| 19 | 9 | 916 | 3 | 772 | 25 | 916 |
| 20 | 10 | 918 | | | 36 | 953 |
| 21 | 11 | 919 | | | 26 | 919 |
| 22 | 12 | 922 | | | 39 | 956 |
| 23 | | | 114 | 923 | 29 | 923 |
| 24 | 13 | 929 | | | 30 | 929 |
| 25 | 14 | 943 | | | 32 | 943 |
| 26 | 15 | 947 | | | 33 | 947 |
| 27 | 16A | 950 | | | 34 | 950 |
| 28 | 17 | 950 | | | 35 | 950 |
| 29 | 18 | 954 | | | 37 | 954 |
| 30 | 19 | 954 | 103 | 954 | 38 | 954 |
| 31 | 20 | 956 | | | 27 | 922 |
| 32 | 21 | 959 | | | 41 | 960 |
| 33 | | | 82 | 968 | 43 | 968? |
| 34 | 22A | 969 | | | 136 | 989 |
| 35 | 22B | 969 | | | 136 | 989 |
| 36 | 23 | 969 | | | | |
| 37 | 24 | 973 | | | 47 | 973 |
| 38 | 16B | 973 | | | 46 | 973 |
| 39 | 25 | 974 | | | 48 | 974 |
| 40 | 26 | 975 | | | 49 | 975 |
| 41 | 27 | 975 | | | 50 | 975 |
| 42 | 28 | 976 | | | 133 | 976 |
| 43 | 29 | 977 | | | 51 | 977 |
| 44 | 30 | 979 | | | 54 | 979 |
| 45 | 31 | 980 | | | 55/134 | 980 |
| 46 | 32 | 980 | | | | |
| 47 | 33 | 982 | | | 56 | 982 |
| 48 | 34 | 987 | | | | |
| 49 | | | 128 | 989 | 58 | 989 |
| 50 | 35 | 989 | | | 59 | 989 |
| 51 | 36 | 991 | | | 60 | 991 |
| 52 | 37 | 991 | 14 | 991 | 61 | 991 |
| 53 | 38 | 992 | | | 73 | 1000 |
| 54 | | | 141 | 995 | 64 | 995 |

| # | Lugo | Date | Tumbo Viejo | Date | Cañizares | Date |
|---|------|------|-------------|------|-----------|------|
| 55 | 39 | 996 | | | 140 | 996 |
| 56 | 40A | 993 | | | 137 | 993 |
| 57 | 40B | 995 | | | 139 | 995 |
| 58 | | | | | 65 | 996 |
| 59 | | | | | 66 | 996 |
| 60 | | | 135 | 997 | 67 | 997 |
| 61 | 40C | 998 | | | 68 | 998 |
| 62 | | | 102 | 998 | 69 | 998 |
| 63 | | | 15 | 998 | 70/142 | 998 |
| 64 | | | | | 72/144 | 900–1000/900–1100 |
| 65 | 41 | 1000 | | | | |
| 66 | 42 | 1002 | | | 74 | 1002 |
| 67 | 43 | 1003 | | | | |
| 68 | 44 | 1004 | | | 75 | 1004 |
| 69 | 45 | 1005 | | | 76 | 1005 |
| 70 | 46 | 1009 | | | 79 | 1009 |
| 71 | 47 | 1010 | | | | |
| 72 | 48 | 1011 | | | | |
| 73 | 49 | 1016 | | | 80 | 1016 |
| 74 | 50 | 1016 | 127 | 1016 | 81 | 1016 |
| 75 | 51 | 1017 | | | | |
| 76 | 52 | 1017 | | | | |
| 77 | 53 | 1017 | | | 82 | 1017 |
| 78 | | | 136 | 1017 | 83 | 1017 |
| 79 | 54 | 1019 | | | 148 | 1019 |
| 80 | 55 | 1019 | | | 146 | 1019 |
| 81 | 56 | 1019 | | | 145 | 1018 |
| 82 | 57 | 1023 | | | | |
| 83 | | | | | 149 | 1024 |
| 84 | | | | | 150/1 | 1025 |
| 85 | 58 | 1027 | 10 | 1027 | 153/4 | 1027 |
| 86 | | | | | 155 | 1027 |
| 87 | | | 16 | 1029 | 156 | 1029 |
| 88 | | | | | 157 | 1030 |
| 89 | | | 111 | 1030 | 158 | 1030 |

**Appendix 5**  Portugal: Concordance of Editions and Dates of Charters

| # | PMH | Date | Edition | Number | Date |
|---|-----|------|---------|--------|------|
| 1 | | | Braga | 12/141 | 830/2 |
| 2 | | | Braga | 17/18 | 835 |
| 3 | 6 | 870 | Floriano | 97 | 870 |
| 4 | | | Braga | 16 | [873] |

*Continued*

**Appendix 5** Continued

| # | *PMH* | Date | Edition | Number | Date |
|---|-------|------|---------|--------|------|
| 5 | 7 | 874 | *Floriano* | 109 | 874 |
| 6 | 8 | 875 | *Porto* | N/A | 875 |
| 7 | 9 | 882 | *ChLA* 114 | 31 | 882 |
| 8 | 10 | 883 | *Floriano* | 129 | 883 |
| 9 | 11 | 883 | *Coimbra* | 12 | 883 |
| 10 | | | *Braga* | 13 | 899 |
| 11 | | | *Braga* | 174 | 900 |
| 12 | 1 | 773 | *Coimbra* | 454 | [902] |
| 13 | | | *Braga* | 175 | 904 |
| 14 | 13A | 906 | *Coimbra* | 356 | 906 |
| 15 | 13B | 906 | *Coimbra* | 354 | 906 |
| 16 | 13C | 906 | *Coimbra* | 355 | 906 |
| 17 | 14 | 907 | *Santos* | 2 | 907 |
| 18 | 15 | 907 | *Lorvão* | 19 | 907 |
| 19 | 16 | 908 | *Floriano* | 190 | 908 |
| 20 | | | *Tumbo C* | 1 | 908 |
| 21 | 5 | 870 | *Guimarães* | 65 | 873–910 |
| 22 | 3 | 850–66 | *Lorvão* | 47 | 811/911 |
| 23 | 17 | 911 | *Braga* | 19 | 911 |
| 24 | | | *Tumbo A* | 21 | 911 |
| 25 | 4 | 867–912 | *Coimbra* | 360 | 867–912 |
| 26 | 18 | 915 | *Tumbo A* | 26 | 915 |
| 27 | 19 | 915 | *Tumbo A* | 27 | 915 |
| 28 | 20 | 915 | *Coimbra* | 169 | 915 |
| 29 | 21 | 915 | | | 915 |
| 30 | | | *Braga* | 14 | 915 |
| 31 | | | *Costa,* 2 | 1 | 917 |
| 32 | 22 | 919 | | | 919 |
| 33 | 23 | 919 | *Lorvão* | 50 | 919 |
| 34 | 24 | 921 | | | 921 |
| 35 | 25 | 922 | *Coimbra* | 81 | 922 |
| 36 | 26 | 922 | *Grijó* | 130 | 922 |
| 37 | 2 | 850–66 | *Lorvão* | 41 | [924] |
| 38 | 27 | 924 | | | 924 |
| 39 | 28 | 924 | *Coimbra* | 514 | 924 |
| 40 | 29 | 924 | *Guimarães* | 16 | 924 |
| 41 | 30 | 925 | | | 925 |
| 42 | 31 | 926 | *Guimarães* | 9 | 926 |
| 43 | 32 | 927 | *Lorvão* | 72 | 927 |
| 44 | 33 | 927 | *Lorvão* | 40 | 927 |
| 45 | 34 | 928 | *Lorvão* | 33 | 928 |
| 46 | 35 | 929 | | | 929 |
| 47 | 37 | 933 | *Lorvão* | 1 | 933 |
| 48 | 38 | 933 | | | 933 |
| 49 | 39 | 933 | *Lorvão* | 7 | 933 |
| 50 | 40 | 935 | *Lorvão* | 4 | 935 |

| # | PMH | Date | Edition | Number | Date |
|---|---|---|---|---|---|
| 51 | 41 | 936 | | | 936 |
| 52 | 42 | 936 | *Lorvão* | 36 | 936 |
| 53 | 43 | 937 | | | 937 |
| 54 | 44 | 937 | *Lorvão* | 12 | 937 |
| 55 | 45 | 937 | *Lorvão* | 69 | 937 |
| 56 | 46 | 938 | *Paço de Sousa* | 121 | 938 |
| 57 | 47 | 938 | *Lorvão* | 34 | 938 |
| 58 | 48 | 938 | | | 938 |
| 59 | | | *Ramiro II* | 42 | 941 |
| 60 | 50 | 943 | *Lorvão* | 3 | 943 |
| 61 | 51 | 943 | *Lorvão* | 22 | 943 |
| 62 | 52 | 943 | *Lorvão* | 56 | 943 |
| 63 | 53 | 943 | *Arouca* | 1 | 943 |
| 64 | 54 | 944 | *Coimbra* | 526 | 944 |
| 65 | 55 | 946 | *Lorvão* | 45 | 946 |
| 66 | 56 | 946 | | | 946 |
| 67 | 57 | 946 | | | 946 |
| 68 | 12 | 897 | *ChLA* 114 | 32 | [947] |
| 69 | 58 | 949 | | | 949 |
| 70 | 59 | 949 | *Guimarães* | 29 | 949 |
| 71 | 36 | 931–50 | *Guimarães* | 10 | 950 |
| 72 | 60 | 950 | | | 950 |
| 73 | 61 | 950 | *Guimarães* | A1 | 950 |
| 74 | 62 | 950 | *Lorvão* | 18 | 950 |
| 75 | 71 | 957 | *Guimarães* | 49 | 950–1 |
| 76 | 63 | 951 | *Arouca* | 2 | 951 |
| 77 | | | *Costa*, 1 | 127n75 | 951 |
| 78 | 64 | 952 | | | 952 |
| 79 | 65 | 952 | *Lorvão* | 66 | 952 |
| 80 | 66 | 952 | *Guimarães* | 4 | 952 |
| 81 | 67 | 953 | *Guimarães* | 53/A2 | 953 |
| 82 | 68 | 954 | *Lorvão* | 73 | 954 |
| 83 | 100 | 969 | *Coimbra* | 56 | 951–5 |
| 84 | 69 | 955 | | | 955 |
| 85 | | | *Pedro* | 1 | post-955 |
| 86 | | | *Arouca* | 51 | 956 |
| 87 | 78 | 960 | *Guimarães* | 14 | 960/56 |
| 88 | 72 | 957 | | | 957 |
| 89 | 73 | 957 | *Coimbra* | 111 | 957 |
| 90 | 74 | 957 | *Lorvão* | 17 | 957 |
| 91 | 75 | 957 | *Coimbra* | 368 | 957 |
| 92 | 49 | 939 | *Lorvão* | 54 | 959 |
| 93 | 76 | 959 | *Guimarães* | 1A/A3 | 959 |
| 94 | 77 | 959 | *Guimarães* | 54 | 959 |
| 95 | 70 | 956 | *Guimarães* | 15 | 956/60 |
| 96 | 79 | 960 | | | 960 |
| 97 | 80 | 960 | | | 960 |

*Continued*

**Appendix 5** Continued

| # | PMH | Date | Edition | Number | Date |
|---|-----|------|---------|--------|------|
| 98 | 81 | 960 | *Guimarães* | 3 | 960 |
| 99 | | | *Lorvão* | 74 | 954–61? |
| 100 | 82 | 961 | *Guimarães* | 62/A4 | 961 |
| 101 | 83 | 961 | *Lorvão* | 46/75 | 961 |
| 102 | 84 | 961 | *Lorvão* | 61 | 961 |
| 103 | 85 | 961 | *Lorvão* | 23 | 961 |
| 104 | 86 | 964 | *Santos* | 3 | 964 |
| 105 | 87 | 964 | *Coimbra* | 139 | 964 |
| 106 | 88 | 964 | *Guimarães* | 50 | 964 |
| 107 | 89 | 965 | | | 965 |
| 108 | 90 | 965 | | | 965 |
| 109 | 91 | 965 | | | 965 |
| 110 | 92 | 966 | *Lorvão* | 5 | 966 |
| 111 | 93 | 967 | *Coimbra* | 530 | 967 |
| 112 | 94 | 967 | *Lorvão* | 2 | 967 |
| 113 | 95 | 968 | *Lorvão* | 8 | 968 |
| 114 | 97 | 968 | *Guimarães* | 1B/A5 | 968 |
| 115 | 98 | 968 | | | 968 |
| 116 | 99 | 968 | *Guimarães* | 67 | 968 |
| 117 | 101 | 970 | *Lorvão* | 57 | 970 |
| 118 | 102 | 971 | | | 971 |
| 119 | 104 | 972 | *Lorvão* | 16 | 972 |
| 120 | 105 | 972 | | | 972 |
| 121 | | | *Arouca* | 84 | 972 |
| 122 | 107 | 973 | *Lorvão* | 58 | 963/73 |
| 123 | 106 | 973 | *Lorvão* | 13 | 973 |
| 124 | 108 | 973 | *Lorvão* | 53 | 973 |
| 125 | 109 | 973 | *Coimbra* | 205 | 973 |
| 126 | 110 | 973 | *Junqueira* | 1 | 973 |
| 127 | 111 | 973 | *Guimarães* | 63 | 973 |
| 128 | 112 | 974 | *Coimbra* | 187 | 974 |
| 129 | 113 | 974 | *Lorvão* | 21 | 974 |
| 130 | 114 | 974 | *Coimbra* | 2 | 974 |
| 131 | | | *Braga* | 25 | 974 |
| 132 | 115 | 976 | | | 976 |
| 133 | 116 | 976 | *Lorvão* | 32 | 976 |
| 134 | 117 | 976 | *Lorvão* | 6 | 976 |
| 135 | 118 | 976 | *Lorvão* | 24 | 976 |
| 136 | 119 | 976 | | | 976 |
| 137 | 120 | 977 | *Coimbra* | 291 | 977 |
| 138 | 121 | 977 | *Lorvão* | 76 | 977 |
| 139 | 122 | 978 | *Lorvão* | 55 | 978 |
| 140 | 123 | 978 | *Lorvão* | 70 | 978 |
| 141 | 124 | 978 | | | 978 |
| 142 | 125 | 978 | *Lorvão* | 25 | 978 |
| 143 | 126 | 979 | | | 979 |
| 144 | 127 | 980 | *Lorvão* | 43 | 980 |

| # | PMH | Date | Edition | Number | Date |
|---|-----|------|---------|--------|------|
| 145 | 128 | 980 | *Lorvão* | 68 | 980 |
| 146 | 129 | 980 | | | 980 |
| 147 | 130 | 981 | *Lorvão* | 60 | 981 |
| 148 | 131 | 981 | *Lorvão* | 28 | 981 |
| 149 | 132 | 981 | *Lorvão* | 29 | 981 |
| 150 | 133 | 981 | *Lorvão* | 26 | 981 |
| 151 | 134 | 982 | *Guimarães* | 23 | 982? |
| 152 | 135 | 982 | *Coimbra* | 524 | 982 |
| 153 | 136 | 982 | *Lorvão* | 27 | 982 |
| 154 | | | *Lorvão* | 30 | 982 |
| 155 | | | *Braga* | 26 | 982 |
| 156 | 137 | 983 | | | 983 |
| 157 | 138 | 983 | *Guimarães* | 68/A6 | 983 |
| 158 | 139 | 984 | *Lorvão* | 48 | 984 |
| 159 | 140 | 984 | | | 984 |
| 160 | 141 | 984 | | | 984 |
| 161 | 142 | 984 | | | 984 |
| 162 | 143 | 984 | *Lorvão* | 44 | 984 |
| 163 | | | *Lorvão* | 35 | 966–85 |
| 164 | 144 | 985 | | | 985 |
| 165 | 145 | 985 | *Lorvão* | 49 | 985 |
| 166 | 146 | 985 | | | 985 |
| 167 | 147 | 985 | *Coimbra* | 1 | 985 |
| 168 | 148 | 985 | *Lorvão* | 51 | 985 |
| 169 | 149 | 985 | | | 985 |
| 170 | 150 | 985 | | | 985 |
| 171 | | | *Coruña* | 96 | 985 |
| 172 | 151 | 986 | | | 986 |
| 173 | 153 | 987 | *Coimbra* | 515 | 987 |
| 174 | 217 | 1012 | *Lorvão* | 39 | [987] |
| 175 | 154 | 988 | *Lorvão* | 52 | 988 |
| 176 | 155 | 988 | | | 988 |
| 177 | 156 | 989 | *Coimbra* | 208 | 989 |
| 178 | 157 | 989 | | | 989 |
| 179 | 158 | 990 | | | 990 |
| 180 | 159 | 990 | *Coimbra* | 366 | 990 |
| 181 | | | *Braga* | 27 | 990 |
| 182 | 160 | 991 | | | 991 |
| 183 | 161 | 991 | | | 991 |
| 184 | 162 | 991 | | | 991 |
| 185 | 163 | 991 | Wright, 'Scribes' | N/A[3] | 991 |
| 186 | 164 | 991 | | | 991 |
| 187 | 165 | 992 | *Lorvão* | 42 | 992 |
| 188 | 166 | 992 | *Guimarães* | 20 | 992 |
| 189 | 167 | 993 | | | 993 |
| 190 | 168 | 994 | *Guimarães* | 60 | 994 |

[3] See Wright, 'Scribes', 74–6.

*Continued*

**Appendix 5** Continued

| # | *PMH* | Date | Edition | Number | Date |
|---|-------|------|---------|--------|------|
| 191 | 169 | 994 | *Paço de Sousa* | 132 | 994 |
| 192 | 170 | 994 | *Coimbra* | 517 | 994 |
| 193 | 171 | 994 | *Coimbra* | 194 | 994 |
| 194 | 172 | 994 | | | 994 |
| 195 | 173 | 995 | *Coimbra* | 200 | 995 |
| 196 | 174 | 995 | | | 995 |
| 197 | 175 | 995 | | | 995 |
| 198 | 176 | 995 | | | 995 |
| 199 | 177 | 995 | | | 995 |
| 200 | | | *Braga* | 406 | 995 |
| 201 | 178 | 998 | | | 998 |
| 202 | 179 | 998 | *Lorvão* | 37 | 998 |
| 203 | 182 | 999 | | | 999 |
| 204 | 183 | 999 | *Guimarães* | 24 | 999 |
| 205 | 184 | 999 | | | 999 |
| 206 | | | *Braga* | 28 | 999 |
| 207 | | | *Paço de Sousa* | 26 | 1000 |
| 208 | | | *Braga* | 29 | 1000 |
| 209 | 185 | 1001 | *Coimbra* | 522 | 1001 |
| 210 | 188 | 1002 | | | 1002 |
| 211 | 189 | 1002 | *Lorvão* | 31 | 1002 |
| 212 | 191 | 1002 | *Coimbra* | 126 | 1002 |
| 213 | 192 | 1003 | *Coimbra* | 191 | 1003 |
| 214 | | | *Braga* | 399 | 1003 |
| 215 | 193 | 1004 | *Coimbra* | 212 | 1004 |
| 216 | 194 | 1005 | *Coimbra* | 135 | 1005 |
| 217 | 195 | 1006 | *Coimbra* | 518 | 1006 |
| 218 | 196 | 1006 | *Coimbra* | 72 | 1006 |
| 219 | | | *Braga* | 30 | 1006 |
| 220 | | | *Coimbra* | 206 | 973–1008 |
| 221 | | | *Azevedo* | 1 | 1003–8? |
| 222 | 197 | 1008 | | | 1008 |
| 223 | 198 | 1008 | | | 1008 |
| 224 | 199 | 1008 | *Coimbra* | 523 | 1008 |
| 225 | 200 | 1008 | *Guimarães* | 66 | 1008 |
| 226 | 201 | 1008 | *Guimarães* | 7 | 1008 |
| 227 | 202 | 1008 | *Coimbra* | 155 | 1008 |
| 228 | 203 | 1008 | *Coimbra* | 204 | 1008 |
| 229 | 204 | 1008 | *Coimbra* | 207 | 1008 |
| 230 | | | *Pedro* | 2 | 1008 |
| 231 | 206 | 1009 | | | 1009 |
| 232 | 207 | 1009? | | | 1009? |
| 233 | 208 | 1009 | *Coimbra* | 529 | 1009 |
| 234 | 209 | 1009 | *Coimbra* | 193 | 1009 |
| 235 | 210 | 1009 | | | 1009 |

| # | *PMH* | Date | Edition | Number | Date |
|---|---|---|---|---|---|
| 236 | 212 | 1009 | *Guimarães* | 8 | 1009 |
| 237 | 213 | 1010 | *Coimbra* | 211 | 1010 |
| 238 | 214 | 1010 | | | 1010 |
| 239 | 215 | 1010 | *Coimbra* | 527 | 1010 |
| 240 | 216 | 1011 | | | 1011 |
| 241 | 219 | 1012 | *Junqueira* | 2 | 1012 |
| 242 | | | *Crasto* | 27 | 1012 |
| 243 | | | *Braga* | 31 | 1012 |
| 244 | 952 | 1000–100 | *Guimarães* | 55 | 959–1013? |
| 245 | 952 | 1000–100 | *Guimarães* | 56 | 959–1013? |
| 246 | 952 | 1000–100 | *Guimarães* | 57 | 959–1013? |
| 247 | 220 | 1013? | | | 1013? |
| 248 | 221 | 1013 | *Guimarães* | 58 | 1013 |
| 249 | 223 | 1014 | *Guimarães* | 46 | 1014 |
| 250 | 224 | 1014 | *Coimbra* | 197 | 1014 |
| 251 | 225 | 1014 | *Guimarães* | 51 | 1014 |
| 252 | 237 | 1018 | *Coimbra* | 118 | 1014 |
| 253 | 226 | 1015 | *Paço de Sousa* | 142 | 1015 |
| 254 | 227 | 1016 | *Coimbra* | 124 | 1016 |
| 255 | 228 | 1016 | *Coimbra* | 202 | 1016 |
| 256 | 230 | 1016 | *Lorvão* | 9 | 1016–17 |
| 257 | 96/229 | 968/1016 | *Lorvão* | 10 | 1016–17 |
| 258 | 231 | 1017 | | | 1017 |
| 259 | | | *Braga* | 1 | 1017 |
| 260 | 233 | 1018 | *Coimbra* | 123 | 1018 |
| 261 | 234 | 1018 | *Coimbra* | 129/61 | 1018 |
| 262 | 238 | 1018 | *Coimbra* | 120 | 1018 |
| 263 | 239 | 1018 | *Coimbra* | 122 | 1018 |
| 264 | 240 | 1018 | *Lorvão* | 15 | 1018 |
| 265 | 246 | 1021 | *Coimbra* | 156 | 1018 |
| 266 | | | *Azevedo* | 2 | 1018 |
| 267 | | | *Braga* | 68 | 1018 |
| 268 | 241 | 1019 | *Coimbra* | 121 | 1019 |
| 269 | 242 | 1019 | *Coimbra* | 134 | 1019 |
| 270 | 243 | 1019 | | | 1019 |
| 271 | 244 | 1020 | | | 1020 |
| 272 | 245 | 1020 | *Coimbra* | 91 | 1020 |
| 273 | | | *Braga* | 67 | 1020 |
| 274 | 247 | 1021 | *Guimarães* | 39 | 1021 |
| 275 | 248 | 1021 | *Coimbra* | 142 | 1021 |
| 276 | 249 | 1021 | | | 1021 |
| 277 | 250 | 1021 | | | 1021 |
| 278 | 251 | 1022 | *Guimarães* | 61 | 1022 |
| 279 | 103/272 | 971/1032 | *Junqueira* | 3 | 1022 |
| 280 | 252 | 1023 | *Coimbra* | 128 | 1023 |
| 281 | 253 | 1023 | *Coimbra* | 143/4 | 1023 |

*Continued*

**Appendix 5** Continued

| # | *PMH* | Date | Edition | Number | Date |
|---|---|---|---|---|---|
| 282 | | | Braga | 185 | 1023 |
| 283 | | | Coimbra | 109 | 1023? |
| 284 | 254 | 1024 | | | 1024 |
| 285 | 255 | 1024 | | | 1024 |
| 286 | 256 | 1025 | | | 1025 |
| 287 | 257 | 1025 | | | 1025 |
| 288 | 258 | 1025 | Coimbra | 203 | 1025 |
| 289 | 259 | 1025 | Guimarães | 22 | 1025 |
| 290 | 260 | 1025 | Coimbra | 359 | 1025 |
| 291 | | | Braga | 22 | 1025 |
| 292 | 261 | 1026 | | | 1026 |
| 293 | | | Fernando I | 4 | 1026 |
| 294 | | | Braga | 76 | 1026 |
| 295 | 262 | 1027 | | | 1027 |
| 296 | 232/63 | 1017/27 | Junqueira | 4 | 1027 |
| 297 | | | Braga | 176 | 1027 |
| 298 | 264 | 1028 | Guimarães | 36 | 1028 |
| 299 | | | Braga | 32 | 1028 |
| 300 | 266 | 1029 | | | 1029 |
| 301 | 267 | 1030 | | | 1030 |
| 302 | 268 | 1030 | | | 1030 |
| 303 | 269 | 1030 | Grijó | 169 | 1030 |
| 304 | | | Braga | 33 | 1030 |
| 305 | 270 | 1031 | | | 1031 |
| 306 | 271 | 1031 | | | 1031 |
| 307 | | | Braga | 34 | 1031 |
| 308 | | | Braga | 69 | 1031 |
| 309 | | | Braga | 35 | 1031 |
| 310 | | | Braga | 70 | 1031 |
| 311 | | | Braga | 36 | 1031 |
| 312 | | | Braga | 178 | 1031 |
| 313 | | | Braga | 177 | 1031 |
| N/A | 152 | 986 | Guimarães | 27 | 1036? |
| N/A | 222 | 1013 | Coimbra | 147 | 1027–37 |
| N/A | 265/361 | 1028/47 | Junqueira | 10 | 1047 |
| N/A | 180 | 998 | | | 1048 |
| N/A | 181 | 998 | | | 1048 |
| N/A | 218/381 | 1012/52 | Junqueira | 18 | 1052 |
| N/A | 235/408 | 1018/58 | Junqueira | 19 | 1058 |
| N/A | 186 | 1001 | Coimbra | 416 | 1101 |
| N/A | 187 | 1002 | Coimbra | 435 | 1102 |
| N/A | 190 | 1002 | Coimbra | 495 | 1102 |
| N/A | 211 | 1009 | Coimbra | 496 | 1109 |
| N/A | 205 | 1009 | Grijó | 182 | 1109? |
| N/A | 236 | 1018 | Grijó | 119 | 1118? |

**Appendix 6** Career Scribes (5+ Charters)

| Name | Collection | Date | Charters |
| --- | --- | --- | --- |
| Petrus *presbiter* | *León* | 990–1031? | 25? |
| Fulgentius *presbiter* | *León, Sahagún* | 995–1030 | 22 |
| Citi *presbiter* | *León, Otero* | 1008–29 | 18 |
| Cidi *presbiter* | *León, Otero* | 1006–30 | 17 |
| Sampiro *quasi presbiter* | *León, Sahagún, Celanova, Coruña, San Pelayo* | 977–1019 | 17 |
| Vivi *presbiter* | *León* | 1005–31 | 16 |
| Felix *diaconus et notarius* | *León, Sahagún* | 939–79? | 11? |
| Sandinus *presbiter* | *León, Otero, Astorga* | 993–1022 | 11 |
| Adulfus *diaconus* Gendoni | *León, Sahagún, Santiago* | 918–77? | 10? |
| Baroncellus *presbiter* | *León* | 952–61 | 10 |
| Iohannes *presbiter* | *León* | 965–1009? | 10? |
| Aloytus *diaconus et notarius* | *Celanova, Coruña* | 932–59 | 9 |
| Iohannes | *Santillana* | 1019–26 | 9 |
| Migael *presbiter* | *León, Otero* | 992–1030 | 9 |
| Velasco *scriptor*\*[4] | *San Juan* | 1014–31 | 9 |
| Bellitus *presbiter* | *León, Sahagún* | 1006–26 | 8 |
| Ciprianus *presbiter* | *León* | 952–94? | 8? |
| Ermegildo | *Santillana* | 1017–26 | 8 |
| Possidonius *notarius*\* | *Oviedo, Sahagún, Santiago, Ourense, VDJ* | 883–906 | 8 |
| Servandus *presbiter* | *León* | 1000–29 | 8 |
| Sescuto *presbiter* | *Otero* | 1021–2 | 8 |
| Aspidius *presbiter et notarius* | *León, Sahagún, San Isidro* | 918–45 | 7 |
| Iohannes *presbiter* | *León* | 914–59? | 7? |
| Petrus *presbiter* | *Sobrado* | 959–84 | 7 |
| Sandinus *presbiter* | *PMH, Coimbra, Grijó* | 1008–30 | 7 |
| Sisivertus *diaconus* | *Sahagún, Eslonza* | 985–91 | 7 |
| Songeri *presbiter* | *Sobrarbe* | 1024 | 7 |
| Stephanus *presbiter* | *León* | 942–60 | 7 |
| Adulfus *diaconus* | *Oviedo* | 896–921 | 6 |
| Cesarius *indignus* | *León, Oviedo, Sahagún* | 974–8 | 6 |
| Cissilani | *Santillana* | 980–1001 | 6 |
| Felix *presbiter* | *León* | 985–1011 | 6 |
| Ferro *presbiter* | *León, Sahagún* | 937–67 | 6 |
| Fredenandus *presbiter* | *León* | 932–66 | 6 |
| Fredmundo *presbiter* | *Sahagún, Otero* | 947–62 | 6 |
| Gaudinas | *Celanova* | 1001–18 | 6 |
| Gomessanus *exarator*\* | *San Millán* | 945–57 | 6 |
| Iohannes | *Sahagún* | 932–71? | 6? |
| Iustus | *Sahagún* | 966–98 | 6 |
| Monnius *presbiter et notarius*\* | *Sahagún* | 950–1001 | 6 |
| Felix Cromaciz, *frater* Munnio *iudex* | *León, Oviedo, Otero* | 980–94 | 6 |

[4] An asterisk denotes false or anachronistic attestations.

*Continued*

## Appendix 6 Continued

| Name | Collection | Date | Charters |
|---|---|---:|---:|
| Onorio *presbiter* | Otero | 1017–19 | 6 |
| Ordonius *presbiter* | León | 1013–30 | 6 |
| Seniorinus, Fagildus *presbiter* | Celanova | 983–1003 | 6 |
| Stephanus *presbiter* | León | 1001–29 | 6 |
| Teodemirus *notarius** | León | 920–34 | 6 |
| Addaulfus *presbiter* | Sobrado | 943–76 | 5 |
| Amphilocius *presbiter* | Celanova, Coruña, Sahagún | 911–25 | 5 |
| Armentarius *presbiter* | León, Otero | 978–1009 | 5 |
| Baltarius *presbiter* | León, Sahagún | 951–74 | 5 |
| Braolio *presbiter* | Otero | 974–97 | 5 |
| Christoforus *presbiter* | Otero | 1019–28 | 5 |
| Dominico *presbiter* | Otero | 995–1026 | 5 |
| Ecta *presbiter* | León, Otero | 1008–28 | 5 |
| Ermegildus *presbiter* | León | 961–1001? | 5? |
| Eterus *presbiter* | Otero | 1024–7 | 5 |
| Felix *diaconus* | Sahagún | 996–1030? | 5? |
| Fidelis *frater* | Celanova | 999–1020 | 5 |
| Florentius *scriba* | Arlanza, Covarrubias | 937–78 | 5 |
| Froila *presbiter* | León | 951–4 | 5 |
| Froila Odoariz *presbiter* | León | 999–1021 | 5 |
| Garsea *presbiter* | León | 992–1030 | 5 |
| Gudesteus *presbiter* | León | 1030–1 | 5 |
| Iohannes *presbiter* | Sobrado | 929–36 | 5 |
| Iuannes *presbiter* | Otero | 994–1026 | 5 |
| Iulianus | León | 1002–17 | 5 |
| Marino *presbiter* | Sahagún, Otero | 1002–27 | 5 |
| Martinus *presbiter* | Sahagún | 925–76? | 5? |
| Scemenus *diaconus, presbiter* | León | 963–97? | 5? |
| Sisebutus *presbiter** | San Millán | 944–97 | 5 |
| Umbertus *scriba** | San Juan | 828–994 | 5 |

## Appendix 7 Institutional and Individual (Ecclesiastical and Lay) Archives

| Institution | Collection | Region | Charters |
|---|---|---|---:|
| San Salvador de Celanova | Celanova | West | 280 |
| Sahagún | Sahagún, Valladolid | Centre | 260 |
| Santos Cosme y Damián de Abellar | León, Sahagún | Centre | 180 |
| San Pedro de Cardeña | Cardeña | East | 146 |
| Santos Justo y Pastor de Ardón | León, Sahagún | Centre | 86 |
| San Xulián de Samos | Samos | West | 82 |
| Santiago de Compostela | Santiago, Sobrado, PMH | West | 71 |

| Institution | Collection | Region | Charters |
|---|---|---|---|
| Lorvão | *PMH, Lorvão, Coimbra* | West | 68 |
| San Millán de la Cogolla | *San Millán* | East | 67 |
| Santa María de León | *León, Sahagún* | Centre | 56 |
| San Lourenzo de Carboeiro | *Coruña* | West | 55 |
| Santiago de León | *León* | Centre | 53 |
| San Juan y San Millán de Hiniestra | *San Millán* | East | 47 |
| Santa María de Astorga | *Astorga* | Centre | 39 |
| Santillana del Mar | *Santillana, Piasca* | Centre | 39 |
| Sobrado dos Monxes | *Sobrado* | West | 36 |
| San Salvador de Oviedo | *Oviedo* | Centre | 35 |
| San Pedro de Eslonza | *Eslonza, Sahagún* | Centre | 29 |
| San Martín de Turieno | *Liébana, Piasca* | Centre | 28 |
| San Miguel Arcángel de la Vega de León | *León* | Centre | 28 |
| Santa María de Valpuesta | *Valpuesta* | East | 28 |
| San Juan de la Peña | *San Juan* | East | 25 |
| San Salvador de Matallana | *León* | Centre | 25 |
| San Vicente de León | *León, Sahagún* | Centre | 25 |
| Santa María de Lugo | *Lugo, Tumbo Viejo, Cañizares, Braga* | West | 25 |
| Santiago y Santa María de Valdevimbre | *León* | Centre | 25 |
| Santa Maria de Guimarães | *PMH, Guimarães* | West | 24 |
| San Adrián del Valle | *Astorga* | Centre | 23 |
| San Martín de Albelda | *Albelda, Irache* | East | 21 |
| San Salvador de Leire | *Leire, Pamplona* | East | 20 |
| San Dictino de Astorga | *Astorga, Valladolid* | Centre | 19 |
| Santa María de Piasca | *Sahagún, Piasca* | Centre | 18 |
| Vacariça / Leça | *PMH, Coimbra* | West | 18 |
| San Isidro de Dueñas | *San Isidro* | Centre | 17 |
| San Cipriano de Valdesaz | *León* | Centre | 16 |
| San Juan Apóstol de Corniero | *Sahagún* | Centre | 15 |
| San Martiño Pinario | *Coruña* | West | 15 |
| Santiago de Cellariolo | *León, Sahagún* | Centre | 15 |
| San Martín de Valdepueblo | *León* | Centre | 14 |
| San Miguel de Pedroso | *San Millán* | East | 14 |
| San Millán y San Esteban de Salcedo | *San Millán* | East | 14 |
| San Paio de Antealtares | *Coruña* | West | 14 |
| San Cosme y San Damián de Burbia | *Astorga* | Centre | 13 |
| San Miguel de Camarzana | *Astorga* | Centre | 13 |
| San Pedro de Montes | *Montes, Diócesis* | Centre | 13 |
| San Salvador de Villeña | *Liébana* | Centre | 13 |
| Buezo de Bureba | *Valpuesta* | East | 12 |
| San Felices de Oca | *San Millán* | East | 12 |

*Continued*

**Appendix 7** Continued

| Institution | Collection | Region | Charters |
|---|---|---|---|
| San Julián y Santa Basilisa de Villagonzalo Pedernales | *Cardeña* | East | 12 |
| San Pedro de Arlanza | *Arlanza* | East | 12 |
| San Salvador de Oña | *Oña* | East | 12 |
| Santa Leocadia de Castañeda | *Astorga* | Centre | 12 |
| San Andrés de Pardomino | *León* | Centre | 11 |
| San Martiño de Mondoñedo | *Mondoñedo, VDJ, Floriano, Braga* | West | 11 |
| San Pedro de Siresa | *Huesca, Navarra* | East | 11 |
| Santiago de Peñalba | *Astorga* | Centre | 11 |
| San Martín de Castañeda | *Castañeda* | Centre | 10 |
| San Salvador de Villar | *Celanova* | West | 10 |
| Santa Marta de Tera | *Astorga* | Centre | 10 |
| Santiago de Valdávida | *Sahagún* | Centre | 10 |
| Covarrubias | *Covarrubias, Burgos* | East | 9 |
| Santa María de Husillos | *Husillos* | East | 9 |
| San Cristóbal de Astorga | *Astorga* | Centre | 8 |
| San Juan de Ardón | *León* | Centre | 8 |
| San Martín de Torres | *Astorga* | Centre | 8 |
| San Vicente de Oviedo | *San Vicente* | Centre | 8 |
| San Xoán de Caaveiro | *Caaveiro* | West | 8 |
| Santa Eugenia y Santa Marina de Marmellar de Arriba | *Cardeña* | East | 8 |
| San Pedro de Zamudia | *Astorga* | Centre | 7 |
| Santa María de Obona | *Obona, Vermudo III* | Centre | 7 |
| San Andrés de Villalbilla | *Cardeña* | East | 6 |
| San Martín de Cillas | *San Juan* | East | 6 |
| San Martín de Villabáscones | *Cardeña* | East | 6 |
| San Salvador de Vilanova de Lourenzá | *Lourenzá* | West | 6 |
| Saelices de Mayorga | *Sahagún, Vega* | Centre | 5 |
| San Cipriano del Condado | *León* | Centre | 5 |
| San Juan Bautista de Cerezal | *Astorga* | Centre | 5 |
| San Julián de Lavasal | *San Juan* | East | 5 |
| San Mamés de Obarenes | *San Millán* | East | 5 |
| San Sebastián do Pico Sacro | *Coruña, Santiago* | West | 5 |
| Santa Cruz | *Astorga* | Centre | 5 |
| Santa María de Rezmondo | *Cardeña* | East | 5 |
| Santiago de Meilán | *Lugo, Tumbo Viejo* | West | 5 |

| Institution | Collection | Region | Charters |
|---|---|---|---|
| San Andrés de Argutorio | *Astorga* | Centre | 4 |
| San Cebrián de Pinza | *Astorga* | Centre | 4 |
| San Juan de Tabladillo | *Arlanza* | East | 4 |
| San Julián y Santa Basilisa de Bezares | *Cardeña* | East | 4 |
| San Martín de Cercito | *San Juan* | East | 4 |
| San Miguel de Silos | *Silos* | East | 4 |
| San Salvador de Bárcena | *Astorga* | Centre | 4 |
| San Salvador de Cinis | *Coruña* | East | 4 |
| Santa Eufemia de Cozuelos | *Cozuelos* | East | 4 |
| Santa Maria de Coimbra | *PMH, Coimbra* | West | 4 |
| Santa María de Pamplona | *Pamplona* | East | 4 |
| Compludo | *Astorga* | Centre | 3 |
| San Acisclo de Astorga | *Astorga* | Centre | 3 |
| San Emeterio y San Celedonio de Taranco | *San Millán* | East | 3 |
| San Juan Bautista | *León* | Centre | 3 |
| San Juan de Edrada | *Celanova* | West | 3 |
| San Pedro de Berlangas | *Burgos, Covarrubias* | East | 3 |
| San Salvador | *León* | Centre | 3 |
| San Salvador de Astorga | *Astorga* | Centre | 3 |
| San Salvador de Boñar | *Sahagún* | Centre | 3 |
| San Sebastián de Silos | *Silos* | East | 3 |
| San Vicente de Fiéstoles | *Floriano* | East | 3 |
| San Vicenzo de Pombeiro | *Pombeiro* | West | 3 |
| Santa Comba de Chamoso | *Lugo* | West | 3 |
| Santa Cristina de Ribas de Sil | *Santa Cristina* | West | 3 |
| Santa María de Carracedo | *Carracedo* | Centre | 3 |
| Santa María de Ferreira de Pallares | *Lugo* | West | 3 |
| Santa María de Fontfrida | *San Juan* | East | 3 |
| Santa María de Puerto | *Puerto* | Centre | 3 |
| Santa Marina | *Otero* | Centre | 3 |
| Santa Teodosia de Arenas de Iguña | *Santillana* | Centre | 3 |
| Santo Estevo de Chouzán | *Chouzán* | West | 3 |
| Miscellaneous Institutions (1-2 Charters) | | | 239 (6%) |
| **West** | | | **868 (21%)** |
| **Centre** | | | **1337 (33%)** |
| **East** | | | **613 (15%)** |
| **Institutional Total** | | | **2818 (69%)** |

*Continued*

## Appendix 7 Continued

| Individual (Ecclesiastical) | Collection | Region | Charters |
|---|---|---|---|
| Melic *presbiter* | *Sahagún* | Centre | 13 |
| Munnio *presbiter* | *León* | Centre | 10 |
| Servandus *presbiter* | *León* | Centre | 8 |
| Vincimalo *presbiter* | *León, Sahagún* | Centre | 6 |
| Bishop Tudemiro | *Albelda* | East | 5 |
| Braolio *presbiter* | *Otero* | Centre | 5 |
| Vincentio *presbiter* | *San Vicente* | Centre | 5 |
| Lalano *presbiter* | *Otero* | Centre | 4 |
| Nantemiru *presbiter* and Alcedonia | *Braga* | West | 4 |
| Sampiro *presbiter* | *León* | Centre | 4 |
| Savaricus *diaconus* | *León* | Centre | 4 |
| Abbot Falconius | *Cardeña* | East | 3 |
| Arzisclus *presbiter* | *León* | Centre | 3 |
| Ihoannes *frater* | *Cardeña* | East | 3 |
| Valite *presbiter* | *León* | Centre | 3 |
| Vermudo *presbiter* | *Liébana* | Centre | 3 |
| Zuleiman *frater* | *León* | Centre | 3 |
| Absalon *presbiter* | *Celanova* | West | 2 |
| Adulfo *diaconus* | *León* | Centre | 2 |
| Crescentius and Gamil *monachi* | *León* | Centre | 2 |
| Enneco *frater* and sister Totaduenna | *San Millán* | East | 2 |
| Enneco *presbiter* | *Cardeña* | East | 2 |
| Felix *diaconus* | *León* | Centre | 2 |
| Gutier *presbiter* | *León* | Centre | 2 |
| Iohannes *presbiter* | *Liébana* | Centre | 2 |
| Iuliano *presbiter* | *Cardeña* | East | 2 |
| Iustus *presbiter* | *León* | Centre | 2 |
| Micahel *diaconus* | *León* | Centre | 2 |
| Modesto *presbiter* | *San Vicente* | Centre | 2 |
| Pasuri *presbiter* | *Cañizares* | West | 2 |
| Sabbarico *diaconus* | *León* | Centre | 2 |
| Segemaru *presbiter*, Antinu, Aliarigu | *Lugo* | West | 2 |
| Sereniano *presbiter* | *Lugo* | West | 2 |
| Stephanus *presbiter* | *León* | Centre | 2 |
| Tellu *presbiter* | *Cardeña* | East | 2 |
| Vimara *presbiter* | *Celanova* | West | 2 |
| Vislavara *conversa* | *León* | Centre | 2 |
| Zamarius *presbiter* and Farega *deovota* | *PMH, Guimarães* | West | 2 |

| Individual (Lay) | Collection | Region | Charters |
|---|---|---|---|
| Count Pedro Flaínez and wife Bronildi | *León, Otero* | Centre | 59 |
| Count Fruela Muñoz and wife Amuna | *Otero* | Centre | 53 |
| Count Hermegildo and wife Paterna | *Celanova, Coruña, Sobrado* | West | 45 |
| Count Munio Fernández and wife Elvira | *León, Astorga, Otero* | Centre | 21 |
| Munio Flaínez and wife Froileuva | *Sahagún, Otero, León* | Centre | 20 |
| Ansur *majordomo* and wife María | *Sahagún* | Centre | 16 |
| Count Gutier and wife Ilduara | *Celanova* | West | 15 |
| Bagaudano and wife Faquilona | *Liébana* | Centre | 14 |
| Cidi Domínguez and wife Oria | *León* | Centre | 12 |
| Tructesindo Osorediz and wife Unisco | *PMH, Coimbra, Paço de Sousa* | West | 11 |
| Eldebuani and wife Kisxilu | *Sobrarbe* | East | 8 |
| Flaíno Muñoz and wife Iusta | *Otero* | Centre | 8 |
| Fruela Velaz and wife Jimena | *León, Sahagún* | Centre | 8 |
| Iuzef and wife Iusta | *León* | Centre | 8 |
| Count Pedro Fernández and wife Sancha | *León* | Centre | 7 |
| Donani Zalamizi and wife Trudilo | *PMH, Azevedo* | West | 7 |
| Ederonio Alvitiz and wife Crastina | *PMH, Coimbra* | West | 6 |
| María Velázquez | *León, Sahagún* | Centre | 6 |
| Menicio and wife Avola | *León* | Centre | 6 |
| Arias and wife Flora | *León* | Centre | 5 |
| Count Munio Muñoz | *León, Astorga, Otero* | Centre | 5 |
| Fruela Vimarédiz and wife Adosinda | *Otero* | Centre | 5 |
| Mumadona Dias | *PMH, Guimarães* | West | 5 |
| Vimara Kagitiz | *Celanova* | West | 5 |
| Izila Christovaliz and wife Creusa | *PMH* | West | 4 |
| Nuño Sarracinez and wife Gudigeva | *León* | Centre | 4 |
| Petro Lovesendiz and wife Aragunti | *Braga* | West | 4 |
| Sandino Muñoz and wife Eilo | *Celanova* | West | 4 |
| Taurello and wife Principia | *León* | Centre | 4 |
| Vela Vermúdez and wife Gontina | *Sahagún* | Centre | 4 |
| Anderquina | *Cardeña* | East | 3 |
| Argemundo and wife Recoire | *Sahagún* | Centre | 3 |
| Atriano and wife Ermesenda | *Otero* | Centre | 3 |
| Count Pelayo Muñoz and wife Sancha | *León* | Centre | 3 |
| Countess Ilduara | *Braga* | West | 3 |

*Continued*

**Appendix 7** Continued

| Individual (Lay) | Collection | Region | Charters |
|---|---|---|---|
| Didacu Danielliz and wife Vislavara | *Otero* | Centre | 3 |
| Elena | *Sahagún* | Centre | 3 |
| Framilde | *León* | Centre | 3 |
| Fredesinde | *León* | Centre | 3 |
| Gundulfo | *Coruña* | West | 3 |
| Lazaro and wife Lempeda | *PMH* | West | 3 |
| Munio and wife Gulatrudia | *Liébana* | Centre | 3 |
| Pelayo and wife Crementina | *PMH, Coimbra* | West | 3 |
| Savarico and wife Vistrilli | *Liébana* | Centre | 3 |
| Sunila and wife Gudilo | *PMH, Coimbra* | West | 3 |
| Vermude and Pascuale | *León* | Centre | 3 |
| Vermudo Núñez | *Sahagún* | Centre | 3 |
| Advocatus and wife Leovilli | *PMH, Coimbra* | West | 2 |
| Agodin and wife Bonilde | *León* | Centre | 2 |
| Agube and wife Auria | *León* | Centre | 2 |
| Aloito and wife Gotina | *PMH* | West | 2 |
| Auriolo | *San Vicente* | Centre | 2 |
| Bonello and wife Arcadie | *San Vicente* | Centre | 2 |
| Cidi Domneliz | *León* | Centre | 2 |
| Count Fafila Fernández and wife Adosinda | *León, Sahagún* | Centre | 2 |
| Dominico and wife Matre | *León* | Centre | 2 |
| Eileuva | *PMH, Arouca* | West | 2 |
| Ermorigu and wife Nantela | *Braga* | West | 2 |
| Fafila Petriz | *Otero* | Centre | 2 |
| Fafilane and Penetrudie | *Sobrado* | West | 2 |
| Fernando Núñez | *León* | Centre | 2 |
| Flaíno and wife Bronildi Velasquita | *León* | Centre | 2 |
| Fromarigu iben Egas and wife Adosenda | *PMH* | West | 2 |
| Fruela and wife Eleuva | *PMH* | West | 2 |
| Fruela and wife Gundilu | *PMH* | West | 2 |
| Fruela and wife Trastalo | *PMH* | West | 2 |
| Fruela Ansaloniz | *PMH* | West | 2 |
| Fruela Gutiérrez | *Celanova* | West | 2 |
| Fruela Sendínez and wife Rosla | *Otero* | Centre | 2 |
| Godesteo Menéndez and wife Ledegundia | *León* | Centre | 2 |
| Gómez | *León* | Centre | 2 |
| Gonzalo Fernández and wife Ermesinda | *PMH* | West | 2 |
| Hermegildo and Paterna | *Sobrado* | West | 2 |
| Lalano and wife Iusta | *Otero* | Centre | 2 |
| Maurele Velázquez and wife Gudina | *León* | Centre | 2 |
| Menendo | *Celanova* | West | 2 |

| Individual (Lay) | Collection | Region | Charters |
|---|---|---|---|
| Michael, Gomeiro, and mother Framille | *León* | Centre | 2 |
| Munio Flaínez | *León* | Centre | 2 |
| Munio Núñez and wife Paterna | *León* | Centre | 2 |
| Nunno | *León* | Centre | 2 |
| Oveco Díaz / Queen Jimena | *San Millán* | East | 2 |
| Paterna | *León* | Centre | 2 |
| Paterno Velázquez | *Sahagún* | Centre | 2 |
| Peitro | *Otero* | Centre | 2 |
| Pelayo Danieliz | *Astorga* | Centre | 2 |
| Roderico and Elvira | *Sobrado* | West | 2 |
| Salbator | *León* | Centre | 2 |
| Sallo | *Sahagún* | Centre | 2 |
| Saracino and wife Iusta | *León* | Centre | 2 |
| Sarrazino Arias and wife Froilo | *León* | Centre | 2 |
| Semena | *Otero* | Centre | 2 |
| Semena Muñoz | *Otero* | Centre | 2 |
| Sintila and wife Gontina | *León* | Centre | 2 |
| Trastalum | *PMH* | West | 2 |
| Tructesindo Guimiriz | *PMH* | West | 2 |
| Vermudo Vegilaz | *Lugo* | West | 2 |
| Vita | *Cardeña* | East | 2 |
| Zondai and wife Aurie | *León* | Centre | 2 |
| **Ecclesiastical Total** | | | 128 (3%) |
| **Lay Total** | | | 532 (13%) |
| Miscellaneous Individuals (1 Charter) | | | 606 (15%) |
| **West** | | | 410 (10%) |
| **Centre** | | | 747 (18%) |
| **East** | | | 109 (3%) |
| **Individual Total** | | | 1266 (31%) |
| Unallocated (Uncertain) | | | 11 |

# Bibliography

## Abbreviations: Primary Sources

*Aguilar*    J. L. Rodríguez de Diego, *Colección diplomática de Santa María de Aguilar de Campoo (852–1230)* (Salamanca, 2004).

*Albelda*    A. Ubieto Arteta, *Cartulario de Albelda* (2nd ed., Zaragoza, 1981).

*Alfonso V*    J. M. Fernández del Pozo, 'Alfonso V, rey de León', in *León y su historia* 5 (León, 1984), 9–262.

*Arlanza*    L. Serrano, *Cartulario de San Pedro de Arlanza, antiguo monasterio benedictino* (Madrid, 1925).

*Arouca*    F. A. S. Silva, *Cartulário de D. Maior Martins (século XIII). Estudo introductório, edição diplomática, índices* (Arouca, 2001).

*Astorga*    G. Cavero Domínguez and E. Martín López, *Colección documental de la catedral de Astorga, I (646–1126)* (León, 1999).

*Azevedo*    R. P. de Azevedo, 'A expedição de Almançor a Santiago de Compostela em 997, e a de piratas normandos à Galiza em 1015–16', *Revista Portuguesa de História*, 14 (1974), 73–93.

*Benevívere*    L. Fernández, *Colección diplomática de la abadía de Santa María de Benevívere (Palencia), 1020–1561* (Madrid, 1967).

*Bóveda*    M. Lucas Álvarez, 'El patrimonio del monasterio de San Miguel de Bóveda anexo al San Clodio do Ribeiro de Avia', *Compostellanum*, 40.3–4 (1995), 501–86.

*Braga*    A. de Jesus da Costa, *Liber Fidei Sanctae Bracarensis Ecclesiae*, rev. J. Marques (2 vols, Braga, 2016).

*Burgos*    J. M. Garrido Garrido, *Documentación de la catedral de Burgos (804–1183)* (Burgos, 1983).

*Caaveiro*    J. I. Fernández de Viana y Vieites, M. T. González Balasch, and J. C. de Pablos Ramírez, 'El Tumbo de Caaveiro', *Cátedra*, 3 (1996), 267–437, 4 (1997), 221–385.

*Cañizares*    V. Cañizares del Rey, *Colección diplomática I (569–1463)*, ed. M. Rodríguez Sánchez and Ó. González Murado (Lugo, 2012), docs 1–86.

    V. Cañizares del Rey, *Colección diplomática II (857–1380)*, ed. M. Rodríguez Sánchez and Ó. González Murado (Lugo, 2014), docs 130–58.

*Cardeña*  J. A. Fernández Flórez and S. Serna Serna, *El Becerro Gótico de Cardeña. El primer gran cartulario hispánico (1086)* (2 vols, Burgos, 2017).

*Carracedo*  M. Martínez Martínez, *Cartulario de Santa María de Carracedo, 992–1500* (2 vols, Ponferrada, 1997–9), 1.

*Carrizo*  M. C. Casado Lobato, *Colección diplomática del monasterio de Carrizo* (León, 1983).

*Castañeda*  Á. Rodríguez González, *El Tumbo del monasterio de San Martín de Castañeda* (León, 1973).

*CCCM*  *Corpus Christianorum Continuatio Mediaevalis*

*CCSL*  *Corpus Christianorum Series Latina*

*Celanova*  E. Sáez and C. Sáez, *Colección diplomática del monasterio de Celanova (842–1230), I (842–942)* (Alcalá de Henares, 1996), docs 1–73.

E. Sáez and C. Sáez, *Colección diplomática del monasterio de Celanova (842–1230), II (943–988)* (Alcalá de Henares, 2000), docs 74–204.

E. Sáez and C. Sáez, *Colección diplomática del monasterio de Celanova (842–1230), III (989–1006)* (Alcalá de Henares, 2006), docs 205–301.

J. M. Andrade Cernadas, M. Díaz Tie, and F. J. Pérez Rodríguez, *O Tombo de Celanova: estudio introductorio, edición e índices (ss. IX–XII)* (2 vols, Santiago de Compostela, 1995), docs 302–383 (see Appendix 3).

*ChLA 114*  M. Calleja-Puerta *et al.*, *Chartae Latinae Antiquiores, Part CXIV. Spain III. Portugal* (Dietikon-Zürich, 2018).

*Chouzán*  R. Pichel Gotérrez, *Fundación e primeiros séculos do mosteiro bieito de Santo Estevo de Chouzán (sécs. IX–XIII)* (Noia, 2009).

*Coimbra*  M. A. Rodrigues and A. de Jesus da Costa, *Livro Preto: cartulário da sé de Coimbra. Edição crítica. Texto integral* (Coimbra, 1999).

*Concejo*  E. González Díez, *Colección diplomática del concejo de Burgos (884–1369)* (Burgos, 1984).

*Corniana*  C. E. Prieto Entrialgo, *Coleición diplomática del monasteriu de San Salvador de Corniana (1024–1499)* (Oviedo, 2004).

*Coruña*  C. Sáez and M. V. González de la Peña, *La Coruña. Fondo antiguo (788–1065)* (2 vols, Alcalá de Henares, 2003–4).

*Costa*  A. de Jesus da Costa, *O bispo D. Pedro e a organização da arquidiocese de Braga* (2nd ed., 2 vols, Braga, 1997–2000).

*Covarrubias*  L. Serrano, *Cartulario del Infantado de Covarrubias* (Valladolid, 1907).

*Cozuelos*  M. D. Guerrero Lafuente and M. A. Álvarez Castillo, 'Los inicios del monacato en Palencia. Santa Eufemia de Cozuelos', in

M. V. Calleja González (ed.), *Actas del III Congreso de Historia de Palencia* (4 vols, Palencia, 1995), 2, 173–94, docs 1–4.

M. A. Álvarez Castillo and M. D. Guerrero Lafuente, 'El manuscrito 13.065 de la Biblioteca Nacional', *Cuadernos de Estudios Medievales y Ciencias y Técnicas Historiográficas*, 18–19 (1993–4), 211–47, doc. 5.

*Crasto*          A. Pimenta, *Cartulário do mosteiro de Crasto* (Guimarães, 1938).

*Diócesis*        G. Cavero Domínguez, C. Álvarez Álvarez, and J. A. Martín Fuertes, *Colección documental del Archivo Diocesano de Astorga* (León, 2001).

*Elorrio*         C. Hidalgo de Cisneros Amestoy *et al.*, *Colección documental del Archivo Municipal de Elorrio (1013–1519)* (San Sebastián, 1988).

*Entrepeñas*      J. M. Ruiz Asencio *et al.*, *Colección documental del monasterio de San Román de Entrepeñas (940–1608)—Colección documental del monasterio de San Miguel de Escalada (940–1605)* (León, 2000).

*Escalada*        J. M. Ruiz Asencio *et al.*, *Colección documental del monasterio de San Román de Entrepeñas (940–1608)—Colección documental del monasterio de San Miguel de Escalada (940–1605)* (León, 2000).

*Eslonza*         J. M. Ruiz Asencio and I. Ruiz Albi, *Colección documental del monasterio de San Pedro de Eslonza, I (912–1300)* (León, 2007).

*Fanlo*           C. Laliena Corbera and E. Knibbs, *El Cartulario del monasterio aragonés de San Andrés de Fanlo (siglos X–XIII)* (Zaragoza, 2007).

*Fernando I*      P. Blanco Lozano, *Colección diplomática de Fernando I (1037–1065)* (León, 1987).

*Floriano*        A. C. Floriano, *Diplomática española del período astur. Estudio de las fuentes documentales del reino de Asturias (718–910)* (2 vols, Oviedo, 1949–51).

*FV*              J. Gil, 'Formulae Wisigothicae', in *Miscellanea Wisigothica* (2nd ed., Seville, 1991), 70–112.

*Grijó*           R. Durand, *Le cartulaire Baio-Ferrado du monastère de Grijó (XI$^e$–XIII$^e$ siècles)* (Paris, 1971).

*Guimarães*       L. C. Amaral *et al.*, *Livro de Mumadona. Cartulário do mosteiro de Guimarães. Edição crítica. Portugaliae Monumenta Historica. Diplomata et Chartae. Chartularia 7* (Lisbon, 2016).

*Hispana*         G. Martínez Díez and F. Rodríguez (eds), *La colección canónica Hispana* (6 vols, Madrid, 1966–2002).

*Huesca*          A. Durán Gudiol, *Colección diplomática de la catedral de Huesca* (2 vols, Zaragoza, 1965–69), 1.

*Husillos*        D. Marcos Díez, *La abadía de Santa María de Husillos: estudio y colección documental (904–1608)* (Palencia, 2011).

*Irache*          J. M. Lacarra, *Colección diplomática de Irache, I (958–1222)* (Zaragoza, 1965).

| | |
|---|---|
| *Junqueira* | S. Lira, *O mosteiro de S. Simão da Junqueira* (2 vols, Vila do Conde, 2001–2). |
| *Leire* | Á. J. Martín Duque, *Documentación medieval de Leire: siglos IX a XII* (Pamplona, 1983). |
| *León* | E. Sáez, *Colección documental del Archivo de la Catedral de León (775–1230), I (775–952)* (León, 1987), docs 1–258. |
| | E. Sáez and C. Sáez, *Colección documental del Archivo de la Catedral de León (775–1230), II (953–985)* (León, 1990), docs 259–511. |
| | J. M. Ruiz Asencio, *Colección documental del Archivo de la Catedral de León (775–1230), III (986–1031)* (León, 1987), docs 512–895. |
| | J. M. Fernández Catón and J. M. Ruiz Asencio, *Colección documental del Archivo de la Catedral de León (775–1230), VII. Apéndices e índices* (León, 2002), doc. 1982bis. |
| *Liébana* | L. Sánchez Belda, *Cartulario de Santo Toribio de Liébana. Edición y estudio* (Madrid, 1948). |
| *Lorvão* | J. M. Fernández Catón et al., 'Transcripción del texto del *Liber Testamentorum*—Transcrição do texto do *Liber Testamentorum*', in *Liber Testamentorum Coenobii Laurbanensis* (2 vols, León, 2008), 2, 581–717. |
| *Lourenzá* | Á. Rodríguez González and J. Á. Rey Caiña, 'Tumbo de Lorenzana. Transcripción y estudio', *Estudios Mindonienses*, 8 (1992), 11–324. |
| *Lugo* | A. Castro Correa and M. Rodríguez Sánchez, *Colección diplomática altomedieval de Galicia, II. Documentación en escritura visigótica de la sede lucense* (2 vols, Lugo, 2019), 1, 59–333. |
| *LV* | K. Zeumer, 'Liber Iudiciorum sive Lex Visigothorum', in *Leges Visigothorum. Monumenta Germaniae Historica. Leges Nationum Germanicarum* 1 (Hanover, 1902), 33–456. |
| *Meira* | M. M. Domínguez Casal, *El monasterio de Santa María de Meira y su colección diplomática* (PhD thesis, Universidad Central de Madrid, 2007 [1952]). |
| *Melón* | M. Romaní Martínez and P. S. Otero Piñeyro Maseda, 'La "domus" de Santa Leocadia de Guillade (Ponteareas) en un documento del año 963. Estudio sobre su autenticidad', *Cuadernos de Estudios Gallegos*, 56.122 (2009), 113–37. |
| *Mondoñedo* | E. Cal Pardo, *Colección diplomática medieval do Arquivo da Catedral de Mondoñedo. Transcrición íntegra dos documentos* (Santiago de Compostela, 1999). |
| *Montes* | A. Quintana Prieto, *Tumbo Viejo de San Pedro de Montes* (León, 1971). |
| *Nájera* | M. Cantera Montenegro, *Colección documental de Santa María la Real de Nájera, I (Siglos X–XIV)* (San Sebastián, 1991). |
| *Navarra* | A. Ubieto Arteta, *Documentos reales navarro-aragoneses hasta el año 1004* (Zaragoza, 1986). |

| | |
|---|---|
| *Obona* | M. J. Sanz Fuentes, 'Documentación medieval del monasterio de Santa María de Obona en el Archivo Histórico Diocesano de Oviedo', *Asturiensia Medievalia*, 8 (1995–7), 291–340. |
| *Oña* | J. del Álamo, *Colección diplomática de San Salvador de Oña (822–1284), I. 822–1214* (Madrid, 1950). |
| *Oseira* | M. Romaní Martínez, *Colección diplomática do mosteiro cisterciense de Santa María de Oseira (Ourense) (1025–1310)* (Santiago de Compostela, 1989). |
| *Otero* | J. A. Fernández Flórez and M. Herrero de la Fuente, *Colección documental del monasterio de Santa María de Otero de las Dueñas, I (854–1108)* (León, 1999). |
| *Ourense* | B. Vaquero Díaz and F. J. Pérez Rodríguez, *Colección documental del Archivo de la Catedral de Ourense, I (888–1230)* (León, 2010). |
| *Oviedo* | S. García Larragueta, *Colección de documentos de la catedral de Oviedo* (Oviedo, 1962). |
| *Paço de Sousa* | F. Lopes and M. J. Oliveira e Silva, *Livro dos Testamentos do mosteiro de São Salvador de Paço de Sousa. Edição crítica. Portugaliae Monumenta Historica. Diplomata et Chartae. Chartularia* 5 (Lisbon, 2015). |
| *Pallares* | A. Castro Correa and M. Rodríguez Sánchez, *Colección diplomática altomedieval de Galicia, II. Documentación en escritura visigótica de la sede lucense* (2 vols, Lugo, 2019), 2, 673–87. |
| *Pamplona* | J. Goñi Gaztambide, *Colección diplomática de la catedral de Pamplona, I (829–1243)* (Pamplona, 1997). |
| *Pedro* | S. Pedro, *O Género diplomático 'notícia' na documentação medieval portuguesa (séculos X–XIII)* (PhD thesis, Universidade de Lisboa, 2008). |
| *Peñafiel* | J. Castro Toledo, *Colección diplomática de Peñafiel* (Valladolid, 2014). |
| *Piasca* | J. Montenegro Valentín, *Colección diplomática de Santa María de Piasca (875–1252)* (Santander, 1991). |
| *Pino* | C. Rodríguez Fernández, *La colección diplomática de San Vicente del Pino* (PhD thesis, Universidad de Granada, 1990). |
| *PMH* | *Portugaliae Monumenta Historica a saeculo octavo post Christum usque ad quintumdecimum. Diplomata et Chartae* 1, fasc. 1–2 (Lisbon, 1868–9). |
| *Pombeiro* | M. Lucas Álvarez and P. Lucas Domínguez, *El priorato benedictino de San Vicenzo de Pombeiro y su colección diplomática en la Edad Media* (A Coruña, 1996). |
| *Porto* | J. da Guarda, *Censual do cabido da sé do Porto* (Porto, 1924). |
| *Puerto* | J. Abad Barrasús, *El monasterio de Santa María de Puerto (Santoña), 863–1210* (Santander, 1985). |
| *Ramiro II* | J. Rodríguez Fernández, *Ramiro II, rey de León* (Madrid, 1972). |

| | |
|---|---|
| Rocas | E. Duro Peña, *El monasterio de San Pedro de Rocas y su colección documental* (Ourense, 1972). |
| Sahagún | J. M. Mínguez Fernández, *Colección diplomática del monasterio de Sahagún (siglos IX–X)* (León, 1976), docs 1–360. |
| | M. Herrero de la Fuente, *Colección diplomática del monasterio de Sahagún (857–1230), II (1000–1073)* (León, 1988), docs 361–429. |
| | J. A. Fernández Flórez, *Colección diplomática del monasterio de Sahagún (857–1300), IV (1110–1199)* (León, 1991), docs 1170–2. |
| Samos | M. Lucas Álvarez, *El Tumbo de San Julián de Samos (siglos VIII–XII). Estudio introductorio, edición diplomática, apéndices e índices* (Santiago de Compostela, 1986). |
| San Clodio | M. Lucas Álvarez and P. Lucas Domínguez, *El monasterio de San Clodio do Ribeiro en la Edad Media: estudio y documentos* (A Coruña, 1996). |
| San Esteban | E. Duro Peña, *El monasterio de San Esteban de Ribas de Sil* (Ourense, 1977). |
| San Isidoro | M. E. Martín López, *Patrimonio cultural de San Isidoro de León, A. Serie documental, I/1. Documentos de los siglos X–XIII. Colección diplomática* (León, 1995). |
| San Isidro | C. M. Reglero de la Fuente, *El monasterio de San Isidro de Dueñas en la Edad Media: un priorato cluniacense hispano (911–1478). Estudio y colección documental* (León, 2005). |
| San Juan | A. Ubieto Arteta, *Cartulario de San Juan de la Peña* (2 vols, Valencia, 1962–3), 1. |
| San Millán | D. Peterson, F. García Andreva, *et al.*, *Becerro Galicano Digital* ([online] http://www.ehu.eus/galicano/?l=en). |
| San Pelayo | F. J. Fernández Conde, I. Torrente Fernández, and G. N. Menéndez, *El monasterio de San Pelayo de Oviedo: historia y fuentes, I. Colección diplomática (996–1325)* (Oviedo, 1978). |
| San Vicente | P. Floriano Llorente, *Colección diplomática del monasterio de San Vicente de Oviedo* (Oviedo, 1968). |
| Santa Cristina | V. Rodríguez Muñiz, *O mosteiro de Santa Cristina de Ribas de Sil na Idade Media* (Ourense, 2010). |
| Santiago | M. Lucas Álvarez, *La documentación del Tumbo A de la catedral de Santiago de Compostela: estudio y edición* (León, 1997). |
| Santillana | L. López Ormazábal, C. Díez Herrera, and R. Pérez Bustamente, *Abadía de Santillana del Mar. Colección diplomática* (Santillana del Mar, 1983). |
| Santos | M. J. A. Santos, *Da visigótica à carolina: a escrita em Portugal de 882 a 1172. Aspectos técnicos e culturais* (Lisbon, 1994). |
| Silos | M. C. Vivancos Gómez, *Documentación del monasterio de Santo Domingo de Silos (954–1254)* (Burgos, 1988). |
| Siresa | A. Ubieto Arteta, *Cartulario de Siresa* (Valencia, 1960). |

| | |
|---|---|
| *Sobrado* | P. Loscertales de García de Valdeavellano, *Tumbos del monasterio de Sobrado de los Monjes* (2 vols, Madrid, 1976). |
| *Sobrarbe* | Á. J. Martín Duque, *Colección diplomática del monasterio de San Victorián de Sobrarbe (1000–1219)* (Zaragoza, 2004). |
| *Tumbo B* | M. T. González Balasch, *Tumbo B de la catedral de Santiago: estudio y edición* (Santiago de Compostela, 2004). |
| *Tumbo C* | M. M. Extremadouro Figueroa, *La colección diplomática del Tumbo C. Parte primera* (PhD thesis, Universidade de Santiago de Compostela, 1967). |
| *Tumbo Viejo* | J. L. López Sangil and M. Vidán Torreira, 'Tumbo Viejo de Lugo (transcripción completa)', *Estudios Mindonienses*, 27 (2011), 11–373. |
| *Valladolid* | M. Herrero Jiménez, 'Documentos de la colección de pergaminos del Archivo de la Real Chancillería de Valladolid (934–1300)', in *El Reino de León en la Alta Edad Media* 11 (León, 2004), 11–240. |
| *Valpuesta* | J. M. Ruiz Asencio, I. Ruiz Albi, and M. Herrero Jiménez, *Los Becerros Gótico y Galicano de Valpuesta* (2 vols, Burgos, 2010). |
| *VDJ* | P. Floriano Llorente, 'El fondo antiguo de pergaminos del Instituto "Valencia de Don Juan". Documentos reales, primera serie (año 875–1224)', *Boletín de la Real Academia de la Historia*, 168.3 (1971), 441–514. |
| *Vega* | S. Domínguez Sánchez, *Colección documental medieval de los monasterios de San Claudio de León, Monasterio de Vega y San Pedro de las Dueñas* (León, 2001). |
| *Vermudo III* | L. Núñez Contreras, 'Colección diplomática de Vermudo III, rey de León', *Historia, Instituciones, Documentos*, 4 (1977), 381–514. |

## Primary Sources

R. de Abadal y Vinyals, *Els comtats de Pallars i Ribagorça* (2 vols, Barcelona, 1955).

J. Alturo and T. Alaix, *Chartae Latinae Antiquiores, Part CXII. Spain I* (Dietikon-Zürich, 2017).

J. Alturo and T. Alaix, *Chartae Latinae Antiquiores, Part CXIII. Spain II* (Dietikon-Zürich, 2017).

J. Alturo *et al.*, *Liber iudicum popularis: ordenat pel jutge Bonsom de Barcelona* (Barcelona, 2003).

J. Alvarado Planas and G. Oliva Manso, *Los Fueros de Castilla. Estudios y edición crítica* (Madrid, 2004), 'Fazañas del manuscrito 431 de la Biblioteca Nacional', 615–26.

R. Arbesmann and W. Hümpfner, *Iordani de Saxonia Liber Vitasfratrum* (New York, NY, 1943).

R. del Arco, 'El Archivo de la Catedral de Jaca', *BRAH*, 65 (1914), 47–98.

T. Ayuso Marazuela, *La Vetus Latina Hispana, I. Prolegómenos. Introducción general, estudio y análisis de las fuentes* (Madrid, 1953).

T. Ayuso Marazuela, *La Vetus Latina Hispana, V. El Salterio. Introducción general y edición crítica* (3 vols, Madrid, 1962).

A. Azkarate Garai-Olaun and I. García Camino, *Estelas e inscripciones medievales del País Vasco (siglos VI–XI), I. País Vasco occidental* (Bilbao, 1996).

J. L. Banús y Aguirre, *El Fuero de San Sebastián* (San Sebastián, 1963).

C. W. Barlow (transl.), *Iberian Fathers* (2 vols, Washington, DC, 1969).

J. Baró Pazos, *Fueros locales de la Vieja Castilla (siglos IX–XIV)*, ed. S. M. Coronas González (Madrid, 2020).

X. R. Barreiro Fernández, E. Portela Silva, and M. C. Pallares Méndez, *Inventario das fontes documentais da Galicia medieval* (Santiago de Compostela, 1988).

G. Barrett, 'Book of Testaments of Lorvão', in D. Thomas (ed.), *The Bloomsbury Reader in Christian-Muslim Relations, 600–1500* (London, 2022), 251–4.

M. J. Barroca, *Epigrafia medieval portuguesa (862–1422)* (3 vols, Lisbon, 2000).

J. Bellès i Sallent *et al.* (transl.), *Llibre dels judicis. Traducció catalana moderna del "Liber Iudiciorum"* (Barcelona, 2008).

D. Berger and S. Domínguez Sánchez, *Regesta Pontificum Romanorum. Iberia Pontificia, I–VI* (Göttingen, 2012–22).

D. Berger *et al.*, *Papsturkunden in Spanien. Vorarbeiten zur Hispania (Iberia) Pontificia, III. Kastilien: Urkunden* (Berlin, 2020).

R. M. Blasco, 'Aproximación a la escritura visigótica en Cantabria. Los documentos conservados en Santillana', *Altamira*, 47 (1988), 75–128.

E. Cal Pardo, 'De Viveiro en la Edad Media', *EMin*, 7 (1991), 11–226.

M. Calleja-Puerta, 'Noticias documentales del Archivo Capitular de la Catedral de Oviedo (ss. IX–XII)', *AHAM*, 25 (2003–4), 541–70.

M. Calleja-Puerta and M. J. Sanz Fuentes, 'Fundaciones monásticas y orígenes urbanos: la refacción del documento fundacional de San Vicente de Oviedo', in *Iglesia y ciudad*, 9–41.

J. Campos Ruiz and I. Roca Meliá, *Santos Padres Españoles, II. San Leandro, San Isidoro, San Fructuoso. Reglas monásticas de la España visigoda. Los tres libros de las "Sentencias"* (Madrid, 1971).

A. Castro, *Colección diplomática altomedieval de Galicia, I. Documentación editada en escritura visigótica (662–1234)* (Noia, 2011).

J. M. de Castro, 'Um documento—doação de 875', in L. A. da Fonseca, L. C. Amaral, and M. F. F. Santos (eds), *Os reinos ibéricos na Idade Média. Livro de homenagem ao professor Doutor Humberto Carlos Baquero Moreno* (3 vols, Porto, 2003), 2, 647–52.

J. Castro Toledo, *Colección diplomática de Tordesillas, 909–1474* (Valladolid, 1981).

A. Conde de São Payo, 'Dois documentos anteriores à Nacionalidade. Os Coutos de Paradela e Mazarefes', *O Archeologo Português*, 27 (1929), 136–55.

S. Corcoran, 'The Donation and Will of Vincent of Huesca: Latin Text and English Translation', *AT*, 11 (2003), 215–21.

S. M. Coronas González (ed.), *Fueros locales del reino de León (910–1230): Antología* (Madrid, 2018).

J. L. Corral Lafuente, *Cartulario de Alaón (Huesca)* (Zaragoza, 1984).

A. de Jesus da Costa, *Liber Fidei Sanctae Bracarensis Ecclesiae* (3 vols, Braga, 1965–90).

M. C. Díaz y Díaz, *Index scriptorum Latinorum Medii Aevi Hispanorum* (Madrid, 1959).

F. Diego Santos, *Inscripciones medievales de Asturias* (Oviedo, 1993).

*Documentos de la monarquía leonesa de Alfonso III a Alfonso VI: estudio y edición* (León, 2006).

*Documentos selectos para el estudio de los orígenes del romance en el reino de León, siglos X–XII: edición facsímil* (León, 2003).

C. Domínguez Maestro, *Cartulario latino de San Pedro de Montes: transcripción del texto, comentario morfosintáctico, léxico* (PhD thesis, 2 vols, Universidad de León, 1991).

M. Echániz Sans, *El monasterio femenino de Sancti Spiritus de Salamanca. Colección diplomática (1268–1400)* (Salamanca, 1993).

A. Emiliano, 'O mais antigo documento latino-português (882 a.D.)—edição e estudo grafémico', *Verba*, 26 (1999), 7–42.

A. Emiliano and S. Pedro, 'Inventário de diplomas conservados no Arquivo Nacional da Torre do Tombo contendo documentos notariais dos séculos IX–X', *Origens do Português. Digitalização, edição e estudo linguístico de documentos dos séculos IX–X* (Lisbon, 2006, unpublished: see [online] https://clunl.fcsh.unl.pt/projetos/projetos-concluidos/philologia-filologia-e-linguistica-historica-fontes-para-historia-da-lingua-portuguesa/).

J. Escalona, I. Velázquez Soriano, and P. Juárez Benítez, 'Identification of the Sole Extant Original Charter Issued by Fernán González, Count of Castile (932–970)', *JMIS*, 4.2 (2012), 259–88.

J. A. Estévez Sola, *Chronica Hispana saeculi XII. Pars III. Historia Silensis. CCCM* 71B (Turnhout, 2018).

Á. Fábrega Grau, *Pasionario hispánico (siglos VII–XI)* (2 vols, Barcelona, 1953–5).

J. M. Fernández Catón, 'Documentos leoneses en escritura visigótica. Fondo del archivo del monasterio de Carrizo', *AL*, 72 (1982), 195–291.

J. M. Fernández Catón, 'Documentos leoneses en escritura visigótica. Fondo M. Bravo del Archivo Histórico Diocesano de León', in *LH* 2 (León, 1973), 203–95.

J. M. Fernández Catón, 'Documentos leoneses en escritura visigótica. Fondo Otero de las Dueñas (años 1000 a 1009) del Archivo Histórico Diocesano de León', *AL*, 55–6 (1974), 31–83.

J. M. Fernández Catón, 'Documentos leoneses en escritura visigótica. Fondo Raimundo Rodríguez del Archivo Catedral de León', in *LH* 3 (León, 1975), 469–511.

J. M. Fernández Catón, *Index verborum de la documentación medieval leonesa: monasterio de Sahagún (857–1300)* (2 vols, León, 1999).

J. M. Fernández Catón, *El llamado Tumbo Colorado y otros códices de la iglesia compostelana: ensayo de reconstrucción* (León, 1990).

J. M. Fernández Catón, J. A. Fernández Flórez, and M. Herrero de la Fuente, *Colección diplomática del monasterio de Sahagún (857–1300), VI. Índices* (León, 1999).

F. J. Fernández Conde and X. L. García Arias, 'Forum Legionense y Fueru de Lleón', *LA*, 117 (2017), 207–33.

F. J. Fernández Conde and M. C. Santos del Valle, 'La corte de Pravia: fuentes documentales, cronísticas y bibliográficas', *BIDEA*, 41.123 (1987), 865–932, 42.125 (1988), 59–84.

E. Fernández Vallina, M. J. Sanz Fuentes, and E. E. Rodríguez Díaz, *Liber Testamentorum Ecclesiae Ovetensis* (2 vols, Barcelona, 1994–5).

J. I. Fernández de Viana y Vieites, *Colección diplomática del monasterio de Santa María de Ferreira de Pantón* (Lugo, 1994).

J. A. P. Ferreira, *Livro de Mumadona: cartulário medievo existente no Arquivo Nacional da Torre do Tombo* (Lisbon, 1973).

A. C. Floriano, *Colección diplomática del monasterio de Belmonte. Transcripción y estudio* (Oviedo, 1960).

B. W. Frier (ed.), *The Codex of Justinian: a New Annotated Translation, with Parallel Latin and Greek Text* (3 vols, Cambridge, 2016).

O. Gallego, *El archivo del monasterio de Celanova* (Madrid, 1991).

A. García Leal, *El diploma del rey Silo* (A Coruña, 2007).

M. R. García Álvarez, 'El gallego Ordoño III, rey de León', *CEG*, 22.68 (1967), 281–336.

M. R. García Álvarez, 'Ordoño Adefonsiz, rey de Galicia de 910 a 914 (noticias y documentos)', *CEG*, 21.64 (1966), 217–48.

F. García Andreva, *El Becerro Galicano de San Millán de la Cogolla. Edición y estudio* (Logroño, 2010).

X. L. García Arias and A. Miranda Duque, *Documentos orixinales de los sieglos IX–X de los archivos del monasteriu de San Pelayo y de la catedral d'Uviéu* (Oviedo, 2011).

J. Á. García de Cortázar, J. A. Munita, and L. J. Fortún (eds), *CODIPHIS. Catálogo de colecciones diplomáticas hispano-lusas de época medieval* (2 vols, Santander, 1999).

A. García Leal, *El archivo de los condes Fruela Muñoz y Pedro Flaínez. La formación de un patrimonio nobiliario en la montaña asturleonesa (854–1048)* (León, 2010).

A. García Leal, *Colección diplomática del monasterio de San Juan Bautista de Corias* (Oviedo, 1998).

A. García Leal, 'Un inventario latino del s. XI (a propósito del diploma ACL, Fondo R. Rodríguez, no. 10)', *Veleia*, 15 (1998), 327–42.

A. García Leal, *El Registro de Corias* (Oviedo, 2000).

L. A. García Moreno, 'Sobre un nuevo ejemplar del *Laterculus regum Visigothorum*', *AST*, 47.1 (1974), 5–14.

F. J. García Turza, *Documentación medieval del monasterio de San Prudencio de Monte Laturce (siglos X–XV)* (Logroño, 1992).

F. J. García Turza, *Documentación medieval del monasterio de Valvanera (siglos XI a XIII)* (Zaragoza, 1985).

J. Gil, *Chronica Hispana saeculi VIII et IX. CCCM 65* (Turnhout, 2018).

J. Gil, *Corpus scriptorum Muzarabicorum* (2 vols, Madrid, 1973).

J. Gil, *Scriptores Muzarabici saeculi VIII–XI. CCCM 65A-B* (2 vols, Turnhout, 2020).

J. Gil Fernández, J. L. Moralejo, and J. I. Ruiz de la Peña, *Crónicas asturianas. Crónica de Alfonso III (Rotense y "a Sebastián") y Crónica albeldense (y "profética")* (Oviedo, 1985).

A. W. Godfrey (transl.), 'The Rule of Isidore', *Monastic Studies*, 18 (1988), 7–29.

F. A. González and J. Tejada y Ramiro, *Colección de cánones de la Iglesia española* (5 vols, Madrid, 1849–55).

N. Grau Quiroga, *Roda de Isábena en los siglos X–XIII. La documentación episcopal y del cabildo catedralicio* (Zaragoza, 2010).

R. Gryson and M.-C. de Bièvre, *Beati Liebanensis Tractatus de Apocalipsin. CCCM* 107B-C (2 vols, Turnhout, 2012).

M. Gurruchaga Sánchez, 'La fundación del monasterio de Caaveiro (La Coruña): nueva documentación', *Faventia*, 21.2 (1999), 129–42.

P. Henriet, 'La lettre d'Alphonse III, *rex Hispaniae*, aux chanoines de Saint-Martin de Tours', in S. Gouguenheim *et al.* (eds), *Retour aux sources. Textes, études et documents d'histoire médiévale offerts à Michel Parisse* (Paris, 2004), 155–66.

F. J. Hernández, *Los cartularios de Toledo: catálogo documental* (Madrid, 1985).

E. de Hinojosa, *Documentos para la historia de las instituciones de León y de Castilla (siglos X–XIII)* (Madrid, 1919).

Isidore of Seville, *Etymologiae*, 11, ed.-transl. F. Gasti, *Etimologie. Libro XI. L'uomo e i portenti* (Paris, 2010).

R. Jimeno Aranguren and A. Pescador Medrano, *Colección documental de Sancho Garcés III el Mayor, rey de Pamplona (1004–1035)* (Pamplona, 2003).

P. Juárez Benítez, *La colección diplomática del monasterio de San Pedro de Arlanza. Formación y trayectoria evolutiva* (PhD thesis, Universidad Complutense de Madrid, 2014).

E. Jusué, *Libro de Regla o Cartulario de la antigua abadía de Santillana del Mar* (Madrid, 1912).

P. Kehr, *Papsturkunden in Spanien. Vorarbeiten zur Hispania Pontificia* (2 vols, Berlin, 1926–8).

L. Kéry, *Canonical Collections of the Early Middle Ages (ca. 400–1140). A Bibliographical Guide to the Manuscripts and Literature* (Washington, DC, 1999).

L. Körntgen and F. Bezler, *Paenitentialia Hispaniae. CCSL* 156A (Turnhout, 1998).

J. M. Lacarra, 'Textos navarros del Códice de Roda', *Estudios de Edad Media de la Corona de Aragón*, 1 (1945), 193–283.

C. Laliena Corbera, 'Documentos sobre la servidumbre en la sociedad navarro-aragonesa del siglo XI', *PV*, 58.211 (1997), 371–92.

C. M. Lawson, *Sancti Isidori episcopi Hispalensis De ecclesiasticis officiis. CCSL* 113 (Turnhout, 1989).

A. Linage Conde, *Una regla monástica riojana femenina del siglo X. El Libellus a regula sancti Benedicti subtractus* (Salamanca, 1973).

A. Linder, *The Jews in the Legal Sources of the Early Middle Ages* (Detroit, MI, 1997).

P. Linehan, *España Pontificia: Papal Letters to Spain, 1198–1303* (Washington, DC, 2023).

B. Löfstedt, *Beati Liebanensis et Eterii Oxomensis Adversus Elipandum libri duo. CCCM* 59 (Turnhout, 1984).

F. A. Lorenzana, *Breviarium Gothicum secundum Regulam beatissimi Isidori archiepiscopi Hispalensis* (Madrid, 1775).

M. Lucas Álvarez, 'La colección diplomática del monasterio de San Lorenzo de Carboeiro', *Compostellanum*, 2 (1957), 549–73, 3 (1958), 221–308, 547–638.

M. Lucas Álvarez, '"Colligere fragmenta". Documentos en escritura visigótica del Archivo Histórico y Universitario de Santiago de Compostela', *HID*, 19 (1992), 267–76.

M. Lucas Álvarez, *El monasterio de San Martiño Pinario de Santiago de Compostela en la Edad Media* (Sada, 2003).

M. Lucas Álvarez, 'El monasterio de San Salvador de Camanzo', *AL*, 32.64 (1978), 273–380.

M. Lucas Álvarez, 'El monasterio de San Salvador y San Nicolás de Cis', *EMin*, 20 (2004), 603–728.

M. Lucas Álvarez, *San Paio de Antealtares, Soandres y Toques: tres monasterios medievales gallegos* (A Coruña, 2001).

M. Lucas Álvarez and P. P. Lucas Domínguez, *San Pedro de Ramirás: un monasterio femenino en la Edad Media. Colección diplomática* (Santiago de Compostela, 1988).

A. G. R. Madahil, *Milenário de Aveiro: colectânea de documentos históricos, I. 959–1516* (Aveiro, 1959).

A. Malalana Ureña, *En torno al año mil. Bibliografías de historia de España* 10 (2 vols, Madrid, 2000).

D. Mansilla, *La documentación pontificia hasta Inocencio III (965–1216)* (Rome, 1955).

A. E. Marques, 'Para um inventário da documentação diplomática anterior a 1101 conservada em arquivos portugueses', in Arízaga Bolumburu *et al.* (eds), *Mundos*, 1, 705–18.

J. M. Martí Bonet (ed.), *Guía de los Archivos de la Iglesia en España* (Barcelona, 2001).

Á. J. Martín Duque, *Colección diplomática de Obarra (siglos XI–XIII)* (Zaragoza, 1965).

J. C. Martín-Iglesias, 'Los *Annales Castellani Antiquiores* y *Annales Castellani Recentiores*: edición y traducción anotada', *TSP*, 4 (2009), 203–26.

J. C. Martín-Iglesias, 'El *Iudicium inter Marcianum et Habentium episcopos* (a. 638): estudio, edición crítica y traducción', *Habis*, 49 (2018), 203–31.

J. C. Martín-Iglesias, *Sources latines de l'Espagne tardo-antique et médiévale (V<sup>e</sup>–XIV<sup>e</sup> siècles). Répertoire bibliographique* (Paris, 2010).

J. C. Martín-Iglesias, 'La *Vita Froilanis episcopi Legionensis* (*BHL* 3180) (s. X): introducción, edición crítica y particularidades lingüísticas', in M. Goullet (ed.), *Parva pro magnis munera. Études de littérature latine tardo-antique et médiévale offertes à François Dolbeau par ses élèves* (Turnhout, 2009), 561–84.

M. S. Martín Postigo, *Santa María de Cárdaba, priorato de Arlanza y granja de Sacramenia* (Valladolid, 1979).

G. Martínez Díez, *Colección documental del monasterio de San Pedro de Cardeña* (Burgos, 1998).

G. Martínez Díez, 'El concilio compostelano del reinado de Fernando I', *AEM*, 1 (1964), 121–38.

G. Martínez Díez, 'Diplomatario de San Cristóbal de Ibeas', *BIFG*, 54.185 (1975), 689–720, 55.186 (1976), 845–72.

G. Martínez Díez, *Fueros locales en el territorio de la provincia de Burgos* (Burgos, 1982).

G. Martínez Díez, *Legislación conciliar del reino astur (718–910) y del reino de León (910–1230)* (León, 2009).

G. Martínez Díez, 'La tradición manuscrita del Fuero de León y del Concilio de Coyanza', in *RLAEM* 2 (León, 1992), 116–84.

F. Martínez Llorente and F. Trullén Galve, 'La carta foral de Peñafiel (s. X-XII): vindicación de un derecho de frontera castellano', in F. Martínez Llorente and I. Ruiz Rodríguez (eds), *La historia y el derecho de España: visiones y pareceres. Homenaje al Dr. Emiliano González Díez* (Madrid, 2022), 389–434.

A. Maya Sánchez, *Vitas sanctorum patrum Emeretensium*. *CCSL* 116 (Turnhout, 1992).

A. Millares Carlo, *Corpus de códices visigóticos*, ed. M. C. Díaz y Díaz (2 vols, Las Palmas de Gran Canaria, 1999).

A. Millares Carlo, *El diploma del rey Silo* (Madrid, 1971).

S. Montero Díaz, *La colección diplomática de San Martín de Jubia* (Santiago de Compostela, 1935).

A. M. Mundó, 'La inscripción visigoda del monasterio de Samos', *SMon*, 3.1 (1961), 157–64.

M. Pérez González, 'El latín de las inscripciones mozárabes', in Codoñer and Alberto (eds), *Wisigothica*, 341–84.

E. Pérez Rodríguez, 'El aspecto léxico como auxiliar en la datación de los diplomas medievales: el doc. nº 1 del monasterio de Obona', in C. Macías and S. Núñez (eds), *Virtuti magistri honos. Studia Graecolatina A. Alberte septuagesimo anno dicata* (Zaragoza, 2011), 527–46.

J. Pérez de Urbel, *Sampiro, su crónica y la monarquía leonesa en el siglo X* (Madrid, 1952).

J. Pérez de Urbel and A. González y Ruiz-Zorrilla, *Liber Commicus. Edición crítica* (2 vols, Madrid, 1950–5).

A. Prieto Prieto, 'Documentos referentes al orden judicial del monasterio de Otero de las Dueñas', *AHDE*, 44 (1974), 619–74.

A. Prieto Prieto, 'Documentos referentes al orden judicial del monasterio de Sahagún', *AHDE*, 45 (1975), 489–541.

R. Ramis Barceló and P. Ramis Serra (transl.), *El Libro de los Juicios (Liber Iudiciorum)* (Madrid, 2015).

K. Reinhardt and H. Santiago-Otero, *Biblioteca bíblica ibérica medieval* (Madrid, 1986).

L. Reynolds (ed.), *Texts and Transmission: a Survey of the Latin Classics* (Oxford, 1983).

P. Riesco Chueca, *Pasionario hispánico. Introducción, edición crítica y traducción* (Seville, 1995).

A. Rodríguez Colmenero, S. Ferrer Sierra, and R. D. Álvarez Asorey, *Callaeciae et Asturiae Itinera Romana. Miliarios e outras inscricións viarias romanas do noroeste hispánico (conventos bracarense, lucense e asturicense)* (Santiago de Compostela, 2004).

E. E. Rodríguez Díaz, *El libro de la Regla Colorada de la catedral de Oviedo: estudio y edición* (Oviedo, 1995).

I. Rodríguez de Lama, *Colección diplomática medieval de La Rioja (923-1225), II. Documentos (923-1168)* (Logroño, 1976).

J. Rodríguez Muñoz, A. García Leal, and J. López Álvarez, *Colección de textos y documentos para la historia de Asturias* (2 vols, Gijón, 1990).

M. Romaní Martínez and P. S. Otero Piñeyro Maseda, 'Documentación del Fondo de Oseira (AHN) relacionada con el monasterio San Pedro de Vilanova de Dozón (1015–1295)', *CEG*, 50.116 (2003), 27–77.

I. Ruiz Albi, 'Hallazgo de un documento original del monasterio de Sahagún (año 978)', in *LH* 6 (León, 2000), 141–6.

J. M. Ruiz Asencio *et al.*, *Fuero de Brañosera (estudio y edición crítica)* (Burgos, 2020).

E. Sáez, 'Notas y documentos sobre Sancho Ordóñez, rey de Galicia', *CHE*, 11 (1949), 25–104.

E. Sáinz Ripa, *Colección diplomática de las colegiatas de Albelda y Logroño (Tomo I: 924–1.399)* (Logroño, 1981).

J. M. Salrach i Marès *et al.*, *Justícia i resolució de conflictes a la Catalunya medieval. Col·lecció diplomàtica, segles IX–XI* (Barcelona, 2018).

C. Sánchez-Albornoz, 'Documentos de Samos de los reyes de Asturias', *CHE*, 4 (1946), 147–60.

C. Sánchez-Albornoz, 'Serie de documentos inéditos del reino de Asturias', *CHE*, 1–2 (1944), 298–351.

M. J. Sanz Fuentes, 'El documento de Fakilo (803): estudio y edición', in *Estudos*, 1, 31–40.

S. P. Scott (transl.), *The Visigothic Code (Forum Judicum)* (Boston, MA, 1910).

G. del Ser Quijano, *Colección diplomática de Santa María de Otero de las Dueñas (León) (854–1037)* (Salamanca, 1994).

G. del Ser Quijano, *Documentación de la catedral de León (siglos IX–X)* (Salamanca, 1981).

L. Serrano, *Becerro Gótico de Cardeña* (Valladolid, 1910).

L. Serrano, *Cartulario de San Vicente de Oviedo (781–1200)* (Madrid, 1929).

M. Serrano y Sanz, 'Notas a un documento aragonés del año 958', *AHDE*, 5 (1928), 254–65.

M. Serrano y Sanz, *Noticias y documentos históricos del condado de Ribagorza hasta la muerte de Sancho Garcés III (año 1035)* (Madrid, 1912).

A. Suárez González, 'Memoria de la fundación de San Lorenzo de Carboeiro (una crónica *despistada*)', *Rudesindus*, 7 (2011), 77–93.

G. Tomás-Faci and J. C. Martín-Iglesias, 'Cuatro documentos inéditos del monasterio visigodo de San Martín de Asán (522–586)', *Mittellateinisches Jahrbuch*, 52.2 (2017), 261–86.

M. J. Torrens Álvarez *et al.*, *Documentación del monasterio de San Salvador de Oña, I (822–1280)* (Madrid, 2016).

A. Ubieto Arteta, *Cartulario de San Millán de la Cogolla (759–1076)* (Valencia, 1976).

A. Ubieto Arteta, *Cartulario de Santa Cruz de la Serós* (Valencia, 1966).

A. Ubieto Arteta, *Documentos del monasterio de Obarra (Huesca) anteriores al año 1000* (Zaragoza, 1989).

A. Ubieto Arteta, *Jaca: documentos municipales, 971–1269* (Valencia, 1975).

J. A. Valdés Gallego, *El Liber Testamentorum Ovetensis: estudio filológico y edición* (Oviedo, 2000).

L. Vázquez de Parga, 'Los documentos sobre las presuras del obispo Odoario de Lugo', *Hispania*, 10.41 (1950), 635–80.

B. Velasco Bayón *et al.*, *Colección documental de Cuéllar (934–1492)* (2 vols, Cuéllar, 2010), 1.

I. Velázquez Soriano, *Las pizarras visigodas (Entre el latín y su disgregación. La lengua hablada en Hispania, siglos VI–VIII)* (Burgos, 2004).

B. L. Venarde, *The Rule of Saint Benedict* (Cambridge, MA, 2011).

J. Vives, 'El Oracional mozárabe de Silos', *AST*, 18.1 (1945), 1–25.

J. Vives, T. Marín Martínez, and G. Martínez Díez (eds), *Concilios visigóticos e hispano-romanos* (Barcelona-Madrid, 1963).

A. de Vogüé and J. Neufville, *La règle de saint Benoît* (7 vols, Paris, 1971–7).

J. Williams, *Visions of the End in Medieval Spain. Catalogue of Illustrated Beatus Commentaries on the Apocalypse and Study of the Geneva Beatus*, ed. T. Martin (Amsterdam, 2017).

J. Williams and B. A. Shailor, *A Spanish Apocalypse: the Morgan Beatus Manuscript* (New York, NY, 1991).

V. Yarza Urquiola, *Passionarium Hispanicum. CCSL* 171–171A (2 vols, Turnhout, 2020).

M. Zabalza Duque, *Colección diplomática de los condes de Castilla* (Salamanca, 1998).

M. Zabalza Duque, 'Hallazgo del documento original de la fundación del monasterio de Oña', in *Pasado*, 325–32.

S. Zapke (ed.), *Hispania Vetus. Musical-Liturgical Manuscripts from Visigothic Origins to the Franco-Roman Transition (9th–12th Centuries)* (Bilbao, 2007).

H. Zimmermann, *Papsturkunden, 896–1046* (3 vols, Vienna, 1984–9).

M. Zimmermann, 'Un formulaire du X$^e$ siècle conservé à Ripoll: édition critique', *Faventia*, 4.2 (1982), 25–86.

## Abbreviations: Secondary Literature

| | |
|---|---|
| *AB* | *Anuario Brigantino* |
| *AC* | *Antigüedad y Cristianismo* |
| *AD* | *Archiv für Diplomatik* |
| *AEA* | *Archivo Español de Arqueología* |
| *AEM* | *Anuario de Estudios Medievales* |
| *AESC* | *Annales. Économies, Sociétés, Civilisations* |
| *AFDUC* | *Anuario da Facultade de Dereito da Universidade da Coruña* |
| *AHAM* | *Acta Historica et Archaeologica Mediaevalia* |
| *AHDE* | *Anuario de Historia del Derecho Español* |
| *AHSS* | *Annales. Histoire, Sciences Sociales* |
| *AL* | *Archivos Leoneses* |
| *ALMA* | *Archivum Latinitatis Medii Aevi* |
| *AM* | *Asturiensia Medievalia* |
| *AST* | *Analecta Sacra Tarraconensia* |
| *AT* | *Antiquité Tardive* |
| *BECh* | *Bibliothèque de l'École des Chartes* |
| *BFDUC* | *Boletim da Faculdade de Direito da Universidade da Coimbra* |
| *BICS* | *Bulletin of the Institute of Classical Studies* |
| *BIDEA* | *Boletín del Instituto de Estudios Asturianos* |
| *BIFG* | *Boletín de la Institución Fernán González* |
| *BRIDEA* | *Boletín del Real Instituto de Estudios Asturianos* |

| | |
|---|---|
| *Blaise* | A. Blaise, *Lexicon Latinitatis Medii Aevi* (Turnhout, 1975). |
| *BRAH* | *Boletín de la Real Academia de la Historia* |
| *CA* | *Codex Aquilarensis* |
| *CC* | *Cuadernos del Centro de Estudios Medievales y Renacentistas* |
| *CCM* | *Cahiers de Civilisation Médiévale* |
| *CEG* | *Cuadernos de Estudios Gallegos* |
| *CHD* | *Cuadernos de Historia del Derecho* |
| *CHE* | *Cuadernos de Historia de España* |
| *CM* | *Cuadernos Medievales* |
| *Documentación* | M. Lucas Álvarez, *La documentación real astur-leonesa (718–1072). El Reino de León en la Alta Edad Media* 8 (León, 1995). |
| *Du Cange* | C. du Fresne, Sieur du Cange, *Glossarium Mediae et Infimae Latinitatis* (8 vols, Paris, 1883–7). |
| *ED* | *Estudios de Deusto* |
| *EEM* | *En la España Medieval* |
| *EHF* | *Estudios Humanísticos. Filología* |
| *EHG* | *Estudios Humanísticos. Geografía, Historia y Arte* |
| *EHH* | *Estudios Humanísticos. Historia* |
| *EHR* | *English Historical Review* |
| *EM* | *Edad Media* |
| *EME* | *Early Medieval Europe* |
| *EMin* | *Estudios Mindonienses* |
| *EMir* | *Estudios Mirandeses* |
| *ETF* | *Espacio, Tiempo y Forma. Serie III, Historia Medieval* |
| *GLM* | *Gazette du Livre Médiéval* |
| *GRBS* | *Greek, Roman, and Byzantine Studies* |
| *HID* | *Historia, Instituciones, Documentos* |
| *HS* | *Hispania Sacra* |
| *JMH* | *Journal of Medieval History* |
| *JMIS* | *Journal of Medieval Iberian Studies* |
| *LA* | *Lletres Asturianes* |
| *Léxico* | R. Menéndez Pidal, R. Lapesa, and C. García, *Léxico hispánico primitivo (siglos VIII al XII). Versión primera del Glosario del primitivo léxico iberrománico*, ed. M. Seco (Madrid, 2003). |
| *Lexicon* | M. Pérez González (ed.), *Lexicon Latinitatis Medii Aevi regni Legionis (s. VIII–1230) imperfectum* (Turnhout, 2010). |
| *LH* | *León y su historia* |
| *LVLT* | *Latin vulgaire—latin tardif* |
| *MCV* | *Mélanges de la Casa de Velázquez* |
| *MM* | *Madrider Mitteilungen* |
| *Niermeyer* | J. F. Niermeyer, C. van de Kieft, and J. W. J. Burgers (eds), *Mediae Latinitatis lexicon minus* (2nd ed., 2 vols, Leiden, 2002). |

| PP | Past & Present |
|---|---|
| PV | Príncipe de Viana |
| RABM | Revista de Archivos, Bibliotecas y Museos |
| RHDFE | Revue Historique de Droit Français et Étranger |
| RHJZ | Revista de Historia Jerónimo Zurita |
| RIDA | Revue Internationale des Droits de l'Antiquité |
| RLAEM | El Reino de León en la Alta Edad Media |
| RM | Revue Mabillon |
| RPH | Revista Portuguesa de História |
| SCH | Studies in Church History |
| SE | Sacris Erudiri |
| Settimane | Settimane di studio del Centro italiano di studi sull'alto Medioevo |
| SHHM | Studia Historica. Historia Medieval |
| SMed | Studi Medievali |
| SMon | Studia Monastica |
| SZ | Studia Zamorensia |
| TH | Do Tempo e da História |
| TL | Tierras de León |
| TRHS | Transactions of the Royal Historical Society |
| TSP | Territorio, Sociedad y Poder |

## Secondary Literature

R. de Abadal y Vinyals, *Els primers comtes catalans* (Barcelona, 1958).

A. Abal, 'El monasterio de San Lorenzo de Carboeiro: intervenciones en el patrimonio y teorías de la restauración', *Abrente*, 40–1 (2008–9), 75–106.

*Actas de las III Jornadas de Derecho. La aplicación del derecho a lo largo de la historia* (Jaén, 1998).

J. N. Adams, *The Latin Sexual Vocabulary* (London, 1982).

A. Adamska and M. Mostert (eds), *The Development of Literate Mentalities in East Central Europe* (Turnhout, 2004).

A. Adamska and M. Mostert (eds), *Oral and Written Communication in the Medieval Countryside: Peasants—Clergy—Noblemen* (Turnhout, 2021).

D. Addison, 'Property and "Publicness": Bishops and Lay-Founded Churches in Post-Roman Hispania', *EME*, 28.2 (2020), 175–96.

L. Agúndez San Miguel, 'Escritura, memoria y conflicto entre el monasterio de Sahagún y la catedral de León: nuevas perspectivas para el aprovechamiento de los falsos documentales (siglos X a XII)', *Medievalismo*, 19 (2009), 261–85.

L. Agúndez San Miguel, *La memoria escrita en el monasterio de Sahagún (años 904–1300)* (Madrid, 2019).

L. Agúndez San Miguel, 'La memoria femenina en los diplomas falsificados de San Salvador de Oña: un monasterio dúplice frente a la reforma benedictina', *EM*, 22 (2021), 233–61.

L. Agúndez San Miguel, 'Memoria y cultura en la documentación del monasterio de Sahagún: la respuesta de las fórmulas "inútiles" (904–1230)', *AEM*, 40.2 (2010), 847–88.

L. Agúndez San Miguel, 'Reacción y defensa en la producción de los cartularios de Sahagún', in Furtado and Moscone (eds), *Charters*, 99–117.

L. Agúndez San Miguel, 'El Tumbo de San Pedro de Montes como instrumento de recreación de la memoria institucional', *ETF*, 29 (2016), 17–47.

L. Agúndez San Miguel and J. Á. García de Cortázar, 'Los cartularios monásticos castellanos revisitados: memoria, arquitectura, intertextualidad', in J. V. Cabezuelo, J. A. Barrio, and J. L. Soler (eds), *Entre el Mediterráneo y el Atlántico. José Hinojosa Montalvo y el mundo medieval. Libro homenaje al profesor Hinojosa Montalvo* (Alicante, 2021), 211–27.

C. Aillet, 'Entre chrétiens et musulmans: le monastère de Lorvão et les marges du Mondego (878–1064)', *RM*, 15.76 (2004), 27–49.

F. N. Akinnaso, 'Schooling, Language, and Knowledge in Literate and Nonliterate Societies', *Comparative Studies in Society and History*, 34.1 (1992), 68–109.

M. A. Alba Bueno and M. Rodríguez García, 'La muerte en el Fuero Juzgo y tipos de enterramientos en el reino visigodo de Toledo', *Estudios sobre Patrimonio, Cultura y Ciencias Medievales*, 18 (2016), 81–106.

A. Alberte González and C. Macías Villalobos (eds), *Actas del Congreso internacional "Cristianismo y tradición latina"* (Madrid, 2001).

J. A. Alejandre García, 'El delito de falsedad testimonial en el derecho histórico español', *HID*, 3 (1976), 9–139.

J. A. Alejandre García, 'Estudio histórico del delito de falsedad documental', *AHDE*, 42 (1972), 117–87.

I. Alfonso, 'El formato de la información judicial en la Alta Edad Media peninsular', in Escalona Monge and Sirantoine (eds), *Chartes*, 191–218.

I. Alfonso, 'Judicial Rhetoric and Political Legitimation in Medieval León-Castile', in Alfonso, Kennedy, and Escalona (eds), *Building Legitimacy*, 51–87.

I. Alfonso, 'Litigios por la tierra y "malfetrías" entre la nobleza medieval castellano-leonesa', *Hispania*, 57.197 (1997), 917–55.

I. Alfonso, H. Kennedy, and J. Escalona (eds), *Building Legitimacy: Political Discourses and Forms of Legitimation in Medieval Societies* (Leiden, 2004).

C. A. F. de Almeida, 'Ainda o documento XIII dos "Diplomata et Chartae"', *Revista da Faculdade de Letras. História*, 1 (1970), 97–107.

J. Alturo i Perucho, 'El sistema educativo en la Cataluña altomedieval', *Memoria Ecclesiae*, 12 (1998), 31–61.

J. Alturo i Perucho, 'The Visigothic Script', in F. T. Coulson and R. G. Babcock (eds), *The Oxford Handbook of Latin Palaeography* (Oxford, 2020), 143–84.

J. Alturo i Perucho, M. Torras Cortina, and A. Castro Correa (eds), *La escritura visigótica en la Península Ibérica: nuevas aportaciones. I Jornadas Internacionales Seminari de Paleografia, Codicologia i Diplomàtica* (Barcelona, 2012).

G. Althoff, *Family, Friends, and Followers: Political and Social Bonds in Early Medieval Europe*, transl. C. Carroll (Cambridge, 2004).

G. Althoff, *Rules and Rituals in Medieval Power Games: a German Perspective* (Leiden, 2020).

J. Alvarado Planas, 'A modo de conclusiones: el *Liber Iudiciorum* y la aplicación del derecho en los siglos VI a XI', *MCV*, 41.2 (2011), 109–27.

J. Alvarado Planas, 'Ordalías y derecho en la España visigoda', in *Antigüedad*, 507–617.

J. Alvarado Planas, 'Orígenes de la nobleza en la Alta Edad Media', *AHDE*, 76 (2006), 439–59.

J. Alvarado Planas, 'La pervivencia del "Liber iudiciorum" en el reino de León', in López Valladares (ed.), *Reino*, 141–52.

J. Alvarado Planas, *El problema del germanismo en el derecho español, siglos V–XI. Ordalías y derecho consuetudinario en la España visigoda* (Madrid, 1997).

J. Alvarado Planas, 'El problema de la naturaleza germánica del derecho español altomedieval', in Iglesia Duarte (ed.), *VII Semana*, 121–47.

C. Álvarez Álvarez, 'El monasterio de Valdevimbre (siglos IX–XII)', in *Escritos*, 1, 41–64.

I. Álvarez Borge, *Poder y relaciones sociales en Castilla en la Edad Media. Los territorios entre el Arlanzón y el Duero en los siglos X al XIV* (Valladolid, 1996).

I. Álvarez Borge (ed.), *Comunidades locales y poderes feudales en la Edad Media* (Logroño, 2001).

E. Álvarez Cora, 'Aproximación al derecho contractual visigodo', *AHDE*, 74 (2004), 543–82.

E. Álvarez Cora, 'El contrato de compraventa a la luz de las fórmulas visigodas', *Revista Internacional de Derecho Romano*, 1 (2008), 309–30.

E. Álvarez Cora, 'Derecho sexual visigótico', *HID*, 24 (1997), 1–52.

E. Álvarez Cora, 'Interrelación de los conceptos de término, uso, fuero y costumbre en el derecho medieval ibérico (siglos IX–XII)', *EEM*, 41 (2018), 49–75.

E. Álvarez Cora, 'La noción de la ley postgótica', *HID*, 22 (1995), 1–38.

E. Álvarez Cora, 'Orto del mal. Derecho penal de los siglos X y XI', *Initium*, 18 (2013), 209–36.

E. Álvarez Cora, '*Qualis erit lex*: la naturaleza jurídica de la ley visigótica', *AHDE*, 66 (1996), 11–117.

E. Álvarez Cora, 'Sagradas Escrituras y vías normativas en el Bajomedievo', in G. E. Pinard and A. Merchán Álvarez (eds), *Libro homenaje in memoriam Carlos Díaz Rementería* (Huelva, 1998), 59–73.

M. P. Álvarez Maurín, *Diplomática asturleonesa. Terminología toponímica* (León, 1994).

M. P. Álvarez Maurín, 'Estudio documental del valle de Pardomino (León)', *EHF*, 14 (1992), 95–104.

M. P. Álvarez Maurín, 'El formulismo en la lengua de los documentos notariales altomedievales', *Helmantica*, 46.139–41 (1995), 419–31.

M. P. Álvarez Maurín, 'El léxico de la escritura en la documentación medieval asturleonesa hasta 1230', in Pérez González (ed.), *Actas III*, 2, 523–30.

M. P. Álvarez Maurín, 'El registro lingüístico especial de los documentos notariales medievales', *EHF*, 15 (1993), 23–41.

V. Á. Álvarez Palenzuela, 'La nobleza del reino de León en la Alta Edad Media', in *RLAEM 7* (León, 1995), 151–329.

A. Álvarez Rodríguez, *El testamento de San Genadio, obispo de Astorga y eremita del Valle de Silencio* (Roquetas de Mar, 2018).

B. Anderson, *Imagined Communities: Reflections on the Origin and Spread of Nationalism* (rev. ed., London, 2006).

J. M. Andrade Cernadas, 'Algunos apuntos sobre la *Vita Rudesindi* y los documentos del Tumbo de Celanova', in Domínguez García *et al.* (eds), *Sub luce*, 270–7.

J. M. Andrade Cernadas, 'Aproximación a la figura del prepósito monástico en el monacato gallego medieval: siglos X al XII', *EMin*, 11 (1995), 279–92.

J. M. Andrade Cernadas, 'Baños, claustros y piedras: una aproximación a los escenarios de las asambleas judiciales en la Galicia altomedieval', *SHHM*, 36.1 (2018), 13–30.

J. M. Andrade Cernadas, 'Las edades del hombre en los monasterios benedictinos y cistercienses: de la infancia a la vejez', in J. Á. García de Cortázar and R. Teja (eds), *El ritmo cotidiano de la vida en el monasterio medieval* (Aguilar de Campoo, 2015), 111–41.

J. M. Andrade Cernadas, 'Fuentes documentales para el estudio del rey García de Galicia', *Minius*, 6 (1997), 41–9.

J. M. Andrade Cernadas, 'Hace veinte años: recordando la edición del Tumbo de Celanova', *Rudesindus*, 10 (2014–17), 77–82.

J. M. Andrade Cernadas, 'En el refectorio: la alimentación en el mundo monástico de la Galicia medieval', *Semata*, 21 (2009), 45–64.

J. M. Andrade Cernadas, 'El Tumbo de Celanova: aspectos diplomáticos y de estructuración interna', in Pérez González (ed.), *Actas I*, 75–8.

J. M. Andrade Cernadas, 'La vida cotidiana en un monasterio medieval', *Semata*, 7–8 (1996), 295–306.

J. M. Andrade Cernadas, 'Villas regias y asambleas judiciales entre los siglos X y XI: el caso de Larín', *Signum*, 12.2 (2011), 18–35.

J. M. Andrade Cernadas, 'La voz de los ancianos. La intervención de los viejos en los pleitos y disputas en la Galicia medieval', *Hispania*, 72.240 (2012), 11–34.

M. A. Andrés Sanz, 'Ediciones y versiones altomedievales de la Biblia Latina: el caso de Isidoro de Sevilla', in M. A. Pena González and I. Delgado Jara (eds), *A quinientos años de la Políglota: el proyecto humanístico de Cisneros. Fuentes documentales y líneas de investigación* (Salamanca, 2015), 67–80.

M. A. Andrés Sanz, '*Lectio sanctarum scripturarum* y exégesis en las obras de Isidoro de Seville: teoría y práctica', *MCV*, 49.1 (2019), 19–39.

A. Angenendt, '*Donationes pro anima*: Gift and Countergift in the Early Medieval Liturgy', in Davis and McCormick (eds), *Long Morning*, 131–54.

L. Anta Lorenzo, 'El monasterio de San Martín de Castañeda en el siglo X. En torno a los orígenes y la formación de la propiedad dominical', *SZ*, 3 (1996), 31–52.

*De la Antigüedad al medievo. Siglos IV–VIII. III Congreso de Estudios Medievales* (Madrid, 1993).

N. Ares, 'Roimil, punto de litigio histórico y lingüístico', *Brigantium*, 3 (1982), 243–8.

A. Ares Legaspi, 'Alfabetización y cultura gráfica en Carmona en 1513', in P. Pueyo Colomina (ed.), *Lugares de escritura: la ciudad* (Zaragoza, 2015), 249–63.

M. Arias, 'Informe sobre el archivo del monasterio de Samos', *Actas de las I Jornadas de Metodología Aplicada de las Ciencias Históricas, V. Paleografía y archivística* (Santiago de Compostela, 1975), 163–70.

M. Arias, 'El monasterio de Samos desde sus orígenes hasta el siglo XI', *AL*, 35.70 (1981), 267–350.

M. Arias y Alonso, 'Algunas notas acerca de la denominación de la mujer casada en la diplomática medieval latina', in J. M. Nieto Ibáñez (ed.), *Lógos hellenikós: homenaje al profesor Gaspar Morocho Gayo* (2 vols, León, 2003), 1, 87–96.

M. Arias y Alonso, 'Expresión de las relaciones de fraternidad en la diplomática medieval latina', *EHF*, 26 (2004), 11–35.

B. Arízaga Bolumburu *et al.* (eds), *Mundos medievales: espacios, sociedades y poder. Homenaje al profesor José Ángel García de Cortázar y Ruiz de Aguirre* (2 vols, Santander, 2012).

F. J. Arlinghaus *et al.* (eds), *Transforming the Medieval World: Uses of Pragmatic Literacy in the Middle Ages* (Turnhout, 2006).

F. de Arvizu y Galarraga, *La disposición "mortis causa" en el derecho español de la Alta Edad Media* (Pamplona, 1977).

F. de Arvizu y Galarraga, 'Fianzas en materia civil en la documentación altomedieval', *AHDE*, 88–9 (2018–19), 15–44.

C. Astarita, 'Prácticas del conde y formación del feudalismo. Siglos VIII a XI', *Revista de Historia Medieval. Anales de la Universidad de Alicante*, 14 (2003–6), 21–52.

E. Auerbach, *Literary Language and its Public*, transl. R. Manheim (Princeton, NJ, 1965).

N. Ávila Seoane, M. J. Salamanca López, and L. Zozaya Montes (eds), *VIII Jornadas científicas sobre documentación de la Hispania altomedieval (siglos VI–X)* (Madrid, 2009).

C. de Ayala Martínez, 'Relaciones de propiedad y estructura económica del reino de León: los marcos de producción agraria y el trabajo campesino (850–1230)', in *RLAEM* 6 (León, 1994), 133–408.

C. de Ayala Martínez, 'El yuguero castellano-leonés: problemas en torno a sus orígenes (siglos X–XIII)', *HID*, 20 (1993), 17–46.

C. de Ayala Martínez *et al.*, *Economía y sociedad en la España medieval* (Madrid, 2004).

P. Azcárate Aguilar-Amat *et al.*, 'Volver a nacer: historia e identidad en los monasterios de Arlanza, San Millán y Silos (siglos XII–XIII)', *Cahiers d'Études Hispaniques Médiévales*, 29 (2006), 359–94.

R. de Azevedo, 'O mosteiro de Lorvão na Reconquista cristã', *Arquivo Histórico de Portugal*, 1 (1933), 183–239.

M. J. Bádenas Población, 'El índice del Libro Gótico de San Juan de la Peña: ¿ordenar para administrar?', in Rodríguez Díaz and García Martínez (eds), *Escritura*, 335–58.

M. J. Bádenas Población, '*Manu mea roboravi*. ¿Representaciones medievales del yo? Monasterio de Sahagún, 1000–1100', in A. Castillo Gómez and V. Sierra Blas (eds), *El legado de Mnemosyne: las escrituras del yo a través del tiempo* (Gijón, 2007), 335–54.

R. S. Bagnall, *Everyday Writing in the Graeco-Roman East* (Berkeley, CA, 2011).

R. Baldaquí Escandell (ed.), *Lugares de escritura: el monasterio* (Alicante, 2016).

S. Baldwin, 'On the Meaning of the Term "Liber Commicus"', *Traditio*, 39 (1983), 439–43.

R. Balzaretti, *The Lands of Saint Ambrose: Monks and Society in Early Medieval Milan* (Turnhout, 2019).

R. Balzaretti, 'The Monastery of Sant'Ambrogio and Dispute Settlement in Early Medieval Milan', *EME*, 3.1 (1994), 1–18.

R. Balzaretti, 'Spoken Narratives in Ninth-Century Milanese Court Records', in Tyler and Balzaretti (eds), *Narrative*, 11–37.

I. G. Bango Torviso, 'El espacio para enterramientos privilegiados en la arquitectura medieval española', *Anuario del Departamento de Historia y Teoría del Arte*, 4 (1992), 93–132.

M. Banniard, 'Le lecteur en Espagne wisigothique d'après Isidore de Séville: de ses fonctions à l'état de la langue', *Revue d'Études Augustiniennes et Patristiques*, 21.1–2 (1975), 112–44.

M. Banniard, *Viva voce. Communication écrite et communication orale du IV<sup>e</sup> au IX<sup>e</sup> siècle en Occident latin* (Paris, 1992).

F. Bautista, 'Breve historiografía: listas regias y anales en la Península Ibérica (siglos VII–XII)', *Talia Dixit*, 4 (2009), 113–90.

A. Barbero and M. Vigil, *La formación del feudalismo en la Península Ibérica* (Barcelona, 1978).

J. Barbier, *Archives oubliées du Haut Moyen Âge. Les gesta municipalia en Gaule franque (VI<sup>e</sup>–IX<sup>e</sup> siècle)* (Paris, 2014).

P. S. Barnwell, 'Emperors, Jurists, and Kings: Law and Custom in the Late Roman and Early Medieval West', *PP*, 168 (2000), 6–29.

J. Barreiro Somoza, *El señorío de la iglesia de Santiago de Compostela (siglos IX–XIII)* (A Coruña, 1987).

G. Barrett, 'Conservatism in Language: Framing Latin in Late Antique and Early Medieval Iberia', in A. Mullen and G. Woudhuysen (eds), *Languages and Communities in the Late Roman and Post-Imperial Western Provinces* (Oxford, forthcoming).

G. Barrett, 'God's Librarian: Isidore of Seville and his Literary Agenda', in A. Fear and J. Wood (eds), *A Companion to Isidore of Seville* (Leiden, 2019), 42–100.

G. Barrett, 'Hispania at Home and Abroad', in Barton and Portass (eds), *Beyond the Reconquista*, 52–119.

G. Barrett, 'The Text of Visigothic Law in Practice', *Visigothic Symposia*, 4 (2020–1), 18–63.

G. Barrett and G. Woudhuysen, 'Assembling the *Austrasian Letters* at Trier and Lorsch', *EME*, 24.1 (2016), 3–57.

J. Barrow, 'Churches, Education, and Literacy in Towns, 600–1300', in D. M. Palliser (ed.), *The Cambridge Urban History of Britain, I. 600–1540* (Cambridge, 2000), 127–52.

J. Barthe Porcel, 'Vindigare, obtoricare, redrar y pactar marjadraque (datos para el estudio histórico del saneamiento por evicción)', *Anales de la Universidad de Murcia* (1946–7), 1, 117–22.

D. Barthélemy, 'La mutation féodale a-t-elle eu lieu?', *AESC*, 47.3 (1992), 767–77.

D. Barthélemy, 'Présence de l'aveu dans le déroulement des ordalies (IX<sup>e</sup>–XIII<sup>e</sup> siècle)', in *L'aveu. Antiquité et Moyen Âge* (Rome, 1986), 191–214.

D. Barthélemy, *The Serf, the Knight, and the Historian*, transl. G. R. Edwards (Ithaca, NY, 2009).

R. Barthes, 'Theory of the Text', ed. R. Young, *Untying the Text: a Post-Structuralist Reader* (London, 1981), 31–47.

R. Barthes, 'From Work to Text', in *Image Music Text*, transl. S. Heath (London, 1977), 155–64.

R. Bartlett, *Trial by Fire and Water: the Medieval Judicial Ordeal* (Oxford, 1986).

S. Barton and R. Portass (eds), *Beyond the Reconquista: New Directions in the History of Early Medieval Iberia (711–1085). In Honour of Simon Barton* (Leiden, 2020).

J. Bastardas Parera, 'El latín medieval', in M. Alvar *et al.* (eds), *Enciclopedia lingüística hispánica, I. Antecedentes. Onomástica* (Madrid, 1960), 251–90.

J. Bastardas Parera, *Particularidades sintácticas del latín medieval (cartularios españoles de los siglos VIII al XI)* (Barcelona, 1953).

J. Bastier, 'Le testament en Catalogne du IX$^e$ au XII$^e$ siècle: une survivance wisigothique', *RHDFE*, 51.3 (1973), 373–417.

J. Bastier, 'La vente dans les Asturies du IX$^e$ au XII$^e$ siècle: droit et économie', *RHDFE*, 57 (1979), 569–609.

F. H. Bäuml, 'Varieties and Consequences of Medieval Literacy and Illiteracy', *Speculum*, 55.2 (1980), 237–65.

A. I. Beach and I. Cochelin (eds), *The Cambridge History of Medieval Monasticism in the Latin West* (Cambridge, 2020).

I. Beceiro Pita, *Libros, lectores y bibliotecas en la España medieval* (Murcia, 2007).

L. Becker, *Hispano-romanisches Namenbuch. Untersuchung der Personennamen vorrömischer, griechischer und lateinisch-romanischer Etymologie auf der Iberischen Halbinsel im Mittelalter (6.–12. Jahrhundert)* (Tübingen, 2009).

B. Bedos-Rezak, 'Diplomatic Sources and Medieval Documentary Practices: an Essay in Interpretive Methodology', in J. van Engen (ed.), *The Past and Future of Medieval Studies* (Notre Dame, IN, 1994), 313–43.

F.-M. Beltrán Torreira, 'Algunas reflexiones en torno a las figuras de Coré, Datán y Abirón en las fuentes hispano-visigodas', *Helmantica*, 40.121–3 (1989), 183–94.

I. V. Benavides Monje, 'Algunas fórmulas de contenido religioso en el protocolo de documentación asturleonesa (775–1230)', in Alberte González and Macías Villalobos (eds), *Actas*, 183–9.

I. V. Benavides Monje, 'La presura en León (siglos VIII–X)', in M. Pérez González (ed.), *II Congreso hispánico de latín medieval. Actas* (2 vols, León, 1998), 1, 255–62.

J. Beneyto Pérez, 'Sobre las Fórmulas Visigodas. "Judas, Datan y Abirón"', *BRAH*, 101 (1932), 191–7.

P. Benito i Monclús, A. J. Kosto, and N. L. Taylor, 'Three Typological Approaches to Catalonian Archival Evidence, 10th–12th Centuries', *AEM*, 26.1 (1996), 43–88.

J. C. Bermejo Barrera and M. Romaní Martínez, '*Et per ubi posuerintis vestros pedes iurare*. La cojuración y el posible uso de los signos podomorfos en la Galicia medieval y moderna', *MM*, 55 (2014), 560–95.

M. Á. Bermejo Castrillo, *Parentesco, matrimonio, propiedad y herencia en la Castilla altomedieval* (Madrid, 1996).

M. Bermúdez Beloso, '*Presares: comitatum, commisso, territorio?* Dimensión documental e espacial dun topónimo abandonado', *CEG*, 66.132 (2019), 77–105.

J. Bernaldo, 'Pactual Monasticism? About a Much-Discussed Feature of Early Spanish Monasticism', in A. Härdelin (ed.), *In Quest of the Kingdom: Ten Papers on Medieval Monastic Spirituality* (Stockholm, 1991), 27–63.

C. Bertelli, 'The Production and Distribution of Books in Late Antiquity', in R. Hodges and W. Bowden (eds), *The Sixth Century: Production, Distribution, and Demand* (Leiden, 1998), 41–60.

P. Bertrand, *Documenting the Everyday in Medieval Europe: the Social Dimensions of a Writing Revolution, 1250-1350*, transl. G. R. Edwards (Turnhout, 2019).

A. Besga Marroquín, *Orígenes hispanogodos del reino de Asturias* (Oviedo, 2000).

J. Bianchini, 'Review Article: Re-defining Medieval Spain', *EHR*, 126.522 (2011), 1167–79.

P. Biller and A. Hudson (eds), *Heresy and Literacy, 1000–1530* (Cambridge, 1996).

J. Binns, *Ascetics and Ambassadors of Christ: the Monasteries of Palestine, 314–631* (Oxford, 1994).

C. J. Bishko, 'Salvus of Albelda and Frontier Monasticism in Tenth-Century Navarre', *Speculum*, 23.4 (1948), 559–90.

C. J. Bishko, *Spanish and Portuguese Monastic History, 600–1300* (London, 1984).

C. J. Bishko, *Studies in Medieval Spanish Frontier History* (London, 1980).

R. Blake, 'Squeezing the Spanish Turnip Dry: Latinate Documents from the Early Middle Ages', in R. Harris-Northall and T. D. Cravens (eds), *Linguistic Studies in Medieval Spanish. Studies in Honor of Dennis P. Seniff* (Madison, WI, 1991), 1–14.

R. M. Blasco Martínez, *Los cartularios de Cantabria (Santo Toribio, Santa María del Puerto, Santillana y Piasca): estudio codicológico, paleográfico y diplomático* (Santander, 1986).

R. M. Blasco Martínez, 'El códice cartulario de Oña. Aproximación codicológica', *HID*, 19 (1992), 61–72.

R. M. Blasco Martínez, 'El monasterio como centro emisor y conservador de documentación entre los siglos IX al XII', *Altamira*, 50 (1992–3), 13–26.

M. Blidstein, 'Swearing by the Book: Oaths and the Rise of Scripture in the Roman Empire', *Asdiwal*, 12 (2017), 53–72.

R. Bof and C. Leyser, 'Divorce and Remarriage between Late Antiquity and the Early Middle Ages: Canon Law and Conflict Resolution', in Cooper and Leyser (eds), *Making*, 155–80.

P.-M. Bogaert, 'The Latin Bible, *c.* 600 to *c.* 900', in R. Marsden and E. A. Matter (eds), *The New Cambridge History of the Bible from 600 to 1450* (Cambridge, 2012), 69–92.

H. Böhmer, 'Early Vernacular Literacy in the Iberian Peninsula', in N. Kössinger *et al.* (eds), *Origin Stories: the Rise of Vernacular Literacy in a Comparative Perspective* (Leiden, 2018), 115–64.

P. Bonnassie, *La Catalogne du milieu du X$^e$ à la fin du XI$^e$ siècle. Croissance et mutations d'une société* (2 vols, Toulouse, 1975–6).

Y. Bonnaz, 'Divers aspects de la continuité wisigothique dans la monarchie asturienne', *MCV*, 12 (1976), 81–99.

J. Bono, *Los archivos notariales. Una introducción en seis temas a la documentación notarial y a la catalogación e investigación de fondos notariales* (Seville, 1985).

J. V. Boscá Codina, 'De la voz en el texto: cambios y permanencias en el proceso de afirmación de la escritura (Cataluña, ss. X–XII)', *AHAM*, 20–1 (1999–2000), 139–75.

K. Böse, 'Speaking Books: Ornament and Sensual Perception in Early Iberian Book Illumination', *CA*, 36 (2020), 49–64.

C. B. Bouchard, 'Monastic Cartularies: Organizing Eternity', in A. J. Kosto and A. Winroth (eds), *Charters, Cartularies, and Archives: the Preservation and Transmission of Documents in the Medieval West. Proceedings of a Colloquium of the Commission Internationale de Diplomatique* (Toronto, 2002), 22–32.

C. B. Bouchard, *Rewriting Saints and Ancestors: Memory and Forgetting in France, 500–1200* (Philadelphia, PA, 2015).

F. Bougard, '"Falsum falsorum judicum consilium": l'écrit et la justice en Italie centro-septentrionale au XIe siècle', *BECh*, 155.1 (1997), 299–314.

F. Bougard, 'Jugement divin, excommunication, anathème et malédiction: la sanction spirituelle dans les sources diplomatiques', in G. Bührer-Thierry and S. Gioanni (eds), *Exclure de la communauté chrétienne. Sens et pratiques sociales de l'anathème et de l'excommunication (IVe–XIIe s.)* (Turnhout, 2015), 215–38.

F. Bougard, 'La justice dans le royaume d'Italie aux IXe–Xe siècles', in *Giustizia*, 1, 133–76.

A. I. Boullón Agrelo, *Antroponimia medieval galega (ss. VIII–XII)* (Tübingen, 1999).

A. I. Boullón Agrelo, 'Cronoloxía e variación das fórmulas patronímicas na Galicia altomedieval', *Verba*, 22 (1995), 449–75.

A. I. Boullón Agrelo, 'A edición de textos en Galicia (da Idade Media aos Séculos Escuros)', *LaborHistórico*, 3.1 (2017), 76–92.

P. Bourgain, 'The Circulation of Texts in Manuscript Culture', in M. Johnston and M. van Dussen (eds), *The Medieval Manuscript Book: Cultural Approaches* (Cambridge, 2015), 140–59.

J. A. Bowman, 'Councils, Memory, and Mills: the Early Development of the Peace of God in Catalonia', *EME*, 8.1 (1999), 99–129.

J. A. Bowman, 'From Galicia to the Rhône: Legal Practice in Northern Spain around the Year 1000', in D'Emilio (ed.-transl.), *Culture*, 343–60.

J. A. Bowman, 'Infamy and Proof in Medieval Spain', in T. Fenster and D. L. Smail (eds), *Fama. The Politics of Talk and Reputation in Medieval Europe* (Ithaca, NY, 2003), 95–117.

J. A. Bowman, 'Record, Chronicle, and Oblivion: Remembering and Forgetting Elite Women in Medieval Iberia', in Barton and Portass (eds), *Beyond the Reconquista*, 201–31.

J. A. Bowman, *Shifting Landmarks: Property, Proof, and Dispute in Catalonia around the Year 1000* (Ithaca, NY, 2004).

J. A. Bowman, 'From Written Record to Historical Memory: Narrating the Past in Iberian Charters', in R. A. Maxwell (ed.), *Representing History, 900–1300: Art, Music, History* (University Park, PA, 2010), 173–80.

S. Boynton, 'Restoration or Invention? Archbishop Cisneros and the Mozarabic Rite in Toledo', *Yale Journal of Music & Religion*, 1.1 (2015), 5–29.

M. J. Branco, 'Portugal no reino de León. Etapas de uma relação (866–1179)', in *RLAEM* 4 (León, 1993), 533–625.

M. J. Branco, 'Reis, condes, mosteiros e poderes: o mosteiro de Lorvão no contexto político do reino de Leão (sécs. IX–XII)', in *Liber*, 2, 27–80.

C. F. Briggs, 'Historiographical Essay: Literacy, Reading, and Writing in the Medieval West', *JMH*, 26.4 (2000), 397–420.

R. Britnell, 'Bureaucracy and Literacy', in C. Lansing and E. D. English (eds), *A Companion to the Medieval World* (Chichester, 2007), 413–34.

L. Brouillard, 'The Secular Family in Monastic Rules, 400–700', *Journal of Medieval Monastic Studies*, 8 (2019), 1–46.

C. Brown, 'A Manuscript Present: *Translatio*, Media, and Mediation in Early Medieval Hispanolatin Book Culture', *JMIS*, 14.1 (2022), 28–40.

C. Brown, 'Manuscript Thinking: Stories by Hand', *Postmedieval*, 2.3 (2011), 350–68.

C. Brown, 'Remember the Hand: Bodies and Bookmaking in Early Medieval Spain', *Word & Image*, 27.3 (2011), 262–78.

C. Brown, *Remember the Hand: Manuscription in Early Medieval Iberia* (New York, NY, 2022).

C. Brown, 'Scratching the Surface', *Exemplaria*, 26.2–3 (2014), 199–214.

W. Brown, 'Charters as Weapons. On the Role Played by Early Medieval Dispute Records in the Disputes They Record', *JMH*, 28.3 (2002), 227–48.

W. Brown, *Unjust Seizure: Conflict, Interest, and Authority in an Early Medieval Society* (Ithaca, NY, 2001).

W. Brown, 'The Use of Norms in Disputes in Early Medieval Bavaria', *Viator*, 30 (1999), 15–40.

W. Brown, 'When Documents are Destroyed or Lost: Lay People and Archives in the Early Middle Ages', *EME*, 11.4 (2002), 337–66.

W. C. Brown *et al.* (eds), *Documentary Culture and the Laity in the Early Middle Ages* (Cambridge, 2013).

J. A. Brundage, *The Medieval Origins of the Legal Profession: Canonists, Civilians, and Courts* (Chicago, IL, 2008).

S. H. Brunsch, 'The Authority of Documents in Early-Medieval Italian Pleas', in B. M. Bolton and C. E. Meek (eds), *Aspects of Power and Authority in the Middle Ages* (Turnhout, 2007), 277–87.

P. Buc, *The Dangers of Ritual. Between Early Medieval Texts and Social Scientific Theory* (Princeton, NJ, 2001).

S. Cabezas Fontanilla, 'De la *invocatio* en los documentos altomedievales (718–910)', in Ávila Seoane, Salamanca López, and Zozaya Montes (eds), *VIII Jornadas*, 43–78.

S. Cabezas Fontanilla and N. Ávila Seoane, 'Cómo fechaba la oficina real asturleonesa y castellana hasta el siglo XII', in Galende Díaz and Santiago Fernández (eds), *X Jornadas*, 59–120.

M. Calleja-Puerta, 'Archivos dispersos, fuentes reencontradas. Notas metodológicas al estudio de las elites del reino de León en los siglos centrales de la Edad Media', *Medievalismo*, 12 (2002), 9–36.

M. Calleja-Puerta, 'Cartularios y construcción de la memoria monástica en los reinos de León y Castilla durante el siglo XII', in V. Lamazou-Duplan and E. Ramírez Vaquero (eds), *Les cartulaires médiévaux. Écrire et conserver la mémoire du pouvoir, le pouvoir de la mémoire* (Pau, 2013), 187–97.

M. Calleja-Puerta, 'La catedral de Oviedo como centro de conservación de documentos en la Alta Edad Media', in *Estudos*, 4, 179–92.

M. Calleja-Puerta, 'Conservación y recepción de archivos familiares en cartularios medievales del noroeste ibérico', in V. Lamazou-Duplan (ed.), *Les archives familiales dans l'Occident médiéval et moderne. Trésor, arsenal, mémorial* (Madrid, 2021), 223–34.

M. Calleja-Puerta, 'La delimitación entre las diócesis de Lugo y Oviedo. Escritura diplomática y territorialidad diocesana a mediados del siglo XII', *HS*, 71.143 (2019), 39–57.

M. Calleja-Puerta, 'Ecos de las *fórmulas visigóticas* en la documentación altomedieval astur-leonesa', in O. Guyotjeannin, L. Morelle, and S. P. Scalfati (eds), *Les formulaires: compilation et circulation des modèles d'actes dans l'Europe médiévale et moderne. XIII<sup>e</sup> Congrès de la Commission internationale de diplomatique* (Prague, 2018), 45–63.

M. Calleja-Puerta, 'Notas sobre el aprendizaje de la lectura y la escritura en la Asturias antigua y medieval', in A. Terrón Bañuelos and J. A. Álvarez Castrillón (eds), *La educación en Asturias. Estudios históricos* (Oviedo, 2019), 13–36.

M. Calleja-Puerta, 'Señores sin cancillería. Génesis y validación de los documentos de la aristocracia castellano-leonesa (1100–1250 *ca*.)', in A. Suárez González (ed.), *Escritura y sociedad: la nobleza* (Santiago de Compostela, 2017), 19–57.

M. Calleja-Puerta, 'Les sources documentaires pour l'histoire des familles aristocratiques du royaume de León (X<sup>e</sup>–XII<sup>e</sup> siècle): production, usage et conservation', in M. Aurell (ed.), *Le médiéviste et la monographie familiale: sources, méthodes et problématiques* (Turnhout, 2004), 105–16.

M. Calleja-Puerta, 'El valor de la escritura en los preámbulos de la cancillería de Alfonso VII', in C. M. Reglero de la Fuente (ed.), *Poderes, espacios y escrituras: los reinos de Castilla y León (siglos XI–XV)* (Madrid, 2018), 179–202.

M. Calleja-Puerta *et al.*, 'Edición de documentos en los reinos de Castilla y León', in T. Kölzer, W. Rosner, and R. Zehetmayer (eds), *Regionale Urkundenbücher. Die Vorträge der 12. Tagung der Commission Internationale de Diplomatique* (Sankt Pölten, 2010), 205–20.

S. Cámara Lapuente, 'Testamentary Formalities in Spain', in K. G. C. Reid, M. J. de Waal, and R. Zimmermann (eds), *Comparative Succession Law, I. Testamentary Formalities* (Oxford, 2011), 71–95.

M. Camille, 'Seeing and Reading: Some Visual Implications of Medieval Literacy and Illiteracy', *Art History*, 8.1 (1985), 26–49.

J. Campos, 'El "Libro de la vida"', *Helmantica*, 21.64–6 (1970), 115–47, 249–302.

J. Campos, '"Quietus" y su tradición lingüística en la Hispania latina', *Helmantica*, 34.103–5 (1983), 103–7.

F. J. Campos y Fernández de Sevilla (ed.), *La Desamortización. El expolio del patrimonio artístico y cultural de la Iglesia en España* (Madrid, 2007).

A. Cañade Juste, 'Un milenario navarro: Ramiro Garcés, rey de Viguera', *PV*, 42.162 (1981), 21–38.

Á. Canellas López, 'El Cartulario visigótico de San Juan de la Peña', in *Homenaje Millares Carlo*, 1, 205–39.

Á. Canellas López, *Diplomática hispano-visigoda* (Zaragoza, 1979).

Á. Canellas López, 'El notariado en España hasta el siglo XIV: estado de la cuestión', in *Notariado público y documento privado: de los orígenes al siglo XIV. Actas del VII Congreso Internacional de Diplomática* (2 vols, Valencia, 1989), 1, 101–39.

Á. Canellas López, 'Sigilografía y diplomática', in *Actas del Primer Coloquio de Sigilografía* (Madrid, 1990), 49–58.

Á. Canellas López, J. de Santiago Fernández, and J. M. de Francisco Olmos (eds), *I Jornadas sobre documentación jurídico-administrativa, económico-financiera y judicial del reino castellano-leonés (siglos X–XIII)* (Madrid, 2002).

D. Caner, *Wandering, Begging Monks: Spiritual Authority and the Promotion of Monasticism in Late Antiquity* (Berkeley, CA, 2002).

B. Cañón Dunner, 'Las prácticas judiciales y sus fuentes en el noroeste de la Península Ibérica en el siglo X', *De Medio Aevo*, 10.2 (2016), 37–60.

B. Cañón Dunner, *L'exercice de la justice dans les royaumes du nord-ouest de la Péninsule Ibérique entre le VIII^e et XI^e siècle* (PhD thesis, Université Paris Nanterre, 2020).

F. Cantera Burgos, 'En torno al documento fundacional de Valpuesta', *Hispania*, 10 (1943), 3–15.

F. Cantera Burgos and J. Andrío Gonzalo, *Historia medieval de Miranda de Ebro* (Miranda de Ebro, 1991).

M. Cantera Montenegro and C. Mendo Carmona, 'Antroponimia y advocaciones religiosas en el reino de León (s. X)', in A. I. Boullón Agrelo (ed.), *Actas do XX Congreso internacional de ciencias onomásticas* (2 vols, Santiago de Compostela, 2002), 2, 1329–42.

M. Cantero Mediavilla, 'El cartulario del monasterio dúplice de Santa María de Piasca', in A. M. Aldama Roy (ed.), *De Roma al siglo XX* (2 vols, Madrid, 1996), 1, 499–504.

M. J. Carbajo Serrano, *El monasterio de los Santos Cosme y Damián de Abellar: monacato y sociedad en la época astur-leonesa* (León, 1988).

M. Cardozo, 'O testamento de Mumadona, fundadora do Mosteiro e Castelo de Guimarães na segunda metade do século X', *Revista de Guimarães*, 77.3–4 (1967), 279–98.

M. C. Carlé, '*Boni homines* y hombres buenos', *CHE*, 39–40 (1964), 133–68.

M. C. Carlé, *Del concejo medieval castellano-leonés* (Buenos Aires, 1968).

M. C. Carlé, 'Gran propiedad y grandes propietarios', *CHE*, 57–8 (1973), 1–224.

E. Carrero Santamaría, '*Ecce quam bonum et quam iocundum habitare fratres in unum*. Vidas reglar y secular en las catedrales hispanas llegado el siglo XII', *AEM*, 30.2 (2000), 757–805.

M. Carriedo Tejedo, 'El diploma 3–4 del Archivo de la Catedral de León. Problemas cronológicos que suscita', *AL*, 39.77 (1985), 71–84.

M. Carriedo Tejedo, 'Documentos relativos al "armiger regis" durante los reinos de Alfonso V y Vermudo III (999–1037)', *Compostellanum*, 57.3–4 (2012), 155–203.

M. Carriedo Tejedo, 'Dos fraudes sincrónicos al monasterio de Celanova (en León y en Galicia) a comienzos del siglo XI', *Rudesindus*, 4 (2008), 43–62.

M. Carriedo Tejedo, 'Dos obispos de Segovia en el siglo X: Frunimio de Wamba (927) e Ilderedo de Simancas (960)', *Estudios Segovianos*, 45.102 (2002), 47–78.

M. Carriedo Tejedo, 'La familia de San Rosendo', *EMin*, 23 (2007), 103–23.

M. Carriedo Tejedo, 'La familia gallega del rey Alfonso Froilaz (926–931)', *Rudesindus*, 9 (2013), 109–54.

M. Carriedo Tejedo, 'Iter Sancti Froilani Episcopi (Lugo, Colcorinho, Viseu, Távora, Esla y León)', *Rudesindus*, 6 (2010), 43–103.

M. Carriedo Tejedo, 'Libros, documentos y clérigos (en la época de San Rosendo)', *Rudesindus*, 3 (2008), 33–105.

M. Carriedo Tejedo, 'Un merino leonés impuesto por Castilla: Fromarico Sendíniz (1010–1014)', *TL*, 22.48 (1982), 59–68.

M. Carriedo Tejedo, 'El nacimiento de Alfonso V (¿Pravia, marzo de 996?) y el gobierno del obispo Gudesteo de Oviedo en Astorga (1000–1001)', *BRIDEA*, 51.149 (1997), 145–68.

M. Carriedo Tejedo, 'En torno a los orígenes del monasterio de Sahagún', *TL*, 43.120–1 (2005), 65–87.

M. Carriedo Tejedo, 'El viñedo y el vino en la provincia *Gallaeciae* (*a flumine Pisorga usque ad mare occidentale*)', *Rudesindus*, 7 (2011), 105–52.

F. Carrillo Boutureira, 'La actividad pesquera en la Galicia de los ss. IX–XIII, a través de la diplomática medieval y la toponimia actual', *AB*, 22 (1999), 105–34.

J. Carroll, A. Reynolds, and B. Yorke (eds), *Power and Place in Europe in the Early Middle Ages* (Oxford, 2019).

M. J. Carruthers, *The Book of Memory: a Study of Memory in Medieval Culture* (2nd ed., Cambridge, 2008).

Á. Carvajal Castro, 'Assembly Politics and Conflicting Discourses in Early Medieval León (10th–11th c.)', in K. Mroziewicz and A. Sroczynski (eds), *Premodern Rulership and Contemporary Political Power. The King's Body Never Dies* (Amsterdam, 2017), 21–46.

Á. Carvajal Castro, *Bajo la máscara del regnum. La monarquía asturleonesa en León (854–1037)* (Madrid, 2017).

Á. Carvajal Castro, 'Los castros de la meseta del Duero y la construcción de la monarquía asturleonesa: el caso de Melgar en el siglo X', in A. Cunha, O. Pinto, and R. O. Martins (eds), *Paisagens e poderes no medievo ibérico. Actas do I Encontro ibérico de jovens investigadores em estudos medievais: arqueologia, história e património* (Braga, 2014), 11–29.

Á. Carvajal Castro, 'Collective Action and Local Leaderships in Early Medieval North-Western Iberia', in Quirós Castillo (ed.), *Social Inequality*, 281–99.

Á. Carvajal Castro, 'La construcción de una sede regia: León y la identidad política de los reyes asturleoneses en la crónica de Sampiro y en los documentos', *e-Spania*, 18 (2014 [online] https://journals.openedition.org/e-spania/23714).

Á. Carvajal Castro, 'Local Meetings and Meeting Places in Early Medieval León', *EME*, 25.2 (2017), 186–207.

Á. Carvajal Castro, 'The Monarchy and the Elites in Early Medieval León (Ninth–Eleventh Centuries)', *JMIS*, 7.2 (2015), 232–48.

Á. Carvajal Castro, 'Religious Houses, Violence, and the Limits of Political Consensus in Early Medieval León (NW Iberia)', *Reti Medievali*, 21.2 (2020), 81–103.

Á. Carvajal Castro, 'Resistencias campesinas en el noroeste ibérico altomedieval: confrontando la tragedia', *RHJZ*, 95 (2019), 13–33.

Á. Carvajal Castro, 'Secular Sanctions and Sales in Early Medieval León (9th–11th c.): Beyond Diplomatic Practice', *Al-Masāq*, 29.2 (2017), 151–71.

Á. Carvajal Castro, 'Sociedad y territorio en el norte de León: Valdoré, los Flaínez y el entorno del alto Esla (IX–XI)', *SHHM*, 31 (2013), 105–31.

Á. Carvajal Castro, 'The Use of the Term *uilla* in Early Medieval León: a Review of the Economic Base of the Astur-Leonese Monarchy (Ninth–Eleventh Centuries)', in Escalona Monge, Vésteinsson, and Brookes (eds), *Polity*, 325–49.

Á. Carvajal Castro and J. Escalona, 'The Value of Status: Monetary Penalties in the Charters from León (854–1037)', *JMH*, 46.1 (2020), 23–49.

Á. Carvajal Castro, A. E. Marques, G. Barrett, *et al.*, 'Towards a Trans-Regional Approach to Early Medieval Iberia', *History Compass*, 20.6 (2022), 1–18.

H. P. Carvalho, 'Marcadores da paisagem e intervenção cadastral no território próximo da cidade de Bracara Augusta (Hispania Citerior Tarraconensis)', *AEA*, 85 (2012), 149–66.

M. I. Carzolio de Rossi, 'La antroponimia femenina en la Alta Edad Media: como revelador social: mujeres libres y siervas en el noroeste hispánico', in *Mujeres en escena. Actas de las Quintas Jornadas Historia de las mujeres y estudios de género* (Santa Rosa, 2000), 305–13.

M. I. Carzolio de Rossi, 'La constitución y organización de un dominio monástico benedictino: Celanova (s. X–XI)', *CHE*, 73 (1991), 5–74.

M. I. Carzolio de Rossi, 'Cresconio, prepósito de Celanova. Un personaje gallego al filo del siglo XI', *CHE*, 57–8 (1973), 225–79.

M. I. Carzolio de Rossi, 'Formación y desarrollo de los dominios del monasterio de San Pedro de Cardeña', *CHE*, 45–6 (1967), 79–150.

M. I. Carzolio de Rossi, 'La gran propiedad laica gallega en el siglo XI', *CHE*, 65–6 (1981), 59–112.

M. I. Carzolio de Rossi, 'Participación monástica en el control de la repoblación. El monasterio de San Salvador de Celanova en el siglo X', *CHE*, 70 (1988), 5–59.

M. I. Carzolio de Rossi, 'Reflexiones en torno a esclavitud y servidumbre en la Alta Edad Media gallega. Los siervos de San Rosendo', *Anales de Historia Antigua, Medieval y Moderna*, 31 (1998), 29–50.

L. Casado de Otaola, 'Cultura escrita, dominio y "clases populares" en la Alta Edad Media en Hispania', in A. Castillo Gómez (ed.), *Cultura escrita y clases subalternas: una mirada española* (Oiartzun, 2001), 35–55.

L. Casado de Otaola, 'Escribir y leer en la Alta Edad Media', in A. Castillo Gómez (ed.), *Historia de la cultura escrita del Próximo Oriente Antiguo a la sociedad informatizada* (Gijón, 2002), 113–77.

L. Casado de Otaola, 'Per visibilia ad invisibilia: representaciones figurativas en documentos altomedievales como símbolos de validación y autoría', *Signo*, 4 (1997), 39–56.

B. Casado Quintanilla, 'Melic (†960), presbítero, agricultor y ganadero: datos y conjeturas', *ETF*, 22 (2009), 47–64.

B. Casado Quintanilla, 'Pan, vino y documentos de compraventa en León hasta el año 1300', in *Escritos*, 1, 163–98.

S. Castellanos, *The Visigothic Kingdom in Iberia: Construction and Invention* (Philadelphia, PA, 2020).

S. Castellanos and I. Martín Viso 'The Local Articulation of Central Power in the North of the Iberian Peninsula (500–1000)', *EME*, 13.1 (2005), 1–42.

A. Castillo Gómez, *Escrituras y escribientes: prácticas de la cultura escrita en una ciudad del Renacimiento* (Las Palmas de Gran Canaria, 1997).

A. Castillo Gómez and C. Sáez, 'Paleografía versus alfabetización. Reflexiones sobre historia social de la cultura escrita', *Signo*, 1 (1994), 133–68.

P. Castillo Maldonado, '*In hora mortis*: deceso, duelo, rapiña y legado en la muerte del obispo visigótico', *HS*, 64.129 (2012), 7–28.

E. Castro, 'Aspectos literarios y jurídicos en las *Leges Wisigothorum*', *Minerva*, 13 (1999), 127–39.

A. Castro Correa, 'Leaving the Past Behind, Adapting to the Future: Transitional and Polygraphic Visigothic-Caroline Minuscule Scribes', *AEM*, 50.2 (2020), 631–64.

A. Castro Correa, 'Pedro Kendúlfiz (†1051), Notary of the Royal Chancery of León: Training, Career, and Relationships', in X. Hermand, J.-F. Nieus, and É. Renard (eds), *Le scribe d'archives dans l'Occident médiéval. Formations, carrières, réseaux* (Turnhout, 2019), 103–32.

A. Castro Correa, 'The Regional Study of Visigothic Script: Visigothic Script vs. Caroline Minuscule in Galicia', in M. Schubert and E. Overgaauw (eds), *Change in Medieval and Renaissance Scripts and Manuscripts. Proceedings of the 19th Colloquium of the Comité international de paléographie latine* (Turnhout, 2019), 25–35.

A. Castro Correa, 'Visigothic Script versus Caroline Minuscule: the Collision of Two Cultural Worlds in Twelfth-Century Galicia', *Mediaeval Studies*, 78 (2016), 203–42.

C. G. de Castro Valdés, 'Notas sobre teología política en el reino de Asturias: la inscripción del altar de Santa María de Naranco (Oviedo) y el testamento de Alfonso II', *Arqueología y Territorio Medieval*, 10.1 (2003), 137–70.

C. G. de Castro Valdés and S. Ríos González, 'El origen de Oviedo', *Anejos de Nailos*, 3 (2016), 31–119.

G. Cavero Domínguez, 'Organización eclesiástica de las civitates episcopales de León y Astorga (siglo X)', in *Iglesia y ciudad*, 67–101.

G. Cavero Domínguez, 'Spanish Female Monasticism: "Family" Monasteries and their Transformation (Eleventh to Twelfth Centuries)', in J. Burton and K. Stöber (eds), *Women in the Medieval Monastic World* (Turnhout, 2015), 15–52.

G. Cavero Domínguez, E. Fernández González, and F. Galván Freile, 'Imágenes reales, imágenes de justicia en la catedral de León', *e-Spania*, 3 (2007 [online] https://journals.openedition.org/e-spania/204).

A. Ceballos-Escalera y Gila, *Ordoño III (951–956), Sancho I (956–966), Ordoño IV (958–959), Ramiro III (966–985), Vermudo II (982–999)* (Burgos, 2000).

J. Cerdá Ruiz-Funes, 'En torno a la pesquisa y procedimiento inquisitivo en el derecho castellano-leonés de la Edad Media', *AHDE*, 32 (1962), 483–517.

P. Chalmeta, 'Précisions au sujet du monnayage hispano-arabe (*dirham qāsimī* et *dirham arbaʿīnī*)', *Journal of the Economic and Social History of the Orient*, 24.3 (1981), 316–24.

C. J. Chandler, *Carolingian Catalonia: Politics, Culture, and Identity in an Imperial Province, 778–987* (Cambridge, 2019).

C. J. Chandler, 'Between Court and Counts: Carolingian Catalonia and the *Aprisio* Grant, 778–897', *EME*, 11.1 (2002), 19–44.

T. M. Charles-Edwards, 'Law in the Western Kingdoms between the Fifth and the Seventh Century', in A. Cameron, B. Ward-Perkins, and M. Whitby (eds), *The*

*Cambridge Ancient History, XIV. Late Antiquity: Empire and Successors, A.D. 425–600*, (Cambridge, 2001), 260–87.

R. Chartier, *Forms and Meanings: Texts, Performances, and Audiences from Codex to Computer* (Philadelphia, PA, 1995).

R. Chartier, *Inscription and Erasure: Literature and Written Culture from the Eleventh to the Eighteenth Century*, transl. A. Goldhammer (Philadelphia, PA, 2007).

R. Chartier, 'Le monde comme représentation', *AHSS*, 44.6 (1989), 1505–20.

P. Chastang, 'L'archéologie du texte médiéval. Autour de travaux récents sur l'écrit au Moyen Âge', *AHSS*, 63.2 (2008), 245–69.

P. Chastang, 'Écrire, remployer, archiver. Quelques remarques sur l'évolution de la culture de l'écrit au Moyen Âge central', in *La cultura en la Europa del siglo XIII: emisión, intermediación, audiencia* (Pamplona, 2014), 135–56.

H. J. Chaytor, *From Script to Print: an Introduction to Medieval Literature* (Cambridge, 1945).

A. Christys, *Christians in al-Andalus, 711–1000* (Abingdon, 2002).

S. M. Cingolani, 'L'abat Oliba, el poder i la paraula', *AHAM*, 31 (2013), 115–62.

C. M. Cipolla, *Literacy and Development in the West* (Harmondsworth, 1969).

M. T. Clanchy, *Looking Back from the Invention of Printing: Mothers and the Teaching of Reading in the Middle Ages* (Turnhout, 2018).

M. T. Clanchy, *From Memory to Written Record: England 1066–1307* (3rd ed., Chichester, 2013).

G. Clavería Nadal, 'Latín y romance en el léxico de la lengua jurídica del siglo XIII: observaciones sobre el verbo *otorgar*', in M. Castillo Lluch and M. López Izquierdo (eds), *Modelos latinos en la Castilla medieval* (Madrid, 2010), 113–29.

G. Clavería Nadal, 'Léxico de la vida cotidiana. Oficios y otros menesteres', in *Monarquía*, 1, 531–61.

G. Clavería Nadal and J. Torruella i Boix, 'Historia del léxico y morfología histórica: orígenes del léxico de los cargos y oficios', in J. Rafel Cufí (ed.), *Diachronic Linguistics* (Girona, 2009), 67–114.

*Códice Albeldense (976). Original conservado en la Biblioteca del Real Monasterio de San Lorenzo de El Escorial (D.I.2)* (Madrid, 2002).

D. Codina Giol, 'Oliba: le moine, l'abbé', *SMon*, 51.1 (2009), 79–106.

C. Codoñer, 'Léxico de las fórmulas de donación en documentos del siglo X', *Emerita*, 40.1 (1972), 141–9.

C. Codoñer (ed.), *La Hispania visigótica y mozárabe. Dos épocas en su literatura* (Salamanca, 2010).

C. Codoñer and P. F. Alberto (eds), *Wisigothica. After M. C. Díaz y Díaz* (Florence, 2014).

M. H. C. Coelho, 'Análise diplomática da produção documental do *scriptorium* de Lorvão (séculos X–XII)', in *Estudos*, 3, 387–405.

M. H. C. Coelho, *O mosteiro de Arouca do século X ao século XIII* (Coimbra, 1977).

M. Cole and J. Cole, 'Rethinking the Goody Myth', in Olson and Cole (eds), *Technology*, 305–24.

R. Collins, 'Ambrosio de Morales, Bishop Pelayo of Oviedo, and the Lost Manuscripts of Visigothic Spain', in Codoñer and Alberto (eds), *Wisigothica*, 609–32.

R. Collins, 'Ambrosio de Morales and the *Codex Vetustissimus Ovetensis*', in T. J. MacMaster and N. S. M. Matheou (eds), *Italy and the East Roman World in the Medieval Mediterranean: Empires, Cities, and Elites, 476-1204. Papers in Honour of Thomas S. Brown* (Abingdon, 2021), 49–69.

R. Collins, *The Arab Conquest of Spain, 710–797* (Oxford, 1989).

R. Collins, *Caliphs and Kings: Spain, 796–1031* (Chichester, 2012).

R. Collins, 'Continuity and Loss in Medieval Spanish Culture: the Evidence of MS Silos, Archivo Monástico 4', in R. Collins and A. Goodman (eds), *Medieval Spain: Culture, Conflict, and Coexistence. Studies in Honour of Angus MacKay* (Basingstoke, 2002), 1–22.

R. Collins, *Early Medieval Spain: Unity in Diversity, 400–1000* (2nd ed., New York, NY, 1995).

R. Collins, *Law, Culture, and Regionalism in Early Medieval Spain* (Aldershot, 1992).

R. Collins, 'Literacy and the Laity in Early Mediaeval Spain', in McKitterick (ed.), *Uses*, 109–33.

R. Collins, '"*Sicut lex Gothorum continet*": Law and Charters in Ninth- and Tenth-Century León and Catalonia', *EHR*, 100.396 (1985), 489–512.

R. Collins, 'The Sixth-Century Documents of the Monastery of Asán in Context', in Martin and Larrea (eds), *Chartes*, 19–36.

R. Collins, 'Visigothic Law and Regional Custom in Disputes in Early Medieval Spain', in Davies and Fouracre (eds), *Settlement*, 85–104.

R. Collins, *Visigothic Spain, 409–711* (Oxford, 2004).

J. P. Conant, 'Literacy and Private Documentation in Vandal North Africa: the Case of the Albertini Tablets', in A. H. Merrills (ed.), *Vandals, Romans, and Berbers: New Perspectives on Late Antique North Africa* (Aldershot, 2004), 199–224.

I. de la Concha Martínez, 'La "presura"', *AHDE*, 14 (1943), 382–460.

R. Conde and J. Trenchs Odena, 'Signos personales en las suscripciones altomedievales catalanas', in Rück (ed.), *Graphische Symbole*, 443–52.

K. Cooper and C. Leyser (eds), *Making Early Medieval Societies: Conflict and Belonging in the Latin West, 300–1200* (Cambridge, 2016).

E. Córcoles Olaitz, 'About the Origin of the *Formulae Wisigothicae*', *AFDUC*, 12 (2008), 199–221.

E. Córcoles Olaitz, 'El contrato de compraventa a la luz de las fórmulas visigodas', *Revista Internacional de Derecho Romano*, 1 (2008), 309–30.

E. Córcoles Olaitz, *Las Formulae Wisigothicae. Aproximación a la práctica jurídica visigoda* (Lecce, 2010).

E. Córcoles Olaitz, *El hurto en el derecho visigodo* (Bilbao, 2006).

E. Córcoles Olaitz, 'The Manumission of Slaves in the View of the *Formulae Visigothicae*', *Veleia*, 23 (2006), 339–49.

S. M. Coronas González, 'El derecho de Asturias en la Alta Edad Media', in *Libro del I Congreso Jurídico de Asturias* (Oviedo, 1987), 73–95.

S. M. Coronas González, 'El orden constitutivo del reino de Asturias (718-910)', *AHDE*, 70 (2000), 9–35.

F. L. Corral, 'Lugares de reunión, *boni homines* y presbíteros en Valdevimbre y Ardón en la Alta Edad Media', *Medievalista*, 18 (2015 [online] https://journals.openedition.org/medievalista/1093).

F. L. Corral and M. Pérez Rodríguez, 'Negotiating Fines in the Early Middle Ages: Local Communities, Mediators, and the Instrumentalization of Justice in the Kingdom of León', *Al-Masāq*, 29.2 (2017), 172–85.

J. F. Correa Arias, 'Os petroglifos das comarcas do Eume e Betanzos: estudio comparativo', *Cátedra*, 9 (2002), 7–58.

I. Corullón, 'El eremitismo en las épocas visigoda y altomedieval a través de las fuentes leonesas (II)', *TL*, 26.64 (1986), 23–36.

M. Costambeys, 'Disputes and Courts in Lombard and Carolingian Central Italy', *EME*, 15.3 (2007), 265–89.

M. Costambeys, 'Disputes and Documents in Early Medieval Italy', in Cooper and Leyser (eds), *Making*, 125–54.

M. Costambeys, *Power and Patronage in Early Medieval Italy: Local Society, Italian Politics, and the Abbey of Farfa, c. 700–900* (Cambridge, 2007).

M. Costambeys and M. Innes, 'Introduction: a Study in the Education of a Society?', in E. Screen and C. West (eds), *Writing the Early Medieval West: Studies in Honour of Rosamond McKitterick* (Cambridge, 2018), 1–11.

J. F. Cotter, 'The Book within the Book in Mediaeval Illumination', *Florilegium*, 12 (1993), 107–40.

X. L. Couceiro, 'De santo Acisclo', in R. Álvarez *et al.* (eds), *Ao sabor do texto. Estudos dedicados a Ivo Castro* (Santiago de Compostela, 2013), 125–43.

R. Couzin, *Right and Left in Early Christian and Medieval Art* (Leiden, 2021).

D. Cowling, *Building the Text: Architecture as Metaphor in Late Medieval and Early Modern France* (Oxford, 1998).

P. Crain, 'New Histories of Literacy', in S. Eliot and J. Rose (eds), *A Companion to the History of the Book* (Chichester, 2009), 467–79.

J. A. Cromwell, *Recording Village Life: a Coptic Scribe in Early Islamic Egypt* (Ann Arbor, MI, 2017).

G. B. da Cruz, 'Algumas considerações sôbre a "perfiliatio"', *BFDUC*, 14 (1937–8), 407–78.

V. de la Cruz, 'Fray Velasco, procurador del monasterio de Cardeña en Poza de la Sal', *BIFG*, 75.213 (1996), 251–66.

A. J. Cruz and R. Hernández (eds), *Women's Literacy in Early Modern Spain and the New World* (Farnham, 2011).

L. M. de la Cruz Herranz, *El Archivo Histórico Nacional. Los orígenes del medievalismo español (1866–1955)* (Madrid, 2020).

L. M. de la Cruz Herranz, 'El archivo monástico: entre la gestión de su administración y la gestión de su memoria histórica', in Baldaquí Escandell (ed.), *Lugares*, 177–230.

L. M. de la Cruz Herranz, 'El "Libro de las Tablas" del monasterio de San Pedro de Cardeña', in Ruiz Rodríguez and Martínez Llorente (eds), *Recuerdos*, 139–62.

L. M. de la Cruz Herranz, 'La Sección de Clero del Archivo Histórico Nacional', in J. C. Galende Díaz (ed.), *II Jornadas científicas sobre documentación de la Corona de Castilla (siglos XIII–XV)* (Madrid, 2003), 373–432.

E. R. Curtius, *European Literature and the Latin Middle Ages*, transl. W. R. Trask (new ed., Princeton, NJ, 2013).

I. Czeguhn *et al.* (eds), *Wasser—Wege—Wissen auf der iberischen Halbinsel. Vom Römischen Imperium bis zur islamischen Herrschaft* (Baden-Baden, 2018).

T. J. Dadson, 'Literacy and Education in Early Modern Rural Spain: the Case of Villarrubia de los Ojos', *Bulletin of Spanish Studies*, 81.7–8 (2004), 1011–37.

P. David, *Études historiques sur la Galice et le Portugal du VIᵉ au XIIᵉ siècle* (Lisbon-Paris, 1947).

W. Davies, *Acts of Giving: Individual, Community, and Church in Tenth-Century Christian Spain* (Oxford, 2007).

W. Davies, '*Boni homines* in Northern Iberia: a Particularity that Raises Some General Questions', in R. Balzaretti, J. Barrow, and P. Skinner (eds), *Italy and Early Medieval Europe: Papers for Chris Wickham* (Oxford, 2018), 60–72.

W. Davies, 'Buying with Masses: "Donation" *pro remedio animae* in Tenth-Century Galicia and Castile-León', in F. Bougard, C. La Rocca, and R. Le Jan (eds), *Sauver son âme et se perpétuer: transmission du patrimoine et mémoire au Haut Moyen Âge* (Rome, 2005), 401–16.

W. Davies, *Christian Spain and Portugal in the Early Middle Ages: Texts and Societies* (Abingdon, 2020).

W. Davies, 'Competition for Control of Churches in Northern Iberia', in P. Depreux, F. Bougard, and R. Le Jan (eds), *Compétition et sacré au Haut Moyen Âge: entre médiation et exclusion* (Turnhout, 2015), 125–38.

W. Davies, 'Counts in Ninth- and Tenth-Century Iberia', in Barton and Portass (eds), *Beyond the Reconquista*, 143–68.

W. Davies, 'Creating Records of Judicial Disputes in Northern Iberia before the Year 1000', repr. in *Christian Spain*, 53–75.

W. Davies, 'The Early Middle Ages and Spanish Identity', in H. Pryce and J. Watts (eds), *Power and Identity in the Middle Ages. Essays in Memory of Rees Davies* (Oxford, 2007), 68–84.

W. Davies, 'Exchange Charters in the Kingdom of Asturias-León, 700–1000', in I. Fees and P. Depreux (eds), *Tauschgeschäft und Tauschurkunde vom 8. bis zum 12. Jahrhundert. L'acte d'échange, du VIIIᵉ au XIIᵉ siècle* (Köln, 2013), 471–89.

W. Davies, 'Free Peasants and Large Landowners in the West', *Revue Belge de Philologie et d'Histoire*, 90.2 (2012), 361–80.

W. Davies, 'Gardens and Gardening in Early Medieval Spain and Portugal', *EME*, 27.3 (2019), 327–48.

W. Davies, 'Holding Court: Judicial Presidency in Brittany, Wales, and Northern Iberia in the Early Middle Ages', in F. Edmonds and P. Russell (eds), *Tome: Studies in Medieval Celtic History and Law in Honour of Thomas Charles-Edwards* (Woodbridge, 2011), 145–54.

W. Davies, 'The Incidence of *Princeps* in the Ninth- and Tenth-Century Charters of Northern Spain', in H. Oudart, J.-M. Picard, and J. Quaghebeur (eds), *Le prince, son peuple et le bien commun. De l'Antiquité tardive à la fin du Moyen Âge* (Rennes, 2013), 217–32.

W. Davies, 'Judges and Judging: Truth and Justice in Northern Iberia on the Eve of the Millennium', *JMH*, 36.3 (2010), 193–203.

W. Davies, 'The Language of Justice in Northern Iberia before AD 1000', in Carroll, Reynolds, and Yorke (eds), *Power*, 241–52.

W. Davies, 'Local Priests and the Writing of Charters in Northern Iberia in the Tenth Century', in Escalona Monge and Sirantoine (eds), *Chartes*, 29–43.

W. Davies, 'Local Priests in Northern Iberia', in S. Patzold and C. van Rhijn (eds), *Men in the Middle: Local Priests in Early Medieval Europe* (Berlin, 2016), 125–44.

W. Davies, 'Lordship and Community: Northern Spain on the Eve of the Year 1000', in C. Dyer, P. R. Coss, and C. Wickham (eds), *Rodney Hilton's Middle Ages: an Exploration of Historical Themes* (Oxford, 2007), 18–33.

W. Davies, 'Notions of Wealth in the Charters of Ninth- and Tenth-Century Christian Iberia', in J.-P. Devroey, L. Feller, and R. Le Jan (eds), *Les élites et la richesse au Haut Moyen Âge* (Turnhout, 2010), 265–84.

W. Davies, 'Reciprocity or Guarantee? Countergift in Tenth-Century Northern Iberia', in A. Deyermond and M. Ryan (eds), *Early Medieval Spain: a Symposium* (London, 2010), 79–96.

W. Davies, 'Regions and Micro-Regions of Scribal Practice', in Escalona Monge, Vésteinsson, and Brookes (eds), *Polity*, 305–23.

W. Davies, 'Sale, Price, and Valuation in Galicia and Castile-León in the Tenth Century', *EME*, 11.2 (2002), 149–74.

W. Davies, 'On Servile Status in the Early Middle Ages', in M. L. Bush (ed.), *Serfdom and Slavery: Studies in Legal Bondage* (London, 1996), 225–46.

W. Davies, 'Small Worlds beyond Empire: the Contrast between Eastern Brittany and Northern Iberia', *Vorträge und Forschungen*, 87 (2019), 385–409.

W. Davies, 'Summary Justice and Seigneurial Justice in Northern Iberia on the Eve of the Millennium', *Haskins Society Journal*, 22 (2010), 43–58.

W. Davies, 'On Suretyship in Tenth-Century Northern Iberia', in Escalona Monge and Reynolds (eds), *Scale*, 133–52.

W. Davies, 'When Gift is Sale: Reciprocities and Commodities in Tenth-Century Christian Iberia', in Davies and Fouracre (eds), *Languages*, 217–37.

W. Davies, 'Where are the Parishes? Where are the Minsters? The Organization of the Spanish Church in the Tenth Century', in D. Rollason, C. Leyser, and H. Williams (eds), *England and the Continent in the Tenth Century. Studies in Honour of Wilhelm Levison (1876–1947)* (Turnhout, 2010), 379–97.

W. Davies, *Windows on Justice in Northern Iberia, 800–1000* (Abingdon, 2016).

W. Davies and P. Fouracre (eds), *The Languages of Gift in the Early Middle Ages* (Cambridge, 2010).

W. Davies and P. Fouracre (eds), *Property and Power in the Early Middle Ages* (Cambridge, 1995).

W. Davies and P. Fouracre (eds), *The Settlement of Disputes in Early Medieval Europe* (Cambridge, 1986).

W. Davies and D. Peterson, 'The Management of Land-Use in Old Castile: the Early Strands of the *Becerro Galicano* of San Millán de la Cogolla', in Dierkens, Schroeder, and Wilkin (eds), *Penser*, 47–68.

J. R. Davis, *Charlemagne's Practice of Empire* (Cambridge, 2015).

J. R. Davis and M. McCormick (eds), *The Long Morning of Medieval Europe: New Directions in Early Medieval Studies* (Aldershot, 2008).

G. Declercq, 'Between Legal Action and Performance: the *firmatio* of Charters in the Early Middle Ages', in Mostert and Barnwell (eds), *Medieval Legal Process*, 55–73.

G. Declercq, 'Originals and Cartularies: the Organization of Archival Memory (Ninth–Eleventh Centuries)', in K. Heidecker (ed.), *Charters and the Use of the Written Word in Medieval Society* (Turnhout, 2000), 147–70.

J. D'Emilio, 'The Charter of Theodenandus: Writing, Ecclesiastical Culture, and Monastic Reform in Tenth-Century Galicia', in D'Emilio (ed.-transl.), *Culture*, 281–342.

J. D'Emilio, 'The Legend of Bishop Odoario and the Early Medieval Church in Galicia', in T. Martin and J. A. Harris (eds), *Church, State, Vellum, and Stone. Essays on Medieval Spain in Honor of John Williams* (Leiden, 2005), 47–83.

J. D'Emilio (ed.-transl.), *Culture and Society in Medieval Galicia: a Cultural Crossroads at the Edge of Europe* (Leiden, 2015).

T. Denecker, 'Getting the Accent Right: Jerome *in Tit.* 3.9 in Isidore *eccl. off.* 2.11.4', *Vigiliae Christianae*, 73.2 (2019), 138–48.

C. Denoël, 'L'Épiphanie du Verbe. Essai d'une typologie formelle des représentations du livre au premier Moyen Âge dans les portraits des évangélistes', in C. Denoël, A.-O. Poilpré, and S. Shimahara (eds), *Imago libri. Représentations carolingiennes du livre. Bibliologia* 47 (Turnhout, 2018), 15–26.

T. Deswarte, *De la destruction à la restauration. L'idéologie du royaume d'Oviedo-León (VIIIᵉ–XIᵉ siècles)* (Turnhout, 2003).

T. Deswarte, '¿Una nueva metrópoli en Oviedo? Dos falsas bulas del obispo Pelayo (1098/1101–1130)', in M. Aurell and Á. G. de la Borbolla (eds), *La imagen del obispo hispano en la Edad Media* (Pamplona, 2004), 153–66.

T. Deswarte, 'Restaurer les évêchés et falsifier la documentation en Espagne: la suppression du diocèse de Simancas (974) et l'église cathédrale d'Astorga', *RM*, 15.76 (2004), 83–106.

J.-P. Devroey, 'Men and Women in Early Medieval Serfdom: the Ninth-Century North Frankish Evidence', *PP*, 166 (2000), 3–30.

P. B. Dias, 'L'idéal monastique, les moines et les monastères du monde wisigothique', *AT*, 23 (2015), 143–54.

P. B. Dias, 'O lugar da *Regula monastica communis* no monaquismo hispânico', *Humanitas*, 52 (2000), 213–39.

J. M. Díaz de Bustamante, 'Más imágenes del día a día en el reino de León hace mil años', in *Monarquía*, 2, 173–92.

J. M. Díaz de Bustamante, 'De pastores e ovellas: o bispo don Pedro de Lugo e os scrinia do seu arquivo', in E. Corral Díaz, L. Fontoira Suris, and E. Moscoso Mato (eds), *A mi dizen quantos amigos ey. Homenaxe ao profesor Xosé Luís Couceiro* (Santiago de Compostela, 2008), 435–48.

J. M. Díaz de Bustamante, 'Las pizarras visigóticas en el contexto de la documentación diplomática del reino de León: posibilidades de una integración de datos', in B. Díez Calleja (ed.), *El primitivo romance hispánico* (Burgos, 2008), 129–36.

J. M. Díaz de Bustamante, 'Los trabajos y los días: acerca de colecciones y ediciones de documentos latinos de la Edad Media', in *Orígenes*, 2, 349–64.

J. M. Díaz de Bustamante, 'Violence Reflected: High-Medieval Diplomatic *Cautelae* as a Mirror of Society', in M. C. Pimental and N. S. Rodrigues (eds), *Violence in the Ancient and Medieval Worlds* (Leuven, 2018), 447–60.

M. C. Díaz y Díaz, 'Los antiguos Tumbos de Santiago', in *Los Tumbos de Compostela* (Madrid, 1985), 9–24, 103–17.

M. C. Díaz y Díaz, *Asturias en el siglo VIII. La cultura literaria* (Oviedo, 2001).

M. C. Díaz y Díaz, *Códices visigóticos en la monarquía leonesa* (León, 1983).

M. C. Díaz y Díaz, 'El cultivo del latín en el siglo X', *Anuario de Estudios Filológicos*, 4 (1981), 71–81.

M. C. Díaz y Díaz, 'La cultura altomedieval', in Á. Montenegro Duque (ed.), *Historia de Burgos, II. Edad Media* (2 vols, Burgos, 1986–7), 1, 218–40.

M. C. Díaz y Díaz, 'La cultura literaria en la España cristiana en torno al año 1000', in *Península*, 195–204.

M. C. Díaz y Díaz, 'Un document privé de l'Espagne wisigothique sur ardoise', *SMed*, 1 (1960), 52–71.

M. C. Díaz y Díaz, 'La Lex Visigothorum y sus manuscritos: un ensayo de reinterpretación', *AHDE*, 46 (1976), 163–224.

M. C. Díaz y Díaz, *Libros y librerías en La Rioja altomedieval* (2nd ed., Logroño, 1991).

M. C. Díaz y Díaz, *Manuscritos del sur de la Península. Ensayo de distribución regional* (Seville, 1995).

M. C. Díaz y Díaz, 'De manuscritos visigóticos. Nuevos fragmentos en León', *AL*, 53 (1973), 57–97.

M. C. Díaz y Díaz, 'San Rosendo y su época', *Rudesindus*, 2 (2007), 73–84.

M. C. Díaz y Díaz, 'El testamento monástico de San Rosendo', *HID*, 16 (1989), 47–102.

M. C. Díaz y Díaz, 'Titulaciones regias en la monarquía visigoda', *RPH*, 16 (1976), 133–41.

M. C. Díaz y Díaz, '*A veces de chica fabla viene mucha folgura*. Ensayo sobre un documento leonés del año 1000', in *Escritos*, 1, 287–305.

M. C. Díaz y Díaz, 'Vida sexual y léxico marginal', in *Monarquía*, 1, 563–70.

P. C. Díaz Martínez, 'Concilios y obispos en la Península Ibérica (siglos VI–VIII)', in *Chiese locali e chiese regionali nell'alto Medioevo. Settimane* 61 (2 vols, Spoleto, 2014), 2, 1095–158.

P. C. Díaz Martínez, 'Confiscations in the Visigothic Reign of Toledo: a Political Instrument', in P. Porena and Y. Rivière (eds), *Expropriations et confiscations dans les royaumes barbares. Une approche régionale* (Rome, 2012), 93–112.

P. C. Díaz Martínez, 'Discipline and Punishment in 7th-Century Visigothic Monasticism: the Contrast between Isidore's and Fructuosus' Rules', in R. Alciati (ed.), *Norm and Exercise: Christian Asceticism between Late Antiquity and Early Middle Ages* (Stuttgart, 2018), 107–23.

P. C. Díaz Martínez, 'La familia como monasterio: los monasterios dúplices y los familiares en la Hispania de los siglos VI a IX', in J. Á. García de Cortázar and R. Teja (eds), *El monasterio medieval como célula social y espacio de convivencia* (Aguilar de Campoo, 2018), 33–58.

P. C. Díaz Martínez, *Formas económicas y sociales en el monacato visigodo* (Salamanca, 1987).

P. C. Díaz Martínez, 'El legado del pasado: reglas y monasterios visigodos y carolingios', in J. Á. García de Cortázar and R. Teja (eds), *Monjes y monasterios hispanos en la Alta Edad Media* (Aguilar de Campoo, 2006), 9–32.

P. C. Díaz Martínez, 'Monasteries in a Peripheral Area: Seventh-Century *Gallaecia*', in M. de Jong, F. Theuws, and C. van Rhijn (eds), *Topographies of Power in the Early Middle Ages* (Leiden, 2001), 329–59.

P. C. Díaz Martínez, '*Regula communis*: Monastic Space and Social Context', in H. Dey and E. Fentress (eds), *Western Monasticism ante litteram. The Spaces of Monastic Observance in Late Antiquity and the Early Middle Ages* (Turnhout, 2011), 117–35.

P. C. Díaz Martínez, 'Social Plurality and Monastic Diversity in Late Antique Hispania (Sixth to Eighth Century)', in Beach and Cochelin (eds), *Medieval Monasticism*, 195–212.

P. C. Díaz Martínez, 'Sumisión voluntaria: estatus degradado e indiferencia de estatus en la *Hispania* visigoda (*FV* 32)', *Studia Historica. Historia Antigua*, 25 (2007), 507–24.

P. C. Díaz Martínez and M. R. Valverde, 'The Theoretical Strength and Practical Weakness of the Visigothic Monarchy of Toledo', in F. Theuws and J. L. Nelson (eds), *Rituals of Power: from Late Antiquity to the Early Middle Ages* (Leiden, 2000), 59–93.

M. E. Díaz Salvado, 'Los colofones en manuscritos latinos medievales de la Península Ibérica: siglos VII–XII', in Nascimento and Alberto (eds), *Actas IV*, 361–78.

M. E. Díaz Salvado, *Falsos y falsificaciones en documentación latina medieval del reino de León* (PhD thesis, Universidade de Santiago de Compostela, 2011).

A. Dierkens, N. Schroeder, and A. Wilkin (eds), *Penser la paysannerie médiévale, un défi impossible?* (Paris, 2017).

C. Díez Herrera, 'La abadía de Santa Juliana en las Asturias de Santillana (943–1450)', in López Ormazábal, Díez Herrera, and Pérez Bustamente, *Abadía*, 14–68.

C. Díez Herrera, 'La organización social del espacio entre la Cordillera Cantábrica y el Duero en los siglos VIII al XI: una propuesta de análisis como sociedad de frontera', in J. Á. García de Cortázar (ed.), *Del Cantábrico al Duero: trece estudios sobre organización social del espacio en los siglos VIII a XIII* (Santander, 1999), 123–56.

A. Díaz-Plaza Casal, 'La recuperación del poder público en el reino de León: Alfonso V', in Díaz-Plaza Casal, Escudero Manzano, and Villarroel González (eds), *Caída*, 143–60.

A. Díaz-Plaza Casal, G. J. Escudero Manzano, and Ó. Villarroel González (eds), *Caída y ascenso de las estructuras de poder en la Alta Edad Media* (Madrid, 2020).

A. Diem, 'The Carolingians and the *Regula Benedicti*', in R. Meens *et al.* (eds), *Religious Franks. Religion and Power in the Frankish Kingdoms: Studies in Honour of Mayke de Jong* (Manchester, 2016), 243–61.

A. Diem and P. Rousseau, 'Monastic Rules (Fourth to Ninth Century)', in Beach and Cochelin (eds), *Medieval Monasticism*, 162–94.

M. Dietz, *Wandering Monks, Virgins, and Pilgrims: Ascetic Travel in the Mediterranean World, A.D. 300–800* (University Park, PA, 2005).

P. Díez de Revenga, 'Algunas expresiones de la sanctio en cartas medievales', *Voces*, 2 (1991), 63–72.

J. D. Dodds, *Architecture and Ideology in Early Medieval Spain* (University Park, PA, 1990).

M. Domínguez, 'Fórmulas de sanción en documentos del noroeste peninsular hasta al año 1000', in Pérez González (ed.), *Actas I*, 475–80.

M. Domínguez García *et al.* (eds), *Sub luce florentis calami. Homenaje a Manuel C. Díaz y Díaz* (Santiago de Compostela, 2002).

L. Domínguez Guilarte, 'Notas sobre la adquisición de tierras y de frutos en nuestro derecho medieval. La presura o escalio', *AHDE*, 10 (1933), 287–324.

S. Domínguez Sánchez, 'En torno a las puntualizaciones sobre la datación de documentos medievales de la catedral de Astorga', *EHH*, 4 (2005), 297–302.

B. Dumézil, 'Le crime de parjure dans l'Espagne wisigothique du VIIe siècle', in M.-F. Auzépy and G. Saint-Guillain (eds), *Oralité et lien social au Moyen Âge (Occident, Byzance, Islam): parole donnée, foi jurée, serment* (Paris, 2008), 27–42.

M. Durany Castrillo and M. C. Rodríguez González, 'El obispado de Astorga en el primer tercio del siglo XI: de Jimeno a Sampiro', *Semata*, 15 (2003), 187–222.

M. Durany Castrillo and M. C. Rodríguez González, 'Puntualizaciones sobre la datación de algunos documentos de la catedral de Astorga del primer tercio del siglo XI: de Jimeno a Sampiro', *EHH*, 3 (2004), 275–302.

S. N. Dworkin, *A Guide to Old Spanish* (Oxford, 2018).

W. S. van Egmond, *Conversing with the Saints: Communication in Pre-Carolingian Hagiography from Auxerre* (Turnhout, 2006).

E. L. Eisenstein, *The Printing Press as an Agent of Change: Communications and Cultural Transformations in Early Modern Europe* (Cambridge, 1980).

E. L. Eisenstein, *The Printing Revolution in Early Modern Europe* (2nd ed., Cambridge, 2005).

A. Emiliano, 'Latin or Romance? Graphemic Variation and Scripto-Linguistic Change in Medieval Spain', in Wright (ed.), *Latin*, 233–47.

A. Emiliano, 'Representational Models vs. Operational Models of Literacy in Latin-Romance Legal Documents (with Special Reference to Latin-Portuguese Texts)', in R. Wright and P. T. Ricketts (eds), *Studies on Ibero-Romance Linguistics Dedicated to Ralph Penny* (Newark, NJ, 2005), 17–57.

P. Erhart, '*Carta ista amalfitana est et nescitur legere*. The Charters of Cava dei Tirreni and St Gall and their Evidence for Earl Medieval Archival Practice', *GLM*, 50 (2007), 27–39.

P. Erhart, K. Heidecker, and B. Zeller (eds), *Die Privaturkunden der Karolingerzeit* (Dietikon-Zürich, 2009).

J. Escalona Monge, 'Antes de los cartularios: gestión de archivos y transmisión de los documentos de la Castilla condal (siglo IX–1038)', in Escalona Monge and Sirantoine (eds), *Chartes*, 131–52.

J. Escalona Monge, 'Aproximación a un análisis comparativo de la territorialidad en los siglos IX–XI: el Territorium legionensis y el Condado de Castilla', in J. I. de la Iglesia Duarte (ed.), *Monasterios, espacio y sociedad en la España cristiana medieval. XX Semana de Estudios Medievales* (Logroño, 2010), 273–93.

J. Escalona Monge, 'Cartularios, memoria y discurso en la Castilla medieval', in E. López Ojeda (ed.), *La memoria del poder, el poder de la memoria. XXVII Semana de Estudios Medievales* (Logroño, 2017), 163–203.

J. Escalona Monge, 'Community Meetings in Early Medieval Castile', in Carroll, Reynolds, and Yorke (eds), *Power*, 216–37.

J. Escalona Monge, 'Comunidades, territorios y poder condal en la Castilla del Duero en el siglo X', *SHHM*, 18–19 (2000–1), 85–120.

J. Escalona Monge, 'Dense Local Knowledge: Grounding Local to Supralocal Relationships in Tenth-Century Castile', in Escalona Monge, Vésteinsson, and Brookes (eds), *Polity*, 351–79.

J. Escalona Monge, 'Family Memories: Inventing Alfonso I of Asturias', in Alfonso, Kennedy, and Escalona (eds), *Building Legitimacy*, 223–62.

J. Escalona Monge, 'Lucha política y escritura: falsedad y autenticidad documental en el conflicto entre el monasterio de Santo Domingo y el Burgo de Silos (ss. XIII–XIV)', in J. I. de la Iglesia Duarte (ed.), *Conflictos sociales, políticos e intelectuales en la España de los siglos XIV y XV. XIV Semana de Estudios Medievales* (Logroño, 2004), 205–52.

J. Escalona Monge, 'Military Stress, Central Power, and Local Response in the County of Castile in the Tenth Century', in J. Baker, S. Brookes, and A. Reynolds (eds), *Landscapes of Defence in Early Medieval Europe* (Turnhout, 2013), 341–67.

J. Escalona Monge, 'In the Name of a Distant King: Representing Royal Authority in the County of Castile, *c.* 900–1038', *EME*, 24.1 (2016), 74–102.

J. Escalona Monge, 'Organización eclesiástica y territorialidad en Castilla antes de la Reforma Gregoriana', in I. Martín Viso (ed.), *La construcción de la territorialidad en la Alta Edad Media* (Salamanca, 2020), 167–201.

J. Escalona Monge, 'De "señores y campesinos" a "poderes feudales y comunidades". Elementos para definir la articulación entre territorio y clases sociales en la Alta Edad Media castellana', in Álvarez Borge (ed.), *Comunidades*, 117–55.

J. Escalona Monge, 'Territorialidad e identidades locales en la Castilla condal', in J. A. Jara Fuente, G. Martin, and I. Alfonso (eds), *Construir la identidad en la Edad Media* (Cuenca, 2010), 55–82.

J. Escalona Monge, 'Towards an Archaeology of State Formation in North-Western Iberia', in Quirós Castillo (ed.), *Social Inequality*, 33–53.

J. Escalona Monge and P. Azcárate Aguilar-Amat, 'Una fuente "casi" perdida para la historia de la Castilla medieval. Notas en torno al Becerro de San Pedro de Arlanza', *Hispania*, 61.208 (2001), 449–74.

J. Escalona Monge, P. Azcárate Aguilar-Amat, and M. Larrañaga Zulueta, 'De la crítica diplomática a la ideología política. Los diplomas fundacionales de San Pedro de Arlanza y la construcción de una identidad para la Castilla medieval', in Sáez and Castillo Gómez (eds), *Actas VI*, 2, 162–206.

J. Escalona Monge and I. Martín Viso, 'The Life and Death of an Historiographical Folly: the Early Medieval Depopulation and Repopulation of the Duero Basin', in Barton and Portass (eds), *Beyond the Reconquista*, 21–51.

J. Escalona Monge and F. Reyes, 'Scale Change on the Border: the County of Castile in the Tenth Century', in Escalona Monge and Reynolds (eds), *Scale*, 153–83.

J. Escalona Monge and A. Reynolds (eds), *Scale and Scale Change in the Early Middle Ages: Exploring Landscape, Local Society, and the World Beyond* (Turnhout, 2011).

J. Escalona Monge and H. Sirantoine (eds), *Chartes et cartulaires comme instruments de pouvoir. Espagne et Occident chrétien (VIIIᵉ–XIIᵉ siècles)* (Toulouse, 2013).

J. Escalona Monge, O. Vésteinsson, and S. Brookes (eds), *Polity and Neighbourhood in Early Medieval Europe* (Turnhout, 2019).

*Escritos dedicados a José María Fernández Catón* (2 vols, León, 2004).

G. J. Escudero Manzano, 'Los condes de Présaras y la fundación de San Salvador de Sobrado. El intento de una parentela magnaticia por recuperar su preeminencia en *Gallecia*', *SHHM*, 39.1 (2021), 197–213.

G. J. Escudero Manzano, 'La "despoblación" y "repoblación" del Valle del Duero: la problemática de las fuentes y el debate historiográfico', *Estudios Medievales Hispánicos*, 5 (2016), 151–72.

S. Esders, 'Early Medieval Use of Late Antique Legal Texts: the Case of the *Manumissio in ecclesia*', in O. Kano (ed.), *Configuration du texte en histoire* (Nagoya, 2012), 55–66.

S. Esders, 'Der Verjährungstitel des Liber iudiciorum (L. Vis. X, 2) und die politischen Implikationen des Ersitzungsgedankens im Westgotenreich', in Czeguhn *et al.* (eds), *Wasser*, 57–86.

A. do Espirito Santo, 'Los benedictinos en el reino de León', in *Monarquía*, 1, 712–32.

C. Estepa Díez, *Las behetrías castellanas* (2 vols, Valladolid, 2003).

C. Estepa Díez, 'La Castilla primitiva (750–931): condes, territorios y villas', *TSP*, Anejo 2 (2009), 261–78.

C. Estepa Díez, *Estructura social de la ciudad de León (siglos XI–XIII)* (León, 1977).

C. Estepa Díez, 'Formación y consolidación del feudalismo en Castilla y León', in *En torno al feudalismo hispánico. I Congreso de Estudios Medievales* (Ávila, 1989), 157–256.

C. Estepa Díez, 'Hombres de benefactoría y behetrías en León (siglos XI–XIV): aproximación a su estudio', in Rodríguez (ed.), *Lugar*, 113–40.

C. Estepa Díez, 'Poder y propiedad feudales en el período astur: las mandaciones de los Flaínez en la montaña leonesa', in *Miscel·lània en homenatge al P. Agustí Altisent* (Tarragona, 1991), 285–328.

*Estudos em homenagem ao professor doutor José Marques* (4 vols, Porto, 2006).

N. Everett, 'Lay Documents and Archives in Early Medieval Spain and Italy, *c.* 400–700', in Brown *et al.* (eds), *Documentary Culture*, 63–94.

N. Everett, 'Literacy from Late Antiquity to the Early Middle Ages, *c.* 300–800 AD', in D. R. Olson and N. Torrance (eds), *The Cambridge Handbook of Literacy* (Cambridge, 2009), 362–85.

N. Everett, *Literacy in Lombard Italy, c. 568–774* (Cambridge, 2003).

N. Everett, 'Scribes and Charters in Lombard Italy', *SMed*, 41.1 (2000), 39–84.

V. Farías Zurita, 'La sagrera catalana (c. 1025–c. 1200): características y desarrollo de un tipo de asentamiento eclesial', *SHHM*, 11 (1993), 81–123.

V. Farías, R. Martí, and A. Catafau, *Les sagreres a la Catalunya medieval* (Girona, 2007).

C. Faulhaber, *Libros y bibliotecas en la España medieval. Una bibliografía de fuentes impresas* (London, 1987).

L. Febvre and H.-J. Martin, *The Coming of the Book: the Impact of Printing, 1450–1800*, transl. D. Gerard, ed. G. Nowell-Smith and D. Wootton (London, 1976).

J. Fentress and C. Wickham, *Social Memory* (Oxford, 1992).

D. Fernández, 'Property, Social Status, and Church Building in Visigothic Iberia', *Journal of Late Antiquity*, 9.2 (2016), 512–41.

D. Fernández, 'Trial Witnesses, Social Hierarchies, and State Building in the Visigothic Kingdom of Toledo', *EME*, 28.4 (2020), 509–31.

J. Fernández Alonso, *La cura pastoral en la España romano-visigoda* (Rome, 1955).

N. Fernández Cadenas, 'A Critical Review of the Signs on Visigothic Slates: Challenging the Roman Numerals Premise', *JMIS*, 13.1 (2021), 1–27.

J. M. Fernández Catón, 'La documentación del monasterio de Lorvão hasta la muerte del abad Eusebio (1118). Relación de documentos, aportaciones históricas y problemas cronológicos', in *Liber*, 2, 453–579.

J. M. Fernández Catón, 'La *Nodicia de Kesos* y los problemas de la documentación del siglo X sobre el origen de los monasterios independientes de Rozuela y Cillanueva', in *Orígenes*, 1, 35–86.

J. M. Fernández Catón, 'El "Tumbo Legionense". Notas sobre su origen, redacción, estructura, contenido y utilización', in Nascimento and Alberto (eds), *Actas IV*, 415–34.

F. J. Fernández Conde, 'Ganadería en Asturias en la primera Edad Media. Algunas características de la economía castreña y romana', in J. Gómez-Pantoja (ed.), *Los rebaños de Gerión. Pastores y trashumancia en Iberia antigua y medieval* (Madrid, 2001), 139–58.

F. J. Fernández Conde, *El Libro de los Testamentos de la catedral de Oviedo* (Rome, 1971).

F. J. Fernández Conde, *La religiosidad medieval en Espana, I. Alta Edad Media (s. VII–X)* (Oviedo, 2000).

F. J. Fernández Conde and R. Alonso Álvarez (eds), *Los reyes de Asturias y los orígenes del culto a la tumba del apóstol Santiago* (Gijón, 2017).

F. J. Fernández Conde and J. Fernández Fernández, 'Abades, obispos y poder social', *TSP*, 4 (2009), 65–94.

F. J. Fernández Conde and I. Torrente Fernández, 'Los orígenes del monasterio de San Pelayo (Oviedo): aristocracia, poder y monacato', *TSP*, 2 (2007), 181–202.

R. Fernández Espinar, 'La compraventa en el derecho medieval español', *AHDE*, 25 (1955), 293–528.

J. A. Fernández Flórez, 'El *Becerro Gótico* de Cardeña: aproximación a sus características más significativas', in Furtado and Moscone (eds), *Charters*, 21–39.

J. A. Fernández Flórez, 'Un calígrafo-miniaturista del año mil: Vigila de Albelda', *CA*, 16 (2000), 153–80.

J. A. Fernández Flórez, 'Los documentos y sus *scriptores*', in *Monarquía*, 2, 97–140.

J. A. Fernández Flórez, *La elaboración de los documentos en los reinos hispánicos occidentales (ss. VI–XIII)* (Burgos, 2002).

J. A. Fernández Flórez, 'Escribas y miniaturistas en el monasterio medieval: organización y funcionalidad del scriptorium monástico', in J. Á. García de Cortázar and R. Teja (eds), *Las edades del monje: jerarquía y función en el monasterio medieval* (Aguilar de Campoo, 2019), 169–99.

J. A. Fernández Flórez, 'Escribir, en León-Castilla, en la época medieval', in *Viajes y viajeros en la España medieval. Actas del V Curso de Cultura Medieval* (Madrid, 1997), 143–76.

J. A. Fernández Flórez, 'Escribir en los monasterios altomedievales del Occidente peninsular (siglos VIII–XII)', in Baldaquí Escandell (ed.), *Lugares*, 17–67.

J. A. Fernández Flórez, 'El fondo documental del monasterio de Sahagún y sus scriptores (siglos IX–X)', in *Monacato*, 125–46.

J. A. Fernández Flórez, 'La génesis documental: desde las pizarras visigodas y la Lex Romana Wisigothorum al siglo X', in Ávila Seoane, Salamanca López, and Zozaya Montes (eds), *VIII Jornadas*, 89–117.

J. A. Fernández Flórez, 'La huella de los copistas en los cartularios leoneses', in *Orígenes*, 1, 159–228.

J. A. Fernández Flórez, 'Paleografía y diplomática en los documentos altomedievales de León y Castilla: ss. VIII–XII', in H. Perdiguero Villarreal (ed.), *Lengua romance en textos latinos de la Edad Media. Sobre los orígenes del castellano escrito* (Burgos, 2003), 81–94.

J. A. Fernández Flórez, 'Purello en Valdoré (un viejo pergamino recuperado)', in M. Herrero de la Fuente *et al.* (eds), *Alma littera. Estudios dedicados al profesor José Manuel Ruiz Asencio* (Valladolid, 2014), 167–81.

J. A. Fernández Flórez and M. Herrero de la Fuente, 'Copistas y colaboradores en el monasterio de Albelda', in H. Spilling (ed.), *La collaboration dans la production de l'écrit médiéval. Actes du XIII<sup>e</sup> Colloque international de paléographie latine* (Paris, 2003), 105–30.

J. A. Fernández Flórez and M. Herrero de la Fuente, 'Libertades de los copistas en la confección de cartularios: el caso del Becerro Gótico de Sahagún', in E. Cordello and G. de Gregorio (eds), *Scribi e colofoni: le sottoscrizioni di copisti dalle origini all'avvento della stampa* (Spoleto, 1995), 301–19.

C. Fernández Ibáñez and C. Lamalfa Díaz, 'Manifestaciones rupestres de época histórica en el entorno de la cabecera del Ebro', *Munibe*, 57.3 (2005–6), 257–67.

M. Fernández Mier, P. López Gómez, and D. González Álvarez, 'Prácticas ganaderas en la Cordillera Cantábrica. Aproximación multidisciplinar al estudio de las áreas de pasto en la Edad Media', *Debates de Arqueología Medieval*, 3 (2013), 167–219.

J. M. Fernández del Pozo, *Alfonso V (999–1028), Vermudo III (1028–1037)* (Burgos, 1999).

J. M. Fernández del Pozo, 'Alfonso V y Vermudo III: fin de la dinastía astur (999–1037)', in C. Álvarez Álvarez (ed.), *Reyes de León: monarcas leoneses del 850 al 1230* (León, 1996), 85–106.

Á. S. Fernández-Sordo, 'Monasterios y núcleos urbanos en la Asturias medieval. Conflicto, acuerdo, convivencia y simbiosis', in G. Cavero Domínguez (ed.), *Civitas bendita: encrucijada de las relaciones sociales y de poder en la ciudad medieval* (León, 2016), 179–225.

J. I. Fernández de Viana y Vieites, 'Aproximación a las citas bíblicas en los documentos gallegos medievales', in *Jubilatio. Homenaje de la Facultad de Geografía e Historia a los profesores D. Manuel Lucas Álvarez y D. Ángel Rodríguez González* (2 vols, Santiago de Compostela, 1987), 1, 229–37.

J. I. Fernández de Viana y Vieites, 'Caecus non iudicat de coloribus. A propósito de la edición del Tumbo de Celanova', *Signo*, 3 (1996), 227–37.

J. I. Fernández de Viana y Vieites, 'Las fuentes documentales gallegas de la Edad Media. Estado de su publicación', in *Galicia en la Edad Media* (Madrid, 1990), 1–7.

J. I. Fernández de Viana y Vieites, 'Problemas y perspectivas de la diplomática de los reinos asturiano, leonés y castellano leonés en la Alta Edad Media', in Sáez and Castillo Gómez (eds), *Actas VI*, 2, 39–53.

A. Ferreiro, '*Secundum quod sancta synodus*: Advancing the Mission of the Church through Conciliar Legislation after the Third Council of Toledo (589)', *Annuarium Historiae Conciliorum*, 44.1 (2012), 27–46.

J. Ferro Couselo, *Los petroglifos de término y las insculturas rupestres de Galicia* (Ourense, 1952).

T. Finbow, 'Inter- and Intra-Word Spacing Conventions in Early Medieval Iberian Texts – the Implications for Reading and Writing Strategies', in M. van Acker, R. van Deyck, and M. van Uytfanghe (eds), *Latin écrit—roman oral? De la dichotomisation à la continuité* (Turnhout, 2008), 159–85.

T. Finbow, 'Limiting Logographic Latin: (Non-) Separation of Orthographic Words in Medieval Iberian Writing', in R. Wright (ed.), *LVLT VIII. Actes du VIII$^e$ Colloque international sur le latin vulgaire et tardif* (Hildesheim, 2008), 521–31.

R. Finnegan, *Literacy and Orality: Studies in the Technology of Communication* (Oxford, 1988).

R. A. Fletcher, *Saint James' Catapult: the Life and Times of Diego Gelmírez of Santiago de Compostela* (Oxford, 1984).

A. C. Floriano, *Curso general de Paleografía y Paleografía y Diplomática españoles* (2 vols, Oviedo, 1946).

P. Floriano Llorente, 'Crítica documental. Los documentos de la catedral de Oviedo', in *Homenaje a Juan Uría Ríu* (2 vols, Oviedo, 1997), 1, 69–80.

P. Floriano Llorente, 'Los documentos reales del período astur. Su formulario', *AM*, 1 (1972), 157–76.

S. Foot, 'Reading Anglo-Saxon Charters: Memory, Record, or Story?', in Tyler and Balzaretti (eds), *Narrative*, 39–65.

I. Forrest, *Trustworthy Men: How Inequality and Faith Made the Medieval Church* (Princeton, NJ, 2018).

L. J. Fortún Pérez de Ciriza, *Leire, un señorío monástico en Navarra (siglos IX–XIX)* (Pamplona, 1993).

P. Fouracre, '"Placita" and the Settlement of Disputes in Later Merovingian Francia', in Davies and Fouracre (eds), *Settlement*, 23–43.

H. Franco Júnior, 'Les trois doigts d'Adam. Liturgie et métaphore visuelle au monastère de San Juan de la Peña', *AHSS*, 62.2 (2007), 413–39.

S. Franklin, 'Literacy and Documentation in Early Medieval Russia', *Speculum*, 60.1 (1985), 1–38.

S. Franklin, *Writing, Society, and Culture in Early Rus, c. 950–1300* (Cambridge, 2002).

J. Freire Camaniel, 'El Liber Regularum y el Codex regularum del monacato prebenedictino', in Domínguez García *et al.* (eds), *Sub luce*, 350–8.

J. Freire Camaniel, *El monacato gallego en la Alta Edad Media* (2 vols, A Coruña, 1998).

J. Freire Camaniel, 'Los primeros documentos relativos a las iglesias de AnteaRtares y Santiago. Una lectura más', *Compostellanum*, 44.3–4 (1999), 335–92, 45.3–4 (2000), 725–55.

N. Frye, *The Great Code: the Bible and Literature* (New York, NY, 1982).

N. Frye, *Words with Power: Being a Second Study of the Bible and Literature*, ed. M. Dolzani (Toronto, 2008).

R. Furtado, 'Writing History in Portugal before 1200', *JMH*, 47.2 (2021), 145–73.

R. Furtado and M. Moscone (eds), *From Charters to Codex: Studies on Cartularies and Archival Memory in the Middle Ages* (Turnhout, 2019).

J. C. Galende Díaz, 'Elementos y sistemas criptográficos en la escritura visigótica', in Ávila Seoane, Salamanca López, and Zozaya Montes (eds), *VIII Jornadas*, 173–83.

J. C. Galende Díaz and J. de Santiago Fernández (eds), *X Jornadas científicas sobre documentación. El calendario y la datación histórica* (Madrid, 2011).

F. Gallegos Vázquez, 'El delito de traición en el derecho visigodo', in M. Fernández Rodríguez, E. Prado Rubio, and L. Martínez Peñas (eds), *Análisis sobre jurisdicciones especiales* (Valladolid, 2017), 35–60.

F. Gallon, 'Falsifier l'histoire pour tromper le pape. Sur un texte relatif à l'histoire du monastère galicien de Cinis (début du XIIᵉ siècle)', in K. Lennartz (ed.), *Engaños e invenciones. Contribuciones multidisciplinares sobre pseudoepígrafos literarios y documentales. De falsa et vera historia* 4 (Madrid, 2021), 285–301.

F. Gallon, 'Monachisme, pouvoirs et société dans la Péninsule Ibérique du Haut Moyen Âge: autour de Gennade d'Astorga (850-865?-936?)', *RM*, 21.82 (2010), 37–75.

F. Galtier Martí, *Ribagorza, condado independiente: desde los orígenes hasta 1025* (Zaragoza, 1981).

A. Gambra Gutiérrez, 'El "palatium" y la "domus regis" castellanoleoneses en tiempos de la dinastía pamplonesa', in A. Gambra Gutiérrez and F. Labrador Arroyo (eds), *Evolución y estructura de la Casa Real de Castilla* (2 vols, Madrid, 2010), 1, 11–64.

D. Ganz, 'Giving to God in the Mass: the Experience of the Offertory', in Davies and Fouracre (eds), *Languages*, 18–32.

D. Ganz and W. Goffart, 'Charters Earlier than 800 from French Collections', *Speculum*, 65.4 (1990), 906–32.

M. R. García Álvarez, 'Gutier e Ilduara, padres de San Rosendo', *Boletín Auriense*, 7 (1977), 119–53.

M. R. García Álvarez, 'Los libros en la documentación gallega de la Alta Edad Media', *CEG*, 20.62 (1965), 292–329.

M. R. García Álvarez, *San Pedro de Mezonzo. El origen y el autor de la "Salve Regina"* (Madrid, 1965).

F. García Andreva, 'La enseñanza en la Edad Media. Aproximación bibliográfica', in Iglesia Duarte (ed.), *Enseñanza*, 473–506.

J. C. García Cacho, 'Memoria funeraria y prestigio social en San Vicente de León, un monasterio aristocrático y episcopal (1005-1036)', *CM*, 29 (2020), 1–21.

J. Á. García de Cortázar, *El dominio del monasterio de San Millán de la Cogolla (siglos X a XIII): introducción a la historia rural de Castilla altomedieval* (Salamanca, 1969).

J. Á. García de Cortázar, 'Las formas de organización social del espacio del Valle del Duero en la Alta Edad Media: de la espontaneidad al control feudal', in *Despoblación y colonización del Valle del Duero, siglos VIII-XX. IV Congreso de Estudios Medievales* (Ávila, 1995), 11–44.

J. Á. García de Cortázar, 'Memoria y cultura en la documentación del monasterio de Samos: la respuesta de las fórmulas "inútiles" (años 785–1209)', *Inter-American Music Review*, 18.1–2 (2008), 87–97.

J. Á. García de Cortázar, 'Reyes y abades en el reino de León (años 910 a 1157)', in *Monarquía*, 1, 201–63.

J. Á. García de Cortázar (ed.), *La memoria histórica de Cantabria* (Santander, 1996).

J. Á. García de Cortázar and L. Agúndez San Miguel, 'Memoria y cultura en la documentación del monasterio de Celanova: la respuesta de las "fórmulas inútiles" (años 842–1165)', in M. I. V. Valdivieso and P. Martínez Sopena (eds), *Castilla y el mundo feudal. Homenaje al profesor Julio Valdeón* (3 vols, Valladolid, 2009), 3, 251–67.

A. García-Gallo, 'Bienes propios y derecho de propiedad en la Alta Edad Media española. Notas para su estudio', *AHDE*, 29 (1959), 351–87.

A. García-Gallo, 'El carácter germánico de la épica y del derecho en la Edad Media española', *AHDE*, 25 (1955), 583–679.

A. García-Gallo, 'El Concilio de Coyanza. Contribución al estudio del derecho canónico español en la Alta Edad Media', *AHDE*, 20 (1950), 275–633.

A. García-Gallo, 'Consideración crítica de los estudios sobre la legislación y la costumbre visigodas', *AHDE*, 44 (1974), 343–464.

A. García-Gallo, 'Los documentos y los formularios jurídicos en España hasta el siglo XII', repr. in *Estudios de historia del derecho privado* (Seville, 1982), 345–408.

A. García-Gallo, 'El Fuero de León. Su historia, textos y redacciones', *AHDE*, 39 (1969), 5–171.

A. García-Gallo, 'El hombre y la tierra en la Edad Media leonesa (el prestimonio agrario)', *Revista de la Facultad de Derecho de la Universidad de Madrid*, 1.2 (1957), 319–72.

A. García-Gallo, 'Notas sobre el reparto de tierras entre visigodos y romanos', *Hispania*, 4 (1941), 40–63.

A. García-Gallo, 'Del testamento romano al medieval. Las líneas de su evolución en España', *AHDE*, 47 (1977), 425–97.

A. García-Gallo, 'En torno a la carta de población de Brañosera', *HID*, 11 (1984), 1–14.

A. García y García, 'Concilios y sínodos en el ordenamiento jurídico del reino de León', in *RLAEM* 1 (León, 1988), 353–494.

A. García y García, 'Contenidos canónico-teológicos de los diplomas leoneses', in *RLAEM* 6 (León, 1994), 7–132.

A. García y García, 'El derecho canónico medieval en los diplomas del reino de León', *AHDE*, 71 (2001), 704–11.

A. García y García, 'Derecho canónico y vida cotidiana en el medievo', *RPH*, 24 (1988), 189–226.

A. García y García, 'Las imprecaciones en los diplomas leoneses', *Atalaya*, 5 (1994), 57–66.

A. García y García, 'Legislación de los concilios y sínodos del reino leonés', in *RLAEM* 2 (León, 1992), 9–115.

E. García García, 'Pequeños propietarios en Asturias (siglos X y XI)', *AM*, 5 (1986), 33–53.

J. García González, 'Traición y alevosía en la Alta Edad Media', *AHDE*, 32 (1962), 323–45.

A. García Leal, 'El archivo de los condes Fruela Muñoz y Pedro Flaínez (854–1048): una visión nueva de viejos documentos', *Signo*, 13 (2004), 121–47.

A. García Leal, 'La colección fotográfica de los Dres. Emilio Sáez y Carlos Sáez correspondiente a la documentación del monasterio de Santa María de Otero de las Dueñas (León)', in González de la Peña (ed.), *Estudios*, 591–600.

A. García Leal, 'Los condes Fruela Muñoz y Pedro Flaínez: la formación de un patrimonio señorial', *AEM*, 36.1 (2006), 1–110.

A. García Leal, 'La documentación medieval de Asturias: reseña crítica de las colecciones documentales y códices hasta el presente editados', in *I Congreso de Estudios Asturianos* (5 vols, Oviedo, 2007), 2, 73–154.

A. García Leal, 'El sistema judicial en la Asturias altomedieval: derecho romano, germánico y árabe a través de la colección documental de Fruela Muñoz y Pedro Flaínez', in C. E. Prieto Entrialgo (ed.), *Árabes in patria Asturiensium* (Oviedo, 2011), 311–28.

V. García Lobo, 'Calígrafos, códices y bibliotecas en el reino de León', in *Monarquía*, 2, 19–44.

V. García Lobo and M. E. Martín López, 'Las inscripciones diplomáticas de época visigoda y altomedieval (siglos VI a XII)', *MCV*, 41.2 (2011), 87–108.

V. García Lobo and M. E. Martín López, 'La liturgie hispanique dans l'épigraphie (VIIIᵉ–XIIᵉ siècles): la liturgie sacramentelle et la liturgie funéraire', *CCM*, 58.231 (2015), 259–78.

Y. García López, *Estudios críticos y literarios de la "Lex Wisigothorum"* (Alcalá de Henares, 1996).

Y. García López, 'La tradición del Liber Iudiciorum: una revisión', in *Antigüedad*, 383–405.

L. M. García Lozano, 'Typologies of Usufruct in the Visigothic Law: Analysis of the Legal Casuistry', *Vergentis*, 8 (2019), 111–24.

A. García Medina, 'Signos de validación de mujeres en la Alta Edad Media', in González de la Peña (ed.), *Estudios*, 85–94.

E. García Molinos, 'Florencio de Valeránica, calígrafo y notario del siglo X', in *RLAEM* 11 (León, 2004), 243–431.

M. García-Pelayo, *Los mitos políticos* (Madrid, 1981).

A. García-Sanjuán, 'From Islamic to Christian Conquest: *Fatḥ* Invasion and *Reconquista* in Medieval Iberia', in E. M. Gerli and R. D. Giles (eds), *The Routledge Hispanic Studies Companion to Medieval Iberia: Unity in Diversity* (Abingdon, 2021), 185–96.

A. García-Sanjuán, 'Replication and Fragmentation: the Taifa Kingdoms', in M. Fierro (ed.), *The Routledge Handbook of Muslim Iberia* (Abingdon, 2020), 64–88.

P. García Toraño, 'La ejecución de últimas voluntades "pro anima" en el período astur', *BIDEA*, 25.73 (1971), 293–316.

P. García Toraño, 'Notas sobre la cuota de libre disposición en el cartulario de San Salvador de Cornellana', *BIDEA*, 20.58 (1966), 83–90.

P. García Toraño, 'La remisión "sicut lex docet" o cláusula similar en los documentos asturianos de la Reconquista', *BIDEA*, 21.60 (1967), 89–100, 22.64–5 (1968), 401–11.

C. García Turza (ed.), *Los manuscritos visigóticos. Estudio paleográfico y codicológico, I. Códices riojanos datados* (Logroño, 2002).

F. J. García Turza, 'Los espacios de poder en La Rioja medieval', in Iglesia Duarte and Martín Rodríguez (eds), *Espacios*, 483–509.

M. V. García Quintela and Y. Seoane-Veiga, 'La larga vida de dos rocas orensanas', *AEA*, 84 (2011), 243–66.

L. García de Valdeavellano, 'La comunidad patrimonial de la familia en el derecho español medieval', *Acta Salmanticensia. Derecho*, 3.1 (1956), 9–40.

L. García de Valdeavellano, 'Sobre los conceptos de hurto y robo en el derecho visigodo y postvisigodo', *RPH*, 4 (1949), 211–51.

L. García de Valdeavellano, 'La cuota de libre disposición en el derecho hereditario de León y Castilla en la Alta Edad Media', *AHDE*, 9 (1932), 129–76.

L. García de Valdeavellano, *Curso de Historia de las Instituciones españolas. De los orígenes al final de la Edad Media* (7th ed., Madrid, 1984).

L. García de Valdeavellano, 'Escodriñamiento y otorificación (contribución al estudio de la reivindicación mobiliaria en el derecho español medieval)', in *Centenario de la ley de notariado. Sección primera: estudios históricos* (2 vols, Madrid, 1964–5), 2, 125–335.

L. García de Valdeavellano, 'El prestimonio. Contribución al estudio de las manifestaciones del feudalismo en los reinos de León y Castilla durante la Edad Media', *AHDE*, 25 (1955), 5–122.

L. García de Valdeavellano, 'El "renovo". Notas y documentos sobre los préstamos usurarios en el reino astur-leonés (siglos X–XI)', *CHE*, 57–8 (1973), 408–48.

A. Garín, 'Economía y religiosidad. Clérigos propietarios en la diócesis de Astorga en los siglos X y XI', *ETF*, 11 (1998), 231–42.

I. H. Garipzanov, *Graphic Signs of Authority in Late Antiquity and the Early Middle Ages, 300–900* (Oxford, 2018).

I. H. Garipzanov, *The Symbolic Language of Authority in the Carolingian World (c. 751–877)* (Leiden, 2008).

M. Garrison, '"Send More Socks": on Mentality and the Preservation Context of Medieval Letters', in Mostert (ed.), *New Approaches*, 69–99.

M. Garrison, A. P. Orbán, and M. Mostert (eds), *Spoken and Written Language: Relations between Latin and the Vernacular Languages in the Earlier Middle Ages* (Turnhout, 2013).

J. Gautier-Dalché, 'Le domaine du monastère de Santo Toribio de Liébana: formation, structure et modes d'exploitation', *AEM*, 2 (1965), 63–117.

J. Gautier-Dalché, 'Du royaume asturo-léonais à la monarchie castillano-léonaise: une histoire monétaire singulière (VIIIᵉ–XIᵉ siècle)', in *L'argent au Moyen Âge* (Paris, 1998), 77–92.

P. J. Geary, 'Entre gestion et *gesta*: aux origines des cartulaires', in O. Guyotjeannin, L. Morelle, and M. Parisse (eds), *Les cartulaires. Actes de la table ronde organisée par l'École nationale des chartes* (Paris, 1993), 13–26.

P. J. Geary, 'Land, Language, and Memory in Europe, 700–1100', *TRHS*, 9 (1999), 169–84.

P. J. Geary, 'Oblivion between Orality and Textuality in the Tenth Century', in G. Althoff, J. Fried, and P. J. Geary (eds), *Medieval Concepts of the Past: Ritual, Memory, Historiography* (Cambridge, 2002), 111–22.

P. J. Geary, *Phantoms of Remembrance: Memory and Oblivion at the End of the First Millennium* (Princeton, NJ, 1994).

T. Gergen, 'The Peace of God and its Legal Practice in the Eleventh Century', *CHD*, 9 (2002), 11–27.

A. Ghignoli, 'Writing Texts, Drawing Signs. On Some Non-Alphabetical Signs in Charters of the Early Medieval West', *AD*, 62 (2016), 11–40.

R. Gibert, 'Enseñanza del derecho en Hispania durante los siglos VI a XI', *Ius Romanum Medii Aevi*, I 5 b *cc* (Milan, 1967), 1–54.

J. Gilbert and S. Harris, 'The Written Word: Literacy across Languages', in Rold and Treharne (eds), *Companion*, 149–78.

S. Gilsdorf, *The Favor of Friends: Intercession and Aristocratic Politics in Carolingian and Ottonian Europe* (Leiden, 2014).

L. Gitelman, *Paper Knowledge: Toward a Media History of Documents* (Durham, NC, 2014).

*La giustizia nell'alto medioevo (secoli IX–XI). Settimane* 44 (2 vols, Spoleto, 1997).

A. A. Godoy, 'Fraudes, descuidos y daños: consideraciones sobre los conflictos que enfrentaron a los magnates laicos y sus agentes en León en el siglo XI', *SHHM*, 38.1 (2020), 167–94.

A. A. Godoy, '"Et relegendo cognovimus": los escribientes y la palabra escrita en los contextos locales de la región de León, siglos X y XI', *EEM*, 41 (2018), 77–104.

A. A. Godoy, 'Riqueza, circulación de bienes y élites rurales en León en los siglos X y XI', *Sociedades Precapitalistas*, 9 (2019), 1–16.

W. Goffart, *Barbarians and Romans, A.D. 418–584: the Techniques of Accommodation* (Princeton, NJ, 1980).

W. Goffart, *The Le Mans Forgeries: a Chapter from the History of Church Property in the Ninth Century* (Cambridge, MA, 1966).

S. A. Gomes, 'The Editions of Archival Sources and Documents', in J. Mattoso *et al.* (eds), *The Historiography of Medieval Portugal (c. 1950–2010)* (Lisbon, 2011), 25–43.

J. Gómez Gómez and I. Martín Viso, '*Rationes* y *decimas*: evidencias sobre la gestión de las sernas en el siglo XI en el noroeste de la Península Ibérica', *ETF*, 34 (2021), 359–82.

M. Gómez-Moreno, *Iglesias mozárabes. Arte español de los siglos IX a XI. Edición facsímil* (Granada, 1998).

A. Gómez Rabal, 'Lengua especializada en documentos latinos catalanes de la Alta Edad Media: una amenaza bíblica', in Nascimento and Alberto (eds), *Actas IV*, 553–63.

A. Gómez Rabal, 'Mujeres testadoras y herederas en documentos latinos catalanes de la Alta Edad Media', *Euphrosyne*, 33 (2005), 261–77.

E. González Díez, 'Decir el derecho en el Medievo en el reino de León (910–1230)', in *Actas III Jornadas*, 30–53.

E. González Díez, 'El Liber Iudiciorum de Vigiliano', in *Códice*, 163–84.

E. González Díez, 'Monarquía leonesa y conflictos de orden social (siglos X–XII)', in *Monarquía*, 2, 193–234.

E. González Díez, 'Reflexiones histórico-jurídicas apresuradas sobre la documentación de San Pedro de Cardeña', in Ruiz Rodríguez and Martínez Llorente (eds), *Recuerdos*, 175–90.

J. M. González y Fernández Valles, 'Pravia, "capital" del reino asturiano', *AM*, 3 (1979), 87–104.

R. González González, *Bastiones de tradición. Ciudades y aristocracias urbanas en la Alta Edad Media asturleonesa (siglos IX–XI)* (León, 2022).

R. González González, 'La ciudad como proyecto político: las "sedes" del reino de Asturias entre tradición y ruptura', in J. Rodríguez Muñoz (ed.), *Nuevas visiones del reino de Asturias. Actas del Congreso internacional* (Oviedo, 2020), 363–87.

R. González González, 'Cultura escrita y sociedad urbana: los escribas en la ciudad altomedieval', *EEM*, 44 (2021), 193–235.

R. González González, 'Esclavitud y dependencia personal en el país asturleonés (siglos IX–XIII)', *Medievalismo*, 27 (2017), 159–205.

R. González González, 'Los jueces de León en la primera mitad del siglo X: prosopografía de una aristocracia letrada', *CM*, 31 (2021), 1–20.

R. González González, 'The Shifting Status of *Infanzones*: Warrior Identity and Social Mobility in the Kingdom of León', *Intus-Legere Historia*, 15.2 (2021), 331–54.

M. González Jiménez, 'La moralidad en el reino de León (siglos X–XII)', in *Monarquía*, 2, 269–306.

D. L. González Lopo, 'El testamento de San Rosendo', *Rudesindus*, 6 (2010), 217–26.

C. A. González Paz, 'El diácono Rodrigo de Coimbra: fundador de tres ecclesiae en la Galicia del siglo VIII', in *Estudos*, 1, 439–51.

C. A. González Paz, 'Repensando a Lilith: mujer, matrimonio y aristocracia en la Galicia de la Alta Edad Media', in C. A. González Paz (ed.), *As voces de Clío: a palabra e a memoria da muller na Galicia* (Santiago de Compostela, 2009), 17–50.

M. V. González de la Peña (ed.), *Estudios en memoria del profesor Dr. Carlos Sáez* (Alcalá de Henares, 2007).

J. Goody, *The Domestication of the Savage Mind* (Cambridge, 1977).

J. Goody, *The Interface between the Written and the Oral* (Cambridge, 1987).

J. Goody, *The Logic of Writing and the Organization of Society* (Cambridge, 1986).

J. Goody, *Renaissances: the One or the Many?* (Cambridge, 2010).

J. Goody and I. Watt, 'The Consequences of Literacy', in J. Goody (ed.), *Literacy in Traditional Societies* (Cambridge, 1968), 27–68.

M. de Gouveia, 'Inventário de referências a livros litúrgicos na documentação asturiano-leonesa relativa ao Entre-Minho-e-Mondego (séc. IX–XI)', *Lusitania Sacra*, 31 (2015), 167–96.

L. da Graça, 'Prácticas campesinas en un contexto feudalizado: las relaciones de benefactoría (siglos XI y XII)', *EEM*, 34 (2011), 25–60.

H. J. Graff, 'Literacy, Myths, and Legacies: Lessons from the History of Literacy', in H. J. Graff (ed.), *Literacy and Historical Development: a Reader* (Carbondale, IL, 2007), 12–37.

M. de la Granja Alonso, 'El dominio del monasterio de Eslonza en el territorio de Lampreana-Villafáfila durante la Edad Media', *TL*, 36.101 (1997), 1–18.

H. Grassotti, '"Dominus" y "dominium" en la terminología jurídica de Asturias, León y Castilla (siglos IX–XIII)', *AHDE*, 50 (1980), 653–82.

H. Grassotti, 'La ira regia en León y Castilla', *CHE*, 41–2 (1965), 5–135.

D. H. Green, *Medieval Listening and Reading: the Primary Reception of German Literature, 800–1300* (Cambridge, 1994).

D. H. Green, 'Orality and Reading: The State of Research in Medieval Studies', *Speculum*, 65.2 (1990), 267–80.

M. Gretsch, 'Literacy and the Uses of the Vernacular', in M. Godden and M. Lapidge (eds), *The Cambridge Companion to Old English Literature* (2nd ed., Cambridge, 2013), 273–94.

C. Grijuela Gil, 'Santa María de Piasca y Santo Toribio: dos monasterios en el territorio medieval lebaniense', *Altamira*, 86 (2015), 75–104.

H. Grundmann, '*Litteratus-illitteratus*: the Transformation of an Educational Standard from Antiquity to the Middle Ages', in J. K. Deane (ed.), *Herbert Grundmann (1902–1970): Essays on Heresy, Inquisition, and Literacy*, transl. S. Rowan (York, 2019), 56–125.

A. J. R. Guerra, *Os diplomas privados em Portugal dos séculos IX a XII. Gestos e atitudes de rotina dos seus autores materiais* (Lisbon, 2003).

S. Guijarro, 'Masters and Schools in the Castilian Cathedrals during the Spanish Middle Ages, 1000–1300', *Medieval History*, 4 (1994), 218–47.

J. A. Gutiérrez González, 'El Páramo leonés. Entre la Antigüedad Tardía y la Alta Edad Media', *SHHM*, 14 (1996), 47–96.

C. Hahn, 'Letter and Spirit: the Power of the Letter, the Enlivenment of the Word in Medieval Art', in M. Dalbello and M. Shaw (eds), *Visible Writings: Cultures, Forms, Readings* (New Brunswick, NJ, 2011), 55–76.

K. Haines-Eitzen, 'Textual Communities in Late Antique Christianity', in P. Rousseau (ed.), *A Companion to Late Antiquity* (Chichester, 2009), 246–57.

G. I. Halfond, *Archaeology of Frankish Church Councils, AD 511–768* (Leiden, 2010).

S. Hamilton, *Church and People in the Medieval West* (Abingdon, 2013).

S. Hamilton, 'Educating the Local Clergy, *c.* 900–*c.* 1150', *SCH*, 55 (2019), 83–113.

S. Hamilton, 'Inquiring into Adultery and Other Wicked Deeds: Episcopal Justice in Tenth- and Eleventh-Century Italy', *Viator*, 41.2 (2010), 21–43.

C. I. Hammer, 'Land Sales in Eighth- and Ninth-Century Bavaria: Legal, Economic, and Social Aspects', *EME*, 6.1 (1997), 47–76.

M. A. Handley, *Death, Society, and Culture: Inscriptions and Epitaphs in Gaul and Spain, AD 300–750* (Oxford, 2003).

W. V. Harris, *Ancient Literacy* (Cambridge, 1989).

B. Hartmann, *The Scribes of Rome: a Cultural and Social History of the Scribae* (Cambridge, 2020).

P. Heather, 'Literacy and Power in the Migration Period', in A. K. Bowman and G. Woolf (eds), *Literacy and Power in the Ancient World* (Cambridge, 1996), 177–98.

K. Heidecker, 'Charters as Texts and Objects in Judicial Actions: the Examples of the Carolingian Private Charters of St Gall', in Mostert and Barnwell (eds), *Medieval Legal Process*, 39–53.

K. Heidecker, 'Communication by Written Texts in Court Cases: Some Charter Evidence (*ca.* 800–*ca.* 1100)', in Mostert (ed.), *New Approaches*, 101–26.

K. Heidecker (ed.), *Charters and the Use of the Written Word in Medieval Society* (Turnhout, 2000).

P. Henriet and H. Sirantoine, 'L'église et le roi. Remarques sur les cartulaires ibériques enluminés (XIIᵉ siècle), avec une attention particulière au *Liber Testamentorum* de Pélage d'Oviedo', in Escalona Monge and Sirantoine (eds), *Chartes*, 165–88.

P. Herrera Roldán, *Cultura y lengua latinas entre los mozárabes cordobeses del siglo IX* (Córdoba, 1995).

M. Herrero de la Fuente, 'El *Becerro Gótico* de Sahagún', in Furtado and Moscone (eds), *Charters*, 61–80.

M. Herrero de la Fuente, 'Cartularios leoneses: del Becerro Gótico de Sahagún al Tumbo Legionense y al Libro de las Estampas', in Rodríguez Díaz and García Martínez (eds), *Escritura*, 111–52.

M. Herrero de la Fuente, 'Producir documentos y códices en escritura visigótica', in M. E. Martín López (ed.), *De scriptura et scriptis: producir* (León, 2020), 89–129.

M. Herrero de la Fuente and J. A. Fernández Flórez, '*Cidi*, "scriptor" de documentos altomedievales del fondo monástico de Otero de las Dueñas', in *Escritos*, 1, 651–88.

M. Herrero de la Fuente and J. A. Fernández Flórez, 'El códice albeldense (o vigiliano) de la Biblioteca del Real Monasterio de El Escorial, Ms. D.I.2', in García Turza (ed.), *Manuscritos*, 117–74.

M. Herrero de la Fuente and J. A. Fernández Flórez, 'Sobre la escritura visigótica en León y Castilla durante su etapa primitiva (siglos VII–X): algunas reflexiones', in Alturo i Perucho, Torras Cortina, and Castro Correa (eds), *Escritura*, 55–104.

M. Herrero de la Fuente and J. A. Fernández Flórez, 'El "Liber Testamentorum" de Lorvão y sus tipos documentales, en el contexto de los cartularios de los reinos hispánicos occidentales', in *Liber*, 2, 243–304.

M. Herrero Jiménez, 'La arenga en los diplomas leoneses de los siglos IX a XII', in *Orígenes*, 2, 365–406.

M. Herrero Jiménez, 'El valor de los documentos reales en los procesos de la Real Chancillería de Valladolid', *ETF*, 31 (2018), 403–30.

I. Herwegen, *Das Pactum des hl. Fruktuosus von Braga* (Stuttgart, 1907).

A. Hevia Ballina (ed.), *Desamortización y exclaustración en los Archivos de la Iglesia (s. XIX)* (Oviedo, 2003).

J. N. Hillgarth, *The Visigoths in History and Legend* (Toronto, 2009).

E. de Hinojosa, 'El origen del régimen municipal en León y Castilla', in *Estudios sobre la historia del derecho español* (Madrid, 1903), 5–70.

R. Hitchcock, *Mozarabs in Medieval and Early Modern Spain: Identities and Influences* (Aldershot, 2008).

R. Hitchcock, 'El rito hispánico, las ordalías y los mozárabes en el reinado de Alfonso VI', *Estudios Orientales*, 8.1 (1973), 19–41.

R. Hoggart, *The Uses of Literacy: Aspects of Working-Class Life with Special Reference to Publications and Entertainments* (London, 1957).

*Homenaje a Don Agustín Millares Carlo* (2 vols, Las Palmas de Gran Canaria, 1975).

E. Hornby and K. Ihnat, 'Continuous Psalmody in the Old Hispanic Rite', *Scriptorium*, 73.1 (2019), 3–33.

E. Hornby and R. Maloy, *Music and Meaning in Old Hispanic Lenten Chants: Psalmi, Threni, and the Easter Vigil Canticles* (Woodbridge, 2013).

C. Humfress, 'Cracking the *Codex*: Late Roman Legal Practice in Context', *BICS*, 49.1 (2006), 241–54.

C. Humfress, 'Judging by the Book: Christian Codices and Late Antique Legal Culture', in Klingshirn and Safran (eds), *Early Christian Book*, 141–58.

C. Humfress, 'Law and Custom under Rome', in A. Rio (ed.), *Law, Custom, and Justice in Late Antiquity and the Early Middle Ages* (London, 2011), 23–47.

J. H. Humphrey (ed.), *Literacy in the Roman World* (Ann Arbor, MI, 1991).

M. Á. Ibáñez García, 'El privilegio de Alfonso II: introducción al señorío de Valpuesta en los siglos XI–XII', *Sancho el Sabio*, 18 (2003), 149–74.

*Iglesia y ciudad. Espacio y poder (siglos VIII–XIII)* (Oviedo, 2011).

J. I. de la Iglesia Duarte (ed.), *La enseñanza en la Edad Media. X Semana de Estudios Medievales* (Logroño, 2000).

J. I. de la Iglesia Duarte (ed.), *VII Semana de Estudios Medievales* (Logroño, 1997).

J. I. de la Iglesia Duarte and J. L. Martín Rodríguez (eds), *Los espacios de poder en la España medieval. XII Semana de Estudios Medievales* (Logroño, 2002).

A. Iglesia Ferreirós, 'La creación del derecho en Cataluña', *AHDE*, 47 (1977), 99–423.

A. Iglesia Ferreirós, 'Derecho municipal, derecho señorial, derecho regio', *HID*, 4 (1977), 115–97.

A. Iglesia Ferreirós, *Historia de la traición. La traición regia en León y Castilla* (Santiago de Compostela, 1971).

A. Iglesia Ferreirós, 'El proceso del Conde Bera y el problema de las ordalías', *AHDE*, 51 (1981), 1–221.

L. Iglesias Rábade, 'El falso testimonio judicial en el derecho hispánico y anglo-sajón en el medievo. Estudio comparado', *EEM*, 40 (2017), 67–110.

L. Iglesias Rábade, 'Las penas corporales en el derecho hispánico e inglés en la Edad Media: estudio comparado', *Revista de Estudios Histórico-Jurídicos*, 38 (2016), 123–47.

*Iglesia y religiosidad en España: historia y archivos* (3 vols, Guadalajara, 2002).

J. A. Infantes Florido, 'San Agustín y la cuota de libre disposición', *AHDE*, 30 (1960), 89–112.

M. J. Innes, 'Memory, Orality, and Literacy in an Early Medieval Society', *PP*, 158 (1998), 3–36.

M. J. Innes, *State and Society in the Early Middle Ages: the Middle Rhine Valley, 400–1000* (Cambridge, 2000).

M. J. Innes, 'Practices of Property in the Carolingian Empire', in Davis and McCormick (eds), *Long Morning*, 247–66.

A. Isla Frez, *La Alta Edad Media. Siglos VIII–XI* (Madrid, 2002).

A. Isla Frez, 'The Aristocracy and the Monarchy in Northwest Iberia between the Eighth and the Eleventh Century', in D'Emilio (ed.-transl.), *Culture*, 251–80.

A. Isla Frez, 'La construcción de la monarquía regia en León y Castilla: historias y leyes', in P. Martínez Sopena and A. Rodríguez (eds), *La construcción medieval de la memoria regia* (Valencia, 2011), 33–44.

A. Isla Frez, 'Monarchy and Neogothicism in the Astur Kingdom, 711–910', *Francia*, 26.1 (1999), 41–56.

A. Isla Frez, 'La monarquía leonesa según Sampiro', in M. A. Loring García (ed.), *Historia social, pensamiento historiográfico y Edad Media. Homenaje al prof. Abilio Barbero de Aguilera* (Madrid, 1997), 33–57.

A. Isla Frez, 'Nombres de reyes y sucesión al trono (siglos VIII–X)', *SHHM*, 11 (1993), 9–33.

A. Isla Frez, 'La pervivencia de la tradición legal visigótica en el reino asturleonés', *MCV*, 41.2 (2011), 75–86.

A. Isla Frez, 'El proyecto político regio de las leyes de León de 1017', in López Valladares (ed.), *Reino*, 172–5.

A. Isla Frez, *Realezas hispánicas del año mil* (Sada, 1999).

A. Isla Frez, 'Las relaciones de dependencia en la Galicia altomedieval: el ejemplo de la *incomuniación*', *Hispania*, 44.156 (1984), 5–18.

A. Isla Frez, *La sociedad gallega en la Alta Edad Media* (Madrid, 1992).

A. Isla Frez, 'Warfare and Other Plagues in the Iberian Peninsula around the Year 1000', in P. Urbańczyk (ed.), *Europe around the Year 1000* (Warsaw, 2001), 233–46.

A. Ivorra, *Liturgia hispano-mozárabe* (Barcelona, 2017).

J. Jarrett, 'Ceremony, Charters, and Social Memory: Property Transfer Ritual in Early Medieval Catalonia', *Social History*, 44.3 (2019), 275–95.

J. Jarrett, 'Comparing the Earliest Documentary Culture in Carolingian Catalonia', in Jarrett and McKinley (eds), *Problems*, 89–126.

J. Jarrett, 'A Likely Story: Purpose in Narratives from Charters of the Early Medieval Pyrenees', in Barton and Portass (eds), *Beyond the Reconquista*, 123–42.

J. Jarrett, 'Nuns, Signatures, and Literacy in Late Carolingian Catalonia', *Traditio*, 74 (2019), 125–52.

J. Jarrett, 'Settling the Kings' Lands: *Aprisio* in Catalonia in Perspective', *EME*, 18.3 (2010), 320–42.

J. Jarrett and A. S. McKinley (eds), *Problems and Possibilities of Early Medieval Charters* (Turnhout, 2013).

A. Jeannin, 'Le greffier durant le Haut Moyen Âge: quelle réalité?', in O. Poncet and I. Storez-Brancourt (eds), *Une histoire de la mémoire judiciaire. De l'Antiquité à nos jours* (Paris, 2009), 119–31.

A. C. Jennings, *A Linguistic Study of the Cartulario de San Vicente de Oviedo* (New York, NY, 1940).

W. A. Johnson and H. N. Parker (eds), *Ancient Literacies: the Culture of Reading in Greece and Rome* (Oxford, 2009).

E. Johnston, *Literacy and Identity in Early Medieval Ireland* (Woodbridge, 2013).

M. de Jong, *In Samuel's Image: Child Oblation in the Early Medieval West* (Leiden, 1996).

B. Jussen, 'Religious Discourses of the Gift in the Middle Ages: Semantic Evidences (Second to Twelfth Centuries)', in G. Algazi, V. Groebner, and B. Jussen (eds), *Negotiating the Gift: Pre-Modern Figurations of Exchange* (Göttingen, 2003), 173–92.

J. Juster, 'The Legal Condition of the Jews under the Visigothic Kings (I)', *Israel Law Review*, 11.2 (1976), 259–87.

B. Kafka, *The Demon of Writing: Powers and Failures of Paperwork* (New York, NY, 2014).

O. Kano, 'La loi ripuaire et la genèse de l'expression *secundum legem Salicam* dans quelques actes juridiques', *Bulletin de la Société Nationale des Antiquaires de France*, 2013 (2015), 126–36.

O. Kano, 'Procès fictif, droit romain et valeur de l'acte royal à l'époque mérovingienne', *BECh*, 165.2 (2007), 329–53.

R. A. Kaster, *Guardians of Language: the Grammarian and Society in Late Antiquity* (Berkeley, CA, 1988).

J. A. Keen, *The Charters of Christ and Piers Plowman: Documenting Salvation* (New York, NY, 2002).

M. J. Kelly, *Isidore of Seville and the Liber Iudiciorum: the Struggle for the Past in the Visigothic Kingdom* (Leiden, 2021).

S. Kelly, 'Anglo-Saxon Lay Society and the Written Word', in McKitterick (ed.), *Uses*, 36–62.

K. Kennelly, 'Sobre la Paz de Dios y la sagrera en el condado de Barcelona (1030–1130)', *AEM*, 5 (1968), 107–36.

S. Keynes, 'Church Councils, Royal Assemblies, and Anglo-Saxon Royal Diplomas', in G. R. Owen-Crocker and B. W. Schneider (eds), *Kingship, Legislation, and Power in Anglo-Saxon England* (Woodbridge, 2013), 17–182.

W. Kienast, 'La pervivencia del derecho godo en el sur de Francia y Cataluña', *Boletín de la Real Academia de Buenas Letras de Barcelona*, 35 (1973–4), 265–95.

P. D. King, *Law and Society in the Visigothic Kingdom* (Cambridge, 1972).

T. Klausmann, 'Book Communities', in Arlinghaus *et al.* (eds), *Transforming*, 71–88.

E. N. van Kleffens, *Hispanic Law until the End of the Middle Ages* (Edinburgh, 1968).

W. E. Klingshirn and L. Safran (eds), *The Early Christian Book* (Washington, DC, 2007).

S. Koon and J. Wood, 'Unity from Disunity: Law, Rhetoric, and Power in the Visigothic Kingdom', *European Review of History*, 16.6 (2009), 793–808.

A. J. Kosto, 'Laymen, Clerics, and Documentary Practices in the Early Middle Ages: the Example of Catalonia', *Speculum*, 80.1 (2005), 44–74.

A. J. Kosto, 'The *Liber feudorum maior* of the Counts of Barcelona: the Cartulary as an Expression of Power', *JMH*, 27.1 (2001), 1–22.

A. J. Kosto, *Making Agreements in Medieval Catalonia: Power, Order, and the Written Word, 1000–1200* (Cambridge, 2007).

A. J. Kosto, 'Reasons for Assembly in Catalonia and Aragón, 900–1200', in P. S. Barnwell and M. Mostert (eds), *Political Assemblies in the Earlier Middle Ages* (Turnhout, 2003), 133–49.

A. J. Kosto, 'Reconquest, Renaissance, and the Histories of Iberia, *ca.* 1000–1200', in T. F. X. Noble and J. Van Engen (eds), *European Transformations: the Long Twelfth Century* (Notre Dame, IN, 2012), 93–116.

A. J. Kosto, '*Sicut mos esse solet*: Documentary Practices in Christian Iberia, *c.* 700–1000', in Brown *et al.* (eds), *Documentary Culture*, 259–82.

A. J. Kosto, 'What about Spain? Iberia in the Historiography of Medieval European Feudalism', in S. Bagge, M. H. Gelting, and T. Lindkvist (eds), *Feudalism: New Landscapes of Debate* (Turnhout, 2011), 135–58.

G. Koziol, *The Politics of Memory and Identity in Carolingian Royal Diplomas: the West Frankish Kingdom (840–987)* (Turnhout, 2012).

D. Kremer, 'De antroponimia asturiana y leonesa medieval', *LA*, 36 (1990), 7–22.

D. Kremer, '(R)espigando en la documentación altomedieval de León', *LA*, 104 (2011), 15–44.

J. Kristeva, *Desire in Language: a Semiotic Approach to Literature and Art*, ed. L. S. Roudiez, transl. T. Gora, A. Jardine, and L. S. Roudiez (New York, NY, 1980).

A. Kurt, 'Lay Piety in Visigothic Iberia: Liturgical and Paraliturgical Forms', *JMIS*, 8.1 (2016), 1–37.

J. M. Lacarra, *Historia del reino de Navarra en la Edad Media* (2nd ed., Pamplona, 2000).

J. M. Lacarra, 'Panorama de la historia urbana en la Península Ibérica desde el siglo V al X', repr. in *Estudios de la Alta Edad Media española* (Valencia, 1971), 25–89.

L. Laffón Álvarez, 'Arenga hispana: una aproximación a los preámbulos documentales de la Edad Media', *HID*, 16 (1989), 133–232.

C. Lagunas, 'Abadesas, sorores y presbíteros en el monasterio dúplice de Santiago de León, siglos X–XI', *Hispania*, 51.179 (1991), 809–33.

J. Lalinde Abadía, 'Los pactos matrimoniales catalanes (esquema histórico)', *AHDE*, 33 (1963), 133–266.

P.-Y. Lambert, 'Exempla bibliques comme précédents judiciaires: les sanctions dans les chartes "celtiques"', *Pecia*, 12 (2007), 45–61.

T. Lambert, *Law and Order in Anglo-Saxon England* (Oxford, 2017).

W.-D. Lange, 'Anmerkungen zur Skripta lateinischer Urkunden des portugiesischen Mittelalters', *Zeitschrift für Romanische Philologie*, 83.1–2 (1967), 32–42.

W.-D. Lange, *Philologische Studien zur Latinität westhispanischer Privaturkunden des 9.–12. Jahrhunderts* (Leiden, 1966).

A. I. Lapeña Paul, *El monasterio de San Juan de la Peña en la Edad Media desde sus orígenes hasta 1410* (Zaragoza, 1989).

J. J. Larrea Conde, 'Construir iglesias, construir territorio: las dos fases altomedievales de San Román de Tobillas (Álava)', in J. López Quiroga, A. M. Martínez Tejera, and J. Morín de Pablos (eds), *Monasteria et territoria. Elites, edilicia y territorio en el Mediterráneo medieval (siglos V–XI)* (Oxford, 2007), 321–36.

J. J. Larrea Conde, 'Construir un reino en la periferia de al-Ándalus. Pamplona y el Pirineo occidental en los siglos VIII y IX', in F. J. Fernández Conde and C. G. de Castro Valdés (eds), *Symposium Internacional. Poder y simbología en Europa, siglos VIII–X* (Gijón, 2009), 279–308.

J. J. Larrea Conde, 'La documentación de San Martín de Cillas: un ensayo de crítica de las fuentes altomedievales', *RHJZ*, 61–2 (1990), 7–44, 63–4 (1991), 253–5.

J. J. Larrea Conde, 'Estudiar el estado para comprender las sociedades altomedievales: a propósito de un libro reciente', *SHHM*, 37.2 (2019), 181–98.

J. J. Larrea Conde, 'De la invisibilidad historiográfica a la apropiación del territorio: aldeas y comunidades en la España cristiana (siglos X y XI)', in J. I. de la Iglesia Duarte (ed.), *Cristiandad e Islam en la Edad Media hispana. XVIII Semana de Estudios Medievales* (Logroño, 2008), 169–207.

J. J. Larrea Conde, *La Navarre du IV<sup>e</sup> au XII<sup>e</sup> siècle. Peuplement et société* (Paris, 1998).

J. N. H. Lawrance, 'The Spread of Lay Literacy in Late Medieval Castile', *Bulletin of Hispanic Studies*, 62.1 (1985), 79–94.

S. Lay, *The Reconquest Kings of Portugal: Political and Cultural Reorientation on the Medieval Frontier* (Basingstoke, 2009).

B. Layton, *The Canons of Our Fathers: Monastic Rules of Shenoute* (Oxford, 2014).

M. Lázaro Ruiz, 'El monasterio de San Martín de Albelda: estrategias en la ocupación del territorio y valoración socioeconómica (925–1094)', in Iglesia Duarte (ed.), *VII Semana*, 353–84.

F. S. Lear, 'The Public Law of the Visigothic Code', *Speculum*, 26.1 (1951), 1–23.

N. Lenski, 'Slavery among the Visigoths', in C. L. de Wet, M. Kahlos, and V. Vuolanto (eds), *Slavery in the Late Antique World, 150–700 CE* (Cambridge, 2022), 251–80.

R. Létinier, '*Abrogata legis illius sententia*. A propósito del enigma contenido en la ley *Dum inlicita* de Chindasvinto (*LV* IV, 5, 1)', *AHDE*, 69 (1999), 367–88.

R. Létinier, 'Juicios monásticos: la apelación del monje en el Pactum de San Fructuoso', *AHDE*, 68 (1998), 467–73.

R. Létinier, 'Naturaleza jurídica y originalidad de los pactos monásticos', in *Monacato*, 49–66.

R. Létinier, 'Les *Pacta* monastiques en Espagne wisigothique et du Haut Moyen Âge: précisions sur leur signification juridique et leur singularité', *RHDFE*, 95.3 (2017), 281–306.

E. Levy, *West Roman Vulgar Law: the Law of Property* (Philadelphia, PA, 1951).

E. Levy, *Weströmisches Vulgarrecht: das Obligationenrecht* (Weimar, 1956).

Á. Líbano Zumalacárregui, 'Génesis y difusión del léxico de mercado en el medioevo peninsular', *CC*, 9 (2001), 25–53.

*Liber Testamentorum Coenobii Laurbanensis* (2 vols, León, 2008).

J. M. Lieu, *Christian Identity in the Jewish and Graeco-Roman World* (Oxford, 2004).

A. Linage Conde, 'Los caminares de la benedictinización', in *RLAEM* 9 (León, 1997), 39–217.

A. Linage Conde, 'El monacato visigótico, hacia la benedictinización', *AC*, 3 (1986), 235–59.

A. Linage Conde, *Los orígenes del monacato benedictino en la Península Ibérica* (3 vols, León, 1973).

A. Linage Conde, 'La repoblación diocesana de Juan de Valpuesta', *EMir*, 24 (2004), 213–28.

A. Linage Conde, 'En torno a la benedictinización. La recepción de la regla de San Benito en el monacato de la Península Ibérica vista a través de Leyre y aledaños', *PV*, 46.174 (1985), 57–92.

P. Linehan, *History and the Historians of Medieval Spain* (Oxford, 1993).

P. Linehan, *The Ladies of Zamora* (University Park, PA, 1997).

P. Linehan, 'León, ciudad regia, y sus obispos en los siglos X–XIII', in *RLAEM* 6 (León, 1994), 411–57.

P. Linehan, 'The Toledo Forgeries, c. 1150–c. 1300', in *Fälschungen im Mittelalter. Internationaler Kongreß der Monumenta Germaniae Historica* (5 vols, Hanover, 1988), 1, 643–74.

L. K. Little, 'La morphologie des malédictions monastiques', *AESC*, 34.1 (1979), 43–60.

G. Lopetegui Semperena, 'Preámbulos y fórmulas de inicio en donaciones reales del monasterio de Leire: retórica e ideología', *EM*, 21 (2020), 353–83.

F. López Alsina, *La ciudad de Santiago de Compostela en la Alta Edad Media* (2nd ed., Santiago de Compostela, 2013).

F. López Alsina, 'Millas in giro ecclesie: el ejemplo del monasterio de San Julián de Samos', *Estudos Medievais*, 10 (1993), 159–87.

F. López Alsina, 'Reyes y obispos en el reino de León', in *Monarquía*, 1, 85–102.

T. López Mata, *Geografía del Condado del Castilla a la muerte de Fernán González* (Madrid, 1957).

J. López Ortiz, 'El proceso en los reinos cristianos de nuestra Reconquista antes de la recepción romano-canónica', *AHDE*, 14 (1942–3), 184–226.

C. López-Rendo Rodríguez, 'Autonomía de la voluntad y arras en la compraventa: fuentes jurídicas romanas y su regulación en los textos legales medievales', *CHD*, 12 (2005), 57–98.

J. A. López Sabatel, 'Apuntes para el estudio de la jurisdicción monástica en la Galicia medieval: renta señorial, sujeción a la tierra y justicia (siglos X–XIII)', *Madrygal*, 23 (2020), 215–32.

J. A. López Sabatel, 'La villa altomedieval gallega: núcleo de estructuración social y escenario de feudalización', *Historia Social y de la Educación*, 2.1 (2013), 78–100.

E. López Salas, 'Decoding the Planning Rules of the Monastic Urban and Rural Forms around Samos Abbey', in M. Abel (ed.), *Medieval Urban Planning: the Monastery and Beyond* (Newcastle upon Tyne, 2017), 46–74.

E. López Salas, 'El papel del clero regular en la ordenación del paisaje. El caso del monasterio de San Julián de Samos', *HS*, 69.139 (2017), 19–29.

R. López Valladares (ed.), *El reino de León hace mil años. El Fuero de 1017* (Madrid, 2018).

J. M. López Villalba, 'Normas españolas para la transcripción y edición de colecciones diplomáticas', *ETF*, 11 (1998), 285–306.

A. Lorenzo-Rodríguez, '*Concubare sine mea volumtate*: denuncias y procesos por violación en el noroeste ibérico (siglos VIII–XII)', *SHHM*, 39.2 (2021), 103–30.

A. Lorenzo-Rodríguez, '"Cosas que no son de decir": violaciones y agresiones colectivas en la plena Edad Media ibérica (XI–XIII)', in M. M. L. de Araújo, C. Contente, and A. Esteves (eds), *As mulheres nos caminhos da história* (Braga-Guimarães, 2021), 308–19.

A. Lorenzo-Rodríguez, 'La culpa y la propiedad: repercusiones del delito sobre la propiedad en Sobrado dos Monxes y Celanova (ss. X–XI)', in Díaz-Plaza Casal, Escudero Manzano, and Villarroel González (eds), *Caída*, 127–41.

A. Lorenzo-Rodríguez, '*Per violentiam*: usos y funciones del estudio de la violencia en el noroeste ibérico (ss. IX–XI)', *Incipit*, 7 (2018), 8–20.

M. I. Loring García, *Cantabria en la Alta Edad Media. Organización eclesiástica y relaciones sociales* (Madrid, 1988).

M. I. Loring García, 'Nobleza e iglesias propias en la Cantabria altomedieval', *SHHM*, 5 (1987), 89–120.

M. I. Loring García, 'Poder económico y relaciones sociales en las Asturias de Santillana en los siglos X y XI', *EEM*, 8 (1986), 603–15.

K. A. Lowe, 'Lay Literacy in Anglo-Saxon England and the Development of the Chirograph', in P. Pulsiano and E. M. Treharne (eds), *Anglo-Saxon Manuscripts and their Heritage* (Aldershot, 1998), 161–204.

F. J. Lozano Sebastián, *La penitencia canónica en la España romano-visigoda* (Burgos, 1980).

M. Lucas Álvarez, 'Paleografía gallega. Estado de la cuestión', *AEM*, 21 (1991), 419–70.

C. Maas-Chauveau, 'Nombres de oficios y apellidos', in A. M. Cano González (ed.), *IX Dictionnaire historique des noms de famille romans* (Berlin, 2011), 83–116.

T. Major, 'The Number Seventy-Two: Biblical and Hellenistic Beginnings to the Early Middle Ages', *SE*, 52 (2013), 7–46.

R. Maloy, *Songs of Sacrifice: Chant, Identity, and Christian Formation in Early Medieval Iberia* (Oxford, 2020).

J. Maldonado y Fernández del Torco, *Herencias en favor del alma en el derecho español* (Madrid, 1944).

J. Maldonado y Fernández del Torco, 'Líneas de influencia canónica en la historia del proceso español', *AHDE*, 23 (1953), 467–93.

J. Maldonado y Fernández del Torco, 'Las relaciones entre el derecho canónico y el derecho secular en los concilios españoles del siglo XI', *AHDE*, 14 (1943), 227–381.

M. Mallo Viesca, 'Los grabados de Pendilla (Villamanín, León): documentación de un conjunto rupestre inédito en las estribaciones de la Cordillera Cantábrica', *Nailos*, 4 (2017), 17–53.

R. Manchón Gómez, 'Tradición cristiana latina y diplomas medievales: las fórmulas conminatorias en los documentos del reino de León (s. VIII–1230)', in Alberte González and Macías Villalobos (eds), *Actas*, 365–75.

E. Manzano Moreno, *La corte del califa. Cuatro años en la Córdoba de los omeyas* (Barcelona, 2019).

M. Marcela Mantel, 'El problema de la evolución de las arras y la dote en el derecho y uso hispanomedieval (siglos VI al XII)', *Fundación*, 2 (1999–2000), 63–72.

T. Marín Martínez, 'Confirmación real en documentos castellano-leoneses', in *Estudios dedicados a Menéndez Pidal* (7 vols, Madrid, 1950–62), 3, 583–93.

T. Marín Martínez, *Paleografía y Diplomática* (2 vols, Madrid, 1998).

D. Mariño-Veiras, 'Las religiosas en las comunidades del medio ciudadano de la iglesia regio-aristocrática o del *regnum* leonés (principios del siglo X–mediados del siglo XI)', in F. J. Campos y Fernández de Sevilla (ed.), *La clausura femenina en España. Actas del simposium* (2 vols, San Lorenzo de El Escorial, 2004), 1, 118–40.

O. Marlasca Martínez, 'Los actos jurídicos documentados en los textos legales visigodos', *ED*, 58.1 (2010), 79–113.

O. Marlasca Martínez, 'Algunos aspectos sobre la invasión de inmuebles: fuentes jurídicas de la época visigoda', *RIDA*, 50 (2003), 206–13.

O. Marlasca Martínez, 'Algunos requisitos para la validez de los documentos en la *Lex Visigothorum*', *RIDA*, 45 (1998), 563–84.

O. Marlasca Martínez, 'Algunos supuestos de infamia y sus consecuencias jurídicas en las fuentes romanas y medievales', *ED*, 61.1 (2013), 247–70.

O. Marlasca Martínez, 'El préstamo de géneros en la sociedad romana, visigoda y en algunos reinos cristianos de la Alta Edad Media', *AFDUC*, 12 (2008), 599–613.

O. Marlasca Martínez, 'La regulación de la falsificación de los documentos en el derecho romano y en la Ley de los Visigodos', *ED*, 47.1 (1999), 209–33.

O. Marlasca Martínez, 'Tala ilícita de árboles y otro tipo de daños en la Lex Visigothorum', in A. Murillo Villar (ed.), *La responsabilidad civil de Roma al derecho moderna. IV Congreso Internacional y VII Congreso Iberoamericano de Derecho Romano* (Burgos, 2001), 553–60.

A. E. Marques, 'Between the Language of Law and the Language of Justice: the Use of Formulas in Portuguese Dispute Texts (Tenth and Eleventh Centuries)', in J. Benham, M. W. McHaffie, and H. Vogt (eds), *Law and Language in the Middle Ages* (Leiden, 2018), 128–64.

A. E. Marques, *Da representação documental à materialidade do espaço. Território da diocese de Braga (séculos IX–XI)* (Porto, 2015).

A. E. Marques, Á. Carvajal Castro, and G. Barrett (eds), *Before and Beyond Charters: Inventories and List-Making in Early Medieval Iberia (8th–11th Centuries)* (Turnhout, forthcoming).

J. Marques, 'O *Liber Fidei* da catedral de Braga e o norte de Portugal', *Bracara Augusta*, 57 (2009–12), 453–500.

J. Marques, 'Le rôle concret des chartes en différentes circonstances de la vie quotidienne', *AD*, 57 (2011), 237–74.

H.-I. Marrou, *A History of Education in Antiquity*, transl. G. Lamb (New York, NY, 1964 [1956]).

C. Martin, 'Le *Liber Iudiciorum* et ses différentes versions', *MCV*, 41.2 (2011), 17–34.

C. Martin and J. J. Larrea (eds), *Nouvelles chartes visigothiques du monastère pyrénéen d'Asán* (Bordeaux, 2021).

J. C. Martín, 'Isidorus Hispalensis ep., 11. *Regula monachorum*', in P. Chiesa and L. Castaldi (eds), *La trasmissione dei testi latini del medioevo. Mediaeval Latin Texts and their Transmission. Te.Tra.* 2 (Florence, 2005), 379–86.

J. L. Martín, 'Utilidad de las fórmulas "inútiles" de los documentos medievales', in *Semana de historia del monacato cántabro-astur-leonés* (Gijón, 1982), 81–6.

R. Martín, 'L'ensagrerament: l'adveniment de les sagreres feudals', *Faventia*, 10.1–2 (1988), 153–82.

Á. J. Martín Duque, '"Señores" y "siervos" en el Pirineo occidental hispano hasta el siglo XI', in *Señores, siervos, vasallos en la Alta Edad Media. XXVIII Semana de Estudios Medievales* (Pamplona, 2002), 363–412.

F. Martín Escudero, 'Calendario judío e islámico, ¿dataciones exóticas en la Península?', in Galende Díaz and Santiago Fernández (eds), *X Jornadas*, 221–47.

M. E. Martín López, 'Las cláusulas penales espirituales en la documentación leonesa del siglo XII por un estudio de la sanctio', *EHG*, 12 (1990), 111–18.

M. E. Martín López, 'De léxico diplomático: nomenclaturas del documento medieval en el occidente peninsular (siglos VIII–XII)', *EHG*, 13 (1991), 131–43.

P. Martín Prieto, 'Elementos de participación de la comunidad en la producción normativa medieval: acuerdo, petición y consejo en torno a la elaboración de los fueros (siglos X–XIII)', *AHDE*, 84 (2014), 15–43.

I. Martín Viso, 'Authority and Justice in the Formation of the Kingdom of Asturias-León', *Al-Masāq*, 29.2 (2017), 114–32.

I. Martín Viso, 'Commons and the Construction of Power in the Early Middle Ages: Tenth-Century León and Castile', *JMH*, 46.4 (2020), 373–95.

I. Martín Viso, *Fragmentos del Leviatán. La articulación política del espacio zamorano en la Alta Edad Media* (Zamora, 2002).

I. Martín Viso, 'Huellas del poder: pizarras y poblados campesinos en el centro de la Península Ibérica (siglos V–VII)', *Medievalismo*, 25 (2015), 285–314.

I. Martín Viso, 'The Memory of the "Holy Men" in Hispanic Monasticism: the Case of the Bierzo Region', *Imago Temporis. Medium Aevum*, 6 (2012), 165–90.

I. Martín Viso, 'Monasterios y redes sociales en el Bierzo altomedieval', *Hispania*, 71.237 (2011), 9–38.

I. Martín Viso, 'Poder político y estructura social en la Castilla altomedieval: el condado de Lantarón (siglos VIII–XI)', in Iglesia Duarte and Martín Rodríguez (eds), *Espacios*, 533–52.

I. Martín Viso, 'Tributación y escenarios locales en el centro de la Península Ibérica: algunas hipótesis a partir del análisis de las pizarras "visigodas"', *AT*, 14 (2006), 263–90.

I. Martín Viso, 'Unequal Small Worlds: Social Dynamics in Tenth-Century Leonese Villages', in Quirós Castillo (ed.), *Social Inequality*, 255–79.

I. Martín Viso, 'The "Visigothic" Slates and their Archaeological Contexts', *JMIS*, 5.2 (2013), 145–68.

M. J. Martínez Alfaro, 'Intertextuality: Origins and Development of the Concept', *Atlantis*, 18.1–2 (1996), 268–85.

G. Martínez Díez, 'La colección canónica "Hispana"', in *Códice*, 135–61.

G. Martínez Díez, *El Condado de Castilla (711–1038). La Historia frente a la leyenda* (2 vols, Valladolid, 2005).

G. Martínez Díez, 'Los fueros leoneses: 1017–1336', in *RLAEM* 1 (León, 1988), 283–352.

G. Martínez Díez, 'Las instituciones del reino astur a través de los diplomas (718–910)', *AHDE*, 35 (1965), 59–167.

G. Martínez Díez, 'El monasterio de San Millán y sus monasterios filiales. Documentación emilianense y diplomas apócrifas', *Brocar*, 21 (1998), 7–53.

G. Martínez Díez, *El patrimonio eclesiástico en la España visigoda. Estudio histórico-jurídico* (Palencia, 1959).

G. Martínez Díez, 'El primer fuero castellano: Brañosera, 13 octubre 824', *AHDE*, 75 (2005), 29–65.

G. Martínez Díez, 'San Emeterio de Taranco', *CHE*, 76 (2000), 7–16.

G. Martínez Díez, 'Servidumbre, ingenuidad y privilegio. Notas a la condición jurídica de las personas en el reino de León: 910–1157', in *Monarquía*, 1, 573–674.

G. Martínez Díez, 'Terminología jurídica en la documentación del reino de León. Siglos IX–XI', in *Orígenes*, 1, 229–72.

L. Martínez García, 'Los pactos de *benefactoria* en la formación de la red feudal leonesa y castellana (siglos X–XII)', *Hispania*, 70.235 (2010), 325–58.

J. Martínez Gázquez, 'Las imprecaciones jurídicas del mundo clásico a la Edad Media', *Revista de Estudios Clásicos*, 37 (2010), 101–23.

J. Martínez Gázquez *et al.*, 'Las fórmulas de imprecación en Cataluña en los siglos IX al XI', *Faventia*, 27.1 (2005), 73–96.

F. Martínez Llorente, 'La aplicación del derecho en la Castilla altomedieval (s. IX–XIII)', in *Actas III Jornadas*, 56–93.

F. Martínez Llorente, 'Justicia divina y justicia humana: ordalías, juramentos y duelos judiciales en el alto medievo', in P. L. Huerta Huerta (ed.), *Mágico y sobrenatural. Creencias y supersticiones en la época del románico* (Aguilar de Campoo, 2021), 13–43.

F. Martínez Llorente (ed.), *En el milenario del Fuero de León, 1017–2017. La ciudad de León y su derecho* (León, 2018).

F. Martínez Martínez, '*De verborum significatione*: notas sobre las acepciones medievales de la voz "foro"', *Boletín do Museo Provincial de Lugo*, 11.2 (2003–4), 247–64.

F. Martínez Martínez, '*Et cum Juda traditore Domini*: lenguaje bíblico como lenguaje jurídico en el derecho altomedieval hispánico', repr. in *Literatura y derecho* (Mexico City, 2010), 165–316.

R. Martínez Peñín, 'Los orígenes de la iglesia cristiana: Marialba de La Ribera in suburbio legionense. Fuentes documentales y datos arqueológicos', in *Iglesia y ciudad*, 103–36.

P. Martínez Sopena, 'Herederos, conquistadores y colonos. Sobre el imaginario de las fuentes castellano-leoneses de los siglos IX–XII', *CC*, 14 (2006), 79–110.

P. Martínez Sopena, 'La justicia en la época asturleonesa: entre el *Liber* y los mediadores sociales', in Rodríguez (ed.), *Lugar*, 239–55.

P. Martínez Sopena, 'Palabras para delimitar y describir espacios y paisajes: León en los siglos X–XII', in Pérez Rodríguez (ed.), *Palabras*, 133–54.

P. Martínez Sopena, '*Prolis Flainiz*. Las relaciones familiares en la nobleza de León (siglos X–XII)', *SZ*, 17 (2018), 69–102.

P. Martínez Sopena, 'La Reforma de la Iglesia y las comunidades campesinas: León y Castilla en el siglo XI', in Dierkens, Schroeder, and Wilkin (eds), *Penser*, 347–61.

P. Martínez Sopena, 'Reyes, condes e infanzones. Aristocracia y *alfetena* en el reino de León', in *Ante el milenario del reinado de Sancho el Mayor. Un rey Navarro para España y Europa. XXX Semana de Estudios Medievales* (Pamplona, 2004), 109–54.

P. Martínez Sopena, 'Reyes y nobles en León (*ca.* 860–1160)', in *Monarquía*, 1, 149–200.

P. Martínez Sopena, *La Tierra de Campos occidental. Poblamiento, poder y comunidad del siglo X al XII* (Valladolid, 1985).

P. Martínez Sopena, 'El uso de la Ley Gótica en el reino de León', in P. Toubert and P. Moret (eds), *Remploi, citation, plagiat. Conduites et pratiques médiévales (Xe–XIIe siècle)* (Madrid, 2009), 97–114.

P. Martínez Sopena (ed.), *Antroponimia y sociedad. Sistemas de identificación hispano-cristianos en los siglos IX a XIII* (Santiago de Compostela-Valladolid, 1995).

P. Martínez Sopena and M. J. Carbajo Serrano, 'Notas sobre la colonización de Tierra de Campos en el siglo X: Villobera', in *Pasado*, 113–25.

A. M. Martínez Tejera, 'Cenobios leoneses altomedievales ante la europeización: San Pedro y San Pablo de Montes, Santiago y San Martín de Peñalba y San Miguel de Escalada', *HS*, 54.109 (2002), 87–108.

M. Martinón-Torres, 'Los megalitos de término. Crónica del valor territorial de los monumentos megalíticos a partir de las fuentes escritas', *Trabajos de Prehistoria*, 58.1 (2001), 95–108.

M. A. Martos Calabrús, *Aproximación histórica a las solemnidades del testamento público* (Almería, 1998).

M. Maskarinec, 'Monastic Archives and the Law: Legal Strategies at Farfa and Monte Amiata at the Turn of the Millennium', *EME*, 29.3 (2021), 331–65.

L. Maté Sadornil, 'El padre Liciniano Sáez: archivero de la Cámara de Comptos Reales', *PV*, 39.150–1 (1978), 93–110.

J. M. D. Mateu Ibars, ' "Signa" sur les parchemins du monastère de Sant Cugat del Vallés (X<sup>e</sup>–XIII<sup>e</sup> siècles)', in Rück (ed.), *Graphische Symbole*, 479–90.

F. Mateu y Llopis, 'Las cláusulas penales pecuniarias de los "Documentos para la historia de las instituciones de León y de Castilla (siglos X–XIII)" ', *AHDE*, 23 (1953), 579–93.

F. Mateu y Llopis, '*Solidos… in aderato pretio*. Notas sobre documentación goda y condal (siglos VI–X)', *Nummus*, 9.1–2, 29–30 (1968), 63–8.

R. W. Mathisen, '*Et manu papae*: Papal Subscriptions Written *sua manu* in Late Antiquity', in G. Schmeling and J. D. Mikalson (eds), *Qui miscuit utile dulci. Festschrift Essays for Paul Lachlan MacKendrick* (Wauconda, IL, 1998), 243–51.

A. C. Matthews, 'Within Sacred Boundaries: the Limitations of Saintly Justice in the Province of Narbonne around the Year 1000', *JMH*, 46.3 (2020), 284–305.

J. Mattoso, 'As famílias condais portucalenses dos séculos X e XI', repr. in *A nobreza medieval portuguesa. A família e o poder* (Lisbon, 1981), 101–57.

J. Mattoso, 'O monaquismo ibérico e Cluny', *TH*, 2 (1968), 79–95.

J. Mattoso, 'S. Rosendo e as correntes monásticas da sua época', *TH*, 5 (1972), 5–27.

J. Mattoso, 'Sanctio (875–1100)', repr. in *Religião e cultura na Idade Média portuguesa* (Lisbon, 1982), 394–440.

J. Maxwell, 'Popular Theology in Late Antiquity', in L. Grig (ed.), *Popular Culture in the Ancient World* (Cambridge, 2017), 277–95.

M. P. McGlynn, 'The Seven Laws of Fernán González: Castile's Tenth-Century Legislative Beginnings', *Confluencia*, 25.1 (2009), 93–100.

R. McKitterick, *Books, Scribes, and Learning in the Frankish Kingdoms, 6th to 9th Centuries* (Aldershot, 1994).

R. McKitterick, *The Carolingians and the Written Word* (Cambridge, 1989).

R. McKitterick, *Charlemagne: the Formation of a European Identity* (Cambridge, 2008).

R. McKitterick, 'Charters, Languages, and Communication: Recent Work on Early Medieval Literacy', in R. Gallagher, E. Roberts, and F. Tinti (eds), *The Languages of Early Medieval Charters: Latin, Germanic Vernaculars, and the Written Word* (Leiden, 2021), 22–67.

R. McKitterick, 'The Church and the Law in the Early Middle Ages', *SCH*, 56 (2020), 7–35.

R. McKitterick, 'A King on the Move: the Place of an Itinerant Court in Charlemagne's Government', in J. Duindam, T. Artan, and M. Kunt (eds), *Royal Courts in Dynastic States and Empires: a Global Perspective* (Leiden, 2011), 145–69.

R. McKitterick, 'Latin and Romance: an Historian's Perspective', in Wright (ed.), *Latin*, 130–45.

R. McKitterick, 'Some Carolingian Law-Books and their Function', repr. in *Books*, VIII.

R. McKitterick, 'Women and Literacy in the Early Middle Ages', repr. in *Books*, XIII.

R. McKitterick (ed.), *The Uses of Literacy in Early Mediaeval Europe* (Cambridge, 1990).

M. McLuhan, *Understanding Media: the Extensions of Man* (Cambridge, MA, 1994 [1964]).

L. Melve, 'Literacy—Aurality—Orality: a Survey of Recent Research into the Orality/Literacy Complex of the Latin Middle Ages (600–1500)', *Symbolae Osloenses*, 78.1 (2003), 143–97.

C. Mendo Carmona, 'El cartulario como instrumento archivístico', *Signo*, 15 (2005), 119–37.

C. Mendo Carmona, 'Consideraciones sobre el concepto de documento privado', *Signo*, 3 (1996), 11–23.

C. Mendo Carmona, 'Cuatro escribas leoneses en el siglo X', in C. Sáez and J. Gómez-Pantoja (eds), *Las diferentes historias de letrados y analfabetos* (Alcalá de Henares, 1994), 27–32.

C. Mendo Carmona, *La escritura como vehículo de cultura en el reino de León (siglos IX–X)* (2 vols, Madrid, 2001 [1994]).

C. Mendo Carmona, 'La escritura de los documentos leoneses en el signo X', *Signo*, 8 (2001), 179–210.

C. Mendo Carmona, 'El pensamiento archivístico medieval. Una página de la historia de la cultura a través del fondo documental de la catedral de León', in J. M. Soto Rábanos (ed.), *Pensamiento medieval hispano. Homenaje a Horacio Santiago-Otero* (2 vols, Madrid, 1998), 1, 591–626.

C. Mendo Carmona, 'Signos y autógrafos reales en la documentación de la catedral de León: el caso de los monarcas de nombre Ordoño', in D. Chieta and L. Pinelli (eds), *Gli autografi medievali. Problemi paleografici e filologici* (Spoleto, 1994), 77–101.

C. Mendo Carmona, 'La suscripción altomedieval', *Signo*, 4 (1997), 207–27.

C. Mendo Carmona, 'Los tumbos medievales desde la perspectiva archivística', in Canellas López, Santiago Fernández, and Francisco Olmos (eds), *I Jornadas*, 165–89.

F. Menéndez Pidal, *Los sellos en nuestra historia* (Madrid, 2018).

F. Menéndez Pidal, 'Los sellos en los reinos de León y Castilla durante los siglos X al XIII', in Canellas López, Santiago Fernández, and Francisco Olmos (eds), *I Jornadas*, 245–82.

R. Menéndez Pidal, *Orígenes del español: estado lingüístico de la Península Ibérica hasta el siglo XI* (9th ed., Madrid, 1980 [1950]).

S. Menzinger, 'Legal Profession', in E. Conte and L. Mayali (eds), *A Cultural History of Law in the Middle Ages* (London, 2019), 125–39.

P. Merêa, 'A doação *per cartam* no direito romano vulgar e no direito visigótico', *BFDUC*, 17 (1940–1), 115–33.

P. Merêa, 'O dote nos documentos dos séculos IX–XII', repr. in *Estudos de direito*, 1, 59–77.

P. Merêa, *Estudos de direito hispânico medieval* (2 vols, Coimbra, 1952–3).

P. Merêa, 'Da minha gaveta (silva histórico-jurídica) (I)', *BFDUC*, 32 (1956), 160–94.

P. Merêa, 'Nota sobre a Lex Visigothorum, II, I, 23 (juramento subsidiário)', *AHDE*, 21–2 (1951–2), 1163–8.

P. Merêa, 'Origens do executor testamentário', repr. in *Estudos de direito*, 2, 1–54.

P. Merêa, 'Para um glossário do nosso latim medieval: gasalianes', *Biblos*, 16 (1940), 55–64.

P. Merêa, 'Perfilhação', *Revista Portuguesa de Filologia*, 7 (1956), 119–26.

P. Merêa, 'Sobre as origens do concelho de Coimbra (estudo histórico-jurídico)', *RPH*, 1 (1940), 49–69.

P. Merêa, 'Sobre a revogabilidade das doações por morte', repr. in *Estudos de direito*, 1, 173–98.

R. Meyer-Hermann, 'El cambio de OV a VO en latín medieval y romance dentro de las construcciones auxiliares de la *sanctio* en documentos notariales del siglo VIII a 1250', *Aemilianense*, 2 (2010), 245–89.

P. Miceli, 'El derecho consuetudinario en Castilla. Una crítica a la matriz romántica de las interpretaciones sobre la costumbre', *Hispania*, 63.213 (2003), 9–27.

P. Miceli, *Derecho consuetudinario y memoria. Práctica jurídica y costumbre en Castilla y León (siglos XI–XIV)* (Madrid, 2012).

P. Miceli, 'Entre formulismo y enumeración: reflexiones sobre las nociones de espacio y límite en los notarios medievales castellano-leoneses (siglos XI–XIII)', *Revista de Historia Social y de las Mentalidades*, 20.1 (2016), 37–51.

F. Millar, *The Emperor in the Roman World (31 BC–AD 337)* (2nd ed., London, 1992).

A. Millares Carlo and J. M. Ruiz Asencio, *Tratado de Paleografía española* (3rd ed., 3 vols, Madrid, 1983).

D. Millet-Gérard, *Chrétiens mozarabes et culture islamique dans l'Espagne des VIIIᵉ–IXᵉ siècles* (Paris, 1984).

J. M. Mínguez Fernández, 'La despoblación del Duero: un tema a debate', in S. Aguadé Nieto and J. Pérez (eds), *Les origines de la féodalité. Hommage à Claudio Sánchez-Albornoz* (Madrid, 2000), 169–82.

J. M. Mínguez Fernández, *El dominio del monasterio de Sahagún en el siglo X: paisajes agrarios, producción y expansión económica* (Salamanca, 1980).

J. M. Mínguez Fernández, *La España de los siglos VI al XIII. Guerra, expansión y transformaciones* (San Sebastián, 2008).

J. M. Mínguez Fernández, 'Justicia y poder en el marco de la feudalización de la sociedad leonesa', in *Giustizia*, 1, 491–548.

J. M. Mínguez Fernández, 'La nueva ordenación del poblamiento en la cuenca septentrional del Duero en los inicios de la Edad Media', *Aragón en la Edad Media*, 14–15.2 (1999), 1027–46.

J. M. Mínguez Fernández, 'Pervivencia y transformaciones de la concepción y práctica del poder en el reino de León (siglos X y XI)', *SHHM*, 25 (2007), 15–65.

W. J. T. Mitchell, *What Do Pictures Want? The Lives and Loves of Images* (Chicago, IL, 2005).

*El monacato en los reinos de León y Castilla (siglos VII–XIII). X Congreso de Estudios Medievales* (Madrid, 2007).

*Monarquía y sociedad en el reino de León. De Alfonso III a Alfonso VII* (2 vols, León, 2007).

L. Monteagudo García, 'Sistematización de los petroglifos gallegos', *AB*, 34 (2011), 57–72.

J. Montenegro Valentín, *Santa María de Piasca: estudio de un territorio a través de un centro monástico (857–1252)* (Valladolid, 1993).

L. Moore, 'By Hand and By Voice: Performance of Royal Charters in Eleventh- and Twelfth-Century León', *JMIS*, 5.1 (2013), 18–32.

J. R. Morala Rodríguez, 'Grafías reales, lecturas imposibles', in *Orígenes*, 1, 579–636.

J. R. Morala Rodríguez, 'Léxico de la vida cotidiana. El trabajo en el campo', in *Monarquía*, 1, 377–444.

J. R. Morala Rodríguez, 'Sobre la *Nodicia de Kesos*, de hacia el 980', in C. Company Company and J. G. Moreno de Alba (eds), *Actas del VII Congreso Internacional de Historia de la Lengua Española* (2 vols, Madrid, 2008), 2, 2019–32.

J. J. Moralejo Álvarez, 'Arco(s), busto(s), pazo(s): ¿toponimia de ganadería?', in A. I. Boullón Agrelo (ed.), *As tebras alumeados: estudos filolóxicos ofrecidos en homenaxe a Ramón Lorenzo* (Santiago de Compostela, 2005), 219–38.

H. Mordek, 'Unbekannte Texte zur karolingischen Gesetzgebung. Ludwig der Fromme, Einhard und die Capitula adhuc conferenda', *Deutsches Archiv für Erforschung des Mittelalters*, 42 (1986), 446–70.

D. Moreau, '*Et alia manu*: les notes non autographes dans les actes pontificaux antérieurs à 604', *SE*, 53 (2014), 235–62.

S. Moreta Velayos, *El monasterio de San Pedro de Cardeña: historia de un dominio monástico castellano (902–1338)* (Salamanca, 1971).

M. R. B. Morujão, 'O *Livro Preto* da sé de Coimbra. Estudo do cartulário', *Revista de História da Sociedade e da Cultura*, 8 (2008), 7–43.

M. Mostert, *A Bibliography of Works on Medieval Communication* (Turnhout, 2012).

M. Mostert, 'Forgery and Trust', in P. Schulte, M. Mostert, and I. van Renswoude (eds), *Strategies of Writing: Studies on Text and Trust in the Middle Ages* (Turnhout, 2008), 37–59.

M. Mostert, 'New Approaches to Medieval Communication?', in Mostert (ed.), *New Approaches*, 15–37.

M. Mostert (ed.), *New Approaches to Medieval Communication* (Turnhout, 1999).

M. Mostert and P. S. Barnwell (eds), *Medieval Legal Process: Physical, Spoken, and Written Performance in the Middle Ages* (Turnhout, 2011).

A. M. Mundó, 'I *Corpora* e i *Codices regularum* nella tradizione codicologica delle regole monastiche', in *Atti del 7° Congresso internazionale di studi sull'alto Medioevo* (2 vols, Spoleto, 1982), 2, 477–520.

A. M. Mundó, 'Le statut du scripteur en Catalogne du IXe aux XIe siècle', in M.-C. Hubert, E. Poulle, and M. H. Smith (eds), *Le statut du scripteur au Moyen Âge. Actes du XIIe Colloque scientifique du Comité international de paléographie latine* (Paris, 2000), 21–8.

I. Muñiz López, 'San Rosendo y su familia: bases de poder de la aristocracia asturleonesa en la Asturias de los siglos IX y X', *TSP*, 2 (2007), 221–64.

A. C. Murray, 'So-Called Fictitious Trial in the Merovingian *Placita*', in S. Diefenbach and G. M. Müller (eds), *Gallien in Spätantike und Frühmittelalter. Kulturgeschichte einer Region* (Berlin, 2013), 297–327.

S. T. Nalle, 'Literacy and Culture in Early Modern Castile', *PP*, 125 (1989), 65–96.

A. A. Nascimento, 'Liber Testamentorum Coenobii Laurbanensis: descrição codicológica', in *Liber*, 2, 157–92.

A. A. Nascimento and P. F. Alberto (eds), *Actas do IV Congreso internacional de latim medieval hispânico* (Lisbon, 2006).

K. Nehlsen-von Stryk, *Die boni homines des fruhen Mittelalters unter besonderer Beruäcksichtigung der frankischen Quellen* (Berlin, 1981).

J. L. Nelson, 'The Dark Ages', *History Workshop Journal*, 63.1 (2007), 191–201.

J. L. Nelson, 'Literacy in Carolingian Government', in McKitterick (ed.), *Uses*, 258–96.

J. L. Nelson, 'Review Article. Church Properties and the Propertied Church: Donors, the Clergy, and the Church in Medieval Western Europe from the Fourth Century to the Twelfth', *EHR*, 124.507 (2009), 355–74.

M. R. Niehoff, 'Did the *Timaeus* Create a Textual Community?', *GRBS*, 47.2 (2007), 161–91.

V. Nieto Alcaide, 'La imagen de la arquitectura asturiana de los siglos VIII y IX en las crónicas de Alfonso III', *Espacio, Tiempo y Forma, Serie VII. Historia del Arte*, 2 (1989), 11–34.

K. O'Brien O'Keeffe, 'Listening to the Scenes of Reading: King Alfred's Talking Prefaces', in M. Chinca and C. Young (eds), *Orality and Literacy in the Middle Ages: Essays on a Conjunction and its Consequences in Honour of D. H. Green* (Turnhout, 2005), 17–36.

K. O'Brien O'Keeffe, *Visible Song: Transitional Literacy in Old English Verse* (Cambridge, 1990).

S. Olcoz Yanguas, 'Pampaneto, el monasterio de San Fructuoso y su influencia en la organización del valle riojano del río Leza, bajo la monarquía pamplonesa (siglos X y XI)', *ETF*, 22 (2009), 229–54.

G. Oliva, 'De Roma a Castilla. Evolución de las estructuras municipales', in J. Alvarado Planas (ed.), *El municipio medieval: nuevas perspectivas* (Madrid, 2009), 11–80.

L. Oliver, *The Body Legal in Barbarian Law* (Toronto, 2011).

S. Olmedo Bernal, *Una abadía castellana en el siglo XI. San Salvador de Oña (1011-1109)* (Madrid, 1987).

D. R. Olson, 'The Documentary Tradition in Mind and Society', in Olson and Cole (eds), *Technology*, 289–304.

D. R. Olson, 'Why Literacy Matters, Then and Now', in Johnson and Parker (eds), *Ancient Literacies*, 385–403.

D. R. Olson, *The World on Paper: the Conceptual and Cognitive Implications of Writing and Reading* (Cambridge, 1994).

D. R. Olson and M. Cole (eds), *Technology, Literacy, and the Evolution of Society: Implications of the Work of Jack Goody* (Mahwah, NJ, 2006).

J. P. O'Neill (ed.), *The Art of Medieval Spain, A.D. 500-1200* (New York, NY, 1993).

W. J. Ong, *Orality and Literacy: the Technologizing of the Word* (London, 1982).

*Orígenes de las lenguas romances en el reino de León: siglos IX–XII* (2 vols, León, 2004).

J. Orlandis, 'Sobre el concepto del delito en el derecho de la Alta Edad Media', *AHDE*, 16 (1945), 112–92.

J. Orlandis, 'Las consecuencias del delito en el derecho de la Alta Edad Media', *AHDE*, 18 (1947), 61–166.

J. Orlandis, 'Sobre la elección de sepultura en la España medieval', *AHDE*, 20 (1950), 5–49.

J. Orlandis, 'Huellas visigóticas en el derecho de la Alta Edad Media', *AHDE*, 15 (1944), 644–58.

J. Orlandis, 'Laicos y monasterios en la España medieval', *AEM*, 17 (1987), 95–104.

J. Orlandis, 'Los monasterios dúplices españoles en la Alta Edad Media', *AHDE*, 30 (1960), 49–88.

J. Orlandis, 'Los monasterios familiares en España durante la Alta Edad Media', *AHDE*, 26 (1956), 5–46.

J. Orlandis, 'Notas sobre la "oblatio puerorum" en los siglos XI y XII', *AHDE*, 31 (1961), 163–73.

J. Orlandis, 'La paz de la casa en el derecho español de la Alta Edad Media', *AHDE*, 15 (1944), 107–61.

J. Orlandis, 'La pervivencia de la legislación visigótica sobre la seguridad del reino en la Alta Edad Media', in *Estudios visigóticos*, 3 (Rome, 1962), 125–36.

J. Orlandis, 'La prenda como procedimiento coactivo en nuestro derecho medieval (notas para un estudio)', *AHDE*, 14 (1943), 81–183.

J. Orlandis, '"Traditio corporis et animae". La "familiaritas" en las iglesias y monasterios españoles de la Alta Edad Media', *AHDE*, 24 (1954), 95–279.

N. Orme, *Medieval Children* (New Haven, CT, 2001).

D. Ortiz Espinosa, 'Los doscientos mártires de Cardeña', in R. Sánchez Domingo (ed.), *El monasterio de San Pedro de Cardeña a lo largo de la historia* (Burgos, 2018), 109–34.

E. Osaba García, *El adulterio uxorio en la "Lex Visigothorum"* (Madrid, 1997).

E. Osaba García, '¿De qué se huye? La realidad del asilo en la Antigüedad Tardía', in J. Á. Tamayo Errazquin (ed.), *Cristianismo y mundo romano. V y VI ciclos de conferencias sobre el mundo clásico* (San Sebastián, 2011), 193–217.

E. Osaba García, 'Deudores y derecho de asilo en la Lex Visigothorum', *RIDA*, 53 (2006), 299–322.

E. Osaba García, 'Imagen y represión de la prostitución en época visigoda', *Fundamina*, 20.2 (2014), 658–66.

E. Osaba García, 'El impacto de la edad en la situación jurídica de las mujeres en la Lex Visigothorum', in C. Rubiera Cancelas (ed.), *Las edades vulnerables. Infancia y vejez en la Antigüedad* (Gijón, 2019), 343–66.

M. I. Ostolaza, 'La validación en los documentos del occidente hispánico (s. X–XII). Del signum crucis al signum manus', in Rück (ed.), *Graphische Symbole*, 453–62.

A. Otero Varela, 'Las arras en el derecho español medieval', *AHDE*, 25 (1955), 189–210.

A. Otero Varela, 'El códice López Ferreiro del "Liber iudiciorum" (notas sobre la aplicación del Liber iudiciorum y el carácter de los fueros municipales)', *AHDE*, 29 (1959), 557–73.

A. Otero Varela, *Dos estudios histórico-jurídicos. El riepto en el derecho castellanoleonés. La adopción en la historia del derecho español* (Rome, 1955).

A. Otero Varela, '"Liber iudiciorum 3, 1, 5" (en tema de dote y "donatio propter nuptias")', *AHDE*, 29 (1959), 545–55.

A. Otero Varela, 'Sobre la realidad histórica de la adopción', *AHDE*, 27–8 (1957–8), 1143–9.

R. Oulion, *Scribes et notaires face à la norme dans la Toscane du Haut Moyen Âge (VII<sup>e</sup>-XI<sup>e</sup> siècles)* (Bayonne, 2013).

F. L. Pacheco Caballero, 'Reyes, leyes y derecho en la Alta Edad Media castellano-leonesa', in A. Iglesia Ferreirós (ed.), *El dret comú i Catalunya. Actes del V Simposi Internacional* (Barcelona, 1996), 165–206.

R. Pacheco Sampedro, 'Arqueología archivística y documental', in Sáez and Castillo Gómez (eds), *Actas VI*, 2, 55–91.

R. Pacheco Sampedro, 'El diploma del rey Silo. Datos de semiótica para un estudio diplomático', *Signo*, 8 (2001), 121–78.

R. Pacheco Sampedro, 'La tradición diplomática documental a partir del análisis de los signos y símbolos religiosos', in *Iglesia y religiosidad*, 2, 771–803.

R. Pacheco Sampedro and M. E. Sotelo Martín, 'El "signum regis" (SR) distintivo de la monarquía asturleonesa desde Alfonso III hasta Alfonso VII, y el origen de la cancillería real', in *Orígenes*, 2, 419–38.

É. Palazzo, 'Le livre dans les trésors du Moyen Âge. Contribution à l'histoire de la *memoria* médiévale', *AHSS*, 52.1 (1997), 93–118.

M. C. Pallares Méndez, 'Grandes señoras en los siglos IX y X', in I. Morant (ed.), *Historia de las mujeres en España y América Latina* (2nd ed., 4 vols, Madrid, 2005–6), 1, 423–42.

M. C. Pallares Méndez, *Ilduara: una aristócrata del siglo X* (Sada, 1998).

M. C. Pallares Méndez, *El monasterio de Sobrado: un ejemplo de protagonismo monástico en la Galicia medieval* (A Coruña, 1979).

M. C. Pallares Méndez and E. Portela Silva, 'El lugar de los campesinos. De repobladores a repoblados', in Rodríguez (ed.), *Lugar*, 61–87.

M. C. Pallares Méndez and E. Portela Silva, 'La villa, por dentro. Testimonios galaicos de los siglos X y XI', *SHHM*, 16 (1998), 13–43.

J. T. Palmer, *The Apocalypse in the Early Middle Ages* (Cambridge, 2014).

M. L. Pardo Rodríguez, 'La confirmación en los documentos señoriales de la Baja Edad Media. Aportación a su estudio', *HID*, 12 (1985), 247–76.

M. Parisse, 'Préambules de chartes', in J. Hamesse (ed.), *Les prologues médiévaux. Actes du Colloque international* (Turnhout, 2000), 141–69.

M. B. Parkes, 'The Literacy of the Laity', in D. Daiches and A. Thorlby (eds), *Literature and Western Civilization* (6 vols, London, 1972–6), 2, 555–77.

*El pasado histórico de Castilla y León, I. Edad Media* (Burgos, 1983).

R. Pastor, *Resistencias y luchas campesinas en la época del crecimiento y consolidación de la formación feudal. Castilla y León, siglos X–XIII* (2nd ed., Madrid, 1990).

E. Pastor Díaz de Garayo, *Castilla en el tránsito de la Antigüedad al feudalismo: poblamiento, poder político y estructura social. Del Arlanza al Duero (siglos VII–XI)* (Valladolid, 1996).

E. Pastor Díaz de Garayo, 'Los testimonios escritos del sector meridional de Castilla (siglos X–XI). Ensayo de crítica documental', *HID*, 24 (1997), 355–79.

E. Pastor Díaz de Garayo, 'El uso de la "presura" en el *scriptorium* de la sede de Lugo-Braga durante el siglo XI: el ejemplo de Odoario, el obispo "presor" de la octava centuria', *SHHM*, 37.1 (2019), 79–103.

E. Pastor Díaz de Garayo and A. Castro Correa, *Las presuras de Odoario 'el Africano' en Lugo y Braga. Textos, objetos y contextos para la construcción de la memoria y la legitimación de la dominación personal y política* (Bilbao, 2020).

E. Peña Bocos, 'La aldea como espacio de poder. La Castilla del Ebro en torno al año mil', in Iglesia Duarte and Martín Rodríguez (eds), *Espacios*, 69–96.

F. J. Peña Pérez, 'Las comunidades de aldea en la Alta Edad Media: precisiones terminológicas y conceptuales', in Álvarez Borge (ed.), *Comunidades*, 331–58.

*La Península Ibérica en torno al año 1000. VII Congreso de Estudios Medievales* (Ávila, 2001).

C. Pensado, 'How was Leonese Vulgar Latin Read?', in Wright (ed.), *Latin*, 190–204.

S. Perea Yébenes, 'La mención a Judas Iscariota en epitafios latinos cristianos de la Hispania visigoda y bizantina: el delito sepulcral y la condena mágica', *Myrtia*, 21 (2006), 235–76.

I. R. Pereira, 'Symboles graphiques dans les chartes médiévales portugaises', in Rück (ed.), *Graphische Symbole*, 491–502.

I. Pereira García, 'La epigrafía medieval en España: un estado de la cuestión', *AEM*, 47.1 (2017), 267–302.

M. Pérez, 'Clérigos rurales, comunidades y formación de las estructuras parroquiales en la diócesis de León (siglos XI–XIII)', *ETF*, 31 (2018), 547–74.

M. Pérez, 'El control de lo sagrado como instrumento de poder: los monasterios particulares de la aristocracia altomedieval leonesa', *AEM*, 42.2 (2012), 799–822.

M. Pérez, 'Monasterios, iglesias locales y articulación religiosa de la diócesis de León en la Alta Edad Media', in A. Vanina Neyra and M. Pérez (eds), *Obispos y monasterios en la Edad Media. Trayectorias personales, organización eclesiástica y dinámicas materiales* (Buenos Aires, 2020), 95–124.

M. Pérez, 'Parentesco, prestigio y poder en la Alta Edad Media: la antroponimia aristocrática en el reino de León (siglos X y XI)', *Estudios de Historia de España*, 16 (2014), 73–93.

M. Pérez, 'Posibilidades y límites de los archivos eclesiásticos para el estudio de la nobleza leonesa (siglos X y XI)', *Actas y Comunicaciones del Instituto de Historia Antigua y Medieval*, 9.1 (2013), 1–12.

M. Pérez, 'Proprietary Churches, Episcopal Authority, and Social Relationships in the Diocese of León (Eleventh–Twelfth Centuries)', *JMIS*, 10.2 (2018), 195–212.

M. Pérez, '*Rebelles, infideles, traditores*. Insumisión política y poder aristocrático en el reino de León', *HID*, 38 (2011), 361–82.

M. Pérez González, 'Las bebidas alcohólicas en el medievo asturleonés a través de los textos', *EHH*, 7 (2008), 61–77.

M. Pérez González, 'Características de la documentación diplomática del monasterio de Sahagún', in J. F. Mesa Sanz (ed.), *Latinidad medieval hispánica* (Florence, 2017), 593–629.

M. Pérez González, 'Sobre la edición de textos en latín medieval diplomático', in J. Martínez Gázquez, Ó. de la Cruz Palma, and C. Ferrero Hernández (eds), *Estudios de latín medieval hispánico. Actas del V Congreso hispánico de latín medieval* (Florence, 2011), 1017–39.

M. Pérez González, 'La fórmula "usque ad minimam rem" y sus variantes en la diplomática medieval asturleonesa hasta 1230', in A. M. Aldama, M. F. del Barrio, and A. Espigares (eds), *Nova et vetera. Nuevos horizontes de la filología latina* (2 vols, Madrid, 2002), 1, 525–38.

M. Pérez González, 'Sobre el formulismo en la diplomática medieval', *Iacobus*, 7–8 (1999), 117–39.

M. Pérez González, 'El latín medieval diplomático', *ALMA*, 66 (2008), 47–101.

M. Pérez González, 'Léxico religioso de la cancillería de Alfonso VIII', *Studium Legionense*, 26 (1985), 197–228.

M. Pérez González, 'Néologismes du lexique des tributs et des prestations dans le latin médiéval du royaume des Asturies et de Léon (VIIIᵉ siècle–1230)', *ALMA*, 63 (2005), 127–36.

M. Pérez González, 'Oficios artesanales en el latín medieval de Asturias y León', *ALMA*, 71 (2013), 111–25.

M. Pérez González, 'Originales y copias en la documentación medieval latina', *Minerva*, 3 (1989), 239–65.

M. Pérez González, 'Los protocolos poéticos en la documentación medieval diplomática', in J. Luque, M. D. Rincón, and I. Velázquez (eds), *Dulces Camenae. Poética y poesía latinas* (Jaén-Granada, 2010), 441–9.

M. Pérez González (ed.), *Actas del I Congreso nacional de latín medieval* (León, 1995).

M. Pérez González (ed.), *Actas del III Congreso hispánico de latín medieval* (2 vols, León, 2002).

J. M. Pérez-Prendes y Muñoz de Arraco, 'La frialdad del texto: comentario al prólogo del "Fuero Viejo de Castilla"', *Interpretatio*, 10 (2004), 337–58.

J. M. Pérez-Prendes y Muñoz de Arraco, 'La potestad legislativa en el reino de León', in *RLAEM* 1 (León, 1988), 495–545.

E. Pérez Rodríguez, 'El agua en la documentación medieval asturleonesa (s. VIII–1230) a través de su terminología: panorama general', *CC*, 18 (2010), 81–104.

E. Pérez Rodríguez, 'La descripción de los lindes: estudio de los verbos usados en los diplomas asturleoneses (s. VIII–1230)', in Pérez Rodríguez (ed.), *Palabras*, 253–313.

E. Pérez Rodríguez, '*Primiclerus*: un estudio de un neologismo hispánico', *Voces*, 14 (2003), 77–101.

E. Pérez Rodríguez (ed.), *Las palabras del paisaje y el paisaje en las palabras de la Edad Media. Estudios de lexicografía latina medieval hispánica* (Turnhout, 2018).

J. Pérez de Urbel, 'Cardeña y sus escribas durante la primera mitad del siglo X', in *Bivium. Homenaje a Manuel Cecilio Díaz y Díaz* (Madrid, 1983), 217–37.

J. Pérez de Urbel, *Historia del Condado de Castilla* (3 vols, Madrid, 1945).

J. Pérez de Urbel, 'El monasterio de Valeránica y su escritorio', in *Homenaje Millares Carlo*, 2, 71–90.

J. Pérez de Urbel, *Los monjes españoles en la Edad Media* (2nd ed., 2 vols, Madrid, 1945).

J. Pérez de Urbel, 'San Rosendo y Celanova en el Cartulario de Sobrado', *Signo*, 5 (1998), 99–108.

J. Pérez de Urbel, *Sancho el Mayor de Navarra* (Madrid, 1950).

R. Perry, 'The Sum of the Book: Structural Codicology and Medieval Manuscript Culture', in Rold and Treharne (eds), *Companion*, 106–26.

D. Peterson, 'El *Becerro Gótico* de San Millán. Reconstrucción de un cartulario perdido', *SHHM*, 29 (2011), 147–73.

D. Peterson, 'Estratos vascos y árabes en la onomástica castellana altomedieval. La toponimia del cartulario de Froncea', in E. Ramos and A. Ros (eds), *Onomástica, lengua e historia. Estudios en honor de Ricardo Cierbide* (Bilbao, 2017), 217–36.

D. Peterson, 'Fronteras políticas y espacios culturales en el Alto Ebro (s. VIII–XI)', *EMir*, 35 (2019), 7–35.

D. Peterson, 'El gran incendio castellano de 949. Huella diplomática y memoria histórica de un desastre natural', *SHHM*, 37.1 (2019), 139–64.

D. Peterson, 'Mentiras piadosas: falsificaciones e interpolaciones en la diplomática de San Millán de la Cogolla', in A. García Leal (ed.), *Las donaciones piadosas en el mundo medieval* (Oviedo, 2012), 295–314.

D. Peterson, 'Order and Disorder in the Cartularies of San Millán de la Cogolla', in Furtado and Moscone (eds), *Charters*, 119–34.

D. Peterson, 'Rebranding San Millán: the *Becerro Galicano* as a Rejection of the Monastery's Navarrese Heritage (1192–95)', *JMIS*, 5.2 (2013), 184–203.

D. Peterson, 'Reescribiendo el pasado. El *Becerro Galicano* como reconstrucción de la historia institucional de San Millán de la Cogolla', *Hispania*, 69.233 (2009), 653–82.

C. Petit, '*Consuetudo* y *mos* en la *Lex Visigothorum*', *AHDE*, 54 (1984), 209–52.

C. Petit, 'Crimen y castigo en el reino visigodo de Toledo', in *Visigodos*, 215–38.

C. Petit, 'De negotiis causarum', *AHDE*, 55 (1985), 151–251, 56 (1986), 5–165.

C. Petit, *Fiadores y fianzas en el derecho romanovisigodo* (Seville, 1983).

C. Petit, *Iustitia Gothica. Historia social y teología del proceso en la Lex Visigothorum* (Huelva, 2001).

C. Petit, 'Lex Visigothorum 11,1. De medicis et egrotis', *CHE*, 67–8 (1982), 5–32.

C. Petit, 'Sobre la práctica jurídica del sur peninsular: las fórmulas notariales godas', in L. A. García Moreno (ed.), *Historia de Andalucía, II. Andalucía en la Antigüedad Tardía: de Diocleciano a Rodrigo* (Seville, 2006), 184–9.

P. Petitmengin, 'La Bible à travers les inventaires de bibliothèques médiévales', in P. Riché and G. Lobrichon (eds), *Le Moyen Âge et la Bible* (Paris, 1984), 31–53.

A. Petrucci, 'Literacy and Graphic Culture of Early Medieval Scribes', repr. in *Writers and Readers in Medieval Italy*, transl. C. M. Radding (New Haven, CT, 1995), 77–102.

L. K. Pick, *Her Father's Daughter: Gender, Power, and Religion in the Early Spanish Kingdoms* (Ithaca, NY, 2017).

L. K. Pick, 'Rebel Nephews and Royal Sisters: the Case of Bernardo del Carpio', in M. Bailey and R. D. Giles (eds), *Charlemagne and his Legend in Early Spanish Literature and Historiography* (Cambridge, 2016), 44–65.

J. Pinell, *Liturgia hispánica* (Barcelona, 1998).

M. Pino Abad, *La pena de confiscación de bienes en el derecho histórico español* (Córdoba, 1999).

J. M. Piquer Marí, 'La justicia en la Edad Media: la pervivencia de los principios inquisitivos y de libre aportación de prueba', *Vergentis*, 5 (2017), 261–99.

H. Pirenne, *Mohammed and Charlemagne*, transl. B. Miall (London, 1939).

W. G. von Plettenberg, *Das Fortleben des Liber Iudiciorum in Asturien/León (8.–13.Jh.)* (Frankfurt am Main, 1994).

A. Poiares, 'Nomenclatura monetária medieval portuguesa', *Nummus*, 38 (2015), 7–177.

M. E. Pontieri, 'Una familia de propietarios rurales en la Liébana del siglo X', *CHE*, 43–4 (1967), 119–32.

R. Portass, 'All Quiet on the Western Front? Royal Politics in Galicia from *c.* 800 to *c.* 950', *EME*, 21.3 (2013), 283–306.

R. Portass, 'The Beginnings of Specialised Economic Production in Tenth-Century Iberia', in P. C. Díaz Martínez and I. Martín Viso (eds), *Los procesos de formación del feudalismo. La Península Ibérica en el contexto europeo* (Gijón, forthcoming).

R. Portass, 'Early Medieval Spain, 800–1100: the Christian Kingdoms and al-Andalus', in S. Mossman (ed.), *Debating Medieval Europe: the Early Middle Ages, c. 450–c. 1050* (Manchester, 2020), 176–225.

R. Portass, 'The Middling Sort at Court in Early Medieval Christian Iberia', *Al-Masāq*, 29.2 (2017), 99–113.

R. Portass, 'Rethinking the "Small Worlds" of Tenth-Century Galicia', *SHHM*, 31 (2013), 83–103.

R. Portass, *The Village World of Early Medieval Northern Spain: Local Community and the Land Market* (Woodbridge, 2017).

S. Portela Pazos, *Anotaciones al Tumbo A de la catedral de Santiago* (Santiago de Compostela, 1949).

E. Portela Silva, 'Galicia y la monarquía leonesa', in *RLAEM* 7 (León, 1995), 12–70.

E. Portela Silva, 'El rey y los obispos. Poderes locales en el espacio galaico durante el período astur', *TSP, Anejo* 2 (2009), 215–26.

E. Portela Silva and M. C. Pallares Méndez, 'Elementos para el análisis de la aristocracia altomedieval de Galicia: parentesco y patrimonio', *SHHM*, 5 (1987), 17–32.

E. Portela Silva and M. C. Pallares Méndez, 'Os mosteiros, protagonistas da colonización e do proceso de señorialización na Galicia medieval: o exemplo do mosteiro de Sobrado', *Estudis d'Història Agrària*, 2 (1979), 51–71.

P. Poveda Arias, 'La diócesis episcopal en la Hispania visigoda: concepción, construcción y disputas por su territorio', *HS*, 71.143 (2019), 9–24.

A. Prieto Morera, 'El proceso en el reino de León a la luz de los diplomas', in *RLAEM* 2 (León, 1992), 381–518.

A. Prieto Prieto, 'El conde Fernando Vermúdez', *AL*, 28.55–6 (1974), 197–213.

A. Prieto Prieto, 'El conde Fruela Muñoz: un asturiano del siglo XI', *AM*, 2 (1975), 11–37.

A. Prieto Prieto, 'La potestad judicial de los reyes de León', in *RLAEM* 2 (León, 1992), 519–64.

J. A. Puentes Romay, 'Aproximación a una visión actual del latín documental hispánico', *Euphrosyne*, 31 (2003), 483–9.

J. A. Puentes Romay, 'Caracterización de los rasgos lingüísticos de un notario altomedieval. Problemas y un ejemplo', in Pérez González (ed.), *Actas III*, 2, 679–86.

J. A. Puentes Romay, 'Documentos y notarios leoneses del ámbito de Viñayo', in Nascimento and Alberto (eds), *Actas IV*, 769–80.

J. A. Puentes Romay, 'Un notario leonés del siglo XI', in Domínguez García *et al.* (eds), *Sub luce*, 519–36.

J. A. Puentes Romay, 'Notarios leoneses altomedievales y fórmulas documentales', *Euphrosyne*, 33 (2005), 235–46.

Y. Quesada Morillas, *El delito de rapto en la historia del derecho castellano* (Madrid, 2018).

P. J. Quetglas Nicolau, 'Nota sobre la cultura dels escrivans medievals a Catalunya', in *Humanitas in honorem Antonio Fontán* (Madrid, 1992), 313–19.

M. Quilis Merín, 'Lectura, escritura y enseñanza en la época de orígenes', in M. Aleza-Izquierdo and Á. López-García (eds), *Estudios de filología, historia y cultura hispánicas* (Valencia, 2000), 159–71.

A. Quintana Prieto, 'Fundaciones de S. Genadio', *AL*, 10.19 (1956), 55–118.

A. Quintana Prieto, 'Monasterios astorganos de San Dictino', *AL*, 29.57–8 (1975), 209–309.

A. Quintana Prieto, 'El obispado de Astorga en el siglo IX. Restauración y episcopologio', *HS*, 18.35 (1965), 159–202.

A. Quintana Prieto, *El obispado de Astorga en el siglo XI* (Astorga, 1977).

A. Quintana Prieto, *El obispado de Astorga en los siglos IX y X* (Astorga, 1968).

A. Quintana Prieto, 'San Miguel de Camarzana y su "scriptorium"', *AEM*, 5 (1968), 65–105.

A. Quintana Prieto, 'Tebaida Berciana. San Cosme y San Damián de Burbia', *AL*, 11.22 (1957), 75–109.

J. A. Quirós Castillo (ed.), *Social Inequality in Early Medieval Europe: Local Societies and Beyond* (Turnhout, 2020).

S. Rankovic, L. Melve, and E. Mundal (eds), *Along the Oral–Written Continuum: Types of Texts, Relations, and their Implications* (Turnhout, 2010).

C. Rapp, 'Holy Texts, Holy Men, and Holy Scribes: Aspects of Scriptural Holiness in Late Antiquity', in Klingshirn and Safran (eds), *Early Christian Book*, 194–222.

M. Recuero Astray, 'Relaciones entre la monarquía y la iglesia de León durante la Alta Edad Media', *RLAEM* 7 (León, 1995), 71–148.

K. B. Reeves, *Visions of Unity after the Visigoths: Early Iberian Latin Chronicles and the Mediterranean World* (Turnhout, 2016).

A. M. Reis, 'D. Diogo Gelmires e as terras sob a jurisdição da igreja de Santiago de Compostela entre os rios Minho e Ave', *População e Sociedade*, 18 (2010), 179–95.

J. M. Remolina Seivane, 'Oviedo y León, las ciudades del poder en el reino asturiano en los siglos IX–X. La aplicación del modelo de ciudad clásica en el proyecto urbano', in S. de Maria and M. P. López de Corselas (eds), *El imperio y las Hispanias de Trajano a Carlos V. Clasicismo y poder en el arte español* (Bologna, 2014), 229–42.

K. R. Rennie, *Medieval Canon Law* (Leeds, 2018).

A. Represa, 'Evolución urbana de León en los siglos XI–XIII', in *LH* 1 (León, 1969), 243–82.

T. Reuter, *Germany in the Early Middle Ages, c. 800–1056* (London, 1991).

F. Reyes Téllez, 'Los orígenes del monasterio de San Salvador de Oña: eremitismo y monasterio dúplice', in Sánchez Domingo (ed.), *Oña*, 32–51.

R. E. Reynolds, 'The Civitas Regia Toletana before the Reconquista: a Mozarabic Vision in the Codices Vigilanus and Aemilianensis', in R. Gonzálvez-Ruiz (ed.), *Estudios sobre Alfonso VI y la Reconquista de Toledo. Actas del II Congreso Internacional de Estudios Mozárabes* (4 vols, Toledo, 1987–90), 3, 153–84.

P. Riché, 'Apprendre à lire et à écrire dans le Haut Moyen Âge', repr. in G. Stavridès (ed.), *L'enseignement au Moyen Âge* (Paris, 2016), 54–69.

P. Riché, *Écoles et enseignement dans le Haut Moyen Âge: fin du $V^e$ siècle–milieu du $XI^e$ siècle* (3rd ed., Paris, 1999).

P. Riché, *Education and Culture in the Barbarian West: from the Sixth through the Eighth Century*, transl. J. J. Contreni (Columbia, NC, 1976).

P. Riché, 'Le Psautier, livre de lecture élémentaire d'après les vies des saints mérovingiens', in *Études mérovingiennes* (Paris, 1953), 253–6.

M. Richter, *The Formation of the Medieval West: Studies in the Oral Culture of the Barbarians* (Dublin, 1994).

M. Richter, *The Oral Tradition in the Early Middle Ages* (Turnhout, 1994).

M. Richter, 'The Written Word in Context: the Early Middle Ages', in K. Reichl (ed.), *Medieval Oral Literature* (Berlin, 2012), 103–19.

Á. Riesco Terrero, 'Diplomática eclesiástica del reino de León hasta 1300', in *RLAEM* 7 (León, 1995), 333–589.

Á. Riesco Terrero, 'Notariado y documentación notarial castellano-leonesa de los siglos X–XIII', in Canellas López, Santiago Fernández, and Francisco Olmos (eds), *I Jornadas*, 129–64.

A. Rio, 'Charters, Law Codes, and Formulae: the Franks between Theory and Practice', in P. Fouracre and D. Ganz (eds), *Frankland: the Franks and the World of the Early Middle Ages. Essays in Honour of Dame Jinty Nelson* (Manchester, 2008), 7–27.

A. Rio, *Legal Practice and the Written Word in the Early Middle Ages: Frankish Formulae, c. 500–1000* (Cambridge, 2009).

A. Rio, 'Penal Enslavement in the Early Middle Ages', in C. G. De Vito and A. Lichtenstein (eds), *Global Convict Labour* (Leiden, 2015), 79–107.

A. Rio, *Slavery after Rome, 500–1100* (Oxford, 2017).

M. L. Ríos Rodríguez, 'Las "ecclesiae" dependientes de los monasterios de Jubia, Caaveiro y Monfero (s. XI a XIII)', *Adaxe*, 5 (1989), 105–23.

M. L. Ríos Rodríguez, 'El valor de las escrituras: resolución de conflictos entre señores y campesinos en la Galicia bajomedieval', *EM*, 11 (2010), 151–71.

G. Ripoll and N. Molist Capella, '*Cura mortuorum* en el nordeste de la Península Ibérica, siglos IV al XII d.C.', *TSP*, 9 (2014), 5–66.

J. Rius Serra, 'El derecho visigodo en Cataluña', *Spanische Forschungen der Görres-Gesellschaft, I. Gesammelte Aufsätze zur Kulturgeschichte Spaniens*, 8 (1940), 65–80.

J. Rius Serra, 'Reparatio Scripturae', *AHDE*, 5 (1928), 246–53.

L. Roach, *Forgery and Memory at the End of the First Millennium* (Princeton, NJ, 2021).

L. Roach, 'Public Rites and Public Wrongs: Ritual Aspects of Diplomas in Tenth- and Eleventh-Century England', *EME*, 19.2 (2011), 182–203.

R. P. Robinson, *Manuscripts 27 (S. 29) and 107 (S. 129) of the Municipal Library of Autun. A Study of Spanish Half-Uncial and Early Visigothic Minuscule and Cursive Scripts* (New York, NY, 1939).

M. J. Roca, 'La distinción entre patrimonio eclesiástico y privado de obispos y clérigos en la España visigoda', *e-Legal History Review*, 20 (2015), 1–16.

C.-P. Rodenbusch, 'Liturgical Framing of Trials in 10th- to 11th-Century Catalonia', *Religions*, 13.3 (2022), 1–12.

C. Rodiño Caramés, 'A Lex gótica e o Liber Iudicum no reino de León', *CEG*, 44.109 (1997), 9–52.

M. A. Rodrigues, 'Cartulários portugueses', in *Liber*, 2, 305–42.

A. Rodríguez (ed.), *El lugar del campesino. En torno a la obra de Reyna Pastor* (Valencia, 2007).

M. Rodríguez-Escalona, 'Gestos simbólicos y rituales jurídicos de transferencia y posesión de bienes en la Cataluña altomedieval', *AEM*, 51.2 (2021), 801–22.

A. Rodríguez Baixeras, *A historia de Odoyno. A primeira novela galega* (Noia, 2015).

T.-H. Rodríguez Castillo, 'Monasterios dúplices: religiosos de ambos sexos bajo un mismo techo', *Historia 16*, 370 (2007), 8–21.

E. E. Rodríguez Díaz, 'Notas codicológicas sobre el llamado *Testamento del Rey Casto*', *AM*, 8 (1995–7), 71–8.

E. E. Rodríguez Díaz and A. C. García Martínez (eds), *La escritura de la memoria: los cartularios* (Huelva, 2011).

J. Rodríguez Fernández, 'La monarquía leonesa. De García I a Vermudo III (910–1037)', in *RLAEM* 3 (León, 1995), 131–416.

J. Rodríguez Fernández, *El monasterio de Ardón* (León, 1964).

J. Rodríguez Fernández, 'Notas sobre el alavés Froila Velaz y la "Peña del Rey"', in *Estudios en homenaje a Don Claudio Sánchez-Albornoz en sus 90 años* (6 vols, Buenos Aires, 1983), 2, 145–60.

J. Rodríguez Fernández, *Ordoño III* (León, 1982).

J. Rodríguez Fernández, *Sancho I y Ordoño IV, reyes de León* (León, 1987).

F. S. Rodríguez Lajusticia, 'La presencia de las reinas Jimena y Munia, madre y esposa de Sancho III el Mayor, en sus documentos auténticos', *PV*, 80.274 (2019), 725–51.

V. E. Rodríguez Martín, 'Los salmos bíblicos como enseñanza en el *Manual* de Dhuoda (s. IX)', in Pérez González (ed.), *Actas III*, 2, 447–56.

R. Rojo Carrillo, *Text, Liturgy, and Music in the Hispanic Rite: the Vespertinus Genre* (Oxford, 2021).

O. da Rold and E. Treharne (eds), *The Cambridge Companion to Medieval British Manuscripts* (Cambridge, 2020).

L. Romera Iruela, 'El Becerro Gótico de Sahagún: esbozo de estudio codicográfico', *AEM*, 18 (1988), 23–41.

L. Romera Iruela, 'Refacciones documentales a fines del s. XI: el caso de Sahagún', in *VIII Coloquio del Comité Internacional de Paleografía Latina. Actas* (Madrid, 1990), 185–202.

M. Romero Tallafigo, 'El concepto clásico de usuario de archivo: de Justiniano a los siglos del historicismo', in J. González Cachafeiro (ed.), *9 Jornadas Archivando: usuarios, retos y oportunidades* (León, 2016), 1–35.

B. H. Rosenwein, *Emotional Communities in the Early Middle Ages* (Ithaca, NY, 2006).

B. H. Rosenwein, *Negotiating Space: Power, Restraint, and Privileges of Immunity in Early Medieval Europe* (Ithaca, NY, 1999).

B. H. Rosenwein, *To Be the Neighbor of Saint Peter. The Social Meaning of Cluny's Property, 909–1049* (Ithaca, NY, 1989).

P. Rousseau, *Pachomius. The Making of a Community in Fourth-Century Egypt* (new ed., Berkeley, CA, 1999).

J. A. Rubio, ' "Donationes post obitum" y "donationes reservato usufructu" en la Alta Edad Media de León y Castilla', *AHDE*, 9 (1932), 1–32.

J. A. Rubio, 'La transmisión de la propiedad inmobiliaria en nuestro derecho medieval. Función del documento', *Anales de la Academia Matritense del Notariado*, 7 (1953), 351–71.

L. M. Rubio Pérez, 'La Valduerna: de la dominación romana al señorío jurisdiccional de los Bazán', *TL*, 21.45 (1981), 15–34.

P. Rück (ed.), *Graphische Symbole in mittelalterlichen Urkunden. Beiträge zur diplomatischen Semiotik* (Sigmaringen, 1996).

A. Rucquoi, 'Compostela: a Cultural Center from the Tenth to the Twelfth Century', in D'Emilio (ed.-transl.), *Culture*, 512–42.

A. Rucquoi, 'Ordres religieux et histoire culturelle dans l'occident médiéval', *Lusitania Sacra*, 17 (2005), 299–328.

A. Rucquoi, 'Peregrinos de España a Jerusalén y Roma (siglos X–XIII)', in P. Caucci von Saucken and R. Vázquez Santos (eds), *Peregrino, ruta y meta en las "peregrinationes maiores". VIII Congreso Internacional de Estudios Jacobeos* (Santiago de Compostela, 2012), 41–60.

J. M. Ruiz Asencio, 'Campañas de Almanzor contra el reino de León (981–986)', *AEM*, 5 (1968), 31–64.

J. M. Ruiz Asencio, 'Los copistas del *Liber Testamentorum*, sus escrituras y notas sobre el *scriptorium* de Lorvão para la confección de documentos', in *Liber*, 2, 193–242.

J. M. Ruiz Asencio, 'Escribas y bibliotecas altomedievales hispanos', in Iglesia Duarte (ed.), *Enseñanza*, 151–74.

J. M. Ruiz Asencio, 'La escritura visigótica II: los documentos', in J. A. Fernández Flórez and S. Serna Serna (eds), *Paleografía I: la escritura en España hasta 1250* (Burgos, 2008), 93–118.

J. M. Ruiz Asencio, '*Libellus a regula sancti Benedicti subtractus*. Bibl. Academia de la Historia, Emilianensis, 62', in García Turza (ed.), *Manuscritos*, 175–200.

J. M. Ruiz Asencio, 'Notas sobre la escritura y monogramas regios en la documentación real astur-leonesa', in *Monarquía*, 1, 265–314.

J. M. Ruiz Asencio, 'Notas sobre el trabajo de los notarios leoneses en los siglos X–XII', in *Orígenes*, 1, 87–118.

J. M. Ruiz Asencio, 'Obispos, patrimonio documental y *reparatio scripture* en el reino de León en los siglos X–XII', in F. J. Molina de la Torre, I. Ruiz Albi, and M. Herrero de la Fuente (eds), *Lugares de escritura: la catedral* (Valladolid, 2014), 181–210.

J. M. Ruiz Asencio, 'Rebeliones leoneses contra Vermudo II', *AL*, 45–6 (1969), 215–41.

J. M. Ruiz Asencio, 'Tres cartularios en el Becerro Gótico de Valpuesta. ¿Los más antiguos de los reinos hispánicos occidentales?', in Furtado and Moscone (eds), *Charters*, 1–19.

E. Ruiz García, 'La escritura: una *vox Dei* (siglos X–XIII)', in Canellas López, Santiago Fernández, and Francisco Olmos (eds), *I Jornadas*, 71–92.

S. Ruiz de Loizaga, *Iglesia y sociedad en el norte de España: iglesia episcopal de Valpuesta, Alta Edad Media* (Burgos, 1991).

J. I. Ruiz de la Peña Solar, 'La monarquía asturiana (718–910)', in *RLAEM* 3 (León, 1995), 9–127.

J. I. Ruiz de la Peña Solar, 'El rey y el reino en la monarquía asturiana (718–910)', in *Monarquía*, 1, 37–84.

J. I. Ruiz de la Peña Solar and M. J. Sanz Fuentes, 'Instrumentos, cauces y expresiones de la actividad investigadora', in *La historia medieval en España. Un balance historiográfico (1968–1998). XXV Semana de Estudios Medievales* (Pamplona, 1999), 779–805.

S. Ruiz Pino, *La vertiente iuspublicista de la institución adoptiva en derecho romano y su proyección en el derecho español* (Madrid, 2012).

J. I. Ruiz Rodríguez and F. J. Martínez Llorente (eds), *Recuerdos literarios en honor a un gran historiador de Castilla: Gonzalo Martínez Díez (1924–2015)* (Madrid, 2016).

M. J. Ryan, '"Charters in plenty, if only they were good for anything": the Problem of Bookland and Folkland in Pre-Viking England', in Jarrett and McKinley (eds), *Problems*, 19–32.

H. de Sá Bravo, *El monacato en Galicia* (2 vols, A Coruña, 1972).

N. P. Sacks, *The Latinity of Dated Documents in the Portuguese Territory* (Philadelphia, PA, 1941).

P. Saenger, *Space between Words: the Origins of Silent Reading* (Stanford, CA, 1997).

S. Sáenz-López Pérez, *The Beatus Maps: the Revelation of the World in the Middle Ages*, transl. P. Krakenberger and G. Coldham (Burgos, 2014).

C. Sáez, 'Códices diplomáticos y conservación documental', *AHAM*, 25 (2003–4), 831–48.

C. Sáez, 'Crismones en la documentación particular de la catedral de León del período astur (864–910)', in Rück (ed.), *Graphische Symbole*, 439–42.

C. Sáez, 'Documentos para ver, documentos para leer', *AEM*, 29 (1999), 899–916.

C. Sáez, 'Donaciones "post-obitum" del monasterio de Celanova (936–1000): estudio diplomático', *Estudis Castellonencs*, 6 (1994–5), 1245–54.

C. Sáez, 'Origen y función de los cartularios: el ejemplo de España', *GLM*, 46 (2005), 12–21.

C. Sáez, 'El signo como emblema', *AEM*, 33.1 (2003), 339–63.

C. Sáez and A. Castillo Gómez, 'Del signo a lo escrito: paleografía e historia social de la cultura escrita', *La Corónica*, 28.2 (2000), 155–68.

C. Sáez and A. Castillo Gómez (eds), *Actas del VI Congreso Internacional de Historia de la Cultura Escrita* (2 vols, Madrid, 2002).

C. Sáez and A. García Medina, 'Los otros signos', *CEG*, 51.117 (2004), 207–18.

C. Sáez and A. E. Gutiérrez García-Muñoz, 'De la austeridad a la ostentación: los cartularios de Celanova y Sigüenza', in B. Acinas Lope (ed.), *Silos. Un milenio, III. Cultura* (Burgos, 2003), 211–25.

C. Sáez and A. E. Gutiérrez García-Muñoz, 'Hacia una interpretación del Tumbo de Celanova', in *Iglesia y religiosidad*, 2, 997–1008.

C. Sáez and E. Sáez, 'El diploma de Quiza Gonteríquiz', *Signo*, 3 (1996), 69–86.

E. Sáez, 'Los ascendientes de San Rosendo. Notas para el estudio de la monarquía astur-leonesa durante los siglos IX–X', *Hispania*, 8.30 (1948), 3–76, 8.31 (1948), 179–233.

E. Sáez, 'Inventario de bibliotecas medievales en el Tumbo de Celanova', *La Ciudad de Dios*, 155 (1943), 563–8.

E. Sáinz Ripa, 'El patrimonio documental eclesiástico en La Rioja', *Berceo*, 128 (1995), 291–306.

J. de Salazar Acha, 'El conde Fernando Peláez, un rebelde leonés del siglo XI', *AEM*, 19 (1989), 87–98.

J. M. Salrach, '*Ad reparandum scripturas perditas*. El valor del documento en la sociedad de los condados catalanes (siglos IX y X)', *TSP, Anejo* 2 (2009), 309–30.

J. M. Salrach, *Justícia i poder a Catalunya abans de l'any mil* (Vic, 2013).

J. M. Salrach, 'Prácticas judiciales, transformación social y acción política en Cataluña (siglos IX–XIII)', *Hispania*, 57.197 (1997), 1009–48.

J. M. Salrach, 'La recreación judicial de documentos perdidos. Sobre la escritura y el poder en los condados catalanes (siglos XI–XII)', in Escalona Monge and Sirantoine (eds), *Chartes*, 219–32.

C. Sánchez-Albornoz, 'Las behetrías: la encomendación en Asturias, León y Castilla', repr. in *Viejos y nuevos estudios*, 1, 17–191.

C. Sánchez-Albornoz, 'Contratos de arrendamiento en el reino asturleonés', *CHE*, 10 (1948), 142–79.

C. Sánchez-Albornoz, *Despoblación y repoblación del Valle del Duero* (Buenos Aires, 1966).

C. Sánchez-Albornoz, *Una ciudad de la España cristiana hace mil años. Estampas de la vida en León* (5th ed., Madrid, 2014 [1966]).

C. Sánchez-Albornoz, 'Falsificaciones en Cardeña', *CHE*, 37–8 (1963), 336–45.

C. Sánchez-Albornoz, 'Imperantes y potestates en el reino asturleonés (714–1037)', *CHE*, 45–6 (1967), 352–73.

C. Sánchez-Albornoz, *Investigaciones y documentos sobre las instituciones hispanas* (Santiago de Chile, 1970).

C. Sánchez-Albornoz, 'El "juicio del libro" en León durante el siglo X y un feudo castellano del XIII', *AHDE*, 1 (1924), 382–9.

C. Sánchez-Albornoz, 'Los libertos en el reino asturleonés', *RPH*, 4 (1949), 9–45.

C. Sánchez-Albornoz, 'Notas sobre los libros leídos en el reino de León hace mil años', in *Miscelánea de estudios históricos* (León, 1970), 273–91.

C. Sánchez-Albornoz, 'El "palatium regis" asturleonés', *CHE*, 59–60 (1976), 5–104.

C. Sánchez-Albornoz, 'Pequeños propietarios libres en el reino asturleonés: su realidad histórica', in *Investigaciones*, 178–201.

C. Sánchez-Albornoz, 'El precio de la vida en el reino asturleonés hace mil años', in *Estudio sobre las instituciones medievales españolas* (Mexico City, 1965), 369–410.

C. Sánchez-Albornoz, *El regimen de la tierra en el reino asturleonés hace mil años* (Buenos Aires, 1978).

C. Sánchez-Albornoz, 'Sede regia y solio real en el reino asturleonés', *AM*, 3 (1979), 75–86.

C. Sánchez-Albornoz, 'Los siervos en el noroeste hispano hace un milenio', repr. in *Viejos y nuevos estudios*, 3, 1523–611.

C. Sánchez-Albornoz, 'Tradición y derecho visigodos en León y Castilla', in *Investigaciones*, 114–31.

C. Sánchez-Albornoz, *En torno a los orígenes del feudalismo* (rev. ed., Madrid, 1993).

C. Sánchez-Albornoz, *Viejos y nuevos estudios sobre instituciones medievales* (2nd ed., 3 vols, Madrid, 1976–80).

J. Sánchez-Arcilla Bernal, 'La administración de justicia en León y Castilla durante los siglos X al XIII', in Canellas López, Santiago Fernández, and Francisco Olmos (eds), *I Jornadas*, 13–49.

J. Sánchez-Arcilla Bernal, 'El derecho especial de los fueros del reino de León (1017–1229)', in *RLAEM* 2 (León, 1992), 189–380.

J. J. Sánchez Badiola, 'Terminología vasallática en la documentación altomedieval leonesa (ss. IX–XI)', in Pérez González (ed.), *Actas III*, 2, 687–96.

J. J. Sánchez Badiola, *El territorio de León en la Edad Media. Poblamiento, organización del espacio y estructura social (siglos IX–XIII)* (2 vols, León, 2004).

L. Sánchez Belda, 'Notas de diplomática. La confirmación de documentos por los reyes del occidente español', *RABM*, 59 (1953), 85–116.

A. Sánchez Candeira, 'La reina Velasquita de León y su descendencia', *Hispania*, 10.40 (1950), 449–505.

E. Sánchez Collado, 'Aproximación al testamentum per holographam scripturam', in *O direito das sucessoes: do direito romano ao direito actual* (Coimbra, 2006), 567–86.

A. Sánchez Díez, 'Los estudios sobre códices diplomáticos hispánicos. Confluencias historiográficas, metodológicas y sistémicas durante los ss. XVIII–XX', *Revista de Historiografía*, 14.27 (2017), 239–63.

R. Sánchez Domingo, '*Iudicium Dei* y creencia en la Alta Edad Media', in *Homenaje al profesor Alfonso García-Gallo* (5 vols, Madrid, 1996), 1, 321–30.

R. Sánchez Domingo (ed.), *Oña. Un milenio* (Burgos, 2012).

M. N. Sánchez González de Herrero, 'El campesinado y sus rentas. El léxico', in *Monarquía*, 1, 445–530.

M. N. Sánchez González de Herrero, 'Usos léxicos y negocios jurídicos. Pobladores y habitantes. Tributos y servicios. Juicios y litigios', in J. A. Bartol Hernández and J. R. Morala (eds), *El cartulario gótico de Cardeña. Estudios* (Burgos, 2018), 251–79.

A. Sánchez Mairena, 'Metodología para la investigación de los cartularios medievales: una experiencia a partir del estudio del Tumbo Viejo de la catedral de Lugo (siglo XIII)', in R. Marín López (ed.), *Homenaje al profesor Dr. D. José Ignacio Fernández de Viana y Vieites* (Granada, 2012), 533–48.

A. Sánchez Mairena, 'Propuestas metodológicas para el estudio de los cartularios medievales', in Arízaga Bolumburu *et al.* (eds), *Mundos*, 1, 217–30.

A. Sánchez Mairena, 'Los Tumbos Negro y Blanco: una ventana a los archivos medievales de la Iglesia de Astorga (León)', *Astórica*, 35 (2016), 23–64.

J. C. Sánchez-Pardo, 'Estrategias territoriales de un poder monástico en la Galicia medieval: Celanova (siglos X–XII)', *SHHM*, 28 (2010), 155–78.

A. B. Sánchez Prieto, 'Dónde aprender a leer y escribir en el año mil', *AEM*, 40.1 (2010), 3–34.

A. B. Sánchez Prieto, 'El poder y su representación documental en la Alta Edad Media', in Escalona Monge and Sirantoine (eds), *Chartes*, 101–15.

M. Sánchez Rodríguez, 'Una cláusula penal del "Tumbo Negro" de Zamora: la maldición divina (ensayo metodológico)', in *Homenaje a Fray Justo Pérez de Urbel, OSB* (2 vols, Silos, 1976–7), 1, 339–79.

V. Sandoval Parra, 'Leyes de aguas en la tradición visigoda', in Czeguhn *et al.* (eds), *Wasser*, 209–26.

M. Santos Estévez, *Petroglifos y paisaje social en la prehistoria reciente del noroeste de la Península Ibérica* (Santiago de Compostela, 2007).

I. Santos Salazar, 'Los privilegios de Berbeia y Barrio: elites, memoria y poder en Lantarón durante el siglo X', *SHHM*, 31 (2013), 51–81.

I. Santos Salazar, 'Ruling through Court: the Political Meanings of the Settlement of Disputes in Castile and Álava (ca. 900–1038)', *Al-Masāq*, 29.2 (2017), 133–50.

M. J. Sanz Fuentes, 'La confirmación de privilegios en la Baja Edad Media. Aportación a su estudio', *HID*, 6 (1979), 341–67.

M. J. Sanz Fuentes, 'El lenguaje de los documentos falsos', in *Orígenes*, 1, 119–58.

M. J. Sanz Fuentes, 'Tiempo de leer y escribir: el "scriptorium"', *CA*, 6 (1992), 37–56.

M. J. Sanz Fuentes and M. Calleja-Puerta, *Litteris confirmentur. Lo escrito en Asturias en la Edad Media* (Oviedo, 2005).

R. Sanz Serrano, 'La excomunión como sanción política en el reino visigodo de Toledo', *AC*, 3 (1986), 275–88.

J. Saraiva, 'A data nos documentos medievais portugueses e asturo-leoneses', *RPH*, 2 (1943), 25–220.

P. C. Scales, *The Fall of the Caliphate of Córdoba: Berbers and Andalusis in Conflict* (Leiden, 1994).

U. Schaefer, '*Ceteris imparibus*: Orality/Literacy and the Establishment of Anglo-Saxon Literate Culture', in P. E. Szarmach and J. T. Rosenthal (eds), *The Preservation and Transmission of Anglo-Saxon Culture* (Kalamazoo, MI, 1997), 287–311.

T. Schattner, 'Imagen y texto sobre monumentos del noroeste hispánico en época imperial romana: algunas observaciones arqueológicas', *Palaeohispanica*, 17 (2017), 349–81.

S. Scribner and M. Cole, *The Psychology of Literacy* (Cambridge, 1981).

A. Sennis, 'Destroying Documents in the Early Middle Ages', in Jarrett and McKinley (eds), *Problems*, 151–69.

G. del Ser Quijano, 'La renta feudal en la Alta Edad Media. El ejemplo del cabildo catedralicio de León en el período asturleonés', *SHHM*, 4 (1986), 59–75.

S. Serna Serna, 'Munio y el Becerro Gótico de Sahagún: una muestra de su actividad como copista', in *Monacato*, 425–36.

S. Serna Serna, 'Validations in Cardeña Gothic Cartulary: Signs, Monograms, and Chrismons', in Furtado and Moscone (eds), *Charters*, 41–60.

B. A. Shailor, 'The Scriptorium of San Pedro de Cardeña', *Bulletin of the John Rylands Library*, 61.2 (1979), 444–73.

B. A. Shailor, 'The Scriptorium of San Sahagún: a Period of Transition', in B. F. Reilly (ed.), *Santiago, Saint-Denis, and Saint Peter: the Reception of the Roman Liturgy in León-Castile in 1080* (New York, NY, 1985), 41–61.

L. Sierra Macarrón, 'El aumento de la producción escrita en los tumbos del monasterio de Sobrado de los Monjes (siglos IX–XIII)', in Sáez and Castillo Gómez (eds), *Actas VI*, 2, 119–31.

L. Sierra Macarrón, 'La escritura y el poder: el aumento de la producción escrita en Castilla y León (siglos XI–XIII)', *Signo*, 8 (2001), 249–74.

L. Sierra Macarrón, 'La presencia de la mujer en la documentación del siglo X: Paterna Gundesíndiz y el monasterio de Sobrado', in M. V. González de la Peña (ed.), *Mujer y cultura escrita del mito al siglo XXI* (Gijón, 2005), 47–57.

L. Sierra Macarrón, 'Producción y conservación de la documentación altomedieval: del Cantábrico al Duero (siglos IX–XI)', *Signo*, 13 (2004), 99–120.

L. Sierra Macarrón, 'Tipologías documentales del monasterio de Sobrado de los Monjes', in *Iglesia y religiosidad*, 2, 1027–39.

L. E. da Silveira, 'La Desamortización en Portugal', *Ayer*, 9 (1993), 29–60.

H. Sirantoine, *Imperator Hispaniae. Les idéologies impériales dans le royaume de León (IXᵉ–XIIᵉ siècles)* (Madrid, 2013).

J. P. Small, *Wax Tablets of the Mind: Cognitive Studies of Memory and Literacy in Classical Antiquity* (London, 1997).

J. M. H. Smith, *Europe after Rome: a New Cultural History, 500–1000* (Oxford, 2005).

T. Snijders, 'Textual Diversity and Textual Community in a Monastic Context: the Case of Eleventh-Century Marchiennes', *Revue d'Histoire Ecclésiastique*, 107.3–4 (2012), 897–930.

M. E. Sommar, 'Ecclesiastical Servi in the Frankish and Visigothic Kingdoms', *Zeitschrift der Savigny-Stiftung für Rechtsgeschichte. Kanonistische Abteilung*, 96 (2010), 57–79.

T. de Sousa Soares, 'Notas para o estudo das instituições municipais da Reconquista', *RPH*, 1 (1940), 71–92.

T. de Sousa Soares, 'Um testemunho sobre a presúria do bispo Odoário de Lugo no território bracarense', *RPH*, 1 (1940), 151–60.

J. A. Souto Cabo, 'A propósito da "charte presque célèbre" de Quiza Gonteríquiz', *Verba*, 36 (2009), 215–54.

M. C. Spalding, *The Middle English Charters of Christ* (Bryn Mawr, PA, 1914).

E. Steiner, *Documentary Culture and the Making of Medieval English Literature* (Cambridge, 2003).

J. R. Stenger, 'Learning Cities: a Novel Approach to Ancient *Paideia*', in J. R. Stenger (ed.), *Learning Cities in Late Antiquity: the Local Dimension of Education* (Abingdon, 2019), 1–23.

B. Stock, *The Implications of Literacy: Written Language and Models of Interpretation in the Eleventh and Twelfth Centuries* (Princeton, NJ, 1983).

R. L. Stocking, *Bishops, Councils, and Consensus in the Visigothic Kingdom, 589–633* (Ann Arbor, MI, 2000).

B. V. Street, *Literacy in Theory and Practice* (Cambridge, 1984).

A. Suárez González, 'Un cartulario de cartularios (BNE, MSS/18382)', in J. L. Hernández Luis (ed.), *Sic vos non vobis. Colección de estudios en honor de Florián Ferrero* (Zamora, 2015), 69–101.

A. Suárez González, 'Los *Libri cartarum Superaddi*. Notas para otra lectura (AHN, códices 976 y 977)', in R. Casal García, J. M. Andrade Cernadas, and R. J. López López (eds), *Galicia monástica. Estudos en lembranza da profesora María José Portela Silva* (Santiago de Compostela, 2009), 39–59.

A. Suárez González, 'Volver al cartulario', *Rudesindus*, 9 (2013), 153–70.

M. M. Sueiro Pena, 'Las bibliotecas monásticas en la Galicia medieval: testimonios documentales', in S. Fortuño Llorens and T. Martínez Romero (eds), *Actes del VII Congrés de l'Associació Hispànica de Literatura Medieval* (3 vols, Castelló de la Plana, 1999), 3, 429–45.

S. de Tapia, 'Nivel de alfabetización en una ciudad castellana del siglo XVI: sectores sociales y grupos étnicos en Ávila', *Studia Historica. Historia Moderna*, 6 (1988), 481–502.

S. Tarozzi, 'Spunti di riflessione sulla *diiudicatio* visigota in Form. Visig. 40', *Glossae*, 14 (2017), 917–29.

F. R. Tato Plaza and A. I. Boullón Agrelo, 'Fontes para o estudo da lingua medieval', in R. Álvarez Blanco and A. Santamarina (eds), *(Dis)cursos da escrita. Estudos de filoloxía galega ofrecidos en memoria de Fernando R. Tato Plaza* (A Coruña, 2004), 709–70.

A. Taylor, 'The Judas Curse', *American Journal of Philology*, 42.3 (1921), 234–52.

N. L. Taylor, 'Testamentary Publication and Proof and the Afterlife of Ancient Probate Procedure in Carolingian Septimania', in K. Pennington, S. Chodorow, and K. H. Kendall (eds), *Proceedings of the Tenth International Congress of Medieval Canon Law* (Vatican City, 2001), 767–80.

J. A. Testón Turiel, 'San Genadio, obispo y monje en el reino de León', *Compostellanum*, 63.1–2 (2018), 35–58.

R. Thomas, *Literacy and Orality in Ancient Greece* (Cambridge, 1992).

J. W. Thompson, *The Literacy of the Laity in the Middle Ages* (Berkeley, CA, 1939).

M. M. Tischler, '"Bibliotheca". Die Bibel als transkulturelle Bibliothek von Geschichte und Geschichten', in A. Speer and L. Reuke (eds), *Die Bibliothek—The Library—La Bibliothèque* (Berlin, 2020), 559–80.

M. M. Tischler, 'How Carolingian was Early Medieval Catalonia?', in S. Greer, A. Hicklin, and S. Esders (eds), *Using and Not Using the Past after the Carolingian Empire, c. 900–c. 1050* (Abingdon, 2020), 111–33.

B.-M. Tock, 'Les Pères de l'Église dans les chartes médiévales', in B.-M. Tock (ed.), *'In principio erat verbum': mélanges offerts en hommage à Paul Tombeur par des anciens étudiants à l'occasion de son éméritat* (Turnhout, 2005), 409–29.

G. Tomás-Faci, 'La construcción de la memoria escrita en los archivos eclesiásticos de Ribagorza (ss. XI–XIII)', *EM*, 16 (2015), 89–105.

G. Tomás-Faci, *Montañas, comunidades y cambio social en el Pirineo medieval. Ribagorza en los siglos X–XIV* (Zaragoza, 2016).

G. Tomás-Faci, 'The Transmission of Visigothic Documents in the Pyrenean Monastery of San Victorián de Asán (6th–12th Centuries): Monastic Memory and Episcopal Disputes', *AT*, 25 (2017), 303–14.

M. C. Torre Sevilla-Quiñones de León, 'Munio Fernández y su descendencia. Vida, patrimonio y política familiar de un conde de Astorga', *Astórica*, 14 (1995), 149–72.

A. J. Torrent Ruiz, 'La protección de las legítimas en los procesos de adulterio de la legislación visigótica: *Lex Wisigothorum* 3,4,12 y 13', in M. T. Duplá Marín and P. Panero Oria (eds), *Fundamentos del derecho sucesorio actual* (Madrid, 2018), 725–54.

A. J. Torrent Ruiz, 'La represión del *adulterium* en las leyes romano-barbáras y particularmente en la legislación hispano-visigótica', *Teoria e Storia del Diritto Privato*, 10 (2017), 1–75.

I. Torrente Fernández, 'Relaciones de parentesco en Asturias durante la Edad Media (siglos VIII y IX)', *AM*, 6 (1991), 39–57.

C. Torres Rodríguez, 'El "confessus" y "confessor" de las lápidas sepulcrales y de los cartularios gallegos, residuo tardío de una antigua disciplina penitencial', *CEG*, 17.52 (1962), 154–74.

E. Treharne and C. Willan, *Text Technologies: a History* (Stanford, CA, 2020).

E. M. Tyler and R. Balzaretti (eds), *Narrative and History in the Early Medieval West* (Turnhout, 2006).

P. Tyszka, 'Sexual Violence in the Early Medieval West', *Acta Poloniae Historica*, 104 (2011), 5–30.

A. Ubieto Arteta, *Ciclos económicos en la Edad Media española* (Valencia, 1969).

A. Ubieto Arteta, 'Con qué tipo de letra se escribió en Navarra hace mil años', *RABM*, 63 (1957), 409–22.

A. Ubieto Arteta, '¿Dónde estuvo el panteón de los primeros reyes pamploneses?', *PV*, 19.72–3 (1958), 267–78.

A. Ubieto Arteta, *Historia de Aragón. La formación territorial* (Zaragoza, 1981).

A. Ubieto Arteta, 'Los primeros años del monasterio de San Millán', *PV*, 34.132–3 (1973), 181–200.

A. Ubieto Arteta, 'Los votos de San Millán', in J. Maluquer de Motes (ed.), *Homenaje a Jaime Vicens Vives* (2 vols, Barcelona, 1965), 1, 304–24.

A. M. Udina i Abelló, *La successió testada a la Catalunya altomedieval* (Barcelona, 1984).

C. Urlacher-Becht, 'La doctrine dans les hymnes de la liturgie wisigothique: entre tradition patristique et réécriture biblique', in M. Cutino (ed.), *Poetry, Bible, and Theology from Late Antiquity to the Middle Ages* (Berlin, 2020), 403–23.

J. A. Valdés Gallego, 'La donación otorgada por Alfonso III a San Salvador de Oviedo en el año 908', *BRIDEA*, 51.150 (1997), 243–60.

J. Varela Rodríguez, 'Autores y lecturas en los monasterios femeninos de la Península Ibérica en el siglo X', in E. Corral Díaz (ed.), *Voces de mujeres en la Edad Media. Entre realidad y ficción* (Berlin, 2018), 495–504.

X. Varela Sieiro, *Léxico cotián na Alta Idade Media de Galicia: a arquitectura civil* (Santiago de Compostela, 2008).

X. Varela Sieiro, '*Petras* y *petras mobiles et inmobiles*: constituyentes de enumeraciones formulares en la documentación altomedieval de Galicia', *ALMA*, 58 (2000), 211–18.

B. Vasconcelos e Sousa and S. Boissellier, 'Pour un bilan de l'historiographie sur le Moyen Âge portugais au XXᵉ siècle', *CCM*, 49.195 (2006), 213–56.

A. Vázquez Martínez, C. Rodríguez Rellán, and R. Fábregas Valcarce, 'Petroglifos gallegos, una perspectiva desde el siglo XXI', *Cuadernos de Arte Prehistórico*, 6 (2018), 61–83.

J. M. Vázquez Varela, 'Los petroglifos gallegos', *Zephyrus*, 36 (1983), 43–51.

I. Velázquez Soriano, 'Ardesie scritte di epoca visigota: nuove prospettive sulla cultura e la scrittura', in Erhart, Heidecker, and Zeller (eds), *Privaturkunden*, 31–45.

I. Velázquez Soriano, '*Baselicas multas miro opere construxit* (*VSPE* 5.1.1). El valor de las fuentes literarias y epigráficas sobre la edilicia religiosa en la Hispania visigoda', *Hortus Artium Mediaevalium*, 13.2 (2007), 261–8.

I. Velázquez Soriano, 'La cultura gráfica en la Hispania visigoda: las escrituras anónimas', in J. Arce and P. Delogu (eds), *Visigoti e Longobardi* (Florence, 2001), 185–215.

I. Velázquez Soriano, 'Elementos religioso-bíblicos en fórmulas y documentos de época visigoda', *AC*, 7 (1990), 559–66.

I. Velázquez Soriano, 'La escritura visigótica cursiva en su período primitivo', in Alturo i Perucho, Torras Cortina, and Castro Correa (eds), *Escritura*, 15–53.

I. Velázquez Soriano, 'Jural Relations as an Indicator of Syncretism: from the Law of Inheritance to the *Dum inlicita* of Chindaswinth', in P. Heather (ed.), *The Visigoths from the Migration Period to the Seventh Century: an Ethnographic Perspective* (Woodbridge, 1999), 225–70.

I. Velázquez Soriano, 'Las pizarras visigodas como reflejo de una cultura', in *Visigodos*, 127–40.

I. Velázquez Soriano, 'Reflexiones en torno a la formación de un *Corpus regularum* de época visigoda', *AC*, 23 (2006), 531–67.

I. Velázquez Soriano, 'En torno a la *Dum inlicita* y la herencia en la *Lex Visigothorum*', *Interpretatio*, 6 (1998), 209–54.

M. Vessey, 'Literacy and *Litteratura*, A.D. 200–800', *Studies in Medieval and Renaissance History*, 13.23 (1992), 139–60.

J. Vezin, 'Écritures imitées dans les livres et les documents du Haut Moyen Âge (VIIe–XIe siècle)', *BECh*, 165.1 (2007), 47–66.

J. Vilella, 'A Canonical Latin Collection from Late Antiquity: the Pseudo-Iliberritan Series', in R. Lizzi Testa and G. Marconi (eds), *The Collectio Avellana and its Revivals* (Newcastle upon Tyne, 2019), 388–424.

J. Vilella, 'The Pseudo-Iliberritan Canon Texts', *Zeitschrift für Antikes Christentum*, 18.2 (2014), 210–59.

J. Villaamil y Castro, *Del uso de las pruebas judiciales, llamadas vulgares. Estudio histórico-jurídico* (Madrid, 1881).

A. Viñayo González, *Fernando I, el Magno: 1035–1065* (Burgos, 1999).

*Los visigodos y su mundo* (Madrid, 1998).

E. B. Vitz, 'Liturgy as Education in the Middle Ages', in R. B. Begley and J. W. Koterski (eds), *Medieval Education* (New York, NY, 2005), 20–34.

M. C. Vivancos Gómez, 'Autenticidad de la donación de Fernán González a San Sebastián de Silos (954)', *HID*, 40 (2013), 427–48.

M. C. Vivancos Gómez, 'Documentación en visigótica del monasterio de San Salvador de Oña: originales y copias', in Sánchez Domingo (ed.), *Oña*, 52–81.

M. C. Vivancos Gómez, 'Vida cotidiana de clérigos y monjes: sus cargos y oficios en la documentación leonesa', in *Monarquía*, 1, 675–712.

C. Vogel, *Individuelle und universelle Kontinuitäten. Testamente und Erbverfahren auf der Iberischen Halbinsel im frühen Mittelalter (ca. 500–1000)* (Berlin, 2019).

A. de Vogüé, *Regards sur le monachisme des premiers siècles: recueil d'articles* (Rome, 2000).

B. Ward-Perkins, *The Fall of Rome and the End of Civilization* (Oxford, 2005).

D. Wasserstein, *The Rise and Fall of the Party-Kings: Politics and Society in Islamic Spain, 1002–1086* (Princeton, NJ, 1985).

M. Weber, *Economy and Society: an Outline of Interpretive Sociology*, ed. G. Roth and C. Wittich, transl. E. Fischoff *et al.* (3 vols, New York, NY, 1968).

C. West, 'Meaning and Context: Moringus the Lay Scribe and Charter Formulation in Late Carolingian Burgundy', in Jarrett and McKinley (eds), *Problems*, 71–87.

S. D. White, 'Inheritances and Legal Arguments in Western France, 1050–1150', *Traditio*, 43 (1987), 55–103.

S. D. White, '"*Pactum…legem vincit et amor judicium*." The Settlement of Disputes by Compromise in Eleventh-Century Western France', *American Journal of Legal History*, 22.4 (1978), 281–308.

S. D. White, 'Proposing the Ordeal and Avoiding It: Strategy and Power in Western French Litigation, 1050–1110', in T. N. Bisson (ed.), *Cultures of Power: Lordship, Status, and Process in Twelfth-Century Europe* (Philadelphia, PA, 1995), 89–123.

C. Wickham, *Early Medieval Italy: Central Power and Local Society, 400–1000* (London, 1981).

C. Wickham, *Framing the Early Middle Ages: Europe and the Mediterranean, 400–800* (Oxford, 2005).

C. Wickham, *The Inheritance of Rome: a History of Europe from 400 to 1000* (London, 2009).

C. Wickham, 'Land Disputes and their Social Framework in Lombard-Carolingian Italy, 700–900', in Davies and Fouracre (eds), *Settlement*, 105–24.

C. Wickham, 'Problems in Doing Comparative History', in P. Skinner (ed.), *Challenging the Boundaries of Medieval History. The Legacy of Timothy Reuter* (Turnhout, 2009), 5–28.

L. Wiener, *Commentary to the Germanic Laws and Mediaeval Documents* (Cambridge, MA, 1915).

J. Williams, 'A Contribution to the History of the Castilian Monastery of Valeranica and the Scribe Florentius', *MM*, 11 (1970), 231–48.

K. J. Wireback, 'The Origins of the Portuguese Inflected Infinitive', *Hispania*, 77.3 (1994), 544–54.

I. Wood, 'Disputes in Late Fifth- and Sixth-Century Gaul: Some Problems', in Davies and Fouracre (eds), *Settlement*, 7–22.

I. Wood, 'Entrusting Western Europe to the Church, 400–750', *TRHS*, 23 (2013), 37–73.

S. Wood, *The Proprietary Church in the Medieval West* (Oxford, 2006).

G. Woolf, 'Ancient Illiteracy?', *BICS*, 58.2 (2015), 31–42.

G. Woolf, 'Literacy or Literacies in Rome?', in Johnson and Parker (eds), *Ancient Literacies*, 46–68.

P. Wormald, 'The *Leges Barbarorum*: Law and Ethnicity in the Post-Roman West', in H.-W. Goetz, J. Jarnut, and W. Pohl (eds), *Regna and Gentes. The Relationship between Late Antique and Early Medieval Peoples and Kingdoms in the Transformation of the Roman World* (Leiden, 2003), 21–53.

P. Wormald, '*Lex scripta* and *verbum regis*: Legislation and Germanic Kingship, from Euric to Cnut', repr. in *Legal Culture in the Early Medieval West: Law as Text, Image, and Experience* (London, 1999), 1–43.

P. Wormald, *The Making of English Law: King Alfred to the Twelfth Century, I. Legislation and its Limits* (Oxford, 1999).

P. Wormald and J. L. Nelson (eds), *Lay Intellectuals in the Carolingian World* (Cambridge, 2007).

R. Wright, 'La difusión inmediata del documento: lenguaje y lectura en el siglo X', in Escalona Monge and Sirantoine (eds), *Chartes*, 117–30.

R. Wright, *Early Ibero-Romance: Twenty-One Studies on Language and Texts from the Iberian Peninsula between the Roman Empire and the Thirteenth Century* (Newark, DE, 1994).

R. Wright, 'Gontigius, Sagulfus, Domitria y el hijo de muchos otros buenos', in A. M. Cano González (ed.), *Homenaxe al profesor Xosé Lluis García Arias* (2 vols, Oviedo, 2010), 1, 407–20.

R. Wright, 'How Scribes Wrote Ibero-Romance before Written Romance was Invented', in E.-M. Wagner, B. Outhwaite, and B. Beinhoff (eds), *Scribes as Agents of Language Change* (Berlin, 2013), 71–84.

R. Wright, 'Late and Vulgar Latin in Muslim Spain: the African Connection', in F. Biville, M.-K. Lhommé, and D. Vallat (eds), *LVLT IX. Actes du IX$^e$ Colloque international sur le latin vulgaire et tardif* (Lyon, 2012), 35–54.

R. Wright, *Late Latin and Early Romance in Spain and Carolingian France* (Liverpool, 1982).

R. Wright, 'Late Latin: the Evidence', in A. García Leal and C. E. Prieto Entrialgo (eds), *LVLT XI. Actas del XI Congreso internacional sobre el latín vulgar y tardío* (Hildesheim, 2017), 129–45.

R. Wright, 'El léxico y la lectura oral', *Revista de Filología Española*, 85.1 (2005), 133–49.

R. Wright, 'Reading a Will in Twelfth-Century Salamanca', in H. Petersmann and R. Kettemann (eds), *LVLT V. Actes du V$^e$ Colloque international sur le latin vulgaire et tardif* (Heidelberg, 1999), 505–16.

R. Wright, *A Sociophilological Study of Late Latin* (Turnhout, 2002).

R. Wright, 'Writing and Speaking Late Latin', in *Scrivere e leggere nell'alto medioevo. Settimane 59* (2 vols, Spoleto, 2012), 1, 273–92.

R. Wright (ed.), *Latin and the Romance Languages in the Early Middle Ages* (London, 1991).

M. P. Yáñez Cifuentes, *El monasterio de Santiago de León* (León, 1972).

J. Yarza Luaces, '*Scriptoria* y manuscritos iluminados en los reinos hispanos occidentales en el entorno del año mil', in *Península*, 65–88.

H. C. Youtie, '*Βραδέως γράφων*. Between Literacy and Illiteracy', *GRBS*, 12.2 (1971), 239–61.

H. C. Youtie, 'Pétaus, fils de Pétaus, ou le scribe qui ne savait pas écrire', *Chronique d'Égypt*, 41.81 (1966), 127–43.

E. Zadora-Rio, 'The Making of Churchyards and Parish Territories in the Early-Medieval Landscape of France and England in the 7th–12th Centuries: a Reconsideration', *Medieval Archaeology*, 47.1 (2003), 1–19.

E. Zaragoza i Pascual, 'Abadologio del monasterio de San Millán de la Cogolla (siglos VI–XIX)', *SMon*, 42.1 (2000), 185–223.

B. Zeller, 'Writing Charters as a Public Activity: the Example of the Carolingian Charters of St Gall', in Mostert and Barnwell (eds), *Medieval Legal Process*, 27–37.

B. Zeller *et al.*, *Neighbours and Strangers: Local Societies in Early Medieval Europe* (Manchester, 2020).

M. Zimmermann, 'L'acte privé en Catalogne aux IX$^e$ et X$^e$ siècles: portée sociale, contraintes formelles et liberté d'écriture', in Erhart, Heidecker, and Zeller (eds), *Privaturkunden*, 193–212.

M. Zimmermann, 'Charter Writing and Documentary Memory in the Origins of Catalan History', in F. Sabaté (ed.), *Memory in the Middle Ages: Approaches from Southwestern Europe* (Leeds, 2020), 117–44.

M. Zimmermann, *Écrire et lire en Catalogne (IX<sup>e</sup>–XII<sup>e</sup> siècle)* (2 vols, Madrid, 2003).

M. Zimmermann, 'Protocoles et préambules dans les documents catalans du X<sup>e</sup> au XII<sup>e</sup> siècle: évolution diplomatique et signification spirituelle', *MCV*, 10 (1974), 41–76.

M. Zimmermann, '*Sicut antiquus sancitum est…* Tutelle des anciens ou protection de l'innovation? L'invocation du droit et la terminologie politique dans les représentations médiévales en Catalogne (IX<sup>e</sup>–XII<sup>e</sup> siècle)', in J.-M. Sansterre (ed.), *L'autorité du passé dans les sociétés médiévales* (Rome, 2004), 27–56.

M. Zimmermann, 'L'usage du droit wisigothique en Catalogne du IX<sup>e</sup> au XII<sup>e</sup> siècle: approches d'une signification culturelle', *MCV*, 9 (1973), 233–81.

M. Zimmermann, 'Vie et mort d'un formulaire: l'écriture des actes catalanes (X<sup>e</sup>–XII<sup>e</sup> siècle)', in M. Zimmermann (ed.), *Auctor et auctoritas. Invention et conformisme dans l'écriture médiévale* (Paris, 2001), 337–58.

A. Zumkeller, 'Der Gebrauch der Termini famulus Dei, servus Dei, famula Dei und ancilla Dei bei Augustinus', in G. J. M. Bartelink, A. Hilhorst, and C. H. J. M. Kneepkens (eds), *Eulogia. Mélanges offerts à Antoon R. Bastiaensen à l'occasion de son soixante-cinquième anniversaire* (Turnhout, 1991), 437–45.

C. Zwanzig, 'Heidenheim and Samos: Monastic Remembrance of the "Anglo-Saxon Mission" in Southern Germany and the "Mozarabic Resettlement" of Northern Spain Compared', in J. C. Sánchez-Pardo and M. G. Shapland (eds), *Churches and Social Power in Early Medieval Europe: Integrating Archaeological and Historical Approaches* (Turnhout, 2015), 269–95.

# Index